Managing Services Marketing

FOURTH EDITION

Managing Services Marketing
Text and Readings

John E. G. Bateson
Gemini Consulting, Ltd.

K. Douglas Hoffman
Colorado State University

The Dryden Press
Harcourt Brace College Publishers

Fort Worth   Philadelphia   San Diego   New York   Orlando   Austin   San Antonio
Toronto   Montreal   London   Sydney   Tokyo

Acquisitions Editor: Bill Schoof
Market Strategist: Lisé Johnson
Development Editor: Rebecca Linnenburger
Project Editor: Rebecca Dodson
Art Director: Bill Brammer
Production Manager: Lois West
Permissions Editor: Adele Krause

ISBN: 0-03-022519-1

Library of Congress Catalog Card Number: 98-73895

Portions of this work were published in previous editions.

Address for editorial correspondence:
Harcourt Brace College Publishers
301 Commerce Street, Suite 3700
Fort Worth, TX 76102

Address for orders:
Harcourt Brace & Company
6277 Sea Harbor Drive
Orlando, FL 32887-6777
1-800-782-4479

Website address: http://www.hbcollege.com
THE DRYDEN PRESS, DRYDEN, and the DP Logo are registered trademarks of Harcourt Brace & Company.

Printed in the United States of America
    0 1 2 3 4 5 6   048   9 8 7 6 5 4 3

The Dryden Press
Harcourt Brace College Publishers

In memoriam
Kenneth James Bateson
Elizabeth Bateson

–John E.G. Bateson

To John Bateson and Scott Kelley
. . . many thanks!

–K. Douglas Hoffman

The Dryden Press Series in Marketing

Parente, Vanden Burgh, Barban, and Marra
Advertising Campaign Strategy: A Guide to Marketing Communication Plans

Rosenbloom
Marketing Channels: A Management View
Sixth Edition

Sandburg
Discovering Your Marketing Career CD-ROM

Schaffer
Applying Marketing Principles Software

Schaffer
The Marketing Game

Schellinck and Maddox
Marketing Research: A Computer-Assisted Approach

Schnaars
MICROISM

Schuster and Copeland
Global Business: Planning for Sales and Negotiations

Sheth, Mittal, and Newman
Customer Behavior: Consumer Behavior and Beyond

Shimp
Advertising, Promotion, and Supplemental Aspects of Integrated Marketing Communications
Fourth Edition

Talarzyk
Cases and Exercises in Marketing

Terpstra and Sarathy
International Marketing
Seventh Edition

Weitz and Wensley
Readings in Strategic Marketing Analysis, Planning, and Implementation

Zikmund
Exploring Marketing Research
Sixth Edition

Zikmund
Essentials of Marketing Research

HARCOURT BRACE COLLEGE OUTLINE SERIES

Peterson
Principles of Marketing

About the Authors

John E.G. Bateson is a Senior Vice President with Gemini Consulting. He was Associate Professor of Marketing at the London Business School, England, and a visiting associate professor at the Stanford Business School. Prior to teaching, he was a brand manager with Lever Brothers and marketing manager with Philips.

Dr. Bateson holds an undergraduate degree from Imperial College, London, a master's degree from London Business School, and a doctorate in marketing from the Harvard Business School. He has published extensively in the services marketing literature including the *Journal of Marketing Research*, the *Journal of Retailing*, *Marketing Science*, and the *Journal of Consumer Research*. He is also the author of *Marketing Public Transit: A Strategic Approach* (Praeger).

Dr. Bateson was actively involved with the formation of the services division of the American Marketing Association. He served on the Services Council for four years and has chaired sessions of the AMA Services Marketing Conferences. He also served on the Steering Committee of the Marketing Science Institute. He consults extensively in the services sector.

Dr. Bateson is current managing director of the consumer, retail, and distribution worldwide practice of Gemini Consulting.

K. Douglas Hoffman is an Associate Professor of Marketing at Colorado State University. His primary teaching and research passion is in the Services Marketing area. Doug initiated and taught the first Services Marketing classes at Mississippi State University, The University of North Carolina at Wilmington, and Colorado State University. He has been formally recognized for *Teaching Excellence* at The University of North Carolina at Wilmington and Colorado State University and is a past Education Coordinator for the Services Marketing Special Interest Group of the American Marketing Association.

Doug holds an undergraduate marketing degree from The Ohio State University and master's and doctoral degrees from the University of Kentucky. Prior to his graduate academic career, Doug was actively involved in his father's golf course business, a distribution analyst for Volkswagen of America, and a research analyst for the Parker Hannifin Corporation.

Doug's current research and consulting activities are primarily in the areas of customer service/satisfaction and services marketing education. He is the co-author of two Services Marketing textbooks and has published in the *Journal of Retailing*, *Journal of Personal Selling and Sales Management*, *Journal of Business Ethics*, *Journal of Services Marketing*, *Journal of Professional Services Marketing*, *Journal of Marketing Education*, and *Marketing Education Review*.

Introduction

Managing Services Marketing, Fourth Edition, is designed for an advanced MBA course in the marketing of services and for executive programs geared to managers in service firms. This edition marks the book's "coming of age," in that for the first time it has not been necessary to include readings to support the chapters. The growth in the field over the past few years means that there is now ample material for a standard textbook.

Every textbook on marketing should be based on services with a couple of chapters at the end on "the special case of goods." Chapter 1 gives ample macro-economic data suggesting that the service sector is becoming the primary source of wealth, trade, and growth throughout the developed world. Even these data underrepresents the impact on consumers. The proportion of purchasing effort focused on goods is declining rapidly due to the impact of a number of forces: the commoditization of branded goods; the shattering of the mass market into a mosaic of millions of pieces; and the resultant growing power of the trade.

By comparison, the purchasing of service is becoming increasingly complex. The global communications network will soon provide home shopping, video on demand, and thanks to digital compression, up to 240 channels of television. In other sectors, the world is being colonized by the multisite service firms. Diplomatic relations with China may vary, but the McDonald's close to Tiananmen Square is the world's biggest with 28,000 square feet of space, more than 700 seats, and a staff of 900. The restaurant is not only changing consumer habits but is also changing the work ethic of its staff. Recently, Union Bank of Switzerland rated the cost of living in various worldwide sectors using the Big Mac Scale: percentage of the weekly wage needed to buy a Big Mac.

Economic prosperity means that service transactions are becoming a trade-off between the benefits obtained and the cost incurred in terms of time and control, with price becoming irrelevant. Services provide opportunities to both generate and consume discretionary time. Services also require the giving up of that sense of control that is becoming a key decision criterion after time and before price.

Economists and consumers know we are in a service world, and marketing textbooks should reflect this. This textbook, therefore, is dedicated exclusively to the problems of marketing services.

The title of the textbook reflects its orientation. It is concerned with the management problems of services marketing managers. The concepts and tools developed in the package goods and industrial marketing areas apply to services. The problems of services marketing, however, are more complex. The service product is more difficult to design, and introducing marketing orientation into a firm dominated by operations is more difficult.

Organization

The book is divided into three parts. Part I covers the basic building blocks that are needed before going on to consider the management of the services experience in Part II. Part III adopts a firm-wide viewpoint and discusses alternative ways service firms can compete.

Part I

The four chapters in Part I cover the service consumer, the service operation, and the service provider. A chapter devoted to understanding consumer behavior is not unexpected in a marketing book, but one on operations management is surprising. Because the operation is the product, it is important to understand not only the needs of the consumer but also the needs of the operation. Equally important is the understanding of the service providers, their motivations, and their role.

Chapter 1 provides an overview of the theoretical framework of the textbook, as well as background on the importance of services. Chapter 2, the consumer chapter, builds on the experiential nature of the service product to suggest that a number of emerging theories from environmental psychology may provide additional insights into the consumer choice process.

Chapter 3 opens with an operation management perspective and sets forth the requirements for an efficient operation. These requirements are then compared with the operational demands of service, and several major threats to efficiency are identified. A number of concepts and theories, which were developed in operations management to overcome these problems, are then described. Throughout the textbook, the emphasis is on understanding the operation and its interdependence with marketing.

Chapter 4 focuses on the service providers, those individuals who sit on the boundaries of the service firm and provide day-to-day contact with consumers. They are the product for many service firms, and yet they are often at the bottom of the organizational hierarchy. Because of their low position in the hierarchy, they are sometimes caught between the consumer and the firm and have to resolve the conflicts produced.

Part II

These five chapters deal with the creation and management of the service experience, which constitutes the product the consumer buys, under the heading *Configuring the Service Firm*. The complexity of the service product is one of the key differentiating features of service marketing. The creation of experiences (service) that take place in real time poses many problems that differ from those faced in the creation of mere physical good. Chapter 5 deals with the configuration of the operation. Chapter 6, new for this edition, deals with the design of the physical setting of the service operation, itself a key part of the service for many firms. Chapter 7 discusses the design of human resource policies necessary to motivate the contact personnel successfully. In particular, it deals with who uses and how to use empowerment and enforcement.

A unique characteristic of services is that consumers are part of the production process and actually coproduce their own experience. Chapters 8 and 9 look at pricing and communication from this perspective. Instead of looking at the traditional theories in both areas, they look instead at how these traditional tools can influence consumer behavior in the service experience.

Part III

This part takes the much broader perspective of the services firm and discusses alternative competitive strategies. Chapter 10 provides an overview for this section of the book and provides a framework of different kinds of competition: for share, reach, and geography. By far the most complex is competition for share, and ideas in Chapter 10 are developed in the rest of the chapters.

Chapter 11 discusses customer satisfaction as a competitive strategy. Chapter 12 shows how service recovery, the recovery from failed service encounters, can be used competitively. Chapter 13 argues that existing customers are far more valuable than prospective customers and shows how this can be built into a strategy. Chapters 14 and 15 then look at the related topics of service quality and creating customer focus.

Key Features

- "Services in Action" boxed features integrate real-world service examples in every chapter.

- Text emphasizes contemporary ethical and international issues in services marketing.

- Bateson's classic structure is seen through the coverage of key topics in services marketing combined with state of the art readings in the field.

- An excellent variety of articles have been selected from areas such as marketing, organizational behavior, operations management, and strategy literature. The marketing implications of all topics are emphasized in the textual material.

New to this Edition

- 95% of articles included are new to this edition.

- Increased focus on textual portion

- Completely rewritten Chapter 3 Understanding the Service Operation

- New Chapters!
  Chapter 5 The Service Operation
  Chapter 6 The Physical Setting
  Chapter 10 Competing as a Service Firm
  Chapter 11 Customer Satisfaction System
  Chapter 12 Service Recovery
  Chapter 13 The Customer Retention System

Ancillary Material

The **Instructor's Manual** and **Transparency Masters** serve as a comprehensive and valuable teaching aid including advice for teaching this emerging course including suggested course outlines, article summaries, suggested cases in services marketing with case notes and transparency masters.

NEW! Don't forget to visit our website at **www.dryden.com.** This resource will provide you with more information about Services Marketing as well as other HOT topics in marketing.

Acknowledgments

I am indebted to all the faculty members using the book throughout the world who have taken the time to share their feedback with me. I am particularly indebted to Doug Hoffman, whose enthusiasm for the textbook reignited my own. As a contributing author to both the last edition and this one, he provided insights, material, and the beginning of the new structure that has come to fruition in this, the fourth edition.

To Earl Sasser, Daryl Wykoff, and Christopher Lovelock, from whom I took my first courses in services at the Harvard Business School, thanks for sowing the seeds that grew into my burning interest in the service.

To Eric Langeard and Pierre Eiglier, truly the pioneers who led the way, thanks for showing me the power of conceptualization in services.

To the Marketing Science Institute, whose Consumer Service Project nurtured my interest in services, supported my first ideas, and created in Christopher Lovelock, Eric Langeard, and Pierre Eiglier a great team of project colleagues, I extend my gratitude.

To Leonard Berry, Valerie Zeithaml, Greg Upah, Ven Venkatesen, Mary Jo Bitner, Bernard Booms, Ben Schneider, Christian Gronroos, Dick Chase, Carol Congram, and all the others who attended those early American Marketing Association service marketing conferences, thanks for the company. If one is going to wander into the wilderness of a new area and be a pioneer, it is good to have friends around to protect your back.

We would also like to thank our colleagues whose insights helped shape *Managing Services Marketing*, 4/e:

Scott Kelley
University of Kentucky

Sue Wild
Manchester Metropolitan University

George Hozier
University of New Mexico

Dean Headly
Wichita State University

Judy Philips
Mississippi State University

Bob Young
Northeastern University

Al Rosenbloom
Benedictine University

Eberhard Scheuing
St. John's University

Larry Cunningham
University of Colorado Denver

Gary Brunswick
University of Michigan Dearborn

Finally, Doug and I are immensely grateful to Bill Schoof, Rebecca Linnenburger, and Becky Dodson for their work on the fourth edition; to Morgen Witzel, who has dealt so efficiently with the administration and organization that such an undertaking demands, and to L. A. Mitchell for her work and dedication in constructing the Instructor's Manual . . . thank you all.

John E.G. Bateson
London

CONTENTS

Chapter 7

Chapter 8

Chapter 9

Article 2.1

Article 2.2

Article 2.3

Chapter 11

Chapter 12

Chapter 13

Chapter 14
Competing as a Service Firm: Service Quality

Chapter 15
Competing as a Service Firm: Building a Customer-Focused Service Organization

Article 3.1

Article 3.2

Article 3.3

Article 3.4

Article 3.5

Article 3.6

Managing Services Marketing

I

The Basic Building Blocks

This part of the book describes the concepts, frameworks, and tools needed to understand service businesses from a marketing perspective. Chapter 1 introduces the conceptual framework of the whole book as well as provides an economic view of the role of service firms. The chapter covers the debate over the classification of services, but focuses on the fact that services exist to create experiences for consumers in which they are active participants. From this experiential nature arise many of the managerial problems of services, and this provides the framework and structure of this book.

Chapter 2, "Understanding the Service Consumer," starts from the experiential nature of the service product to suggest that a number of emerging theories may provide additional insight into consumer behavior. It separates the consumer choice process—"Which service firm shall I go to?" from the evaluation process—"Am I satisfied with the experience I have just received?" Particularly in the discussion of the evaluation process, it draws from the related field of environmental psychology to find interesting and insightful theories.

Article 1.1 by Keith Murray should be read in conjunction with Chapter 2. This article tests empirically some of the theories introduced around the consumer choice process. In particular, it tests the idea that in the choice of services consumers will acquire different sorts of information than they would normally use in the selection of goods. This is generally believed to be due to the higher perceived risk in the purchase of services. The empirical study confirms that services consumers are less likely to prefer outright purchase and to use observation or trial in the purchase process. However, they are more likely to use personal sources of information.

Chapter 3, "Understanding the Service Operation," is perhaps at first sight a surprising topic for a marketing text. However, in services the operation is the product. It is therefore important to understand the needs of the operator as well as the needs of the consumer. Every company needs to trade-off operational efficiency with the needs of the consumer, but for service firms this trade-off is acute, and it takes place in real time, all the time.

The chapter starts, therefore, with a delineation of the requirements of an efficient operation irrespective of whether we are discussing goods or services. It then discusses the traditional approaches to driving manufacturing efficiency and their applicability to service operations. It concludes that they are more difficult to apply as many operational changes will have a direct impact on the consumer because the consumer is an integral part of the process. Conversely, the presence of the consumer can sometimes be used to improve efficiency by, for example, getting the consumer to do more of the work in a typical "self-service" operation.

The final chapter in this part of the book deals with "Understanding the Service Worker." This chapter discusses the key role that the service provider plays in nearly all services, not only as a "factory worker," but as the human face of the organization. Being in such a position puts enormous stress on the service providers since they span the boundary between the organization and the consumers. This means they are frequently subject to conflicting demands and to extremely ambiguous situations. The chapter draws on the general theories of organization behavior to show that such stress has many detrimental effects for the individual. Moreover, many of the strategies that service providers can, and do, use to overcome this stress reduce the quality of the service experience for the consumer.

Articles 1.2 and 1.3 should be read in conjunction with Chapter 4. Article 1.2 by Mary Jo Bitner and her colleagues explores the service provider's perception of when consumers receive satisfactory and unsatisfactory experiences. It uses the critical incident technique, an approach which is growing in popularity and which is used in a number of other articles in this book. The article's interest is that it compares the results of this study with service providers in conjunction with an earlier study which used consumers. The primary finding when comparing the two groups is that the "customer is always right" is not a correct summary. Many unsatisfactory service encounters may be due to inappropriate customer behaviors.

Article 1.3 by Kristopher Weatherly and David Tansik investigates empirically the strategies used by service providers to respond to conflicting demands in their role. In particular, it looks at the impact of role conflict and ambiguity. Conflict in roles implies that the service provider faces conflicting demands from the consumer and the organization; in other words, the "can't win" situation. Ambiguity, by comparison, implies that a service provider is unsure about the role that they should be playing. Other research has shown that conflict and ambiguity are positively related to the levels of job satisfaction and intention to leave.

This study shows that, for service providers, ambiguity and conflict are related to job dissatisfaction. The study also looks at the relationship with commonly used tactics: working hard, negotiating, preempting, and avoiding. Negotiating relates to attempts to clarify the role by negotiating with the "role seekers," in this case, the organization and the consumer. Preempting involves taking over the encounter to ensure that the consumer "does as they are told" and hence cannot be a source of conflicting demands. Avoiding involves the service provider trying not to engage in the service encounter by, for example, ignoring consumers when they arrive.

1

The Service Revolution

- **The Service Economy**
- **Service at the Firm Level**
- **What Is a Service?**
- **Classification of Services**
- **The Basic Model**
  Services Cannot Be Inventoried
  Services in Action 1.1   Rainforest Cafe
  Services Are Time Dependent
  Services Are Place Dependent
  Consumers Are Always Involved in the Factory
  Changes in the Factory Mean Changes in
  Consumer Behavior
  Services in Action 1.2   Domino's Pizza
  Changes in the Benefit Concept Mean
  Changes in the Factory
  Everyone and Everything That Comes into
  Contact with the Consumer Is Delivering the
  Service
  Contact Persons Are Products
  Services Cannot Be Quality Controlled at the
  Factory Gate
  A Different Concept of Marketing as an
  Organizational Function
- **Sequence of the Book**
  Part I: The Basic Building Blocks
  Part II: Configuring the Service Firm
  Part III: Competing as a Service Firm
- **Notes**

The Service Economy

Services permeate every aspect of our lives. We use transportation services when we travel, often to and from work; when we travel away from home, we use restaurant services to feed us and hotels to put roofs over our heads. At home, we rely on services such as electricity and telephones; at work, we need postal, courier, and maintenance services to keep our work places running. We use the services of hairdressers to maintain our personal self-image, and our employers use the services of public relations and advertising firms to maintain their corporate images. Lawyers, physicians, dentists, stockbrokers, and insurance agents look after our personal and financial health. In our leisure time, we use a battery of services ranging from movie theatres to swimming pools to Disney-style theme parks for amusement and relaxation. And when we do buy goods, such as a new car or a washing machine, we often still rely on services to keep them running and repair them when they break down.

Services allow us to budget our time as well as our money. We use some services to generate increased discretionary time in order to buy other services. A family might, for example, eat at McDonald's to save the time that would have been spent cooking a meal at home. That "extra" time might then be "spent" at a movie or at a theme park, using another service to provide recreation. A company might buy a service, such as advertising or research or catering, rather than spending its own valuable time in the field, and then be free to concentrate on its core business.

Many of these services have always been present to some degree, but the complexity and diversity of services have increased dramatically over the past century. Contrary to popular belief, services, not manufactured goods, have fueled modern economic growth. The Industrial Revolution of the 18th century involved changes not only in production, but also in financial structures and in transportation and communication networks. It is no coincidence that two of the biggest service sectors, banks and railroads, boomed at the same time as the Industrial Revolution. Without the emergence of these and other services, the economic benefits of large-scale production units could never have been realized.[1]

Economic growth has in its turn fueled the growth of the service sector, as increasing prosperity means that companies, institutions, and individuals increasingly have become willing to trade money for time and to buy services rather than spend time doing things for themselves. New technology has led to considerable changes in the nature of many services and in the development of new services. Higher disposable incomes have led to a proliferation of personal services, particularly in the entertainment sector. Growth has meant an increase not only in the overall volume of services, but in the variety and diversity of services offered.

The result has been phenomenal growth in service industries, shown clearly in economic and trade statistics (see Figure 1.1). In economic terms, the service sector now accounts for 58 percent of worldwide gross national product (GNP); in 1980, service business worldwide was valued at $350 billion and accounted for 20 percent of all world trade, whereas by 1992 that figure had nearly tripled to $1,000 billion.[2] All developed economies now have large service sectors, and Japan and Germany in particular have service economies at least as developed as that of the United States. Many service firms now operate internationally, and exports of services are also increasing. The United States remains the world's leading service exporter, with exports valued at $148.5 billion, or 10.5 percent of total worldwide service exports in 1991; service imports amounted to $100 billion in the same year. Given that the American balance of payments deficit in manufactured goods is nearly $130 billion year, the $50 billion trade surplus in services is obviously vital to the American economy.[3]

The difference in trade figures shows distinctly the growing importance of services and the parallel decline of manufacturing. In 1970, manufacturing accounted for 26 percent of American gross domestic product (GDP); by 1991, it accounted for only

FIGURE 1.1   SERVICE ECONOMICS AND EMPLOYMENT

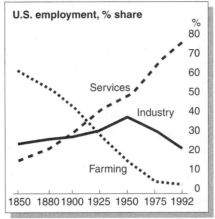

U.S. employment, % share

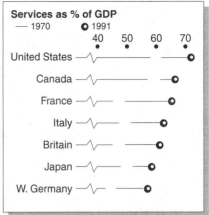

Services as % of GDP

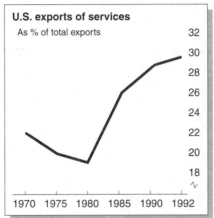

U.S. exports of services

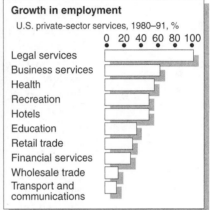

Growth in employment

SOURCE: *The Economist*, February 20, 1994, 20.

21 percent. Even more dramatic declines can be seen in the other two traditional manufacturing nations: in the former West Germany, manufacturing as a percentage of GDP fell from 41 percent in 1970 to 28 percent in 1991, and in Japan the figures show a drop from 36 percent to 29 percent. Yet the idea that an economy cannot survive without relying on manufacturing to create wealth continues to dominate business and political thinking in the West. *The Economist* magazine noted in 1992: "That services cannot thrive without a strong manufacturing 'base' is a claim rarely challenged. The opposite argument—that manufacturing needs services—is hardly ever put."[4]

In fact, the American economy is becoming heavily reliant on services; it is hard to avoid the conclusion that it is services, not manufacturing, that are the real creators of wealth in America. In 1993, services accounted for 74 percent of the American GNP.[5] Services also provide the bulk of employment. In 1900, 30 percent of the United States' workforce was employed in the service sector; by 1984, service industries employed 74 percent of the workforce; and by 1992, that figure had risen to nearly 80 percent. At the same time, the proportion of the workforce engaged in agriculture declined from 42 percent to just 3 percent.[6] In 1948, 20.9 million persons were employed in goods production of all kinds in America, and 27.2 million persons were employed in services; by 1992, employment in goods production was 19.9 million (with no increase in more than two decades), whereas service employment (including wholesale and retail trade and financial services) had risen to 81.1 million, far more than the total number of persons employed in all sectors 30 years earlier.[7]

The service industries not only have grown in size, but they also have absorbed all the jobs shed by traditional industries, such as agriculture, mining, and manufacturing, along the way. The Bureau of Labor Statistics expects service occupations to account for all net job growth through the year 2005. And the same pattern is being repeated in the European Community and Japan. In 1990, services accounted for 58 percent of GDP in Japan and 60 percent of total GDP in the European Community. The service sector employs 133 million persons, or 60 percent of the workforce, in the European Community, whereas industrial employment has declined steadily to 32 percent. Only in Japan has industrial employment continued to increase.[8]

Even these numbers conceal the true contribution of services to economic growth, because service employees on the direct payroll of goods companies are counted as goods industry employees. The service division of IBM, one of the largest worldwide service organizations, is counted as being in the goods, not the service, sector because IBM's core business is computers and electronics. A truer picture can be obtained by looking at the combination of persons employed formally in the services sector—such as independent architectural or accounting firms—and persons employed in the same jobs but working for firms based in goods sectors. Ginzberg and Vojta state that the number of the latter rose from 4.7 million to 12.7 million between 1948 and 1978. They go on to suggest that the value added to the economy by these producer services alone exceeded the value added by all of manufacturing in 1977, and this is without counting the formal service sector and its value.[9]

One of the consequences of this change has been an alteration in the shape of the workforce itself. Ginzberg and Vojta point out how the bulk of new jobs created in the previous 30 years were white-collar jobs, in higher-level professional, technical, administrative, and sales positions. Not all service jobs are necessarily white-collar jobs, but Ginzberg and Vojta contend that, in the United States, as services have replaced goods as the most dominant force in the economy, "human capital" has replaced physical capital as the important source of investment. "Americans must unshackle themselves from the notion," the authors declare, "that goods alone constitute wealth, whereas services are nonproductive and ephemeral. At the same time, they should act on Adam Smith's understanding that the wealth of a nation depends on the skill, dexterity, and knowledge of its people."[10]

Service at the Firm Level

Interest in the problems of marketing in service organizations is growing rapidly. This may be explained in part by rising levels of competition in many parts of the service sector. Services marketing emerged late because of a perceived lack of need for it in times when demand exceeded supply and competitive pressures were few. Now, however, competition is increasing, and consumers are demanding more and better services. Growing sophistication among consumers means that service standards are changing steadily, and there were fears that American service firms were failing to keep up.

American firms—of all kinds, not just pure service firms—face a challenge, in the words of Henkoff, to treat service as "the ultimate strategic imperative, a business challenge that has profound implications for the way we manage our companies, hire employees, develop careers, and craft policies."[11] It seems clear that this challenge is being met. Again, in Henkoff's words, "Product quality is no longer a source of competitive advantage." He cites one American CEO as saying: "Everyone has become better at developing products. The one place you can differentiate yourself is in the service you provide."[12]

There are numerous examples of firms using the "service imperative" to differentiate themselves from the market and to increase profits. In the highly competitive, low-margin auto insurance market, one company, Progressive Corp., has made policyholder service a major part of its competitive strategy. Four years ago, Progressive introduced its Immediate Response Program, in which clients who need to make claims can contact the company at any time of day or night. Progressive representatives make contact with 80 percent of clients who have been involved in accidents within nine hours of the event; sometimes they arrive at the scene of the accident. Most claims are settled in less than one week. Automated claims management systems streamline the process and keep costs down. Customers are impressed by the service, and Progressive's profits are increasing at a rate of 20 percent a year.[13]

It is clear that services in America are no longer manufacturing's poor cousin. Services provide the bulk of the country's wealth and are an important source of employment and exports. American companies have woken up to the potential of using service as a source of competitive advantage, both at home and abroad. There are countless other examples of American firms using the service imperative to drive their businesses forward to profit and growth. And the service boom looks set to continue; it seems likely that by the time the 21st century arrives, there will be no successful business that does not make service the foundation of its competitive strategy.

Within organizations, the growth in the importance of service has been reflected in the changing role of the service department. For an organization that competes on the basis of goods, the service department is a necessary evil. Fixing the computer or the durable represents making good on a failed production promise. As service becomes a source of differentiation, however, it grows in importance. If the premium price of a Xerox machine is justified by the quality of the service, then the importance of the service department becomes much greater.

At some point, the value-added pendulum swings across to emphasize the service over the good. The major computer companies learned a long time ago that the bulk of their profit comes from their after-sales service contracts, not from the sale of the "boxes" themselves. Being in the service department is now the place to be, rather than a punishment as it may once have been. At the extreme of the pendulum's swing, the organization is faced with the choice of becoming a pure service business. Offering service contracts on competitor products finally separates the "box" from the service.

In 1996, GE took on a global servicing contract for Columbia/HCA Healthcare whereby the former would service all the latter's imaging machines and equipment, even those made by GE's competitors. Later, the contract was expanded to include virtually all medical equipment, including many product lines in which GE has no involvement. Service contracts for aircraft engines, power generation plants, and transportation equipment have followed. Says Welch, "We're in the service business to expand our pie." For GE, the switch to emphasizing services is a response to slow growth and tight competition at home and abroad; services represent a way to break the deadlock of a mature market.[14]

What Is a Service?

It is extremely difficult to define a pure good or a pure service. A pure good implies that the consumer obtains benefit from the good alone, without any added value from service; concurrently, a pure service assumes that there is no "goods" element to the service that the customer receives. In reality, most services contain some goods element. At McDonald's, the customer receives a hamburger; the bank provides a bank statement; the garage that repairs cars adds new parts to those cars; and so on. And most goods offer some service—even if it is only delivery.

The goods/service dichotomy is a subtly changing spectrum, with firms moving their position within that spectrum over time.[15] In fact, an exact definition of services is not really necessary to understand services and the marketing problems associated with them. That there are different problems associated with the two is readily apparent; Mills and Moberg describe two factors that set service operations apart from goods operations, namely, differences in process and differences in output.[16] It is probably of greater practical value to focus on these kinds of differences rather than on ultimate definitions. Certainly the line between goods and services can be drawn in different places for different companies. James L. Schorr, who went from Procter & Gamble to be vice president of marketing for Holiday Inns, provides his own rough definition: "Simply defined, in our terms, a product is something a consumer purchases and takes away with him or consumes, or otherwise uses. If it is not physical, not something that they can take away or consume, then we call it a service."[17]

When asked which he was selling in the hotel business, however, Schorr's answer put the goods/service dichotomy firmly in the realms of the theoretical: "What I am really selling, in terms of what people are buying is a hotel experience. I'm selling the room, the way they treat you at the front desk, the way the bellman treats you, the way the waitress treats you—it's all mixed together in a consumer's mind when he makes a hotel decision."[18]

Another good example of a goods/service dichotomy is Domino's Pizza, the national home delivery pizza chain. Domino's sells a product that is clearly visible (and indeed, edible), but an important element in Domino's business was its home delivery service, which originally guaranteed that the customer's pizza would arrive within 30 minutes of the order being placed. Is the customer buying a good or a service? Clearly, in practical terms, he or she is buying both. The service offering, which is what any marketing proposition must consider, is a mix of services and goods.

We still can speak of goods and services, and indeed, this book will continue to use them, but the word *service* should be read with the following caveat: *to the extent that the benefits are delivered to the consumer by a service rather than a good.* As will become apparent when our basic model is developed, there is an implicit assumption made here that service benefits are delivered through an interactive experience involving the consumer to a greater or lesser extent. In real terms, however, it is necessary to remember that the product delivered to the consumer is usually a bundle of benefits that can include, as in the Holiday Inn example above, both goods and services in a variety of combinations.

Classification of Services

Even more contentious than the goods/service dichotomy is the question of classification of services. Classification has a long tradition within science; of all classification systems, perhaps the most powerful is the periodic table of elements developed by Mendeleyev to analyze elements in chemistry. By classifying the properties of the elements, the Russian chemist was able to show that the elements could be organized into groups having common properties. This schematic representation was sufficiently powerful to allow scientists to identify "missing" elements that were later formally discovered. Subsequent developments in atomic physics were able to verify the entire table by using the subatomic characteristics of the individual elements.

Those classifications for services that have emerged so far compare poorly with such a benchmark. Most of these schemes attempt to combine organization with classification, and they are not based on empirically testable properties of services. As with the goods/services dichotomy, they tend to focus on opposites and produce categories such as people-based versus equipment-based (services that are delivered by individuals or by machines), high-contact versus low-contact, individual versus collective. In each set, many examples can be produced that fit cleanly into neither category but are somewhere in the middle.

Too many of these classifications focus on the operational aspect of services and fail to take the marketing problems into account. For example, one traditional dichotomy is that of for-profit versus not-for-profit services. The not-for-profit sector of the economy is huge, particularly if the various levels of government are included, but many not-for-profit organizations share common problems with their for-profit brethren, far more so than with other not-for-profit organizations. For example, a not-for-profit health care chain has more in common with a for-profit health care chain such as Humana than with a government department. Such a distinction is of little value when assessing the marketing problems of the organizations concerned. In fact, virtually all this book is as relevant to not-for-profit organizations as it is to for-profit businesses.

Lovelock argues that classification schemes can only be of value if they offer strategic insights into the services themselves. It is important, he says, for such schemes to highlight the characteristics that certain types of service have in common and to analyze the implications of these common factors for marketing managers. Lovelock suggests that the following questions be asked to determine which category a service fits into:

1. What is the nature of the service act?

2. What type of relationship does the service organization have with its customers?

3. How much room is there for customization and judgment on the part of the service provider?

4. What is the nature of demand and supply for the service?

5. How is the service delivered?[19]

The thrust of Lovelock's argument is that services should be considered not for the factors that set them apart, but for the factors that draw them together. His concern is less to provide an organizational scheme than to provide a series of guidelines for marketing managers. Identifying factors that different types of service have in common helps marketing managers to better understand their products, their organizations, and the relationships their organizations have with their customers.

Recognizing that the products of service organizations previously considered as "different" actually face similar problems or share certain characteristics in common can yield valuable managerial insights. Innovation in marketing, after all, often reflects a manager's ability to seek out and learn from analogous situations in other contexts.[20]

Commonalities rather than differences between services are the focus of this book. Zeithaml, Parasuraman, and Berry sum up four common factors that characterize all services: intangibility, inseparability of production and consumption, heterogeneity, and perishability. Services are said to be intangible because they are performances rather than objects, and they cannot be touched or seen in the same manner as goods; rather, they are experienced, and consumers' judgments about them tend to be more subjective than objective. Inseparability of production and consumption refers to the fact that whereas goods are first produced, then sold, and then consumed, services are sold first and then produced and consumed at one and the same time. A passenger on an airplane first purchases a ticket and then flies, consuming the in-flight service as it is produced. Heterogeneity refers to the potential for variability in the performance of services and problems of lack of consistency that cannot be eliminated in services as they frequently can be with goods. Finally, perishability means that services cannot be saved, unused capacity in services cannot be claimed, and services themselves cannot be inventoried.[21]

The Basic Model

All products, whether goods or services, deliver a bundle of benefits to the consumer. The benefit concept is the encapsulation of these benefits in the consumer's mind. For a detergent brand, such as Tide, that benefit concept might simply be cleaning; the consumer wants clean clothes and buys a product that will achieve this goal. On a more detailed level, this benefit concept might include attributes built into the product that go beyond the powder or liquid itself; extending the benefit concept might produce attributes such as cleanliness, whiteness, or even parenthood. The determination of what constitutes the bundle of benefits purchased by the consumer is at the heart of marketing, and it transcends any distinction between goods and services.

When a consumer purchases a service, he or she purchases an experience created by the delivery of that service. In other words, services deliver a bundle of benefits to the consumer through the experience that is created for that consumer, such as the one created for Rainforest Cafe customers described in Services in Action 1.1. The way in which the consumer receives the benefits package is thus very different for services than for goods. With goods, the benefits package is intimately connected to the actual goods and remains a part of it, generally disappearing once the good has been consumed or is not being used.

With services, however, the different parts of the bundle of benefits can come from a variety of sources at once. The model of the servuction system, shown in Figure 1.2, illustrates this simply and effectively. First, we break the service firm into two parts, that which is visible to the consumer and that which is not. The invisible portions of the firm—the kitchen in a restaurant or the room-cleaning department of a hotel—affect the visible part of the organization, which is, in turn, broken into two parts, the inanimate physical environment in which the service encounter takes place and the contact personnel who actually provide the service.

Finally, the model suggests that customer A, who is purchasing the service, also will be affected by customer B, who is in contact with the service organization at the same time. In practical terms, customers in a restaurant may find their service experience spoiled if other customers are loud or rude; conversely, passengers on an airline may come away with a favorable outlook on the service they have just received if they were sitting next to an interesting fellow passenger who made stimulating conversation and helped pass the time.

The benefits package, therefore, is derived from an interactive process or experience. The visible components of the organization are supported by the invisible components that provide the administration and maintenance of the physical facilities; further, as service usually is delivered to groups of customers simultaneously, benefits are derived from interaction with other customers.

The servuction system model not only shows the different elements of the service experience, but it shows how the service experience as a whole is created. If services are experiences, as has been demonstrated above, then it is inappropriate to speak of delivering them, a term that in some way implies their transportation. The servuction system model, first developed by Langeard and Eiglier, shows how consumers interact with the visible part of the system and with other consumers to create the service experience. The whole of the servuction system creates the experience, and the experience, in turn, creates the benefit to the consumer.[22] Such a simple perspective has profound implications. Looking at the model, a number of conclusions can be drawn about services in general, conclusions that are of direct importance to the problems of services marketing.

Services Cannot Be Inventoried

Perhaps the most far-reaching implication of the servuction system model is that to receive the benefit, the consumer must be part of the system. It is thus impossible to

Rainforest Cafe

The Rainforest Cafe is one of a new genre of restaurant in the United States. Building on earlier concepts such as the Hard Rock Cafe and the Fashion Cafe, described sometimes as "museums with food," the Rainforest Cafe and similar venues offer food as part of an interactive experience.

With an average floorspace of 23,000 square feet, Rainforest Cafe venues feature aquariums, live parrots, a waterfall, a mechanical crocodile, fiberglass monkeys, a video screen, a talking tree, and a regularly timed thunderstorm, complete with lightning. The concept began in the Midwest but has since spread to locations in Florida, Virginia, and Las Vegas.

The environmental theme features strongly in the chain's decor and products. The restaurants make a point of not serving beef from deforested land or fish caught in nets. The talking trees give messages about the environment to customers waiting in line. However, the restaurants place a great deal of focus on their core business, the food, and work to ensure quality in this area. Management believes that no matter how strong the themes are, if the food is not good, the customers will not come back. Currently, the estimate is that about 68 percent of customers are repeat visits, meaning the firm has been successful in this area.

So far, Rainforest Cafes have been located in centers where they are available to large crowds, primarily as attachments to large shopping centers. These high-volume traffic areas are able to generate the traffic the cafes need, in terms not only of number but also of demographic profile.

One important aspect of the Rainforest Cafe concept is that not all its turnover is generated by food sales. Each site also contains a 5,000-square-foot retail space selling merchandise ranging from private-label merchandise such as T-shirts and embroidery to the spices and sauces featured in items on the restaurant menu. About 25 percent of annual sales currently come from these retail units, and that percentage is expected to grow.

inventory services. For example, a British Airways flight from London to New York that leaves this morning has empty seats, whereas the afternoon flights are overbooked. The flight experience of the passengers cannot be moved from morning to afternoon; their decisions to fly at a particular time of day are part of their own decision-making process and are outside the airline's ability to control.

Some service firms find it is possible to inventory part of the service process. McDonald's, for example, can inventory hamburgers for a limited period of time. However, a McDonald's outlet cannot inventory the entire service experience. Spare capacity in the system on a Thursday evening cannot be saved for the Friday evening peak, nor can the hamburgers.

This inability to inventory creates profound difficulties for marketing. In goods, the ability to create an inventory of the good that eventually will be purchased by the consumer means that production and consumption of the good can be separated in time and space. A good can be produced in one locality in the United States and transported for sale in another; a good can be produced in January and not released into the channels of distribution until June. Most services, however, are consumed at the point of production. From a goods-marketing manager's point of view, concerns about when and where the consumer consumes the product are important in understanding consumer behavior and motivation but are largely irrelevant in day-to-day operations.

The existence of inventory also greatly facilitates quality control in goods-producing organizations. Statistical sampling techniques can be used on warehouse stock to select individual items for testing, to the point of destruction if necessary. The sampling process can be set up to ensure minimum variability in the quality of the product released for distribution. Quality control systems also provide numerical targets against which managers can work. It is thus possible for Procter & Gamble to produce tens of millions of packages of Tide that are all essentially identical. James L. Schorr, speaking about the differences between Procter & Gamble and Holiday Inns, notes, "A major difference between product marketing and services marketing is that we can't control the quality of our product line as well as a P&G control engineer on a production line can control the quality of his product. When you buy a box of Tide,

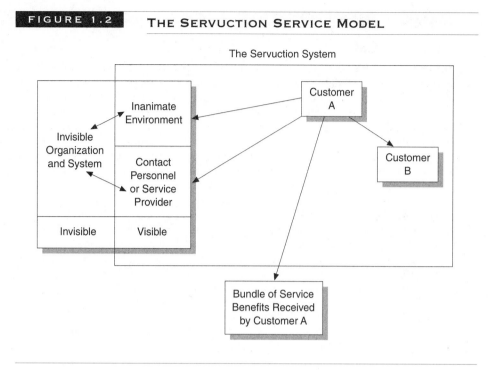

FIGURE 1.2   THE SERVUCTION SERVICE MODEL

you can reasonably be 99 and 44/100 percent sure that the stuff will work to get your clothes clean. When you buy a Holiday Inn room, you're sure at some lesser percentage that it will work to give you a good night's sleep."[23]

Finally, in goods-producing businesses, inventory performs the function of separating the marketing and production departments. In many organizations, stock actually is sold at a transfer price from one department to another. The two parts of the firm have what amounts to a contract on quality and volumes. Once this contract has been negotiated, each department is able to work relatively independently of the other. In service firms, however, marketing and operations constantly are interacting with one another—owing to the inability to inventory the product.

Services Are Time Dependent

In theory, a marketing manager in a service firm does not care when individuals consume a service because they are part of the system while they are consuming it.

The American Automobile Association (AAA) offers a 24-hour roadside emergency service to its members across the United States. Because drivers may have an emergency at any time, the AAA cannot "plan ahead"; service is delivered when the customer asks for it. Nor can Domino's Pizza make and deliver its pizzas ahead of time; service delivery is confined to the narrow space of time between the customer placing the order and the firm's delivery.

In aggregate terms, customers often tend to use a service more frequently at certain peak times. In these cases, generating further customer demand can be more of a disadvantage than an advantage, placing strain on contact staff and resources and creating a poor customer experience through overcrowding of the physical site. Restaurants may experience a rush of customers at lunch time, filling the site to capacity, and then can be nearly empty for the rest of the afternoon; holiday resorts may be booked full in summer and stand empty all winter. One service that suffers especially from this peak time phenomenon is public transit. Transit services in many large cities are full to capacity at morning and evening rush hours, often causing delays due to overcrowding and breaking down of overstressed equipment. For the large part of the middle of the day, however, transit facilities are heavily underused. In these cases, marketing can attempt to move customer demand out of peak times and into slack times. This kind of movement can be very profitable.[24]

Services Are Place Dependent

Where the service experience takes place is also largely dependent on the consumer. The AAA is perhaps an extreme example of this; when a customer calls for roadside emergency service, that service has to be delivered wherever the customer is; the customer cannot move his or her vehicle to a place of the AAA's choosing. Again, Domino's Pizza undertakes to provide a pizza delivered to the place of the customer's choosing, usually a private residence.

All that the service provider can do in each case is to try to ensure that the service operation is widespread enough to cover the areas where service demand is likely.

Even when customers come into a shop or to an airport for service, hence narrowing the geographic focus of the service experience, the service organization still is required to provide products across a variety of locations. McDonald's cannot follow the lead of Ford or Procter & Gamble and build a huge capital-intensive factory to produce 1 billion hamburgers a year in Michigan, because the consumers who want food are scattered all over the world. The huge factory has to be broken up into what Levitt calls "factories in the field."[25] Each service location has to be its own factory, and in the instance of delivered services, such as the AAA's repair service, the factory in the field literally extends down to the scale of the repair person and a van.

Consumers Are Always Involved in the Factory

As the servuction model clearly demonstrates, consumers are an integral part of the service process. Their participation may be active or passive, but their role cannot be ignored. Put simply, the role of the consumer in the factory has four principal ramifications for services marketing.

- If we change the factory, then we have to change consumer behavior.

- If we change the benefit concept, then we have to change the factory.

- Everyone who comes into contact with the consumer is delivering the service.

- Everything that comes into contact with the consumer is delivering the service.

Changes in the Factory Mean Changes in Consumer Behavior

Logically, if changes are made in the factory and the consumer is involved in the factory, then consumer behavior will have to be changed as well. Changes made to the visible part of the service firm at the least will be apparent to the consumer and may affect his or her decision-making and purchasing processes; and frequently, changes will demand that the consumer alter his or her behavior.

Lovelock and Young[26] cite the change from full-service to self-service gas stations as one example of how changes in the factory necessitate changes in consumer behavior. The switch to self-service was made largely for operational reasons, to save on labor costs and to increase profitability, and the gas station owners assumed that by keeping prices down they would continue to attract customers who valued price over service quality. However, the behavioral change required from full-service (wait in the

Domino's Pizza

Domino's Pizza is a pizza delivery chain consisting of about 5,000 stores, based mostly in the United States. About 70 percent of the locations are franchises, nearly all owned by former Domino's employees who purchased with the company's assistance.

Unlike other pizza chains, Domino's has no sit-down restaurant facilities. The target market consists of individuals who are, for one reason or another, unwilling to go out for a meal and prefer to have food delivered to them at a time and place of their choosing. To narrow the market still further, Domino's relies on individuals who prefer pizza to other forms of fast food, and the only thing on the menu besides pizza is soft drinks, breadsticks, and chicken wings. Generally speaking, however, the customers are expecting the service as much as the food itself. To secure its position, Domino's offers delivery within 30 minutes of the time the order is placed, with the customer receiving the pizza free if the delivery takes longer.

The operation is designed to meet this goal. Individual stores are built according to the same design, and simple, efficient internal systems are instituted. Domino's employees fall into five basic categories: drivers, order-takers, pizza-makers, oven-tenders, and routers, the last having responsibility for ensuring that orders and deliveries are correctly matched. The object is to achieve an assembly line-style production, in which the customer is only directly involved at two points, the initial order and the moment of delivery.

If one part of the organization breaks down, then the entire service operation can be in jeopardy. Because of limited customer contact, there is little room for service personnel to attempt to reassure customers or offer them alternative services. If the pizza arrives late, giving away a free product costs the firm money and may not always mollify a hungry customer. The actual delivery process is particularly important because a cooked pizza rapidly grows cold and inedible. Small matters such as finding traffic-free routes to allow drivers to avoid congestion can become crucial to operations.

Establishing this service operation requires strict control, first when establishing the location of a store and determining its service radius and then over employee training, product quality, operations, and routing. Constant monitoring of both customer satisfaction and employees' performance establishes whether the service goal is being met. In 1987, the average delivery time for a Domino's pizza was 23.08 minutes.

car and be warm and comfortable while an attendant pumped the gas) to self-service (get out of the car no matter what the weather and handle a dirty, smelly gas pump) was one that some consumers were not willing to make. To get consumers to accept self-service stations, gas station owners had to make a number of other amendments to the stations, such as better equipment and weather protection. Even so, some consumers still prefer not to use self-service stations.

The involvement of the consumer in the factory is one of the most important aspects of services marketing. Consumer behavior in the service process becomes the core of any marketing analysis. Understanding consumer behavior and consumer decision-making processes is discussed in much greater detail in Chapter 2, but it is important to understand from the very beginning that the experiential nature of services requires a different perspective for consumer behavior. The focus here must be on an understanding of evaluation processes as well as choice processes; theories must address the interactive nature of services and the involvement of the consumer in the production process.

One idea, discussed in more detail in Chapter 2, is that consumers will have a script for frequently used services. That script is analogous to a theatrical script and governs the experience in much the same way. Consumers may have a wide variety of scripts to cover the different kinds of service encounters that they might have in the course of a day: putting gas in the car, eating a meal, buying a ticket and riding on a train, or using operator assistance to make a long-distance telephone call. But although consumers themselves will have different scripts for different services, a group of consumers coming to use the same service will not necessarily have homogeneous scripts.[27] A wide variety of variables can affect the script; clearly changing the factory changes the consumers' script.

Similar examples abound in other services, particularly those where the customer comes to a set location, such as a store or restaurant, to receive service. Changes in the layout of a bank, for example, or in the table arrangement of a restaurant can affect consumers. Banks in particular believe that they can substitute products for personal service, with technological improvements such as automatic tellers; more than half of all Citibank's customers in the New York area say they now no longer have any need to go into the bank to transact their business.[28] In this case, changes in the factory have met with customer approval and the customers have altered their behavior accordingly. However, in the airline industry it has long been known that, in the event of a crash, fatalities can be reduced sharply by having passengers sit facing backward rather than facing forward. But even this simple change in the layout of a service operation can affect passenger behavior, and so far no airline has been able to risk flying aircraft with backward-facing passenger seats.

Changes in the Benefit Concept Mean Changes in the Factory

Changes in the benefit concept mean alterations in the factory for both goods and services. A goods firm might have to change its factory procedures, developing new specifications and retooling to produce a different product. Most of these changes will be invisible to the consumer, who will see only the different benefits package in the finished product. With services, changes in the benefit concept usually mean change in both the visible and invisible parts of the factory.

Shostack cites changes in barbering services through the 1970s as an example of a service becoming both more diverse and more complex. Barbers began adapting techniques borrowed from women's hair salons, transforming themselves into "hair stylists" and offering a broader range of services other than just basic hair cutting. In the process, they tapped into a new market segment—men willing to pay higher prices for a more elaborate service than that offered by old-fashioned barbers.[29] Changing benefits concepts can result in changes to the factory that are off-putting to customers— witness the quiet family restaurant that transforms itself into an upscale cafe, alienating its family customers—but they can also be used to reposition the service operation into a new market.

The relationship between changes in the benefits concept, changes in the factory, and the changes in consumer behavior raise real issues for innovation and for the relationship between marketing and operations in service organizations. Innovation coming from either the factory or the consumer implies major changes in the consumer script, which in turn implies changes for the contact personnel. Trade-offs then have to be made between operational efficiency and marketing effectiveness, a series of choices that is discussed in greater detail in Chapter 3. Strategic changes that are made to increase the efficiency of the operating system often can reduce the quality of the product; part of the marketing challenge is to find ways of improving the efficiency of the servuction system while, at the same time, improving the service experience for customers.

Everyone and Everything That Comes into Contact with the Consumer Is Delivering the Service

The servuction system is a simple model, but identifying that model in practice turns out to be more difficult than it first appears. Many firms underestimate the number of points of contact between them and their customers. Many forget or underestimate the importance of telephone operators or accounting departments. The AAA delivers service principally through its roadside repair persons who come out to repair the stranded motorist's car. But the AAA also has to pay attention to the service offered by its telephone operators, who are the first personnel to come into contact with a frequently agitated motorist, and dispatchers, whom the customer does not see at all but who are responsible for ensuring the repair persons get to the motorist in time.

One way of assessing the level of contact between customers and the service organization is to understand the process through which the organization delivers service to the customers. Chapter 4 describes the key figures in this system, the boundary-spanning personnel who link the customer with the organization and deliver the service. Chapter 5 then looks at the service process in some detail and introduces the use of flowcharts to analyze a service and to create a service blueprint that plugs gaps and controls implementation. Mapping out current levels of customer contact can help show deficiencies in the service organization and point the way toward improvement.[30] Chapter 6 focuses on designing the physical setting of the service firm to be operationally efficient and to add value for the consumer.

Contact Persons Are Products

Just as customers are part of the service process, so contact personnel are part of the experience. Unlike goods, contact personnel are not inanimate objects, and being human, they exhibit variances that cannot be controlled by the service process. The feelings and emotions of contact personnel are apparent to the customer and can affect the service experience for better or for worse.

Robert L. Catlin, a senior vice president with N.W. Ayer ABH International in New York, describes his business as "dealing with something that is primarily provided by people to people. Your people are as much your product in the consumer's mind as any other attribute of that service. People's performance day in and day out fluctuates up and down. Therefore, the level of consistency that you can count on and try to communicate to the consumer is not a certain thing."[31] Surly or unhappy employees can affect the customers with whom they come into direct contact and also can affect other employees. However, a bright, well-motivated employee can create a more pleasant service experience for everyone who comes into contact with that person. Certainly, a large percentage of consumer complaints about service focus on the action or inaction of employees. Critics of service quality have focused on "robotic" responses by staff and on staff who have been trained to use technology but have no training in how to deal with different types of customers.[32]

Contact personnel are frequently in positions that cause personal stress, which adds a further complication to the service process (Chapter 4). Marketing can play a role in this area and can help to ameliorate stress, which can lead to excessive turnover in both staff and customers, and should be involved in discussions about the human resources policies that are used to manage contact personnel (Chapter 7).

Services Cannot Be Quality Controlled at the Factory Gate

One of the most frequently stressed differences between goods and services is the lack of ability to control service quality before it reaches the consumer. Service encounters occur in real time, and consumers already are involved in the factory; if something goes wrong during the service process, it is too late to institute quality control measures before the service reaches the customer. Indeed, the customer or another customer may be part of the quality problem. If, in a restaurant, something goes wrong during a meal, that service experience for a customer is bound to be affected; the manager cannot logically ask the customer to leave the restaurant, reenter, and start the meal over again.

Almost by definition, therefore, it is impossible for a service to achieve 100 percent perfect quality on an ongoing basis. Manufacturing operations also may have problems achieving this sort of target, but they can isolate mistakes and correct them over time, as mistakes tend to be recurring parts of the process. Many errors in service operations are one-time events; in the restaurant above, the waiter who drops a plate creates a technical problem that neither can be foreseen nor corrected ahead of time.

Interestingly enough, such mistakes often can be used to create customer satisfaction by recovering the situation in an excellent fashion. Chapter 12, which discusses service recovery, develops this logic and shows how recovery can become a competitive advantage.

Chapter 14 focuses on the problems of service quality and suggests that the key may be to build quality into all the processes of the firm. Because mistakes cannot be corrected as they occur, the only answer is to attempt to eradicate them at the source. Again, as the consumer is both part of the process and the person who ultimately determines service quality, understanding consumer behavior must be a basic part of the quality process. Service quality is an integrated function, which needs inputs from all parts of the service organization.

A Different Concept of Marketing as an Organizational Function

This chapter has outlined some of the factors that characterize services marketing in general and some of the problems that service marketers face. Marketing, it is clear, plays a very different role in service-oriented organizations than it does in pure goods organizations. The servuction system model shows how closely interwoven the different components of the service organization are; the invisible and visible parts of the organization, the contact personnel and the physical environment, the organization and its customers, and indeed, customers themselves are all bound together by a complex series of relationships.

Accordingly, the marketing department must maintain a much closer relationship with the rest of the service organization than is customary in many goods businesses. The concept of operations being responsible for producing the product and marketing being responsible for selling it, which is starting to disappear in goods firms in any case, cannot work in service firms. Channels of distribution are either very short—from the kitchen to the dining room in our restaurant example—or nonexistent, with production and consumption being simultaneous. Gronroos argues that marketing is a key function in the service sector: "Even if the term marketing is not used in connection with the activities in the buyer/seller interaction, managing these activities is a marketing function."[33] The role of marketing in the service firm is discussed in more detail in Chapter 15.

Sequence of the Book

This book is divided into three parts. Part I covers the basic building blocks of services marketing, key concepts that need to be understood before going on to consider the management of the service experience in Part II. Part III takes a broader perspective and considers the various ways service firms try to create competitive advantage.

Part I: The Basic Building Blocks

The next three chapters focus on the services consumer, the services operation, and the service provider. The consumer is, of course, important, and it is vitally necessary to understand the consumer and to gain insights into consumer behavior. The second is equally important because, in services, the operation is the product. It is therefore important to understand the needs of the operation as well as the needs of the consumer. Every company faces a trade-off between consumer needs, technology, and economics, but the servuction system model implies that this trade-off is more pronounced for service firms. If the provider is the product, then a deep understanding of the role and motivation of service employees is a necessary building block.

Chapter 2, "Understanding the Service Consumer," builds on the experiential nature of the service product to suggest that a number of emerging theories may provide additional insights into the consumer choice and evaluation processes. These include the dramaturgical perspective as well as role theory and script theory. The perceived control theory, which suggests that, in any situation, individuals like to feel in control, is also discussed.

Chapter 3, "Understanding the Service Operation," then turns to the perspective of operations management and seeks to determine the requirements for an efficient operation. These requirements are compared with the operational demands of services, a comparison that allows the identification of several major threats to operational efficiency. Several concepts and theories that have been developed in operations management to overcome these problems are described. Throughout this chapter, the emphasis is on understanding the service operation and on coming to terms with its interdependence with marketing.

Chapter 4, "Understanding the Service Worker," looks at the final element of the service experience, the service provider. This chapter discusses the key role that the service provider can play, not only as part of an operation, but as an individual. However, such roles are extremely stressful because they are boundary-spanning roles, bridging the gap between the environment and the firm. The role stress and conflict caused by boundary spanning are described, as are the strategies adopted by contact personnel to overcome that stress.

Part II: Configuring the Service Firm

The five chapters in this section describe the service marketing mix, the variables available to the firm to manage the service experience. "Product policy" issues discussed in Chapters 5, 6, and 7 include the configuration of the operation, the physical environment, and the personnel who provide the service. The complexity of the service product is one of the key differentiating features of service marketing, as the creation of a real-time experience poses many problems that differ significantly from the problems arising from the creation of a mere physical good.

Chapter 5, "The Service Operation," focuses on the configuration of the operating system. Starting from the strategy or policy level, it uses a modified version of the manufacturing strategy paradigm to set the parameters of a service strategy. These can then be put into operation using processes, flowcharting, and process reengineering as a framework.

Chapter 6, "The Physical Setting," focuses on the creation of the physical setting characteristic of many services. It moves from an operational to a marketing perspective. Operationally, the physical setting provides the infrastructure in which the operation itself takes place. The marketing perspective is much richer and draws on environmental psychology to suggest how the physical setting can support the benefit concept.

Chapter 7, "The Service Employees," looks at the human resources policies of the service firm as being the key means of influencing the service provider. In particular, it looks at two emerging issues, empowerment and enfranchisement. Varying degrees of empowerment have been shown to be highly motivating for service providers. In the retail area, firms such as Nordstrom have combined empowerment with payment by results to enfranchise their employees.

Chapters 8 and 9 cover the problems of service communications strategy and service pricing. In these chapters, there is a sizeable overlap with existing models and theories in marketing. The emphasis in these chapters is on the unique characteristics of the service communications and pricing processes and how these influence the service experience. Chapter 8, "Communications Strategy," shows how the management of expectations is crucial to service communications and how misdirected communications can have a noticeable effect on services and on customers. Communications, moreover, can be aimed at employees as well as external customers. Chapter 9, "Service Pricing Policy," focuses on the three characteristics of services that affect pricing: the nature of service costs, time-dependent capacity, and the role of the customer as part of the process.

Part III: Competing as a Service Firm

This section of the book refocuses on the potential sources of competitive advantage for the service firm. The topics covered include the competition for space or sites as firms spread geographically and internationally; this section discusses the role of franchising in this type of competition. Competition to attract different consumer segments to the same service site and competition by offering more services through the same sites are also covered in Chapter 10, "Competing as a Service Firm: Generic Competitive Strategies." This chapter also provides an overview for other chapters in this section.

Customer satisfaction as a service strategy is discussed in Chapter 11, "The Customer Satisfaction System." It suggests that the measurement of customer satisfaction is not enough. It is important also to create an economic justification for investment in satisfaction and a system to understand and manage the factors that drive satisfaction.

A competitive strategy based on service recovery is described in Chapter 12, "Service Recovery." No service business can deliver 100 percent of the time. Failure, however, can be turned to advantage if correct recovery plans are in place. Enhanced levels of customer satisfaction often can be the result. Chapter 13, "The Customer Retention System," then focuses on customer retention as a service strategy.

Service quality as a way of competing has been a popular topic in the past three to five years. A successful quality program touches every part of the organization and can have a profound effect on consumers. Chapter 14, "Competing as a Service Firm: Service Quality," describes a service quality model and shows how it can be applied.

Finally, Chapter 15, "Competing as a Service Firm: Building a Customer-Focused Service Organization," takes up the question of building customer focus into service organization as a way of competing. This chapter discusses how marketing often can be sidelined in service businesses and goes on to outline the actions necessary to reestablish customer focus.

Notes

[1] See Dorothy I. Riddle (1986), "Service-Led Growth," International Trade 1991/92 (Westpoint, CT: Praeger, 1993); GATT publication. GATT acknowledge that it is difficult to estimate precisely the total value of the service production worldwide as some countries do not report statistics on many service items and many service transactions are not registered; the real figure is probably well over $1,000 billion.

[2] Ibid.

[3] *International Trade 1991/92* (1993).

[4] *The Economist*, February 20, 1992.

[5] See Ronald Henkoff, "Service Is Everybody's Business," *Fortune*, June 27, 1994, 26–31.

[6] See Peter Mills, *Managing Service Industries* (Cambridge, MA: Ballinger, 1986), 3.

[7] *Statistical Abstract of the United States, 1993.*

[8] Sernos, *Annual Statistics 1990, Eurostat, 1993.*

[9] Eli Ginzberg and George J. Vojta, "The Service Sector of the U.S. Economy," *Scientific American* 244, no. 3 (March 1981): 31–39.

[10] Ibid.

[11] Henkoff, "Service Is Everybody's Business," 26.

[12] Ibid., 27.

[13] Ibid.

[14]"Jack Welch's Encore: How GE's Chairman Is Remaking His Company—Again," *Business Week*, October 28, 1996, 43–50.

[15]The idea of a goods/service spectrum has existed for many years (see John M. Rathmell, *Marketing in the Services Sector* [Cambridge, MA; Winthrop, 1974] and Lynn G. Shostack, "Breaking Free from Product Marketing," *Journal of Marketing* 41 (April 1977): 73–80. In fact, any attempt to define this spectrum leads to more examples that are exceptions than that fit the rule.

[16]Peter K. Mills and Dennis J. Moberg, "Perspectives on the Technology of Service Operations," *Academy of Management Review* 7, no. 3 (1982): 467–478.

[17]Gary Knisely, interviewing James L. Schorr in *Advertising Age*, January 15, 1979, 10–13.

[18]Ibid.

[19]Christopher H. Lovelock, "Classifying Services to Gain Strategic Marketing Insights," *Journal of Marketing* 47 (Summer 1983): 9–20.

[20]Ibid.

[21]Valarie A. Zeithaml, A. Parasuraman, and Leonard L. Berry, "Problems and Strategies in Services Marketing," *Journal of Marketing* 49 (1985): 33–46. The authors include a review of previous literature on the characteristics of services.

[22]The servuction system model originally was developed by Eric Langeard and Pierre Eiglier in an article published in a French journal. More detailed descriptions of the model appear in E. Langeard, J. Bateson, C. Lovelock, and P. Eiglier, *Marketing of Services: New Insights from Consumers and Managers*, report 81-104 (Cambridge, MA: Marketing Sciences Institute, 1981) and in Pierre Eiglier and Eric Langeard, *Servuction* (Paris: McGraw Hill, 1987), Chap. 1.

[23]Knisely, *Advertising Age*, 12.

[24]Langeard et al., "Marketing of Services."

[25]Theodore Levitt, "Production-Line Approaches to Services," *Harvard Business Review* 50, no. 5 (September–October 1972): 41–52.

[26]Christopher H. Lovelock and Robert F. Young, "Look to Consumers to Increase Productivity," *Harvard Business Review* (May–June 1979): 168–178.

[27]Michael R. Solomon, Carol Surprenant, John A Czepiel, and Evelyn G. Gutman, "A Role Theory Perspective on Dyadic Interactions: The Service Encounter," *Journal of Marketing* 49 (Winter 1985): 99–111.

[28]Stephen Koepp, "Pul-eeze! Will Somebody Help Me?" *Time*, February 2, 1987, 28–34.

[29]G. Lynn Shostack, "Service Positioning through Structural Change," *Journal of Marketing* 51 (January 1987): 34–43. Shostack's ideas are discussed in more detail in Chapter 5.

[30]Shostack, "Breaking Free."

[31]Knisely, *Advertising Age*, 11.

[32]Koepp, "Pul-eeze."

[33]Christian Gronroos, "Designing a Long-Range Marketing Strategy for Services," *Long-Range Planning* 13 (1980): 36–42.

2

Understanding
the Service Consumer

Chapter Overview

The heart of the marketing concept lies in consumer orientation. As marketers, we are required to understand our consumers and to build our organizations around them. This requirement is particularly important for services, which in the past have tended to be operations dominated rather than marketing led.

Today, it is more important than ever to understand consumers and to understand how consumers choose between alternative services offered to them and how they evaluate these services once they have received them. Understanding the link between choice and evaluation processes is particularly important, as satisfied customers are necessary for repeat business.

The Three-Stage Model of Services Consumer Behavior

To market services effectively, marketing managers need to understand the thought processes used by consumers during each of the three stages of purchase: the prepurchase choice between alternatives, the consumers' reactions during consumption, and the postpurchase evaluation of satisfaction. In the first stage, the objective is to understand why a consumer chooses to use a particular service or service outlet. In the second stage, it is necessary to understand consumers' reactions to the interactive process; and, in the last stage, we need to understand the sources of customer satisfaction or dissatisfaction.

The Prepurchase Stage

The prepurchase stage refers to all consumer activities occurring before the acquisition of the service. This stage begins when an individual realizes a need or problem. The recognition of a problem demands a solution from the individual, and it usually implies a potential purchase. The individual then searches for relevant information from both internal and external sources, arrives at a set of solutions to the recognized problem, and, finally, selects the option that he or she considers to be most satisfactory.

For example, consider a consumer trying to decide which restaurant to go to for lunch. The first question to be considered might be "What is the occasion?" It is often possible to segment consumers into homogeneous groups based on the occasion of the purchase. Clearly, in our example, the choice of restaurant will be different if our consumer is planning to eat alone and in a hurry rather than have a business lunch with colleagues and a client. Often, the same individuals who eat in McDonald's at lunch eat in a French restaurant in the evening.

Once the occasion for a meal has been specified, the next question becomes "Which restaurants are on the list?" Similar questions can be posed for other services. For banking, this question might become "Which banks in which locations are on the list?" It is clear that in all consumer decision making, consumers seldom consider all feasible alternatives. Instead, they have a limited list of options chosen on the basis of past experience, convenience, and knowledge. This list often is referred to by theorists as the evoked set—the set of "brands" that will be evoked by the consumer and from which the choice will be made.

Even if the occasion and the evoked set have been specified, the consumer still has to choose from that set a specific restaurant to go to for lunch. We can never truly know the thought process used by the individual when making that choice. As discussed later, however, we need a model on which to structure our thinking and to guide our market research.

The Consumption Stage

An important outcome of the prepurchase stage is a decision to buy a certain brand of the service category. This decision is accompanied by a set of expectations about the performance of the product. In the case of goods, the consumer then uses the product and disposes of any solid waste remaining. The activities of buying, using, and disposing are grouped together and labeled as the consumption process.[1]

For services, this stage is more complex. The servuction system concept introduced in Chapter 1 suggests that the benefits bought by a customer consist of the experience that is delivered through an interactive process. Even when a service is rendered to an individual's possession (e.g., auto repair) rather than to the individual's person, the service production/consumption process often involves a sequence of personal interactions (face-to-face or by telephone) between a customer and a service provider.[2]

Furthermore, interactions between the customer and the company's facilities and personnel are also inevitable. It is from these interpersonal and human–environment interactions that the service experience is acquired. "Differences in kind"[3] between the services and goods-purchasing processes can be attributed largely to this extended client–company interface.

Perhaps the most important outcome of the consumption stage is the contradiction of the idea that postchoice evaluation occurs only at a certain point in time after use.[4] The use of goods is virtually free from any kind of direct marketer influences. An individual customer can choose when, where, and how he or she will use a good. However, service firms play an active role in the customer consumption activities because services are produced and consumed simultaneously. No service can be produced or used with either the customer or the service firm absent. Due to the extended service delivery process, some authors have hypothesized that postchoice evaluation occurs both during and after, rather than just after, the use of services. Customers evaluate the service while they are interacting with the service provider.

From a marketer's point of view, this opens up the prospect of being able to influence that evaluation directly. The restaurant manager who visits diners' tables and asks, "How is the meal?" is able to catch problems and change evaluations in a way that the manufacturer of a packaged good never could.

Postpurchase Evaluation

Customer satisfaction is the key outcome of the marketing process. It is an end in itself, but it is also the source of word-of-mouth recommendations and thus can stimulate further purchases. As discussed later, there is considerable evidence to suggest that buying service represents a major risk to the consumer, and this makes word-of-mouth recommendation very valuable. But how is this satisfaction created? Several approaches have been suggested, but perhaps the simplest and most powerful is the disconfirmation of expectations model. The concept of this model is straightforward. Consumers evaluate services by comparing the service they perceive they have received with their expectations. If the perceived service is equal to or better than the expected service, then the consumer is satisfied.

It is crucial to point out that this entire process takes place in the mind of the consumer. It is perceived service that matters, not the actual service. Once this simple idea is established, two subsidiary questions emerge: What is it that drives expectations, and what is it that drives perceptions?

What Is It That Drives Expectations? The nature and source of expectations have been the subject of much recent theoretical and empirical research. Current thinking discriminates between many different standards. In Figure 2.1, Zeithaml et al.[5] focus on customer expectations. Expectations, it is clear, come in various forms: There are

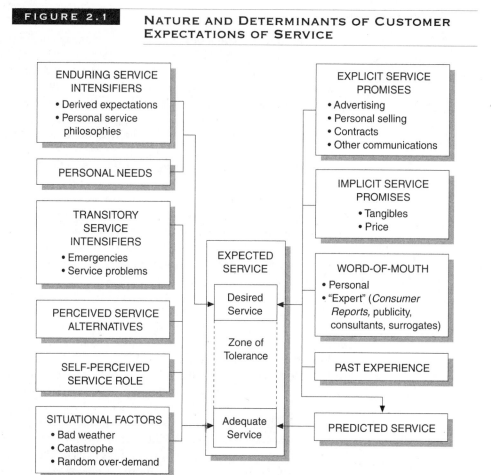

FIGURE 2.1   NATURE AND DETERMINANTS OF CUSTOMER EXPECTATIONS OF SERVICE

SOURCE: Adapted from V. Zeithaml, L. Berry, and A. Parasuraman, "The Nature and Determinants of Customer Expectations of Service," *Journal of the Academy of Marketing Science*, Winter 1993, 1–12.

expectations as predictions (what benefits do I think I will receive if I purchase this service?), expectations as ideals (what, in a perfect world, would I like to receive as benefits from this service?), expectations based on experience (what, given what I already know about this brand or service, am I likely to receive?), minimum tolerable expectations (what is the least I can expect from purchasing this service?), deserved expectations (what benefits am I likely to receive given the investment I have put into making this purchase?), comparative expectations (having experienced other similar services, what can I now expect from this service?), and so on.

Further, the expectation process is a complex one, and it is entirely possible, even likely, that more than one form of expectation will be functioning simultaneously. A customer going into a restaurant for a hasty meal may well have an expectation of what quality of meal he or she is going to receive (expectation as prediction). However, the customer may also be aware that the food or service in this restaurant is of lesser quality than what he or she would ideally like (expectation as ideal). This may be based on previous meals at this restaurant (expectation based on experience) or on a meal at another restaurant in this particular chain (comparative expectation). Therefore, the decision to eat here may be based on factors such as value for money (deserved expectation) and an assurance that at least the place will be comfortable and the food edible (minimum tolerable expectation).

Based on these varying types of expectation, Zeithaml and colleagues concluded that customers assess service performance by using two standards.[6] First, there is the level of service they desire, what might be called maximum acceptable service; second, there is the level of service that they deem adequate, what might be called minimum acceptable service. In between these, there is what they call the "zone of tolerance," not quite perfect but acceptable in circumstances. Of course, circumstances can change; further, not only will different customers have different levels of desired and acceptable service, but the same customer will have different levels for different services. A gourmand not interested in fashion will set the levels of desired and acceptable service far higher when buying a meal than when getting a haircut, for example. The zone of tolerance can therefore be seen to be both variable between customers and fluctuating according to customer purchases. A final point to be noted is that the desired or maximum service level often remains relatively fixed, whereas the adequate or minimum level rises and falls according to customer circumstances (a restaurant customer wanting a quick lunch will set a lower standard of adequate service than will the same customer wanting a romantic candlelit dinner).

Desired service levels are ultimately set by personal needs and wants. These in turn can stem from a variety of social, physical, and psychological sources. An obvious example is the needs of shoppers in wheelchairs to have access to ramps to enter stores. Less obvious examples might be the desire of a restaurant customer to have a quiet background in which to enjoy the food, the need by a customer at a hairdresser to have a hair style that will exactly fit their own self-image, or the need of a grocery store shopper to buy only organic fruit and vegetables. At all events, it is the person's personal circumstances and outlooks that go to formulate the desired service levels.

However, desired service levels can be increased by what Zeithaml et al. call "enduring service intensifiers."[7] These are factors that lead customers to be more than usually sensitive to a particular service. One example is service customers who are also service providers. These can be found in industrial and professional services and tend to demand very high service levels, as this affects in turn the service they provide their own customers. Customers may also have personal service philosophies, particularly if they have personal experience of working in the service sector in question; restaurant owners, food critics, wine writers, and so on will tend to have higher desired service levels when eating out than will ordinary diners.

Adequate service levels, however, are influenced by five factors. Zeithaml et al. define these as transitory service intensifiers, perceived service alternatives, customer self-perceived service roles, situational factors, and predicted service.[8]

Transitory service intensifiers are short-term factors that temporarily raise the minimum acceptable level of service. They are typically associated with crises or emergencies. When the family car breaks down on holiday, the customer typically needs the car to be repaired much more quickly, to avoid wasting precious holiday time, than when at home when alternatives such as public transport may be available.

Perceived service alternatives can either raise or lower the minimum standard. Take the restaurant customer described above. If he or she is standing in a street full of many busy cafes and diners, there is likely to be a perception that at least some of these will be serving good food; expectations go up, and the customer becomes more choosy about which service offering to accept. If there is only one cafe, however, and time is limited, the customer is more likely to settle for less; the only alternative then would be to go hungry.

The self-perceived service role defines the extent to which customers are aware that they too are part of the servuction process. For example, customers are often aware that the quality of the service they get depends to some degree on their own attitude toward the service provider personnel; being polite and friendly to a bank teller will usually be rewarded with better service than shouting or pounding one's fist on the counter. Customers may also be aware that they need to define their needs carefully and let the providers know exactly what they want. Awareness that they have failed to carry out their own role may lead customers to accept a lower level of service ("It's my fault, I should have told the waiter what I wanted"); whereas conversely, awareness that they have fulfilled their own roles can lead customers to raise their levels of expectation ("I said very clearly that I wanted the steak medium rare").

Situational factors represent circumstances in which the customer is aware that there are problems beyond the service provider's ability to control. In effect, these can be seen as the opposite of temporary service intensifiers; they are critical or crisis situations in which the provider is unable to fulfil the normal offering, and they lead customers to temporarily lower their minimum level of expectation. Generally, situational factors must be clearly understandable by the customer. An airline that delays a flight because a member of the crew has not reported for duty will be regarded much less favorably than one that delays a flight because of unforeseen mechanical problems with the aircraft.

Finally, there is the level of predicted service. As noted above, customers to some extent set their level of desired service according to the standard of service they believe they are likely to get. In other words, customers consciously try to adapt their expectations to their previously performed perceptions of the service offering. Their ability to do this is obviously limited by their own experience of this particular service and their knowledge of the services on offer. Customers are much better able to predict service when they are in familiar places, a fact that influences the service offerings of firms in the travel and tourism sectors. In general, high levels of predicted service result in high levels being established for minimum acceptable service and a correspondingly narrow zone of tolerance.

This leads us to the importance of the service promise, that is, the level of service that the provider promises to deliver to the customer. These come in two forms: explicit (formal statements about the service delivered through media such as advertising) and implicit (signals about service quality sent through factors such as the appearance of the shop or restaurant). Evaluation of the service offering is also affected by word-of-mouth communication from friends, family, and others who have used the service in the past and the customer's own past experience with the service. The whole picture is described by Zeithaml et al. as follows: "A positive relationship exists between levels of past experience with a service and the levels of desired service and predicted service."[9]

What Is It That Drives Perceptions?   The nature of service perceptions, in turn, is driven not merely by the technical quality of the service. Technical quality is important and can be thought of as the reality that is measurable using a stopwatch or television camera. It is the real and objective world in which the operations personnel of the service firm operate. Unfortunately, it is the consumers' perceptions of that reality that are crucial. Waiting time in a bank may well have been reduced by 30 seconds, but there is no reason why consumers should perceive the difference when past experience may have shown them that there is always a long wait. Further, the staff members may be surly and rude, and this will be reflected in the perception of service time. Many things can interfere with the perception.[10]

Many factors can influence a consumer's perceptions of service, including most of those hypothesized to influence expectations: word of mouth, advertising, and past experience. To these must be added the full complement of the servuction system. The dress and behavior of the contact personnel, the physical environment, and the other customers are all bound to have an impact on how the service experience is perceived (see Chapters 6 and 7).

As noted earlier, the consumption of goods can be divided into three activities: buy, use, and dispose. The three activities occur in a definite buy-use-dispose order and have clear boundaries between them. The customer buys a box of detergent at a

Riverside Methodist Hospital

Hospitals are unique among service providers in that they provide services that most individuals need but not everyone necessarily wants. Relatively few persons use the services of a hospital out of pure choice.

A number of factors set hospitals apart. In the first place, levels of risk are higher; a poor service choice can endanger health or life, not just create an unpleasant impression of the experience. Second, because many patients lack proper knowledge about how a hospital functions and the nature of the treatment they are receiving, even a merely unpleasant service experience can be genuinely frightening.

Riverside Methodist Hospital in Columbus, Ohio, is a part of U.S. Health Corporation, a small for-profit hospital chain. A key part of Riverside's competitive strategy revolves around changing the image of the hospital and the service experience in the eyes of patients and potential patients. Reducing the patient's sense of inferiority changes the nature of patient evaluation of the experience before, during, and after the hospital visit.

Understanding patient demands is an important part of this strategy. First, not all patients are the same, and the needs of different groups can contain important variables. For example, the presence of a large Honda automobile plant nearby means that the hospital regularly takes in Japanese-speaking patients and visitors. On a different scale, Riverside Methodist has developed the Elizabeth Blackwell Centre, a separate facility dealing specifically with women's needs for health care.

Once patients are in the hospital, the principal objective is to reduce patient anxiety and insecurity. The physical facilities of the hospital, the attitude and demeanor of nursing and medical staff, and the perceived quality and frequency of care can all have an impact, as can more peripheral factors such as frequency and duration of family visits to patients. The question is not one of improving patient care but of improving patient perception of care by making an otherwise unpleasant experience as comfortable as possible.

---

supermarket, uses it at home in the washing machine, and disposes of the empty box after the detergent is used up.

This scenario does not apply to the consumption of services, however. First of all, there does not exist a clear-cut boundary or definite sequence between acquisition and use of services because there is no transfer of ownership. Because of the prolonged interactions between the customer and the service provider, the production, acquisition, and use of services often become entangled and appear as a single process.[11] Furthermore, the concept of disposition is obviously irrelevant because of the intangibility and experiential nature of services.

In short, the postchoice evaluation of services is a complex process. It begins soon after the customer makes the choice of the service firm he or she will be buying and continues throughout the consumption and postconsumption stages. The evaluation is influenced by the unavoidable interaction of a substantial number of social, psychological, and situational variables. Service satisfaction relies not only on the properties of the four elements of the servuction system—contact personnel, physical support and environment, clients, and internal organization system—but also on the synchronization of these elements in the service production/consumption process.

The success or failure of a service firm can be at least partly attributed to management's ability or inability to manipulate the customer experience as the output of a collection of interpersonal interactions (client versus client, client versus employee) and human–environment interactions (employee versus working environment and supporting facilities, customer versus service environment and supporting facilities).

Models of Consumers' Decision-Making Process

In both the prepurchase choice and postconsumption evaluation, the consumer must be using a process or model to make his or her decision. There are many versions of those models, but it is important to point out before going further that no model is wholly correct. The consumer's mind is still closed to us; it is a "black box" that remains sealed. We can observe inputs to the box and decisions taken as a result, but we never can know how the process truly happens.

Why then bother with such models? The problem remains that the heart of marketing is consumer orientation. Whether marketing managers like it or not, every time they make marketing decisions they are basing them on some model of how the consumer will behave. Often these models are implicit and seldom are shared with others, representing in effect the marketing manager's own experience. However, every time a price is changed, a new product is launched, or advertising is shown, some assumption has been made about how the consumer will react.

Models therefore are needed as a way of structuring marketing decisions. They may not be totally real, but many are the result of much research in marketing and psychology and they allow us at least to make logical deductions about consumer behavior when making marketing decisions. Models also can provide frameworks and formats for the structuring of market research, which is the core of the marketing process.

Because all the perspectives described here have both strengths and weaknesses, they therefore should be considered as complementary rather than mutually exclusive. Some, such as the risk-taking perspective and the multiattribute model, are more relevant to the prepurchase choice process. Others are more powerful when trying to understand customer satisfaction: These include the control and script theory models. Managerial insights can be developed more effectively through a combination of these various perspectives.

The Consumer as a Risk Taker

The concept of perceived risk as an explanation for customer purchasing behavior was first suggested in the 1960s.[12] The central theory is that consumer behavior involves risk in the sense that any action of a consumer will produce consequences that he or she cannot anticipate with any certainty, and some of which are likely to be unpleasant. Bauer, who first suggested this idea, proposed that perceived risk is actually composed of two structural dimensions:

Consequence, the degree of importance and/or danger of the outcomes derived from any consumer decision.

Uncertainty, the subjective possibility of occurrence of these outcomes.

As the idea was developed, four types of perceived risk were identified based on four different kinds of outcomes: financial, performance, physical, and social.[13] Performance risk relates to the idea that the item or service purchased will not perform the task for which it was purchased. Financial risk assumes there may be financial costs if the purchase goes wrong or fails to operate. The physical risk of a purchase can emerge if something does go wrong and injury is inflicted on the purchaser. Social risk suggests that there might be a loss of personal social status associated with a particular purchase (a fear that one's peer group will react negatively, e.g., "Who bought this?")

Several authors have shown that services have a higher perceived risk of purchase than goods, for several reasons. Much already has been made of the fact that it is extremely difficult to standardize the service product.[14] Because a service is an experience involving highly complex interactions, it is not surprising that it is very difficult to replicate the experience from customer to customer or from day to day. As a result of this, however, the customer may find that it is difficult to predict precisely the quality of the service he or she will be buying. The fact that Brown's Auto Repair shop did a good tune-up for your neighbor does not mean it will perform to the same level for you. Perceived risk, therefore, may be high.

Other authors have argued that the higher risk level is due to the very limited information available before the purchase decision is made. Parasuraman, Zeithaml, and Berry,[15] for example, draw on economics literature to suggest three different properties of goods and services:

- Search attributes are those that can be evaluated before purchase.

- Experience attributes are those that cannot be evaluated until after a service has been received.

- Credence attributes are those that cannot be evaluated confidently, even immediately after receipt.

Because of the nature of services, it is often extremely difficult for consumers to evaluate a service objectively before it is bought. Services thus have very low search attributes. Rather, a large proportion of the properties of the service (how friendly are the air hostesses and hosts of a particular airline?) can only be discovered by consumers after the consumption of the service and are thus experience attributes. Finally, some of the properties of many services (how well a car has been repaired by the garage) may not be assessed even after the service is completed and are thus credence attributes.

The involvement of the consumer in the "production process" of services is another source of increased perceived risk. Unlike goods, which can be purchased and taken away, services cannot be taken home and used in private where the buyer's mistakes will not be visible. Instead, the consumer must take part in the ritual of the service itself. To be part of such a process and not to know exactly what is going on clearly increases the uncertainty about the consequences, particularly the social consequences of doing the wrong thing.

Risk-Reduction Strategies for Consumer Services

If we start from the premise that consumers do not like taking risks, then it would seem obvious that they will try when possible to reduce risk during the purchase process. Much research has been done on how consumers will attempt to reduce high perceived risk.

One strategy is for a consumer to be brand or store loyal; having been satisfied in one high-risk purchase, consumers are less likely to experiment with others. This is an obvious trade-off between the risk inherent in returning to one possibly uncertain service business and the even greater risk of trying something new.

Research also has shown that, in the area of communications, word-of-mouth references often take on increased importance over company-controlled communication. A reference from a friend becomes more important when the purchase to be made has a greater risk. For example, a visit to a new hairdresser can be stressful because the outcome of the service will be highly visible. That stress can be reduced by a prior recommendation from someone whose judgment the consumer trusts. The consumer then will feel more confident about the outcome. Murray empirically tests these ideas and shows that consumers do use different information search procedures for goods and services.[16] This provides the basis of the discussion of services communications strategies (see Chapter 8).

Similarly, there is some evidence to suggest that opinion leaders play an important role in the purchase of services. An opinion leader in a community is an individual who is looked up to for advice. Within the perceived risk framework, an opinion leader can be viewed as a source of reduced social risk. The consumer, referred to above, who visited a hairdresser for the first time may feel uncertain about the quality of the

Fidelity Investments

Fidelity Investments is a high-volume investment house that, since 1986, has offered a toll-free telephone dealing service on a 24-hour, 7-days-a-week basis. Fidelity's basic operation revolves around providing information about certain investment products to its customers and potential customers and then inviting them to purchase those products either by telephone or in person through Fidelity's network of offices.

Many of Fidelity's clients are individuals with money to invest in stocks or other investment products. They themselves lack the time and facilities, particularly the technology, to monitor the markets and make buying decisions. Fidelity provides that service for them and with the service comes a form of security for the customer, who knows that his or her investment funds are in safe hands. In effect, Fidelity does the job the customer cannot do him- or herself.

Fidelity's position is that it has no direct control over the products it sells but can only configure them into packages that make them more desirable to customers. Part of that package is the service that Fidelity itself can offer. For investment customers, factors such as accurate information, instant communications, and investment security are of prime importance.

To meet the first two demands, Fidelity has invested heavily in systems, including automated telephone services, computerized information management, dealing support for customers who use home computers, and even telecommunications devices for the deaf. The basic telephone dealing service offers fast service, promising that the telephone will be answered within three rings and connection at all times to a licensed dealer who can provide information and arrange trades. The Black Friday stock market crash of October 1987 changed the nature of the service operation. Whereas the telephone system normally logged 80,000 to 100,000 calls per day, by the end of that particular day nearly 600,000 calls had been logged. In this case, Fidelity's customers suddenly perceived the risk to their investments to be much higher and equated security with direct communications with the investment firm. Customer expectations and perceptions had changed overnight. The problem for Fidelity Investments on Black Friday became one of adapting its existing service operations to provide a different, more intense service experience.

outcome. However, the consumer may be reassured by the fact that the friend who recommended the service is well known to have good judgment in such matters and will tell others in his or her social group this fact. In this way, the opinion leader's judgment partially substitutes for the consumer's own.

Risk-Reduction Strategies for Industrial and Professional Services

Several authors have used the risk idea to study the purchase of industrial services. Their approach is summarized in Table 2.1. This model considers the risk-reduction strategies available through reducing uncertainty and/or consequences. The vertical axis focuses on how the reduction of uncertainty or consequences is to occur, breaking it down into sources internal to the firm and those that are external.

Minimizing uncertainty requires the collection of information. That information can come from both inside and outside the organization. Information can be of a general nature, such as an appraisal of a "general reputation," or as specific as a reference from a current user of the service.

Strategies for reducing consequence also can involve internal and external approaches. External reduction of consequences is relatively straightforward. It can involve, for example, the minimization of the financial consequences by making financial purchases small. This implies trials and pilot projects for professional service firms. Such a strategy also can be thought of as one of the key reasons for using multiple sources, because in this way the consequences of the failure of any one supplier is minimized.

The reduction of consequences internally can be used as an explanation of the buying committee or decision-making unit (DMU). This unit often consists of a for-

TABLE 2.1	RISK-REDUCTION STRATEGIES FOR INDUSTRIAL AND PROFESSIONAL SERVICES	
	Uncertainty	**Consequences**
External	Reputation	Pilot projects
	Advertising	Investigations
	References	
	Articles	
Internal	Past experiences	The decision-making unit

mal or informal committee involved in the purchase of goods or services in organizations. The rational explanation for the emergence of such committees is the need to assemble interested parties with relevant information or expertise. Users need to be involved, as do engineering, finance, and other relevant departments within the firm.

From the risk perspective, however, a different explanation can be hypothesized. It is the committee, or DMU, that makes the decision, and therefore it suffers the consequences of a bad decision. An individual DMU member, if necessary, can deny involvement in the decision or at least claim that involvement was only minor. Alternatively, each member of the committee, in turn, can claim, for example, that they wanted to buy professional services from firm X but were overruled when the service of firm Y was contracted.

Recognizing this risk perspective, it is important for the supplier to offer as many opportunities as possible for the client to reduce risk. Competitively, it could be argued that the client will choose the supplier with the lowest risk. This implies either low consequences or low uncertainty. Buying from a well-known firm can help, but clients always are seeking for other ways to reduce their risk.

The Consumer as a Rational Mathematician

Marketing theorists have made extensive use of multiattribute models to simulate the evaluation process of the purchase of tangible goods. According to these models, several salient attributes or dimensions are used by consumers as the basic references for the evaluation of a service. Consumers compute their preference for the service by combining the scores of the product on each individual attribute.

In the prepurchase evaluation process, consumers are assumed to create a table similar to that shown in Table 2.2. This example uses the choice of an airline for travel across the North Atlantic. Across the top of the table are two types of variables. The first is the evoked set of brands that will be evaluated. Generally, this evoked set will, for various reasons, be less than an exhaustive list of all possible brands; in this case, it includes British Airways (BA), United, American, and El Al. (This evoked set idea was discussed earlier.) The second type of variable is an importance rating with which the consumer is supposed to rank the various attributes that constitute the vertical axis of the table. In Table 2.2, the consumer rates safety as the most important attribute, followed by time of flight, and so on. To complete the table, the consumer rates each brand on safety, followed by time of flight, and so on. This particular consumer gives BA top marks for safety, type of aircraft, and cabin crew but perceives the airline to be less good on time of flight and flight time.

Given such a table, various choice processes have been suggested with which the consumer can use the table to make a decision. The linear compensatory model proposes that the consumer creates a global score for each brand or airline by multiplying

| TABLE 2.2 | A TYPICAL MULTIATTRIBUTE CHOICE MATRIX |

	Evoked Set of Brands				Importance Weights
Attributes	**British Airways**	**United**	**American**	**El Al**	
Safety	10	10	10	9.9	**10**
Time of flight	9	10	10	9.0	**9**
Type of aircraft	10	8	8	10.0	**8**
Flight time	9	9	8	9.0	**7**
Cabin crew	10	8	8	10.0	**6**

the rating of the airline on each attribute by the importance attached to that attribute and adding the scores together. British Airways would score 10 × 10 (safety) plus 9 × 9 (time of flight) plus 10 × 8 (aircraft), and so on. The result of such a process would be that British Airways would be chosen with a score of 384, followed by El Al (383), United (365), and American (358).

Perhaps the most intriguing process that has been suggested is the lexicographic model. This rather pedantic term in fact describes lazy decision makers who try to minimize the effort involved. They look at each attribute in turn, starting with the most important, and try to make a decision. The individual whose preferences are shown in Table 2.2 would look first at safety and rule out El Al. Next, time of flight would rule out BA. The choice is thus reduced to American and United; type of aircraft does not help, as it produces a tie in the scoring. Managerially, this highlights a key problem, because consumers cannot actually make a choice based on aircraft type, but managers cannot change aircraft type either, because they then no longer would be at parity. The type of aircraft thus becomes a minimum requirement. Finally, the choice can be made in favor of United based on the next attribute, flight time. Thus, a different decision rule results in a different choice: United under the lexicographic model and BA under the linear compensatory model.

The same kind of model can be applied to the postpurchase evaluation process. In this case, the brands are replaced by two columns. The first is the score expected by the consumer on each attribute. The second is the perceived score on each attribute obtained by the consumer after purchase. The satisfaction score then is derived by creating a global score of the comparisons between perceptions and expectations weighted by the importance of each attribute. This is shown in Table 2.3.

In this example, the customer has chosen to fly on BA by using the multiattribute choice matrix shown in Table 2.2 and a linear compensatory model. The expected levels on each attribute therefore are taken from that matrix. This is, in fact, a gross oversimplification of the expectation. There are many sources of expectation, as discussed earlier. However, there must be a link between the choice process and the satisfaction process. The multiattribute model implies a ranking of different choices, and such a ranking must include an expectation that the brand or service can satisfy an individual's needs on a particular attribute. That expectation, developed for the choice process, in some way must be carried over into the satisfaction process. In reality, the flight was delayed and the cabin crew was not very helpful under the circumstances. The consumer therefore downgraded his or her evaluation on those attributes.

Given the popularity of the multiattribute models, it is not unexpected that they have been used to describe and explain the consumers' service decision processes. The merit of these multiattribute models lies in their simplicity and explicitness. The attributes identified cover a wide range of concerns related to the service experience

TABLE 2.3	A POSTPURCHASE EVALUATION MODEL FOR A FLIGHT TAKEN ON BRITISH AIRWAYS		
Attributes	Expected Score	Perceived Score	Importance Weights
Safety	10	10.0	**10**
Time of flight	9	8.0	**9**
Type of aircraft	10	10.0	**8**
Flight time	9	9.0	**7**
Cabin crew	10	8.0	**6**

and are understood easily by service managers. The tasks for management when using this model are relatively straightforward.

First, it is necessary to identify the criteria used by consumers. This often can be done by using focus groups during which customers are asked to talk about a particular service. The kinds of words consumers use and the dimensions they use for choice and evaluation become apparent. Importance scores, evoked sets, and brand scores are elicited directly. It should be stressed that such a model must be thought of at the individual level, for groups of consumers cannot be combined for these purposes. Different consumer segments can be created, however, by combining individuals who rate attributes with the same importance weights.

Once managers understand the process, there are obvious actions that can be taken to improve the firm's competitive positions, through improving the firm's share of consumers' choices. If the service package does not contain the appropriate mixture of attributes, then clearly a new service ought to be developed. To return to our airline example, if consumers demand an executive cabin, this ought to be built into the aircraft and the system.

Alternatively, advertising can be used to stress a particular attribute on which the firm's service appears to be weak in the mind of the consumers. An airline may have had a bad punctuality record in the past but still may be perceived as punctual by consumers. If necessary, advertising also can be used to try to reduce the attribute scores obtained by competitors by engaging in competitive advertising. For example, Federal Express, when it was first launched, featured the results of market research regarding "on-time delivery," which showed that it outperformed existing competitors.

The same logical process can be applied to managing customer satisfaction. Because satisfaction is the result of the comparison of expectations with perceptions, two different routes are open to improve satisfaction. Consumer perceptions of service can be improved by stressing in communications how good the service is, relative to the competition, on key attributes. Alternatively, care can be taken in communications to ensure the accuracy of customers' expectations on the same key attributes. Returning to the Federal Express example, care would need to be taken when advertising to ensure that a clear distinction was made between Priority Service (guaranteed overnight delivery) and Standard Air (second-day delivery).

Shortcomings of the Multiattribute Model for Services

Although the multiattribute model has been used widely in the analysis of services, it does have a number of shortcomings that are specific to services. The first shortcoming of such models is that they adopt a static perspective on an experience that consists of a series of dynamic interactions. A defect in one aspect of the service encounter may affect adversely the customers' perceptions on a wide array of attributes, and thus there is no way to find and tackle the real source of the problem.

For instance, a crowded bank may not only give its customers a perception of a poor service environment but also may jeopardize the relationship between the tellers and the customers. The customers may feel that the tellers are unfriendly and unhelpful when actually they are trying to speed up their work pace to cope with the large crowd of customers.

However, the tellers may feel that the customers are too demanding of tellers when they are working under pressure. In this case, it may not be the best strategy for the management of the bank to focus solely on training and regulating their tellers' manner and behavior; rather, the managers also may have to tackle in some way the real source of the trouble, the crowded environment.

In a similar way, researchers in the area of human touch have demonstrated the existence of a "Midas touch."[17] In a library setting, researchers manipulated whether the librarian touched borrowers' hands when they checked out the books. They controlled for the sex of the librarian and the borrower, and the touch was so casual that only 57 percent of the respondents who actually had been touched claimed that they had when asked. Intercepted after leaving the library, respondents were asked for their evaluation of the librarian and the library environment and their own emotional state. All those touched, independent of whether they noticed it, responded more positively on all scales. A single touch, therefore, was able to influence apparently concrete attributes of the environment as well as customers' emotional states.

Relating Consumers' Attributes to Managerial Actions

The second major shortcoming is the lack of correspondence between a service company's effort to improve its operational standards (e.g., increase the number of branches of a bank) and its customers' rating of the service attributes (e.g., convenience). One reason for this is that the attributes are often abstract in nature, such as reliability or friendliness. Second, the attributes are rarely under the full control of the service organization. The service delivery process is open to the influence of the customers and to environmental factors that are predominantly beyond the service manager's control.

As a response to the insufficiency of the multiattribute-type models, theorists recently have proposed a number of new perspectives on the service encounter. New concepts, originally developed in various disciplines of the behavioral sciences, have been suggested.

The Consumer as a Searcher for Control

The concept of control has drawn considerable attention from psychologists. They argue that, in modern society in which people no longer have to bother about the satisfaction of primary biologic needs, the need for control over situations in which one finds oneself is a major force driving human behavior.[18]

Perceived control, in this context, refers to the ways in which persons perceive that they have the ability to manage their environments. Psychologists define control in several forms: behavioral control, in which persons seek to control stimuli that cause pleasure or pain by modifying their own behavior (not sticking your hand in the fire when you realize it burns you is a simple example), cognitive control, in which persons seek to gain information about and analyze elements in their environment to learn how to control them, and decisional control, which involves changing one's own goals can afford a measure of control, either actual or imaginary. For example, the decision to stop trying to complete one's Christmas shopping can dramatically affect one's feelings in a crowded department store.

Perceived control has important ramifications for the service encounter, from the perspective of both provider and customer. Rather than being treated as a service attribute, as implied by multiattribute models, perceived control can be conceptualized as a super-factor, a global index that summarizes an individual's experience in the service. The basic premise of this perspective is that, during the service experience, the higher the level of control over the situation perceived by the consumers, the stronger will be their satisfaction with the service. A similar positive correlation is proposed between the service providers' experience of control and their job satisfaction.

It is equally important to recognize that service providers, that is, the front-line service personnel who interact with customers in the servuction process, also have their own perceived control needs. They too are affected by stress and uncertainty, in different ways from the customer.

When control is withdrawn from the server, the outcomes can be negative. Certain service jobs, such as janitor or parking lot attendant, are characterized by lack of control and are accordingly stigmatized; no matter how well the job is performed, those working in these jobs feel this stigma. Studies have shown that the perceived lack of control is primarily responsible for the stigma.

Ultimately, neither server nor customer can ever have complete control. This is due not only to the demands of the other but also to those of the service environment itself, as embodied in the rules and procedures laid down by the service-providing firm, the effective determinant of the environment. All three parties—customer, server, and firm—are partially in conflict, and all service encounters can be seen as a compromise by the three that attempts to overcome that conflict. The three-cornered fight between these parties is shown in Figure 2.2.

One of the problems that service providers face is getting that compromise right. Letting any one party have too much power can have negative consequences. For example, if the service providing firm has too much power, the result may well be an operation characterized by rules, procedures, and "form-filling." These rules and procedures may well be necessary for efficiency; in some sectors, such as banking, they are also important for security. Nevertheless, they are off-putting for customers, who may perceive an atmosphere of red tape and obstruction, and for service staff, who may be as frustrated as customers but unable to explain to customers why they cannot have the service they want. In extreme cases, customers and servers may actually ally against the organization.

If the customer is dominant, then the customer may well have very strong perceived behavioral control over the situation and will be correspondingly satisfied. However, the pressures of living up to customer expectations can create an inefficient service operation—for example, large numbers of staff may have to be on duty at all times to cope with possible customer demand—and will be less profitable. Servers will also have little control, being there primarily to satisfy customer demand.

Finally, if the contact personnel are dominant, a situation may result in which servers are able to order the encounter to their satisfaction but not to that of the customer, who may resent being "bossed around" by the server. There are also problems with servers adopting their own independent systems, which leads to problems for the back office trying to administer the company and can also diffuse the company's image and confuse customers about the nature of the service offering.

The ideal service encounter, therefore, should seek to harmonize the aims of all three parties to as great an extent as is possible and should balance the control needs of customer and server against the efficiency needs of the operation. To do this, we need to look again at the various levels of perceived control. If we assume the behavioral control idea alone, then the problem is clearly impossible; the behavioral control needs of customers and servers can never be matched, as it is impossible for both to do what they want. Much work has been done to suggest that cognitive control is also important. Thus, when consumers perceive they are in control, or at least that what is

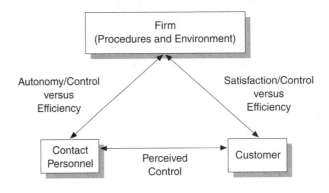

FIGURE 2.2 THE PERCEIVED BEHAVIORAL CONTROL CONFLICTS IN THE SERVICE ENCOUNTER

SOURCE: John E. G. Bateson, "Perceived Control and the Service Encounter," in John A. Czepiel, Michael R. Solomon, and Carol F. Surprenant, eds., *The Service Encounter* (Lexington, MA: Heath, 1985), 67–82.

happening to them is predictable, the effect can be the same as that achieved by behavioral control. In other words, it is the perception of control that is important, not the reality.

However the compromise is ultimately worked out, though, it is clear that the customer must give up some control. From a managerial perspective, the service transaction can be seen as an event in which the customer gives up money and some control and receives benefits in return. Managerially, this raises a number of interesting ideas. The first is the value of information given to the consumers during the service experience, to increase their sense that they are in control and that they know what will happen next. This is particularly important for professional service firms, which often assume that simply because they are doing a good job, their clients will be happy. They forget that their clients have not heard from them for over a month and are frantic from lack of information. It is equally important to the airline that delays the flight after boarding but fails to let the passengers know what is happening. In the same way, if the firm is due to make changes to the operation that will have an impact on the consumers, it is important that those consumers are forewarned. If not, they may perceive themselves to be "out of control" and may be dissatisfied with the service received to the extent that they may change suppliers. In general, for customers, the following points are worth considering:

Can the manager increase the perceived control of the customer, thereby increasing the customer's perceived value of the service?

How does the customer view the encounter in terms of perceived control, both on its own terms and in comparison with the services offered by competitors?

Can information be offered to the customer to increase cognitive control, by suggesting that the service offering is predictable and of a constant standard?

Is it possible to analyze the various elements of the service encounter and understand how each individually affects customer-perceived control? And having done so, is it possible to build customer-perceived control into the system?

Likewise, the following should be considered when discussing the role of the contact personnel:

How do contact personnel currently view their control? Are they satisfied with present control levels, or do they desire more control?

Can more control be given to contact personnel, thus allowing them to serve the customer better?

Can more real or apparent control be given to contact personnel to satisfy their own personal needs for control?

What factors in the firm's operating environment and procedures are perceived by contact personnel as limiting their control?

If more control is given to contact personnel, what will be the impact on operating efficiency? Are the gains in marketing and personnel effectiveness such as to make this efficiency worth sacrificing?

The control perspective raises interesting issues about the trade-off between predictability and choice. Operationally, one of the most important strategic issues is the amount of choice to give to the consumer. Because both choice and predictability (standardization) can contribute to a sense of control, it is crucial to determine which is the most powerful source of control for the relevant consumers.

The Consumer as an Actor within a Script

A number of alternative theories within psychology and sociology can be brought together under the idea of a script and a role. A role is generally defined as "a set of behavior patterns learned through experience and communication, to be performed by an individual in a certain social interaction in order to attain a maximum effectiveness in goal accomplishment."[19] The principal idea proposed is that, in a service encounter, customers will perform roles, and their satisfaction is a function of "role congruence"—whether or not enacted behaviors by customers and staff are consistent with the expected roles.

One consequence of the servuction system model, proposed in Chapter 1, is the importance this places on the encounter between contact personnel and customer during the course of the transaction. The transaction or exchange is one of the key elements in any marketing activity. Ultimately, the service experience revolves around this single, person-to-person encounter. In some services, such as consulting services and medical services in which the primary benefit purchased by the consumer is the service itself, this "dyadic interaction" dominates the service encounter. In other cases, in which the service is provided along with a good (e.g., sales of industrial equipment, clothing, or insurance), the dyadic encounter is less crucial but still important.

So, service encounters are, to a greater or lesser extent, human interactions. They are also reciprocal, in that there is interplay between customer and server throughout the encounter; neither consumer nor server is static (even automatic teller machines are capable of limited interaction, providing menus and information to users).

The dyadic encounter is important precisely because it is personal and therefore not ultimately controllable. The service firm can write rules and procedures that the server and customer are to follow, but as noted above, if these procedures and rules become too restricting, customer and server both may feel dissatisfied. There is always space in which customers and servers can "do their own thing" in an attempt to customize the service to their own satisfaction. One way of overcoming this problem is the development of the concepts of *role* and *script*.

Solomon et al. have commented that "a distinguishing feature of service encounters as a class of human interaction is the purposive, task-oriented nature of the interaction."[20] In other words, each transaction is oriented toward a certain mutual goal, and each party—customer and contact personnel—has a role to play in achieving that goal. Depending on their prior knowledge or experience of the service, the customer will be familiar with the role he or she is expected to play (although again, travelers in foreign environments for the first time may have little or no knowledge of the expected role). Servers will also be familiar with their role, usually through a mix of experience and training.

One of the most important aspects of role is the concept of *role expectation*, which Solomon et al. define as "the privileges, duties, and obligations of any occupant of a social position."[21] Role expectation is, in effect, the definition of one's role or position. In service encounters, role expectation defines the behaviors of both staff and customer; it sets the parameters within which each is expected to perform. In addition, it creates predictions about how the other party will behave and about how the third party in the service experience, the service firm, will attempt to intervene.

Problems can arise when participants in the service experience see their own role, or that of the other, incorrectly. The employee's perception of what his or her job entails may be quite different from that of the customer; in turn, this perception may be because the employee has not defined the job correctly or because the service firm has failed to define the job correctly for the customer. To take a simple example, a customer at a gas station reading the sign "full service" may think this entitles him or her to a free window wash as well as filling up the gas tank. The attendant, however, may define full service as simply filling up the tank. Is the attendant wrong, or did the gas station fail to define what full service means?

Similarly, the customer's perception of his or her own role can differ from that of the employee. It is entirely possible for customers to define their roles "wrongly" from the perspective of the service firm. At McDonald's restaurants in the United States, it has always been common for customers to clear away their own trays when they have finished eating. When McDonald's first arrived in Europe, they found that European customers did not do so; they were more used to eating in restaurants and cafes where a waiter cleared the tables and "wrongly" assumed that this would happen in McDonald's as well.

Role is assumed to be extraindividual. Every individual is expected to display the same predetermined set of behaviors when he or she takes up a certain role, either as a customer or as a service provider. Role theory is not concerned directly with the perception of the participants in the service encounter and is therefore incompatible with the concepts of service evaluation and customer satisfaction. For example, two different customers, one introvert and one extrovert, may have completely different perceptions and evaluations of interactions with the same chatty provider. In this case, intraindividual variables have to be used to explain the differences in customer evaluation and satisfaction.

The role idea can, however, be adapted for use in service situations. This adaptation draws on the psychological idea of a script. The script theory and role theory perspectives appear, on the surface, to be extremely similar. Script theory argues that rules, mostly determined by social and cultural variables, exist to facilitate interactions in daily repetitive events, including a variety of service experiences.[22] These rules shape the expectation of the participants in this type of event.

Furthermore, the rules have to be acknowledged and obeyed by all participants if satisfactory outcomes are to be generated; if one participant deviates from the rules, the other co-actors will be uncomfortable. Therefore, a satisfied customer is unlikely with a dissatisfied service provider, whereas a dissatisfied customer is unlikely a satisfied service provider.

Figure 2.3 shows a script developed by one researcher for the process of going for a job interview at the end of an MBA program. Through individual interviews, it was possible to develop a script for what had become a frequently occurring experience for many MBAs.

Despite the similarity of the role theory and script theory perspectives, two basic differences exist between them. First, the script theory perspective has a wider range

| FIGURE 2.3 | A SCRIPT FOR AN MBA JOB INTERVIEW |

As a business student in your final semester at the University of Wisconsin-Madison, you are using the business placement office in your search for a permanent position after graduation. Earlier this semester, you checked the master list of firms that would be recruiting at Wisconsin and chose a group of companies to interview whose requirements matched your qualifications. Also at that time, you picked up a supply of computerized interview request forms at the placement office.

Shortly after the recruiters from one of the firms you had selected were scheduled to be on campus, you carefully prepared a college interview form and an interview request form in order to obtain an interview with that company. Since the firm was one in which you were especially interested, you used one of your priorities. Exactly seven days before the firm's visit, you turned one of these forms in at the placement office.

The next day, you checked the company's interview schedule to confirm that you had an appointment. Over the next several days, you researched the firm, using materials available in the placement office and from other sources. Based on this information, you prepared a list of questions for the interviewer, and formulated your answers to the questions you expected to be asked.

You purchased a good business suit to wear to the interview, and the day before your appointment, you assembled all the materials you wanted to take with you, including a copy of your resume. That evening, you attended a pre-interview reception at the Union-South which was sponsored by the firm. At the reception, you had an opportunity to talk with some of the company's representatives, and you expressed your enthusiasm for the firm.

On the day of the interview, you dressed appropriately and arrived at the placement office about 15 minutes before your appointment. You checked "Today's Interviews" for the location of your interview, and wrote down the name, title, and address of the recruiter you would meet. You were pleased to discover that your interviewer was Mr. James Moore, with whom you had talked at the previous evening's reception.

You then found a seat outside the interview room, and waited for Mr. Moore to call you. At exactly the scheduled time, he emerged from the interview room with another student. After bidding good-bye to the previous interviewee, he called your name, and you stood up, shook hands, and then followed Mr. Moore into the interview room. During the next half-hour, you responded to his questions about your career goals and accomplishments, and asked him several questions about the company. Finally, you thanked the recruiter for the opportunity to talk, and left the interview room as Mr. Moore welcomed the next student on his schedule.

You immediately found a quiet spot to sit and collect your thoughts about the meeting. You made notes about the critical points that had been discussed, and the instructions Mr. Moore had given you for following up on the preliminary interview. You also noted your impressions of the firm, and your feelings about further pursuing employment opportunities there.

That evening, you composed a formal letter of thanks to Mr. Moore, expressing your continued interest in a position with the company, and briefly summarizing the main points discussed in the interview. You then began the tedious wait to hear about the firm's decision, hoping you would be invited for a second interview. You decided that if you had not heard within a reasonable interval, you would follow up with a letter or phone call to Mr. Moore.

SOURCE: Ruth A. Smith, "An Investigation of the Measurement and Explanatory Potency of Cognitive Scripts as an Element in Satisfaction with Services," unpublished doctoral dissertation (Madison, WI: University of Wisconsin, 1983). Reprinted with permission.

of concerns (e.g., the impact of the service setting) and hence is concerned with the whole service experience rather than only with the interpersonal service encounter. Second, scripts are by definition intraindividual and are a function of the individual's experience and personality. Part of the job of the service provider is to uncover the script and either enact it, if appropriate, with the customer, or revise it with the customer. However, the content of a role is defined in a more objective sense, by means of a social position or title (physician, waiter) rather than the perception and cognition of an individual. Part of the job of the service provider who has a defined role is to manage the customers' expectations by educating them about the service process.

When customers and servers both know what is expected of them and are capable of carrying out their roles, then customer satisfaction is usually the result. However, there are also implicit dangers. Too much standardization and efficiency, which are

Safeway

Point-of-sale scanning devices, or scanners, are the latest innovation in supermarket store technology. Scanners, which read a bar code on the back of each item and compute the price automatically, are now in use by nearly all large supermarket chains. Stores have noticed considerable increases in the number of customers processed per hour (and hence profitability) and considerable decreases in lines waiting to be served at check-outs. There was some initial public opposition to the scanners, which meant that they could not actually see checkers inputting the price, and customers expressed fears that they could be overcharged without their knowing it. By and large, however, scanners have been accepted by the public.

In September 1990, Safeway stores in Maryland took the innovation a step farther and introduced do-it-yourself checkers for grocery store customers. Instead of waiting while a checker ran each item through the scanner, shoppers were now invited to use the scanners themselves at check-out points. Safeway maintained the original system of staffed check-outs, but set up several lanes to allow those shoppers who wished to check themselves through.

Each self-check-out machine comes with a video terminal, a keyboard, and a bar scanner with a simple set of controls. The system has advantages over the staffed check-outs in that customers can see prices much more easily. Customers can also subtotal at will, keeping a running tab on how much their order is before actually paying. Once the order has been run through the scanner and totaled, customers then take their receipt to a central cashiers booth to pay before leaving the store.

Customer reactions have so far been mixed. Some customers expressed satisfaction when making a quick purchase of a few items but maintained the system would be cumbersome when making a large grocery purchase. Others expressed worry about the difficulties of simultaneously running groceries through the scanner and looking after small children.

One customer complained that Safeway was now making him do the work normally done by staff but still charging the original price and suggested that the service he now received was worth less: "Safeway should give me a 10 percent discount now, since I'm doing all the work." Another customer complained that the routine of buying groceries had been disturbed, and while scanning her own groceries, she had no opportunity to write out the check to pay for them. This operation was normally performed while the staff manning the original check-outs were running the groceries through the scanner.

Many people appeared to miss the personal touch of having staff serve them at the check-outs. Safeway's answer to this has been to have a cashier appear on the check-out video screen at the end of each transaction, to thank the customer for his or her business.

necessary components of a script, can conflict with the need to treat each customer as a unique person and each service encounter as a unique event. Overscripting an encounter can lead to loss of involvement and thus of perceived control, with the consequences noted above. In high-involvement services in particular, such as hairdressing or medical services, there may need to be more room for customization. Less scripting can lead to less efficiency and less exact definition of roles, in which case the service staff need to be particularly adept at both customizing their own roles and assisting customers to learn theirs as they go along.

The Consumer as a Partial Employee

A more radical view of consumers' behavior in services is to consider them as partial employees. Consumers derive the benefit they receive from service from an interactive experience of which they are a part. Following the script analogy, consumers must obey the script, otherwise they will negate the entire experience. Classic examples of this occur when "novice consumers" appear in services. Foreign tourists who are on their first visit to McDonald's or the tourist new to a bank does not know the script. As a result, they can impair the experience, not only for themselves but also for those individuals trying to serve them and for other customers

Such a perspective opens up an opportunity for marketing to improve the profitability of service firms in nontraditional ways. At the heart of marketing is the idea that consumer behavior can be changed to induce more consumers to buy and/or each consumer to buy more. In service, a third option appears—to change the consumer's behavior as a partial employee. This can involve asking consumers to do more work, as with self-service gas stations for example, or just asking them to behave differently during the interaction with the firm. Consumers, for example, might be asked to behave differently by using a single line for customers to wait in, which "snakes" as those seen in amusement parks, rather than using multiple lines, which can cause anger in a consumer who gets stuck in one line that is moving more slowly than another.

Consumer Behavior and Management Decisions

Several authors have pointed out an analogy between marketing and warfare. The enemy is the competition. The market is the battlefield; but what are the weapons? At one level, they can be thought of as the elements of the marketing mix: product, price, promotion, and channels. At a much more basic level, firms compete with their knowledge of the consumers. The competitor that best understands the consumer wins. As mentioned earlier, all marketing managers have models of consumers, but they do not always make these models explicit. The purpose of this chapter has been to suggest a number of alternative models, each of which can be used in conjunction with others. These models permeate the remainder of this book, and it is important that they are understood before proceeding farther. The next chapter, for example, reconciles the conflicting needs of operational efficiency and marketing effectiveness by using a deep understanding of the consumer. Chapters 5 and 6 on configuring the setting and the operation draw on the models suggested here, particularly when considering the design of the physical environment.

Chapter 7 revisits many of these themes from the perspective of the service provider. Although employees can be viewed from the organizational behavior perspective, they also can be viewed as partial consumers who are part of the servuction process. Chapter 8 draws directly on both the models of consumer choice and evaluation to position the role of communications. Finally, Chapter 14 approaches quality from the consumer's perspective and suggests the first cause of a quality problem may be an inappropriate model of consumer behavior.

Questions

1. Apply the role theory, script theory, and perceived-control concepts to a common service of your choice. What insights could you give that would be useful to management?

2. What are the implications of script theory and perceived-control theory for the design and introduction of a new form of home banking that allows customers to access their accounts from a personal computer in their own homes?

3. Describe two or three instances of a service experience with which you were dissatisfied. Interpret your dissatisfaction using script theory or perceived-control theory.

4. Imagine tourists encountering a McDonald's for the first time. How would they learn the script? What are the clues that would allow them to deduce what to do?

5. "The art of being a tourist is to go some place where you don't know the script." Discuss this statement and suggest why individuals might want to pursue this art.

6. Collect two or three print advertisements for services. What are they promising? What expectations are they raising in the mind of the consumer? In the context of the disconfirmation model of satisfaction, is the firm wise to raise such expectations?

7. For a service experience with which you are familiar, write a role specification for the actions and behaviors expected of you as a consumer.

Notes

[1] F. Nicosia and R.N. Mayer, "Toward a Sociology of Consumption," *Journal of Consumer Research* 3, no. 2 (1976): 65–75.

[2] Christopher Lovelock has argued for a distinction between services performed to oneself versus those performed to one's possessions; C. Lovelock, "Classifying Marketing Services to Gain Strategic Insights," *Journal of Marketing* 47 (Summer 1983): 9–20.

[3] Alan Andreason, "Consumer Research in the Service Sector," in L. Berry, G.L. Shostack, and G. Upah, eds., *Emerging Perspectives on Services Marketing* (Chicago, IL: American Marketing Association, 1984): 63–64.

[4] Raymond Fisk, "Towards a Consumption/Evaluation Process Model for Services," in J. Donnelly and W. George, eds., *Marketing of Services* (Chicago, IL: American Marketing Association, 1981), 191.

[5] Valerie A. Zeithaml, Leonard L. Berry, and A. Parasuraman, "The Nature and Determinants of Customer Expectations of Service," *Journal of the Academy of Marketing Science* 21, no. 1(1993): 1–12.

[6] Ibid., 6.

[7] Ibid., 7.

[8] Ibid., 8.

[9] Ibid., 11.

[10] Shirley Taylor, "Waiting for Service: The Relationship between Delays and Evaluation of Service," *Journal of Marketing* 58 (April 1994): 56–69.

[11] Bernard Booms and Jody Nyquist, "Analyzing the Customer/Firm Communication Component of the Services Marketing Mix," in J. Donnelly and W. George, eds., *Marketing of Services* (Chicago, IL: American Marketing Association, 1984), 172; and Fisk, "Towards a Consumption/Evaluation Process Model."

[12] D. Guseman, "Risk Perception and Risk Reduction in Consumer Services," in James H. Donnelly and William R. George, eds., *Marketing of Services* (Chicago, IL: American Marketing Association, 1981), 200–204; and R.A. Bauer, "Consumer Behavior as Risk Taking," in R.S. Hancock, ed., *Dynamic Marketing for a Changing World* (Chicago, IL: American Marketing Association, 1960), 389–398.

[13] L. Kaplan, G.J. Szybillo, and J. Jacoby, "Components of Perceived Risk in Product Purchase: A Cross-Validation," *Journal of Applied Psychology* 59 (1974): 287–291.

[14] Guseman, "Risk Perception and Risk Reduction."

[15] A. Parasuraman, V. Zeithaml, and L. Berry, "A Conceptual Model of Service Quality and Its Implications for Future Research," *Journal of Marketing* 49 (Fall 1985): 41–50.

[16] Keith B. Murray, "A Test of Services Marketing Theory: Consumer Information Acquisition Models," *Journal of Marketing* 55 (1991): 10–25.

[17] Jeffrey Fisher, Martin Rytting, and Richard Neslin, "Hands Touching Hands: Affective and Evaluative Effects on Interpersonal Touch," *Sociometry* 39, no. 4 (1976): 416–421.

[18] John E.G. Bateson, "Perceived Control and the Service Encounter," in John A. Czepiel, Michael R. Soloman, and Carol F. Surprenant, eds., *The Service Encounter* (Lexington, MA: Lexington Books, 1984), 67–82.

[19] Michael R. Soloman, Carol F. Surprenant, John A. Czepiel, and Evelyn G. Gatman, "A Role Theory Perspective on Dyadic Interactions: The Service Encounter," *Journal of Marketing* 1, no. 49 (Winter 1985): 99–111.

[20] Ibid.

[21] Ibid., 103.

[22] Ruth A. Smith and Michael Houston, "Script-Based Evaluations of Satisfaction with Services," in L. Berry, G.L. Shostack, and G. Upah, eds., *Emerging Perspectives in Services Marketing* (Chicago, IL: American Marketing Association, 1982), 59–62.

3

Understanding
the Service Operation

Chapter Overview

One way of viewing the marketing task is to conceptualize it as the marrying of consumers' needs with the technology and manufacturing capabilities of the firm. Such a marriage obviously will involve compromises because consumers' needs seldom can be met completely and economically. Within a goods firm, this marriage requires marketing's understanding of the capabilities of manufacturing and of research and development. The task of marketing is made somewhat easier because the different functions can be separated by means of inventory.

In a service firm, this problem is magnified. Significant aspects of the operation are the product, because these aspects create the interactive experience that delivers the benefit to the customer. A successful compromise between operations efficiency and marketing effectiveness is therefore that much more difficult to achieve. Success in services marketing demands a much greater understanding of the constraints and opportunities posed by operations.

To introduce these complexities, in this chapter we first adopt the perspective of an operations manager and ask, "What would be the ideal way to run the system from the operations perspective?" The impact on marketing and the opportunities for marketing to assist in the creation of this ideal then are developed. The major topics discussed are the prerequisite for manufacturing efficiency and alternative strategies for achieving it, the application of this model to services, potential solutions to service operations problems, and marketing and operations interdependence. Many of these topics are discussed from different perspectives in later chapters. They are introduced here to show their relationship to the operational demands of services.

As pointed out in Chapter 1, the key distinctive characteristic of services is that the product is an experience. That experience is created by the operating system of the firm interacting with the customer. Thus the operating system of the firm, in all its complexity, is the product. For a marketing manager, this fact imposes constraints on the strategies that can be used, but it also presents new and challenging opportunities for improving the profitability of the firm.

Chapter 2 provided one base on which to build an understanding of the product-design problem for services. An understanding of consumer behavior always has been a necessary condition for successful marketing. One way of viewing the product design process is to think of it as the process of combining such an understanding with the technological and manufacturing skills of the organization. A knowledge of consumer behavior is not sufficient in itself to produce economically successful products.

As pointed out in Chapter 1, in a goods firm it is possible to separate the problems of manufacturing and marketing by the use of inventory. Even so, there are many areas of potential conflict.[1] These problems are summarized in Table 3.1. Although the issues have been characterized as conflicts, they can be reconceptualized as opportunities. In each area, it is clear that a better integration of marketing and manufacturing plans could yield a more efficient and profitable organization. For example, the determination of the extent of the product line should be seen as a compromise between the heterogeneous demands of the market and the manufacturing demand for homogeneity. Too large a marketing bias will mean many products and an inefficient operation. As long as this is compensated for by higher prices, then a successful strategy can ensue. Too large a manufacturing bias will mean a single product, which may be less attractive to the market. As long as this is compensated for by lower costs and hence lower prices, a successful strategy can emerge.

The purpose of this chapter is to extend to services the logic of this type of compromise. In the service sector, the possible areas of conflict or compromise are much broader because the operation itself is the product. Again, there are no single solutions because operational efficiency and marketing effectiveness may push in opposite direc-

Arby's

Armed with a slew of high-tech innovations, Arby's is starting to look like a fast-food joint straight out of *The Jetsons*. The roast beef sandwich chain is testing automated systems for food selection and payment and has some revolutionary plans for its kitchens. All the changes are the result of consumer demand, said George Nadvit, executive vice president of operations for Arby's Inc., Atlanta.

As menus at fast-food restaurants have increased in size, service has slowed down, and consumers don't like that. Technology can help speed things up and cut labor needs.

"The predicted labor crisis of the 90s occupies the mind of every fast-food operator," says Nadvit. "Arby's is developiong automated systems as potential cost-effective solutions to provide faster service and thus allow personnel to focus on providing hospitality."

Technology can do all the mundane and repetitive tasks, such as slicing roast beef, while employees help customers at the counter or in the dining room. Arby's is not alone. Many fast-food chains are taking a closer look at technology. Some are having more success than others, he says, but they have to stick with it. If not, they'll be in big trouble. "They have to continue to look at better and new ways of doing business, or they aren't going to be around in a few years," he stresses.

Arby's is testing Touch 2000, a computerized system that allows customers to order food from a touch-sensitive display screen. As the food selection is touched on the screen, it is processed through an IBM PS/2 Model 30 computer and displayed on IBM monitors in the food-preparation area. The machine's screen automatically indicates the selections made and keeps a running tab of the order. Some of the restaurants in Southwestern markets are using bilingual machines, allowing customers to order in English or Spanish.

Touch 2000 saves labor and food costs, Nadvit claims, providing faster service and allowing personnel to focus on the consumer. "We don't want to lose the human touch in fast food. We just want to provide the best service possible. Touch 2000 allows us to have the best of both worlds."

Arby's has found that Touch 2000 helps to increase sales by proposing the purchase of other items. If a customer doesn't order dessert, for example, the system will suggest a little something. Nadvit said the average check increased 4 percent on chains using the system.

Although Arby's thought it would be the younger customers using the machines, the chain is finding that use runs across the board and even includes some senior citizens. A recent study by Arby's found that 77 percent of its customers prefer ordering through Touch 2000. Ninety percent said the system was easy to use, and 54 percent said using the computer was faster than the traditional means. But some customers prefer the old-fashioned way. They give their orders to a cashier who then enters the data through a similar device behind the counter.

The system is used in more than 30 locations, and because 90 percent of the 2,300 Arby's restaurants are franchised, Nadvit said he expects the innovative franchisees to help move the customer-activated system forward.

Arby's also announced its plans to integrate its credit-card program into the Touch 2000 system. The chain is accepting payment by Visa and MasterCard credit cards at its company-owned restaurants in Cleveland and Phoenix, and has been testing acceptance of the Discover card in 50 company and franchised locations in Pittsburgh and Youngstown, Ohio. Accepting credit also stimulates add-on purchases, Nadvit said. The average cash purchase in Arby's restaurants is about $2.80, he said, but the credit-card average has been between $5 and $6.

In Phoenix, Arby's recently expanded its credit-card program with a new satellite broadcasting system that lets restaurants obtain credit-card authorization in less then three seconds. Nadvit said the chain is using the same satellite technology for other communications between the point-of-sale and regional and corporate offices. Arby's can move financial information as well as audio and visual information. Videos, for example, can be sent from corporate headquarters to individual restaurants.

Even the kitchens at Arby's restaurants will be going high-tech. "Customers will be seeing more extensive use of 'smart kitchens,' which control the cooking process based on analysis of sales volume," said Nadvit. "These systems will cook according to projected demand and continuously track food stocks to prevent shortages."

Arby's is working on a really nifty slicer for its roast beef. Linked to the point of sale, the machine turns on and delivers the current number of portions to the assembling area according to orders. Arby's wants to resolve some safety considerations and make the unit self-heating so the beef can be kept at the proper temperature.

The chain also plans to make some changes in the actual cooking process, so that the meat is cooked more evenly and doesn't have to be watched so closely. Arby's is testing ovens that feature temperatures that can be preset and monitored throughout the cooking process to see how long the meat took to cook and how much weight was lost. All the employee has to do is put the beef in, and the oven's probing system will send a signal when it's done.

The chain also is looking at a prototype of a product that would toast sandwich buns in one-third less time than its current model. And the Arby's self-service beverage area will be getting a make over, he said, opting for a new long-profile look so "there's not as much ugly equipment showing."

SOURCE: *Marketing Week* 24, no. 23 (November 12, 1990).

TABLE 3.1	MARKETING/MANUFACTURING AREAS OF NECESSARY COOPERATION BUT POTENTIAL CONFLICT	
Problem Area	**Typical Marketing Comment**	**Typical Manufacturing Comment**
Capacity planning and long-range sales forecasting	"Why don't we have enough capacity?"	"Why didn't we have accurate sales forecasts?
Production scheduling and short-range sales forecasting	"We need faster response. Our lead times are ridiculous."	"We need realistic customer commitments and sales forecasts that don't change like wind direction."
Delivery and physical distribution	"Why don't we ever have the right merchandise in inventory?"	"We can't keep everything in inventory."
Quality assurance	"Why can't we have reasonable quality at reasonable cost?"	"Why must we always offer options that are too hard to manufacture and that offer little customer utility?"
Breadth of product line	"Our customers demand variety."	"The product line is too broad—all we get are short, uneconomical runs."
Cost control	"Our costs are so high that we are not competitive in the marketplace."	"We can't provide fast delivery, broad variety, rapid response to change, and high quality at low cost."
New-product introduction	"New products are our lifeblood."	"Unnecessary design changes are prohibitively expensive."
Adjunct services, such as spare parts inventory support, installation, and repair	"Field service costs are too high."	"Products are being used in ways for which they weren't designed."

SOURCE: Reprinted by permission of the *Harvard Business Review*. An exhibit from "Can Marketing and Manufacturing Coexist?" by Benson P. Shapiro (September/October 1977), 105. Copyright © 1977 by the President and Fellows of Harvard College; all rights reserved.

tions. By its very nature, this chapter is operations oriented rather than marketing oriented. To polarize the issues, the perspective adopted in this chapter is that of the operations manager, just as in Chapter 2 the consumer's position was taken. The focus is on the requirements for operational efficiency and the ways that marketing can help to achieve those requirements. It should be stressed that, in the drive for competitive advantage in the marketplace, marketing demand may in the end mean less operational efficiency.

Prerequisites for Manufacturing Efficiency

The starting point for this discussion is the work of J.D. Thompson.[2] Thompson, who started from an organizational perspective, introduced the idea of a "technical core," that is, the technical heart of the organization. He specified that, to operate efficiently, the firm must be able to operate "as if the market will absorb the single kind of product at a continuous rate and as if the inputs flowed continuously at a steady rate and with specified quality." At the center of his argument was the idea that uncertainty creates inefficiency. In the ideal situation envisaged by Thompson, the technical core is able to operate without uncertainty on both the input and output side, thereby creating many advantages for management.

The absence of uncertainty means that decisions within the core can become programmed and individual discretion can be replaced by rules; the removal of individual discretion means that jobs are deskilled and lower-quality labor is used. Alternatively, the rules can be programmed into machines and labor can be replaced with capital. Because output and input are fixed, it is very easy to plan capacity and to run at the high levels of utilization needed to generate the most efficient operations performance.

A system without uncertainty is very easy to control and manage. Performance can be measured by using objective standards. Because the system is not subject to disturbances from the outside, it is also very easy to diagnose the causes of any problems.

Clearly, such an ideal world is virtually impossible to create, and even in goods companies, the demands of procurement and marketing management have to be traded off against the ideal operations demands. Within goods manufacturing, Skinner has operationalized this concept with his idea of the focused factory.[3] He argues for focusing a factory on a particular job; once this is achieved, the factory does a better job because repetition and concentration in one area allow the workforce and managers to become effective and experienced in the task required for success. He broadens Thompson's concept in that he argues that focus generates effectiveness as well as efficiency. In other words, the focused factory can meet the demands of the market better whether the demand is low cost through efficiency, or quality, or any other criterion.

Alternative Strategies for Achieving Manufacturing Efficiency

Skinner extends the idea of the focused factory in another direction with his concept of a "plant within a plant" (PWP). Because there are advantages to having production capability at a single site, Skinner introduces the concept of breaking up large unfocused plants into smaller units buffered from each other so that they each can be focused separately.

In goods manufacturing, the concept of buffering is a very powerful one. Thompson expressed the idea as decoupling: "Organizations seek to buffer environmental influences by surrounding their technical core with input and output components."[4] A PWP thus can be operated close to Thompson's ideal if buffer inventories are created on the input and output sides. On the input side, the components needed within a plant can be inventoried and quality controlled before they are needed; in this way, it can appear to the PWP that "inputs flow continuously at a steady rate and with specified quality." In a similar way, the PWP can be separated from downstream plants or from the market by creating finished goods inventories.

The alternatives to buffering proposed by Thompson were smoothing, anticipating, and rationing. Smoothing and anticipating focus on the uncertainty introduced into the system by the flow of work; smoothing involves managing the environment to reduce fluctuations in supply and/or demand, and anticipating mitigates the worst effects of those fluctuations by anticipating them. Finally, rationing involves resorting to triage when the demands placed on the system by the environment exceed its ability to handle them.

Applying the Efficiency Model to Services

We saw in Chapters 1 and 2 that the application of operations concepts to services is fraught with difficulty. The problem can be understood easily by thinking about the servuction system model discussed in Chapter 1 and illustrated in Figure 1.2. From an operations point of view, the key characteristics of the model are that the customer is an integral part of the process and that the system operates in real time. Because the system is interactive, it can be (and often is) used to customize the service for each individual.

It is clear from this simplified model that services, by their very nature, do not meet the requirements of the Thompson model. The closest the servuction model comes to the Thompson ideal is that part of the system is invisible to the customer. Even here, however, the customization taking place may introduce uncertainty into the system. Providing that all customization can take place within the servuction system itself, then the part invisible to the customer can be run separately. It often can be located in a place different from the customer contact system.[5] However, when the customization cannot be done within the servuction system, it can introduce uncertainty into the back office.

The servuction system itself is an operations nightmare, because it is impossible to use inventories and impossible to decouple the system from the market. Instead of measuring demand "at a continuous rate," the system is linked directly to a market that frequently varies dramatically from day to day, hour to hour, and even minute to minute. This creates massive problems in capacity planning and utilization.

Instead of "the single kind of product" specified by Thompson, the system can be called on to make a different "product" for each customer. Indeed, it could be argued that, because each customer is different, each customer is an integral part of the process, and each experience or product is unique, this creates massive task uncertainty.

Thompson specifies inputs that flow continuously and at a steady rate with specified quality. Consider the inputs to the servuction system: the physical environment, the contact personnel, the other customers, and the individual customer. The environment may stay constant, but the other three inputs are totally variable, not only in their quality but also in their rate of arrival in the process.

Contact personnel are individuals, not inanimate objects. They have emotions and feelings and, like all other persons, are affected by what is happening in their lives outside work. If they arrive at work in a bad mood, this can influence their performance throughout the day. And that bad mood directly affects the customer, because the service worker is part of the experience being purchased. This problem is discussed again in Chapter 4, which is concerned with the service provider.

Customers also can be subject to moods that can affect their behavior toward the service firm and toward each other. Some moods are predictable, like that caused when a home team wins and the crowds hit the local bars. Other moods are individual, specific, and totally unpredictable until after the customer is already part of the servuction system.

Customers arrive at the service firm at unpredictable rates, making smoothing and anticipation very difficult. One minute a restaurant can be empty, and in the next few minutes it can be full. Analysis often can show predictable peaks that can be planned for; but even this precaution introduces inefficiency, because the firm ideally would prefer that customers arrive in a steady stream. Worse still are the unpredictable peaks. Planning for these peaks produces large amounts of excess capacity at most times. They strain the entire system, undermining the experience for the customer and the contact personnel alike.

Potential Solutions to Service Operations Problems

Within the operations management literature of the past decade, there is a growing body of ideas about how to overcome some of the problems of service operations. These ideas can be classified into four broad areas: isolating the technical core; minimizing the servuction system; production-lining the whole system, including the servuction system; and creating flexible capacity. Other solutions, such as moving the time of demand and increasing customer participation, have been suggested in the marketing literature.

These solutions are not operations solutions alone. To make any of them work requires a marketing input, and to ignore that marketing input is to risk increasing efficiency at the expense of the effectiveness of the system in the mind of the customer. It is this characteristic that differentiates services marketing from any other type of marketing. We discuss each solution from an operations perspective and then from a marketing viewpoint.

Isolating the Technical Core and Minimizing the Servuction System

The Operations Perspective

Isolating the technical core and minimizing the servuction system have been combined because they are closely related from an operations point of view and their marketing implications are similar. Both of these approaches have been suggested by Richard B. Chase's "customer contact model."[6] Following Thompson, Chase advocates the clear separation of the servuction system from the back office. Once this is achieved, he argues, completely different management philosophies should be adopted for each entity.

Chase proposes a classification of services ranging from high contact through low contact. At the high-contact end of the spectrum, he lists "pure services" such as hotels, public transport, restaurants, and schools. At the low-contact end, he puts manufacturing operations. In between are "mixed services" and "quasimanufacturing" operations. Low-contact firms are characterized by the fact that they can easily isolate or "seal off" the technical core from the service component of the operation. Banks, for example, Chase describes as mixed services because the technical core, the head office, can be easily isolated (from the customer's perspective, at least) from the branches, where the service encounters take place. Most bank customers never see the head office; their only contact is with branches. With high-contact services, however, either it is more difficult to isolate the technical core or the technical core is much smaller.

Chase maintains that high-contact systems should sacrifice efficiency in the interest of the customer but that low-contact systems need not necessarily do so. High-contact systems find it difficult to predict demand and so may have to keep unnecessarily high numbers of staff on duty. They are unable to batch production or make use of schedules to create full efficiency. The high levels of uncertainty mean that what schedules they do make are also prone to disruption. Low-contact services can usually avoid these problems; if customers are required to make appointments, for example, then production and scheduling can be planned and appropriate numbers of staff placed on duty. The differences between these two types of systems are summarized in Figure 3.1.

In the servuction system, Chase argues against the use of traditional production-lining approaches, focusing instead on optimizing the experience for the customer. Conversely, once the technical core has been isolated, it should be subjected to all these procedures. This is precisely the approach that has been adopted in some areas of banking.[7] Thus, large-scale banking networks have been consolidated, and the traditional administrative tasks associated with a branch have been brought together in one location. This frees up the branch itself to focus on customer service. The resulting "paper factory" offers all the same characteristics as any other factory and can be subject to the same kind of logic.

Later, Chase extends his ideas,[8] arguing for the minimization of the customer contact component; he expresses this argument in the form of an equation:

$$\text{Potential operating efficiency} = \int \left(1 - \frac{\text{Customer contact time}}{\text{Service creation time}}\right)$$

FIGURE 3.1	MAJOR DESIGN CONSIDERATIONS IN HIGH- AND LOW-CONTACT SYSTEMS	
Decision	**High-Contact System**	**Low-Contact System**
Facility location	Operations must be near the customer.	Operations may be placed near supply, transportation, or labor.
Facility layout	Facility should accommodate the customer's physical and pyschological needs and expectations.	Facility should enhance production.
Product design	Environment as well as the physical product define the nature of the service.	Customer is not in the service environment, so the product can be defined by fewer attributes.
Process design	Stages of production process have a direct immediate effect on the customer.	Customer is not involved in the majority of processing steps.
Scheduling	Customer is in the production schedule and must be accommodated.	Customer is concerned mainly with completion.
Production planning	Orders cannot be stored, so smoothing production flow will result in loss of business.	Both backlogging and production smoothing are possible.
Worker skills	Direct workforce comprises a major part of the service product and so must be able to interact well with the public.	Direct workforce need only have technical skills.
Quality control	Quality standards are often in the eye of the beholder and hence variable.	Quality standards are generally measureable and hence fixed.
Time standards	Service time depends on customer needs, and therefore time standards are inherently loose.	Work is performed on customer surrogates (e.g., forms), and time standards can be tight.
Wage payment	Variable output requires time-based wage systems.	"Fixable" outputs permit output-based wage systems.
Capacity planning	To avoid lost sales, capacity must be set to match peak demand.	Storable output permits setting capacity at some average demand level.
Forecasting	Forecasts are short term, time-oriented.	Forecasts are long term, output-oriented.

SOURCE: Richard. B. Chase, "Where Does the Service Customer Fit in a Service Operation," *Harvard Business Review* (November–December 1978): 137–142.

Operating efficiency thus is reduced by the uncertainty introduced into the system by the customer. Another author has similarly argued that "clients . . . pose problems for organizations . . . by disrupting their routines, ignoring their offers for service, failing to comply with their procedures, making exaggerated demands, and so forth."[9] This latter problem is illustrated well by two empirical studies that show that one of the key causes of service failure is the unrealistic expectations of the customers.[10]

Chase suggests a number of ways of decoupling the technical core. For example, only exceptions should be handled on a face-to-face basis, with routine transactions being handled as much as possible by telephone or, even better, by mail. Mail transactions have the great advantage of being able to be inventoried.[11]

Chase's final refining of the concept was done with a number of colleagues.[12] Together, they suggest that the degree of customer contact should be matched to customer requirements and that the extent of high-contact service offered should be the minimum acceptable to the customer. This approach is summarized in Table 3.2. Operational efficiency always favors low-contact systems, but effectiveness from the customer's point of view favors the correct matching.

Each cell in the table shows the extent to which marketing effectiveness has been met and the extent to which operational efficiency has been achieved. Offering high-contact services to customers who demand low contact is both inefficient and ineffective and is clearly the least-desirable quadrant. Low-contact requirement and delivery

TABLE 3.2	MATCHING CUSTOMER AND FIRM	
	Customer Requirement	
Firm Provision	High Contact	Low Contact
High Contact	Inefficient	Inefficient
	Effective	Ineffective
Low Contact	Efficient	Efficient
	Ineffective	Effective

offer the opportunity to be both efficient and effective. The other two quadrants represent the classic marketing/operations compromise, and the choice would be determined best by the competitive environment.

The Marketing Perspective

At this point, the need for a marketing involvement in this approach becomes clear, as a decision about the extent of customer contact favored by the customer is clearly a marketing issue. In some cases, a high degree of customer contact can be used to differentiate the service from its competitors; in these cases, the operational costs have to be traded against the competitive benefits.

Conversely, in some situations the segment of the firm that the operations group views as the back office is not actually invisible to the customer. For example, in some financial services, the teller operation takes place in the administrative offices. Operationally, this means that staff members can leave their paperwork to serve customers only when needed. Unfortunately, customers frequently view this operationally efficient system very negatively. A customer waiting to be served can see a closed teller window or service point and observe staff who apparently do not care because they sit at their desks and do not serve. In fact, they are extremely busy, but the nature of administrative work is such that this may not be the impression given.

Even if it is decided that part of the system can be decoupled, marketing has a major role in evaluating and implementing alternative approaches. Any change in the way in which the servuction system works implies a change in the behavior of the customer. A switch from a personal service to a combined mail and telephone system clearly requires a massive change in the way the customer behaves in the system. Marketing always has been the function that understands and modifies consumer behavior, and this must be the case here.

Perhaps the easiest way to understand this problem is in terms of script theory, which was described in Chapter 2. If this perspective is accepted, then clearly any change in the operations of a service business that impacts on the customer requires a change in the script. If the change of script is not managed, then it will be perceived by the customer as a breakdown compared with expectations. It is marketing's task to ensure the correct education of the customer to the new script.

Production-Lining the Whole System

Theodore Levitt advocates a "production-line approach,"[13] which involves the application of hard and soft techniques to both the "front" and the "back" of the house. In his examples of McDonald's, he draws from both the servuction system and the back of house. This kind of solution is relatively rare and, indeed, the fast-food firms provide a classic example, together with dry cleaners and some auto maintenance firms. Their rarity stems largely from the marketing demands imposed on such systems. Those demands mean minimal customization, large-volume throughput, and high levels of customer participation. Even Burger King, with its "Have It Your Way" approach, still has minimal customization.

The generation of any kind of operational efficiency in such a servuction system implies a very limited product line—in this case, the menu. Moreover, customization must be kept to a minimum, because the whole operating system is linked straight through to the customer. Several authors have discussed precisely this problem of how to provide efficient, standardized service at some acceptable level of quality, while simultaneously treating each customer as a unique person.[14] Their conclusions show the complexity of the problem, because attempts at a routine personalization—the "have-a-nice-day syndrome"—have positive effects on perceived friendliness but have negative effects on perceived competence. Thus, an apparently simple operations decision can have complex effects on customer perceptions.

The servuction system of a restaurant also depends for its success on large volumes of customers available to take the food that is produced. Because the invisible component is not decoupled and food cannot be prepared to order, the operating system has to run independently of individual demand and assume that, in the end, aggregate demand will absorb the food produced.

Such a servuction system is also extremely demanding of its customers. They must preselect what they want to eat. They are expected to have their order ready when they reach the order point. They must leave the order point quickly and carry their food to the table. Finally, they are expected to bus their own table.

Creating Flexible Capacity

The Operations Perspective

As pointed out earlier, the servuction system creates major capacity-planning problems. Rather than tackle the cause directly, Sasser[15] suggests alternative strategies for matching supply and demand, one of which is the creation of flexible capacity. To meet the fluctuating demand, he advocates the use of:

Part-time employees

A strategy that focuses on customer service jobs during peak demand

Shared capacity with other firms

In the first strategy, part-time employees can be used to provide extra capacity at peak times without increasing the costs at off-peak times. The second strategy suggests that, during peak demand, personnel focus only on those parts of the operation needed to serve customers. Chase, in a similar way, advocates the use of roving greeters to channel away from service employees purely informational tasks and hence to keep the main operation performing at maximum capacity.[16] Finally, Sasser suggests the sharing of capacity with other firms—firms that have different peak demands and can share facilities.

The Marketing Perspective

Part-time employees appear to be a useful strategy from an operations point of view. There are, however, a number of marketing implications inherent in this approach that Sasser does not discuss. Part-time employees may deliver a lower-quality service than full-time workers; their dedication to quality may be less, as probably will be their training. They are used at times when the operation is at its worst, and this may be reflected in their attitude. As Schneider has shown, such attitudes can be very visible to the customer and are likely to influence negatively the perceptions they have of the service.[17]

In a similar way, the two other approaches suggested by Sasser have major marketing implications. Focusing on customer-serving jobs during peak demand presupposes that it is possible to identify the key part of the service from the customer's point of view. From a marketing perspective, the dangers with sharing capacity are numerous. Confusion may be produced in the customer's mind over exactly what the service facility is doing, and this could be particularly acute during changeover times when customers from two different firms are in the same facility, each group with different priorities and different scripts.

Increasing Customer Participation

Increasing customer participation has been discussed by a number of marketing researchers, among them Lovelock and Young.[18] The essence of the idea is to replace the work done by the employees of the firm with work done by the customer. Unlike the other strategies discussed, this approach is not necessarily an efficiency argument, but rather a cost-based argument. It moves the operation no closer to the ideal suggested by Thompson,[19] but it reduces the costs, no matter what the state of the operation.

Following the script-theory analogy, it is clear that such an approach demands a major change in the script. Moreover, the customers are called on to take a greater responsibility for the service they receive. For example, the automatic teller machine (ATM) is seen by many operations personnel as a way of saving labor. The substitution of capital for labor is a classic operations approach, and the ATM can be viewed in that light. From the customer's point of view, such ATMs provide added convenience in terms of the hours during which the bank is accessible. However, it has been shown that, for some customers, this represents increased risk, less control of the situation, and a loss of human contact.[20]

Such a switching of activities to the customer clearly has major marketing implications, because the whole nature of the product received is changing. Such changes in the customer's script therefore require much customer research and detailed planning.

Moving the Time of Demand to Fit Capacity

To overcome the capacity-utilization problem outlined earlier, Sasser suggests that marketing should be used to smooth the peaks in demand. Perhaps the classic example of this problem is the mass transit system that needs to create capacity to deal with the rush hour and, as a consequence, has much of its fleet and labor idle during the nonrush hours. A number of authorities have tried to reduce the severity of the problem by inducing passengers to travel in nonrush periods. Unfortunately, because much travel is a derived demand and is based on work hours, little success can be expected.

Summary: The Marketing/Operations Interdependence

The purpose of this discussion has been to highlight the fact that operations-management problems in services often cannot be solved by the operations function alone. The search for operations efficiency can be crucial to long-run competitiveness.

Unfortunately, efficiency has to be balanced against the effectiveness of the system from the customer's point of view, as discussed in the next chapter.

Frequently, it is too easy to view the customer as a constraint: "If we could just get rid of these customers, we could run a good service!" Such a negative perspective ignores the golden opportunity. Customers in a service operation can be used to help service operations. Such a positive view, however, does require that operations personnel recognize the importance of their marketing counterparts.

More important, such a view also requires that marketing personnel have an intimate knowledge of the operating system and its problems. It is not enough to propose new products that can be delivered through the system. The impact of such products on the whole system needs to considered.

Questions

1. Using the framework in this chapter, categorize the various ways Arby's has tried to industrialize its service.

2. Describe a recent example familiar to you in which operational demands have necessitated a change in script for the consumer. How was that change managed?

3. A local bank is considering the introduction of a single-line queuing system to replace its current multiline system. Advise the bank's management from both operations and marketing perspectives, discussing the advantages and disadvantages of this change.

4. Choose one of the operations-based strategies discussed in this chapter and discuss its impact on the service providers—the contact staff members.

Notes

[1] Benson P. Shapiro, "Can Marketing and Manufacturing Coexist?" *Harvard Business Review* (September–October 1977): 107–117.

[2] J.D. Thompson, *Organizations in Action* (New York: McGraw-Hill, 1967).

[3] W. Skinner, "The Focused Factory," *Harvard Business Review* 52, no. 3 (May–June 1974): 113–121.

[4] Thompson, *Organizations in Action*, 69.

[5] For the application of this idea to banking, see R.J. Matteis, "The New Back Office Focuses on Customer Service," *Harvard Business Review* 57, no. 3 (May–June 1979): 146–159.

[6] Richard B. Chase, "Where Does the Service Customer Fit in a Service Operation," *Harvard Business Review* (November–December 1978): 137–142.

[7] R.J. Matteis, "The New Back Office Focuses on Customer Service," *Harvard Business Review* 57, no. 3 (May–June 1979): 146–159.

[8] These extensions of the customer contact model are developed in Richard B. Chase, "The Customer Contact Approach to Services: Theoretical Base and Practical Extensions," *Operations Research* 29, no. 4 (July–August, 1981): 698–706; and Richard B. Chase and David A. Tansik, "The Customer Contact Model for Organization Design," *Management Service* 29, no. 9 (1983): 1037–1050.

[9] B. Danet, "Client-Organization Interfaces," in P.C. Nystrom and W.N. Starbuck, eds., *Handbook of Organization Design*, vol. 2 (New York: Oxford University Press, 1981), 384.

[10] These studies employed the critical incident technique to look at service encounters that fail. They are described in Mary J. Bitner, Jody D. Nyquist, and Bernard H. Booms, "The Critical Incident Technique for Analyzing the Service Encounter," in Thomas M. Block, Gregory D. Upah, and Valarie A. Zeithaml, eds., *Service Marketing in a Changing Environment* (Chicago: American Marketing Association, 1985), 48–51; and Jody D. Nyquist, Mary J. Bitner, and Bernard Booms, "Identifying Communications Difficulties in the Service Encounter: A Critical Incident Approach," in J. Czepiel, M. Solomon, and Carol Surprenant, eds., *The Service Encounter* (Lexington, MA: Heath, 1984).

[11] Chase, "The Customer Contact Approach to Services."

[12]For detailed descriptions, see Richard B. Chase and Gerrit Wolf, "Shaping a Strategy for Savings and Loan Branches," Working Paper, Department of Management, College of Business and Public Administration, University of Arizona, 1982; and Richard B. Chase, Gerrit Wolf, and Gregory B. Northcroft, "Designing High Contact Service Systems: Applications to Branches of Savings and Loans," Working Paper, Department of Management, College of Business and Public Administration, University of Arizona, 1983.

[13]T. Levitt, "Production-Line Approach to Services," *Harvard Business Review* 50, no. 5 (September–October 1972): 41–52.

[14]Carol F. Surprenant and Michael Solomon, "Predictability and Personalization in the Service Encounter," *Journal of Marketing* 51 (April 1987): 86–96.

[15]W. Earl Sasser, "Match Supply and Demand in Service Industries," *Harvard Business Review* 54, no. 5 (November–December 1976): 61–65.

[16]Chase, "The Customer Contact Approach to Services."

[17]Benjamin Schneider, "The Service Organization: Climate Is Crucial," *Organizational Dynamics* (Autumn 1980): 52–65.

[18]Christopher M. Lovelock and Robert F. Young, "Look to Consumers to Increase Productivity," *Harvard Business Review* (May 1979): 168–178. See also J.E.G. Bateson, "Self-Service Consumer: An Exploratory Study," *Journal of Retailing* 61, no. 3 (Fall 1986): 49–74.

[19]Thompson, *Organizations in Action*, 69.

[20]Bateson, "Self-Service Consumer."

4

Understanding
the Service Worker

Chapter Overview

The public faces of the service firm are the contact personnel, the service workers in day-to-day contact with the customers from hell described in this chapter. Part factory workers, part administrators, part servants, theirs is a complex and difficult job. Despite this, they are often the lowest-status persons in the organization, and often in society.

This chapter highlights the importance of the contact personnel to the firm and their particular role in creating customer satisfaction. It goes on to explain the pressures and tensions on the service workers as they try to play a boundary-spanning role. They are the permeable surface of the organization, interfacing outward with the environment and inward with the organization itself. They thus have a complex role to play, and the impact of the resulting stress on the individuals occupying these roles has been explored extensively in the literature of organizational behavior.

To alleviate that stress, several alternative strategies are open to boundary spanners. Unfortunately, many of these strategies have negative consequences for customers.

The Importance of Contact Personnel

Strategically, contact personnel can be the source of product differentiation. One way to consider the problem of product differentiation is to break the service firm into three parts: the benefit concept, the servuction system, and the service level. The benefit concept is the bundle of benefits received by the customer, and it can be measured only in the mind of that customer. The basis of the service-level idea is that the operating system itself should be separated from the way it operates. This rather arbitrary separation allows for the separation of systems design from the operating performance of that design.

It is often impossible for a service organization to differentiate itself from other similar organizations in regard to the benefit bundle it offers or its delivery servuction system. For example, one extreme view is that many airlines offer similar bundles of benefits and fly the same planes from the same airports. Their only hope of a competitive advantage is therefore from the service level—the way things are done. Some of this differentiation can come from staffing levels or the physical systems designed to support the staff. Often, however, the deciding factor that distinguishes one airline from another is the attitude of the service providers.[1]

This problem is well highlighted by Bitner and colleagues[2] in an interesting analysis of the sources of satisfaction and dissatisfaction for service consumers. The approach used is the critical incident procedure, which is a powerful tool for gaining insights into complex phenomena. Respondents were asked to recall a time when, as customers, they had a particularly satisfying or dissatisfying interaction with an employee of an airline, hotel, or restaurant; and then they were asked a series of questions:

When did the incident happen?

What specific circumstances led to this situation?

Exactly what did the employee say or do?

What was the result?

Do you feel the interaction was satisfying or dissatisfying?

The result was 699 descriptions of specific incidents (347 satisfactory and 352 unsatisfactory) from customers who had interacted with airlines, restaurants, and hotels. Through a process of classification, the incidents were sorted according to the

TABLE 4.1	CLASSIFICATION OF TYPE OF INCIDENT AND OUTCOME	
	Outcome	
	Percent Satisfactory	**Percent Dissatisfactory**
Group 1: Employee Responses to Service Delivery Failure		
Response to unavailable service	7	8
Response to unreasonably slow service	5	15
Response to other core service failure	11	20
Subtotal	23	43
Group 2: Employee Responses to Customer Needs and Requests		
Response to "special needs" customers	10	2
Response to customer preferences	15	11
Response to admitted customer error	6	2
Response to potentially disruptive others	2	1
Subtotal	33	16
Group 3: Unprompted and Unsolicited Employee Actions		
Attention paid to customer	14	13
Truly out-of-the-ordinary employee behavior	6	12
Employee behaviors in the context of cultural norms	5	12
Gestalt evaluation	16	4
Performance under adverse circumstances	3	—
Subtotal	44	41

source of satisfaction and dissatisfaction and a simplified version of the results is shown in Table 4.1.

Several things become immediately apparent from this table. The first is that service failures, such as unavailable service or slow service, do not automatically lead to dissatisfied customers. If handled correctly by contact personnel, they can lead to satisfaction—as they did with 23 percent of the incidents.

Customers do not always obey the rules (see "Customers from Hell"). Their personal preferences, behavior, and mistakes can place demands on contact personnel that fall outside the scope of standard procedures and practices. Again, the way the employee responds to these needs and requests can influence the satisfaction level of the customer dramatically.

Finally, and most important, nearly half of satisfied and dissatisfied customers described incidents in which the primary action was an unprompted employee action. These ranged from positive actions ("The bus boy ran after us to return a $50 bill my boyfriend had dropped under the table)" to negative actions ("I needed a few more minutes to decide on a dinner. The waitress said, 'If you would read the menu and not the road map, you would know what you wanted to order.'")

All these actions are outside the scope of normal operating procedures. Each represents an independent positive or negative action by a contact person. Part of designing a service is to understand what it is that influences individuals to behave as they do.

The Customers From Hell

The Crown of Creation

Call him *Egocentric Edgar*. This is the guy Carly Simon had in mind when she sang, "You're so vain, you probably think this song is about you." Stand in line? Him? My dear, his time is much too valuable. "Excuse me, I'm in a hurry here! Coming through!"

It turns out, of course, that Edgar's big emergency involves buying a plane ticket—for a flight next month. Or a sudden need to cash 97 savings bonds—except he doesn't have them signed and his checking account is in another bank and there is only one teller on duty. "You *do* advertise that you believe in service to the customer, *n'est-ce pas?*" Then again, he may simply be in urgent need of directions to the nearest hot comb.

Edgar *will* speak to the owner, the president, the chairman, "the man in charge," as he will never fail to put it. Actually, he doesn't care if the individual in charge is male, female, or a Swiss mountain goat as long as there is a chance it's someone he can intimidate through some judicious name-dropping. And he'll delight in walking over a front line person to get there.

Edgar is the one who loudly demands that your organization stop the hurricane, quell the civil insurrection, or create the replacement part out of thin air so his flight can leave on time. "Don't tell me this airplane can't be moved! I want it moved!" Me first, me last, me only—that's his creed. You? You're just a bit player, an extra, an extraneous piece of scenery in his grandest of all productions. "Edgar: The Greatest Story Ever Told."

The Breath of Spring

Bad-Mouth Betty: Her mother would be proud. Such an extensive vocabulary! It takes timing, talent, and a total lack of shame to walk into a department store or a bank lobby and cuss like a drunken stevedore, but Betty makes it look easy.

You: "Good morning, Ms. Coupon Clipper."

Betty: "Don't good morning me, you ————! I know what you ————s are doing. You're holding on to my ————ing money so you can get rich on the ————ing float!"

You: "But Ms. Clipper, the payment isn't due until the first of the month and this is only the 25th."

Betty: "———— you, you little ————! I know your game, you ————ing lousy, two-bit ————. You were two days late last ————ing month. Let it happen again and I'll have your ————s in court, you ————ing ————s!"

If she can't be right, she'll be caustic, crude, cruel, and as foul as a pigpen in July.

The Air Raid Siren

Hysterical Harold is a screamer. The Harolds of the world blow their corks higher and faster than an agitated bottle of cheap champagne—and come down a lot slower. The second Harold senses a possible deviation from the plan—his plan—he goes off at 10,000 decibels.

Allen Funt would love this guy: he's so animated and photogenic. Harold is likely to turn vein-popping purple and jump up and down on the hood of his own car when the service manager tells him a part is out of stock and has to be emergency ordered—for the next day. Naturally, Harold expects the dents he inflicted to be fixed at the dealership's expense, during the same visit.

And wouldn't you know it, Harold is *always* the guy who gets the banana split without any banana in it. All of his friends think this is hilarious. Harold does his rabid-dog impersonation while everyone else is doubled over laughing.

If it's true that there is a child in all of us yearning to break free, Harold demonstrates the dark side of that happy thought. He is the classic tantrum-thrower, the adult embodiment of the terrible twos. Only louder. Much louder.

The Pride of the Reich

"Und you *will* follow orders, und you *will* do it my vay! *Macht schnell!*" That's *Dictatorial Dick*. Any wonder that this guy gets dose after dose of malicious obedience? People follow his mandates to the letter, even those that make no sense.

Suspected of being Edgar's even-eviler twin, Dick often shows up with written marching orders: a copy for the service person, a copy for the service person's manager, a copy for himself. The original will have been dated, time-stamped, and sent to his lawyer by registered letter.

By a happy coincidence, Dick "used to be in this business" and knows all the little tricks of the trade that you, you sneaky peon, were planning to pull on him. As soon as you hear his plan for how the impending transaction is going to work, you realize why he isn't in the business any more.

Dick issues ultimatums, sets arbitrary deadlines, and tells everyone exactly how to do their jobs. And when his plan doesn't work? It's your company's fault, of course. Better still, it's *your* fault. Obviously, you were incompetent. Either that or you were trying to sabotage his brilliant plan.

(Continued)

(Continued)

The Soul of Charity

A material girl in a material world, *Freeloading Freda* wants her dollar's worth—and yours, and mine, and anyone else's she can get. If the deal is "Buy one, get one free," she wants two for nothing. If the offer is buy the Jumbo Stuperific size and get a small for free, she wants a regular. She orders the small drink, complains that it's too small, and demands a large. She orders the wild boar stew, inhales nine of the ten ounces in the bowl, then calls the waitress over and pronounces it too gamy. "Take it back and bring me a hamburger instead." If asked to pay for either the stew or the burger, she carries on like the victim of a stock swindle.

If it wears out, breaks or begins to bore her, Freda takes it back. Her kid dribbles the portable TV down the basement stairs; she takes it back. She buys a fancy dressing gown, wears it to the company Christmas party (where she rolls in the punchbowl), and takes it back. There is not a store in town she hasn't hit up for a cash refund for that cuckoo clock Aunt Sarah sent from France in 1955. But don't you dare accuse her of taking advantage. She will scream lawsuit, slander, Eyewitness News, and Better Business Bureau at the top of her lungs.

SOURCE: Ron Zemke and Kristin Anderson, "Customers from Hell," *Training* 26 (February 1990), 25–31.

Benjamin Schneider[3] argues that measurements of staff effectiveness cannot focus solely on short-term statistical factors such as number of transactions processed or number of errors made. More general factors also need to be included; he argues that, at the very least, courtesy and style of performance should be assessed as indicators of effectiveness.

In Schneider's view, management has a strong role to play in creating a climate in which good service is the norm. Managers who establish policies and procedures that emphasize style of service performance are service enthusiasts; those who stress routinization and maintenance of the system are service bureaucrats. The consequences of the latter can be lack of fit between the employees' own service orientation and that of management, role ambiguity, and role conflict, followed by feelings of dissatisfaction and frustration on the part of employees. However, if procedures are used to create a "climate for service" (see Figure 4.1), an environment can result in which employees are encouraged and supported in their wish to give good service.

Schneider starts from the perspective that most employees desire to give good service and have a service orientation; if they did not, they would not be in their jobs in the first place. His surveys of service employees show that the most important creator of job dissatisfaction is lack of managerial support; likewise, an important determinant of satisfaction by employees is the availability of support in areas such as personnel, central processing, marketing, and equipment. Parallel research conducted with customers, aimed at eliciting their views on good service, found many areas of customer satisfaction were contingent on the presence or absence of these same systems. Courtesy and competence on the part of staff, adequate numbers of staff, promptness and convenience, and a general air of being well managed and run were all given as determinants of satisfaction. Schneider's research showed strong correlation between employee and customer dissatisfaction and satisfaction.[4] His conclusion is that when employees think there is a strong service orientation and that they are being supported in their desire to give good service, then customers are offered a higher standard of service, notice this, and reflect back a corresponding increase in satisfaction.

The Boundary-Spanning Role

The boundary-spanning role has been defined as one that links an organization with the environment within which it operates.[5] Participants in such a role create these

FIGURE 4.1   ANTECEDENTS AND CONSEQUENCES OF "CLIMATE FOR SERVICE" IN BANKS

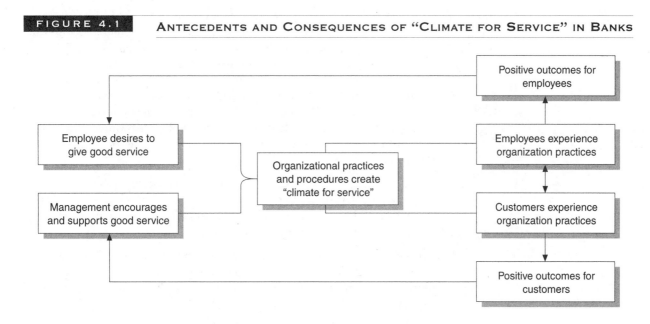

SOURCE: Benjamin Schneider, "The Service Organization: Climate Is Crucial," *Organizational Dynamics*, Autumn 1980, 52–65.

links for the organization by interacting with nonmembers. Persons in such roles have two purposes: information transfer and representation.[6] Boundary spanners collect information from the environment and feed it back into the organization, and they communicate with the environment on behalf of the organization. They are also the organization's personal representatives. Such roles often carry high status and are filled by highly trained personnel; salespersons are a classic example.

Boas Shamir[7] suggests that there are two types of roles in service firms—subordinate service roles and service roles based on professional expertise. In reality, there is not a dichotomy of roles but a spectrum. At one extreme are the "subordinate service roles" existing at the bottom of the organization. Persons in these roles work for service firms where the customer's purchase decision is entirely discretionary. They are subordinate to the organization and to the customer. These are the waiters, porters, drivers, and the like who operate at the very base of the organization and yet are the organization's contact personnel with the outside world.

At the other extreme are the professionals. They, too, are boundary spanners, and yet their status is very different. Because of their "professional" qualifications, they have a status that is independent of their place in the organization. Customers, or (as they more often are called) clients, are not superior to them because they acknowledge the professional's expertise on which they wish to draw.

Regardless of the type of role, however, conflicts can occur when role expectations do not fit with either the overall service orientation of the firm, or the contact person's own standards and values. Individuals' own views of themselves may not necessarily be what the firm expects of them, or indeed what is appropriate for the job they are doing.

Role Stress in Boundary-Spanning Roles

Rafaeli[8] provides a detailed observational study of one such contact role, the supermarket cashier. This qualitative study highlights the sources of stress faced by the cashier as well as the paradoxes of the role. Customers have the major influence on cashiers because their influence is instantaneous, continuous, and simultaneous with the performance of the job. The manager, by comparison, who holds the legitimate influence, can only create the environment and set the stage for employee performance. It is the customers who directly create the stress in this role.

Rafaeli suggests that there are four main sources of stress:

- An inability of contact personnel to develop a strong social network among co-workers because of a discipline imposed by the customers who do not want the staff to be too "chatty" while they are working. This is obviously an idiosyncrasy of the supermarket situation, but occurs to a greater or lesser extent in other settings as well.

- The constrained nature of the customer–cashier relationship means that cashiers often are denied the freedom to engage in normal social interaction with customers. This, combined with the inability to socialize with other staff, makes this particular contact role a lonely one.

- Role conflict and ambiguity are just as prevalent within this boundary-spanning role as in any other. Conflict and ambiguity are organization behavior concepts that have been discussed at considerable length in the literature on this field.

- The fight for control. Everyone needs to believe that they are in control, and in service settings this is a source of much tension.

The latter two sources of stress are addressed by other authors, notably Shamir[9] and Bateson.[10]

Sources of Conflict in Boundary-Spanning Roles

Shamir develops a long list of potential conflicts imposed on subordinate personnel because they have boundary-spanning roles. This list can be applied to a greater or lesser extent to professionally oriented roles as well.

1. Inequality dilemmas. Although it is important to put the customer first, this can sometimes result in the service personnel feeling belittled or demeaned. These feelings can be magnified if customers make a point of establishing their personal superiority over the server.

2. Feelings versus behavior. Contact personnel are often required to hide their true feelings and present a "front" or "face" to the customer. This can result in role stress as the server does not identify with the role he or she is acting out.

3. Territorial conflict. Contact personnel will often try to establish their own personal space, which they will defend against clients and other servers. Trespass on this space can lead to reactions that conflict with the server's own role.

4. Organization versus client. Contact personnel can sometimes receive conflicting instructions, one set from the client who wants a service performed in a particular way, the other from the organization that wants that service performed in a different way. Chapter 2 referred to the "three-cornered fight" between customer, server, and organization, which must essentially be resolved by compromise. However, such compromises can, if mishandled, leave the server feeling badly treated.

5. Interclient conflicts. These conflicts occur when two or more customers have different and opposing demands; for example, one customer may want the window open while another may demand it be closed. In such cases, the

Holding It for Eight Hours I

The following conversations with waitresses in London illustrate how the boundary-spanning role creates stress.

ANNA HAMILTON:

Silly things happen—you know, you have to pretend as if everything they do is OK. If drunk people come along, particularly when they start eating off the flowers and throwing glasses on the floor. "It's quite all right sir; don't worry about it," you know, and you have to pretend that everything they do is fine.

ANNE LEVER:

I was approaching this woman and she was there, calmly reading her Listener, I think it was; I just plonked the whole thing on her dress (laughs), you know, and it just completely fell and, you know, did a nice neat turnover, you know, so no savory, I mean no dough side—it had to be all the toppings . . . weeeraaarghhh.

SHEILA COLE:

The difficulty is to keep smiling of course. I always remember at the end of a long shift someone saying to me "Smile!" You know, why don't you smile, and you just feel like saying no, you smile—now hold it for eight hours.

EVA MILENSKA:

If you really wish something bad to happen to your friend, just wish her to be a waitress! (laughs)

SHEILA:

I play sort of little games sometimes. I suppose to relieve the boredom of the monotony of the job, but I go to a table and I'll be really, really, you know, over the top or really, um, jolly and witty and whatever and then other times I'll be sort of slightly different. You know, it's just sort of interesting how people react to you and you also look at people you're going to serve and I think that has a lot to do with how you are as well. Um, sometimes I'm overwhelmed by peoples' shyness. You know that sometimes I feel that I'm very overpowering and I haven't meant to be. You realize that from the way they've reacted to you you're coming across as very different to how you really are or you've been misinterpreted somehow.

BERNADETTE GEIFER:

Sometimes, I'd prefer challenging customers if the challenge is all right. There was a woman who came in who wasn't happy with anything at all and she didn't like anything on the menu, and your first response was to just slam down things down and be very snippy towards her. But, in the end, I felt no, she was looking to find something wrong with the place and with me and I thought no, I'm not going to give her the satisfaction. And I was so brilliant towards her and so polite; in the end she, you know, she was brilliant, hugged me when I left, and all that.

ANNE KOVAL:

I find that because a lot of the customers are young and, um, they are involved in jobs where they're making lots of money and they bring their friends around to the wine bar, er, they tend to, um, use you—the waitress—as a servant. It's the closest I've ever become to being a servant, um, for someone. It's quite disturbing at times when they treat you, in front of their friends, as a non-human being in a lot of ways. I went up to a table and a group of gentlemen and, um, I think they were probably estate agents or something of that genre, and, um, one of the gentlemen had, um, one of those portable telephones and it rang while he was talking to me or doing some ordering, and, um, he was talking on the telephone and the other gentlemen didn't take up the initiative and finish the order, so they expected me to wait around. It was very busy at that moment, so I walked away and was waiting for him to complete his phone call, and then I'd return to the table and when I did return to the table, he, um, he was quite put out—the fact that I hadn't waited around until he'd finished his conversation on his portable telephone.

SHEILA:

People can be incredibly rude, unbelievably rude. We had an instance a few weeks ago that happened here; a waitress, who's since left the profession, and she was dealing with a man who was just outrageous and she just couldn't stand any more, come to her wits' end, and he said the classic one-liner, "This food isn't fit for a pig!"—which had only one retort which was "I'll get you some that is, sir," and I think when you get to that, you're on your way out. That's it and you know you won't keep going unless you keep up the performance. In a way, waitressing is a kind of performing thing where you're putting on an act in a way. So I think that's why you find so many people within the arts involved in waitressing, partly because of the hours, but partly because they can put on different roles and no one's going to know whether it's them or not them.

BERNADETTE:

I write fiction, mostly short stories, and, I mean, obviously, I would like to do that full time for a living if I could make enough money at it, but it's one of those things where you obviously can't make enough money in the beginning, you know. So you try and get a few stories out to publications, and while you're waiting to hear from them, or, you know, you write three hours a day or four hours a day, you know you obviously need to be doing something else as well. I do find that I like meeting people, um, I just like talking to people; I'll basically talk to anyone and, in some ways, that's quite a good . . . I never think about writing stories about the people I meet, but some of the things they say to me make me stop and think, and some of the things that happen, um, would make a humorous story. So that's one of the aspects that I like about that is that it keeps me in contact with more than just, you know, a bunch of office people that I know every day. I mean, I'm constantly meeting people I've never met before.

SOURCE: BBC Radio, "Holding It for Eight Hours," September 8, 1988.

contact personnel often have to serve as arbitrators or referees. This may not have been specified as part of their role, and stepping outside the role in this fashion can produce additional stress.

Such conflicts are exacerbated if the BSP (boundary-spanning personnel) agrees with the customer. Schneider found that contact personnel in a subordinate role do know whether they are giving good or bad service; moreover, they are well aware when the rules and procedures prevent them from delivering good service.[11] This is precisely the organization/client conflict suggested by Shamir. Often, it is aggravated by BSP's siding with the customer.

For subordinate service personnel, this kind of conflict is very stressful, because they have no status with the customer or the organization and no power to alter the situation. They cannot change the rule or procedure, and often they cannot tell the customer the reason for the rule or procedure. Professionals, with their higher status, are more able to control what happens.

Conflicts between clients arise because many servuction systems have within them a number of clients, some of whom may be operating with conflicting standards. In a sense, these individuals have completely different scripts for themselves, the contact personnel, and the other customers. When customers come into conflict, it is usually the BSP who is called on to resolve it. For example, it is the airline cabin attendant who generally is summoned to ask one's neighbor not to smoke in a nonsmoking section. Moreover, any attempt to satisfy all the clients involved can escalate the conflict or bring the BSP into the battle. A restaurant customer requesting speedy service and receiving it can cause complaints from other tables about the unevenness of the service. Once again, those in subordinate roles start from the weakest position because they have low status with the clients. Professionals may face the same problems; for example, consider the patient in the hospital waiting room demanding preferential treatment. In this case, however, the professional can invoke his or her status and expertise to resolve the situation.

The Fight for Control

In Chapter 2, it was suggested that the service encounter can be viewed as a fight for control. This model, which applies equally to customers and to contact personnel, suggests that individuals like to feel in control of what happens to them. Therefore, there is a fight between these two parties for control of the encounter. An early study of restaurants, for example, found that waitresses coped with the pressures of their jobs by managing their customers. They were able to wrest control away from the customer by suggesting menu items and telling customers how long they would have to wait.[12] This is precisely the strategy used by many professionals who use their status, and the fact that the client is not in a position to leave, to take control.

This is not simply a two-cornered fight, however; the organization itself also wishes to establish control of the encounter. The procedures and systems established by the organization are not always created for sheer bureaucratic pleasure, as implied by Schneider. Often the procedures and systems are the heart of the economics of the organization. Deviation can jeopardize profitability.

The Implications of Role Stress for Boundary-Spanning Personnel

The consequences of role conflict and stress have been investigated extensively. Generally, such stress produces dissatisfaction, frustration, and turnover intention in personnel. Schneider[13] shows that organization/client conflict in service organizations can lead to such outcomes. He shows that contact personnel, who are more service

Holding It for Eight Hours II

The following conversations with waitresses in London further illustrate how the boundary-spanning role creates stress.

SHEILA:

Of course it's great having regular customers, but sometimes it can be a bit difficult. I remember one chap used to come in an awful lot, every week, you know, sometimes twice a week, and he would always come in with a different woman every time. I mean, it was phenomenal, but he used to start off by kissing them across the table and it would get more and more involved until he was practically making love in quite an offensive way. I mean, people around would be quite put off until, in the end, we had to, you know, say I'm sorry, but we can't have this any more, and he was asked to leave, which is awful for him, but we haven't seen him since.

BERNADETTE:

Arguments are very difficult—when a couple's having an argument—because you inevitably go up at the very wrong time and say, you know, would you like to see a dessert menu or something stupid. And, you know, you're trying to wait for a point to break in, and you can't do it very easily and you can see them fuming and, er, some of that gets very difficult. Because once there was a friend of mine—instead of saying "Would you like to see a dessert menu?" he said, "Would you like to see a divorce menu?" and they went . . . !

SHEILA:

Oh yes, yes, there's been a few divorces over, um, dinner, um, yes, and people, um, flirting with each other. Er, it's very very amusing; I mean, obviously, you don't mean to listen, but you know some man shooting off about how brilliant he is all night—you know, every time you go up it's I, I, I, and the girl's sort of slowly . . . or some woman who's talking so much, I mean, you can see the nervousness of people, you know, and when they've blown it or when they haven't.

BERNADETTE:

Oh, you smell when you come out a lot of times. You go out after work—if it's an afternoon shift—you go out for an evening and you bring your clothes in, but you want to hide them somewhere—because any time you leave your good clothes somewhere they always smell—and you want to hide them in the office, and you want to put them in bags, and, er, so that you don't smell like the restaurant when you go out. Or you want to bring lots of perfume or something to make you get away from that smell, whatever smell that is. I mean, certain restaurants smell worse or different than others, but it's, just, it's one of those feelings where you wish that you could go in to a job, you know, clean and come out still smelling of perfume and still smelling clean and you can't.

SHEILA:

There's no doubt about it—you just feel so grimy all the time. I just find it really unromantic, you know.

Especially—it's all right if you go out with someone you work with and you both go home together or whatever, and you go out and you're both smelly. It's sort of, you don't notice, but if you, um, if you go out with someone who doesn't work in a restaurant, it's, er, you know, if they meet you for tea . . . I always remember one story I, um, an old boyfriend of mine, we went back for tea at his mother's. He'd met me after lunch time, after I'd been working lunch time, 'cause we had to go for tea. And, um, we were sitting down, and she said, "What is that smell?" And we were all sort of, I didn't think it was me to start with, you know; I didn't know what it was. Anyway, it came down to it that it was my hair, because the oil, it was sometimes the oil. I don't know what it is, but it gets . . . I suppose if it's near the end when it just needs changing it gets much a bit smellier, like more oniony or something, and my hair absolutely stunk of this oily . . . And it was the most embarrassing thing. I thought after that I never go out after work. I mean, I won't go out after work like to a club or anything unless I can change and wash, and I won't go out straight from work in the afternoon. I'll have to go home and wash before and change.

BERNADETTE:

My back aches, my arms ache, um, you just feel drained. I mean, it's not mentally drained, but in a way it is, if you've been dealing with, you know, with sort of horrendous customers all day, you're just exhausted—completely exhausted physically as well as mentally. Though, because you are dealing with people and having to understand how they're feeling and what sort of mood they're in and what they want and what they don't want, um, but it's the sort of thing where, when you've finished, you can't very easily go home and go straight to bed. You can't just collapse somewhere, because you're still buzzing—whether it's from a really good night—say you've made, you know, brilliant tips and it's a brilliant night, or it's been a very bad night and, you know, you're very upset about things that happened or customers that you've had. You're still buzzing. You can't just collapse and fall asleep; you have to unwind. It's one of those things where you just you need at least an hour before you go to bed to, sort of, become normal again.

SHEILA:

I've always had lots and lots of energy, physical energy. And you have to almost have that nervous energy, you know; you have to have an element of that. Everyone who does it has to be highly energetic and very healthy; obviously, you can't do it if you've got a bad back or whatever. I feel, when it gets to about twelve o'clock in the evening, especially if it's been a busy night, I just feel like I could go to sleep there and then on the table.

(Continued)

(Continued)

ANNE KOVAL:

But when you climb into your bed at the end of a long night, um, your bones ache and it always helps to have a, um, a hot bath. Er, I usually find that it's very difficult to wind down, um, it's a bit like any sort of job which requires a lot of energy. At the end of it, you just, you keep, you know, even when you're sleeping, you're still going. And I, when I'm waitressing a lot, I find that I have a lot of waitress dreams which are sort of notorious, um, dreams where you're constantly going crazy serving people and somehow your orders are always getting confused. And, um, it's, you know, sort of a typical nightmare, which is a waitress's dream. And I always know when I get those dreams too much that I'm obviously working too hard!

SHEILA:

When I get in the cab at the end of a long shift, I mean, I'm on my feet for eight hours and I just, I think what I'm going to be doing tomorrow. And all my friends, we all think the same. We're all doing our acting or our designing or our painting and it's like another little world, and you have to shut out what you've just been doing, and the danger is, of course, that you lose sight of what you should be doing because you work so much. And you're at the restaurant more than you're at the recording studio and, in the end, you know, you don't become that dancer or singer or actress any more. You're just left with being a waitress.

SOURCE: BBC Radio, "Holding It for Eight Hours," September 8, 1988.

enthusiastic than their management, find the rules and procedures frustrating and have higher intentions of quitting.

When faced with such role stress in their jobs, individuals do not accept it passively but rather attempt to ameliorate the stress. The simplest way of avoiding conflict is to avoid the customer. This is exemplified by the waiter who refuses to notice a customer who wishes to place an order. This strategy also allows the waiter to increase his sense of control over the encounter. An alternative strategy is to move into "people-processing mode,"[14] in which customers are treated as inanimate objects to be processed rather than as individuals. This reduces the requirement for the BSP to associate or empathize with the individual.

Many strategies are used by the BSP to maintain a sense of control of the encounter. Physical symbols and furniture are often used to boost the BSP's status and, hence, his or her control.[15] In the extreme case, the BSP overacts the role and forces the customer into the subservient role, as is the case with many waiters and waitresses.

An alternative strategy used by BSPs to reduce organization/client conflict is to side completely with the customer. When forced to obey a rule with which they disagree, BSPs will proceed to list for the customer all the other things about the organization with which they disagree. In this way, they attempt to reduce stress by seeking sympathy from the customer.

Managing the Customer–Contact Personnel Interface

Chapter 7 deals with the problem of how to design the human resources policies of the organization to maximize the likelihood of success in the service encounter. A study by Sutton and Rafaeli[16] describes an analysis of the results of an in-store initiative in a chain of convenience stores. The stores had used a variety of local and corporatewide practices to reward clerks who acted in a friendly fashion during transactions with customers, including mystery shoppers and in competitions. To assess the results of the initiative, a sample of 576 stores was observed to look at the behavior of the staff. In each store, 20 transactions were coded for four features: greeting ("Hello," "How are you today?"), thanking, smiling, and eye contact.

The subsequent analysis attempts to relate the behaviors of the staff to total sales. Given the variations to be found between stores, control variables were introduced to allow for customer gender compensation, store ownership, store supervision cost, etc. The surprising finding was a negative and significant relationship between store sales and the positive display of emotion by staff.

Only after detailed qualitative analysis was it possible to understand the complexity of the relationship. Qualitative comparisons of stores during slow and busy times suggest that pace of business is a cue for norms of expressed emotions. The norm or script for a busy time is that both customers and staff expect customers to be processed rapidly. Any attempt to display emotions during the service period is seen as a waste of time. Busy times are stressful times, and expressing irritation toward individuals who hamper efficiency was found to be especially legitimate during busy times.

During normal or nonbusy times, customer processing can be a source of entertainment. Staff are more likely to display emotions, and customers are more likely to be friendly because the script is now different. Thus, the pace of the store, reflected in levels of store sales, fixes the norms of behavior. High pace and, hence, high sales are associated with a nonfriendly processing model.

Summary: People as the Product

Much has been written about the fact that, for many service firms, personnel constitutes the bulk of their product. It is thus important that the place of the personnel within the organization be understood.

Marketing theory is ill equipped to provide insights into the problem of where contact personnel fit into the hierarchy of the service firm. Organizational behavior, by comparison, is a field focused on this and similar problems. By drawing on the concepts of organizational behavior and, in particular, on the concept of a boundary-spanning role, this chapter has provided a solid framework on which to develop the marketing implications of individuals as the product. This approach has served to stress the increased levels of interdependence among the various functions within a service firm.

Questions

1. In designing a new restaurant, management must decide whether to add a service charge to the bill or encourage patrons to tip the staff directly. What are the implications of tipping for the role conflict of the subordinate service personnel?

2. Provide examples of marketing programs that you believe have served to increase the role stress for service providers. Why do you believe that these programs have increased the stress?

3. Describe an instance in which you have received particularly good or bad service from a service provider. Using the boundary-spanning concept, analyze the interaction and the role played by yourself and the provider.

4. Give examples of the organization/client role conflict you have witnessed or experienced. Could that conflict have been removed for the service provider? How? Why do you think the organization has not taken the steps you describe?

5. What is the role of the uniforms worn by many service providers? What is their impact on the relationship between the provider and the customer? As a service provider, would you rather be in uniform or not in uniform when interacting with customers?

Notes

[1] This idea was originally suggested in a slightly different form in W. Earl Sasser, P. Olsen, and D. Daryl Wyckoff, *Management of Service Operations: Text, Cases, and Readings* (Boston: Allyn and Bacon, 1978).

[2] Mary Jo Bitner, Bernard H. Booms, and Mary Stanfield Tetreault, "The Service Encounter: Diagnosing Favorable and Unfavorable Incidents," *Journal of Marketing* 54 (January 1990): 71–84.

[3] Benjamin Schneider, "The Service Organization: Climate Is Crucial," *Organizational Dynamics* (Autumn 1980): 52–65.

[4] Ibid., 58.

[5] J.D. Thompson, "Organization and Output Transactions," *American Journal of Sociology* 68 (1967): 309–324.

[6] See U. Aldrich and D. Huber, "Boundary-Spanning Roles and Organization Structure," *Academy of Management Review* 2 (1977): 217–230, which discusses the role of boundary spanners as information processors and filters; and J.D. Thompson, *Organizations in Action* (New York: McGraw-Hill, 1967), which discusses the representation aspect of the boundary-spanning role.

[7] Boas Shamir, "Service and Servility: Role Conflict in Subordinate Service Roles," *Human Relations* 33, no. 10 (1980): 741–756.

[8] Anat Rafaeli, "When Cashiers Meet Customers: An Analysis of the Role of Supermarket Cashiers," *Academy of Management Journal*, 32, no. 2 (1989): 245–273.

[9] Shamir, "Service and Servility."

[10] John Bateson, "Perceived Control and the Service Encounter," in John A. Czepiel, Michael R. Solomon, and Carol F. Surprenant, eds., *The Service Encounter* (Boston: Lexington Books, 1985), p. 67.

[11] Schneider, "The Service Organization."

[12] See W. Foote White, *Men at Work*, Dorsey Series in Behavioral Sciences (Homewood, IL: Dorsey Press and Irwin, 1949).

[13] Schneider, "The Service Organization."

[14] Peter Klaus, "The Quality Epiphenomenon," in John Czepiel, Michael R. Solomon, and Carol F. Surprenant, eds., *The Service Encounter* (Lexington, MA: Heath, 1983), 15.

[15] Charles T. Goodsell, "Bureaucratic Manipulation of Physical Symbols: An Empirical Investigation," *American Journal of Political Science* 21 (February 1977): 79–91.

[16] Robert I. Sutton and Anat Rafaeli, "Untangling the Relationship between Displayed Emotions and Organizational Sales," *Academy of Management Journal* 31, no. 3 (1988): 461–487.

A Test of Services Marketing Theory
Consumer Information Acquisition Activities

KEITH B. MURRAY
Northeastern University

The author explores the information needs of service consumers. In the purchase decision process, search behavior is motivated in part by perceived risk and the consumer's ability to acquire relevant information with which purchase uncertainty can be addressed. Marketing theory suggests that consumer use information sources in a distinctive way to reduce the uncertainty associated with services. Hence, six hypotheses are developed to test the information acquisition of service buyers. An experimental approach is employed to compare, in a pre-purchase contest, the information sources used by consumers of service and those used by consumers of goods. The resulting data support the predictions offered and extend marketing theory.

Though the marketing discipline has directed attention to the field of services marketing in recent years, much of the work in that area has centered on the development of conceptual models with an emphasis on managerial paradigms. Considerably less attention has been given to understanding the behavior of the service consumer, though efforts to examine consumer activity (e.g., Surprenant and Solomon 1987; Vredenburg and Wee 1986) are noteworthy and highlight the linkage between service consumer behavior and the management task. An area of particular importance to managers is an understanding of the prepurchase information acquisition process used by service customers. Knowledge of information acquisition strategies is vital to both marketing managers and scholars because information search is an early influential stage in the purchase decision process.

In general, the greater the degree of perceived risk of a prepurchase contest, the greater the consumer propensity to seek information about the product. The role of risk in the consumption of services has been addressed both conceptually (e.g., Eiglier and Langeard 1977; Zeithaml 1981) and empirically (e.g., Brown and Fern 1981; Davis, Guiltinan, and Jones 1979; George, Weinberger, and Kelly 1985; Guseman 1981; Murray and Schlacter 1990), with theory and evidence suggesting that services are perceived to be riskier than goods. Comparatively little attention, however, has been directed to understanding the impact of the riskier nature of services on the purchase process and the information "needs" of services consumers.

The research reported here explores the use of information sources by service consumers. The aim of this article is to present a theoretical, empirical, and managerial perspective on consumer preferences for information in the consumption decision process involving services. In particular, the study examines the information acquisition of consumers in light of heightened perceived risk associated with service products. First, relevant consumer information acquisition literature is reviewed. Then six hypotheses are offered on information sources and consumer behavior related to services in comparison with goods. The method and experimental procedures used to test these predictions are described and the study results are reported. Finally, the findings and their implications are discussed.

Keith B. Murray is Assistant Professor of Marketing, College of Business Administration, Northeastern University. The author thanks four colleagues at Arizona State University, Stephen W. Brown, Lawrence Crosby, Michael Hutt, and John L. Schlacter, for their detailed comments on drafts of the article and the three anonymous JM reviewers for their helpful suggestions. A previous version of the article was part of the First Interstate Center for Services Marketing working paper series.

Source: Keith B. Murray, "A Test of Services Marketing Theory: Consumer Information Acquisition Activities," reprinted with permission from the Journal of Marketing, *January 1991, vol. 55, pp. 10-25, published by the American Marketing Association, Chicago, IL 60606.*

Overview of Perceived Risk and Information Acquisition

Despite difficulties in precisely defining what a service is, marketing literature reflects broad agreement in terms of both conceptual description and empirical substantiation as to what characterizes services (e.g.,

Zeithaml, Parasuraman, and Berry 1985). Generalizations that have widespread acceptance among scholars and practitioners in the field as being characteristic of services include intangibility, simultaneity of production and consumption, and nonstandardization. In both theory and practice, marketers have recognized that the fundamental, qualitative differences between goods and services, in addition to requiring special management paradigms, may elicit distinctive behavior on the part of consumers. That services are not directly perceptible, are frequently experimental, and typically are unpredictable in their outcomes for the buyer implies that they would influence purchasing behavior of consumers. Though varying degrees of perceived risk characterize all consumer purchases, evidence suggests that by their fundamental nature services may be perceived to be particularly risky (Guseman 1981; Murray and Schlacter 1990). Furthermore, because of the transitory and varied nature of services, product evaluation may occur primarily *after* purchase and consumption (Young 1981), heightening prepurchase uncertainty.

The concept of risk implies that most individuals make purchase decisions under some degree of uncertainty about a particular product and/or brand. Conceptualized as the likelihood of negative consequences (i.e., danger, loss, etc.), perceived risk represents consumer uncertainty about loss or gain in a particular transaction and has six components (e.g., Brooker 1984; Jacoby and Kaplan 1972; Roselius 1971): financial, performance, social, psychological, safety, and time/convenience loss. Overall perceived risk represents the aggregate impact of these various factors. Given the level of aggregation for goods and services, this study focuses on inherent risk (Bettman 1972, 1973), the latent risk a generic product category holds for a consumer.

Marketing theorists long have argued that consumers seek information from a variety of sources when faced with risk or uncertainty (e.g., Cox 1967). Because services appear to create particularly uncertain and risky purchase situations, it is logical to expect that consumers acquire information as a strategy of risk reduction in the face of this specific uncertainty. Zeithaml (1981) argues that services are more difficult to evaluate than goods and that, as a consequence, consumers may be forced to rely on different cues and processes when evaluating services. Indeed, service marketing scholars suggest that consumers evaluate information about services in a more complex and distinctive way (e.g., Bateson 1977; Booms and Nyquist 1981; Davis, Guiltinan, and Jones 1979) and often demand increased information for predominantly service-type products (Deshpande and Krishnan 1977).

The following discussion briefly identifies a simple typology of information sources and reviews the relevant literature on risk and information sources.

Sources of Information

Consumer information sources can be classified into two broad types, internal and external; both types are used by consumers to gather information and cope with perceived risk. Internal search is fundamentally linked to memory scan (Bettman 1979a, b; Leigh and Rethans 1984; Lynch and Srull 1982), though understanding of internal search dynamics is largely speculative (Hansen 1972). When faced with a purchase decision, the consumer first examines information in memory about past purchase experience, including experiences in a product class and previous learning about the environment. Experience creates knowledge, which in turn leads to internal search in subsequent decision situations (Jacoby, Chestnut, and Silberman 1977; van Raaij 1977). Hence, internal search can be viewed as an important source of information available to the consumer.

The marketing literature is replete with evidence suggesting that external information search represents a motivated and conscious decision by the consumer to seek new information from the environment (e.g., Berning and Jacoby 1974; Furse, Punj, and Stewart 1984; Moore and Lehmann 1980; Winter 1975). Though sources of external information can be classified in terms of whether the source is marketer-dominated or whether information comes for personal or impersonal communication (e.g., Engel, Blackwell, and Miniard 1986), other typologies encompass a wide range of information sources that are amendable to empirical operationalization and classification (Andreasen 1968; Luta and Reilly 1973), including forms of personal, impersonal, and direct experience information sources.

Role of Perceived Risk

Depending on the level of risk perception, several risk-handling strategies may be adopted by the consumer, one of which is the search for further information and evaluation of alternatives. Other risk-handling strategies include risk adoption and reduction of aspiration levels, but here the focus is solely on information sources as they may be associated with a risk-reduction strategy by consumers. Cox (1967, p. 604) argues that the "amount and nature of perceived risk will define consumers' information needs, and consumers will seek out sources, types, and amounts of information that seem most likely to satisfy their particular information needs." Evidence supports this position in relation to depth of search, types of sources, types of risk, and personality factors (e.g., Capon and Burke 1977; Locander and Hermann 1979; Lutz and Reilly 1973), but none of the studies examined risk associated with services per se or risk reduction specifically by service consumers.

Several findings point to the use of specific strategies by the consumer to diminish prepurchase uncertainty. First, as total risk of the purchase situation increases, an individual's direct observation and experience become a preferred information source (Lutz and Reilly 1973), suggesting that as risk increases, the search pattern for information expands and the tendency simply to buy without prepurchase deliberation decreases (Locander and Hermann 1979). Second, consumers appear to use information or personal channels primarily in situations in which perceived risk and uncertainty have not been reduced sufficiently by formal information sources and in which uncertainty and involvement are high enough to justify seeking information through informal channels (Cox 1963a). Perry and Hamm (1969) show that the greater the perceived risk of purchase decision, the greater the importance of personal influence. These findings support those of several studies (e.g., Arndt 1967; Lutz and Reilly 1973) showing that word-of-mouth is the most important source of risk-reducing information and has a greater impact on consumers than mass media communications because of clarification and feedback opportunities. Midgley (1983) notes that both the nature and degree of risk distinguish between different sources of interpersonal information, suggesting that for products dominant in social aspects, information from other individuals rather than from objective or impersonal sources is likely to be preferred by consumers. These conclusions are supported by the findings of Price and Feick (1984) that point to interpersonal influence as an important component of information acquisition. Hence, evidence suggests that types of information used by consumers to reduce prepurchase uncertainty vary across levels of perceived risk and that as perceived risk increases, personal sources are the most preferred *external* source of information, second only to direct observation and product trial (Locander and Hermann 1979; Lutz and Reilly 1973).

Third, Lutz and Reilly (1973) note that consumers use more sources of information when faced with increasing levels of perceived performance risk and that consumers' relative preference for various information sources shifts dramatically, depending on performance risk factors. Over a wide range of products that are low or moderate in performance risk, the most

frequently used method of information acquisition is simply to *buy* the product, conceivably on a "trial" basis. However, as performance risk increases, trial purchase becomes less preferred. Furthermore, Lutz and Reilly (1973) observe that direct observation and/or experience with a product is generally preferred to any secondary source of product information. Of various information sources external to the individual, word-of-mouth is particularly useful and independent impersonal sources may be preferred under conditions of high performance risk.

In short, consumers use various amounts and types of information sources to reduce perceived risk, depending on the amount and type of risk. Though consumer decision models identify information search as a prominent aspect of the purchase decision process, the literature has a critical gap in terms of examining risk specifically associated with services and concomitant types of information sources. In the following discussion, extant services marketing and risk theory is used, as well as information acquisition knowledge, to develop research hypotheses for subsequent verification.

Research Hypotheses

Several predications can be made about acquisition of prepurchase information on services. The following hypotheses seek to test and extend service marketing and information acquisition theory by examining the differences in search behavior and information source usage by consumers contemplating the purchase of goods and services.

Internal Sources and Prepurchase Information Acquisition

As services are associated, *ceteris paribus*, with greater perceived risk, it follows that service consumers would use more information sources as a risk-coping strategy than would consumers of less risky products. This rationale suggests an extended information acquisition process, which may mean that consumers are more likely to defer a service purchase because the information search is more time-consuming. One approach to conceptualizing this phenomenon is to examine the proclivity of service consumers to make an outright purchase as a way to learn more about the product. Hence,

H_1: The incidence of outright purchase as a consumer information strategy is lower for services than for goods.

Types of External Information Sources and Risk Reduction

Services are conceptualized as *experiential* (e.g., Booms and Bitner 1981; Lovelock 1981; Young 1981; Zeithaml 1981) and as such are difficult to specify or evaluate precisely in advance of the purchase event. Consequently, consumers wanting to reduce prechoice uncertainty may be compelled to seek information from other individuals who have experienced the service directly of indirectly. Information from individuals with previous product experience is subjective and evaluative. It logically reduces the prospective consumer's uncertainty by means of vicarious learning and approximates direct experience with the product. Consistent with Nelson's (1974) theory of information and consumer behavior and Urbany and Weilbaker's (1987) prediction that personal sources are more important for consumers in the purchase of experience-type products, the second hypothesis is:

> H$_2$: Consumers choose more personal sources of information for services than for goods.

Effectiveness of Information Sources Used by Service Consumers

In view of the distinguishing characteristics of services (i.e., intangibility, nonstandardization, and inseparability), Zeithaml (1981) argues that services are more difficult to evaluate prior to initial purchase than goods. Hence, service prospects may simple engage fewer *prepurchase* information sources than consumers contemplating goods, consistent with an attribution-dissonance model (Ray 1973) positing that nonmarketing communication sources precipitate consumer purchase choice, subsequently followed by attitude change and learning. The absolute number of information sources an individual uses, however, may not be the most useful measure of the extent of information acquisition. Source *effectiveness* is more relevant to understanding source usage (e.g., Engel and Blackwell 1982; May 1965), reflecting the *decisive* influence of a source and its importance in relation to exposure. Decisiveness implies that some types of sources are more instrumental than others in providing meaningful information to an individual (e.g., Davis, Guiltinan, and Jones 1979; Houston 1979).

For many services, physical and point-of-purchase cues typically associated with tangible products are not available. Indeed, Young (1981) argues that consumers acquire only limited evaluative information prior to the initial service purchase, suggesting that service consumption is highly personal and difficult to comprehend until directly experienced. Even if prior information exists for services, mass media are not expected to be particularly conducive to effective communication of service attributes (Shostack 1977). Instead, non-marketer-dominated information sources are expected to play a particularly important role in the consumer decision process for services. Consistent with primary research reported by Engel, Blackwell, and Miniard (1986), the expectation is that service consumers would prefer the opinions and experiences of other comparable individuals in making service purchase decisions. Hence,

> H$_3$: Personal independent sources of information are more effective for services than for goods.

The Effect of Subjective Information about Services

That consumers' use of information sources is related to confidence in the source has long been established. Cox (1963b), for example, supports the notion that source trustworthiness and expertise are important and appear to influence source usage. Though virtually any type of information can provide some degree of instrumental utility to the consumer in terms of risk reduction, particular *types* of information sources are known to be sought by consumers for specific utilities (Hansen 1972, Houston 1979). The ephemeral nature of services, coupled with the absence of an objective and uniform product, suggests that experiential and subjective data are likely to be more relevant and offer greater prepurchase evaluative utility than other types of informational data.

Objective and technical product specifications may be feasible for a service (e.g., dentist A is licensed to perform root canals and can do so tomorrow at 3:30 p.m. for less than $300), but information of an interpretive subjective, and affective nature may address key customer information needs more directly (e.g., dentist A, is a very competent professional and also does not want his patients to suffer a lot of pain), allaying expected prepurchase apprehensions. Bateson (1989) suggests, for example, that a static, multiattribute model is insufficient in assisting the consumer to understand services. Instead, he argues that such models afford a static perspective on an experience that consists essentially of a series of dynamic interactions. This observation leads to the prediction that personal sources engender relatively greater levels of consumer confidence for service products than for nonservice products.

H_4: Consumers have greater confidence in personal sources of information for services than for goods.

Trialability as a Source of Information For Service Consumers

As perceived risk of a purchase increases, consumers engage in risk-reduction by means of direct observation and product trail (Locander and Hermann 1979; Lutz and Reilly 1973). However, that strategy may not work for services because of their experiential nature (e.g., Booms and Bitner 1981; Young 1981; Zeithaml 1981). In addition to the limited opportunities for direct experience or product observation, "trialability" of the service is problematic. For example, consumers can visit a retail location and examine a nonservice product directly for fit, styling, structural integrity, package information, and/or expressed warranties; occasionally, consumers alter the perceived uncertainty of some nonservice purchases by buying a small quantity or a popular brand. Such prepurchase strategies, however, are rarely possible in the case of services because they are typically ephemeral and intangible. It is reasonable to argue that service consumers will make a service purchase decision on some basis other than observation or trial. Therefore,

H_5: Service consumers use direct observation and/or trial as a source of prepurchase information less often than consumers of goods.

Prior Experience and Information Acquisition of Service Consumers

Service consumers' prepurchase information search activities can be analyzed in terms of costs and benefits (Moore and Lehmann 1980). Though consumers may perceive services to be inherently more risky and otherwise may be inclined to acquire more prepurchase information, accessing information sources may not be feasible or accomplished without considerable effort. Indeed, impersonal information for services may not be easily organized by brand or attribute, implying decreased search processes (Olander 1975). Furthermore, personal sources are inconvenient to acquire, thus increasing the costs of information search and decreasing the number and types of sources used (Staelin and Payne 1976). Marketing literature suggests that because less information is available for services (Booms and Bitner 1981; Lovelock 1981; Young 1981; Zeithaml 1981), the cost of an extended search

will be elevated, and, as the cost of acquiring information increases, less information will be sought and acquired (e.g., Jacoby, Speller, and Berning 1974). Consequently, the internal information search made possible by prior learning from past purchase experiences in a product class and/or previous learning about the environment is particularly instrumental in providing useful product information in the case of services.

H_6: Consumers with prior experience have a greater preference for internal sources of information for evaluating services than for evaluating goods.

The hypotheses were examined empirically in terms of the experimental framework and procedures described in the following section.

Method

To test the hypotheses, an experimental context was developed to examine the information needs of service consumers. The research objective was to assess the effect of varying levels of perceived service attributes on consumer behavior in terms of information sources used in a prepurchase context. In this section, the pre-experimental procedures, methodological choice considerations, research design, procedures, dependent measures, statistical approach, and sample are described.

To operationalize the independent variable (i.e., the service construct) more precisely, an extensive pretest process was followed to establish control over key aspects of the experimental treatment, specifically in relation to "serviceness," expected cost, and respondent familiarity. Briefly, 146 subjects, drawn from the population of interest for the study, used a 7-point interval scale to evaluate a sample of 235 products in terms of product familiarity, expected cost, and perceived characterization as a service, good, or some combination of the two. The pretest ratings by this separate and independent group of subjects were used to eliminate products with which respondents were unfamiliar and to array products hierarchically on the basis of expected cost and relative perceived service attributes. In view of the association between expected financial cost and overall risk (Jacoby and Kaplan 1972), selection of products was limited to those within the expected cost range of $20 to $50. Consistent with Park's (1976) work, only those products with which respondents expressed at least moderate familiarity were included in the final sample.

Products within this specified familiarity and monetary value range were arrayed along a goods–service continuum on the basis of mean scores, from those relatively high in service attributes (i.e., "pure" services) to those relatively low in service attributes (i.e., goods), with products of a "mixed" nature being at midpoint on the continuum (i.e., those sharing both service *and* goods qualities). The relative product attribute rating values derived from this pre-experimental procedure were used to choose a sample of five products from those that were rated extremely high, midlevel, and extremely low in service content. These three samples, consisting of five products each and drawn from three disparate points along the product continuum, constituted the manipulations of the independent variable (i.e., the degree of service attributes characterizing a product). This empirical approach to operationalizing the service construct is consistent with the call by Shostack (1977) to use consumer judgments to define the "image" of products and is described in greater detail by Murray and Schlacter (1990). The use of multiple product stimuli in the study was intended to contribute to generalizability of the findings beyond any single product class (see Richins 1983).

Methodological Choice Considerations

Several methods for examining the information needs and source usage of consumers were considered before a purchase scenario approach was selected. Retrospective questioning of subjects is a nonexperimental approach and thus implies little capacity to control key factors, either theoretical or extraneous. Similarly, techniques involving observation of purchase behavior and/or eye movement analysis were deemed deficient. Two other approaches were considered—protocol analysis and information display board (IDB) technique. In view of problems associated with protocol analysis (see Bettman 1977; Bettman and Zins 1977), IDB initially seemed to hold considerable promise by way of analytic precision and quantitative rigor, rivaling the purchase scenario approach. However, in the context of this particular study, specific shortcomings of artificiality and demand effects were evident with the use of an IDB technique (see Lehmann and Moore 1980). Though IDB research to date has involved subjects in the *actual selection* of products in the experimental setting (thus comparing favorably with other approaches in achieving "mundane realism"), products typically have been limited to *inexpensive goods within a single product class* (e.g., Bettman and Jacoby 1976; Hofacker 1984; Hoyer and Jacoby 1983; Jacoby, Chestnut, and Fisher 1978; Lehmann and Moore 1980). Given the study's focus on nontrivial products,

however, the absence of actual purchase behavior by subjects in the experimental setting implied forfeiture of a major appeal of the IDB paradigm. Also, with a conventional IDB brand-by-attribute format, services potentially represent a range of products for which directly comparable *brands* typically do not exist, further diminishing the direct applicability of the method. In terms of demand effects, an IDB imposed an unrealistic task environment for examining perceptions and use of information sources for services, which are expected to be relatively low in "search" qualities and high in "experience" qualities (see Zeithaml 1981). Consequently, an IDB technique for services implied the provision of information that, in an actual purchase setting, may be either nonexistent or accessible to buyers only at great relative difficulty.

Hence, though a projective scenario approach was potentially subject to similar drawbacks, the limitations associated with IDB—given the research objectives—were sufficiently compelling to justify use of a hypothetical purchase task technique. To the degree that reactivity and demand properties were feasible with a projective method, however, two observations are relevant. First, the study represents a controlled, comparative analysis of sources in terms of their perceived utility, consumers' preferences, and relative efficacy to address the implicit information needs of consumers in a service purchase context. Inferences about a precise delineation of information search, *per se*, simply go beyond the method and the data. Instead, the research seeks to examine what, in a relative sense, consumers' information needs are and which sources (and types of sources) address those needs in the context of services. Second, to the degree that the experimental conditions do promote reactivity, it would be expected to be distributed across both types of sources and types of products; given the experimental design and nature of the study, one could reasonably assume that reactivity would influence all treatment levels and dependent measures uniformly.

Research Design

The specific experimental layout used in the study was completely balanced block, repeated-measure with nested factors in a hierarchical arrangement whereby all respondents were presented one factor (of five possible) from each of three levels of the independent variable, ranging from pure good to pure service. Because information seeking is, in part, a function of individual factors (Moore and Lehmann 1980), this design was selected to control for between-subject error variance and to obtain a more precise estimate of treatment effects, thereby obtaining a more powerful

FIGURE 1
Layout of the Balanced Complete Block Design with Repeated Measures

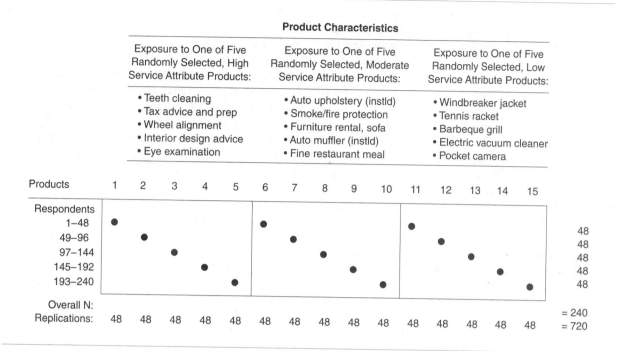

NOTE: Five product stimuli were selected from three disparate portions of a goods-services continuum composed of 235 products, each rated by a comparable consumer sample for their relative service attribute level. Products represent empirically determined stimuli which operationalize the independent variable. Subjects were exposed to one product stimulus from each sample of five for each of three levels of the experimental variable.

test of a false null hypothesis (Kirk 1982). The decision to operationalize the independent variable in the context of a purchase scenario was predicated on the increasing number of studies that use scenarios to manipulate variables and contexts that cannot be easily replicated in a real-life setting (e.g., Jackson, Keith, and Burdick 1984; Puto, Patton, and King 1985). The specific merits of this approach are not discussed here, but have been identified by Eroglu (1987).

The experimental treatments consisted of three levels of the independent variable—high, moderate, and low service attribute products. Five product stimuli were associated with each treatment level, resulting in a total sample of 15 hypothetical purchase decision situations. As noted previously, all treatments were controlled for respondent familiarity and economic risk and were identical (as indicated by manipulation checks) except for the product to be "purchased."

Subject reactivity to the experimental procedures and the data collection method was assessed. Specifically, subjects were tested for order effects of the independent variable administration as well as order effects of the questionnaire items (constituting the dependent measures). Dependent measures under contrasting conditions for each potential reactivity factor were analyzed statistically. No statistical differences in the dependent measures were found for either order

effects in terms of administration of the independent variable or for the sequence of items constituting the data collection instrument. These findings suggest that experimental reactivity attributable to treatment order of the independent variable or dependent measures was not significant. Figure 1 shows the research design.

Procedures

Consistent with established experimental practices involving scenarios (e.g., Jackson, Keith, and Burdick 1984; Mowen et al. 1985; Puto, Patton, and King 1985), the procedures consisted of presenting to subjects a randomly preassigned sequence of three hypothetical purchase scenarios. Each scenario described the purchase of a specific product and constituted the administration of one level of the independent variable. Subjects were encouraged to read each hypothetical scenario twice. After exposure, each scenario was removed from view. Subjects were asked to respond to a questionnaire in the presence of the experimenter. They were queried about three types of dependent variable: type of preferred prechoice information source and confidence in and importance of each respective information source. In addition, covariate measures of respondent age, sex, and experience with the product were taken. Manipulation checks of perceived service attributes, risk, and respondent familiarity with the product also were employed. (See Appendix A for the scenario stimulus and specific product stimuli varied by levels of perceived service attributes.)

This approach to examining information sources for products that are varied in service attributes was viewed to be most desirable in terms of several critical research factors. Specifically, the administration of a projective purchase task allowed experimental control of key elements of interest, namely the purchase context and the prior selection of subjects. This approach had the advantage of incorporating extant operationalizations and accepted measures (as well as an assessment of the validity and reliability of such dependent measures) within the context of a within-subjects design. A within-subjects design, in turn, maximizes the degree of experimental and statistical control over a wide range of important consumer purchase determinants not previously found in the literature on this topic.

The hypothetical purchase scenario was adapted from previous contributions in the field (Locander and Hermann 1979; Lutz and Reilly 1973), reflecting Bettman's (1972) concept of inherent risk for products having varied service attributes. As purchase decisions reflecting emergency circumstances may involve atypical information-seeking processes by consumers (Wright 1974), the decision context of the purchase scenario was a nonemergency one. The scenarios across all levels of the independent variable (the degree of perceived service attributes of the product being purchased) were identical except for the mention of the specific product embedded in the stimulus.

Dependent Measures, Item Reliability Estimates, and Manipulation Checks

Information Sources   A 25-item rating scale derived from Andreasen (1968) served to operationalize the following seven sources of consumer information: impersonal advocate, impersonal independent, personal independent, personal advocate, direct observation, personal experience, and outright purchase. This typology is similar to that advocated by Kotler (1980) and Anderson and Engledow (1981) and included response items that did not "force" respondents to consult external sources of information in a purchase situation. In effect, these items gave subjects response alternatives that sought to tap internal search predispositions and consumer inclinations not to engage in extended external search behaviors. All dependent measures for information acquisition had multiple items. This 25-item set was employed to collect data

on sources accessed, source effectiveness, and source confidence. (See Appendix B for information sources used in the study).

Measure of Information Effectiveness and Confidence   Source effectiveness is a function of the importance of an information source in relation to the exposure value of that source (Engel and Blackwell 1982). In this study, source importance was measured on a 7-point importance scale ranging from "most important" to "not important at all" for each source examined in the study. Variable scores for importance were obtained by summing across each type of information source (e.g., personal advocate, impersonal independent, etc.). Effectiveness was determined by a ratio value of the summated importance scores for a particular source type to the subjects' reported exposure scores for that information source (e.g., Engel and Blackwell 1982). The confidence variable was operationalized by a 7-point interval scale ranging from "extreme confidence" to "extreme lack of confidence" across 7- and 9-item measures of personal and impersonal sources of information, respectively. Dependent variable data were computed as the net positive difference between confidence in personal sources and confidence in impersonal sources of information.

Other data collected included multiple-item scales to measure confidence in specific information sources, a covariate addressing extent of respondent product experience, and respondent age and gender.

Estimates of Item Reliability   The reliability of each type of dependent variable measurement scale was assessed, consistent with the assumptions of domain sampling theory (Churchill 1979) and the coefficient alpha calculations of Peter (1979). All dependent measures had acceptable correlations with true scores, consistent with Nunnally's (1967) suggested reliability estimates for this type of research.

Analysis of the Experimental Condition and Manipulations   Though extensive products led to the isolation of independent variable with considerable face validity, a manipulation of the independent variable was recorded by respondents for each experimental factor. On a 7-point scale, the ratings of perceived service attributes across all factors were 6.32, 3.77, and 1.75 for high, moderate, and low levels of the independent variable, respectively. The MANOVA F-value for significant difference among the three levels of the manipulation check of the independent variable was statistically significant ($F = 254.00$, $p < .000$). Bonferroni multiple comparison t-test statistics for contrasts among the three means were all significant at the α< .001 level. These data suggest that the levels of the independent variable were manipulated successfully in terms of service attributes to test the proposed hypotheses adequately.

Consistent with previous marketing literature, an underlying assumption of the research is that services are characterized by higher levels of perceived risk. To minimize the opportunity for any potentially significant research findings to be attributed to other factors, a manipulation check was incorporated in the data collection instrument to verify that the factors of the independent variable (i.e., product stimuli varied in service attributes) were significant in terms of expected risk differences. Specifically, respondents were asked to rate each product stimulus on a 6-item, 7-point scale as "not risky at all" to "extremely risky," consistent with the six types of perceived risk (e.g., Jacoby and Kaplan 1972; Peter and Tarpey 1975; Roselius 1971) previously noted. Perceived risk measures were summated to reflect an overall measure of perceived risk. Across all factors of the independent variable, the MANOVA F-value for differences among the three levels of the independent variable in terms of perceived risk was statistically significant (F = 15.449, p < .000). Bonferroni multiple comparison t-test statistics for contrasts among the three means for perceived risks were significant for contrasts between the low and high and between the moderate and high operationalizations of the independent variable at the α<.0001 level. These findings suggest that perceived risk associated with levels of the independent variable was in the expected direction as predicted by the literature.

Though expected cost of each experimental operationalization (i.e., each product stimulus) was not examined specifically in the experimental setting because of questionnaire length and subject fatigue considerations, pretest data indicated that the mean perceived cost for products high, moderate, and low in service attributes was $34.66, $34.16, and $35.00, respectively. However, tests for economic risk and familiarity in relation to the product factors were conducted during the experimental procedures. Perceived financial risk was analyzed statistically for significant differences across all levels of the independent variable. The results were not statistically significant at conventional levels (F = 2.106; p < .124), indicating that financial risk was held constant across all levels of the independent variable. Mean product familiarity scores were analyzed for evidence of respondent unfamiliarity with experimental stimuli. On the basis of a 7-point interval measure, mean familiarity values for low, moderate, and high service product levels were 4.85, 4.44, and 4.42, indicating greater than average familiarity across all respondents for products used in

the study. These data provide evidence that economic risk and familiarity across all factors associated with the levels of the independent variable were sufficiently controlled to minimize their contamination of the study results.

Statistical Procedures

Respondent questionnaire ratings on the dependent measures were analyzed within the framework of a repeated-measures design in which dependent measures were within-factor and product service attributes between-factor elements. The research design was a 1 × 3 factor design. Subjects' responses to questionnaire items were analyzed by the SPSS^X multivariate analysis of variance (MANOVA) procedure for repeated measures.

Subjects

A total of 273 experimental forms were administered to university students at a large, urban university in the southwestern United States. However, 17 questionnaire sets were incomplete, leaving 256 acceptable response sets for tabulation and analysis. Of the sample, 120 subjects were men (46.9%) and 136 were women (53.1%). The average of the respondent population was 23.8 years, with a standard deviation of 3.4 years.

Results

The data collected in the experimental setting were analyzed statistically and are described here in terms of the stated hypotheses.

Consistent with marketing evidence showing services to be more risky than goods, H_1 proposes that respondents would indicate a relative preference to defer an outright purchase of a service. This variable was operationalized by a 3-item measure assessing respondent preferences for making a product purchase without engaging information sources. The MANOVA F-statistic for the variable is significant at the α< .05 level (F = 100.465, p < .000), with the mean values of the independent variable in support of the predicted hypothesis. In a planned Bonferroni t-test (α< .05) of mean differences, significant differences are found between moderate and high (t = 4.080, p < .000) and between low and high (t = 3.700, p < .000) levels of the independent variable. These results support the stated hypothesis, suggesting that consumers engage in comparatively less outright purchase of products high in service attributes and implying that extended information acquisition may be preferred for services.

H_2 states that personal sources of information are more preferred by service consumers than by goods consumers. Preference for personal and impersonal sources of information was measured by 7- and 9-item measures, respectively. Dependent variable data were computed as the net difference in the preference for personal sources over impersonal sources of information at each level of the independent variable. MANOVA procedures yield significant findings ($F = 5.897$, $p < .003$) in the expected direction for the effect of service attributes on the preference for personal sources of information. Bonferroni t-tests ($\alpha < .05$) for differences among the means are significant for differences between high and low factors of the independent variable ($t = 3.315$, $p < .000$). The data support the prediction that respondents have a greater prepurchase preference for personal sources of information for services than for goods.

H_3 predicts that personal, independent sources of information are more effective to service consumers than to goods consumers. Computation of information effectiveness values from respondent data was consistent with Engel and Blackwell's (1982) approach, whereby source effectiveness is "controlled for" by exposure and use. The information sources range from ineffective to decisively effective. When this index is less than 1.0, the exposure to a source exceeds importance of that source; when the index is greater than 1.0, importance exceeds exposure and the effectiveness of that source in consumer decision-making processes increases (Katz and Lazarsfeld 1955). MANOVA procedures were run to test for differences in effectiveness for all external sources of information at different levels of the independent variable. Only personal independent sources show significant differences in effectiveness ($F = 4.275$, $p < .008$), with mean effectiveness scores in the predicted direction. In a Bonferroni t-test ($\alpha < .05$) of differences between treatment levels, statistically significant differences were found between low and moderate levels and low and high levels of the independent variable.

H_4 predicts that respondents would indicate a greater confidence in personal sources of information for services. MANOVA F-procedures yield significant findings ($F = 14.226$, $p < .000$) in support of the predicted outcome. Bonferroni t-tests for planned comparisons ($\alpha < .05$) among the means are significant for contrasts between low and high levels ($t = 4.593$, $p < .000$) and moderate and high levels ($t = 5.039$, $p < .000$) of the independent variable. Thus, the findings are consistent with the prediction that respondents have greater confidence in personal sources of information for services and corroborate Cox's (1963b) finding that source trustworthiness and expertise are

important and that consumer confidence influences types of sources used. The confirmation of H_2, H_3, and H_4 substantiates the predictions of services marketing theory and suggests a need for promotional strategies for services that stimulate and/or simulate personal sources of information.

Consumer behavior theory suggest that as perceived risk of a purchase increases, consumers will engage in risk-reduction behavior by means of direct observation and trial. However, the relative lack of tangible cues may preclude this alternative for consumers. H_5 predicts that direct product observation and/or product trial will be preferred to a greater extent for goods than for services. This hypothesis is confirmed by the data. The variable was composed of a 3-item measure that addressed direct product inspection and/or limited product involvement prior to purchase. The MANOVA F-value for these data is significant ($F = 14.823$, $p = .000$), with mean scores in the predicted direction. Bonferroni t-test statistics ($\alpha < .05$) for planned contrasts among the means are significant for mean differences between low and moderate ($t = 3.176$, $p < .000$) and low and high ($t = 5.364$, $p < .000$) levels of the independent variable. Thus, the data support the prediction that respondents indicate less preference for the use of direct observation and/or trial for services than they do for goods.

H_6 states that consumers with product experience have greater preference for internal sources of information for evaluating services than for evaluating goods. This variable was operationalized by employing 3-item measure tapping respondents' preference to using previous knowledge and information in a prepurchase situation. MANOVA procedures are significant ($F = = 3.805$, $p < .027$). Thus, the data support the prediction that experience is a more preferred source of information for consumers in the purchase of services than in the purchase of goods. Bonferroni t-tests of differences ($\alpha < 0.5$) between the levels of the independent variable are statistically significant between low and moderate and low and high treatment levels. Descriptive statistics pertaining to the six hypothese are summarized in Table 1.

Discussion

This article identifies an area of relevance and interest to both marketing scholars and practitioners. The fundamental thesis of the research is that because services are higher in perceived risk, they may create distinctive information needs in consumers. The service construct is operationalized and employed in the context of a controlled experiment examining important consumer

TABLE 1

Statistical Results for Effects of Service Attributes on Consumer Information Acquisition Behavior

Hypothesis	Level of Service Content	n	Mean	F Score	Probability	r2	Contrast	t Score	Probability	Empirical Conclusions
In comparison with purchasers of goods, consumers contemplating the purchase of services:										
—show a decreased preference for outright purchase (H_1)	Low Moderate High	252	5.431 5.429 5.772	10.47	.000	.04	L-M M-H L-H	0.190 4.080 3.700	.500 .000 .000	Confirmed
—prefer personal over impersonal sources (H_2)	Low Moderate High	231	.044 .159 .299	.590	.003	.03	L-M M-H L-H	1.753 2.028 3.315	.039 .023 .000	Confirmed
—find personal independent sources more effective (H_3)	Low Moderate High	242	1.027 1.095 1.105	4.28	0.15	.02	L-M M-H L-H	2.610 0.180 2.860	.005 >.250 .002	Confirmed
—have more confidence in personal sources (H_4)	Low Moderate High	241	.127 .118 .375	14.23	.000	.06	L-M M-H L-H	0.176 5.039 4.593	>.250 .000 .000	Confirmed
—depend less on observation and/or trial (H_5)	Low Moderate High	253	3.035 3.414 3.685	14.82	.000	.05	L-M M-H L-H	3.176 2.117 5.364	>000 .020 .000	Confirmed
—prefer internal sources over all others when they have experience in the product category (H_6)	Low Moderate High	68	1.922 1.931 1.627	3.81	0.27	.06	L-M M-H L-H	2.642 1.137 2.491	.005 >.100 .010	Confirmed

decision-making phenomena. In this section, the limitations as well as the contributions and implications of the study are discussed.

Contributions and Limitations of the Research

This study contributes to marketing and information acquisition literature by specifically addressing the information needs of service consumers. Service scholars have proposed that prior evaluation is more difficult for services than for goods (Zeithaml 1981) and that consumers may evaluate them differently than they do goods (Young 1981). Several findings of the study converge to support this prediction. First, the data provide evidence of consumers' inclination to deter making an outright purchase of services. This finding is consistent with the prediction of risk theory that in the face of greater uncertainty and loss, consumers engage in an extended decision process. Second, the role of personal sources of information is noteworthy. The data show that for services, personal sources are preferred over impersonal sources of information, more so than for goods. Similarly, consumers indicate greater confidence in personal sources when contemplating a service purchase. Further, personal independent sources are

more effective for services than for goods. These findings provide indirect support for the notion that products with service attributes are largely subjective and experiential. Third, the data suggest that internal sources, in contrast to external ones, are particularly relevant to service consumers.

These data point to a distinctive information acquisition pattern for service consumers. Specifically, the findings suggest a greater need for risk-reducing information and an extended consumer decision process for services. However, in view of the intangible, ephemeral, and experimental nature of services, there may be less opportunity to diminish uncertainty by direct observation and/or trial for services, suggesting a prolonged consumer adoption process and, ultimately, a more lengthy diffusion process for services. The conclusions from this research have important implications for a better understanding of consumer behavior and marketing management

Because of such factors as intangibility, variability, and consumer-provider interaction, service phenomenology is not conducive to controlled empirical operationalizations. Indeed, despite the continued interest in the services marketing area, the number of experimental studies involving services has been limited. The research reported here sought to test theory-derived hypotheses by controlling the experimental setting, randomly assigning subjects, and collecting data on service phenomenology in a context advocated by Calder, Phillips, and Tybout (1981). This research was an exploratory effort to understand better the information needs of service consumers and their use of sources. To put the findings into proper perspective, however, limitations of the study must be noted. Given the degree of experimental control sought, the findings are necessarily subject to the criticism that a real-world context is lacking in the experimental setting. Further, demand effects may have exerted some influence on the dependent measures. For example, the scenario instructions may have biased the subsequent behavior of subjects. Though steps were taken to minimize and subsequently identify (via debriefing procedures) these effects, the degree to which they occurred in this specific study is not definitely known. In general, however, a projective purchase task poses several threats, including spurious effects stemming from instructions to subjects, setting artificiality, occurrence of novel behavior, and the desire of subjects to accommodate the experimenter. Clearly, these factors may have affected the dependent measures.

On balance, we have ample reason to believe that there is some *a priori* validity to a role-playing technique as a research procedure in that numerous real-life purchase situations are, implicitly, role playing situations for consumers. To the extent that role-playing behavior tracks behavior intention, indications in the literature suggest that behavior intention does predict actual behavior of consumers (e.g., Bonfield 1974; Vinokur-Kaplan 1978), with positive correlation having been shown to be present (e.g., Ryan and Bonfield 1980). In any event, information acquisition can be viewed as probabilistic. Though it is feasible that the task characteristics may have influenced the absolute level of intention to acquire information, the consistent confirmation of theoretical predictions in a relational, comparative sense (of services vs. goods) generally supports the decision to employ this particular approach. When asked to indicate their likely response to the hypothetical purchase scenarios, subjects had no prior knowledge of the experimental intent or predictions, and debriefing did not reveal any awareness of those factors. Hence they had limited opportunity to please the experimenter.

Nonetheless, the robustness of the results across different environments can only be determined empirically. In view of this demonstration of replicable laboratory behavior, other approaches, including information process monitoring, protocol, and script-based methods should be explored to provide con-

vergent and complementary evidence in marketing strategy development and theory for services. Confirmatory research, based on theoretical underpinnings but characterized by greater external validity, should be conducted to facilitate further conceptual development in services. Furthermore, it is entirely fitting and necessary now to field test the hypotheses in more complex environments. The present study is hoped to prompt such research on consumer information needs and behavior.

Research Implications

The study highlights the need to explore more fully the decision-making process associated with the purchase of services. The testing of hypotheses grounded in extant theory affords empirical evidence that consumers use information sources distinctively in evaluating services. Further study should be conducted to address issues raised here. First, the research data imply that service consumers are inclined to seek additional prepurchase information. For services, this finding appears to contradict the expectation that as information sources become more scarce, difficult to access, and "costly" in terms of consumer expenditures of time and effort, consumer preference for seeking additional information decreases. What heuristics affect the service prepurchase situation is not readily apparent and warrants further research attention.

The study results also appear to contradict previous findings suggesting that as perceived risk of a purchase increases, individuals seek to reduce risk by direct observation and trial. Two considerations must be noted. First, risk and information acquisition theory has been based exclusively on empirical research involving tangible goods and characterized by an objective reality. Risk and information acquisition for services may not necessarily conform to previous research conclusions based exclusively on nonservice products. Second, given the fundamental nature of services, the opportunity for consumer observation and trial is logically limited and findings divergent from the ones in this study would be difficult to explicate fully. Though the unique nature of services is precisely what might heighten risk perceptions, it also appears to prevent the consumer from carrying out the same information strategies they employ for goods. More research is needed to identify how prospective service consumers make observations from visible cues and service trial.

The hypothesis that consumers with direct prior knowledge would have grater preference for internal sources of information when evaluating services than when evaluating goods is consistent with that proposed in Young's (1981) hierarchy of effects model for service promotion and is supported by the study data. In view of the limitations associated with the direct application of an IDB brand-by-attribute analytic framework to many services, subsequent research might examine how prior experience is organized.

Managerial Implications

The research results suggest that the consumer's increased information need is for information from *particular types of sources.* Beyond consumers' general proclivity for personal sources of information, those sources are even more preferred and appear to have an even greater degree of consumer confidence than impersonal sources in the context of service purchases than in purchase contexts involving goods. Personal independent sources are particularly more effective for services than goods. Influence exerted by those sources appears to confirm service marketing theory, which suggests that consumers desire subjective and experiential information. Consequently, the study conclusions point to a prominent role for opinion leaders and reference group members who may be early service adopters. These types of sources, however, have been viewed by managers as largely beyond the direct control of the marketing function. Nonetheless, the prominence of word-of-mouth (WOM) generally and for services in particular has received renewed attention and interest (e.g., Midgley 1983; Reingen and Kernan 1986). There is reason to believe that WOM may be particularly relevant to services (e.g., Brown and Reingen 1987), and cost to a firm that neglects negative WOM has been noted (Richins 1983). Consequently, several approaches may be possible that specifically address prospective service consumers' need for word-of-mouth information.

First, the study findings show that managers should not only train and equip service employees to carry out their service functions *per se,* but also ensure their knowledgeability and understanding of the service product and process. Managers' ability to influence contact employees' knowledge and understanding of the service encounter—and hence their ability and willingness to communicate that to customers—may directly enhance customer satisfaction or mitigate dissatisfaction. These positive effects are achieved by service providers who are prepared and able to offer WOM information to customers, depending on the demands of different encounters. Early evidence from other research supports this view (Bitner, Booms, and Tetreault 1990). Second, service providers should equip customers with information (from both personal and impersonal sources) about the service, thereby making them more informed and potentially more likely and effective transmitters of information to other prospects. Third, WOM between service customers and prospective service customers could be motivated by the provision of incentives for referral of new customers to the firm.

In terms of marketing strategy development, during the services' introductory stage a decision to encourage early service adoption by likely service prospects implies that increased numbers of service personnel may be necessary at the service or purchase site to address consumer information needs. Throughout the life cycle of the service, the firm should take measures to provide specially trained service personnel who can respond to the heightened information needs of the first-time service customer. The findings suggest that for customers with product experience, internal sources play a key role in providing information. Thus, it is particularly important that early service encounters be informative and satisfactory ones because of the role experience in addressing the information needs of service consumers.

Finally, the provider of services may be able to engage in marketing activities beyond word-of-mouth communication to encourage the adoption process. The preference of consumers for personal information suggests that persuasive communication strategies should stress experiential rather than technical or objective dimensions of the offering. Similarly, WOM simulation may be an effective promotional approach, particularly when spokespersons and endorsers are selected carefully for their perceived similarity to the service customer prospect. Incentives to induce trial are likely to motivate prospects to acquire relevant experience and "information" that would provide the basis for continued service usage. The banking industry's use of contests to encourage consumer use of ATMs is an example of how incentives can promote patronage of a particular service. Finally, the data underscore the need for the firm to "tangibilize the offer" by providing visible or explanatory cues that prospective service consumers can use to evaluate the ultimate benefits and quality of the product. This notion has been noted in the literature (e.g., Levitt 1981) as a useful heuristic, and the present research provides some empirical basis for its particular relevance.

In summary, the study findings suggest that the information needs of service consumers warrant special attention from both marketing scholars and practitioners. The data suggest that the information requirements of prospective service buyers result in unique information acquisition strategies by consumers and point to special marketing and communication strategies on the part of marketers. The theoretical and managerial implications should be tested further to provide confirmation of the study data.

APPENDIX A
Form of the Hypothetical Purchase Scenario

_____ Purchase Situation

You plan to purchase_____. However, when you consider all possible alternatives of _____ with which you are familiar, none are available. In fact, the only alternatives are ones which you are not familiar with.

Assume that you plan to purchase _____ and will make a choice in the near future.

For you to make a decision without any information about the options available would be virtually the same as making a selection at random. Therefore, you are asked to indicate what your strategy would be before making a final selection . . .

THE SPECIFIC PRODUCT STIMULI ASSOCIATED WITH THE THREE LEVELS OF THE INDEPENDENT VARIABLE AND INCORPORATED INTO PURCHASE SCENARIOS

High Service Attribute Products	Moderate Service Attribute Products	Low Service Attribute Products
Teeth cleaning by a dentist or hygienist	Auto reupholstery (including installation)	Windbreaker jacket
Income tax advice and preparation	Smoke detector/alarm protection	Tennis racket
Auto wheel alignment	Furniture rental, sofa	Barbecue grill
Professional interior decoration advice	Auto muffler (including installation)	Small electric vacuum cleaner
Eye exam	Fine restaurant meal	Pocket camera

APPENDIX B
Source Items Used in the Study: 25 Items Tapping Information Sources Used in a Purchase Situation

Circle the number below that best describes your reaction when considering the purchase of a

definitely would
   generally would
      would be inclined to
         may or may not
           would not be inclined to
              generally would not
                definitely would not

I . . .	1	2	3	4	5	6	7 . . . ask for a demonstration of the product or service
I . . .	1	2	3	4	5	6	7 . . . think about my previous involvement with this type of product or service.
I . . .	1	2	3	4	5	6	7 . . . try to remember what alternative my friends use.
I . . .	1	2	3	4	5	6	7 . . . ask the opinion of the salesperson.
I . . .	1	2	3	4	5	6	7 . . . pay attention to magazine ads about the product before buying.
I . . .	1	2	3	4	5	6	7 . . . ask member of my family or a relative for their opinion.
I . . .	1	2	3	4	5	6	7 . . . pay attention to radio commercials for the product or service.
I . . .	1	2	3	4	5	6	7 . . . check some type of printed consumer information source for objective product ratings, i.e., *Consumer Reports*, etc.
I . . .	1	2	3	4	5	6	7 . . . rely on past personal experience.
I . . .	1	2	3	4	5	6	7 . . . consider what a magazine article may say about the product.
I . . .	1	2	3	4	5	6	7 . . . pay attention to newspaper ads about the product before buying.
I . . .	1	2	3	4	5	6	7 . . . simply go ahead and make a selection of the product or service without additional information or further pre-purchase deliberation.

I . . .	1	2	3	4	5	6	7	. . . ask the opinion of a friend or someone I know.
I . . .	1	2	3	4	5	6	7	. . . try to recall relevant events which I can associate with this product or service.
I . . .	1	2	3	4	5	6	7	. . . ask to try to sample the product before purchasing.
I . . .	1	2	3	4	5	6	7	. . . pay attention to TV commercials about the product before buying.
I . . .	1	2	3	4	5	6	7	. . . buy the first purchase alternative I found.
I . . .	1	2	3	4	5	6	7	. . . ask the opinion of the owner or manager of the store, office, or retail outlet.
I . . .	1	2	3	4	5	6	7	. . . try to experience first-hand all I could about the product or service.
I . . .	1	2	3	4	5	6	7	. . . see a written description of the product or service or study a detailed descriptive analysis of the product or service.
I . . .	1	2	3	4	5	6	7	. . . read available information such as printed brochure, pamphlet, point-of-purchase display, or other information provided by the seller.
I . . .	1	2	3	4	5	6	7	. . . ask the opinion of an employee of the firm offering the product such as a receptionist, delivery person, etc.
I . . .	1	2	3	4	5	6	7	. . . be ready to make a purchase selection and not worry about acquiring more information prior to buying.
I . . .	1	2	3	4	5	6	7	. . . read a report written by a knowledgeable third party, such as a critic, authority in the field, or product specialist.
I . . .	1	2	3	4	5	6	7	. . . pay attention to what previous customers had to say about the product or service.

References

Anderson, Ronald D., and Jack L. Engledow (1981), "Perceived Importance of Selected Product Information Sources in Two Time Periods by United States and West German Consumers," *Journal of Business Research*, 9 (December), 339–351.

Andreasen, A. R. (1968), "Attitudes and Customer Behavior: A Decision Model," in *Perspectives in Consumer Behavior*, H. H. Kassarjian and T. S. Robertson, eds. Glenview, IL: Scott, Foresman and Company, 498–510.

Arndt, Johan (1967), "Word of Mouth Advertising and Information Communication," in *Risk-Taking and Information Handling in Consumer Behavior*, D. F. Cox, ed. Boston: Harvard University Press, 188–239, 289–316.

Bateson, John E. G. (1977), "Do We Need Service Marketing?" in *Marketing Consumer Services: New Insights*, Pierre Eiglier et al., eds. Cambridge, MA: Marketing Science Institute, 1–30.

—— (1989), *Managing Services Marketing*, Hinsdale, IL: Dryden Press.

Berning, Carol, A. Kohn, and Jacob Jacoby (1974), "Patterns of Information Acquisition in New Product Purchases," *Journal of Consumer Research*, 1 (September), 18–22.

Bettman, James R. (1972), "Perceived Risk: A Measurement Methodology and Preliminary Findings," in *Proceedings, Third Annual Conference of the Association for Consumer Research*, M. Venkatesan, ed. College Park, MD: Association for Consumer Research, 394–403.

—— (1973), "Perceived Risk and Its Components: A Model and Empirical Test," *Journal of Marketing*, 10 (May), 184–189.

—— (1977), "Data-Collection and Analysis Approaches for Studying Consumer Information Processing," in *Advances in Consumer Research*, Vol. 4, William D. Perreault, Jr., ed. Chicago: Association for Consumer Research, 342–348.

—— (1979a), *An Information Processing Theory of Consumer Choice*. Reading, MA: Addison-Wesley Publishing Company.

—— (1979b), "Memory Factors in Consumer Choice: A Review," *Journal of Marketing*, 43 (Spring), 37–53.

—— and Jacob Jacoby (1976), "Patterns of Processing in Consumer Information Acquisition," in *Advances in Consumer Research*, Vol. 3, B. B. Anderson, ed. Urbana, IL: Association for Consumer Research, 315–320.

—— and Michael A. Zins (1977), "Constructive Processes in Consumer Choice," *Journal of Consumer Research*, 3 (September), 75–85.

Bitner, Mary Jo, Bernard H. Booms, and Mary Stanfield Tetreault (1990), "The Service Encounter: Diagnosing Favorable and Unfavorable Incidents," *Journal of Marketing*, 54 (January), 71–84.

Bonfield, E. H. (1974), "Attitude, Social Influence, Personal Norms, and Intention Interactions as Related to Branch Purchase Behavior," *Journal of Marketing Research*, 11 (November), 379–389.

Booms, Bernard H., and Mary J. Bitner (1981), "Marketing Strategies and Organization Structures for Service Firms," in *Marketing of Services*, James H. Donnelly and William R. George, eds. Chicago: American Marketing Association, 47–51.

—— and Jody L. Nyquist (1981), "Analyzing the Customer/Firm Communication Component of the Services Marketing Mix," in *Marketing of Services*, James H. Donnelly and William R. George, eds. Chicago: American Marketing Association, 172–177.

Brooker, George (1984), "An Assessment of an Expanded Measure of Perceived Risk," in *Advances in Consumer Research*, Vol. 11, Thomas C. Kinnear, ed. Urbana, IL: Association for Consumer Research, 439–441.

Brown, Jacqueline Johnson, and Peter H. Reingen (1987), "Social Ties and Word-of-Mouth Referral Behavior," *Journal of Consumer Research*, 14 (December), 350–362.

Brown, James R., and Edward F. Fern (1981), "Goods vs. Services Marketing: A Divergent Perspective," in *Conceptual and Theoretical Developments in Marketing*, O. C. Ferrell, S. W. Brown, and C. W. Lamb, Jr., eds. Chicago: American Marketing Association, 205–207.

Calder, Bobby J., Lynn W. Phillips, and Alice M. Tybout (1981), "Designing Research for Application," *Journal of Consumer Research*, 8 (September), 197–207.

Capon, Donald, and Marian Burke (1977), "Information Seeking Behavior in Consumer Durable Purchases," in *Contemporary Marketing Thought, 1977, Educators Proceedings*, Barnett A. Greenberg and Danny N. Bellenger, eds., Chicago: American Marketing Association, 110–115.

Churchill, Gilbert A., Jr. (1979), *Marketing Research*. Hinsdale, IL: Dryden Press.

Cox, Donald F. (1963a), "The Audience as Communicators," in Toward Scientific Marketing, *Proceedings of the Winter Conference of the American Marketing Association*, Stephen A. Greyser, ed. Chicago: American Marketing Association, 58–72.

——— (1963b), "The Measurement of Information Value: A Study in Consumer Decision-Making," in *Emerging Concepts in Marketing*, W. S. Decker, ed., Chicago: American Marketing Association, 413–421.

——— (1967), *Risk-Taking and Information Handling in Consumer Behavior*. Boston: Harvard University.

Davis, Duane L., Joseph P. Guiltinan, and Wesley H. Jones (1979), "Service Characteristics, Consumer Search, and the Classification of Retail Services," *Journal of Retailing*, (Fall), 3–23.

Deshpande, Rohit, and S. Krishnan (1977), "A Consumer-Based Approach for Establishing Priorities in Consumer Information Programs: Implications for Public Policy, *Contemporary Marketing Thought, 1977, Educators' Proceedings*, Barnett A. Greenberg and Danny N. Bellenger eds. Chicago: American Marketing Association, 338–341.

Eiglier, Pierre, and Eric Langeard (1977), "A New Appraoch to Service Marketing," in *Marketing Consumer Services Insights*, Pierre Eiglier et al., eds. Cambridge Marketing Science Institute, 33–58.

Engle, James F., and Roger D. Blackwell (1982), *Consumer Behavior*. New York: Dryden Press.

Eroglu, Sevgin (1987), "The Scenario Method: A Theory Not Theoretical, Approach," in *AMA Educators' Proceedings*, Susan P. Douglas et al., eds. Chicago: American Marketing Association, 220.

Furse, David H., Girish N. Punj, and David W. Stewart (1984), "A Typology of Individual Search Strategies among Purchasers of New Automobiles," *Journal of Consumer Research*, 10 (March), 417–431.

George, William R., Marc G. Weinberger, and J. Patrick Kelly (1985), "Consumer Risk Perceptions: Managerial Tool for the Service Encounter," in *The Service Encounter: Managing Employee/Customer Interaction in Service Businesses*, John A. Czepiel, Michael R. Solomon, and Carol F. Surprenant, eds. Lexington, MA: Lexington Books, 83–100.

Guseman, Dennis S. (1981), "Risk Perception and Risk Reduction in Consumer Services" in *Marketing of Services*, John H. Donnelly and William R. George, eds. Chicago: American Marketing Association, 200–204.

Hansen, Flemming (1972), *Consumer Choice Behavior*. New York: The Free Press.

Hofacker, Thomas (1984), "Identifying Consumer Information Processing Strategies: New Methodologies of Analyzing Information Display Board Data," in *Advances in Consumer Research*, Vol. 11, Thomas C. Kinnear, ed. Provo, UT: Association for Consumer Research, 579–584.

Houston, Michael J. (1979), "Consumer Evaluations and Product Information Sources," in *Current Issues & Research in Advertising*, 1979, James H. Leigh and Claude R. Martin, Jr., eds. Ann Arbor, MI: University of Michigan, 135–144.

Hoyer, Wayne D., and Jacob Jacoby (1983), "Three Dimensional Information Acquisition: An Application to Contraceptive Decision Making," in *Advances in Consumer Research*, Vol. 10, Richard P. Baggozi and Alice M. Tybout, eds. Ann Arbor, MI: Association for Consumer Research, 618–623.

Jackson, Donald W., Jr., Janet E. Keith, and Richard K. Burdick (1984), "Purchasing Agents' Perceptions of Industrial Buying Center Influence: A Situational Approach," *Journal of Marketing*, 48 (Fall), 75–83.

Jacoby, Jacob, Robert W. Chestnut, and William Fisher (1978), "A Behavioral Process Approach to Information Acquisition in Nondurable Purchasing," *Journal of Marketing Research*, 15 (November), 532–544.

———, ———, and William Silberman (1977), "Consumer Use and Comprehension of Nutrition Information," *Journal of Consumer Research*, 4 (September), 119–128.

——— and Leon B. Kaplan (1972), "The Components of Perceived Risk," in *Proceedings, Third Annual Conference of the Association for Consumer Research*, M. Venkatesan, ed. College Park, MD: Association for Consumer Research, 382–393.

———, Donald E. Speller, and Carol Kohn Berning (1974), "Brand Choice Behavior as a Function of Information Load: Replication and Extension," *Journal of Consumer Research*, 1 (June), 33–42.

Katz, Elihu, and Raul F. Lazarsfeld (1955), *Personal Influences*. New York: The Free Press.

Kirk, Roger E. (1982), *Experimental Design: Procedures for the Behavioral Sciences*. Belmont, CA: Brooks/Cole Publishing.

Kotler, Philip (1980), *Marketing Management*. Englewood Cliffs, NJ: Prentice-Hall, Inc.

Lehmann, Donald R., and William L. Moore (1980), "Validity of Information Display Boards: An Assessment Using Longitudinal Data," *Journal of Marketing Research*, 17 (November), 450–459.

Leigh, Thomas W., and Arno J. Rethans (1984), "A Script-Theoretic Analysis of Industrial Purchasing Behavior," *Journal of Marketing*, 48 (Fall), 22–32.

Levitt, Theodore (1981), "Marketing Intangible Products and Product Intangibles," *Harvard Business Review*, 59 (May–June), 94–102.

Locander, William B., and Peter W. Hermann (1979), "The Effects of Self-Confidence and Anxiety on Information Seeking in Consumer Risk Reduction," *Journal of Marketing Research*, 16 (May), 268–274.

Lovelock, Christopher L. (1981), "Why Marketing Management Needs to Be Different for Services," in *Marketing of Services*, James H. Donnelly and William R. George, eds. Chicago: American Marketing Association, 5–9.

Lutz, Richard J., and Patrick J. Reilly (1973), "An Exploration of the Effects of Perceived Social and Performance Risk on Consumer Information Acquisition," in *Advances in Consumer Research*, Vol. 1, Scott Ward and Peter Wright, eds. Urbana, IL: Association for Consumer Research, 393–405.

Lynch, John G., Jr. and Thomas K. Srull (1982), "Memory and Attentional Factors in Consumer Choice: Concepts and Research Methods," *Journal of Consumer Research*, 9 (June), 18–37.

May, Fredrick C. (1965), "An Appraisal of Buying Behavior Research," in *Marketing and Economic Development*, Peter D. Bennett, ed. Chicago: American Marketing Association, 392.

Midgley, David F. (1983), "Patterns of Interpersonal Information Seeking for the Purchase of a Symbolic Product," *Jouranl of Marketing Research*, 20 (February), 74–83.

Moore, William L., and Donald R. Lehmann (1980), "Individual Differences in Search Behavior for a Nondurable," *Journal of Consumer Research*, 7 (December), 296–307.

Mowen, John C., Janel E. Keith, Stephen W. Brown, and Donald W. Jackson, Jr. (1985), "Utilizing Effort and Task Difficulty Information in Evaluating Salespeople," *Journal of Marketing Research*, 22 (May), 185–191.

Murray, Keith B., and John L. Schlacter (1990), "The Impact of Services versus Goods on Consumers' Assessment of Perceived Risk and Variability," *Journal of the Academy of Marketing Science*, 18 (1), 51–65.

Nelson, P. (1974), "Advertising as Information," *Journal of Political Economy*, 81 (July/August), 729–754.

Nunnally, Jum C. (1967), *Psychometric Theory*. New York: McGraw-Hill Book Company.

Olander, Folke (1975), "Search Behavior in Non-Simultaneous Choice Situations: Satisficing or Maximizing," in *Utility, Probability and Human Decision Making*, D. Wendt and C. A. J. Ulek, eds., Dordrecht, Holland: D. Reidel.

Park, C. Whan (1976), "The Effect of Individual and Situation-Related Factors on Consumer Selection of Judgmental Models," *Journal of Marketing Research*, 13 (May), 144–151.

Perry, Michael, and B. Curtis Hamm (1969), "Canonical Analysis of Relations between Socioeconomic Risk and Personal Influence in Purcahse Decisions," *Journal of Marketing Research*, 6 (February), 351–354.

Peter, John Paul (1979), "Reliability: A Review of Psychometric Basics and Recent Marketing Practices," *Journal of Marketing Research*, 16 (February), 6–17.

———— (1981), "Construct Validity: A Review of Basic Issues and Marketing Practices," *Journal of Marketing*, 18 (May), 133–145.

———— and Lawrence X. Tarpey (1975), "A Comparative Analysis of Three Consumer Decision Strategies," *Journal of Consumer Research*, 2 (June), 29–37.

Price, Linda L., and Lawrence F. Feick (1984), "The Role of Interpersonal Sources in External Search: An Informational Perspective," in *Advances in Consumer Research*, Vol. 11, Thomas C. Kinnear, ed. Provo, UT: Association for Consumer Research, 250–255.

Puto, Christopher P., Wesley E. Patton III, and Ronald H. King (1985), "Risk-Handling Strategies in Industrial Vendor Selection Decisions," *Journal of Marketing*, 49 (Winter), 89–98.

Ray, Michael L. (1973), "Marketing Communications and Hierarchy of Effects," in *New Models for Mass Communication Research*, Peter Clarke, ed. Beverly Hills, CA: Sage Publications, Inc., 147–176.

Reingen, Peter H., and Jerome B. Kernan (1986), "Analysis of Referral Networks in Marketing: Methods and Illustration," *Journal of Marketing Research*, 23 (November), 370–378.

Richins, Marsha L. (1983), "Negative Word-of-Mouth by Dissatisfied Consumers: A Pilot Study," *Journal of Marketing*, 47 (Winter), 68–78.

Roselius, Ted (1971), "Consumer Rankings of Risk Reduction Methods," *Journal of Marketing*, 35 (January), 56–61.

Ryan, Michael J., and E. H. Bonfield (1980), "Fishbein's Intention Model: A Test of External Pragmatic Validity," *Journal of Marketing*, 44 (Spring), 82–95.

Shostack, G. Lynn (1977), "Breaking Free from Product Marketing," *Journal of Marketing*, 41 (April), 73–80.

Staelin, Richard, and John W. Payne (1976), "Studies of the Information Seeking Behavior of Consumers," in *Cognition of Social Behavior*, J. Carroll and J. W. Payne, eds. New York: Lawrence Erlbaum Associates, 185–202.

Surprenant, Carol F. and Michael R. Solomon (1987), "Prediction and Personalization in the Service Encounter," *Journal of Marketing*, 51 (April), 86–96.

Urbany, Joel E., and Dan C. Weilbaker (1987), "A Critical Examination of Nelson's Theory of Information and Consumer Behavior," in *AMA Educators' Conference Proceedings*, Susan P. Douglas et al., eds. Chicago: American Marketing Association, 220.

Van Raaij, W. Fred (1977), "Consumer Information Processing for Different Structures and Formats," in *Advances in Consumer Research*, Vol. 10, William D. Perreault, ed. Atlanta: Association for Consumer Research, 176–184.

Vinokur-Kaplan, Diane (1978), "To Have—Or not to Have—Another Child: Family Planning Attitudes, Intention, and Behavior," *Journal of Applied Social Psychology*, 8 (January-March), 29–46.

Vredenburg, Harrie, and Chow-Hou Wee (1986), "The Role of Customer Service in Determining Customer Satisfaction," *Journal of the Academy of Marketing Science*, 14 (Summer), 17–26.

Winter, Fredrick W. (1975), "Laboratory Measurement of Response to Consumer Information," *Journal of Marketing Research*, 12 (November), 390–401.

Wright, P. (1974), "The Harassed Decision Maker: Time Pressures, Distractions, and the Use of Evidence," *Journal of Applied Psychology*, 59 (October), 55–61.

Young, Robert F. (1981), "The Advertising of Consumer Services and the Hierarchy of Effects," in *Marketing of Services*, James H. Donnelly and William R. George, eds., Chicago: American Marketing Association, 196–199.

Zeithaml, Valarie A. (1981), "How Consumer Evaluation Processes Differ between Goods and Services," in *Marketing of Services*, James H. Donnelly and William R. George, eds. Chicago: American Marketing Association, 186–190.

————, A. Parasuraman, and Leonard L. Berry (1985) "Problems and Strategies in Services Marketing," *Journal of Marketing*, 49 (Spring), 33–46.

Critical Service Encounters: The Employee's Viewpoint

MARY JO BITNER
BERNARD H. BOOMS
LOIS A. MOHR

ABSTRACT *In service settings, customer satisfaction is often influenced by the quality of the interpersonal interaction between the customer and the contact employee. Previous research has identified the sources of satisfaction and dissatisfaction in service encounters from the customer's point of view; this study explores these sources in service encounters from the contact employee's point of view. Drawing on insights from role, script, and attribution theories, 774 critical service encounters reported by employees of the hotel, restaurant, and airline industries are analyzed and compared with previous research. Results generally support the theoretical predictions and also identify an additional source of customer dissatisfaction—the customer's own misbehavior. The findings have implications for business practice in managing service encounters, employee empowerment and training, and managing customers.*

The worldwide quality movement that has swept the manufacturing sector over the last decade is beginning to take shape in the service sector (*Business Week* 1991; Crosby 1991). According to some, the shift to a quality focus is essential to the competitive survival of service businesses, just as it has become essential in manufacturing (Heskett et al. 1994; Schlesinger and Heskett 1991).

Service quality researchers have suggested that "the proof of service [quality] is in its flawless performance" (Berry and Parasuraman 1991, p. 15), a concept akin to the notion of "zero defects" in manufacturing. Others have noted that "breakthrough" service managers pursue the goal of 100% defect-free service (Heskett, Sasser, and Hart 1990). From the customer's point of view, the most immediate evidence of service occurs in the service encounter or the "moment of truth" when the customer interacts with the firm. Thus, one central goal in the pursuit of "zero defects" in service is to work toward 100% flawless performance in service encounters. Here, flawless performance is not meant to imply rigid standardization, but rather 100% satisfying performance from the customer's point of view. The cost of not achieving flawless performance is the "cost of quality," which includes the costs associated with redoing the service or compensating for poor

service, lost customers, negative word of mouth, and decreased employee morale.

Although more firms are realizing the importance of service quality and customer satisfaction, it is not always clear how to achieve these goals. Situations arise in which quality is low and the problem is recognized by both the firm (i.e., employees) and the customer, but there may be disagreement on the causes of the problem and the appropriate solutions. In service encounters such disagreements, sure to diminish customer satisfaction, underscore the importance of understanding the types of events and behaviors that cause customers to be satisfied or dissatisfied. Because the service encounter involves at least two people, it is important to understand the encounter from multiple perspectives. Armed with such understanding, firms are better able to design processes and educate both employees and customers to achieve quality in service encounters.

Previous research in the context of the restaurant, hotel, and airline industries identified categories of events and behaviors that underlie critical service encounters from the customer's point of view (Bitner, Booms, and Tetreault 1990; hereafter BBT). The primary purpose of this study is to examine the contact employee's perspective of critical service encounters and to understand, in the context of the same three industries, the kinds of events and behaviors that employees believe underlie customer satisfaction. The employee perspective is then compared with BBT to gain insight into any disparities in perspectives. A second purpose of the study is to evaluate the usefulness of the classification scheme developed by BBT (1990). If the scheme is conceptually robust, it should hold for different respondent groups.

Mary Jo Bitner is an Associate Professor of Marketing, Arizona State University. Bernard H. Booms is a Professor, Business Program, University of Washington–Tacoma. Lois A. Mohr is an Assistant Professor of marketing, Georgia State University. The authors gratefully acknowledge the support of the First Interstate Center for Services Marketing and the College of Business, Arizona State University, in conducting this research. The helpful comments of three anonymous *JM* reviewers are also appreciated.

The research is guided by the following questions:

- From the contact employee's point of view, what kinds of events lead to satisfying service encounters for the customer? What causes these events to be remembered favorably?

- From the contact employee's point of view, what kinds of events lead to dissatisfying service encounters for the customer? What causes these events to be remembered with distaste?

- Do customers and employees report the same kinds of events and behaviors leading to satisfaction and dissatisfaction in service encounters?

Before presenting the empirical study, we discuss relevant research and theory.

Customer and Contact Employee Viewpoints

Frontline personnel are a critical source of information about customers. There are two basic ways that customer knowledge obtained by contact employees is used to improve service: (1) Such knowledge is used by the contact employees themselves to facilitate their interactions with customers and (2) It is used by the firm for making decisions. First, employees often modify their behavior from moment to moment on the basis of feedback they receive while serving customers. Schneider (1980) argues that people who choose to work in service occupations generally have a strong desire to give good service. To the extent that this is true, contact personnel can be expected to look frequently for cues that tell them how their service is received by customers. The more accurate their perceptions are, the more likely their behavioral adjustments are to improve customer satisfaction.

Second, because contact personnel have frequent contact with customers, they serve a boundary-spanning role in the firm. As a result, they often have better understanding of customer needs and problems than others in the firm. Researchers have theorized and found some evidence that open communication between frontline personnel and managers is important for achieving service quality (Parasuraman, Berry, and Zeithaml 1990; Zeithaml, Berry, and Parasuraman 1988). Schneider and Bowen (1984) argue that firms should use information gathered from contact personnel in making strategic decisions, especially decisions regarding new service development and service modifications.

It seems reasonable to conclude that accurate employee understanding of customers enables both the employee and the firm to adjust appropriately to customer needs. However, previous research correlating customer and employee views of service is sparse and offers mixed conclusions. Schneider and Bowen (1985) and Schneider, Parkington, and Buxton (1980) found high correlations (r = .63 and r = .67, respectively) between employee and customer attitudes about overall service quality in a bank setting. Their results are contradicted, however, in a study by Brown and Swartz (1989). These researchers gathered data on patient experiences with their physicians and compared them with the physicians' perceptions of their patients' experiences. The differences they found were rather large and inversely related to overall patient satisfaction.

Another study of 1300 customers and 900 customer service professionals conducted by Development Dimensions International found differences in perceptions between the two groups (*Services Marketing Newsletter 1989*). Customer service professionals in that study consistently rated the importance of particular service skills and competencies and their actual performance higher than customers rated the same skills and competencies. Similarly, Langeard and colleagues (1981) found that field managers at two banks tended to overestimate (compared with customer ratings) the importance of six broad service delivery dimensions. Other studies have found differences when comparing customer and employee evaluations of business situations using scenarios and role playing in product failure contexts (Folkes and Kotsos 1986), a complaint context (Resnik and Harmon 1983), and the context of retailer responses to customer problems (Dornoff and Dwyer 1981).

We would therefore expect, on the basis of these studies, to find similarities in employee and customer views of the service encounter, but we would expect significant differences as well. Role, script, and attribution theories provide conceptual bases for these expectations.

Theoretical Explanations

Role and Script Theories

Similarities in how customers and employees view service encounters are most likely when the two parties share common role expectations and the service script is well defined (Mohr and Bitner 1991; Solomon et al. 1985). A *role* is the behavior associated with a socially defined position (Solomon et al. 1985), and *role expec-*

tations are the standards for role behavior (Biddle 1986). In many routine service encounters, particularly for experienced employees and customers, the roles are well defined and both the customer and employee know what to expect from each other.

In addition, many types of service encounters, such as seating customers in a restaurant, are repeated frequently throughout a person's life, resulting in strong, standardized, and well-rehearsed scripts (i.e., structures that describe appropriate sequences of role behaviors) (Schank and Abelson 1977). When service encounters have strong scripts, the employee and customer are likely to share expectations about the events that will occur and the order of occurrence. They are less likely to share ideas about subscripts, which are prescriptions for handling what Schank and Abelson describe as "obstacles and errors," two types of interferences that may occur in otherwise predictable scripts.

Role and script theory, combined with the routine nature of many service encounters, suggests that customers and employees are likely to share a common perspective on service experiences. It is also clear that differences in perspective may arise when roles are less defined, a participant is unfamiliar with expected behaviors, or interferences require the enactment of complex or less routine subscripts.

Attribution Theory

Dissimilarities in viewpoint may arise when service encounter partners have conflicting views of the underlying causes behind the events, that is, when their attributions differ. Research shows that there are many biases in the attribution process (Fiske and Taylor 1984). Most clearly relevant for the perceptions of service providers and customers is the self-serving attribution bias. This is the tendency for people to take credit for success (i.e., to give internal attributions for their successes, a self-enhancing bias) and deny responsibility for failure (i.e., to blame failure on external causes, a self-protecting bias). Given these biases we would expect employees to blame the system or the customer for service failures, whereas the customer would be more likely to blame the system or the employee. The result would be different views of the causes of service dissatisfaction. It is less clear that this bias would operate in the case of a service encounter success. Although the desire for self-enhancement might lead both the employee and customer to give themselves credit for the success, the fact that the customer is paying the firm for a service would probably preclude the bias on the customer's side. Overall, then, the self-serving attribution bias leads to the expectation that the perspectives of the employee and cus-

tomer will differ more in service failure than in service success situations.

Both empirical research and theory suggest that similarities as well as differences in perspective are likely to occur between service encounter participants. Role and script theories suggest that in relatively routine situations such as the ones studied, there will be strong similarities in perspective. However, attribution biases suggest that there will also be significant differences in viewpoint. We explore to what extent the perspectives of contact personnel and those of customers are different. And, to the degree that they are different, the data provide insight into the nature of these disparities.

Method and Analysis

Data Collection

Data were collected using the critical incident technique (CIT), a systematic procedure for recording events and behaviors that are observed to lead to success or failure on a specific task (Ronan and Latham 1974), in this case, satisfying the customer. (For more detailed discussions of the method, see BBT; Flanagan 1954; Wilson-Pessano 1988). Using the CIT, data are collected through structured, open-ended questions, and the results are content analyzed. Respondents are asked to report specific events from the recent past (within 6 to 12 months). These accounts provide rich details of firsthand experiences in which customers have been satisfied or dissatisfied. Because respondents are asked about specific events rather than generalities, interpretation, or conclusions, this procedure meets criteria established by Ericsson and Simon (1980) for providing valuable, reliable information about cognitive processes. Researchers have concluded that when used appropriately (Flanagan 1954; Wilson-Pessano 1988), the critical incident method is reliable in terms of stability of the categories identified across judges, valid with respect to the content identified, and relevant in that the behaviors illuminated have proven to be important to the success or failure of the task in question (Ronan and Latham 1974; White and Locke 1981).

Hotel, restaurant, and airline employees were interviewed and asked to recall critical service encounters that caused satisfaction or dissatisfaction for customers of their firms. Thirty-seven trained student interviewers collected the data—781 total incidents. Each one recruited a minimum of ten employees from among the same three industries studied in BBT, asking each employee to describe one incident that was satisfactory and one that was dissatisfactory from the customer's point of view.

Because all the interviewers were employed in the hospitality sector, they recruited fellow employees and employees of establishments with which they were familiar. They were instructed not to interview fellow students. The refusal rate was negligible. The incident sample represented 58 hotels, 152 restaurants, and 4 airlines. On average, the employees providing the incidents had 5.5 years of working experience in their respective industries. The employees ranged in age from 16 to 65 (mean age 27) and were 55% female and 45% male. The instructions to the employees being interviewed were as follows:

> Put yourself in the shoes of customers of your firm. In other words, try to see your firm through your customers' eyes.

> Think of a recent time when a customer of your firm had a particularly satisfying (dissatisfying) interaction with yourself or a fellow employee. Describe the situation and exactly what happened.

They were then asked the following questions:

1. When did the incident happen?

2. What specific circumstances led up to this situation?

3. Exactly what did you or your fellow employee say or do?

4. What resulted that made you feel the interaction was satisfying (dissatisfying) from the customer's point of view?

5. What should you or your fellow employee have said or done? (for dissatisfying incident only)

To be used in the analysis, an incident was required to (1) involve employee-customer interaction, (2) be very satisfying or dissatisfying from the customer's point of view, (3) be a discrete episode, and (4) have sufficient detail to be visualized by the interviewer. Seven incidents failed to meet these criteria, leaving 774 incidents (397 satisfactory and 377 dissatisfactory).

Classification of Incidents

The incident classification system developed by BBT was used as a starting point for sorting the data with the assumption that, to the degree that customers and employees remember satisfying and dissatisfying encounters in the same way, the same classification

system should be appropriate. Incidents that could not be classified within the original scheme would then provide evidence for differences in perspective.

One researcher trained in the classification scheme coded the incidents. Any that did not fit into the scheme were put aside. This researcher and a second then worked together on categorizing this group of 86 incidents (11% of the total). These incidents were read and sorted, combined, and resorted until a consistent coding scheme was developed that combined similar incidents into distinct, meaningful categories. When the new categories were labeled and the two researchers achieved consensus on assignment of the incidents, the new categories (one major group with four sub-categories) were added to the original classification system.

A set of complete coding instructions was then written (see Appendix A). They included general instructions for coders, operational definitions of each category, and decision rules for assigning incidents to categories. These are procedures recommended by Perreault and Leigh (1989) for improving the reliability of judgment-based data. The coding instructions were used to train a third researcher who had not participated in the categorization decisions. This researcher then coded the 774 employee incidents, providing an interjudge reliability check on the classification system. Discrepancies between the first and third researchers' assignments were resolved by the second researcher.

The interjudge agreement between the first and third researchers was 84% for the satisfying incidents and 85% for the dissatisfying incidents. These figures are respectably high, especially considering that the classification system in this study contains 16 categories. The percentage agreement statistic probably underestimates interjudge reliability in this case because this statistic is influenced by the number of coding categories (i.e., the more categories, the lower the percentage agreement is likely to be) (Perreault and Leigh 1989). For this reason, two other measures of interjudge reliability were calculated. Cohen's K, which corrects for the likelihood of chance agreement between judges, was found to be .816 for the satisfying and .823 for the dissatisfying incidents. Perreault and Leigh (1989) argue, however, that K is an overly conservative measure of reliability because it assumes an a priori knowledge of the likely distribution of responses across categories. To correct for this they designed an alternative index of reliability, I_r, appropriate for marketing data. Rather than contrasting interjudge agreement with an estimate of chance agreement, I_r is based on a model of the level of agreement that might be expected given a true (population) level of reliability. Furthermore, the index focuses on the reliability of the whole coding process, not just on the agreement between judges. I_r was found to be .911 and .914 for the satisfying and dissatisfying incidents, respectively.

Results and Discussion

The categories of events and behaviors that employees believe underlie their customers' satisfaction and dissatisfaction in service encounters are identified and discussed first. Then the results are compared with customer perceptions using the BBT data.

Classification of Employee-Reported Incidents

The critical incident classification system based on incidents gathered from customers (BBT) consists of three major groups of employee behaviors that account for all satisfactory and dissatisfactory incidents: (1) employee response to service delivery system failures, (2) employee response to customer needs and requests, and (3) unprompted and unsolicited employee actions. Of the 774 employee incidents, 668 were classified into one of these three groups and the 12 categories within them. The incidents were very similar in detail to those provided by customers. (See BBT for detailed descriptions of the groups and categories and sample incidents.)

Eighty-six encounters (11% of the total) did not fit any of the predetermined groups. These incidents were categorized into one major group labeled "problem customer behavior," and they were added to the categorization scheme as "Group 4." In these cases, the coders could not attribute the satisfaction and dissatisfaction to an action or attitude of the employee—instead, the root cause was the customer. Such customers were basically uncooperative, that is, unwilling to cooperate with the service provider, other customers, industry regulations, and/or laws. These situations created problems for the employees, and rarely were they able to deal with them in such a way as to bring about customer satisfaction; only 3 of these incidents were satisfactory.

Within the problem customer behavior group, four categories emerged (Table 1 provides examples of incidents from the four new categories):

1. *Drunkenness*—The employee perceives the customer to be clearly intoxicated and creating problems such as harassing other customers nearby, giving the employee a hard time, or disrupting the atmosphere of the establishment;

2. *Verbal and physical abuse*—The customer verbally and/or physically abuses either the employee or other customers;

3. *Breaking company policies or laws*—The customer refuses to comply with policies or laws, and the employee attempts to enforce compliance; and

4. *Uncooperative customers*—The customer is generally rude and uncooperative or unreasonably demanding. From the employee's perspective, the customer is unwilling to be satisfied, no matter what is done for him or her.

The Employee's View of Satisfactory versus Dissatisfactory Encounters

Here we examine the frequencies and proportions of employee accounts in the four groups and 16 categories as shown in Table 2. It should be noted that the frequencies and proportions shown in the table reflect numbers of reported events. The actual frequency of occurrence of the type of event represented by a particular group or category cannot be inferred from the data. Nor can greater importance be inferred by greater frequencies in a particular category (Wilson-Pessano 1988). The data are shown in full in Table 2; however, our discussion focuses on the four major groups. To facilitate understanding, the employee-reported incidents are summarized and ranked according to the percentage of incidents in the four major incident groups:

Distribution of Dissatisfactory Incidents

Rank Order	Group #	Percentage
1	Group 1—Response to failures	51.7
2	Group 4—Problem customers	22.0
3	Group 2—Response to requests	16.4
4	Group 3—Unprompted action	9.8

Distribution of Satisfactory Incidents

Rank Order	Group #	Percentage
1	Group 2—Response to requests	49.4
2	Group 1—Response to failures	27.5
3	Group 3—Unprompted action	22.4
4	Group 4—Problem customers	.8

When employees were asked to report incidents resulting in customer dissatisfaction, they tended to describe problems with external causes such as the delivery system or inappropriate customer behaviors. By far the largest number of dissatisfactory incidents were categorized in Group 1 (response to delivery sys-

TABLE 1
Group Four Sample Incidents: Problem Customers

Incident	
Dissatisfactory	**Satisfactory**
A. Drunkenness	
An intoxicated man began pinching the female flight attendants. One attendant told him to stop, but he continued and then hit another passenger. The copilot was called and asked the man to sit down and leave the others alone, but the passenger refused. The copilot then "decked" the man, knocking him into his seat.	A person who became intoxicated on a flight started speaking loudly, annoying the other passengers. The flight attendant asked the passenger if he would be driving when the plane landed and offered him coffee. He accepted the coffee and became quieter and friendlier.
B. Verbal and Physical Abuse	
While a family of three was waiting to order dinner, the father began hitting his child. Another customer complained about this to the manager who then, in a friendly and sympathetic way, asked the family to leave. The father knocked all the plates and glasses off the table before leaving.	None
C. Breaking Company Policies or Laws	
Five guests were in a hotel room two hours past checkout time. Because they would not answer the phone calls or let the staff into the room, hotel security staff finally broke in. They found the guests using drugs and called the police.	None
D. Uncooperative Customer	
When a man was shown to his table in the nonview dining area of the restaurant, he became extremely angry and demanded a window table. The restaurant was very busy, but the hostess told him he could get a window seat in a half hour. He refused to wait and took his previously reserved table, but he complained all the way through the dinner and left without tipping.	None

tem failures), with the next largest proportion falling into Group 4 (problem customers). These results are not unexpected given what attribution theory suggests. When things go wrong, people are more likely to blame external, situational factors than to attribute the failure to their own shortcomings. A modest number of dissatisfactory incidents were found in Group 2. In many of these cases, the employees implied that they were unable to satisfy customer needs due to constraints placed on them by laws or their own organization's rules and procedures, again placing the blame on an external source. The smallest percentage of dissatisfactory incidents were classified in Group 3, which reflects spontaneous negative employee behaviors (e.g., rudeness, lack of attention). Again, this is consistent with the bias toward not blaming oneself for failures.

The largest proportion of satisfactory incidents, from the employee's point of view, occurred in response to customer needs and requests (Group 2). Almost half of particularly satisfying customer encounters reported by employees resulted from their ability to adjust the system to accommodate customer needs and requests. Success is attributed in these cases to the employee's own ability and willingness to adjust. The next largest proportion of satisfactory incidents were categorized in Group 1. This is an interesting set of incidents, because each one began as a failure but ended as a success because of the ability of the employee to recover. Employees clearly remember their ability to recover in failure situations as a significant cause for ultimate customer satisfaction. A relatively modest (when compared with the customer view) number of satisfactory incidents were categorized as unprompted and unsolicited employee actions (Group 3). Perhaps employees do not view their own behaviors as "spontaneous," but they instead remember them in association with a specific external cause

TABLE 2

Group and Category Classification by Type of Incident Outcome (Employees Only)

| | Type of Incident Outcome | | | | | |
| | Satisfactory | | Dissatisfactory | | Row Total | |
Group and Category	No.	%	No.	%	No.	%
Group 1. Employee Response to Service Delivery System Failures						
A. To unavailable service	31	7.8	37	9.8	68	8.8
B. To unreasonably slow service	23	6.0	48	12.7	71	9.2
C. To other core service failures	55	13.9	110	29.2	165	21.3
Subtotal, Group 1	109	27.5	195	51.7	304	39.3
Group 2. Employee Response to Customer Needs and Requests						
A. To "special needs" customers	80	20.2	14	3.7	94	12.1
B. To customer preferences	99	24.9	43	11.4	142	18.3
C. To admitted customer error	11	2.8	0	0.0	11	1.4
D. To potentially disruptive others	6	1.5	5	1.3	11	1.4
Subtotal, Group 2	196	49.4	62	16.4	258	33.3
Group 3. Unprompted and Unsolicited Employee Actions						
A. Attention paid to customer	43	10.8	6	1.6	49	6.3
B. Truly out-of-the-ordinary employee behavior	25	6.3	28	7.4	53	6.8
C. Employee behaviors in the context of cultural norms	7	1.8	3	.8	10	1.3
D. Gestalt evaluation	0	0.0	0	0.0	0	0.0
E. Performance under adverse circumstances	14	3.5	0	0.0	14	1.8
Subtotal, Group 3	89	22.4	37	9.8	126	16.3
Group 4. Problematic Customer Behavior						
A. Drunkenness	3	.8	16	4.2	19	2.5
B. Verbal and Physical Abuse	0	0.0	9	2.4	9	1.2
C. Breaking company policies or laws	0	0.0	16	4.2	16	2.1
D. Uncooperative customer	0	0.0	42	11.1	42	5.4
Subtotal, Group 4	3	.8	83	22.0	86	11.1
Column Total	397	51.3	377	48.7	774	100%

(e.g., a customer need, a service failure). Finally, there were virtually no satisfactory incidents categorized in the problem customer group (Group 4). This makes sense, because it is difficult to imagine a very problematic customer leaving the encounter feeling satisfied except under highly unusual circumstances.

Comparing Customer and Employee Views

Table 3 combines data from the current study with the original BBT data for purposes of comparison. Because the employees and customers in these two studies all described different incidents, conclusions from employee-customer comparisons are exploratory, and the explanations are somewhat speculative. Although we rely on role and attribution theories to explain the differences we observed, it is possible that these differences could be due to sampling variations or differences in the incident pool from which the two groups drew. However, given the care taken in collecting the data to avoid systematic biases, that both studies were conducted in the same city using the same

three industries, and that many of the same firms were the source of incidents in both studies, we have confidence in our theoretical explanations of the results.

A large majority of the employee incidents from the current study could be categorized in the original three groups and 12 categories, suggesting strong similarities in the way employees and customers report the sources of satisfaction and dissatisfaction in service encounters. Recall that these are relatively routine service encounters and in both studies the respondents were experienced service participants. Even so, the addition of a fourth group and the significant differences in frequencies and proportions of incidents found in the groups suggest that there are dissimilarities in what they report as well. Hierarchical log-linear analysis of Table 3 shows a significant three-way interaction between group (1, 2, 3, or 4), type of outcome (satisfactory or dissatisfactory), and incident source (employee or customer) (L.R. χ^2 change = 8.17; p = .04). There is also a significant two-way interaction between group and incident source (L.R. χ^2 change = 263.31; p < .0001). Because of the significant three-

TABLE 3

Comparison of Employee and Customer Responses: Incident Classification by Type of Incident Outcome[a]

| | Type of Incident Outcome | | | | | |
| | Satisfactory | | Dissatisfactory | | Row Total | |
Groups	No.	%	No.	%	No.	%
Group 1. Employee Response to Service Delivery System Failures						
Employee Data	109	27.5	195	51.7	304	39.3
Customer Data	81	23.3	151	42.9	232	33.2
Group 2. Employee Response to Customer Needs and Requests						
Employee Data	196	49.4	62	16.4	258	33.3
Customer Data	114	32.9	55	15.6	169	24.2
Group 3. Unprompted and Unsolicited Employee Actions						
Employee Data	89	22.4	37	9.8	126	16.3
Customer Data	152	43.8	146	41.5	298	42.6
Group 4. Problematic Customer Behavior						
Employee Data	3	.8	83	22.0	86	11.1
Customer Data	0	0.0	0	0.0	0	0.0
Column Total						
Employee Data	397	51.3	377	48.7	774	100%
Customer Data	347	49.6	352	50.4	699	100%

[a]Customer response data from Bitner, Booms, and Tetreault (1990)

way interaction, the results are discussed separately for satisfactory and dissatisfactory incidents.

Within the dissatisfactory incident classifications, customers and employees have relatively similar proportions in Groups 1 and 2. The significant interaction is caused by Group 3, which is dominated by customer incidents, and Group 4, which contains incidents reported by employees only. These results are very consistent with expectations based on attribution biases. Employees are highly unlikely to describe customer dissatisfaction as being caused by their own predispositions, attitudes, or spontaneous behaviors. Customers, on the other hand, will be likely to blame the employee rather than anything they themselves might have contributed. This is clearly reflected in the observation that customers report no dissatisfactory incidents caused by their own problem behaviors (Group 4).

The differences in how customers and employees report satisfactory encounters are provocative as well, albeit less extreme. Again, this is consistent with attribution theory, which predicts larger differences in perceptions in failure than in success situations. Within the satisfactory incidents, Groups 1 and 4 are equally represented for both customers and employees. The significant interaction is the result of Group 2 being dominated by employee incidents and Group 3 being dominated by customer incidents.

Implications for Researchers

Generalizability of the Service Encounter Classification Scheme

The importance and usefulness of robust classification schemes for theory development and practical application have been discussed by social scientists (e.g., McKelvey 1982) and marketing scholars (e.g., Hunt 1991; Lovelock 1983). Yet we have few such frameworks in marketing, primarily because the classification schemes that have been proposed have rarely been subjected to empirical validation across times and contexts.

This study represents one contribution in a program of research designed to test the validity and generalizability of a scheme for categorizing sources of service encounter satisfaction and dissatisfaction (BBT). If the scheme holds in different settings (e.g., different industry contexts, or in internal as well as external encounters) and across different respondents (e.g., customers versus providers, customers in different cultures), then the scheme can be viewed as more robust and of greater theoretical as well as practical value. Other studies have reported that the three major groups of behaviors identified by BBT are also found in a retail context (Kelley, Hoffman, and Davis 1993) and a study of 16 consumer services (Gremler and Bitner 1992). Through replication, the framework becomes more valuable in identifying generalizable "service behaviors."

The results of our research indicate that all the categories found in the original customer-perspective study were also found when employees were asked to report except "problem customers." The addition of this new group provides a more complete classification system that can be further examined in other contexts.

Problem Customers

A primary contribution of this research effort is the empirically based finding that unsatisfactory service encounters may be due to inappropriate customer behaviors—the notion that sometimes customers are wrong. Others have suggested the existence of problem customers (e.g., Lovelock 1994; Schrage 1992; Zemke and Anderson 1990). Lovelock, for example, suggests the term "jaycustomers" to label customers who "misconsume" in a manner similar to jaywalkers who cross streets in unauthorized places. Our research provides empirical evidence that these difficult customer types do exist and in fact can be the source of their own dissatisfaction.

Although no one really believes customers are always right, firms have policies that pretend this is so, and managers urge and demand that customer contact employees treat customers as if they are always right. Needless to say, such avoidance leads to stresses and strains for managers and frontline personnel alike and potentially bigger problems for firms. (See Hochschild 1983 for a discussion of personal and organizational impacts of nonauthentic ways of dealing with customers.) With a better understanding of problem customers can come better methods for eliminating or dealing with the underlying causes of the problems.

This area is ripe with important research questions, such as the following: What types of problems do customers cause? What are the most frequent problems? What types of customers tend to be problem customers? Under what circumstances do customers create either more or fewer problems? And, from a management viewpoint, what can be done to identify problem customers, and how can and should employees deal with them?

This initial research represents a start at addressing some of these questions and the beginnings of a typology of problem customer behaviors. The categories of behaviors discovered are not surprising given the nature of the industries studied. Each service involves the possible serving of food and drink—including alcoholic beverages. In each service the customers are in close physical proximity for extended periods of time. Restaurant, airline, and hotel cus-

tomers are many times in tight public spaces that put them cheek to jowl with other customers. Personal social interactions are carried out in front of other customers who are most often strangers. And, as mentioned previously, the types of encounters studied here are all relatively routine and commonly experienced. Finally, customers frequently have transaction-based encounters with the service personnel rather than long-term relationship-based encounters. It is assumed that these circumstances influenced the nature of the subcategories of problems identified in Group 4. Thus, although we believe that the major problem customer group will surface whenever employees are asked to relate instances of dissatisfactory encounters, further research is needed to identify other subcategories within the group and relate problem types to service industry conditions, circumstances, and customer segments.

Although we have identified problem customers by exploring the sources of customer dissatisfaction, there may be other types of "wrong customers." For example, even when customers do not misbehave, they may not be good relationship customers for the organization because they do not meet the target market profile, they are not profitable in the long term, or in some cases they may not be compatible with the service provider in terms of personality or work style (Lovelock 1994; Zeithaml and Bitner 1995). It is beyond the scope of this article to discuss the full conceptualization of wrong customers, but it may be fruitful for researchers in the future to incorporate the misbehaving customers we have identified into this more extensive conceptual scheme.

Theory Implications

Role and script theories suggest that customers and employees in routine, well-understood service transactions will share parallel views of their roles and the expected sequence of events and behaviors. The types of service encounters studied here and in the original study do represent frequently encountered and routine services. Shared views of the encounter should result in common notions of the sources of customer satisfaction and dissatisfaction. The fact that 89% of the employee incidents could be classified in the original classification scheme suggests that customers and employees do indeed report incidents with most of the same sources of satisfaction and dissatisfaction.

An interesting issue for further research is whether the overall strong similarity of views between customers and employees would result if the industries studied were ones in which the scripts were less routine and well practiced.

Results of the study indicate that though employees and customers do report many of the same sources of customer satisfaction and dissatisfaction, there are also significant differences. These disparities show up in the distribution of incidents across the major groups, and the differences were most dramatic for the dissatisfactory service encounters. The self-serving attribution bias suggests explanations for why some of these differences were observed.

Managerial Implications

Using the Classification Scheme

One purpose of this study was to evaluate the soundness of the classification scheme developed by BBT in a distinctive context. Through the addition of the problem customer grouping, the framework is now more complete, and the scheme itself can provide a starting point for a company or industry to begin identifying with greater specificity the events and behaviors peculiar to its own setting. For example, the framework has been used for proprietary purposes in medical and travel agent contexts. In these cases, the companies began with the existing groups in the classification scheme and fleshed out the categories with useful specifics that could be employed in service training or service redesign.

The Customer Is Not Always Right

In the industries studied here, problem customers were the source of 22% of the dissatisfactory incidents. This group may be even larger in industries in which the customer has greater input into the service delivery process (e.g., health care, education, legal services).

Several implications are suggested by the problem customer group. First, managers must acknowledge that the customer is not always right, nor will he or she always behave in acceptable ways. Contact employees who have been on the job any period of time know this, but frequently they are being told that the "customer is king" and are not given the appropriate training and tools to deal with problem customers. Employees need appropriate coping and problem-solving skills to handle customers as well as their own personal feelings in these situations. Employees can also be taught to recognize characteristics of situations (e.g., unexpected peaks in demand, inordinate delays) and anticipate the moods of their customers so that some potential problem situations can be avoided completely or alleviated before they accelerate.

To provide employees with the appropriate training and skills for working with problem customers, the organization must clarify its position regarding such customers. A basic problem customer strategy might be conceptualized as ranging along a continuum from "refuse to serve them" to "satisfy them at all costs." For example, some car rental companies have attempted to refuse customers with bad driving histories by checking records in advance and rejecting bad-risk drivers (Dahl 1992). In a different context, some Madison Avenue ad agencies say that "some accounts are so difficult to work with that they simply cannot—or will not—service them." (Bird 1993). Although organizations have intuitively recognized that not all customer segments are right for the firm and that each individual customer is not right all the time, some are beginning to acknowledge these facts more explicitly and are attempting to quantify the impact of problem or "wrong" customers on profitability and organizational stress.

Beyond the need to develop employee skills, there is the need for "training" customers so that they will know what to expect and appropriate behaviors in given situations. For example, some upscale resorts that offer highly discounted rates in nonpeak seasons find that their discount customers, who may not be accustomed to the "rules of behavior," appreciate information on what to wear and other expected behaviors while at the resort. In other more complex and less familiar service situations (e.g., professional services), customers may truly appreciate knowing more about their role in the service process and the behaviors and information that are needed from them to make the service succeed (Bloom 1984). It has been suggested that by treating customers as "partial employees" they can learn to contribute to the service in ways that will enhance their own satisfaction (Bowen 1986).

Employees as Sources of Customer Data

Previous research has suggested that contact employees are good sources of information on customer attitudes (Schneider and Bowen 1985; Schneider, Parkington and Buxton 1980). Our study confirms these findings insofar as employees of hotels, restaurants, and airlines report all the same categories of customer satisfaction and dissatisfaction reported by customers in the same industries. However, we would caution against relying too much on contact employee interpretations of customer satisfaction for two reasons. First, although they report the same basic categories, the proportions of incidents found in the categories are significantly different from those reported by customers. Second, in some industries in which service encounters are less routine, contact employees may not be as accurate in their assessment of customer expectations and satisfaction (see Brown and Swartz 1989).

Employee Desire for Knowledge and Control

It is apparent in reading the incidents that contact employees *want* to provide good service and are very proud of their abilities to do so. This pride comes through in the large percentage of satisfactory incidents found in Group 2, in which employees' own skills, abilities, and willingness to accommodate customer needs were the sources of customer satisfaction. Balancing out this sense of pride are a large number of frustrating incidents in which employees believe they cannot for some reason recover from a service failure or adjust the system to accommodate a customer need. These reasons usually stem from lack of basic knowledge of the system and its constraints, inability to provide a logical explanation to the customer, cumbersome bureaucratic procedures, poorly designed systems or procedures, or the lack of authority to do anything.

Reliability Is Critical

The data show that a majority of the dissatisfactory incidents reported by employees resulted from inadequate responses to service delivery system failures. This result, together with other research reporting service reliability as the single most important dimension used by consumers to judge service quality (Parasuraman, Zeithaml, and Berry 1988, 1990), implies a need for service process and system analysis to determine the root causes of system failures (Kingman-Brundage 1989; Shostack 1984, 1987). Systems can then be redesigned and processes implemented to ensure higher reliability from the customer's point of view. The best way to ensure satisfaction, however, is not to have a failure in the first place.

Conclusion

The research suggests that many frontline employees do have a true customer orientation and do identify with and understand customer needs in service encounter situations. They have respect for customers and a desire to deliver excellent service. Oftentimes the inability to do so is governed by inadequate or poorly designed systems, poor or nonexistent recovery strategies, or lack of knowledge. When employees have the skills and tools to deliver high-quality service, they are proud of their ability to do so.

We also learned from employees that customers can be the source of their own dissatisfaction through inappropriate behavior or being unreasonably demanding. We suspect that this new group of dissatisfactory incidents caused by problem customers would surface in any service industry and that its existence represents a strategic challenge for the organization as well as an operational, real-time challenge for service employees. In a time when "customer is king" is the stated philosophy of most forward-thinking organizations, acknowledgment that wrong customers exist, coupled with creative thinking about customer roles and management of customer expectations, may considerably deepen understanding of and ability to cultivate customer relationships.

APPENDIX A
Instructions for Coders

Overview

1. You will be provided with a set of written critical service encounter events. Each "story" or "event" is recorded on a standardized questionnaire. Two types of questionnaires were used, one for satisfying interactions and one for dissatisfying interactions.

2. Each service encounter questionnaire reflects the events and behaviors associated with an encounter that is memorable because it is either particularly satisfying or particularly dissatisfying. The respondents were employees of restaurants, airlines, and hotels. However, they were asked to take the customer's point of view in responding to the questions. Thus, the data reflect employees' remembrances of times when customers had particularly dis/satisfying encounters with their firms.

3. You will be asked to categorize each incident into one of 16 categories, based on the key factor that triggered the dis/satisfactory incident. Sorting rules and definitions of categories are detailed below.

4. It is suggested that you read through each entire service encounter before you attempt to categorize it. If an incident does not appear to fit within any of the 16 categories, put it aside. In addition, do not attempt to categorize incidents that do not meet the basic criteria. An incident must: (A) include employee-customer interaction, (B) be very satisfying or dissatisfying from the cus-

tomer's point of view, (C) be a discrete episode, and (D) have sufficient detail to be visualized by the interviewer.

Coding rules

Each incident should be categorized within one category only. Once you have read the incident, you should begin asking the following questions in order to determine the appropriate category. Definitions of the categories are attached.

1. Is there a service delivery system failure? That is, is there an initial failure of the core service that causes the employee to respond in some way? Is it the employee's response that causes the event to be remembered as highly satisfactory or dissatisfactory?

If the answer is *yes*, place the incident in Group 1. Then ask, what type of failure? (A) unavailable service; (B) unreasonably slow service; (C) other core service failures.

If the answer is *no*, go on to question 2.

2. Is there an explicit or implicit request or need for accommodation or extra service(s)? That is, is the customer asking (either explicitly or implicitly) that the system be somehow adjusted to accommodate him/her? Is it the employee's response that causes the event to be remembered as highly satisfactory or dissatisfactory?

If the answer is *yes*, place the incident in Group 2. Then ask what type of need/request is triggering the incident: (A) "special needs" customer; (B) customer preferences; (C) admitted customer error; (D) potentially disruptive other customers.

If the answer is *no*, go on to question 3.

3. Is there an unprompted and unsolicited action on the part of the employee that causes the dis/satisfaction? That is, does a spontaneous action or attitude of the employee cause the dis/satisfaction? (Since this follows rules 1 and 2, it obviously implies that there is no service failure and no explicit/implicit request.)

If the answer is *yes*, place the incident in Group 3. Then, ask what type of unprompted and unsolicited action took place: (A) attention paid to customer; (B) truly out-of-the-ordinary action; (C) employee behaviors in the context of cultural norms; (D) gestalt evaluation; (E) exemplary performance under adverse circumstances.

If the answer is *no*, go to question 4.

4. Does the dis/satisfaction stem from the actions/attitudes/behaviors of a "problem customer"? That is, rather than the dis/satisfaction being attributable to an action or attitude of the employee, is the root cause actually the customer?

If the answer is *yes*, place the incident in Group 4. Then, ask what type of behavior is causing the problem: (A) drunkenness; (B) verbal/physical abuse; (C) breaking/resisting company policies or laws; (D) uncooperative customer.

If the answer is *no*, put the incident aside.

CIT Classification System—Definitions

Group 1. Employee response to service delivery system failure (failure in the core service, e.g., the hotel room, the restaurant meal service, the flight, system failures).

A. Response to unavailable service (services that should be available are lacking or absent, e.g., lost hotel room reservation, overbooked airplane, unavailable reserved window table).

B. Response to unreasonably slow service (services or employee performances are perceived as inordinately slow). (Note: When service is both slow and unavailable, use the *triggering* event.)

C. Response to other core service failures (e.g., hotel room not clean, restaurant meal cold or improperly cooked, damaged baggage).

Group 2. Employee response to customer needs and requests (when the customer requires the employee to adapt the service delivery system to suit his/her unique needs; contains either an explicit or inferred request for customized [from the customer's point of view] service).

A. Response to "special needs" customers (customers with medical, dietary, psychological, language, or sociological difficulties; children; elderly customers).

B. Response to customer preferences (when the customer makes "special" requests due to personal preferences; this includes times when the customer requests a level of service customization clearly beyond the scope of or in violation of policies or norms).

C. Response to admitted customer error (triggering event is a customer error that strains the service encounter, e.g., lost tickets, incorrect order, missed reservations).

D. Response to potentially disruptive others (when other customers exhibit behaviors that potentially strain the encounter, e.g., intoxication, rudeness, deviance).

Group 3. Unprompted and unsolicited employee actions (events and behaviors that are truly unexpected from the customer's point of view, not triggered by a service failure, and show no evidence of the customer having a special need or making a special request).

A. Attention paid to customer (e.g., making the customer feel special or pampered, ignoring or being impatient with the customer).

B. Truly out-of-the-ordinary employee behavior (particularly extraordinary actions or expressions of courtesy, or profanity, inappropriate touching, violations of basic etiquette, rudeness).

C. Employee behaviors in the context of cultural norms (norms such as equality, honesty, fairness, discrimination, theft, lying, or refraining from the above when such behavior was expected).

D. Gestalt evaluation (no single feature stands out; instead "everything went right" or "everything went wrong").

E. Exemplary performance under adverse circumstances (when the customer is particularly impressed or displeased with the way an employee handles a stressful situation).

Group 4. Problematic customer behavior (customer is unwilling to cooperate with laws, regulations, or the service provider; this includes rudeness, abusiveness, or a general unwillingness to indicate satisfaction with the service regardless of the employees' efforts).

A. Drunkenness (in the employee's perception, the customer is clearly intoxicated and creating problems, and the employee has to handle the situation).

B. Verbal and physical abuse (the customer verbally and/or physically abuses either the employee or other customers, and the employee has to handle the situation).

C. Breaking/resisting company policies or laws (the customer refuses to comply with policies [e.g.,

showing airplane ticket to the flight attendant before boarding] or laws [e.g., use of illegal drugs in the hotel room], and the employee has to enforce compliance).

D. Uncooperative customer (customer is generally rude and uncooperative or extremely demanding; any efforts to compensate for a perceived service failure are rejected; customer may appear unwilling to be satisfied; and the employee has to handle the situation).

References

Berry, Leonard L. and A. Parasuraman (1991), *Marketing Services*. New York: The Free Press.

Biddle, B. J. (1986), "Recent Developments in Role Theory," *Annual Review of Sociology* 12, 67–92.

Bird, Laura (1993), "The Clients That Exasperate Madison Avenue," *Wall Street Journal* (November 2), B1.

Bitner, Mary Jo, Bernard H. Booms, and Mary Stanfield Tetreault (1990), "The Service Encounter: Diagnosing Favorable and Unfavorable Incidents," *Journal of Marketing* 54 (January), 71–84.

Bloom, Paul N. (1984), "Effective Marketing for Professional Services," *Harvard Business Review* (September/October), 102–10.

Bowen, David E. 91986), "Managing Customers as Human Resources in Service Organizations," *Human Resource Management*, 25 (3), 371–83.

Brown, Stephen W. and Teresa A. Swartz, (1989) "A Gap Analysis of Professional Service Quality," *Journal of Marketing*, 53 (April), 92–98.

Business Week (1991), Special Issue on Quality.

Crosby, Lawrence A. (1991), "Expanding the Role of CSM in Total Quality," *International Journal of Service Industry Management*, 2 (2), 5–19.

Dahl, Jonathan (1992), "Rental Counters Reject Drivers Without Good Records," *Wall Street Journal* (October 23), B1.

Dornoff, Ronald J. and F. Robert Dwyer, (1981) "Perceptual Differences in Market Transactions Revisited: A Waning Source of Consumer Frustration," *The Journal of Consumer Affairs*, 15 (Summer), 146–57.

Ericsson, K. Anders and Herbert A. Simon (1980), "Verbal Reports as Data," *Psychological Review*, 87 (May), 215–50.

Fiske, Susan T. and Shelley E. Taylor (1984), *Social Cognition*, Reading, MA: Addison-Wesley.

Flanagan, John C. (1954), "The Critical Incident Technique," *Psychological Bulletin*, 51 (July), 327–58.

Folkes, Valerie S. and Barbara Kotsos (1986), "Buyers' and Sellers' Explanations for Product Failure: Who Done It?" *Journal of Marketing*, 50 (April), 74–80.

Gremler, Dwayne and Mary Jo Bitner (1992), "Classifying Service Encounter Satisfaction Across Industries," in *Marketing Theory and Applications*, Chris T. Allen et al., eds. Chicago: American Marketing Association, 111–18.

Heskett, James L., Thomas O. Jones, Gary W. Loveman, W. Earl Sasser, Jr., and Leonard A. Schlesinger (1994), "Putting the Service-Profit Chain to Work," *Harvard Business Review* (March/April), 164–72.

————, W. Earl Sasser, Jr., and Christopher W. L. Hart (1990), *Service Breakthroughs*. New York: The Free Press.

Hochschild, Arlie Russell (1983), *The Managed Heart*. Berkeley, CA: University of California Press.

Hunt, Shelby (1991), *Modern Marketing Theory*. Cincinnati, OH: South-Western Publishing Company.

Kelley, Scott W., K. Douglas Hoffman, and Mark A. Davis (1993), "A Typology of Retail Failures and Recoveries," *Journal of Retailing*, 69 (4), 429–52.

Kingman-Brundage, Jane (1989), "The ABC's of Service System Blueprinting," in *Designing a Winning Service Strategy*, Mary Jo Bitner and Lawrence A. Crosby, eds. Chicago: American Marketing Association, 30–33.

Langeard, Eric, John E.G. Bateson, Christopher H. Lovelock, and Pierre Eiglier (1981), *Services Marketing: New Insights from Consumers and Managers*. Cambridge, MA: Marketing Science Institute.

Lovelock, Christopher (1983), "Classifying Services to Gain Strategic Marketing Insights," *Journal of Marketing*, 47 (Summer), 9–20.

———— (1994), *Product Plus*. New York: McGraw-Hill.

McKelvey, Bill (1982), *Organizational Systematics: Taxonomy, Evolution, Classification*. Berkeley, CA: University of California Press.

Mohr, Lois A. and Mary Jo Bitner (1991), "Mutual Understanding Between Customers and Employees in Service Encounters," in *Advances in Consumer Research*, Vol. 18, Rebecca H. Holman and Michael R. Solomon, eds. Provo, UT: Association for Consumer Research, 611–17.

Parasuraman, A., Leonard L. Berry, and Valarie A. Zeithaml (1991), "Refinement and Reassessment of the SERVQUAL Scale," *Journal of Retailing*, 67 (4), 420–50.

————, Valarie Zeithaml, and Leonard L. Berry (1988), "SERVQUAL: A Multiple-Item Scale for Measuring Consumer Perceptions of Service Quality," *Journal of Retailing*, 64 (Spring), 12–40.

————, ————, and ———— (1990), "An Empirical Examination of Relationships in an Extended Service Quality Model," Report No. 90–122. Cambridge, MA: Marketing Science Institute.

Perreault, William D., Jr. and Laurence E. Leigh (1989), "Reliability of Nominal Data Based on Qualitative Judgments," *Journal of Marketing Research*, 26 (May), 135–48.

Resnik, Alan J. and Robert R. Harmon (1983), "Consumer Complaints and Managerial Response: A Holistic Approach," *Journal of Marketing*, 47 (Winter), 86–97.

Ronan, William W. and Gary P. Latham (1974), "The Reliability and Validity of the Critical Incident Technique: A Closer Look," *Studies in Personnel Psychology*, 6 (Spring), 53–64.

Schank, Roger C. and Robert P. Abelson (1977), *Scripts, Plans, Goals and Understanding*. New York: John Wiley and Sons, Inc.

Schlesinger, Leonard A. and James L. Heskett (1991), "The Service-Driven Service Company," *Harvard Business Review* (September/October), 71–81.

Schneider, Benjamin (1980), "The Service Organization: Climate Is Crucial," *Organizational Dynamics* (Autumn), 52–65.

———— and David E. Bowen (1984), "New Services Design, Development and Implementation and the Employee," in *Developing New Services*, William R. George and Claudia Marshall, eds. Chicago: American Marketing Association, 82–101.

———— and ———— (1985), "Employee and Customer Perceptions of Service in Banks: Replication and Extension," *Journal of Applied Psychology*, 70 (3), 423–33.

————, John J. Parkington, and Virginia M. Buxton (1980), "Employee and Customer Perceptions of Service in Banks," *Administrative Science Quarterly*, 25 (June), 252–67.

Schrage, Michael (1992), "Fire Your Customers," *Wall Street Journal* (March 16), A8.

Services Marketing Newsletter (1989), "Recent Study Shows Gap Between Customers and Service Employees on Customer Service Perceptions," 5 (Summer), 1.

Shostack, G. Lynn (1984), "Designing Services That Deliver," *Harvard Business Review* (January/February), 133–39.

———— (1987), "Service Positioning Through Structural Change," *Journal of Marketing*, 51 (January), 34–43.

Solomon, Michael R., Carol Surprenant, John A. Czepiel, and Evelyn G. Gutman (1985), "A Role Theory Perspective on Dyadic Interactions: The Service Encounter," *Journal of Marketing*, 49 (Winter), 99–111.

White, Frank M. and Edwin A. Locke (1981), "Perceived Determinants of High and Low Productivity in Three Occupational Groups: A Critical Incident Study," *Journal of Management Studies*, 18 (4), 375–87.

Wilson-Pessano, Sandra R. (1988), "Defining Professional Competence: The Critical Incident Technique 40 Years Later," American Institutes for Research, invited address to the Annual Meeting of the American Educational Research Association, New Orleans.

Zeithaml, Valarie A., Leonard L. Berry, and A. Parasuraman (1988), "Communication and Control Processes in the Delivery of Service Quality," *Journal of Marketing*, 52 (April), 35–48.

———— and Mary Jo Bitner (1995), *Services Marketing*. New York: McGraw-Hill.

Zemke, Ron and Kristin Anderson (1990), "Customers From Hell," *Training* (February), 25–33.

Managing Multiple Demands:

A Role-Theory Examination of the Behaviors of Customer Contact Service Workers

KRISTOPHER A. WEATHERLY

DAVID A. TANSIK

ABSTRACT *This paper presents the results of an empirical field survey which investigated the strategies used by service industry customer contact workers in response to role demands. Four strategies emerged: Effort, Negotiating, Preempting and Avoiding. Negotiating was positively related to role conflict and role ambiguity. Job satisfaction was positively related to Effort and negatively related to Preempting and Avoiding. Implications of the findings for service-industry managers and researchers are discussed.*

I couldn't stand for one minute longer being at the beck and call of every sonofabitch just because he had three cents in his pocket.

WILLIAM FAULKNER

The American novelist was explaining why he quit his job as postmaster of Oxford, Mississippi, in 1924 (Humes 1975, p. 261). The feeling described by Faulkner is what organizational researchers refer to as role stress (Katz and Kahn 1978; Kahn et al. 1964). Faulkner is not unique in his reaction to the stress which accompanies many service jobs. Role stress refers to uncertain or conflicting demands placed on an organizational member and their psychological and physiological consequences (French and Caplan 1972; Kahn et al. 1964). Parkington and Schneider (1979) demonstrated that employees' feelings of role stress in front-line service jobs are negatively correlated with employee job satisfaction and customer perceptions of service quality and positively correlated with customer intentions to switch to other service providers. Meta-analyses of the role-stress literature demonstrate that role stress is negatively correlated with organizational commitment, job involvement and satisfaction with pay, coworkers and supervisors, and positively correlated with anxiety and propensity to leave the organization (Fisher and Gitelson 1983; Jackson and Schuler 1985). Service workers' responses to role stress have

important consequences for workers, their organizations and their customers.

The boundary-spanning nature of customer contact service jobs frequently leads to role conflict for service workers (Parkington and Schneider 1979). Role conflict can be defined as "the simultaneous occurrence of two or more role expectations such that compliance with one would make compliance with the other more difficult" (Katz and Kahn 1978, p. 204). Several researchers have indicated that role conflict in boundary-spanning service jobs can impact the behavior of employees and the attitudes and intentions of customers and employees (cf. Parkington and Schneider 1979; Rafaeli 1989a; Shamir 1980; Sutton and Rafaeli 1988). Role conflict and role stress may account for some of the poor service decried in Stephen Koepp's 1987 *Time* article, "Why is Service So Bad? Pul-eeze! Will Somebody Help Me?"

Consequently, the purpose of this research is to examine the specific behavioral tactics and strategies used by customer contact workers when they experience role stress and to examine the relationship of these behaviors to contextual factors which may predict them. This research adds to the emerging body of literature on the service encounter (cf. Bitner, Booms and Tetreault 1990; Czepiel, Solomon and Surprenant 1985). The importance of this stream of research to service industries has been argued by Tansik (1990), who asserts that service organizations are often dependent on customer contact employees—usually the most recently hired, lowest paid members of the organization—for the service firm's reputation and cash flow.

Advances in Services Marketing and Management, *Volume 2, pages 279–300. Copyright © 1993 by JAI Press Inc. All rights of reproduction in any form reserved. ISBN: 1-55938-656-8.*

Background and Theoretical Framework

Organizational Role Theory

As used by organizational researchers, a role is "the summation of the requirements with which the system confronts the individual member" (Katz and Kahn 1978, p. 186). We will use the role of a purchasing manager to illustrate role theory.

A role-set refers to the people in an organization who are directly associated with the role (Katz and Kahn 1978; Merton 1957). For example, the purchasing manager's role-set might include the manager's supervisor and secretary, the organization's comptroller, the total-quality manager and the production manager.

Individuals in the role-set develop beliefs and expectations about appropriate behavior for the focal person (e.g., how much can be spent for an item, when the item should be ordered, when paperwork should be completed, etc.). Combined, these beliefs and expectations define the role (Katz and Kahn 1978).

Role expectations are communicated to the focal person through attempts to influence the focal person. These communications are referred to as the "sent-role" (Katz and Kahn 1978, p. 195). Examples of the sent-role might include comments or memos from the role-set. The "received-role," on the other hand, refers to the focal person's perception and understanding of the expectations being communicated (Katz and Kahn 1978, p. 195). For example, the purchasing manager might interpret a request from the total-quality manger for "improvement in the purchasing system" as a request for higher-quality parts when the total-quality manager may have wanted more timely delivery of raw materials.

Finally, the focal person's responses to role expectations are referred to as "role behaviors" (Katz and Kahn 1978, p. 195). In the case of the purchasing manager, role behaviors are simply what the purchasing manager does as a result of the received role. Together, role expectations, the sent-role, the received-role and role behaviors make up what can be called a "role episode" (Katz and Kahn 1978, p. 194).

When the expectations in a role episode are "such that compliance with one would make compliance with the other more difficult," role conflict occurs (Katz and Kahn 1978, p. 204). Again using the example of a purchasing manager, role conflict might result when the comptroller insists on cutting costs while the total-quality manager insists on improving the quality of raw materials. Role ambiguity results from a lack of clear information about appropriate role behaviors and about resources available to do a job properly (Kahn et al. 1964, pp. 21–22). The purchasing manager would experience role ambiguity when s/he was not sure what was expected or when s/he was not fully aware of the resources available to do the job correctly.

Kahn and his colleagues (1964) described role conflict and role ambiguity as different facets of role stress. Role stress has been positively correlated with employees' propensity to leave the organization and negatively correlated with job satisfaction, performance, organizational commitment and job involvement (Fisher and Gitelson 1983; Jackson and Schuler 1985). In 1979, Parkington and Schneider reported similar results in their study of customer contact workers in the banking industry.

Literally hundreds of published articles have demonstrated a strong positive correlation between role conflict and turnover intentions and a strong negative correlation between role conflict and job satisfaction (Fisher and Gitelson 1983; Jackson and Schuler 1985). However, research on role ambiguity is equivocal. While some researchers have found the same relationship between role ambiguity, job satisfaction and turnover intentions as they found for role conflict (French and Caplan 1972), others have found directly opposite relationships (Katz and Kahn 1978). Furthermore, Hollander (1964) has suggested that some degree of role ambiguity might be necessary to facilitate the management of role conflict.

Role Stress, Boundary Spanning and Customer Contact Workers

The Customer Contact Model (Chase and Tansik 1983) defines organizational contact with customers in service industries as the presence of the customer in the production system of the organization. In other words, customers are present during—*and often participate in*—the production of the service. This interface between the customer and the organization is facilitated by a blend of technology and human resources. In a low-contact service encounter (when a customer uses a bank's automatic teller machine, for example), the interface is mediated by technology. In a high-contact service encounter (when a customer's transaction is processed by a bank teller, for example) the interface is mediated by organizational human resources. The organizational members who interface with customers can be described as customer contact workers.

Because customer contact workers interact with both the organization and the organization's environment, they occupy what organizational researchers have identified as boundary-spanning roles (Bowen and Schneider 1985). These are roles which "involve resource acquisition and disposal, political legitimacy and hegemony, and . . . social legitimacy and organizational image" (Aldrich and Herker 1977, p. 220).

A review (Van Sell, Brief and Schuler 1981) and two meta-analyses (Fisher and Gitelson 1983; Jackson and Schuler 1985) of the role-stress literature indicated that boundary spanning is highly correlated with both role conflict and role ambiguity. Thus, it seems reasonable that customer contact workers experience high levels of role stress.

The nature of role conflict and role ambiguity in customer contact jobs in service organizations is illustrated by the example of a retail store which sells low-cost footwear. The business is designed to be mostly self-service, which means that the store rarely has enough personnel on the sales floor to provide high levels of personalized service to customers. Generally, the employees show the customers where to look to find the shoes they want. Occasionally, customers request more specialized service from the store's personnel, for example, measuring a child's foot, offering suggestions on styles, lacing an athletic shoe, assisting the customer in putting the shoes on his/her feet and checking how well the shoe fits. Meanwhile, the store's manager has assigned store personnel the task of rearranging the merchandise on the shelf to make it easier for customers to find the shoes they want. The company's training program emphasizes both types of tasks as important elements of "good" customer service. On a busy day, an employee must choose between completing the merchandising tasks assigned by management and fulfilling customer requests for specialized attention. Both tasks are legitimate aspects of customer service. The conflict inherent in this type of situation led one store employee to remark,

> I'm damned if I do; damned if I don't. You just can't win. Either Tom [a pseudonym for the boss] is mad at me, or the customer is. If I don't get my work done, Tom's going to yell at me. But if I don't help the customers, *they* get pissed at me (Weatherly 1991, p. 21).

Conflict of this nature is especially troublesome to customer contact workers who are caught between the demands of legitimate authority (their boss, organizational policy, and so forth) and the demands of customers with whom they usually identify psychologically (Rafaeli 1989a). In service jobs which allow tipping of the customer contact worker, the identification of the worker with the customer is typically even stronger (Shamir 1983; 1984).

As a result of this conflict, Bateson (1985, p. 72) has suggested that a service encounter be viewed as "a three-cornered fight" with the customer, the server and the service firm all vying for control. He argued that customer contact workers seek to control the service encounter as a means of guarding their own mental and physical health. Yet, customers also seek to control the encounter since they not only consume the service but also help to produce the service (Chase and Tansik 1983; Mills 1986; Tansik and Chase 1988). Meanwhile, the organization itself seeks to control the encounter through its system of policies, procedures and supervision (Schneider, Parkington and Buxton 1980). By working together, all three actors benefit: the consumer seeks to exchange money for satisfaction; the customer contact worker exchanges job performance for job satisfaction and pay; the organization provides the resources necessary for the encounter to transpire in hopes of earning a profitable return of capital. Nevertheless, conflict over control of the service encounter can prevent the actors from working together (Bateson 1985).

Similarly, in a study of service workers in Israel, Shamir (1980, p. 748) referred to the conflict experience by customer contact workers as "the organization vs. the client: the two bosses dilemma." For example, the loyalty of employees who receive tips is often divided between customers and the organization.

In a 1978 review of job stress, employee health and organizational effectiveness, Beehr and Newman stated, "Job stress researchers, however, generally ignored the decision-making or response selection process of employees who have experienced a stressful situation" (p. 683). However, Rafaeli (1989a), Shamir (1980), and Weatherly (1991) have noted several different strategies customer contact workers use to gain control of their interactions with customers. Weatherly's (1991) typology of the tactics used by customer contact workers is presented in Table 1; a more detailed definition of the tactics appears in the Appendix.

Several studies of employees' behavioral responses to role stress have indicated that employees are likely to engage in behaviors which they believe will reduce the amount of strain they experience as a result of their work environment. For example, van de Vliert (1981) proposed that employees seek to fulfill the obligations of their received role, negotiate the demands of the received role with the role senders or avoid the role senders in an attempt to prevent them from communicating any new expectations. Burke and Belcourt (1974) surveyed 137 managers and managerial trainees employed by the Federal Government of Canada. Nearly all of the respondents (95%) listed at least one technique for coping with work-related stress, and the mean was 2.4 techniques per respondent. Sixty-five

TABLE 1

Weatherly's (1991) Typology of Tactics Used by Customer Contact Workers in Service Industries

Effort: Tactics to Satisfy Role Demands
    Effort

Negotiating: Tactics to Alter Role Demands
    Delegating
    Explaining
    Rewarding
    Punishing

Preempting: Tactics to Avoid the Sent Role
    Ingratiating
    Distracting

Avoiding: Tactics to Avoid the Received Role
    Reinterpreting
    Ignoring

percent of coping responses were grouped into five categories: (1) talking to others, (2) working harder and longer, (3) changing to an engrossing nonwork or play activity, (4) analyzing the situation and changing the strategy of attack and (5) withdrawing physically from the situation. Investigations of workers in service industries have also indicated that customer contact workers are likely to use a variety of tactics in an attempt to manage their interactions with customers (cf. Rafaeli 1989a; Shamir 1980; Weatherly 1991).

These studies suggest that customer contact workers are likely to respond to role conflict by seeking to fulfill the obligations placed on them, by seeking to negotiate and satisfy lesser demands or by avoiding the demands placed on them. The following hypotheses are offered based on the past research:

    Hypothesis 1. Role conflict is positively related to customer contact workers' effort in satisfying role demands.

    Hypothesis 2. Role conflict is positively related to customer contact workers' use of negotiation tactics.

    Hypothesis 3. Role conflict is positively related to customer contact workers' use of avoidance tactics.

Inasmuch as role ambiguity provides employees opportunities for creatively managing their role stress (Hollander 1964), similar relationships are hypothesized for role ambiguity:

    Hypothesis 4. Role ambiguity is positively related to customer contact workers' effort in satisfying role demands.

    Hypothesis 5. Role ambiguity is positively related to customer contact workers' use of negotiation tactics.

    Hypothesis 6. Role ambiguity is positively related to customer contact workers' use of avoidance tactics.

Job Satisfaction and Customer Contact Workers

A meta-analysis of studies linking job satisfaction and performance suggested that the actual population correlation between job performance and job satisfaction is fairly low (about .17) (Iaffaldano and Muchinsky 1985). Vroom (1964) also suggested a low correlation between job satisfaction and performance (about .14) based on his review of the literature. Iaffaldano and Muchinsky (1985, p. 270) concluded as a result of their analysis of the literature:

> Our results indicate, similar to the findings reported in the earlier review published over 20 years ago, that satisfaction and performance are only slightly related to each other. . . . It is almost as is the satisfaction-performance relation is itself [only] a perceived relation between two variables that we logically or intuitively think should interrelate, but in fact do not.

Nevertheless, a new discussion of the link between job satisfaction and performance is emerging around the nature of the role of customer contact workers in service industries. For example, Schneider and his colleagues (Bowen and Schneider 1985: Parkington and Schneider 1979: Schneider 1980: Schneider and Bowen 1985) have demonstrated in studies of bank employees that organizational human resource practices and employee job satisfaction are related to customer perceptions of service quality and customer satisfaction. When employees viewed their branch's policies as employee oriented, the bank's *customers* reported higher levels of satisfaction with the bank's service.

In addition, the popular management press is replete with anecdotes and prescriptions which emphasize the links between employee satisfaction, job performance and customer satisfaction (cf. Peters and Austin 1986; Peters and Waterman 1982). Davidow and Uttal (1989), for example, have extolled the virtues of the employee-oriented management practices of Embassy Suites and credited these practices as being the major reason behind the company's success in the hospitality industry. Wal-Mart is another example of a company which seeks to provide excellent customer service through highly satisfied "associates" (Johnston and Moore 1991).

Albrecht and Zemke (1985) define a "motivating environment" as an environment where "service people can find personal reasons for committing their energies to the benefit of the customer" (p. 107). They assert that a motivating environment is created by four factors: (1) quality of work life, which includes job satisfaction, job security, pay and benefits, and opportunities for advancement; (2) morale, which they define as the essence of high commitment; (3) energy level, which provides customer contact workers with the emotional fuel to provide good customer service; and (4) optimism, a belief in new possibilities, new challenges and new opportunities (pp. 108–109).

One of the most compelling arguments for a relationship between customer contact workers' job satisfaction and their performance has been articulated by Davidow and Uttal (1989): "Since service is intangible, customers judge its quality by the quality of their interactions with service providers" (p.119). As a result, they stated that customer contact workers should be treated as "performers" rather than as "1950s style assembly line" workers (p. 120). The reason for the difference in treatment is that customer contact workers "must perform a kind of emotional labor that's entirely foreign to production-line workers" (p. 121). Clearly, displayed emotions are an integral part of the customer contact worker's role (Hochschild 1983; Rafaeli and Sutton 1987).

To illustrate the importance of emotion in high-contact service jobs, Davidow and Uttal (1989) quote Wesley Henry, a researcher in the hospitality industry:

> Most people who deal with paperwork feel the customer is a pain in the ass. They have resentment. It shows up in the voice. And if a customer hears that he's a bother, he'll be reluctant to ask for service again (p. 120).

The marketing literature on service quality and customer satisfaction confirms Henry's statement. In a study of the determinants of consumer satisfaction in retail outlets, Westbrook (1981) found that the most important factor in determining the customer's overall satisfaction with a large conventional department store was the customer's satisfaction with the salespeople in the store. The salespeople were evaluated on dimensions of helpfulness, friendliness, politeness and availability. The customer's satisfaction with the salespeople accounted for 26.7% of the variance in overall satisfaction compared with the next highest factor, store environment (layout, spaciousness, ease in find-

ing things, and cleanliness), which only accounted for 9.4% of the variance.

Parasuraman, Zeithaml and Berry (1985) conducted in-depth interviews with 14 service industry executives and conducted 12 focus groups with service consumers to develop a model of service quality. "Courtesy" was one of the dimensions of service quality mentioned by the informants in the study. Courtesy refers to "politeness, respect, consideration, and friendliness of contact personnel" (p.47).

As a follow-up to their earlier work, Parasuraman, Zeithaml and Berry (1988) developed a multiitem scale to measure customers' perceptions of service quality. Three of the five dimensions of service quality measured by the instrument are "responsiveness," which refers to "willingness to help customers and provide prompt service"; "assurance," which is defined as "knowledge and courtesy of employees and their ability to inspire trust and confidence"; and "empathy," which means "caring, individualized attention the firm provides its customers" (p. 23).

The impact of customer contact workers' job satisfaction on customer satisfaction is further argued by Schneider and Bowen (1984). Drawing on the fields of organizational behavior and consumer behavior, they admonish organizations to treat "employees as highly valued customers" as a means of encouraging "employees to, in turn, treat customers better" (p. 98). The same notion is reflected in "The Service Profit Chain" proposed by Schlesinger and Heskett (1991a). The chain suggests that employee satisfaction is related to overall organizational profit through the following links: employee satisfaction contributes to employee retention and employees' desire to give good service, both of which contribute to customer satisfaction. Customer satisfaction, in turn, contributes to customer retention, which has a major impact on an organization's long-term profitability.

Schlesinger and Heskett (1991b) have criticized service industry managers who view profitability in the same manner as their manufacturing industry counterparts. Traditionally, profitability is viewed as a function of marketing strategies driving revenue and unit-level managers keeping operating costs low. "But what these assumptions omit is the role that workers who are in direct contact with customers play in enhancing or diminishing customer satisfaction and therefore profits" (p. 75). As a result, Schlesinger and Heskett urge service industry managers to rethink the impact of employee job satisfaction on customer satisfaction and organizational profitability.

In the present study, it is argued that customer contact workers who are satisfied with their jobs are more likely to work hard to satisfy customers than are their less satisfied co-workers. Also it is argued that dissatisfied employees are more likely to engage in behaviors which seek to avoid satisfying customer and organizational demands, and dissatisfied workers are more likely to engage in behaviors which seek to prevent customers and organizational members from making demands. While no a priori hypotheses about the relationship between job satisfaction and negotiation tactics are made, the following hypotheses are offered concerning job satisfaction, customer contact workers' effort toward fulfilling role demands and customer contact workers' use of avoidance tactics:

> **Hypothesis 7.** Job satisfaction is positively related to customer contact workers' effort in satisfying role demands.

> **Hypothesis 8.** Job satisfaction is negatively related to customer contact workers' use of avoidance tactics.

Method

The purpose of the present research is to investigate how customer contact workers respond to the multiple demands they experience as a result of the role stress in their front-line service jobs. To gain insight into this issue, a field survey was conducted to examine the relationships between key role variables, employee job satisfaction and employee behaviors. A survey was used because it provided an economical means of assessing specific behaviors of actual customer contact workers.

Sample

The field survey was conducted in a regional division of a large international convenience store chain. Convenience stores were chosen as the context for the field survey for several reasons. First, the convenience store (c-store) industry is a fast-paced industry with front-line workers who typically have many contacts with customers during their regular business day. Second, the workload on c-store employees is quite tough: managers often work 60 to 80 hours per week in an attempt to fulfill their responsibilities (Weatherly 1991). Third, c-stores have proven to be valuable for studying service industries by other researchers (Rafaeli 1989b; Rafaeli and Sutton 1990; Sutton and Rafaeli 1988). In addition, the role of c-store employees shares common elements with the role of supermarket cashiers studied by Rafaeli (1989a). Finally, conducting the survey in a company with 132 locations in a single metropolitan area allowed the data to be collected under tight economic and time constraints.

Store managers were chosen as respondents for the survey because of their multiple roles. C-store managers have administrative and operations responsibilities, supervision and human resources responsibilities, and merchandising and marketing responsibilities. Also, c-store managers interact directly with customers, making them customer contact workers as well as supervisors. Thus, the roles of these managers have critical strategic implications for operations, marketing and human resources management in addition to their impact on customer perceptions of service quality.

The survey questionnaire was first pilot-tested with several academic colleagues and three retail sales clerks. The survey was then presented to the senior managers of the regional division of the c-store chain for their review and approval. Next, questionnaires, cover letters and postage-paid return envelopes were distributed through the company's courier service to 132 store managers in a large metropolitan area in the southwestern United States, The cover letter explained that the purpose of the survey was to find out "how people handle demanding situations at work," and assured the respondents of complete confidentiality. The cover letter also encouraged the respondents to mail their completed surveys directly to the first author at the university using the self-addressed, stamped envelope. To increase the response rate, a follow-up letter was also delivered to the store managers two weeks after they received the initial letter and survey.

Of the 132 questionnaires delivered to store managers, 45 usable questionnaires were returned for a response rate of 34%. Although the response rate is marginal, managers from each of the 11 zones included in the sample participated in the study, and we believe that the returned questionnaires adequately represent the sample.

One of the dilemmas of studying individuals in highly demanding occupations is the threat that they may be "too busy" to participate. McGrath, Martin and Kulka (1982) stated that data collection is often a process of compromise between suitability and accessibility argued that researchers may choose at times to forego some of the usually desired characteristics of scientific research (e.g., randomness, sample size, response rate) in exchange for mundane considerations such as how well the respondent pool typifies the behavior under study or how accessible the respondents are.

Measures

Role conflict and role ambiguity were assessed using the abridged 14-item instrument developed by Rizzo, House and Lirtzman (1970; see also Murphy and

Gable 1988). The survey included eight role-conflict items (Cronbach's α = 0.87) and six role-ambiguity items (Cronbach's α = 0.78) with seven-point Likert-type scales.

Job satisfaction was measured using a two item facet-free job satisfaction measure taken from the University of Michigan Quality of Employment Survey (Quinn and Staines 1979). The two item job satisfaction measure was adapted by Gutek and has been used in several of her studies (cf. Gutek and Winter, in press; 1990) The two items provided a fairly reliable estimate of job satisfaction (Cronbach's α = 0.59).

Employees' use of tactics was measured with 17 questions based on Weatherly's (1991) typology of tactics used by customer contact workers. The items represented the respondent's use of a specific tactic on a specific target. Response options included "never, seldom (less than once a month), occasionally (once or twice a month), moderately often (once or twice a week), very often (nearly every day)." Analysis of the basic structure of respondents' use of tactics was evaluated with factoring based on principal-components analysis. Based on an examination of the scree plot of eigenvalues and theoretical considerations, the items were constrained to three factors. The question relating to the employee's use of effort as a tactic ("I work extra hard to get everything done without neglecting the customer's needs") related to each of the factors negatively, with factor loading being relatively equal for each of the factors (−0.47, −0.33, and −0.35). Effort was then separated from the other tactics (which represent tactics the respon-

dent would choose as alternatives to effort), and the factor analysis was repeated. Various orthogonal and oblique rotations were examined, with the factor loading remaining fairly consistent. However, oblique promax rotation provided the most interpretable factor structure.

Given our sample size of 45 and the number of items we used in principal-components analysis (17), several of the assumptions for this procedure have been violated. However, the results make sense intuitively, and we are not suggesting that our structure is definitive and unequivocal; thus, the procedure is suitable for our purposes (Kim and Mueller 1978). Together, the three factors accounted for 8.16% of the total variation of the items.

The factor structure of the items is shown in Table 2. Factor loadings above 0.3 are shown in bold type. The first factor appears to be a preemptive strategy which uses tactics designed to prevent role senders from communicating their expectations to the customer contact worker. Factor 2 appears to be a negotiation strategy which seeks to alter the demands of the role senders by either adjusting the level of the role senders' expectations ("explaining") or by enlisting the help of others to satisfy the demands ("delegating"). Factor 3 appears to be an avoidance strategy which uses tactics to ignore the demands by pretending not to have received the sent-role ("reinterpreting" and "ignoring").

Using factor loadings above 0.30, factor-based scales were created for Negotiating, Preempting and Avoiding by calculating the weighted sum of the factor

TABLE 2
Factor Analysis of Use of Tactics

	Factor 1 Preempting	Factor 2 Negotiating	Factor 3 Avoiding
Reinterpreting → Boss	**0.82**	0.12	0.02
Punishing → Boss	**0.82**	0.19	−0.12
Distracting → Boss	**0.72**	0.03	−0.05
Ingratiating → Boss	**0.68**	0.11	−0.13
Distracting → Customer	**0.30**	0.10	0.03
Ingratiating → Customer	0.20	0.03	−0.15
Delegating → Customer	−0.02	**0.79**	−0.24
Rewarding → Customer	0.15	**0.79**	−0.23
Rewarding → Boss	0.26	**0.76**	−0.10
Explaining → Customer	**0.32**	**0.66**	0.20
Explaining → Boss	**0.31**	**0.50**	**0.32**
Punishing → Customer	−0.14	**0.41**	0.11
Delegating → Boss	−0.29	**0.33**	0.21
Reinterpreting → Customer	−0.04	−0.12	**0.93**
Ignoring → Boss	0.02	−0.09	**0.91**
Ignoring → Customer	−0.14	0.07	**0.63**
Percentage of Total Variance	2.87	2.84	**2.45**

TABLE 3
Intercorrelations Among Study Variables

	1	2	3	4	5	6	7
1. Role Conflict	—						
2. Role Ambiguity	0.511*	—					
3. Job Satisfaction	−0.388*	n.s.	—				
4. Effort	n.s.	n.s.	.331	—			
5. Negotiating	n.s.	0.325	n.s.	n.s.	—		
6. Preempting	n.s.	n.s.	−0.386	−0.547*	0.318	—	
7. Avoiding	n.s.	n.s.	−0.358	−0.522*	n.s.	0.618*	—

Notes: *α < .01.
    All other correlations are significant at α <.05.

correlations with the individual variable (Kim and Mueller 1978). All of the variables were standardized prior to statistical analysis. In all, four specific variables were used to indicate the behavioral responses of customer-contact workers to the demands of their roles: Effort (from the questionnaire item), Negotiating, Preempting and Avoiding. Both Preempting and Avoiding appear to be different aspects of a strategy of not responding to role-senders' expectations. Therefore, both of these variables will be used to analyze the hypotheses relating to avoidance strategies (Hypotheses 3, 6, and 8).

Results

The data from the survey were analyzed using simple correlational analysis since the hypotheses represent statements of associations between constructs. The intercorrelations among the study variables are displayed in Table 3.

Role Conflict, Role Ambiguity and Job Satisfaction

In the present study, role conflict and role ambiguity were intercorrelated (r = 0.511, α < .01). In addition, role conflict was negatively related to employee job satisfaction (r = −0.388, α < .01). These findings are consistent with the role-stress literature (cf. Fisher and Gitelson 1983; Jackson and Schuler 1985). However, role ambiguity and employee job satisfaction were not significantly related. This result is not surprising since the literature on role ambiguity and satisfaction is equivocal (Katz and Kahn 1978). If the respondents were experiencing a high degree of role conflict, they may have welcomed some role ambiguity which would allow the role incumbent latitude to maneuver (Hollander 1964).

Role Conflict, Role Ambiguity and Customer Contact Workers' Use of Tactics

There were no significant relationships between role conflict and the use of the four tactics (Effort, Negotiating, Preempting and Avoiding). Thus, Hypotheses 1, 2, and 3 were not supported. One significant relationship was found between role ambiguity and the customer contact workers' use of tactics. Role ambiguity and Negotiating were positively related (r = 0.325, α < .05), supporting Hypothesis 5. Hypotheses 4 and 6 were not supported.

Job Satisfaction and Customer Contact Workers' Use of Tactics

Job satisfaction was significantly related to the employees' use of effort to satisfy multiple role demands (r = 0.331, α < .05), supporting Hypothesis 7. Also, job satisfaction was negatively related to the use of preempting tactics (r = −0.386, α < .05) and was negatively related to the use of avoidance tactics (r = −0.358, α < .05). Therefore, Hypothesis 8 was also supported. No a priori relationship was predicted for job satisfaction and the use of negotiation tactics, and no relationship was found.

Discussion

The purpose of this research was to investigate how customer contact workers manage the multiple demands they experience as a result of their front-line service jobs. Weatherly's (1991) typology of nine tactics was reduced to four basic strategies: working hard (Effort), Negotiating, Preempting and Avoiding. These strategies were examined in relation to three other variables: role conflict, role ambiguity and job satisfaction. These relationships provided some insight into the behaviors of customer contact workers.

Apparently, customer contact workers use a variety of tactics—"tricks of the trade," perhaps—in an attempt to control their work environment. The battle waged for control by service industry workers has been described by Bateson (1985), Rafaeli (1989a) and Shamir (1980). The four strategies which emerged from factor analyzing Weatherly's (1991) typology were working harder (Effort), Negotiating, Preempting and Avoiding. In response to role demands, a customer contact worker may simply work harder in an attempt to get everything done and still have time to serve customers. Another option, however, is negotiating the demands of the environment. Negotiating provides customer contact workers a way to satisfy role demands without requiring them to fulfill all of the demands themselves. Negotiating involves bargaining with the role senders for lessened demands and/or getting someone else to satisfy the role expectations. Customer contact workers are likely to enlist co-workers, bosses and customers in producing the service. Preempting refers to tactics which seek to prevent role senders from communicating their expectations to the customer contact worker. For example, customer contact workers might try to keep their boss or their customers busy and distracted in order to prevent them from making any demands. Avoiding, on the other hand, relates to customer contact workers' response *after* the expectations have been communicated: they pretend not to have noticed. They might act as if they misunderstood the original request and instead do something similar but less demanding, or they might ignore the person's request altogether. One example of the "playing dumb" strategy would be when a customer contact worker says to his/her boss, "Oh, I didn't realize you wanted me to rearrange all of the merchandise in this section. I just thought you wanted me to switch the peanuts and the cashews."

Although customer contact workers use a variety of tactics to control their environment (Rafaeli 1989; Shamir 1980; Weatherly 1991), these tactics are apparently not in response to role conflict. However, the use of negotiation tactics does appear to be related to role ambiguity. In other words, customer contact workers who perceive that there is flexibility in their roles may attempt to use the flexibility to satisfy multiple demands by either getting someone else to satisfy the demands or by obtaining agreement on more easily satisfied, reduced demands.

Although job satisfaction was not related to customer contact workers' use of negotiation tactics, job satisfaction was related to their use of effort and hard work to satisfy role demands. Job satisfaction was also negatively related to service workers' use of avoidance

tactics. The data in the present study suggest that satisfied customer contact workers may be more likely to work hard to satisfy organizational and customer expectations, and dissatisfied customer contact workers my be more likely to "play dumb" and act as if they were unaware of the expectations incumbent in their role as front-line service workers. The results of the present research provide tentative support for a link between job satisfaction and attributes of employee performance for front-line service workers.

Limitations

Meaningful results have been obtained from field surveys with a variety of response rates. Depending on the nature of the population investigated, response rates typically range "from as low as 10% to as high 90 percent" for mail surveys (Kalton 1983, p. 66). Although the present response rate (34%) is adequate for the type of analysis conducted, there is a possibility that respondents and nonrespondents are different in a way which could limit the generalizability of the findings from the present study. Unfortunately, no objective data were available to compare respondents with nonrespondents; however, company executives stated that the demographic profile of the respondents was not dissimilar to their perception of the population of c-store managers.

The marginal reliability of the satisfaction measure may also have attenuated the results of the correlational analysis. As a result, the correlations between job satisfaction and the other items may be higher than the present study suggests, or the relationships could be spurious due to measurement error (Cohen and Cohen 1983). In addition, social-desirability bias may have influenced the way respondents answered the questions about their use of tactics. If the same respondents were also biased to report higher levels of job satisfaction, the correlations obtained may have been due to common methods variance (Cohen and Cohen 1983).

Implications and Conclusions

The present research has implications for service industry managers and researchers for job design, employee training, performance appraisal, quality of work-life and marketing. As proposed in the Customer Contact Model (Chase and Tansik 1983), customer contact jobs are different from jobs which have no customer contact. In designing jobs for customer contact workers, organizations need to clearly identify and separate customer service tasks and noncustomer service tasks. Although there may be some efficiency in having customer contact workers completing "back-office" tasks, there may also be a negative impact on customer service. If customer contact workers will be doing both customer service tasks *and* tasks which are not immediately related to serving the customer, clear direction needs to be given to the front-line employee about which tasks have higher priority under different circumstances.

In addition, it appears that customer contact workers learn and use several tactics for managing their job demands. Some of the tactics may not be what the organization prefers. For example, some customer contact workers indicate that they ignore or avoid the bosses and customers. Results from the present study suggest that organizations may want to include in their training programs *positive* alternative strategies for managing multiple demands. For example, enhancing an employee's communication skills might encourage the employee to give feedback to his/her boss about having too much to do instead of avoiding the boss or the customer. In addition, when new customer contact employees are hired into an organization, the company might want to use the new-employee orientation program to indoctrinate the incoming employees with a corporate value system that would sanction the use of some strategies and censure the use of others.

Organizations may also want to develop performance-appraisal systems which take into account customer contact workers' use of various tactics. For example, employees may be evaluated negatively for their use of tactics, like ignoring customers or pretending to misunderstand the boss, and positively evaluated for their use of tactics which enhance and strengthen the service-production system, such as providing feedback to supervisors when too many demands are made on the worker or delegating some of their tasks to other individuals in the system. Likewise, customer contact workers could be evaluated positively for their use of tactics which enhance the company's marketing efforts by creating goodwill with the customers. Empirical research needs to be conducted on the effect of using various human resource management practices (e.g., socialization and performance appraisal) on the behaviors of customer contact workers.

Also, managers need to pay attention to creating what Albrecht and Zemke (1985, p. 107) call a "motivating environment" in which "service people can find personal reasons for committing their energies to the benefit of the customer." Respondents in this study indicated that their willingness to work hard to satisfy the demands placed on them was positively related to their overall sense of job satisfaction. Job satisfaction has been related to factors such as pay, supervision and opportunity for advancement (Quinn and Staines 1979). Consequently, companies should build oppor-

tunities for advancement and pay increases into the career ladders of customer contact workers, and supervisors should treat their employees as they want their employees to treat their customers. Likewise, service industry researchers may want to take a new look at an old question: "What is the relationship—if any—between employee satisfaction and performance?" This study has suggested a rationale for such a link in the service industry context and has provided tentative support for such a relationship.

Service industry managers need to recognize the marketing consequences of their human resource practices. Parkington and Schneider (1979) noted a relationship between employee satisfaction and customer satisfaction. One explanation for this relationship may be that satisfied employees choose positive strategies to control their environment while dissatisfied employees choose negative strategies.

Clearly, more research is needed to untangle the dynamic nature of service encounters. Also, interdisciplinary research from the organizational behavior and consumer behavior perspectives could help us understand the impact on customers of various behaviors of customer contact workers.

APPENDIX

Weatherly's (1991) Typology of Tactics Used by Customer Contact Workers in Service Industries

---

Effort: Tactics to Satisfy Role Demands

Effort. Attempting to perform various tasks efficiently enough to please organizational and customer demands (e.g., becoming so familiar with routine facets of the job that they can be done simultaneously with other tasks; putting merchandise on a shelf while answering a customer's question).

Negotiating: Tactics to Alter Role Demands

Delegating. Getting other organizational members (including supervisors) and/or customers to perform some of the aspects of the service (e.g., asking another waiter to "refill the iced tea at table 4"; asking the customer to put the laces in the athletic shoe while the employee measures another child's foot).

Explaining. Giving reasons why certain expectations cannot be fulfilled (e.g., "company policy only allows us to give refunds under these circumstances . . .", "the manufacturer is out of this item, and we don't know when to expect any more"; "if we do what you are suggesting, we won't have time to complete this other project").

Rewarding. Doing extra favors or providing unusually good service to customers or other organizational members in return for their requests of not creating role stress for the employee (e.g., telling favored customers of special deals; calling other stores to find out where the customer can find a certain product; doing tasks normally outside the scope of the employee's position).

Punishing. Penalizing supervisors or customers who add to the worker's role conflict (e.g., sabotage in the extreme case; making a customer wait while finishing another task).

Preempting: Tactics to Avoid the Sent-role

Ingratiating. Seeking to put the customer or supervisor in a good mood or in a state of mind in which they think favorably of the employee so that he or she will not want to overload the employee with expectations (e.g., complimenting a customer's sense of fashion; talking with the supervisor about his/her favorite sports team).

Distracting. Engaging customers or supervisors to prevent them from having the opportunity to express expectations (e.g., talk about the weather, the "big game," the latest fashions; asking the customer or supervisor to do something which keeps him/her too busy to ask the employee to do something).

Avoiding: Tactics to Avoid the Received-role

Reinterpreting. Pretending to comprehend the customers' or organization's expectations in a way which minimizes role stress (e.g., the customer asks a retail sales clerk to find a certain product, and the sales clerk acts as if s/he believes the customer is asking for general directions and tells the customer that "the item should be on the left side of aisle 6").

Ignoring. Providing no feedback to customers who try to get the employee's attention (e.g., a bank teller keeping his or her eyes focused on paperwork and acting as if the customer or supervisor is speaking to someone else; a waiter pretending not to see a patron motioning for service).

Acknowledgment

This article is based on the senior author's master's thesis which was submitted in partial fulfillment of the requirement for a degree at the University of Arizona. The assistance of Lee Roy Beach, Terry Connolly and Barbara A. Gutek is gratefully acknowledged. In addition, we owe a special thanks to the customer-contact workers and their managers who participated in the research.

References

Albrecht, Karl and Ron Zemke (1985), *Service America!* New York: Warner Books.

Adrich, Howard E. and Diane Herker (1977), "Boundary-Spanning Roles and Organizational Structure," *Academy of Management Review*, 2, 217-230.

Bateson, John E. G. (1985), "Perceived Control and the Service Encounter," in *The Service Encounter*, John A. Czepiel, Michael R. Solomon and Carol F. Surprenant, eds. Lexington, MA: Lexington Books, 67–82.

Beehr, Terry A. and John E. Newman (1978), "Job Stress, Employee Health, and Organizational Effectiveness: A Facet Analysis, Model, and Literature Review," *Personnel Psychology*, 31, 665–699.

Bitner, Mary Jo, Bernard H. Booms and Mary S. Tetreault (1990), "The Service Encounter: Diagnosing Favorable and Unfavorable Incidents," *Journal of Marketing*, 54, 71–84.

Bowen, David E. and Benjamin Schneider (1985), "Boundary-Spanning-Role Employees and the Service Encounter: Some Guidelines for Management and Research," in *The Service Encounter*, John A. Czepiel, Michael R. Solomon and Carol F. Surprenant, eds. Lexington, MA: Lexington Books, 127–147.

Burke, Ronald J. and Monica L. Belcourt (1974), "Managerial Role Stress and Coping Responses," *Journal of Business Administration*, 5 (2), 55–68.

Chase, Richard B. and David A. Tansik (1983), "The Customer Contact Model for Organization Design," *Management Science*, 29, 1047–1050.

Cohen, Jacob and Patricia Cohen (1983), *Applied Multiple Regression/Correlation Analysis for the Behavioral Sciences* (2nd edn.) Hillsdale, NJ: Lawrence Erlbaum Associates.

Czepiel, John A., Michael R. Solomon and Carol F. Surprenant, eds. (1985), *The Service Encounter*, Lexington, MA: Lexington Books.

Davidow, William H. and Bro Uttal (1989), *Total Customer Service: The Ultimate Weapon*. New York: Harper and Row.

Fisher, Cynthia D. and Richard Gitelson (1983), "A Meta-Analysis of the Correlates of Role Conflict and Ambiguity," *Journal of Applied Psychology*, 68, 320–333.

French, John R. P. and Robert D. Caplan (1972), "Organizational Stress and Individual Strain," in *The Failure of Success*, Alfred J. Marrow, ed. New York: AMACOM, 30–66.

Gutek, Barbara A. and Susan J. Winter (1990), "Computer Use, Control Over Computers, and Job Satisfaction," in *People's Reactions to Technology in Factories, Offices, and Aerospace*, Stuart Oscamp and Shirlynn Spacapan, eds. Newbury Park, CA: Sage, 121–144.

———— and ———— (In Press), "Consistency of Job Satisfaction across Situations: Fact or Artifact?" *Journal of Organizational Behavior*.

Hochschild, Arlie R. (1983), *The Managed Heart*. Berkeley: University of California Press.

Hollander, Edwin P. (1964), *Leaders, Groups, and Influence*. New York: Oxford University Press.

Humes, James C. (1975), *Podium Humor*. New York: Harper and Row.

Iaffaldano, Michelle T. and Paul M. Muchinsky (1985), "Job Satisfaction and Job Performance: A Meta-Analysis," *Psychological Bulletin*, 97, 251–273.

Jackson, Susan E. and Randall S. Schuler (1985), "A Meta-Analysis and Conceptual Critique of Research on Role Ambiguity and Role Conflict in Work Settings," *Organizational Behavior and Human Decision Processes*, 36, 16–78.

Johnston, Von and Herff Moore (1991), "Pride Drives Wal-Mart to Service Excellence," *HR Magazine*, 36 (10), 79–82.

Kahn, Robert L., Donald M. Wolfe, Robert P. Quinn, J. Diedrick Snoek and Robert A. Rosenthal (1964), *Organizational Stress: Studies in Role Conflict and Ambiguity*. New York: John Wiley and Sons.

Kalton, Graham (1983), *Introduction to Survey Sampling*. Beverly Hills, CA: Sage.

Katz, Daniel and Robert L. Kahn (1978), *The Social Psychology of Organizations* (2nd edn.). New York: John Wiley and Sons.

Kim, Jae-On and Charles W. Mueller (1978), *Factor Analysis: Statistical Methods and Practical Issues*. Newbury Park, CA: Sage.

Koepp, Stephen (1987), "Why Is Service So Bad? Pul-eeze! Will Somebody Help Me?" in *Managing Services: Marketing, Operations, and Human Resources*, Christopher H. Lovelock, ed. (1988), Englewood Cliffs, NJ: Prentice-Hall, 208–215.

McGrath, Joseph, E. Joanne Martin and Richard A. Kulka (1982), *Judgment Calls in Research*. Newbury Park, CA: Sage.

Merton, Robert K. (1957), *Social Theory and Social Structure* (rev. edn.) New York: Free Press.

Mills, Peter K. (1986), *Managing Service Industries*. Cambridge, MA: Ballinger.

Murphy, Christine A. and Robert K. Gable (1988), "Validity and Reliability of the Original and Abridged Role Conflict and Ambiguity Scales," *Educational and Psychological Measurement*, 48, 743–751.

Parasuraman, A., Valerie A. Zeithaml and Leonard L. Berry (1985), " A Conceptual Model of Service Quality and its Implications for Future Research," *Journal of Marketing*, 49, 41–50.

——, ——, and —— (1988), "SERVQUAL: A Multiple-Item Scale for Measuring Consumer Perceptions of Service Quality," *Journal of Retailing*, 64 (1), 12–40.

Parkinton, John J. and Benjamin Schneider (1979), "Some Correlates of Experienced Job Stress: A Boundary Role Study," *Academy of Management Journal*, 22, 270–281.

Peters. Thomas J. and Nancy Austin (1986), *A Passion for Excellence*. New York: Warner Books.

—— and Robert H. Waterman Jr. (1982), *In Search of Excellence*. New York: Harper and Row.

Quinn, Robert P. and Graham L. Staines (1979), *The 1977 Quality of Employment Survey*. Ann Arbor, MI: Institute for Social Research.

Rafaeli, Anat (1989a), "When Cashiers Meet Customers: An Analysis of the Role of Supermarket Cashiers," *Academy of Management Journal*, 32, 245–273.

—— (1989b), "When Clerks Meet Customers: A Test of Variables Related to Emotional Expressions on the Job," *Journal of Applied Psychology*, 74, 385–393.

—— and Robert I. Sutton (1987), "Expression of Emotion as Part of the Work Role," *Academy of Management Review*, 12, 23–37.

—— and —— (1990), "Busy Stores and Demanding Customers: How Do They Affect the Display of Positive Emotion," *Academy of Management Journal*, 33, 623–637,

Rizzo, John R., Robert J. House and Sidney I. Lirtzman (1970), "Role Conflict and Ambiguity in Complex Organizations," *Administrative Science Quarterly*, 15, 150–163.

Schlesinger, Leonard A. and James L. Heskett (1991a), "Customer Satisfaction is Rooted in Employee Satisfaction," *Harvard Business Review*, 69 (6), 148–149.

—— and —— (1991b), "The Service-Driven Service Company," *Harvard Business Review*, 69 (5), 71—81.

Schneider, Benjamin (1980), "The Service Organization: Climate is Crucial," *Organizational Dynamics* (Autumn), 52–65.

—— and David E. Bowen (1984), "New Services Design, Development and Implementation and the Employee," in *Developing New Services*, William R. George and Claudia Marshall, eds. Chicago: American Marketing Association, 82–101.

—— and —— (1985), "Employee and Customer Perceptions of Service in Banks: Replication and Extension," *Journal of Applied Psychology*, 70, 423–433.

——, John J. Parkington and Virginia M. Buxton (1980), "Employee and Customer Perceptions of Service in Banks," *Administrative Science Quarterly*, 25, 252–267.

Shamir, Boas (1980), "Between Service and Servility: Role Conflict in Subordinate Service Roles," *Human Relations*, 33, 741–756.

—— (1983), "A Note on Tipping and Employee Perceptions and Attitudes," *Journal of Occupational Psychology*, 56, 225–259.

—— (1984), "Between Gratitude and Gratuity: An Analysis of Tipping," *Annals of Tourism Research*, 11, 59–78.

Sutton, Robert I. and Anat Rafaeli (1988), "Untangling the Relationship between Displayed Emotions and Organizational Sales: The Case of Convenience Stores," *Academy of Management Journal*, 31, 461–487.

Tansik, David A. (1990), "Managing Human Resources Issues for High-Contact Service Personnel," in *Service Management Effectiveness*, David E. Bowen, Richard B. Chase and Thomas G. Cummings, eds. San Francisco: Jossey-Bass, 152–176.

—— and Richard B. Chase (1988), "The Effects of Customer Induced Uncertainty on the Design of Service Systems," Paper presented at the annual meeting of the Academy of Management, Anaheim, CA.

van de Vliert, Evert (1981), "A Three-Step Theory of Role Conflict Resolution," *The Journal of Social Psychology*, 113, 77–83.

Van Sell, Mary, Arthur P. Brief and Randall S. Schuler (1981), "Role Conflict and Role Ambiguity: Integration of the Literature and Directions for Future Research," *Human Relations*, 34, 43–71.

Vroom, Victor H. (1964), *Work and Motivation*. New York: John Wiley and Sons.

Weatherly, Kristopher A. (1991), "Managing Multiple Demands: Examining the Behaviors of Customer-Contact Workers in Service Industries," Unpublished M.A. thesis, University of Arizona, Tucson.

Westbrook, Robert A. (1981), "Sources of Consumer Satisfaction with Retail Outlets," *Journal of Retailing*, 57,(3), 68–85.

II

Configuring the Service Firm

The five chapters and seven articles in this part of the book describe the "service marketing mix," the components that have to be put together to create a meaningful service experience from the viewpoint of the customer and the firm. Using the concepts and frameworks from the first part of the book, Chapters 5, 6, and 7 cover the configuration of the operation, the physical environment, and the service providers. Chapters 8 and 9 cover the problems of service communication and pricing. In these chapters, there is a sizable overlap with existing models and theories in goods marketing. The emphasis, however, is on the unique characteristics of service communications and pricing and on how these influence the service experience.

Chapter 5, "The Service Operation," focuses on configuring the operating system. The chapter first describes the typical life cycle of a service operation's competitiveness as it moves from "available for service" to "world-class service delivery." It goes on to use a modified version of the manufacturing strategy paradigm to show how firms can migrate to a "world-class" position.

This discussion leads on to the use of flowcharting to design the interactive process that takes place in the service experience. This can be done from both the company's and the consumer's perspective, but it is the combination of the two that is the most powerful approach.

Chapter 6, "The Physical Setting," looks at the different roles that the physical setting has to play in the service experience. This is a big part, for retail services, of the benefit delivered to the consumer. The physical setting has a role to play in the operational efficiency of the firm, since it provides a framework for the service delivery process. At a more subtle level, the physical setting can socialize both customers and employees to their roles. Altogether, the physical setting can be a source of competitive advantage.

The chapter starts by discussing the role of the physical environment in operation efficiency and in socializing customers and employees to their roles. To understand how this can work, it is necessary to understand how individuals respond to physical settings. A simple framework known as the "Servicescape Model" is introduced to discuss the impact of sight, size, color, sound, and scent on consumers. This model is then used to review the potential solutions to two commonly occurring service problems: crowding and queues.

Articles 2.1, 2.2, and 2.3 should be read in conjunction with this chapter, since they illustrate different empirical studies on the impact of the physical environment. Julie Baker and her colleagues in Article 2.1 manipulate different aspects of the physical environment of a retail outlet to create a "Prestige Image" or a "Discount Image." They then look at the impact of these factors on consumers' inferences about merchandise and service quality. Their factors included ambient factors such as music and lighting; design factors such as color and layout; and social factors such as the greetings given by salespeople and the dress code of the sales staff.

All of these changes were simulated using videotapes of a card and gift store. The results showed the impact particularly of ambient factors and social factors on perceived merchandise quality, perceived service quality, and perceived store image.

Michael Hui and David Tse in Article 2.2, and Shirley Taylor in Article 2.3, look at a different problem, that of managing queues in retail services. There is ample evidence to show that waiting has negative effects on service evaluation. To reduce these negative effects, service organizations can either provide faster service by modifying their service delivery system, or take actions designed to reduce the negative effects without changing the real waiting-time duration. These two empirical studies address this latter approach. Hui and Tse look at the impact of information about expected waiting times, that is, information about the expected length of a wait and queuing information that shows the customer's position in a queue with continuous updates. Taylor looks at the impact of the extent to which the service provider was perceived to have control over the delay and whether the customer's waiting time was filled. She also looks at the different impacts when waiting time is filled with activity related to the service, and when unrelated.

The Hui and Tse study is more complex but offers more insights, since it also looks at how these factors might influence customers' evaluation. In particular, they suggest three intermediate variables: "perceived waiting duration"; "affective response to the wait"; and "acceptability of the wait." They show that under certain circumstances, these variables can have a mediating effect linking the giving of information and the service evaluation.

Chapter 7, "The Service Employees," looks at the human resources policies of the service firm and how they can influence the service provider. It starts by showing the evidence linking human resources policies to the service provider's behavior and the consumer's evaluation of the service. It then shifts to the issues of empowerment and even enfranchisement of service employees. It reviews both the need for empowerment and the requirements to make empowerment successful.

Articles 2.4 and 2.5 can be read with Chapter 7. Hartline and Ferrel in Article 2.4 ask how a manager's commitment to service quality could be reflected in customers' perceptions of service quality. They build a model and test it empirically. They propose that a manager committed to service quality is likely to empower service providers and evaluate employees based on their behavior, not just their output. Empowerment and measuring behavior are in turn postulated to influence role conflict and ambiguity, employees' job satisfaction, belief in their ability to perform their job, and ability to adapt to different service encounters. These in turn are meant to influence consumers' service quality perceptions. In an elegant empirical study, based on hotel data, they test the various models.

Article 2.5, by comparison, focuses on the different dimensions that are likely to determine the nature of the service encounter. Price and her colleagues suggest three dimensions of "the moment of truth" in the service encounter: (1) temporal duration, or how long the encounter lasts; (2) affective or emotional context, or the extent to which the encounter is emotionally charged; and (3) spatial proximity of the service provider and consumer, or how physically close the service encounter requires them to be. They go on to use a white-water river rafting experience to study the most extreme encounter on each end of their dimensions and the appropriate measures for service provider performance under these conditions.

Chapter 8, "Communications Strategy," shows how the management of expectations is a crucial role in service communications, since it is expectations that provide a standard against which perceived service performance is evaluated. The chapter goes on to show how misdirected communications can negatively influence the encounter by socializing the wrong script or upsetting the service employees.

Article 2.6 by Turley and Kelley looks at the differences in advertising content in business-to-business services versus consumer services. They review the content of nearly 200 advertisements to test a series of hypotheses relating to communications strategies needed by business-to-business rather than consumer services. They suggest that business-to-business advertising should be more rational, more focused on benefits, use quality claims more frequently, provide price information more often, and provide Internet addresses more often.

Chapter 9, "Pricing Policy," focuses on the three characteristics of services that affect pricing: the nature of service costs, time-dependent capacity, and the role of the consumer as part of the process. The experiential nature of the service product means that cost measurement is very difficult. Many costs are both fixed and shared across a variety of services. This, combined with the shared nature of demand in such services, creates the opportunity for price bundling—that is, the bundling together of different services at a combined price.

The time-dependent nature of the service experience means that there is ample opportunity for charging different prices for the same "ticket" depending on the time of booking or the time of use. Such price discrimination is often used in the yield management systems of airlines or in hotel pricing.

Pricing can be used to influence the consumer's behavior in the service encounter in order to improve efficiency. A simple example is to use pricing to move peak demand and hence smooth the required capacity. More subtle models include pricing to encourage consumers to use the "self-service" option.

5

The Service Operation

Chapter Overview

Throughout the 1980s and 1990s, the distribution center of L.L. Bean was a required stop for companies engaged in benchmarking exercises. Many companies, including Nike, Disney, Gillette, and Chrysler, came to see how Bean could fill orders so effectively. In fact, the center they visited is no more; it has been replaced by a completely new approach.

Driven by ever-increasing volumes—12 million orders in 1996—increasingly global reach, and a growing variety of customized products, the old system had to be taken apart and rebuilt. The old system would build up orders from the telephone operations and then issue them every 12 hours to the pickers. The pickers would assemble the orders from around the center and then deliver them to the packers, who prepared them for dispatch.

The new Wave Pick Technology operates differently. Orders come straight from the telephones and are allocated dynamically to pickers with capacity. Moreover, the orders are broken down by item and assigned to different pickers, who themselves are assigned to different parts of the warehouse. The items are placed on a conveyor belt and bar coded. Scanners then automatically assemble the orders for packing. As a result, 100 percent of orders can be serviced within 24 hours; from order to delivery to the on-site Federal Express depot takes only two hours.

The operations of a service firm are the heart of the "product." Without a successful operation, the firm is out of business, because it will have nothing to offer to the customer. However, firms setting out to construct a service operation can choose from a large range of operational options.

Strategically, the service firm can choose to use its operations as the key component of its competitive strategy. Associating the firm in the mind of the consumer with service operational excellence can create a competitive advantage, but doing this also places considerable demands on the organization. This chapter discusses the strategic choices and the design criteria in terms of the organization and the operation itself.

Once the strategic choices have been made, they can be operationalized by using a flowchart to describe the detailed operations of the service. There need to be both consumer and operational versions of the flowchart. The chapter uses the flowcharting approach to understand the design of new services and to show how operations strategy can be tied back to a detailed flowchart.

The Four Stages of a Service Firm's Operational Competitiveness

Chase and Hayes[1] argue that there are four operational stages in the competitiveness of service firms: "available for service," "journeyman," "distinctive competence achieved," and "world-class service delivery." Along this dimension of competitiveness, clearly the key determinants are the customers and their perspectives. The different stages relate to varying degrees of preference for the firm, as shown in Figure 5.1. The primary focus of Chase and Hayes, however, is the operational capabilities of firms that are different stages of competitiveness.

Stage 1: Available for Service

Operations for a firm with this level of competitiveness are a "necessary evil." Operations are at best reactive to the needs of the rest of the organization and deliver the service as specified. As its mission, the operations department attempts primarily to avoid mistakes. Back office support is minimized to keep costs down. Technological investment is also minimized, as is investment in training for front-line personnel.

| FIGURE 5.1 | THE FOUR STAGES OF SERVICE FIRM COMPETITIVENESS |

Stage	Available for Service	Journeyman	Distinctive Competence Achieved	World-Class Service Delivery
Consumer Reaction	Customers patronize for reasons other than performance	Customers neither seek nor avoid the firm	Customers seek out the firm based on its sustained reputation for meeting customers' expectations	Company's name is synonymous with service excellence; it does not just satisfy customers, but delights them

Management designs skill out of the work done by these personnel and pays them the minimum wage whenever possible.

Stage 2: Journeyman

This level of competitiveness is often provided by the arrival of competition. It is no longer enough just to have an operation that works. The firm must now seek feedback from its customers on the relative costs and perceived qualities of the service. At this point, the operations department becomes much more outward-looking and often becomes interested in benchmarking.

Technology for firms at this stage tends to be justified based on the cost savings possible. The back office is now seen as a contributor to the service but tends to be treated as an internal service function. In the management of front-line employees, the emphasis shifts from controlling workers to managing processes. Employees are often given procedures to follow, and management consists of ensuring that these procedures are followed.

Stage 3: Distinctive Competence Achieved

By this stage, operations have reached a point where they continually excel, reinforced by the personnel management function and systems that support the customer focus. By this time, the firm has mastered the core service and understands the complexity of changing such operations. The back office is now seen to be as valuable as the front-of-house personnel. Technology is no longer seen as a source of cost advantage alone, but also as a way of enhancing the service to customers.

Perhaps the biggest changes come about in the workforce and in the nature of front-line management. As described in detail in Chapter 7, the need now is for empowerment. Front-line workers are allowed to select from alternative procedures and are not tied down in the same way. The role of front-line management is to listen to customers and become coaches to the front-line workers.

Stage 4: World-Class Service Delivery

To sustain this level of performance, operations not only have to continually excel but also become a fast learner and innovator. The back office, once seen as a second-class citizen, now must be proactive, develop its own capabilities, and generate opportunities. Technology is seen as a way to break the paradigm—to do things competitors cannot do.

The workforce itself must be a source of innovators, not just operators. To achieve this, the front-line supervisors must go beyond coaching to mentoring. As mentors, they need to be accountable for the personal development of the workforce so that employees can develop the skills necessary for them to innovate for the firm.

FIGURE 5.2 **THE MANUFACTURING STRATEGY PARADIGM APPLIED TO SERVICE**

SOURCE: Richard B. Chase and Robert H. Hayes, "Beefing Up Operations in Service Firms," *Sloan Management Review* (Fall 1991), 15–26.

The Manufacturing Strategy Paradigm Applied to Service

These stages represent a combination of stages in philosophy as much as anything else. Operations move from being a necessary evil to a key source of competitive advantage. The workforce moves from mechanical robots to sources of innovation. Management moves from command and control to empowerment and mentoring. To implement such a change also requires a systematic logic. Chase and Hayes[2] suggest the application of the Manufacturing Strategy Paradigm, shown in Figure 5.2, to service.

Baselining Performance

This is effectively an audit of operational performance. However, instead of just looking at a cost-based criteria, baselining looks also at those things that are important to the customer. This can be a complex topic, because operational activities do not necessarily match with the kind of attributes used by consumers to evaluate services in a one-to-one way. If a customer rates "reliability" and friendliness highly, what are the analogous operational dimensions? Customers can be asked to rate performance in operational terms, but this does not necessarily relate to their decision-making processes. Even if it does, the competitive environment must be included and absolute performance is irrelevant to customers, who will always compare alternative supplies.

Setting Priorities and Achieving Coherence

It is here that the baseline data must be used to make choices. In a typical manufacturing strategy, the choices are between such things as cost-price, flexibility, quality, and dependability. For services, to these choices must be added the degree of customer contact, the degree of customer participation, and the degree of staff empowerment. The company must choose a limited set of things to do well, and it must choose the

---

SERVICES IN ACTION 5.1

Citicorp

Between 1975 and 1985, the major American bank Citicorp completely overhauled its consumer banking services. Prior to that time, Citicorp's personal banking services had been very much operations oriented. The bank had strict but traditional measures of good performance. Unfortunately, these measures of good performance did not match what the bank's customers perceived to be good service, with the result that the personal banking arm of the company was losing money.

Money is the same no matter what bank it comes from, and banks can only market themselves on the basis of the services they offer. For Citicorp, the challenge became one of finding a marketing perspective. At the same time, the company could not afford to give service at any expense or it would lose still more money. There was thus a second challenge—of matching a marketing perspective to the operations perspective and making the two work together.

Personal banking customers, it was found, wanted services delivered efficiently and quickly, without having to wait in long lines. One possible solution was the automated teller machine (ATM). The advantages of the machine were several: It could be open when the bank itself was closed; it could be set up to operate quickly; and it could be configured to perform a variety of functions, depending on consumer needs. Later, Citicorp ATMs included multilingual versions and had keyboards that allowed customers to issue more complex instructions.

ATMs thus could satisfy both marketing and operations requirements by increasing capacity, production, and profitability while also extending the available range of services and extending capacity to meet demand over a greater range of time. However, such an innovation was easy to copy and Citicorp's widespread introduction of ATMs quickly was imitated by other banks.

Nationally, all bank customers use ATMs for just under one-half of their transactions: In the New York area, where Citicorp has more than 1,000 "banking centers," Citicorp's customers use ATMs for more than 80 percent of all transactions. It is also worth noting that Citicorp's personal banking arm made a profit of $548 million in 1987. However, rival banks offering the same types of services were unlikely to let Citicorp retain this position without a struggle. The next challenge was to improve the ATM and the service it offered while continuing to keep both the marketing and operations perspectives.

---

right set. The criteria for that choice include consumer needs and the technology and capabilities of the organization. It cannot be based on internal criteria alone.

The unique characteristics of a service firm all stem from the interface with the customer: the servuction system. Variations in this system are predominantly driven by the customer, but as discussed in Chapter 3, the resultant complexity is what should drive the choice of operations strategy. Larson and Bowen[3] suggest a three-stage mechanism for designing a service operation: (1) defining the nature of input uncertainty; (2) match input uncertainty to alternative interdependence patterns; and (3) adopt appropriate coordinating mechanisms (see Figure 5.3).

What the authors call "input uncertainty" has already been alluded to in Chapter 2. Input uncertainty stems from lack of information. Larson and Bowen use the term to refer to incomplete information on the part of the service organization about how, when, and where customers will require a particular service; this can be the result of uncertainty about the intentions of individual customers, a diversity of customer demand that makes prediction impossible, or both. This concept can easily be extended to include lack of information on the part of the customer about the nature of the service offering. This would tend to make customer behavior more unpredictable, as noted in Chapter 2, because of role uncertainty. However, the basic concept remains that customers introduce uncertainty into the service operation.

To illustrate how to use this idea, Larson and Bowen use a simple matrix. On one axis, they place "diversity of demand," although this can be best understood in terms of standardization. High level of diversity represents low levels of standardization, with customization driven by consumers' requests. Low levels of diversity are represented by much more standardized services. The second axis is the degree to which the

FIGURE 5.3	FRAMEWORK FOR THE DESIGN AND COORDINATION OF SERVICE INTERDEPENDENCIES

Input Uncertainty

Contingent upon:
—Diversity of demand
—Customer disposition
to participate

First
Match

Interdependence Patterns

—Division of work:
Front-office employees
Back-office employees
Customers
—Customized vs.
standardized inter-
dependencies

Second
Match

Portfolios of Coordination Mechanisms

—Different mechanisms
—Main locus of portfolio

SOURCE: Richard Larson and David E. Bowen, "Organization and Customer-Managing Design and Coordination of Services," *Academy of Management Review* 14, no. 2 (1989); 213–233.

FIGURE 5.4	DIVERSITY OF DEMAND AND CUSTOMER DISPOSITION TO PARTICIPATE

	Customer Disposition to Participate	
Diversity of Demand	**Low**	**High**
High (nonstandardized)	Appliance cleaning Car repair "sequential customized"	Psychotherapy Medical care Higher education "reciprocal service"
Low (standardized)	Banks Theaters Fast food "pooled service"	Laundromats Supermarkets "sequential standard"

customers are disposed to participate in the production of services and/or to provide information input. Figure 5.4 shows typical examples from each quadrant.

From such a typology, it is relatively easy to define:

The division of work between the front-line employees and the customers, the servuction system, and the back office.

The extent to which customization and standardization take place in the different linkings of the service firm model.

1. *Sequential standardized* service design. Here, employees provide the goods required for customers to serve themselves; examples include laundromats, self-service stores, and car rental agencies. Demand diversity is low, but customer intentions are uncertain. The division of labor is very clear, and there is little customization.

2. *Reciprocal* service design. These are very high-contact services with necessarily high levels of customization and contact; the division of labor sees contact staff playing a major role. Customer diversity is high, and customer intentions

TABLE 5.1			

PORTFOLIOS OF COORDINATION MECHANISMS FOR ALTERNATIVE DESIGNS OF SERVICE INTERDEPENDENCE PATTERNS

	Area of Coordination		
Design of Service Interdependence Patterns	**Front-Office Coordination of Service Interaction**	**Front/Back-Office Coordination of Service Support**	**Back-Office Coordination of Support Processing**
Sequential standardized service design (customer dominated)	**Customer self-adjustment to presupply** **Large, tightly specified scripts**	Routines for presupply Decoupling	Logistic planning
Reciprocal service design (customized customer/ employee interactive)	**Customer/employee mutual adjustment** **Large, loosely specified scripts**	Communication Limited decoupling	Programming
Sequential customized service design (front/back-office employee interactive)	Communication and agreement Limited, loosely specified scripts	**Adjusting customer orders and input to agreed performance**	Planning
Pooled service design (standardized back-office dominated)	Standardization Limited, tightly specified scripts	Information systems Decoupling	**Standardized pooling**

SOURCE: Richard Larson and David E. Bowen, "Organization and Customer-Managing Design and Coordination of Services," *Academy of Management Review* 14, no. 2 (1989); 213–233.

are uncertain. Examples are consulting services, medical care, legal advice, and higher education.

3. *Sequential customized* service design. Here, diversity of demand is high, but customer intentions can be predicted; therefore, there is the opportunity to safely customize the service. The division of labor is biased heavily toward the staff. Car repair, cleaning, and gardening are examples of this kind of interdependence.

4. *Pooled* service design. Here, diversity of demand is low, and customer intentions are more likely to be known. There is low customization and a fairly even division of labor, with much of the service work being carried out by back office staff (the technical core) and then delivered through contact personnel. Examples are banks, airlines, and fast-food restaurants.

From this typology, Larson and Bowen go on to describe the coordinating mechanisms that can be used to manage these interdependencies. It should be stressed that no single coordination mechanism is capable of doing this and that several mechanisms may need to be used in conjunction. They describe three different coordination mechanisms:

1. Front-office coordination of service interaction.

2. Front/back-office coordination of service support.

3. Back-office coordination of support processing.

Table 5.1 shows the role that each coordinating mechanism has to play in each of the interdependence patterns described above. In the sequential standardized service design, for example, it can be seen that the front office, the contact personnel, have primary responsibility for the service, working to tightly specified scripts; the role of

The Chubb Group of Insurance Companies

The Chubb Group is one of the larger financial service organizations in the United States. About two-thirds of its turnover is handled by 11 wholly owned subsidiary insurance companies in the United States and Canada, all of which are diversified operations, handling insurance for a variety of large industrial concerns as well as for personal and homeowner insurance.

The regulations surrounding the insurance industry require, on the whole, a considerable amount of attention to operational detail. A customer cannot simply walk into an office, purchase an insurance product, consume it, and walk out again. In addition to offering different policies, companies frequently offer different premiums on the same policy to different customers (e.g., nonsmokers pay lower life insurance premiums than smokers). All of this means that insurance companies must collect and process a great deal of data from their customers.

For the Chubb Group, with its highly diversified insurance-industry and customer base, making the collection of data more efficient became a major goal. The aim was to develop a data collection system that would allow brokers and agents to spend less time filling in forms and filing them. As well as saving operational time, such a process also would save on the amount of training necessary for staff. At the same time, it was felt that a simpler, more user-friendly method of collecting data would reduce perceived risk and would attract customers.

In the personal insurance sector, the Chubb Group's answer to the problem was a new personal insurance package called Masterpiece. The goal of Masterpiece was to reduce the amount of data needed to complete a policy from more than 300 questions to the number that would fit on a single sheet of paper. Through the use of computers, the layout and type of questions on the sheet could be customized, depending on the customer and the nature of the policy. Each form contains only the premium amount and other information relevant to that particular policy. The form was designed to apply to all personal insurance policies, including automobile, home, personal liability, and valuables.

To back up this system, Chubb also instituted a centralized toll-free telephone service to deal with any alterations, such as changes of address, thereby relieving agents and customers of the necessity of filling out new forms. The goal was to reduce the amount of paperwork and thus to create operational efficiency and service attractive to consumers at the same time.

---

back office is limited to logistics support and planning. In the sequential customized service design, however, the major service operation takes place as a coordinating mechanism between front and back office; front-office staff, working with limited but loosely configured scripts (due to the customizable nature of the service), are responsible primarily for ascertaining customer needs and then delivering the completed service (e.g., repaired car, cleaned clothes) back to the customer.

For the highly interactive and customized reciprocal service design, it is the mutual adjustment of the customer and the front-line employee that delivers the service with long, complex, and loosely-specified scripts. The role of the back office is limited to programming and scheduling, and the linkage between front and back office allows for limited decoupling because "client" records and requests can be prepared "off-line."

Thus, the nature of the customer interface and, in particular, the uncertainty it causes drive the relative importance of the different components of the service firm. Moreover, it is the key determinant of the role played by the back office and the nature of the interaction between the customer, the contact personnel, the front office, and the back office.

Incorporating Learning

Incorporating learning requires both gathering and disseminating new roles obtained from analyzing the operations. A true learning organization does not just learn on an ad hoc basis. Rather, it learns systematically, often experimenting formally with the operation to learn more. In manufacturing, such experiments are commonplace and focus on "yield"; with services, they need to focus on both cost and customer satisfaction.

Designing the Interactive Process

The heart of the service process is the experience of the consumer, which takes place in real time. This interaction can take place in a building or in an environment created by the service firm, but it need not necessarily do so. It is the interactive process itself that creates the benefits desired by the consumer. Designing that process therefore becomes key to the product design for a service firm.

The interactive process visible to the consumer constitutes the product. However, as the servuction model, discussed in Chapter 1, demonstrates, the visible part of the operations process with which the consumer interacts has to be supported by an invisible process.

One of the most commonly used operations management techniques is flow-charting. It is used to analyze and manage complex production processes, because it involves the identification of flows, stocks, costs, and bottlenecks. The flowcharting of service operations can also serve a number of purposes, not only for operations management but also for marketing management. This concept has been renamed *blueprinting* by G. Lynn Shostack, who has written a number of papers advocating its use.[4]

As pointed out in Chapter 3, because services are delivered by an interactive process involving the consumer, a marketing manager in a service firm must have a detailed knowledge of the operation. Flowcharting provides a useful analytical way of acquiring that knowledge. Flowcharting also allows the manager to understand which parts of the operating system are visible to the consumer and hence are part of the servuction process.

The search for operational efficiency is not unique to services, but it does pose interesting problems in this field. A shift in the underlying process may be more efficient, for example, but it may also change the nature of the interaction with the consumer. A detailed flowchart provides communication between operations and marketing that can highlight the potential problems that were discussed in Chapter 3.

Figure 5.5 shows a simple process in which, for now, it is assumed that the entire system is visible to the customer. It covers the stages involved in getting a meal in a cafeteria-style restaurant. The diagram illustrates the various components in the process. In this example, each task is represented in a box. The "raw material" flowing through the process is the customers. There are no inventories in the process, but clearly there would be an inventory of persons in the form of a line in front of each stage. A restaurant run in such a fashion would be a single long chain of counters, with customers progressing along the chain and emerging after paying. In Figure 5.5, the cost figure by stage represents the cost of providing personnel to service each counter; the service cost per meal is computed by dividing the total cost of the personnel per hour by the maximum number of individuals that can be served per hour.

The Service Operations Manager's Perspective

The first thing that the flowchart does is provide a check on the logical flow of the whole process. Clearly, a flowchart makes it immediately apparent if a task is being performed out of sequence. In this case, we shall further assume that only the cashier stage is fixed (because paying the cashier has to be the last stage) and that the other tasks can be performed at other times.

Once the different steps have been identified, it is relatively easy to identify the potential capacity bottlenecks. The hot-food counter stage is an obvious bottleneck because it represents the longest process time (i.e., the longest time to process one individual through that stage). A balanced production line is one in which the process times of all steps are the same. The process time is calculated by dividing the activity time (the time required to perform the activity) by the number of stations or locations

FIGURE 5.5	SIMPLE PROCESS FLOWCHART OF A CAFETERIA-STYLE RESTAURANT

	Stations	Activity Time	Process Time	Maximum Output/Hour
Appetizer Counter	1	15 secs.	15 secs.	240
↓ $3.00/hour				
Salad Counter	1	30 secs.	30 secs.	120
↓ $3.00/hour				
Hot-Food Counter	1	60 secs.	60 secs.	60*
↓ $3.00/hour				
Dessert Counter	1	40 secs.	40 secs.	90
↓ $3.00/hour				
Drinks Counter	1	20 secs.	20 secs.	180
↓ $3.00/hour				
Cashier	1	30 secs.	30 secs.	120
$6.00/hour				

*Capacity Bottleneck

$$\text{Service cost per meal} = \frac{\$21.00}{60} = \$0.35$$

performing the activity. In Figure 5.5, the process and activity are the same because there is only one station for each activity.

To solve this particular bottleneck problem, we could consider adding one extra station, in this case an extra counter, to the hot-food stage. The process time would then drop to 30 seconds (60 seconds divided by two). The bottleneck would then become the dessert counter, which has process time of 40 seconds and a maximum capacity of 90 persons per hour. Costs would go up by $3.00 per hour for the extra counter, but because the number of customers would go up to 90 persons per hour, the service cost per meal would go down to $0.27 per meal.

The creative use of additional staff may produce a model such as that shown in Figure 5.6, which combines certain activities and uses multiple stations. This process is capable of handling 120 customers per hour, compared with 60 in the process shown in Figure 5.5. Although costs rise, the service cost per meal falls because of this increase in capacity.

The Service Marketing Manager's Perspective

A marketing manager dealing with the process illustrated in Figure 5.5 has some of the same problems as his or her operations colleague. The process as defined is designed to operate at certain production levels, and these are the service standards that customers should perceive. But, if the process is capable of processing only 60

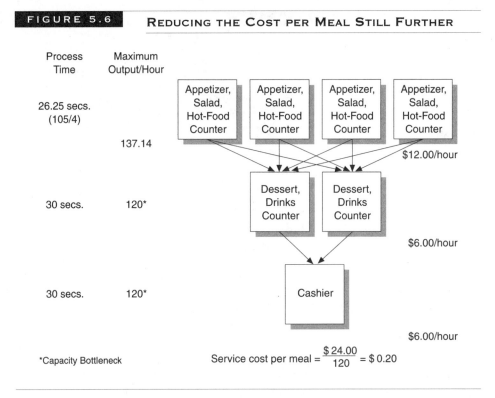

FIGURE 5.6   REDUCING THE COST PER MEAL STILL FURTHER

Process Time	Maximum Output/Hour	
26.25 secs. (105/4)	137.14	Appetizer, Salad, Hot-Food Counter (×4) — $12.00/hour
30 secs.	120*	Dessert, Drinks Counter (×2) — $6.00/hour
30 secs.	120*	Cashier — $6.00/hour

*Capacity Bottleneck

$$\text{Service cost per meal} = \frac{\$24.00}{120} = \$0.20$$

customers per hour, there may be a problem. Also, it is clear that the bottleneck at the hot-food counter will produce queues within the line.

The marketing manager should recognize the capacity benefits immediately. However, what the chart also shows is the change in consumer behavior required for the system to operate. In Figure 5.5, the consumer goes from counter to counter, has only one choice at each counter, and probably will queue at each station but will wait for a longer time at the hot-food counter. Moreover, the wait at each station almost certainly will far exceed the time spent in each activity. In the process proposed in Figure 5.6, the consumer visits fewer stations but frequently is faced with a choice between different stations. Clearly, the script to be followed by consumers will be different; indeed, the restaurant will look completely different. This obviously will impose different marketing demands.

The use of the flowcharting approach allows the marketing and operations personnel to analyze in detail the process that they are jointly trying to create and manage. Flowcharting can easily highlight the kind of conflicts discussed in Chapter 3 and can provide a common language for their discussion and for the resolution of their problems.

Using Flowcharts to Identify the Servuction Process

Flowcharts may also be used for a different purpose. Consider Figure 5.7, which shows a much more detailed flowchart for the production of a discount brokerage service. This chart is designed to identify the points of contact between the service firm and the customer. The points above the line are visible to the consumer, and those below are invisible. In assessing the quality of the service received, according to the servuction model, the customer refers to the points of contact.

To illustrate, let us consider the consumers as being proactive rather than reactive. Consider them as worried individuals looking for clues that they have made the right

Lands' End

Lands' End is a catalog retail company operating nationally from a base in Wisconsin. The company sells mainly clothing, along with accessories and luggage, to a mostly young, affluent, well-educated, and quality-oriented customer base. The Lands' End catalog, which offers about 600 distinct items with a total option range of more than 10,000, provides customers with information about products. Some customers order by mail, but about 75 percent use the Lands' End toll-free telephone number to place their orders by phone. This telephone line is open 24 hours a day every day except Christmas.

Operations management for catalog retailers involves, first, having stock on hand to meet demand and, second, managing a system in which orders are filled and processed quickly to avoid delays to the customers. Service management depends on being able to meet each customer's inquiry individually and, because customers cannot actually see or try on garments over the telephone, offer as much guidance as possible. Success overall entails the resolving of the contradiction between personal service and assembly-line production.

The focus of this effort is on the customer sales representatives who answer the telephones. In the case of Lands' End, these representatives are well trained and are able to give full descriptions of all items in the catalog to supplement the information given in print. The customer sales representatives are further supported by a team of "specialty shoppers" who can give even more detailed information and advice and who can attempt to provide more service than the customer expects.

The front-line operation then needs systems backup to provide the second half of the service—the fast dispatch of goods. This is accomplished at Lands' End by providing customer service representatives with links to the computer mainframe so that they can check stock, look up credit ratings, and place delivery orders while the customer is still on the phone. Automation, particularly in the distribution center, has served to decrease order processing time to less than 24 hours for most orders.

Lands' End so far has succeeded by remaining relatively small and keeping all systems simple and free from bureaucracy. In 1987, when executives began thinking about expanding the company, one of the prime considerations was how to increase volume and at the same time maintain service quality.

decision, rather than as inanimate objects to which things are done. The points of contact are the clues. In a recent article, Levitt talks about the "tangible clues" and argues that the intangible nature of services makes it important to manage the tangible clues provided to the customer.[5] These tangible clues constitute the servuction process.

Besides demonstrating a more complicated process, the chart in Figure 5.7 has a number of added features. First, each of the main features is linked to a target time. In the top right-hand corner, for example, the time to mail a statement is targeted as five days after month-end. In designing a service, these target times initially should be set by marketing, and they should be based on consumers' expected levels of service. If the service is to be offered in a competitive marketplace, then it may be necessary to set standards higher than those of services currently available. Once the standards have been set, however, the probability of achieving them must be assessed. If the firm is prepared to invest enough time and money, it may be feasible to meet all the standards set by marketing; doing so, however, would affect the costs and therefore the price of the service. Hence, the process should be an interactive one.

The chart also highlights potential fail points "F." These key points have two characteristics: the potential for operations malfunction is high, and the result of such a malfunction becomes visible. Such points also represent stages in which a malfunction would be regarded by consumers as particularly significant.

A Marketing or an Operations Flowchart?

Although the idea of a flowchart is attractive to both marketing and operations, it may well be that a marketing flowchart should be prepared in a different way. The

FIGURE 5.7 FLOWCHART OF A DISCOUNT BROKERAGE SERVICE

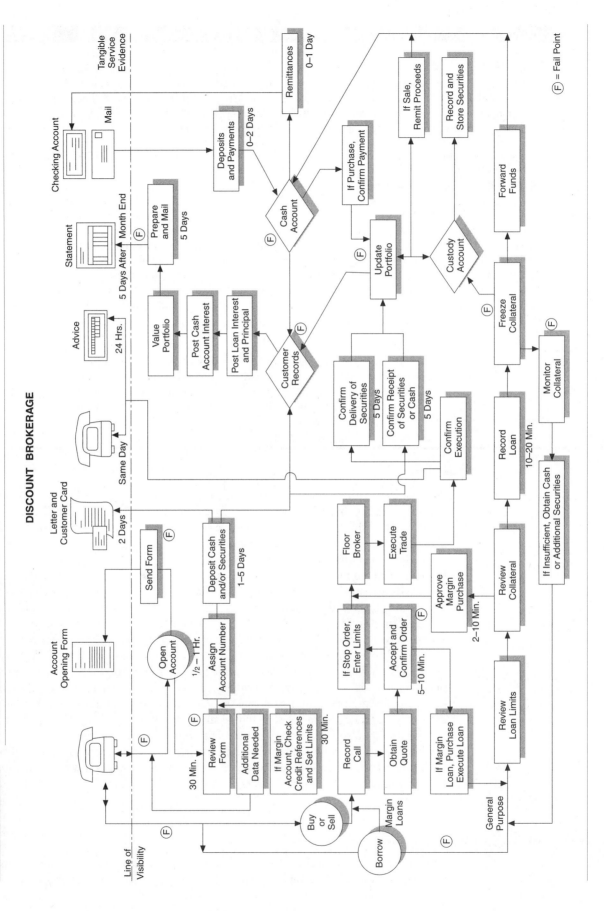

DISCOUNT BROKERAGE

charts used in this chapter have an internal focus: although they identify clearly the tangible points of contact with the client, they start from the organization and look outward.

An alternative way to develop a flowchart would be to start from a consumer protocol. Respondents, individually or in groups, can be asked to describe the process or the script they follow in using the service. Clearly, such an approach cannot cover the invisible parts of the service firm, but it can provide a much better understanding of the points of contact. The process, as described by the consumer, may well differ greatly from that perceived by the firm.

Respondents asked to describe a flight on United Airlines, for example, might start with their experience with the travel agent. They then might proceed to describe the process of getting to the airport, parking, and entering the terminal. If the signs for United and the entrance to the specific terminal are confusing, this will reflect on the airline. A parking lot that is filthy, poorly lit, and inhabited by vagrants will also deter customers. Although the airline may not have direct control over these points of contact, it could be a wise investment to use its own staff to improve the parking lot. McDonald's long ago learned the value of removing litter not only from its own property but also from the adjoining roadways.

Flowcharting for New Product Development

Flowcharts may also be used in new product development. Once the process has been documented, choices can be made that will produce "new" products. Although the processes in Figures 5.5 and 5.6 are for the same task, from the consumer's point of view they are very different. The charts define alternatives that are operationally feasible; the choice between them is one for marketing.

Strategically, the decision may be made to move the line separating visibility and invisibility. Operationally, arguments have been made for the minimization of the visible component. From a marketing point of view, however, more visibility may create more differentiation in the mind of the consumer. For example, a restaurant can make its kitchen into a feature by making it visible. This poses constraints on the operational personnel, but it may add value in the mind of the consumer.

G. Lynn Shostack suggests an alternative view of using flowcharts by introducing the concepts of complexity and divergence as a means of classifying the charts.[6] Complexity is a measure of the number and intricacy of the steps and sequences that constitute the process—the more steps, the more complex the process. Divergence is defined as the executional latitude or variability of those steps and sequences. As examples, Shostack develops, for two alternative florists, flowcharts that differ dramatically in their complexity and divergence. Although they perform equivalent tasks operationally, they can be very different from a marketing viewpoint and hence constitute separate products.

Figures 5.8 and 5.9 show the two florists, both capable of delivering a bouquet of flowers. For the first—and more traditional—florist, the process is linear and involves a limited number of steps. It has low complexity. However, the generation of bouquets under such a system calls for considerable discretion to be allowed for the florist at each stage—in the choice of vase, flowers, and display—and produces a heterogeneous output. The system therefore has high divergence. Interestingly, the flowchart tells us little about the interactive part of the process.

For the second florist in Figure 5.9, the process can be viewed as an attempt to "production-line the system," as discussed in Chapter 3. Because the objective is to deskill the job, the system is designed to generate a limited number of standardized bouquets. The divergence of the system is therefore reduced, but to achieve this the complexity of the process is increased significantly.

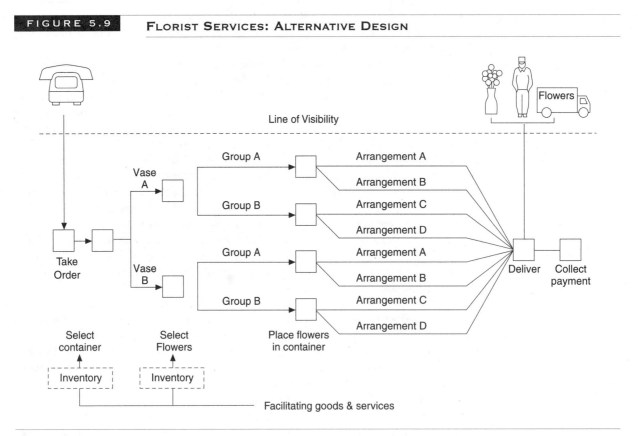

FIGURE 5.8   **PARK AVENUE FLORIST**

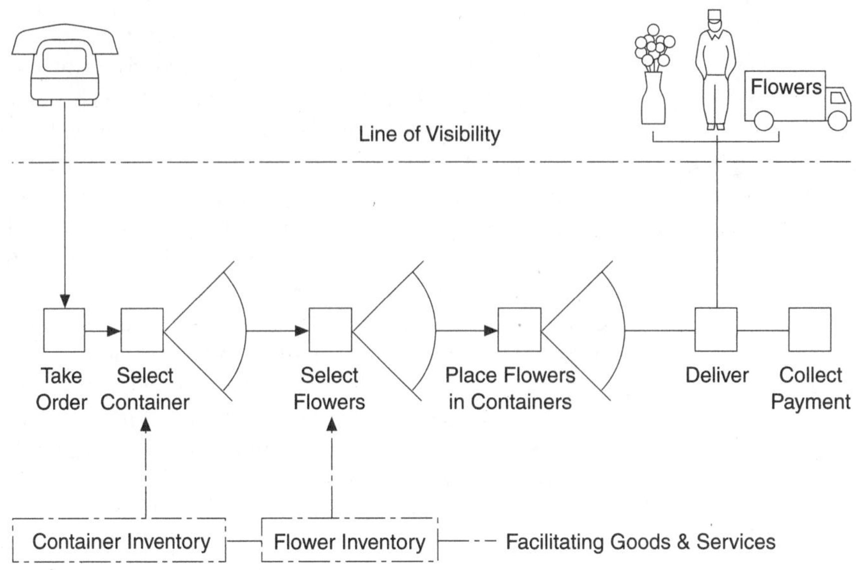

FIGURE 5.9   **FLORIST SERVICES: ALTERNATIVE DESIGN**

SOURCE G. Lynn Shostack, "Service Positioning through Structural Change," *Journal of Marketing* 51 (January 1987), 34–43. Reprinted by permission of the American Marketing Association.

Intercontinental Florist

Intercontinental Florist, founded in 1993 and based in Orlando, Florida, is a rapidly growing floral retailer that uses advanced communications technologies, including the Internet, to market its products. In just three years, turnover has grown from more than $100,000 to $11 million. Although the firm has just five physical outlets, all in the Orlando area, 90 percent of sales now come from outside Florida.

The firm's owner, William J. Marquez, first learned the value of technology in marketing when he acquired a stock of 10,000 bonsai trees on the assumption that these could be sold through his firm's usual channel, a mail-order catalogue. However, it quickly became apparent that this would not work. After acquiring the trees, Marquez learned that they require expensive and time-consuming care; for example, each tree needs to be soaked three times a week. Marquez needed to dispose of the stock quickly before he lost either money or the trees themselves.

Intercontinental then launched an advertising blitz, using faxes to regular clients, an 800 telephone number,

and an electronic catalogue on the Internet to promote the bonsai trees. Within two months, the firm had disposed of the entire stock, made a profit, and acquired valuable new customers.

Using the lessons learned from this incident, Intercontinental has gone on to develop a large and steady customer base, all of whom can be reached quickly no matter what their physical location may be. A fax service has been developed that can reach 25,000 clients overnight; detailed logs of sales via 800 numbers allow advertising to be directed at market segments in which high responses have been received in the past. Marquez, not technologically minded himself, has also come to appreciate the power of the Internet; Intercontinental's Web site began to break even after just six months. Later plans include expanding telemarketing efforts to include a nationwide database of telephone numbers. For Intercontinental, technology offers the key to yet further rapid expansion.

Shostack argues that in developing products in the service sector, manipulation of complexity and divergence are two of the key choices. Reducing divergence creates uniformity that can reduce costs, but it does so at the expense of increasing conformity and inflexibility in the system. However, increasing divergence creates flexibility in tailoring the experience to each customer, but it does so at increased expense. Reducing complexity is a specialization strategy often involving the unbundling of the different services offered.

Process Reengineering and Service Businesses

Process reengineering has become one of the hottest topics in consulting in the past three years. Firms are encouraged to reengineer all their processes to improve efficiency and effectiveness. For service businesses, process reengineering can be just as effective, providing the uniqueness of the service provider is understood.

Process reengineering starts with a simple inconsistency in modern organizations. To preserve functional excellence, organizations are structured around departments, and yet the organization actually runs on cross-functional processes. The new product development process crosses the functional boundaries of research and development, marketing, manufacturing, logistics, and sales. Even the simple order-fulfillment process needs to coordinate sales, logistics, and manufacturing. It is a sad fact that as a result, most processes were not designed but just "happened." "We've always done it this way" is often the epitaph on the gravestone of a sinking process.

Reengineering is a conceptually simple process but is extremely difficult to implement. The existing processes are first defined as they actually happen, not as they are supposed to happen. This involves everyone in the organization helping to create a huge diagram of the processes, often called a "brown paper" because of the huge sheets of brown paper sometimes used. Once this has been done, teams highlight wasted steps and inefficiencies and design new processes. The skill of the consultants is in creating the change climate necessary to get from the old model to the new one.

Such a process is analogous to many of the things already described in this chapter. Clearly, service processes are more difficult to redesign, as they involve or, at least, influence the consumer. If processes are "visible," then both marketing and operations must be involved in any redesign.

Summary

The design of the operational strategy of a service firm is a crucial decision. This chapter first suggests that the relative emphasis given to operations must first be determined. Once the priority is set, the normal manufacturing strategy paradigm can be used, provided the importance of the customer interface is recognized. An operations strategy can be visualized and operationalized through a flowchart. In goods companies, there is only one flowchart, that for operations. For service businesses, there must be two flowcharts, because the customer also has a flowchart or script. Differences in manufacturing or operational strategy are reflected in both types of flowchart.

Questions

1. Describe a recent example familiar to you in which operations demands have necessitated a change of script for the consumer. How is the change managed?

2. Create a consumer flowchart for a service with which you are familiar. Would the managers of the firm find the flowchart surprising? If so, in what way?

3. How can information technology be used to balance the conflicting needs of operations and marketing in a service business? Give an example and show how it has helped with the aid of a flowchart.

Notes

[1]Richard B. Chase and Robert H. Hayes, "Beefing Up Operations in Service Firms," *Sloan Management Review* (Fall 1991): 15–26.
[2]Ibid.
[3]Richard Larson and David E. Bowen, "Organization and Customer-Managing Design and Coordination of Services," *Academy of Management Review* 14, no. 2 (1989): 213–233.
[4]See, for example, G. Lynn Shostack, "Services Positioning through Structural Change," *Journal of Marketing* 51 (January 1987): 34–43.
[5]Theodore Levitt, "Marketing Intangible Products and Product Intangibles," *Harvard Business Review* (May–June 1981): 94–102.
[6]Shostack, "Services Positioning."

6

The Physical Setting

Chapter Overview

A jaunty accordion tune inspired British supermarket shoppers to buy French wine, whereas bierkeller music had them reach for German wine. In a study in a UK supermarket, the shelf facings of German and French wines were equalized, as were the price range and the placing of the bottles on shelves. The only thing that changed during the day was the music played in the shopping aisle.

The surprising result was that French music ensured that French wine outsold German wine by 3.3 to 1. Playing German music reversed the ratio, with German wine outselling French by 2.75 to 1. Only a small proportion of shoppers acknowledged or recognized that the music influenced their choice. *(Based on a study led by Adrian North of Leicester University.)*

The physical setting of a service firm has many different roles to play. It is a big part of the service delivered to the consumer. It has a role to play in the operational efficiency of the firm, coordinating and providing a framework for the service delivery process. At a more subtle level, the physical setting can socialize the customers and employees to their roles. Finally, the physical setting can be a source of competitive advantage by differentiating the firm from its competitors.

This chapter discusses these different roles and shows that the consumer and, to a lesser extent, the contact personnel must be the key determinants of the structure and form of the physical setting. The chapter uses frameworks from environmental psychology to explain how the physical setting influences the consumer.

Physical Setting and Different Types of Service Delivery

The servuction model provides a highly simplified view of a service business. However, even at this level it is clear that for many services the physical setting, or evidence, is a key part of the process. Moreover, it is clear that for the contact personnel, the physical evidence is just as important. Whatever the physical infrastructure and artifacts the service entails, they are experienced by both the consumer and the contact personnel; indeed, the contact personnel are exposed for far longer than the average consumer. And, because we know that the attitude and behavior of the contact personnel can have a major impact on the consumer (Chapter 4), the physical setting can therefore have a large secondary effect on the consumer through the contact personnel.

However, not all service businesses have the same mix of physical setting or evidence and contact personnel. Figure 6.1 shows a simple spectrum highlighting the different levels of importance to the consumer of physical evidence for different types of service.

Under the general heading of "retail services" are those consumer services in which the physical presence of the consumer in the service setting is a key component of the service delivered. Hospitals, resorts, child care, and so on all have a physical environment, which is a key part of their service offering. Conversely, there are consumer services that involve very little physical evidence, such as insurance firms or express mail. Here, the "back office" of the firm provides the bulk of the service, and the tangible clues are very limited.

In industrial markets, the dominant model is limited physical evidence. The service provided to repair and service copying machines, for example, requires no retail space and the tangible clues are limited to the telephone answering system and the tools and appearance of the engineer. For professional service firms, the physical environment can sometimes be used as physical evidence. Advertising agencies, for example, will invest in offices that help to create the correct image of the firm. Advertising

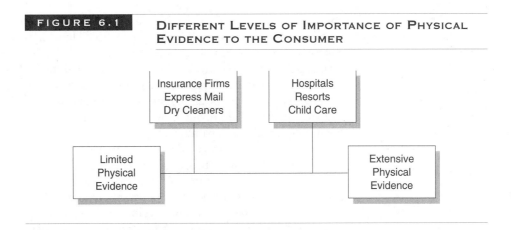

FIGURE 6.1   DIFFERENT LEVELS OF IMPORTANCE OF PHYSICAL EVIDENCE TO THE CONSUMER

agencies are the exception rather than the rule, because most professional service firms "deliver" to the clients' premises rather than in their own offices.

For the contact personnel, the physical environment is their personal working environment, and this will always condition their behavior. The relative emphasis given to the consumer in designing the evidence and environment will therefore depend on the opportunity to use that evidence as part of the service delivery and to create a competitive advantage in that way.

Physical Evidence and Operational Efficiency

The translation of an operations flowchart into a physical design is relatively straightforward. For example, flowcharts like those given in Chapter 5 (Figures 5.5 and 5.6) can be used to forecast the lines expected at various stations. The lengths of the lines and the physical equipment needed by each station then can be used to work out the square footage required. To a large extent, the logical sequencing of the stages defines the physical layout. All of this, of course, is constrained by the size and shape of the building available.

Chase and Stewart[1] suggest that many common failures caused by contact personnel and staff can be avoided through restructuring of the physical environment. Failures on the part of staff to deliver the basic service can be solved by creating physical aids. Cash drawer keys can be color-coded and change trays provided on the tops of the drawers to improve both the speed and accuracy of taking cash from customers. The ways in which staff interact with customers also can be built into the systems and facilities. A mirror facing a telephone operator will produce a smiling voice; a request for bank tellers to record the color of their customers' eyes will result in eye contact. Finally, the facilities themselves can be made fail-safe. Uncomfortable chairs stop staff from sleeping, and mirrors in strategic points remind staff to check their appearance.

Intriguingly, the same logic can be applied to making customers' behavior fail-safe. Checklists sent to customers can ensure that they are prepared before calling in for a service request. Door locks on airline lavatories that turn on lights ensure doors are locked and occupied signs are illuminated. In fast-food restaurants, strategically located tray-return stands and trash receptacles remind customers to return their trays.

Socializing Employees and Customers

Organizational socialization is the process by which an individual adapts to and comes to appreciate the values, norms, and required behavior patterns of an organization.[2] The firm's physical evidence plays an important part in the socialization process by conveying expected roles, behaviors, and relationships among employees and between employees and customers. The purpose of socialization is to project a positive and consistent image to the public. However, the service firm's image is only as good as the image each employee conveys when interacting with the public.[3]

Physical evidence, such as the use of uniforms, facilitates the socialization of employees toward accepting organizational goals and affects consumer perceptions of the quality of service provided. Studies have shown that the use of uniforms aids in identifying the firm's personnel, presents a physical symbol that embodies the group's ideals and attributes, implies a coherent group structure, facilitates the perceived consistency of performance, provides a tangible symbol of an employee's change in status (e.g., military uniforms can change as personnel move up through the ranks), and assists in controlling the behavior of errant employees.[4]

One classic example of how tangible evidence affects the socialization process of employees involves women in the military. Female military personnel were originally permitted to wear civilian clothing during pregnancy, in lieu of their traditional military uniforms. However, it was soon noticed that discipline and morale problems emerged among these servicewomen, as they began to lose their identification with their roles as soldiers. "Maternity uniforms are now standard issue in the Air Force, Army, and Navy as well as at US Air, Hertz, Safeway, McDonald's, and the National Park Service."[5]

Physical Setting as a Source of Differentiation

As competition increases in a particular part of the service sector, opportunities for differentiating the firm become increasingly difficult to find. The physical evidence of the firm can be used as a means of service differentiation. The physical appearance of personnel and facilities often have a direct impact on how consumers perceive that the firm will handle the service aspects of its business. Numerous studies have shown that well-dressed individuals are perceived as more intelligent, better workers and more pleasant to engage in interactions.[6] Similarly, nicely designed facilities are going to be perceived as having the advantage over poorly designed and decorated alternatives.

Differentiation can also be achieved by using physical evidence to reposition the service firm in the eyes of its customers. Upgrading the firm's facilities often upgrades the image of the firm in the minds of consumers and may also lead to the attraction of more desirable market segments, which further aids in differentiating the firm. However, a too-elaborate upgrade can alienate some customers, who believe the firm may be passing on the costs of the upgrade to consumers through higher prices.

Finally, differentiation can be achieved by using physical evidence to influence the attitude and behavior of contact personnel. The nature of the physical work environment and its impact on worker attitudes and performance has long been studied; numerous studies of the workplace spanning many decades have shown that lighting, temperature, noise, music, and color can all influence employee performance and job satisfaction.[7]

At the heart of such a set of differentiation strategies, there must be an understanding of how individuals, both consumers and service providers, interpret and react to their physical environment. The next section of this chapter draws on the field of environmental psychology to provide a framework for this understanding.

Individuals' Responses to Physical Settings

The study of how environments influence people provides the rationale for the field of environmental psychology. It is impossible, of course, to consider, within the context of this chapter, the whole of the literature on environmental psychology. In

Surreal but So Real

Not content to represent the vanguard of TV, movies, and literature, Beavis and Butt-head are out to change the world of retailing.

At Viacom's new flagship entertainment store in Chicago, America's fame deadbeats appear on licensed merchandise and as life-size replicas sitting on a couch. Shoppers can sit next to them to hear such insights as, "This is starting to hurt my butt," then commemorate the special moment by buying a photo of it.

It is all part of Viacom's entry into the often surreal world of entertainment retailing. Divided into individually branded boutiques, the 30,000-square-foot, two-level Michigan Avenue store sells more than 2,000 products. Consumers can buy "Clueless" nail polish in the Paramount Pictures area or wander over to the Nick at Nite boutique and buy that Lucille Ball original costume. Viacom actually sells what it calls its "showstoppers," collectibles including an original *Breakfast at Tiffany's* movie poster or a $2,800 Nickelodeon bed that comes with a hidden locker.

There are also more than 30 "experiential hooks," designed to draw consumers in and let them "experience and connect with the brand directly." On entering the Nickelodeon area, for example, shoppers are greeted with a loud belching noise. There's also a "Rant Room" where consumers can voice their opinions on videotape, to be sent to MTV for possible broadcasting.

"These flagship stores are about having to become retail theme parks, and the products are the souvenirs that consumers take home," said Scott Smith, vice president of design at Design Forum in Dayton, Ohio.

The challenge with "all this gee-whiz type of interactivity is that it has to work," he said. Indeed, during a news conference for the Viacom store opening, one of the highly hyped displays was out of commission.

"Since Viacom's brands are about attitude and lifestyle, we decided our strategy should reflect that," said Thomas C. Byrne, president of Viacom Retail Group. "So everything about the store—each brand's environment, the exclusive fashion and merchandise, the events that will take place in the stores—were designed to reflect the attitudes and lifestyles of the people who are drawn to these brands. Our overall objective was to take entertainment retailing, and retailing in general, to the next level."

Adapted from "Surreal but So Real," *Marketing News*, June 23, 1997.

general, however, the theory can be summarized in the following grossly simplified model:

$$\text{Physical Characteristics} \rightarrow \text{Intervening Cognitive/Affective Response} \rightarrow \text{Behavior or Behavioral Intention}$$

The physical characteristics of the environment generally are hypothesized to create or influence some internal state of the consumer, which in turn influences behavior within the setting or the behavioral intention toward it.

The Mehrabian-Russell Model

There is considerable variation in the nature of the hypothesized intervening variable and in the way in which the physical characteristics are conceptualized. One of the most commonly used theories in environmental psychology, the Mehrabian-Russell Model, proposes that three basic emotional states mediate behavior in environmental situations: pleasure/displeasure, arousal/nonarousal, and to a lesser extent, dominance/submissiveness. In the researchers' development, the dominance dimension has been dropped to give a framework for environments, as shown in Figure 6.2.

Recent developments suggest that the dominance dimension is in some way a cognitive rather than an affective dimension. As such, it should be viewed as precursor to the other dimensions, thereby influencing the extent to which it can explain behavioral intention.

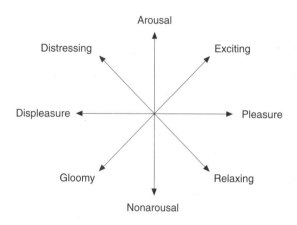

FIGURE 6.2   MEHRABIAN-RUSSELL MODEL

Mehrabian and Russell conceptualize physical characteristics at a relatively abstract level, and they conceptualize the environment in terms of the load on the individual. They argue that the load of the environment can be thought of in terms of its novelty, complexity, and spaciousness.

The Servicescapes Model

From this simple model, Bitner[8] has developed the "Servicescapes Model," shown in Figure 6.3.

This model uses the simple framework but greatly increases its power by modifying it to fit the nature of the service encounter. Most important of all, the model includes both the customer and the employee. Because services are interpersonal interactions taking place often in the same physical environment, this is logical. The output of the model is also expanded to include not only the behaviors of the individual but the nature of the social interaction. A great deal of research has been carried out on this issue, showing that physical layout especially can have a huge impact on the social interactions taking place.[9]

Finally Bitner[10] adds to the model the idea that responses to the environment can be modified by internal response moderators. Studies have, for example, shown that individual personality traits can influence a person's reaction to his or her physical surroundings.[11] Arousal-seeking is one such trait. Arousal seekers enjoy and look for high levels of stimulation. Such a trait is bound to influence an individual's perception of a servicescape.

Apart from the structural dimensions of the model, Bitner[12] also defines the different attributes in terms relevant to service firms. In terms of the physical environment dimensions, the cognitive, emotional, and physiologic responses, and the individual behaviors, she uses definitions relevant to the service firm.

In terms of the physical environmental dimension, three basic dimensions are defined: ambient conditions; space/function; and signs, symbols, and artifacts. These are the tools that marketing and operations managers can use to create the servicescape.

Ambient Conditions   Ambient conditions include background characteristics of the environment such as temperature, lighting, noise, music, and scent. As a general rule, ambient conditions affect the five senses but may not be perceived directly by the consumer or the service provider.

FIGURE 6.3 **SERVICESCAPES MODEL**

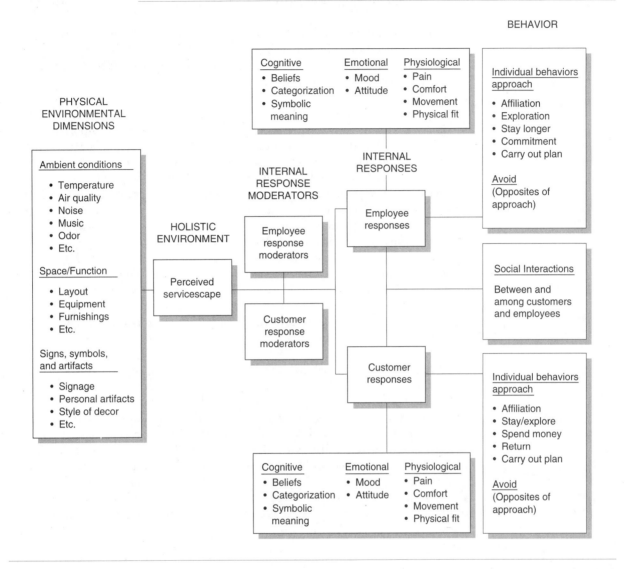

SOURCE: Mary J. Bitner, "Servicescapes: The Impact of Physical Surroundings on Customers and Employees," *Journal of Marketing* 56, 2 (April 1992), 60. Reprinted with permission of the American Marketing Association.

Just as the firm cannot be all things to all people, so the atmosphere developed will likely not appeal to all customers. Therefore, firms should develop facilities with a particular target market in mind. Experts suggest answering the following questions before implementing an atmosphere development plan:[13]

1. Who is the firm's target market?

2. What does the target market seek from the service experience?

3. What atmospheric elements can reinforce the beliefs and emotional reactions that buyers seek?

4. How do these same atmospheric elements affect employee satisfaction and the firm's operations?

5. Does the suggested atmosphere development plan compete effectively with competitors' atmospheres?

Ultimately, individuals base their perceptions of a firm's facilities on their interpretation of sensory cues. The following section discusses how firms can use the senses of sight, sound, scent, touch, and taste in creating sensory appeals that enhance customer and employee attraction response.[14]

Sight Appeals   The sense of sight conveys more information to consumers than does any other sense and, therefore, should be considered as the most important means available to service firms when developing the firm's atmosphere. Sight appeals can be defined as the process of interpreting stimuli, resulting in perceived visual relationships.[15] On a basic level, the three primary visual stimuli that appeal to consumers are size, shape, and colors. Consumers interpret visual stimuli in terms of visual relationships, consisting of perceptions of harmony, contrast, and clash. Harmony refers to visual agreement and is associated with quieter, plusher, and more formal business settings. By comparison, contrast and clash are associated with exciting, cheerful, and informal settings. Hence, based on the size, shape, and colors of the visual stimuli used and the way consumers interpret the various visual relationships, extremely differing perceptions of the firm emerge. For example, consider how different target markets might respond to entering a "Chucky Cheese" restaurant for the first time. Some segments would find the environment inviting, whereas others might be completely overwhelmed by too much stimuli.

Size Perceptions   The actual size of the firm's facility, signs, and departments conveys different meanings to different markets. In general, the larger the size of the firm and its corresponding physical evidence, the more consumers associate the firm with importance, power, success, security, and stability. For many consumers, the larger the firm, the lower the perceived risk associated with the service purchase. Such consumers believe that larger firms are more competent and more likely to engage in service recovery efforts when problems do arise. Still other customers enjoy the prestige often associated with conducting business with a larger, well-known firm. On the flip side, other customers may view large firms as impersonal and uncaring and seek out smaller, niche firms that they view as more personal, intimate, and friendly. Hence, depending on the needs of the firm's target market, size appeals differently to different categories.

Shape   Shape perceptions of a service firm are created from a variety of sources, such as the use and placement of shelves, mirrors, and windows, and even the design of wallpaper if applicable. Studies show that different shapes arouse different emotions in consumers. Vertical shapes or vertical lines are perceived as "rigid, severe, and lend[ing] a masculine quality to an area. It expresses strength and stability . . . gives the viewer an up-and-down eye movement . . . tends to heighten an area, and gives the illusion of perceived space in this direction."[16] In contrast, horizontal shapes or lines evoke perceptions of relaxation and restfulness. Diagonal shapes and lines evoke perceptions of progressiveness, proactiveness, and movement. Curved shapes and lines are perceived as feminine and flowing. Using similar and/or dissimilar shapes in facility design will create the desired visual relationship of harmony, contrast, or clash. For example, the use of several different shapes in one area might be used to distinguish an area of emphasis.[17]

Color Perceptions   The color of the firm's physical evidence often makes the first impression, whether seen in the firm's brochure, the business cards of its personnel, or the exterior or interior of the facility itself. The psychological impact of color on indi-

| TABLE 6.1 | PERCEPTIONS OF COLORS |

Warm Colors			Cool Colors		
Red	**Yellow**	**Orange**	**Blue**	**Green**	**Violet**
Love	Sunlight	Sunlight	Coolness	Coolness	Coolness
Romance	Warmth	Warmth	Aloofness	Restfulness	Shyness
Sex	Cowardice	Openness	Fidelity	Peace	Dignity
Courage	Openness	Friendliness	Calmness	Freshness	Wealth
Danger	Friendliness	Gaiety	Piety	Growth	
Fire	Gaiety	Glory	Masculinity	Softness	
Sin	Glory		Assurance	Richness	
Warmth	Brightness		Sadness	Go	
Excitement	Caution				
Vigor					
Cheerfulness					
Enthusiasm					
Stop					

SOURCE: Dale M. Lewison, *Retailing*, 4th ed. (New York: Macmillan, 1991), 277.

viduals is the result of three properties: hue, value, and intensity. Hue refers to the actual family of the color, such as red, blue, yellow, or green. Value defines the lightness and darkness of the colors. Darker values are called shades and lighter values are called tints. Intensity defines the brightness or the dullness of the hue.

Hues are classified into warm and cool colors. Warm colors include red, yellow, and orange hues, whereas cool colors include blue, green, and violet hues. Warm and cool colors symbolize different things to different consumer groups, as presented in Table 6.1 In general, warm colors tend to evoke consumer feelings of comfort and informality. For example, red commonly evokes feelings of love and romance, yellow evokes feelings of sunlight and warmth, and orange evokes feelings of openness and friendliness. Studies have shown that warm colors, particularly red and yellow, are a better choice than cool colors for attracting customers in retail settings. Warm colors are also said to encourage quick decisions and work best for businesses in which low-involvement purchase decisions are made.

In contrast to warm colors, cool colors are perceived as aloof, icy, and formal. For example, the use of too much violet may dampen consumer spirits and depress employees who have to continuously work in the violet environment. Although cool colors do not initially attract customers as well as warm colors, cool colors are favored when the customer needs time to make decisions, such as the time needed for high-involvement purchases. Despite their differing psychological effects, when used together properly, combinations of warm and cool colors can create relaxing, yet stimulating atmospheres.

The value of hues also psychologically affects the firm's customers. Offices painted in lighter colors tend to look larger, whereas darker colors may make large, empty spaces look smaller. Lighter hues are also popular for fixtures such as electrical face plates, air conditioning vents, and overhead speaker systems. The lighter colors help the fixtures blend in with the firm's environment. However, darker colors can be used to grab consumers' attention. Retailers are often faced with the problem that only 25 percent of their customers ever make it more than halfway into the store. Some retailers have had success in attracting more customers further into the store by painting the back wall in a darker color that attracts more attention.

The intensity of the color also affects perceptions of the service firm's atmosphere. For example, bright colors make objects appear larger than do duller colors. However,

TABLE 6.2	IMPACT OF BACKGROUND MUSIC ON RESTAURANT PATRONS	
Variables	Slow Music	Fast Music
Service time	29 min.	27 min.
Customer time at table	56 min.	45 min.
Customer groups leaving before seated	10.5%	12.0%
Amount of food purchased	$55.81	$55.12
Amount of bar purchases	$30.47	$21.62
Estimated gross margin	$55.82	$48.62

SOURCE: R. E. Milliman, "The Influences of Background Music on the Behavior of Restaurant Patrons," *Journal of Consumer Research* 13 (September 1986), 288; see also R. E. Milliman, "Using Background Music to Affect the Behavior of Supermarket Shoppers," *Journal of Marketing* (Summer 1982), 86–91.

bright colors are perceived as harsher and "harder," whereas duller colors are perceived as "softer." In general, children appear to favor brighter colors, and adults tend to favor softer colors.

Sound Appeals   Sound appeals have three major roles: mood setter, attention grabber, and informer.

One common example of a sound appeal is music. Studies have shown that background music affects sales in at least two ways. First, background music enhances the customer's perception of the store's atmosphere, which, in turn, influences the consumer's mood. Second, music often influences the amount of time spent in stores.[18] In another study, firms that played background music in their facilities were thought to care more about their customers.[19] The study described in the introduction suggests that music can have even more direct impact on product choice in retail settings.[20]

Studies have shown that in addition to creating a positive attitude, music directly influences consumer buying behavior. Playing faster tempo music increases the pace of consumer transactions. Slowing down the tempo of the music encourages customers to stay longer. Still other studies have indicated that consumers find music distracting when considering high-involvement purchases, yet found that listening to music during low-involvement purchases made the choice process easier. Moreover, employees tend to be happier and more productive when listening to background music, which, in turn, leads to a more positive experience for customers.

Table 6.2 displays the impact of background music on consumer and provider behavior in a restaurant setting. As can be concluded by the table, the pace of service delivered and the pace of consumer consumption is affected by the tempo of the music. Although the estimated gross margin was higher when the restaurant played slow music, the restaurant should also consider the additional number of tables that would turn over if faster-paced music was played throughout the day.

Scent Appeals   The atmosphere of the firm can be strongly affected by scents, and the service marketing manager should be aware of this fact. Scents can be related to particular products in a retail environment, such as the smell of new-baked bread in a supermarket. Such smells are, however, not truly ambient. An ambient smell pervades an environment, may or may not be noticed by consumers, and is not related to any specific product. The impact of such ambient smells has been the subject of articles in the popular press. The *Wall Street Journal* reported that pleasant scents increased lingering time in stores,[21] and it was also reported that one Marriott Hotel scents its lobby to alleviate stress.[22] Furthermore, proprietary research purportedly shows a 45 percent increase in slot machine use in scented casinos.[23]

TABLE 6.3	IMPACT OF SCENT ON STORE EVALUATIONS	
Evaluations	**No Scent**	**Scent**
Store	Mean	Mean
Bad/good	4.49	5.11
Unfavorable/favorable	4.27	5.10
Negative/positive	4.65	5.24
Dislike/like (2-point)	0.10	0.57
Dislike/like (14-point)	0.39	2.81
Image: outdated/modern	3.76	4.72
Store Environment		
Unattractive/attractive	4.12	4.98
Tense/relaxed	5.10	5.38
Uncomfortable/comfortable	4.84	5.17
Depressing/cheerful	4.35	4.90
Closed/open	4.04	4.99
Drab/colorful	3.63	4.72
Negative/positive	4.47	5.11
Boring/stimulating	3.75	4.40
Bad/good	4.22	5.05
Unlively/lively	3.73	4.35
Dull/bright	4.00	4.58
Unmotivating/motivating	3.84	4.40
Uninteresting/interesting	4.03	4.87
Unpleasant/pleasant	4.47	5.15
Merchandise		
Style: outdated/up-to-date	4.71	5.43
Selection: inadequate/adequate	3.80	4.65
Quality: low/high	4.81	5.48
Prices: low/high	5.20	4.93

SOURCE: Eric R. Spangenberg, Ayn E. Crowley, and Pamela W. Henderson, "Improving the Store Environment: Do Olfactory Cues Affect Evaluations and Behaviors?" *Journal of Marketing* 60 (April 1996), 67–80.

A recent study of a simulated shopping experience applied a much more rigorous experimental design to this issue.[24] The researchers manipulated the presence and absence of different ambient scents and tested consumers' evaluations not only of the store environment but also of the store itself and the merchandise within it. Table 6.3 shows the results. The differences between the means are all statistically significant at a high level, with the exceptions of the environmental measure tense/relaxed and the merchandise measure of low/high. The researchers also assessed approach avoidance and found significant differences in intention to visit the store and that respondents in the scented condition perceived that they had spent less time in the store than those subjects in the nonscent condition. Scent has thus been able to influence perceptions of time, and indeed the "no-scent" respondents perceived themselves to have spent considerably *more* time in the store than they actually did.

Spatial Layout and Functionability   Because service encounter environments are purposeful environments (i.e., they exist to fulfill specific needs of consumers), spatial layout and functionability are particularly important.[25] Spatial layout refers to the way in which machinery and other items are arranged, and functionability refers to the ability of those same items to facilitate performance. Much work has been published on spatial layout and functionability as they relate to employees but little as they relate to consumers or indeed to service providers.

SERVICES IN ACTION 6.2

Restaurants Tell All about Their Food

It sometimes seems to restaurant customers that they could eat a meal in the time it takes to describe one. In menu descriptions, especially advertising copy for uniquely ephemeral products, the origin, habitat, and method of capture of the ingredients have become the name of the game. Sophisticated restaurants now describe dishes in excruciating and sometimes inscrutable detail. Olive oil is always extra virgin, vinegar is balsamic, tomatoes are beefsteak, rabbit and trout are "farm-fresh." One Seattle restaurant not only identifies its salmon as line-caught but even names the fisherman.

"We preach that if restaurants are using Vermont maple syrup, they should say they are using Vermont maple syrup," says Gregg Rapp, president of Menu Workshop, a Seattle firm that specializes in "menu engineering." The same applies to Lake Superior fish, Maine lobster, or Florida orange juice. Says Rapp, "It just makes it a better item."

"Restaurants, like any business, are constantly looking for ways to distinguish themselves," says Danny Meyer, proprietor of the Union Square Cafe and Grammercy Tavern, both in New York City. "The quality of the ingredients has become a badge of excellence." Tim Zagat, publisher of the Zagat surveys of restaurants in 35 U.S. cities, agrees that precise descriptions of what goes into a dish are helpful to diners.

Customer opinions seem divided. One woman said she liked the long descriptions; they whet her appetite, and their precise lists of ingredients make her feel as if she could duplicate the dish at home. "It's as though they're letting you in on a secret." But another begs to differ. "There's always one too many things," he says. "It's hype trying to justify the price." Grilled peasant bread? "That's toast."

SOURCE: *The Wall Street Journal*, 1986.

Signs, Symbols, and Artifacts Many items in the physical environment serve as explicit or implicit signals that communicate about the place to its users. Signs and signals can play an important part in communicating firm image as well as helping consumers find their way around the environment.

The physical characteristics of an operating environment provide consumers with the information they need to find their way, in the most general sense, around the environment. Consumers draw meaning from their setting; environmental design sends clear signals and can affect behavior radically, as recent studies of jails have shown. Jails with high levels of violence are able to reduce violence by manipulating the physical environment. Bright wall colors, such as orange, were replaced by pastels. Mirrors on sharp corners reduced congestion and barging.

Disorientation occurs when consumers no longer are able to derive clear signals from their environment. Complex operations can increase consumer fears about "getting lost," and poor legibility can lead to incomprehension or uncertainty about how a system actually works. These problems can be partially offset by consumer experience, but for new consumers, they are likely to lead to delays, anger, and frustration.[26]

Much way-finding literature focuses on the concept of control as the intervening variable. This concept, discussed in Chapter 2, suggests that individuals wish to feel in control of the situations in which they find themselves. Clearly, the sense of "knowing where you are" or "what you are being served" is closely related to the idea of control and to the physical characteristics of the environment.

Crowding, Capacity, and Control

From an operational point of view, one of the key questions is, What is the capacity of the service operation? Capacity management is a key operational task, and Chapter 3 discussed some of the operational and marketing approaches to capacity management. From the perspective of a retail service, the capacity of, for example, a restaurant can be set legally or can depend on the capacity of the kitchen. However, capacity can also be determined by the perceived level of crowding.

The relationship between the density of individuals in a setting and perceived crowding is a classic of the complexity implied by the "servicescapes" model. Crowding is an emotional and psychological response. Individuals experiencing crowding demonstrate signs of stress including palm sweating and find the experience unpleasant. The onset of perceived crowding, however, does not depend only on physical density. Individuals can experience high levels of density at a football game and yet not trigger the crowding response. However, those same individuals will immediately exhibit crowding symptoms if someone yells "fire." The intervening variable again is perceived control. As long as they feel in control, density does not equate to crowding. When control is threatened by the density of the crowd, then the crowding response results.

The capacity of a restaurant can be driven by the density of the customers. However, if they are distracted and/or the situation is clearly signaled and predictable, the crowding response may not occur. Thus, even an apparently objective capacity can be manipulated by the servicescape.

Waiting in Line Blues

The alternative solution to a crowded retail service environment is a queue. Having the consumers "wait in line" provides an operational buffer for the "manufacturing" operation. The unpleasantness of the crowding may, however, be merely replaced by the unsatisfactory waiting experience. Here again, the psychology of queuing shows that even an apparently objective waiting time is actually subjective and influenced by the servicescape.

In one study, the researchers were able to compare actual waiting time with perceived waiting time. Moreover, they manipulated whether the respondents were distracted during the wait and whether the length of wait was known in advance. Distraction was provided by an electronic newsboard placed so that respondents could see it while waiting in line. Predictability was manipulated by changing the newsboard so that it showed the expected time of the wait. Thus the servicescape of the queue was changed and the researchers were able to compare results for three groups: those with no manipulation, those with distraction, and those with predictability.[27]

Newsboard installation did not significantly affect perceived waiting times, nor the amount by which respondents overestimated their waits. Nor did it affect how customers rated the length of the wait on a ten-point scale. What it did do was make the wait more palatable. Interest level increased and perceived boredom while waiting dropped. After the newsboard had been removed, many customers noticed and asked that the bank bring it back.

The electronic clock appeared to influence perceived waiting time and overestimation of the waiting time. Perceived waiting times were lower, and the respondents with the queuing time estimate overestimated their waiting time to a lesser extent.

At a more general level, Maister[28] proposes eight principles that organizations can use to influence customers' satisfaction with waiting times:

- Unoccupied time feels longer than occupied time.

- Preprocess waits feel longer than in-process waits.

- Anxiety makes waits seem longer.

- Uncertain waits are longer than known finite waits.

- Unexplained waits are longer than explained waits.

- Unfair waits are longer than equitable waits.

- The more valuable the service, the longer individuals will wait.

- Solo waiting feels longer than group waiting.

In each case, his principles imply that time is subjective rather than objective and can be manipulated through the servicescape. Other authors have taken these principles and converted them into suggestions for managers.[29]

1. Do not overlook the effects of perceptions management: consumer concern about waiting is growing.

2. Determine the acceptable waiting time for your customers.

3. Install distractions that entertain and physically involve the customer. Keep the content light-hearted.

4. Get customers out of line.

5. Only make individuals conscious of time if they grossly overestimate waiting times.

6. Modify customer arrival behavior.

7. Keep resources not serving customers out of sight.

8. Segment customers by personality types.

9. Adopt a long-term perspective.

10. Never underestimate the power of a friendly server.

Questions

1. What are the main design differences between high customer contact and low customer contact services?

2. What are the negative effects of putting service employees into uniform? Use examples from your own experience as a customer or provider?

3. What is the impact of music on the customer, the provider, and the encounter?

4. Give examples of successful and unsuccessful attempts to create a servicescape.

Notes

[1]Richard B. Chase and Douglas M. Stewart, "Making Your Service Fail-Safe," *Sloan Management Review* 35 (Spring 1994): 35–44.

[2]Edgar Schein, "Organizational Socialization and the Profession of Management," *Industrial Management Review* 9 (Winter 1968): 1–16.

[3]Michael R. Solomon, "Packaging the Service Provider," in Christopher H. Lovelock, ed., *Managing Services Marketing, Operations, and Human Resources* (Englewood Cliffs, NJ: Prentice-Hall, 1988), 318–324.

[4]Ibid.

[5]Ibid.

[6]Ibid.

[7]E. Sundstrom and Mary Graehl-Sundstrom, *Work Places* (Cambridge: Cambridge University Press, 1986).

[8]Mary Jo Bitner, "Servicescapes: The Impact of Physical Surroundings on Customers and Employees," *Journal of Marketing* 56,2 (April 1992): 650.

[9]Joseph L. Fargas, *Social Episodes* (London: Academic Press, 1979).

[10]Bitner, "Servicescapes."

[11]Russel Toms and Jacalyn Snodgrass, "Emotion and the Environment," in Daniel Stokols and Irwin Altman, eds., *Handbook of Environmental Psychology*, Vol. 1 (New York: Wiley, 1997), 245–281.

[12]Bitner, "Servicescapes."

[13]Philip Kotler, "Atmosphere as a Marketing Tool," *Journal of Retailing* (Winter 1973–1974): 48.

[14]Dale M. Lewison, *Retailing*, 4th ed. (New York: Macmillan, 1995).

[15]Ibid.

[16]Kenneth M. Hills and Judith E. Paul, *Applied Visual Merchandising* (Englewood Cliffs, NJ: Prentice-Hall, 1982).

[17]Kenneth M. Hills and Judith E. Paul, *Create Distinctive Displays* (Englewood Cliffs, NJ: Prentice-Hall, 1974).

[18]J. Barry Mason, Morris L. Mayer, and J. B. Wilkinson, *Modern Retailing: Theory and Practice*, 6th ed. (Homewood, IL: Irwin, 1993).

[19]Ronald E. Milliman, "Using Background Music to Affect the Behavior of Supermarket Shoppers," *Journal of Marketing* 56, no. 3 (Summer 1982): 86–91; see also Douglas K. Hawse and Hugh McGinley, "Music for the Eyes, Color for the Ears: An Overview," in David W. Schumann, ed., *Proceedings for the Society for Consumer Psychology* (Washington, DC: Society for Consumer Psychology, 1988), 145–152.

[20]*The Times*, November 18 1997, p. 11.

[21]Joanne Lipman, "Scents That Encourage Buying Couldn't Smell Sweeter to Stores," *Wall Street Journal*, January 9, 1990, B5.

[22]C. Miller, "Research Reveals How Marketing Can Win by a Nose," *Market News* 25 (February 4, 1991): 1–2.

[23]Cyndee Miller, "Scent as a Marketing Tool as Retailers—and even a Casino—Seek Sweet Smell of Success," *Marketing News* 27 (January 18, 1993): 271–272.

[24]Eric R. Spangenburg, Ayn E. Cowley, and Pamela W. Henderson, "Improving the Store Environment: Do Olfactory Cues Affect Evaluations and Behaviors?" *Journal of Marketing* 60 (April 1986): 67–80.

[25]Bitner, "Servicescapes."

[26]Richard E. Wener, "The Environmental Psychology of Service Encounters," in John A. Czepiel, Michael R. Solomon, and Carol F. Surprenant, eds., *The Service Encounter* (Lexington, MA: Lexington Books, 1985), 101–112.

[27]Karen Katz, Blair Larson, and Richard Larson, "Prescription for the Waiting in Line Blues," *Sloan Management Review* (Winter 1991): 44–53.

[28]D. W. Maister, "The Psychology of Waiting in Line," *Harvard Business School Note* 9-684-064 (rev. May 1984): 2–3.

[29]Katz, Larson, and Larson, "Prescription for the Waiting in Line Blues."

7

The Service Employees

Chapter Overview

More than 45 million people (or roughly 42 percent of the U.S. workforce) are employed in serving food, selling merchandise in retail stores, performing clerical work in service industries, cleaning hospitals, schools and offices, or providing some other form of personal service. These are the occupations that accounted for most of the U.S. job growth in the 1980s, a pattern that will continue at least until the turn of the century. Yet for the most part, these jobs are poorly paid, lead nowhere, and provide little if anything in the way of health, pension and other benefits.[1]

The service providers are the human face of the organization and are required to provide excellent service. They are caught between the organization and the customer and are expected to cope with all the ensuing conflicts of their roles (see Chapter 4). In return for achieving this miracle, they are paid virtually nothing and have no career prospects.

It is little wonder therefore that service jobs often have extremely high levels of staff turnover. In 1989, 119,000 sales jobs turned over within the retail network of the Sears Merchandise Group. The cost of hiring and training each new sales assistant was $900, or more than $110 million in total, a sum that represented 17 percent of Sears' 1989 income.[2] Even this figure does not represent the true cost of employee turnover. In a 1990 study, Philips[3] highlighted the additional costs of disruptions to work relationships of high turnover. He quoted the Merck Corporation, which had calculated that combining disruption costs with more traditional transaction costs meant that getting employees on and off the payroll cost an average of 1.5 times an employee's salary and that eliminating turnover therefore had a payback period of less than one year.

The purpose of this chapter is to talk about the management of contact personnel. Human Resources policies can be shown to have a direct relationship with the outcomes experienced by customers and to have an indirect relationship on the climate created within the organization. Despite this, many firms are still stuck in a model of human resources management based on old manufacturing models of cost minimization. Current thinking is looking for ways to break out of this mindset and in particular to use empowerment or enfranchisement to break the mold. Such approaches can be very powerful, but only in certain settings.

Human Resources Policies and the Customer

Schneider[4] argued that service organizations are open systems and that the policies and practices of the organizations, as well as the climate or culture those policies created, would be visible to the consumer. Schneider and Bowen[5] provide even more conclusive proof of this proposition. They relate empirically a range of internal variables to the experience of the consumer. The key relationships are highlighted in Table 7.1.

The data in Table 7.1 relate employees' perception of the organization in terms of both its climate and its procedures to outcomes perceived by customers of that organization. The customer experience indicators are relatively straightforward, but some of the employee perception indicators warrant further explanation. The *managerial behavior* factor listed under service climate includes items relating to branch managerial behavior concerning planning, organizing, and managing service. *Customer attention* includes a number of items to assess the behaviors in the branch demonstrating the importance of customers to the branch.

TABLE 7.1	STATISTICAL SIGNIFICANT CORRELATIONS BETWEEN EMPLOYEE AND CUSTOMER PERCEPTION DATA

Employee Perceptions	Customer Experiences					
	Overall Quality	Courtesy/ Competency	Utility/ Security	Adequate Staff	Employee Morale	Branch Admin
Service Climate						
Managerial behavior	*				*	*
Systems support	*				*	*
Customer attention	*				*	*
Logistics support	*			*		
HRM Practices						
Work facilitation	*	*		*	*	*
Supervision	*				*	*
Organization career facilitation						
Organizational status	*				*	*
New employee socialization	*				*	
Overall quality	*	*	*	*	*	*

The Human Resource Management (HRM) practices are relatively straightforward. *Work facilitation* measures organizational and job attributes that facilitate and inhibit task performance. *Organizational career facilitation* uses factors that assess the organization's practices concerning employee career growth, and *organizational status* includes the image employees believe the organization has in the eyes of outsiders.

The table highlights the crucial role both climate and HRM practices have in determining customers' perception of quality and employee morale. Moreover, customers' assessment of the administration of the organization is related directly to administrative practices and the staff's perception of these practices. For these branches, at least, the organization is an "open system."

Human Resources Policies and Climate or Culture

Schneider and Bowen[6] stress the importance of the climate created within the organization and its importance in supporting or inhibiting good service. Climate is conceptualized as employee perceptions of one or more strategic imperatives. A passion for service within the organization would therefore lead to a climate that sets service as the key strategic imperative.[7]

In previous studies, such a climate has been shown to be strongly associated with positive outcome variables for customers. But what are the signals within the organization that can trigger such a perception for service contact personnel?

When service commitment is high, the service unit reveals a passion for doing things directly related to the provision of service. Employees speak often and favorably about the service delivery process and the product offered to consumers, as well as about the concern for and/or responsiveness of the unit to customer opinions.

HRM issues also feature strongly in creating a passion for service within the organization. When this passion is strong, employees speak favorably about performance feedback, internal equity of compensation, training, and staff quality. Even the physical design of the setting can have an influence, with service passion being associated with excellent office conditions and facilities and automation systems.

SERVICES IN ACTION 7.1

Pre-Opening Training at the Sheraton Palace Hotel

The Sheraton Palace Hotel had been closed for a two-year, $150 million refurbishment and now faced the task of training some 300 staff members to ensure a successful opening. Sheraton's management knew that, after reopening, they would need to increase room rates to recoup their investment. Higher room rates, in turn, would lead to higher service expectations on the part of customers. Sheraton set about trying to meet those expectations.

With the assistance of a professional training consultancy company, Sheraton began working with its department managers and supervisors two and a half months before the reopening. The first step was to develop generic service manuals for some 50 hotel jobs. Next, the trainers began customizing job guidelines based on how each department manager believed the job would work. This meant that managers had to think through the process of staff training *before* staff were hired or even interviewed. The plan was to use bilevel training so that managers would train staff to the standards they themselves had helped develop.

Every job description, from host to front-desk person, was divided up and analyzed in detail. Step-by-step procedures were developed for each procedure that each employee would carry out. Once standards were in place, department managers learned how to walk their staff members through each procedure in "train the trainer" seminars conducted by the training consultants and the hotel's own training director.

Before the hotel finally opened, management arranged a three-day simulated opening with half the managers playing the role of guests and half the staff performing their specified jobs. The management team "guests" received the full range of the hotel's services, including checking in, using room service and the hotel restaurant, using laundry services, and calling an engineer to examine the room thermostat. Each "guest" acted according to a scenario worked out in advance by the human resources department and the trainers. Internal procedures, such as cashiering and accounting, also were tested.

The result was that, by the time the hotel's doors opened for real, all systems had been tested and the bugs had been worked out. Staff knew their roles explicitly and were fully prepared to offer the kind of service that would meet or exceed customer expectations.

SOURCE: Based on Jennifer J. Laabs, "Sheraton Remodels a Hotel and a Service Plan," *Personnel Journal*, 70, no. 8 (August 1991), 35.

Creating the Right Type of Organization

HRM practices are the key levers available to senior management for creating a type of organization that can be a source of sustainable competitive advantage. At the same time, front-line customer contact jobs are designed to be as simple and narrow as possible so that they can be filled by anyone—in other words, idiot-proof jobs. Employers place few demands on employees, selection criteria are minimal, and wages are low.

The result is the classic cycle of failure.[8] Fewer and less knowledgeable contact persons are available, and hence the customer gets less and lower-quality help. The customers vent their feelings of impatience and dissatisfaction on the staff, which in turn demotivates the employees, especially the most conscientious ones because they are already aware of the poor service they are being forced to give. The best staff leave and are replaced with poorly trained recruits, and the cycle continues.

What prevents service firms from breaking out of this cycle? The argument seems to be that they are locked into the old manufacturing logic, which argues that, all things being equal, it is better to rely on machines, systems, and technology than on people.[9] Machines, it is believed, are more efficient and productive and cost less to run. More important, they are easier to manage than people because they do not need to be recruited, supervised, trained, and motivated. This is, of course, the ideal logic for operations (as laid out in Chapter 3) and is applied here to the role of the contact person.

However, it is possible to break out of the old thinking and hence escape from the classic cycle of failure. To do this, the organization must build a new model that[10]

- Values investments in people as much as investments in machines and sometimes more.

Taco Bell Recruitment and Empowerment

Taco Bell's new recruitment model is based on a very simple premise: customers value the food, the service, and the physical appearance of a restaurant, and that is all. Everything that helps the company deliver value to the customers along these lines deserves reinforcement and management support. Everything else is nonvalue-adding overhead.

At the outset, Taco Bell management realized that the company could not execute the new strategy as long as its old, seven-layer organization remained in place. To compete on services and maintain low prices, the stores had to be staffed with talented, motivated individuals.

The management's view was that front-of-house jobs required staff who could take responsibility, manage themselves, and respond well to pressure from customers. Management further assumed that service workers, just like customers, come into the workplace with a wide variety of attitudes, assumptions, and expectations. Some have the potential to reach the goals set by management and to fulfill customer expectations, and some do not. The important task is to differentiate between them.

To do so, Taco Bell uses a selection process that aims to elicit prospective employees' values and attitudes toward responsibility, teamwork, and other values that have been shown to correlate with successful service. One important side effect is that the selection process has been able to identify high-potential candidates regardless of race, gender, or age.

Taco Bell complements these selective hiring policies with detailed training efforts. Revised job descriptions for the company's restaurant managers require them to spend more than half their day, or twice the time they formerly spent, on human resource matters. They now also receive training and communications support, learning about team building, performance management, coaching, and empowerment. They pass these skills on to front-line employees.

Changes in job design and supervisory style have stimulated marked improvements in employee morale. In a recent companywide survey, 62 percent of respondents said they felt more empowered and accountable; 55 percent felt they had more freedom to act independently; 66 percent felt they had the authority they needed to act; and 60 percent felt a strong sense of accountability.

SOURCE: Based on Leonard Schlesinger and James L. Heskett, "The Service-Driven Service Company," *Harvard Business Review* 65, no. 5 (September–October 1991), 71–81.

- Uses technology to support the efforts of men and women on the front line, not just to monitor or replace them.

- Makes recruitment and training as crucial for the sales clerks and housekeepers as for managers and senior managers.

- Links compensation to performance for employees at every level, not just for those at the top.

Thus the organization must use the full battery of HRM policies to break out of this cycle.

Successful companies that use these policies strategically[11] see training, for example, as a means to greater competitive performance. In addition to educating and motivating employees, training sessions typically provide the context in which employees commit themselves to the company and its service expectation. Once committed, employees remain loyal but also provide a source of new employees by referring their friends. Such referrals reduce recruiting costs but also dramatically increase the quality of the applicant.

Empowerment and Enfranchisement

Perhaps one of the most powerful tools to break out of the old logic is the whole area of empowerment and enfranchisement of employees. Empowerment means giving discretion to the contact employees to "turn the front line loose"[12] or as so powerfully expressed by Jan Carlson of Scandinavian Airlines: "To free someone from vigorous control by instructions, policies and orders and to give that person freedom to take responsibility for his ideas, decisions and actions is to release hidden resources that would otherwise remain inaccessible to both the individual and the organization."[13]

Enfranchisement carries this logic even further by first empowering the individual and then coupling this with a compensation method that pays individuals for their performance. The most significant and successful enfranchisement programs have occurred in the field of retailing. Here, advocates argue that it can dramatically improve sales and earnings while at the same time require less supervision from corporate management. Perhaps the most commonly used example is Nordstrom's, which pays salespersons a commission not only on what they sell but on the extent to which they exceed their superiors' projected sales forecasts. At the same time, they free salespersons of normal constraints and celebrate publicly "associates'" outstanding service accomplishments.

Empowerment encompasses a broad range of discretion that can be given to the contact personnel. *Routine discretion* is typified by employees who are given a list of alternatives actions from which to choose. The employees' list may be based on training or previous experience. *Creative discretion*, by comparison, requires the employee to develop the list of alternatives as well as choosing between them.[14] Finally, *deviant discretion* involves the performance of counter-role behaviors. These are behaviors that are not part of the employee's formal job description and are not included in management's role expectations. These are precisely the activities that often delight the customer.

Making Empowerment Work

The various factors that can actively discourage or encourage empowerment or discretion are shown in Figure 7.1. In each case, it identifies which factors are more likely to generate creative or deviant discretion rather than routine discretion. The factors break down into two broad categories: organizational factors and employee-related factors.

Organizational Factors The organizational factors considered in the framework are organizational socialization, organizational structure, organizational culture, and the control system used by the organization.

Organizational socialization is a process that leads to individuals understanding the values, abilities, expected behaviors, and social knowledge necessary for performing organizational roles.[15] In the service organization that has effectively socialized its employees, a clear understanding of the context and process characteristics associated with the employees' role will facilitate the exercise of routine discretion.

When employees become comfortable with the role and processes, they are more able to cope with novel and different tasks and to exercise creative discretion. The self-confidence of socialization creates the capacity to act outside of the role, to do what is best for the customer.

Organizational structure is considered in three aspects: formalization, centralization, and complexity. The more formal the organization, the more likely it is that service-worker discretion will be confined to the routine, because in highly formalized organizations, even creative discretion would be seen as deviant. As organizations decentralize, they have the opportunity to become less formal, and therefore the probability of creative and deviant discretion increases. In general, greater organizational complexity is characterized by greater specialization of labor, narrower spans of control, and longer chains of command.[16] Each of these is more likely to drive employees toward the routine end of the discretion operation.

FIGURE 7.1 ANTECEDENTS OF EMPOWERMENT

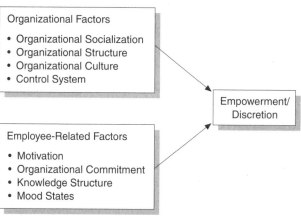

Organizational culture is the shared set of assumptions about the functioning of the organization.[17] The culture provides the service manager with an ad hoc means of conveying expected service delivery standards to employees. Culture is closely related to the ideas of Schneider,[18] and in fact, the culture and climate concepts overlap. Using Schneider's distinction between a "climate for services" and a "bureaucratic climate," it is clear that the climate or culture sends some of the strongest signals to the employees about their desired behavior with regard to discretion.

Control systems are one of the key sources of a climate or culture. They are used to monitor, direct, and evaluate performance and can be categorized as either behavior-based or outcome-based. Behavior-based systems involve high levels of activity monitoring, a great deal of managerial discretion, and subjective evaluation of activities. Outcome-based systems, by comparison, are characterized by low levels of monitoring, little managerial discretion, and objective measures of outcomes achieved by individuals.

In service organizations, behavior-based control systems focus on task performance during the process of service delivery. The high levels of activity monitoring are more likely to produce routine rather than creative or deviant discretion from employees. Conversely, outcome-based systems will result in greater discretion.

Employee-Related Factors Several employee-related factors contribute to the level of discretion exercised. These are motivation, organizational commitment, knowledge, and mood states.

Motivation has a direct impact on discretion, because creative and deviant discretion require higher levels of effort. High levels of motivation should therefore be associated with high levels of activity.

Organizational commitment can be defined as the strength of an individual's involvement and identification with an organization.[19] It is generally believed to result in the acceptance of organizational goals and values. As service employees become more committed to an organization, it is therefore possible for managers to allow them more discretion, because they are more committed to the goals of the organization.

Knowledge clearly has an impact on both the ability of the service provider to use routine discretion and the self-confidence to use higher-level discretion. High levels of discretion are logically associated with experienced employees, who have a large repertoire of scripts on which to draw.

Disney World

One of the keys of Disney World's success has been the consistently high quality of service provided by the theme park's many employees. Disney World places a high priority on attracting good people to work for it, training and preparing them thoroughly before they start their jobs, and motivating them to want to do well.

Disney World is an entertainment business, and management has adopted show-business terminology. The personnel department is the "casting" department, employees are "cast members"; those who work in contact with the public are "on stage," and those who work out of sight of the public are "backstage." No difference is made between on-stage and backstage employees; management emphasizes that the skills of both are needed to "put on the show."

Combined with this showbiz metaphor, there is an emphasis on hosting, rather than serving or controlling. All employees in the theme park have the word *host* in their job title; waiters are referred to as "food and beverage hosts," and street cleaners as "custodial hosts." Customers always are referred to as "guests."

When new cast members are hired, they are provided with written information about their training program, telling them when and where to report, what is expected in terms of personal appearance, and the length of each training phase. Every new employee, from junior staff to senior management, must attend the company's training school, Disney University. The first part of the curriculum is called Traditions 1, where new employees learn the Disney philosophy of business, the company's history, and how the various theme-park divisions, such as operations, food and beverage, and entertainment, work together to "put on the show."

Each group attending Traditions 1 has a photograph taken, which is printed on the front page of the weekly employee newspaper, *Eyes and Ears*. The newspaper provides news about employee activities, educational and training offerings, and special benefits, along with a classified section. There are numerous pictures of employees.

Disney also has a policy of using first names only; everyone, regardless of rank or job description, is known by his or her first name, and employee name tags show only first names. To further ensure that management and staff mix and work together, each executive-level manager takes part in an annual one-week "cross-utilization" program, in which he or she works in the theme park doing basic service tasks, such as selling tickets or loading and unloading rides. This program is meant to give managers greater insight into the role of both staff and guests.

Disney World hires many part-time employees for the busy summer season. When the season is over, each of these employees completes an anonymous questionnaire on subjects such as hiring practices, the orientation program, training, communications, wages, and fairness of treatment. These data help Disney World enhance and improve its personnel management policies still further. The result is an organization that, as one observer has commented, owes its success to the ways in which it looks upon people.

SOURCE: Based on N. W. Pope, "Mickey Mouse Marketing," *American Banker*, July 25, 1979, 16; N. W. Pope, "More Mickey Mouse Marketing," *American Banker*, September 12, 1979, 18.

Moods are feelings, generally ranging from positive to negative, that can mediate an individual's propensity to use discretion. Individuals in positive mood states tend to be risk-prone.

This model has direct implications for management action. Clearly, socialization of new employees is a key variable in increasing discretion. The "new starter" program run by the organization must convey the expected behaviors and roles. This provides not only socialization but higher levels of knowledge and motivation. Chapter 4 described how role ambiguity and conflict can lead to low levels of motivation.

The roles and expected behaviors signaled in the socialization process will also have an impact on the culture of the organization. As roles and behaviors become more consistent across the organization, the organization culture will become stronger.

Training can reinforce this process, while at the same time increasing the knowledge level of the service providers. Training can be tailored to the level of discretion required. Organizations aiming at routine discretion would focus training activities on tasks and procedures. Those aiming at higher levels of discretion would focus instead on the goals of the organization.

Management systems must reinforce the desired level of discretion. A "command and control" activity measurement model is unlikely to produce discretion of any kind. This is especially the case when the complicit assumption is also that the employees are in some way dishonest and need to be "policed."

Making Enfranchisement Work

Enfranchisement gives discretion over earnings to the employee as well as discretion over work. It has been shown to be very powerful in retail settings for salespersons. If empowerment changes the organizational relationships, then enfranchisement polarizes them even farther. All the job role changes described in the previous section are even more polarized. To this must be added two other key factors: equity and inadequate conditioning.

Clearly, under enfranchisement, issues such as assignment take on major equity dimensions. A particular assignment within a store or hotel can dramatically influence the income of the individuals concerned. To the extent that participants feel that the enfranchisement program is being managed unfairly, the program is wide open for criticism.

Enfranchisement may seem instantly obvious to management, but it involves large amounts of perceived risk for the participants. It violates many of the normal roles within the organization and changes the risk/reward relationship. Introducing such a program therefore requires a great deal of communication and precondition to ensure that everyone in the organization knows what the new roles are to be.

When to Empower and Enfranchise

Is there a single solution to managing the contact personnel? Do empowerment and enfranchisement always win out against the manufacturing-based models? Consider the examples of Federal Express and UPS:

> In 1990, Federal Express became the first service organization to win the Malcolm Baldridge National Quality Award. . . . Behind its blue, white and red planes and uniforms are self-managed work teams, gainsharing plans, and empowered employees seemingly concerned with providing flexible and creative service to customers with varying needs.
>
> At UPS . . . we find turned on people and profits. But we do not find empowerment. Instead we find controls, rules, a detailed union contract and carefully studied work methods. How do we find a promise to do all things for customers, . . . In fact, rigid operational guidelines help guarantee the customer reliable, low-cost service.[20]

Empowerment clearly brings benefits. Empowered employees are more customer focused and will be much quicker in responding in real time to customer needs. They will customize the product or remix it in real time.[21] Empowered employees are more likely to respond positively to service failures and to engage in Service Recovery (see Chapter 12). Fixing something after doing it wrong the first time can turn a dissatisfied customer into a satisfied, even loyal, customer.

Employees who are empowered tend to feel better about their jobs and themselves. This is reflected automatically in the way they interact with the customers. They will be genuinely warmer and friendlier. Empowerment can therefore not only reduce costs but also improve the quality of the product.

Being close to the front line, an empowered employee is continuously seeing the good and the bad things about the service operation. They can be the key to new ser-

Enfranchisement at Fairfield Inns

Fairfield Inns is a division of the Marriott Corporation with a chain of 135-room inns, the first of which opened in 1987. Rooms are priced economically, often as low as $39 per night. Fairfield's management policy is to "impress" its customers (i.e., deliver service that exceeds expectations). To do so, it carefully selects staff who have what the company considers to be appropriate attitudes and the capability to deliver two things: the friendliest atmosphere and the cleanest rooms.

The company's human resource strategies include excellent systems for selection, performance management, and incentives for employees. The focal point of these strategies is the Scorecard computer-assisted measurement system, which uses guest feedback to assess service quality. Measurement is frequent, and staff rewards and bonuses are based on performance.

Empowerment is an important feature of employment and management practices. Housekeepers, known as guest-room attendants, or GRAs, at Fairfield, are assigned to clean 14 rooms in an eight-hour workday. If the rooms can be cleaned faster, a full day's wage still is paid. On busy days, GRAs can ask for additional rooms to clean and are paid an additional half hour's wages for each room cleaned; this "overtime" is paid in cash at the end of each shift. This policy has two benefits: Fairfield is able to maintain a relatively small core of regular housekeepers, and it has staff who are motivated to increase their workload at peak times.

Housekeepers are also empowered to manage their own schedules over the longer term. They earn paid leave through regular attendance on the job, but they can maintain their attendance record on days they do not work; each housekeeper has the option of finding a trained replacement who can substitute for them.

Each inn in the chain has two discretionary budgets of $150 for each 28-day period. The first is an employee-relations budget that is spent at the discretion of the inn's managers as seen fit. The second, however, is a guest-relations budget, which is managed and spent by the employees themselves. Employees frequently show great creativity in managing customer relations; many keep records of customer preferences for return customers and will go out of their way to see those preferences are met.

Independent surveys of Fairfield Inns suggest that the company has achieved high product quality, high customer loyalty, and high occupancy rates, while maintaining a cost structure that compares favorably with its competitors. Employee turnover is 60 to 70 percent of that of competing firms. Enfranchisement programs are actually reducing recruitment costs. Fairfield further reduces costs by reducing some forms of traditional supervision; housekeeping supervisors, for example, have been eliminated. Operations costs are thus lessened and unit managers are free to spend time on more positive tasks, such as selecting and motivating employees.

SOURCE: Based on Leonard A. Schlesinger and James L. Heskett, "Enfranchisement of Service Workers," *California Management Review*, Summer 1991, 44.

vice ideas and can often be a cheaper source of market research than going to the customers directly.[22]

Unfortunately, empowerment and enfranchisement do carry costs. The balance between benefits and costs determines the appropriateness of the approach. Empowerment increases the costs of the organization. A greater investment is needed in remuneration and recruitment to ensure that the right persons are empowered. A low-cost model using cheap labor and part-time labor cannot cope with empowerment, so the basic labor costs of the organization will be higher.

If costs are higher, then there are also marketing implications. By definition, an empowered employee will "customize" the product. This means that the service received will be inconsistent, varying with the employee. It is also likely to be a slower service because it is customized.

The balance of empowerment and enfranchisement therefore comes down to the benefit concept of the organization. A branded organization that guarantees consistency of product and service dare not empower for fear of the inconsistency it would produce. What would be the implications of empowerment on McDonald's?

An organization that competes on the basis of value driven by a low cost base cannot afford to empower because of the costs involved. Equally, a high-cost service organization using a nonroutine and complex technology almost certainly has to empower because the ability to use a "manufacturing" approach is severely limited.

Implications for Marketing

Although the focus of this chapter has been on human resource policy, the servuction system implies that decisions made within one function will have implications within others. The decisions about the way the contact personnel are to be managed affects marketing at three levels: strategy, mix, and tactics.

Strategically, the role of marketing is to be actively involved in the decision on the benefit concept to be offered to consumers. That decision will determine the feasibility of empowerment or enfranchisement. Therefore, the debate is two-way because the benefit concept may have to adapt to management style preference.

An empowered organization has major implications for the marketing mix, especially for the "product." Empowerment implies high levels of customization, so where is the product designed? Clearly, the marketing group itself must take on the role of coach to the front-line staff, where the product is continually being "remixed."[23] New product development cannot be done without the active and complete involvement of the front line. These contact personnel know the customer and the system and provide a unique resource. More important, they have to be involved to maintain a sense of equity.

Reducing Role Stress with Marketing

Traditionally, marketing can cause or reduce the role stress discussed in Chapter 4, merely by the way it implements its tactics. Marketing can, without making major strategic changes, help to reduce service employee stress levels. It is in the best interests of the marketing department to do so. Clearly, unhappy, frustrated, and disagreeing contact personnel are visible to the customer, and Schneider has shown that such employees will deleteriously affect customers' perceptions of a service's quality.[24]

The contact personnel's use of any of the stress-reducing strategies described in Chapter 4 will also influence customers' perceptions of the quality of the service. Customers obviously do not like being ignored by waiters or treated as if they were inanimate objects. If the contact personnel maintain their sense of control over their encounters, there is every likelihood that it will be at the expense of the sense of control felt by customers. Finally, although we may sympathize with service providers who tell us how the organization stops them from giving good service, such a narration will reflect negatively on our perception of the organization.

Person/Role Conflicts   Conflicts between the individual and the assigned role can often be reduced simply by being sensitive to the issue. A promotional gimmick dreamed up at head office may look great on paper. A medieval theme day in the hotel will almost certainly have great public relations value. But how will the staff feel when called on to wear strange costumes? How will it affect their relationship with the hotel guests?

To improve the quality of the service, a change in operating procedure may be needed. However, it is important to ensure that the service providers are well trained in the new script. Should they not be, they may well be extremely embarrassed in the presence of customers. This situation can be aggravated if the new service is advertised so that the customers are more aware of the new script than the staff.

Organization/Client Conflicts   Marketing can similarly help to reduce conflicts between the organization and its clients. It is crucial, for example, that customer expectations should be consistent with the capabilities of the service system. Customers should not ask for services that the system cannot perform. Advertising is one of the main sources of inflated expectations, as the temptation is to exaggerate claims in advertising to maximize the impact. Consider, for example, the airline that portrayed in its advertising a stewardess reading a story to a child passenger. The ad was designed to demonstrate the friendliness of the airline. Unfortunately, in subsequent weeks a number of passengers took the advertisement literally, either because they believed it or could not resist the temptation, and called on the stewardess to read stories (see also Chapter 8).

Interclient Conflicts   Conflicts between clients can be avoided if the clients are relatively homogeneous in their expectations. In Chapter 8, we shall discuss the importance of segmentation for the success of a service—a concept based on other customers forming part of the service. In this case, however, it is the impact of two disparate groups of customers on the service providers that is crucial. As long as all clients share the same script and expect the same standard of service, the chances of interclient conflict are much reduced.

Services in Transition

Structural changes taking place in both the consumer and the employee marketplaces can have profound effects on service organizations and on their marketing strategies. Consider the case of Singapore Airlines, an organization whose competitive strategy was based on the availability of a pool of "Singapore Girls." Featured in advertising worldwide and a key component of the differentiation of the airline's in-flight service, this was a competitive advantage rooted in the nature of Singapore itself.

Now, however, the world has changed. Even when Singapore Airlines offers higher pay, a labor market crunch created by the island's high growth rate means that the supply of suitable applicants is drying up. The airline is scrambling to stay competitive in a labor-intensive business as a booming economy soaks up workers and raises costs. For the first time, the airline has changed its rules and is now rehiring flight attendants who left the company to have children.

Changes in government regulation can have unforeseen consequences for service organizations. Raising the minimum wage was a controversial issue in the United States; many economists expected this to depress the hiring of low-wage workers. However, one study, by a North Carolina State University economist, showed that the increase in the minimum wage actually increased the labor market for waiters and waitresses.[25] Unlike other workers, waiters derive most of their income from the tips that they earn. Because of this, the regulations allow restaurants to pay a special rate 50 percent below the regular minimum wage. Tip income, in turn, depends on the level of sales per waiter. This is the equation that has reversed the traditional logic.

Businesses seeking to expand will usually find that the average sales per employee falls as they add new employees until sales pick up. Tips will therefore fall, and this is traditionally offset by boosting the basic hourly wages for all such workers. However, when the minimum wage was raised, growing restaurants found they could add waiters without adjusting pay for their current serving staff. As a result, in most states the hiring of waiters and restaurants accelerated significantly in the wake of minimum wage hikes.

Perhaps the most complex set of marketing and employee issues arise when the cost base of the organization gets out of line with the competitive marketplace. For example, Delta Airlines set itself the target of only 7.5 cents per airplane seat per mile by June 1997. That represented a 23 percent reduction on existing costs and would give the airline the second lowest costs of any major airline, after Southwest Airlines.

This was a major change for the airline, which found itself with the wrong human resources policies for the new deregulated world. In the past, it was proud of its policies of lifetime employment, high pay, and high-quality in-flight service. Unfortunately, by April 1994, the airline had not shown a profit since 1990, and the issue had

Northwest Airlines: The Turnaround Bill Arrives

Northwest Airlines CEO John H. Dasburg has been flying high for the past three years. The carrier has posted record profits, paid down billions in debt, and repaired badly damaged relations with its unions. A strong economy and travel-happy consumers certainly helped. But underpinning the turnaround was a three-year employee stock ownership plan (ESOP) that staved off bankruptcy in 1993 by giving employees a 30 percent equity stake in exchange for $886 million in concessions.

Now the ESOP is drawing to a close, and Dasburg suddenly is heading into chop. Wages at Northwest Airlines will "snap back" by 12 percent, to 1993 levels, while rivals hold theirs steady or reduce them. The added cost will crimp cash flow, constraining Northwest's ability to modernize its ageing fleet and pay down the remaining $2.7 billion in debt.

Northwest's harmonious labor relations may be endangered as well. Management is determined to offset any pay hikes with work-rule changes that lift productivity. Yet union leaders want raises on top of the snap-backs already due. Dasburg is optimistic that the problems can be overcome, but management and labor have already begun to clash.

Dasburg's biggest challenge is to establish a new relationship with labor. Northwest's 45,000 employees don't see themselves as worker-owners the way those at majority-owned United Airlines do. Instead, they view the ESOP as an emergency loan to keep the company afloat. Indeed, the unions have said flatly that they do not want to renew the ESOP by taking any more pay cuts.

Nor has Dasburg built a culture of worker participation. Aside from a successful employee suggestion program, there are no task teams to reengineer work or efforts to bring workers into decision making. That is in contrast to United, which has teams tackling everything from cash management to fuel use. While today's cooperative labor relations won't unravel immediately, according to one observer, "the worry is what happens two or three years down the road when all this employee ownership is forgotten."

SOURCE: "Northwest: The Turnaround Bill Arrives," *Business Week*, August 19, 1996, 54.

---

become one of survival. However, the resultant cost-cutting was traumatic: 17,391 jobs were axed.

The marketing problems of such a situation are huge. The image of the airline must be maintained even during downsizing. Every effort must focus on identifying the impact of job cuts on the servuction process. A "climate for service"[26] can quickly become a "we follow the book" climate of bureaucracy when jobs are reduced and service providers lose faith in their employees.

Questions

1. Suggest how empowerment could be introduced into McDonald's and the implications for the customer.

2. Under what situations would you suggest that a service business other than a retailer move to enfranchisement? Why?

3. For a service business with which you are familiar, describe the human resource policies. How do these policies influence the organizational climate?

4. Based on this chapter, decide whether you would recommend empowerment in the following organizations: a repair garage and a health maintenance organization.

Notes

[1] Leonard A. Schlesinger and James L. Heskett, "The Service-Driven Service Company," *Harvard Business Review* (September–October 1991): 71–81.

[2] Dave Ulrich et al., "Employee and Customer Attachment: Synergies for Competitive Advantage," *Human Resource Planning* 14, no. 3 (1991): 89–95.

[3]J. Douglas Philips, "The Price Tag of Turnover," *Personnel Journal* (December 1990): 42–45.

[4]Benjamin Schneider, "The Service Organization: Climate is Crucial," *Organizational Dynamics* 9 (Autumn 1980): 52–65.

[5]Benjamin Schneider and David E. Bowen, "The Service Organization: Human Resources Management Is Crucial," *Organizational Dynamics* 21 (Spring 1993): 39–52.

[6]Ibid.

[7]Benjamin Schneider, Jill K. Wheeler, and Jonathan F. Fox, "A Passion for Service: Using Content Analysis to Explicate Service Climate Themes," *Journal of Applied Psychology* 77, no. 5 (1992): 705–716.

[8]Schlesinger and Heskett, "The Service-Driver Service Company."

[9]Ibid.

[10]Ibid.

[11]Ron Zemke and Dick Schaaf, *The Service Edge: 101 Companies that Profit from Customer Care.*

[12]Ibid.

[13]J. Carlson, *Moment of Truth* (New York: Balligen, 1987).

[14]Scott W. Kelley, "Discretion and the Service Employee," *Journal of Retailing* 69, no. 1 (Spring 1993): 104–126.

[15]Meryl Reis Louis, "Surprise and Sense-Making: What Newcomers Experience in Entering Unfamiliar Organizational Settings," *Administrative Science Quarterly* 25 (June 1980): 226–251.

[16]James L. Gibson, John M. Ivancevich, and James M. Donnelly, *Organizations: Behaviour, Structure, Process*, 7th ed. (Homewood, IL: Richard D. Irwin, 1991).

[17]Rohit Deshpande and Frederick Webster, "Organizational Culture and Marketing: Defining the Research Agenda," *Journal of Marketing* 53 (January 1989): 3–15.

[18]Schneider, "The Service Organization."

[19]Richard M. Steers, "Antecedents and Outcomes of Organizational Commitment," *Administrative Science Quarterly* 22 (March 1977): 46–56.

[20]From David E. Bowen and Edward E. Lawler III, "The Empowerment of Service Workers: What, Why, How, and When," *Sloan Management Review*, Spring 1992, 31–39.

[21]Martin L. Bell, "Tactical Services Marketing and the Process of Remixing," in W. R. George and J. M. Donnelly, eds, *Marketing of Services* (Chicago: American Marketing Association, 1991), 162–165.

[22]Benjamin Schneider and David E. Bowen, "New Service Design, Development, and Implementation and the Employee," in William R. George and Claudia Marshall, eds, *Developing New Services* (Chicago: American Marketing Association, 1984), 82–101.

[23]Ibid.

[24]Schneider, Wheeler, and Fox, "A Passion for Service."

[25]"The Mystifying Minimum Wage," *Business Week*, June 9, 1997, 10.

[26]Schneider, "The Service Organization."

8

Communications Strategy

Chapter Overview

By 1996, according to data from Nielsen Media Research, eight of the top ten TV advertisers in America were service firms. They included the top four—McDonald's, Burger King, Wendy's, and Sears, in that order—as well as MCI Phone Services, Baskin-Robbins, Kmart, and Olive Garden restaurants.[1] Clearly, America's large service firms are well aware of the power of advertising and communications.

Communications can have a profound effect on the service experience. They can be used in the preconsumption choice process to attract new customers, but if used wrongly in this way, they can fill a service setting with incompatible segments of customers each with different expectations and induce operational inefficiency and customer dissatisfaction.

Uniquely, services communications can be used to teach the consumer the consumption script. Communications can educate the consumer to use the service more effectively. This is particularly the case if the script is being changed.

Finally, communications have a major impact on postconsumption evaluation because they can be a source of the expectation against which perceptions are compared. Such expectations can be set by broad-ranging mass media or personal contact.

This chapter uses a single communications strategy framework to highlight the constraints and opportunities of the service experience for this key element of the marketing mix.

Setting Communications Strategy for Services

The setting of a communications strategy follows a common pattern irrespective of whether the firm is producing goods or services (Figure 8.1). The first step is to define a target audience and a clear objective for the complete communications mix. The term *communications mix* is sometimes used to describe the array of communications tools available to marketers. Just as marketers need to combine the elements of the marketing mix (including communications) to produce a marketing program, so they also need to select the most appropriate ingredients for the communications program.

The traditional elements of the communications mix fall into four broad categories: personal selling, media advertising, publicity and public relations, and promotional or information activities at the point of sale. Only personal selling is normally a two-way process. The remainder are one-way communications, from the marketer to the customer only. With services, however, the service providers at the point of communication can also have an important two-way communications role.

In addition to a target audience and a clear objective, it is also important at this stage to determine the likely total communications budget. After this has been established, the target audience or audiences, objectives, and budgets are divided among the different areas of the mix. Each area does not have to have the same task or audience, so long as together they meet the overall objective. Once this has been done, information delivery can be planned and executed and the results monitored

Defining the Target Audience for Service Communication

The target audience should flow from the overall marketing plan and from a sound understanding of consumer behavior. The target audience for the service needs to be decided early in the process or the whole service formula may become malformed. Defining the target customer for the service is thus the foundation of the service formula (see Chapter 10). Unlike goods, however, the target audience has to be much more precisely targeted.

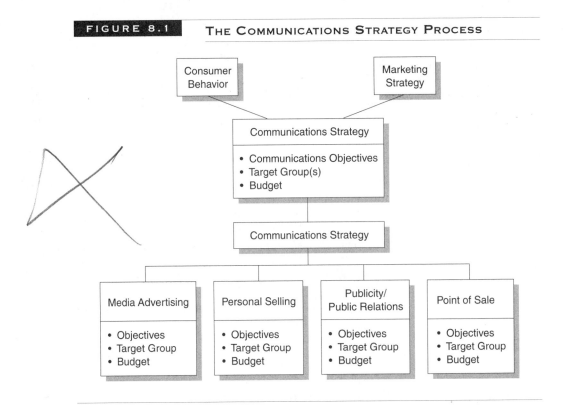

FIGURE 8.1   THE COMMUNICATIONS STRATEGY PROCESS

Although segmentation is applied in both goods and service companies, the consequences of reaching an inappropriate segment with a part of the advertising are far less serious for goods companies than for services. If the wrong group of consumers buys a particular brand of detergent, for example, it does not really affect the company making the detergent; sales are still being generated. A product may have been developed for the youth market, but through some quirk of the advertising execution or the media plan, it has attracted some senior citizens. This group visits the supermarket, buys the product, and uses it in their homes. The negative consequences to the company are few.

Suppose, however, that some of the wrong segment decides to buy a restaurant service. An up-market concept has been developed, but to launch the restaurant, management has a price promotion and the advertising agency develops inappropriate advertising. Or through poor management, publicity activity is unfocused and produces feature articles in the wrong media. The result is that the restaurant gets two types of customers: middle-aged couples and groups of students. The former were the original target; the latter were attracted by inappropriate marketing tactics. Unfortunately for the restaurant, the other customers are part of the product. The result is that neither segment enjoys the experience because of the presence of the other, and neither type of customer returns.

Advertising to Employees

The staff of service firms frequently forms a secondary audience for any advertising campaign. This is distinct from developing communications strategies directed at staff as advocated under the heading "Internal Marketing"[2]; in this case, the target group is clearly the customers. The media are not selective enough to screen out the staff, who indeed may be customers when off duty.

Clearly, advertising seen by the staff, if it empathizes with them, can be highly motivating. However, if the advertising is developed without a firm understanding of the operational problems, it can intimate service performance levels that are technically or bureaucratically impossible; that is, it can set expectation levels unrealistically high. This has a doubly damning effect on the staff because it (1) shows that the personnel who developed the advertising (the marketing department) did not understand the business, and (2) raises the prospect that customers will actually expect the service to operate that way and it will be the staff that will have to tell them that the reality differs from the advertisement. In both cases, the impact will be a negative influence on staff motivation, which will, in turn, negatively influence customer satisfaction.

Setting Communications Objectives for Services

 Communications can be used to influence any stage in the choice and consumption process: choice, consumption, and evaluation. Although communication objectives are traditionally set in terms of choice, getting more consumers to choose our brand, it is a unique characteristic of services that communications can be usefully used to impact all three phases.

The Preconsumption Choice Phase   Setting objectives in the preconsumption choice phase can be thought of as using either the risk-taking model of consumer choice or the rational mathematician model (see Chapter 2). Consumers will try to minimize the risk taken in the purchase phase. Because risk is some combination of consequences and uncertainty, these are the two dimensions along which communication can operate. In each case, the objective must be to ensure that the company's service is the one perceived to be the least risky alternative.

Communications can obviously offer information that is a key factor in reducing the uncertainty component of all risky decisions.[3] It can also seek to offer reassurance. As for consequences, these are generally thought of as being of three basic types: financial, performance, and social. Financial consequences can be reduced by communications that ensure that consumers correctly understand the likely financial consequences of a purchase, particularly if a money-back guarantee is offered. Social consequences can be reduced by highlighting the fact that other persons are using the service and that it would not be embarrassing for them to use the service. Performance consequences need to be made explicit and clearly communicated to ensure that consumers clearly understand what would happen if the performance was not 100 percent successful. Clearly, most services are perceived as more risky on the performance and social dimensions, and communications has a key role to play in reassuring consumers.

The rational mathematician model assumes consumers are rational decision makers by using a choice matrix of attributes, brand or company scores, and importance weights. Services in the evoked set are scored by using the matrix, and the one with the highest score is chosen. Clearly, communications could be used to try to influence the choice process in the following ways:

- To ensure that the firm's service offering is in the evoked set.

- To alter the weights attached to different attributes by consumers to favor those on which the company is strong.

- To alter the score on a given attribute for the company, particularly if there is a gap between performance and consumers' perceptions.

- To alter the score on a given attribute given to a competitor, again particularly if there is a gap between performance and consumers' perceptions.

- If the company is not in the evoked set, to build enough awareness of the offering to arouse inclusion.

Influencing the Preconsumption Choice Process: NASDAQ International

NASDAQ International is a London-based financial services company providing a market for European companies wishing to enter the U.S. capital market. By using several high-tech electronics systems, NASDAQ aims to put European companies into these U.S. markets as efficiently as possible, allowing them access to new sources of capital and new shareholder bases. The following advertisement was placed by NASDAQ in *Business Week* (January 21, 1991).

Targeting communications in this market requires the company to take into account several factors relating to the customer. First, the market, like all capital markets, is uncertain and efficient flows of information are vital. Second, because of the scale of investment, risk levels are likely to be high. The company must understand what customer perceptions of such a service are likely to be and should aim its advertising toward reassuring customers on all counts.

ONLY NASDAQ OFFERS YOUR COMPANY THIS MANY WAYS TO THE US CAPITAL MARKETS.

Why are so many companies entering the US capital markets?

It may be to tap new sources of finance. To take up merger and acquisition opportunities. Or simply to raise the profile of the company and its products in the world's largest market.

But whatever your own company's objectives, you'll almost certainly find that one of the NASDAQ markets is the ideal (and most cost-effective) way to go.

You may decide on a full listing on the main screen-based NASDAQ system — the third-largest stock market in the world, and by far the preferred route for ADRs issued by non-US corporations.

You may prefer PORTAL — the fast-growing electronic debt and equity market targeted specifically at institutional investors, which (under the SEC's Rule 144a) imposes minimal disclosure requirements on issuing companies.

Or you may opt for the OTC Bulletin Board — NASDAQ's automated version of the over-the-counter "Pink Sheet"

market. Here too, with modest disclosure requirements, European companies can build a valuable following among America's 50 million retail investors.

Most importantly, each offers you entry to the US capital markets for a fraction of the cost of traditional stock exchanges.

For more information, please contact Lynton Jones, Managing Director of NASDAQ International, 43 London Wall, London EC2M 5TB. Telephone: 071-374 4499 or 374 6969.

NASDAQ INTERNATIONAL

THE STOCK MARKET FOR THE NEXT 100 YEARS

54 A-E

It is important to stress that there are differences between actual performance and perceived performance. If actual performance is ahead of perceived performance, then communications may be more effective than if the reverse is the case.

Alternatively, advertising can be used to maintain a situation that is favorable to the firm. Consumers need reminding that a firm does well on particular attributes and those attributes should be regarded as important by the consumer.[4]

The Consumption Phase   During this phase, the services consumer is a more or less active participant in the production process. It is important that consumers perform that production role successfully. From the firm's point of view, successful performance will improve the efficiency of the operation and the satisfaction of other customers. From the consumer's point of view, successful performance will ensure a high level of perceived control and, in all probability, a high level of satisfaction in the postconsumption phase.

Communications, in the broadest sense, can be used to ensure successful performance by giving the consumer a clear script. The nature of this script depends on the nature of the service operation and on such factors as the levels of technology used and whether the operation has high or low levels of customer contact. The script for a single point of contact operation such as an insurance company, in which most business is done over the telephone with an agent, will vary greatly from that of an airline, in which the customer is in contact with several different employees over an extended period of time during booking, check-in, flight, and landing. Technology is also important; the script for using a bank ATM is different from that used when seeing a teller face to face over a counter. Service operations need to take these factors into account when designing the script and communicating with the customer.

In times of operational change, the management of the consumers' script takes on even more importance. An example can be seen in a bank that is changing from multiple-line queuing to single-line queuing. No longer may consumers wait in front of an individual teller window. Instead, they must form a single line and go to the first free window available to them when they are at the head of the line. Operationally, this can be shown to offer shorter and more predictable waiting times. No matter which model of consumer behavior choice we adopt, these achievements should be valued by the customer.

However, such a shift requires a change of script. Arriving at the bank without prior warning of the change, the consumer finds a new experience that no longer conforms to the existing script. It is not immediately obvious how the new system works, and the customer may feel a loss of control. The queue seems to be extremely long, and worse still, it is no longer possible to choose a specific favorite teller to provide service. Clearly, the script needs to be modified.

It is fairly obvious how the various elements of the communications mix can be used to achieve modification. Media advertising or leaflets can be used to describe the new process. "Salespersons" positioned outside the bank can explain the new system to customers before they enter. Public relations can be used to generate editorial comment about the benefits of the new system. Inside the branch, the layout and signage must clearly signal the desired customer behavior. Finally, service providers can personally reassure customers and reinforce the new script.

The Postconsumption Evaluation Phase   Chapter 2 introduced the disconfirmation model of consumer satisfaction. This model hypothesizes that consumers judge satisfaction by comparing their prior expectations of performance with the perceived actual performance.

Consumer expectations come from a number of sources, some within the control of the service firm and some outside its control. Expectations arise either from previous experience with the firm and/or its competitors or from some form of

Teaching the Consumer the Script: Wendy's Hamburgers

Wendy's, with McDonald's and Burger King, is one of the big three international hamburger restaurant chains. One of Wendy's strategies was to attempt to differentiate itself from the market leader, McDonald's, by providing made-to-order burgers rather than the standard product range featured by its competitor.

To do so, Wendy's first had to explain to customers what was required of them. The leaflet, reproduced here, was an attempt to tell customers about the servuction system at Wendy's. It presented a new and, to customers won over from McDonald's, possibly unfamiliar script. In making this script change, Wendy's cast both order-taker and customers in different roles.

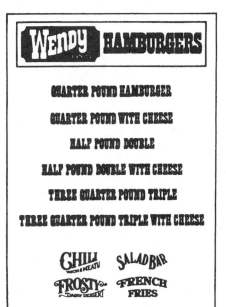

WENDY HAMBURGERS

QUARTER POUND HAMBURGER

QUARTER POUND WITH CHEESE

HALF POUND DOUBLE

HALF POUND DOUBLE WITH CHEESE

THREE QUARTER POUND TRIPLE

THREE QUARTER POUND TRIPLE WITH CHEESE

CHILI   SALAD BAR

FROSTY   FRENCH FRIES

Your recipe for a great Hamburger.

At Wendy Restaurants we don't tell you how to have your hamburger. You tell us.

The order-taker will want to know what size hamburger you'd like. A glance at the menu will help you to make up your mind. With cheese or without?

Then you've a choice of what goes on top. Mayonnaise, Ketchup, Pickle, Fresh Onion, Juicy Tomato, Crisp Lettuce, Mustard. Choose as many as you like - or have the lot - all at no extra charge.

The rest is up to us. In no time at all you'll have a pure beef hamburger that's hot, fresh and juicy - and made just the way you like it.

communication. The latter can encompass all aspects of the communications mix. Advertising, designed to influence prepurchase choice behavior, can set expectations in the customer's mind about the quality of service that will be received. Indeed, setting such an expectation may be a key aspect of a firm's advertising strategy.

Further, and often most important, expectations can be set by service providers. These are real-time expectations created during the service experience itself. They may reinforce preexisting ideas, or they may dramatically alter them. They can be set by something as explicit as a promise ("Your food will be ready in five minutes") or as implicit as a behavior pattern that sets a tone. Often such expectations are created unwittingly, as when a server promises to "be right back." Such a statement can be viewed as a both binding contract by a customer and a farewell salutation by the server.

Perceived service also has many sources. "Technical service quality" is an objective level of performance produced by the operating system of the firm. It is measurable with a stopwatch, temperature gauge, or other measuring instrument. Unfortunately, this is not the level of performance perceived by the consumer. Perception acts as a filter that moves the perceived service level up or down.

Perception is itself influenced by the same factors that dictate expectations. For example, advertising can create warm feelings toward the organization that has raised perceived service levels. Inappropriately dressed and ill-behaving staff can deliver high-quality service but be poorly perceived by the consumer, which will downgrade the perceived service level.

Communications to Influence Choice or Evaluations?

It is clear that many of the sources of expectations are under the direct control of the firm. Given such control, the firm must then determine what should be the objectives of the communications mix.

In the absence of competition, reduced expectations will result in higher satisfaction levels, provided levels of perceived service are maintained. One strategy would therefore be to reduce expectations as much as possible. Irrespective of the service actually delivered, the customer would be satisfied.

Unfortunately, communications must also be called on to play their more traditional role of stimulating demand. It is inconsistent to think of achieving this by promising bad service, even if this might minimize customers' expectations (for the few customers who use the service!).

In competitive terms, firms wish to make promises and build expectations that will differentiate them in the marketplace and cause customers to come to them and not to their competitors. The temptation is therefore to overpromise and to raise expectations to a level that is not realistic and cannot be met. It is perhaps fortunate that the variability of services is well known to consumers and that they therefore discount many such promises. When they do not, however, the result is often dissatisfied customers.

It is probably more effective to attempt to match customers' expectations to the performance characteristics of the servuction system. It is under such circumstances that the match between expectations and perceptions is most likely to be made. In such a scenario, the behavior of the customer is also most likely to conform to the script required by the operating system. There is little point, for example, in encouraging McDonald's customers to specify how well they want their hamburgers done. Not only will they be disappointed, but any attempt to meet their demands could destroy the operating system.

Dividing the Communications Objectives and Target Audiences among the Channels

Once the overall objectives and target audiences for the whole communications mix are set, it is necessary to divide the tasks among advertising, selling, publicity and public relations, and point-of-sale messages. This is a process of matching the tasks to the capabilities of the different communications channels and to the ways consumers use those channels and the different objectives.

Capabilities of Different Channels

One way of assigning tasks across the array of communications channels is to consider the degree to which the message can be targeted at specific audiences. Media advertising itself varies along this dimension. At the broadest "shotgun" level, TV advertising can reach very broad audiences but it is not very selective except in the variation in audiences across channels and by time of day. National print media such as newspapers and magazines offer more selective focus, as they themselves tend to be targeted at more specific segments of consumers.

Trade magazines are even more specific in their readership. Direct mail offers the most focused of the impersonal media. The choice among these media must be made based on the cost per thousand members of the target audience and the risk and cost of reaching the wrong segments. As mentioned at the start of the chapter, the latter is particularly important for services.

When there is a broadly defined audience and little cost of getting the wrong segments, TV advertising may work out to be the cheapest vehicle. However, it is unlikely to be efficient for a specialist service with a tightly defined target audience and a high cost of attracting the wrong segment.

Public relations and publicity can be broad or highly focused, depending on how they are used. Editorial comment can be solicited in broad or narrow media. Public relations carries with it the advantages and disadvantages of not being paid advertising. On the positive side, it is given more credence by the consumer; on the negative side, it is much more difficult to control. The content may not be as designed, or the coverage may be limited.

Both media advertising and public relations and publicity are one-way communications. They cannot respond to consumers enquiries or tailor the message to the characteristics of the receiver. Personal or telephone selling is far more expensive per member of the target audience but does offer that additional facility. If the message is difficult to communicate or a great deal of persuasion is needed, personal communication may be most appropriate: a salesforce can be highly targeted and trained to make complex arguments interactively, responding to the inputs of customers during the process.

Users can be reached through all the channels just discussed and can be further reached by communications through the service provider and the point-of-sale environment.

Understanding Consumer Information Acquisition

There are key differences in information usage between goods and services.[5] These differences are crucial to understanding how to divide the communications objectives, target audiences, and budget between the different channels. As discussed in Chapter 2, services are inherently more risky for prospective purchasers. Cox argued that the "amount and nature of perceived risk will define consumers' information risks and consumers will seek out sources, types and amounts of information that seem most likely to satisfy their particular information needs."[6]

Consumers of services are less likely to purchase without information than those buying goods. This relates to the increased perceived risk associated with services and the need for the consumer to reduce that risk by collecting information before purchasing.[7]

Consumers of services will prefer personal over impersonal sources of information. Because services are experimental, it is extremely difficult to describe or specify the "product" before purchase. It might be possible to use TV advertising to convey the experience, but it is clear that consumers prefer to obtain their information from individuals who have experienced the service directly or indirectly. This is a form of vicarious learning.[8]

Even among personal services, the high levels of risk inherent in the process mean that *consumers will give greater credibility to independent sources of information* rather than those perceived to be controlled by the firm. All this implies that word-of-mouth communication from comparable individuals is far more likely than mass advertising to be used by consumers as a source of information.[9]

However, it is possible to use advertising and other forms of promotion to leverage word-of-mouth communication.[10] Such an approach might imply using advertising and promotional tools to persuade satisfied customers to tell other consumers. Many firms, American Express, for example, have created programs to reward customers who introduce their friends and colleagues to the company. Others create material for customers to give to noncustomers. Finally, word-of-mouth communication can be used directly in media advertising, in the form of testimonials from satisfied customers.

Consumer information sources can be classified broadly into internal and external sources. Both types can be used to help consumers cope with perceived risk. Internal sources are fundamentally linked to memory scan. A study by Murray[11] clearly shows that *consumers who have had prior experience with a service are more likely to turn to their memories first before collecting new external information.*

General Guidelines for Communications Messages

The nature of services and the problems of service firms as described in earlier chapters lead to general guidelines for developing communications messages. Many of these guidelines have developed directly as a result of the intangibility, inseparability, heterogeneity, and perishability inherent in service products.

Promise What Is Possible

In its most basic form, customer satisfaction is developed by customers' comparing their expectations to their perceptions of the actual service delivery process. In times of increasing competitive pressures, firms may be tempted to overpromise. Making promises the firm cannot keep initially increases customer expectations and then subsequently lowers customer satisfaction as those promises are not met.

Two problems are associated with overpromising. First, customers leave disappointed, and a significant loss of trust then occurs between the firm and its customers. Moreover, disappointed customers are sure to tell others of their experience, which increases the fallout from the experience. The second problem directly affects the service firm's employees. Working for firms that make false promises places employees in compromising and often confrontational positions. Front-line personnel have to repeatedly explain to customers why the company cannot keep its promises. Given the link between employee satisfaction and customer satisfaction, creating expectations that cannot be met can have devastating long-term effects.

Tangibilize the Intangible

Chapter 1 described a continuum that assesses the tangible properties of the market entity, ranging from tangible dominant to intangible dominant. Interestingly, tangible-dominant market entities such as perfume use image development in their advertising schemes. From a basic viewpoint, perfume is simply liquid scent in a bottle. The customer can pick it up, try it on, and smell the perfume's fragrance. Hence, the perfume is tangible dominant. As with many tangible-dominant products, the advertising tends to make them more abstract to differentiate one product from another.[12]

By contrast, services are already abstract. Hence, one of the principal guidelines for advertising a service is to make it more concrete. This explains why insurance companies use tangible symbols to represent their companies. The product of insurance is already abstract, so it becomes the advertisement's objective to explain the service in simple and concrete terms. In addition to tangible symbols, other firms have tangibilized their service offerings by using numbers in their advertisements, such as "We've been in business since 1925," or "Nine out of ten customers would recommend us to a friend."

In tangibilizing the intangible, the scale of market entities, which reflects the degree of tangibility among products, should be turned on its ends (see Figure 8.2). The advertising of tangible-dominant products tends to make them more abstract to differentiate them from one another. In contrast, the advertising of intangible-

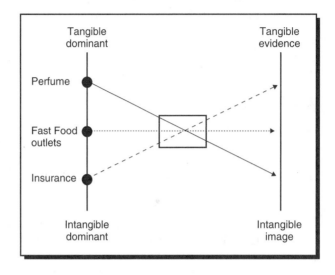

FIGURE 8.2   **THE IMPACT OF INTANGIBILITY: DIFFERENT COMMUNICATION STRATEGIES FOR DIFFERENT PRODUCTS**

SOURCE: Adapted from G. Lynn Shostack, "Breaking Free from Product Marketing," *The Journal of Marketing* (April 1977).

dominant products should concentrate on making them more concrete through the use of physical cues and tangible evidence. The advertising of products in the middle of the continuum often uses both approaches. McDonald's, for example, promotes "food, folks, and fun" in its advertisements. Food and folks are concrete, and fun is abstract.

Feature the Working Relationship between Customer and Provider

Service delivery is an interactive process between provider and customer, and it is therefore appropriate that the firm's advertising should feature, for example, a customer and a company representative working together to achieve a desired outcome. H&R Block advertising commonly shows a service provider and a customer interacting in a friendly and reassuring manner. The advertising of services, in particular, must concentrate not only on encouraging customers to buy but also on encouraging employees to perform. Clearly, advertising that illustrates the inseparability of the service delivery process should target both the customer and the firm's service providers.

Reduce Consumer Fears about Variations in Performance

The firm's advertising can also minimize the pitfalls of heterogeneity in the customer's mind. To enhance the perception of consistent quality, the firm's advertising should provide some sort of documentation that reassures the customer. Typical examples include stating the firm's performance record through numbers as opposed to qualitative testimonials. The use of "hard" numbers in advertisements reduces the consumer's fear of variability and also tangibilizes the service, as mentioned above.

Determine and Focus on Relevant Service Quality Dimensions

The reasons customers choose among competing services are often closely related to the five dimensions of service quality: reliability, responsiveness, assurance, empathy, and the quality of the tangibles associated with the service. However, some features are commonly more important to customers than others. For example, 30 percent of today's airline customers list "safety" as one of their top five considerations when choosing an airline. It would therefore seem appropriate for airlines to emphasize the assurance dimension of service quality by featuring their safety record, maintenance and training programs, and any certified aspects of their particular operations. An example of a campaign that backfired was a hotel that promoted itself as one of the tallest hotels in the world. Although this reinforced the "tangible dimension" of service quality, this particular component was not very important to customers; in fact, many who had even the slightest fear of heights avoided the hotel and the risk of being given a room on an upper floor.

Putting the Communications Mix Together

If the objective is to reach nonusers of the service at the preconsumption phase, then the choice of communications channels is limited. Media advertising can be used either directly or as a way to harness or create word-of-mouth communication in the marketplace. If the number of target customers is limited, it might be possible to use other means such as a personal salesforce or direct marketing. The decision would depend on the cost-effectiveness of the different channels and the complexity of the message to be conveyed.

By the time consumers reach the consumption and postconsumption phases, they are already part of the servuction process. On a cost/audience member basis, it would seem more logical to use the point-of-sale environment or the service provider to handle the communication.

Using the service provider as a communications channel can be very cost-effective, but there may be negative implications for operational efficiency and for levels of stress experienced by the providers themselves. An apparently simple decision, for example, to have a bank teller sell services, can have profound negative consequences. Following the logic of Chapter 4, it could well be that the decision produces role conflict for tellers. There may be role/self conflict caused by the tellers wanting to see themselves not as salespersons but as bankers, or vice versa. There may be direct conflict between the two roles when the operations role demands fast service and a minimization of the time spent with each customer, and the selling role demands the opposite.

As demonstrated in Chapters 2 and 4, there may be a breakdown in the script for both the service provider and the customer as the teller tries to do something new. The customer may be expecting a brisk, businesslike transaction and suddenly the teller wants to build a rapport (before starting to sell) by talking about the weather.

Potentially, such a decision can also diminish operational efficiency as the transaction time per customer rises. This problem is well illustrated by the problems experienced by Federal Express before it centralized its telephone customer contact system. In times of peak demand, especially if these times were unpredicted, everyone in the Federal Express depots answered telephones, including the field salespersons who were based at the depots. The result, as personnel tried to sell instead of deliver service, was that calls took much longer than usual, and the telephone bottleneck consequently worsened.

Questions

1. Collect a series of magazine advertisements for a number of firms within a service industry. What differential advantage is each firm claiming? What service level expectations is each firm setting?

2. From your own experience, choose an advertisement that you believe creates too high an expectation level. Explain why.

3. Identify advertisements that you believe would have a negative effect on the service providers within the particular service firm.

4. Identify a physical environment created by a service firm that you believe communicates the wrong script to consumers. Explain.

5. Is the concept of branding through advertising applicable to services? Why and how?

6. Identify an advertisement that runs the risk of attracting mixed segments to a service business. Explain why this may happen and state what negative consequences, if any, there are likely to be.

Notes

[1] *USA Today*, September 16, 1996, 48.

[2] See Leonard L. Berry, "The Employee as Customer," *Journal of Retail Banking* 11, no 1: 33–40.

[3] William B. Locander and Peter W. Herman, "The Effects of Self-Confidence and Anxiety of Information Seeking in Consumer Risk Reduction," *Journal of Marketing Research* 16 (May 1979): 268–274.

[4] See P. Nelson, "Advertising as Information," *Journal of Political Economy* 81 (July–August 1974): 729–754.

[5] Keith B. Murray, "A Test of Service Marketing Theory: Consumer Information Acquisition Activities," *Journal of Marketing* 55 (1991): 10–25.

[6] Donald Cox, "The Audience as Communicators," in Stephen A. Greyer, ed, *Toward Scientific Marketing*, Proceedings of the Winter Conference of the American Marketing Association (Chicago: American Marketing Association).

[7] Ibid.

[8] See J. Bettman, *An Information Processing Theory of Consumer Choice* (Reading, MA: Addison-Wesley, 1979).

[9] Ibid.

[10] William R. George and Leonard L. Berry, "Guidelines for the Advertising of Services," *Business Horizons* 24, no. 4 (July–August 1981): 52–56.

[11] Murray, "A Test of Services Marketing Theory," 10–25.

[12] G. Lynn Shostack, "Breaking Free from Product Marketing," *Journal of Marketing* 41 (April 1977): 73–88.

9

Service Pricing Policy

Chapter Overview

A group of passengers traveling from London to New York are delayed and, to entertain themselves, decide to compare the price they have paid for their tickets. To their surprise, they discover many different prices. Apart from an expected differential between first, business, and economy class, they find many variations within each class. Some booked early and paid less; others did not book and went stand-by and also paid less. Some are staying for the weekend and paid less; others bought the airfare and hotel as a package and have a different price. Some remember paying a different price when making an identical trip but at a different time of the year.

A group of train travelers discover that they too have paid very different prices for their tickets. Their pricing analysis is complicated further by the fact that some have bought season tickets allowing for unlimited travel for a period of time.

In certain parts of the world, a full-service gas station will charge more for a gallon of gasoline than a self-service station, even though the gasoline and the stations are identical.

The purpose of this chapter is to show how the need to manage the service experience, combined with its time dependency and the nature of service costs, makes the various examples of service prices described above not only logical, but profitable.

Time-Dependent Capacity and Its Impact on Pricing

The idea that services cannot be inventoried was introduced in Chapter 1, and the operations-management problems of services were explained in some detail in Chapter 3. The interaction that creates the service experience, which is what the consumer buys, takes place in real time. It is possible to create an inventory of the physical components of the service experience, but not of the experience itself.

Because consumers, in most cases, must come to the service setting to be part of the experience, this means that capacity utilization depends on when they arrive. For most services, consumers tend to arrive unevenly and unpredictably. The result is often periods of low utilization of capacity, because it is impossible to match capacity to demand.

Capacity, in turn, represents the bulk of the costs for a service. The restaurant has to be open, staffed, and stocked, even at times when it has no customers. As Dearden points out, the result is a very low level of variable costs for services and a high value attributable to incremental customers even at discount prices.[1] As a result, pricing is called on to try to smooth demand in two ways:

1. Creating new demand in off-peak, low-capacity utilization periods.

2. Flattening peaks by moving existing customers from peaks to less busy times.

Price discrimination is essential, however, if a cheap "off-peak" airfare used to shift demand is not to be available to full-fare-paying passengers. If such an exchange is possible, the result will be an overall reduction in revenue, and none of the desired movement to off-peak periods will take place.

The use of time-based price discrimination, therefore, conveys a double benefit. As well as minimizing consumer surplus and maximizing the number of customers, it also maximizes capacity utilization.

The Mass Transit Authority (MTA) in Boston attempted to reduce rush-hour crowding through pricing. The alternative would have been to invest in more capacity, which would stand idle outside the peak periods. The MTA offered a 60 percent fare discount between 10 A.M. and 2 P.M. Although the strategy did generate extra riders, those riders did not come from the peak periods and were new to the system.

The reason is fairly obvious: Most rush-hour travelers have little discretion over their time of travel, because this is dictated by their work. No matter how much they want to save money by traveling at other times, they have to be at work before 9 A.M. The program, therefore, solved one problem by helping to fill low capacity, but it did nothing to solve the underlying peak period problem.

The MTA attempted to alleviate the rush-hour problem by tackling the underlying cause. Working together with the city government and major companies, it created a staggered working-day program. By varying the start and finish of the working day, the MTA was able to smooth demand at key stations. This had economic benefits for the MTA as well as offering the commuters a more pleasant ride to work.

This is the basic argument that will be developed in this chapter and that can explain much of the proliferation of service prices. To complete the argument, the idea of consumer surplus needs to be extended to include the costs of both participation in service production and the cost of ticket acquisition. Each one of the building blocks in the argument now will be elaborated: the low level of variable costs in services, the high level of shared costs, price discrimination, and the ability to price by time of usage or reservation.

The Nature of Service Costs

When deciding on a pricing policy, the seller must be aware that the range of pricing options open to him or her is limited. Demand considerations provide a ceiling to the price that may be charged, whereas cost considerations create a price floor. The difference between what buyers are willing to pay and what sellers can afford to charge creates a vital price discretion.

This price discretion is narrowed at both ends. Sellers must consider corporate objectives, as well as costs, when setting the price floor. Merely covering costs is insufficient, because the firm needs to meet its financial objectives and generate a profit. At the other end, competitive factors usually reduce the price ceiling and often can prevent the firm from charging the full value as it is perceived by the customer.

Calculating the cost of a product raises two problems, according to Dearden:

1. Identifying which of the company's costs are relevant when calculating the profitability of a particular product.

2. Creating methods to assign relevant costs to that product.[2]

Dearden argues that, for services, the best answer to the relevance question is to consider "uniquely attributable costs." These are costs that can be uniquely attributed to the production and sale of a particular service. One way of approaching this concept is to realize that these are costs that disappear if the service is not produced.

The concept of uniquely attributable costs differs from the traditional cost-accounting distinction between variable and fixed costs. Variable costs are those costs that change with volume, assuming that the company continues to produce and market the service. The unique-cost concept assumes that no amount of the product would be produced. At zero volume, many costs can be eliminated that would have to be incurred at higher levels. Revenues minus uniquely attributable costs constitute the total profit contribution of a service for a specific period.

The uniquely attributable cost concept is necessary because of the characteristics of services. Variable costs for goods consist of such things as direct labor, material, and energy costs and some indirect labor and maintenance costs. All these vary directly and proportionately with volume. As a consequence, variable costs tend to range between 60 percent and 90 percent of total manufacturing costs.

By contrast, many service organizations have little or no direct material or labor costs and limited variable overhead costs. As a result, variable costs for these businesses represent a very small proportion of total costs. Because variable costs are so low, the financial impact of most factors affecting the volume of sales in the short run can be estimated by simply calculating the revenue impact. Variable costs, therefore, have little use in setting a pricing floor. Following the uniquely attributable cost idea, however, it is possible for a product's price to exceed its variable cost and the sale of a service to result in a loss of net worth.

Unique-cost analysis is a hierarchical process that starts with the most aggregated definition of the product and breaks this down by stages as the definition of the product is narrowed. Starting with the most aggregate definition—the business unit—the traditional profit and loss statement provides an accurate indication of costs.

The next step is to calculate the profitability of the various product lines. For this figure, it is necessary to separate the total costs into those that can be attributed to specific products and those that are joint costs. The attributable costs are determined by calculating which costs would *not* have been incurred had Service A (e.g., NOW accounts in a bank) not been produced. The difference, then, between total unique costs and total costs are the joint costs. Such a process should be sequential, starting with the business unit, then proceeding to each product group, and then breaking down each product or service into the next divisible unit until it is no longer possible to divide the product or service. It is evident that, as we move down the hierarchy, more costs become joint and, consequently, fewer costs are unique.

Although a uniquely attributable cost is likely to be higher than a simple variable cost, it is still clear that the price floor for many services can be very low. An extra customer usually will generate a large incremental profit. This is logical at an intuitive level if one considers the time-dependent nature of service capacity. However, it should not be surprising that many service firms offering an undifferentiated product can end up in deadly price wars.

Incremental customers are only valuable if the service operation has the capacity to service them. That capacity often is dictated by the quality of the experience that can be provided. There is a steep deterioration in the quality of the experience as the system reaches capacity and queries and crowds become a problem.

The problem for the service firm is that, at times of peak demand, it wants both to charge as much as possible and to be as close to the consumers' reservation prices (the maximum amounts buyers are willing to pay) as possible. Consumers exchange their money, time, and effort for the bundle of benefits offered by the service provider. Economic theory suggests that consumers will have a reservation price that captures the value they place on these benefits. As long as the total cost to the consumer is less than the reservation price, consumers will be prepared to buy. If they can purchase the service for less than their reservation price, there will be a consumer's surplus. However, in nonpeak times, there is a large opportunity to reduce price and return surplus to the consumer, but still make a profit because of the low uniquely attributable costs and the high fixed or shared costs. Such a strategy is only possible if it is possible to price discriminate.

The Nature of Service Demand

Price Discrimination and Time-Based Pricing

The reservation price idea suggests that consumers determine a price that captures the benefits they perceive in a service. The consumer's surplus is then the difference between this price and the reservation price. Such an idea is at the heart of price discrimination and time-based pricing.

Up to this point, we have assumed implicitly that a reservation price is fixed and homogeneous across the market. Segmentation theory would argue that it is more likely that the market will be heterogeneous and that different groups of consumers will put different valuations or reservation prices on a service. For example, when considering the reservation price for an airline shuttle ticket between Boston and New York City, the value placed on that ticket can vary even with the same individual. One reservation price applies to business travel, but when the traveler is paying for the ticket out of his or her own pocket, there will be a different valuation. For the airline, however, the cost of operating a particular flight will not vary because of who its passengers are. Where different groups of customers are willing to pay different prices, price discrimination can be used to set differing prices that do not reflect a proportional difference in marginal cost.

To successfully price discriminate and hence minimize aggregate consumer surplus, the following criteria must be met:

1. Different groups of consumers must have different responses to price (i.e., they must value the service differently).

2. The different segments must be identifiable, and a mechanism must exist to price them differently.

3. There should be no opportunity for individuals in one segment who have paid a low price to sell their tickets to other segments.

4. The segment should be large enough to make the exercise worthwhile.

5. The cost of running the price-discrimination strategy should not exceed the incremental revenues obtained. This is partly a function of item 4 above.

6. The customers should not become confused by the use of different prices.

It is an interesting characteristic of services that these criteria frequently can be met through the time-based nature of demand. Discrimination can be practiced by time of usage of the service or by time of reservation or ticket purchase.

Discrimination by Time of Usage

There are a number of obvious examples of price discrimination by time of usage (Services in Action 9.1). To return to the airline ticket example, it is clearly impossible to identify the business and leisure travelers separately as they approach the ticket counter. Even if they were identifiable, it would be impossible to then offer them differential prices at the same time. The fact that a Hawaiian shirt guaranteed a low ticket price would soon produce a rash of such shirts. Clearly, criterion 2 above would have been violated.

There is, however, a good surrogate for travel occasion in the *time* of travel. Business travelers are unlikely to want to travel at awkward hours (the time costs of the transaction are too high), but leisure travelers may be willing to do so. Hence, airlines can offer inexpensive late-night flights to attract leisure demand without risking price dilution.

Discrimination by Time of Reservation or Ticket Purchase

Price discrimination by time of reservation or ticket purchase has long been used by the hotel industry. Conference or group bookings offer the hotel the advantage of guaranteed demand but usually require cheaper prices. The lone traveler arriving at 6 P.M. without a reservation has, by comparison, little bargaining power and will

Sealink Cross-Channel Ferries

Sealink Ferries is one of four companies that compete in offering ferry services in several major routes across the English Channel. Sealink also operates ferry services from southern England to Brittany and to Ireland. The busiest routes are those across the narrowest point of the channel from Dover, England, to Calais, France—a distance of about 35 miles. Ferries on this route are large roll-on, roll-off vessels capable of carrying several hundred cars and up to a thousand passengers.

As with its competitors, Sealink fine-tunes its fare structure, raising fares during peak periods, such as legal and school holidays, and lowering them in mid-week and in midwinter. The accompanying exhibits show (1) the fare structure used and (2) the times at which various fares are in operation.

By adjusting its fare schedules day by day and sailing by sailing, Sealink attempts to fill both car and passenger berths that otherwise might remain empty. During peak periods, such as summer, the service is used to capacity, but in winter, and especially on the late-night sailings, demand is relatively low. The intention is to try to stimulate demand during the off-peak periods, when fewer persons take holidays and the only steady travelers are individuals going between France and England on business. These travelers obviously prefer to travel during the day.

Sealink, again in line with its major competitors, currently is facing a major challenger. Prior to this time, the only alternatives to cross-channel ferries have been airlines, which are expensive, and water-borne services such as hovercraft and jetfoils, which are at the mercy of rough weather. However, the Channel Tunnel now connects England and France by rail, with uninterrupted service that feasibly can be operated around the clock and with greater frequency than the ferries. The railway link also is considerably faster than the two-hour ferry journey. Sealink's pricing strategy now must take into account this new competition and the variation in demand patterns that it inevitably will bring.

PRICES FOR DOVER-CALAIS AND FOLKESTONE-BOULOGNE.

ALL CAR PRICES NOW INCLUDE DRIVER	STANDARD SINGLE FARE & FARESAVER 2½ DAY RETURN				FARESAVER 5 DAY RETURN			
	E	D	C	B	E	D	C	B
	£	£	£	£	£	£	£	£
CAR / MOTORISED CARAVAN / MINIBUS INCLUDING DRIVER	*FARES INCLUDE DRIVER*				*FARES INCLUDE DRIVER*			
Up to 6.00 metres in length	46.00	71.00	95.00	106.00	69.00	107.00	143.00	162.00
Over 6.00 metres, each additional metre or part metre	7.00	7.00	9.00	11.00	11.00	11.00	14.00	17.00
TOWED TRAILER / CARAVAN								
Up to 3.00 metres in length	10.00	10.00	13.00	15.00	15.00	15.00	19.00	23.00
Up to 6.00 metres in length	20.00	20.00	26.00	35.00	30.00	30.00	39.00	53.00
Over 6.00 metres, each additional metre or part metre	1300	13.00	13.00	15.00	20.00	20.00	20.00	23.00
ADDITIONAL MOTORIST PASSENGERS								
Adult	8.00	13.00	13.00	13.00	16.00	20.00	20.00	20.00
Child (4 but under 14 years)	8.00	8.00	8.00	8.00	12.00	12.00	12.00	12.00
Infant (under 4 years)	FREE	FREE	FREE	FREE	FREE	FREE	FREE	FREE
MOTORCYCLE / SCOOTER AND RIDER	30.00	35.00	40.00	43.00	45.00	52.00	60.00	65.00
BICYCLE / TANDEM (rider charged as foot passengers)	FREE	FREE	FREE	FREE	FREE	FREE	FREE	FREE
FOOT PASSENGERS								
Adult	21.00	21.00	21.00	21.00	31.00	31.00	31.00	31.00
Student	17.00	17.00	-	-	25.00	25.00	-	-
Child (4 but under 14 years)	10.00	10.00	10.00	10.00	15.00	15.00	15.00	15.00
Infant (under 4 years)	FREE	FREE	FREE	FREE	FREE	FREE	FREE	FREE
FAMILY SAVER RETURN —*NEW*								
Car and up to to 2 adults and 2 children	124.00	184.00	232.00	-	-	-	-	-

NOTES

1. FARESAVERS:
2½ DAY AND 5 DAY RETURNS
Both are return fares: The price is determined by the date, time and route of the outward sailing. The return journey may be made on any sailing departing up to a maximum of 2½ days (60 hours) or 5 days as appropriate from the time of arrival in France. (Additional charges become payable if the ticket validity is exceeded).

2. FAMILY SAVER
The price is determined by the tariff band which applies to the date and time of outward travel. The fare shown is for up to 2 adults and 2 children travelling in the same car. Additional adults and children pay the "Additional Motorist Passengers" fare. The special offer is not valid on B tariff sailings in either direction.

happily pay the full rate. Profitable hotel management therefore depends on a balancing act between capacity utilization and yield. Filling the hotel with low-rate guests who have booked six months in advance precludes higher-priced, same-day sales. However, reserving capacity runs the risk that capacity will be unused.

The airline industry uses time of reservation to tap into the leisure and business segments. Few business travelers can risk booking flights weeks in advance and often

(Continued)

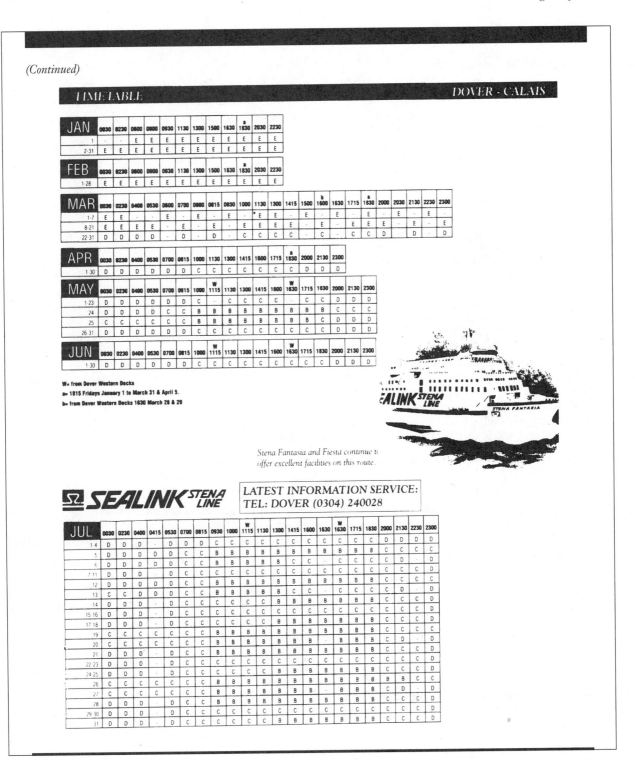

Stena Fantasia and Fiesta continue to offer excellent facilities on this route.

need to book tickets on the day of departure. Leisure travelers, by comparison, plan their trips in advance and are willing to buy tickets in advance. Discrimination is therefore possible, and low prices can be offered for early booking with little dilution of the business-traveler yield.

Both airlines and hotels have an advantage in that tickets are not interchangeable, so that cross-selling of tickets by different segments is impossible. Confusion in the

The Parker House

The Parker House in Boston is the oldest continuously operating hotel in the United States, having first opened its doors in 1855. The Parker House had experienced hard times, but after Dunfey Hotels bought the building, it was completely refurbished between 1973 and 1975, and for a time, it was the undisputed king of the Boston hotel market. The Parker House philosophy was that customers were part of the hotel's ambiance (i.e., part of the product) and great attention was paid to choosing clientele to match the hotel's mission. Management defined the hotel's market very narrowly, looking ideally for professionals and executive travelers either as individuals or companies.

Room-pricing policies were aimed at this segment. Although, because of its 19th-century design, the hotel did have several small single rooms that were low-priced, usually on a contract basis to government employees, the bulk of the rooms were relatively luxurious. The Parker House aimed to keep its prices in the top 10 percent of the local room-rate price spread, to get the right kind of customer rather than simply fill the hotel. This policy was matched closely by a strong sales effort aimed at the executive market.

Matching demand to price involved examination of the room sales efficiency (RSE) rate. Most hotels use some form of discounting to fill rooms. The RSE represents the total occupancy rate at a given time multiplied by the average percentage of the full room rate, after discounting, being paid by all guests (i.e., if occupancy is 90 percent and guests are paying an average of 90 percent of the full rate, the RSE is then 81 percent). This measure, unlike the more generally used occupancy measure, includes both occupancy and yield.

In markets where demand is high, there is a wide spread of potential customers in many different segments. RSE thus also tends to be high, as there is little need for discounting. Strategically, the hotel then tries to move the "bottom up," squeezing out the lower-priced segments by increasing room rates. Dunfey Hotels' strategic principle was that any hotel with an RSE of 85 percent or more needed a rate increase to move farther up in the market.

In 1979, the Parker House was faced with a major challenge. Three new hotels were about to open within a few miles of the hotel, all, like the Parker House, positioned in the top 10 percent price range and almost certainly planning to aim at the same market segments. The challenge facing the Parker House was how to use a combination of physical facilities and price to meet this new competition.

consumer's mind is avoided because the strategies follow an economic logic, which is consistent with the nature of service costs.

The complexity of airline pricing becomes apparent when it is realized that airlines use both of the above forms of discrimination simultaneously. Fares between a single pair of cities vary both by time of day and time of booking. Airline pricing schedules have been made even more complex by the introduction of the stand-by flight. This idea taps into yet another market segment by providing very low prices without any guarantee of a seat. As in many other service businesses, these types of strategies are driven by the nature of costs as well as by demand considerations (SIA 9.2).

Multiple Services and Price Bundling

Most service organizations provide more than one service. In recent years, the practice of bundling services has become more prevalent. *Bundling*, broadly defined, is the practice of marketing two or more products and/or services in a single package. Common examples include hotels putting together weekend packages that include meals, and sometimes entertainment, as well as lodging at an inclusive rate. Airlines routinely price vacation packages that include air travel, car rental, and hotel accommodations.

Such price bundling follows logically from both the nature of service costs and the nature of service demand. Individual services have low uniquely attributable costs and high joint costs, making the incremental cost of adding a service to a bundle very low.

On the demand side, there is interdependence as well. This stems partly from the search theory perspective on demand. Search theory provides a paradigm for examining the elasticity of demand. It argues that price sensitivity depends on the number of alternatives considered for the purchase. The fewer the number of alternatives considered, the more inelastic the demand curve will be. The number of alternatives, however, can be said to depend on the number of alternatives about which the consumer is knowledgeable.

It has been argued that the consumer's ability to obtain knowledge of alternatives depends on the nature of the attributes of the service. Three types of attributes have been defined: search attributes, experience attributes, and credence attributes.

Search attributes are characteristics that can be evaluated before purchase of a service by asking questions or looking up information, such as airline flight durations or the location of a particular restaurant. *Experience attributes* are characteristics that can be evaluated only after purchase; they include such things as the quality of a meal or the quality and speed of photo-processing services. *Credence attributes* often cannot be evaluated until some time after receiving the service and are thus experienced over time; they are particularly common in professional services such as health care or in technical consultancies.

Demand is likely to be most elastic for services that can be evaluated on the basis of search attributes. Consumers will be aware of more alternatives because such information is easier to collect. However, if service personnel themselves dictate the quality or nature of the service and if the service can be customized, consumers will be less able to evaluate the service and thus less sensitive to price differences between alternatives.

Using this framework, consider a financial institution that can create a range of services that could meet different needs for the same individual. If the services are bundled together, the time and effort needed for consumers to find information is reduced. At the same time, the data on several attributes will not be collected, and experience and credence attributes from other services may be pooled. The result is that demand is likely to be inelastic and interdependent.

Generally, services are concerned with mixed bundling, which allows consumers either to buy service A and service B together or purchase one service separately. The simplest argument for bundling is based on the idea of consumer surplus. Bundling makes it possible to shift the consumer surplus from one service to another service that otherwise would have a negative surplus (i.e., would not be purchased). Thus, the combined value of the two services is less than the combined price, even though, separately, only one service would be purchased.

This argument is made more complex if a competitive marketplace is assumed, and if the reservation price, or value, of the combined bundle is not assumed to be merely the sum of its parts. Assuming a competitive market means that the objectives of price bundling can be broadened. The combination of services A and B can be targeted at purchasers of A or B but not both, at A and B separately and concurrently, or at nonpurchasers of either A or B. Each target demands a different perspective.

Relaxing the reservation price additivity assumption is worth further exploration. Three reasons have been suggested for why the sum of the parts would have less value than the whole. First, information theory would argue that there is value to the consumer in easy access to information. Consumers of one financial service from an institution have a lower information cost when buying another service from the same institution than when buying that service from a different institution. A second case argues that the bundling of service B with service A can enhance a consumer's satisfaction with service A. Guiltinan[3] uses the example of a ski resort that offers a ski-rental and lessons package. The reservation price for the lessons is likely to be the same whether or not the skis are rented because the value of the lessons depends on the skills and needs of the skier. However, the reservation price of the ski rental will be enhanced, at least for novices, by lessons. The final argument is that the addition of service B to service A can enhance the total image of the firm. A financial planning service offering both investment advice and tax advice enhances its credibility in both services.

The extent to which there is more incremental value in a bundle than in the parts determines the price that can be charged. Ideally, the reservation prices of the separate services and of the bundle should be measured separately. A number of researchers have argued that it is possible to measure reservation prices directly by asking what is the most that consumers are willing to pay.

Alternative approaches are the utility estimation approaches, such as conjoint analysis. Although these do not attempt to measure reservation prices directly, they do measure utilities for various price/attribute combinations.

Clearly, reservation prices will vary because of institutional factors. Segmentation by occasion will be important because the reservation price of a service will depend on the use to which it is put. An airline ticket will have a different reservation price for the same individual depending on whether it is purchased for a business trip or a leisure trip.

Introducing Nonmonetary Costs into the Analysis

Thus far in this chapter, monetary and information costs have been included in the analysis. Economic theory itself has included the information costs through search theory. One of the key characteristics of services is that they may demand an effort cost from the consumer in the form of effort made during the process and during the purchase as well.

The Self-Service Consumer—Effort During the Process   It has been argued throughout this book that the consumer is, to a greater or lesser extent, part of the servuction process. In addition to providing information as a minimum input to the system, the consumer often, and increasingly, is called on to provide physical effort to aid the process.

The rationale for including the consumer in the servuction system is discussed in Chapter 3. Essentially, it is possible to reduce costs by having the consumer do part of the work. The issue then arises as to whether it is necessary to change the price to reflect the added cost of that effort to the consumer. Is it necessary for self-service gas stations to be cheaper than full-service stations?

At first sight, it would appear that a price cut is necessary to balance the consumer's value equation. However, this assumes that the consumer attaches the same benefit or value to the service delivered in two different ways. There is considerable evidence to suggest that this may not be the case.

Research suggests that consumers' response to such do-it-yourself offerings is variable. One segment of consumers would prefer to "do it themselves" even if no price incentive is offered. Conversely, there is another segment that would not use these kinds of service even for large price discounts. This segmentation is consistent with the consumer behavior discussed in Chapter 2.

The do-it-yourself consumers attach a high value to perceived control and time. They perceive that increasing their participation increases their value through a greater sense of control over the situation and lower time costs. Members of the second group of consumers see these services as equal to full-service options on control and time but lacking in "human content." The value of these services is reduced for them because of the lack of contact with service personnel.

The Effort Cost of Purchasing   Services, like goods, require effort from the consumer to acquire the right to use them. Discussions about goods focus on convenience and ensuring that goods will be "conveniently available." In a similar way, there is a transaction cost for the purchase of services. This cost is compounded in the case of frequently used services, such as transportation, in which the cumulative effort can become very large. In these situations, consumers may be prepared to buy bulk access

TABLE 9.2	FARE PREPAYMENT SCHEMES

		Maximum Number of Uses	
		Fixed	**Unlimited**
Duration of Instrument	**Unlimited**	Trip pass: "Good for 10 Trips" (e.g., Punch Card, Ticket Book)	Nonexpiring pass —Employees —Senior citizens Credit card
	Fixed	Timed trip pass: "10 Trips This Week"	Fixed duration pass Daily/monthly pass

TABLE 9.2	INCREASING AND MAINTAINING PROGRAM USAGE

	Current Regular User	**Current Irregular User**	**Nonuser**
Increasing usage	*Objective:* Get a regular user to travel off-peak more often	*Objective:* Get an irregular user to increase frequency	*Objective:* Generate usage
	Typical program: Unlimited use, fixed time	*Typical program:* Stress discount component of bulk purchase	*Typical program:* Stress reduced monetary and effort costs
Maintaining usage	*Objective:* Avoid losing a regular user because of a system failure	*Objective:* Stop an irregular user from drifting away	
	Typical program: Fixed use or long fixed duration, unlimited usage	*Typical program:* Bulk discount, ensure fixed duration or use to penalize nonuse	Not applicable

to save such costs, particularly if a bulk purchase-price discount is offered. The key components of pricing then become how, when, where, and to whom the price should be paid.

The " who, when, where, and how" of price collection is perhaps best illustrated by certain prepayment programs. These programs, frequently used by services such as transportation, minimize the nonmonetary cost for the consumer and offer bulk discounts, although they also are used to achieve service-related objectives. A simple classification of fare prepayment schemes is shown in Table 9.1. As technology has developed, it has become increasingly possible to use such systems as automatic passes. These passes offer major cost savings in fare collection in that they can be used to operate automatic turnstiles or other entry machines.

In general, the pass program must be designed to minimize the nonmonetary cost to the consumer. However, pass programs also can be used to meet other objectives. Programs can be set up to increase usage or to maintain it. They can be targeted at current regular users, current irregular users, or nonusers. A typical set of objectives is shown in Table 9.2.

Questions

1. How many different airfares would you expect to find for the Los Angeles–New York routes? Consult a price guide and document the range of fares and restrictions. Explain the logic of this fare structure.

2. A hotel will offer discounts from the basic rate for advanced, group, and weekend bookings. Why?

3. Discuss the use of pricing mechanisms to encourage the use of self-service options for consumers. Give examples.

Notes

[1]John Dearden, "Cost Accounting Comes to Service Industries," *Harvard Business Review* 56 (September–October 1978): 132–140.

[2]Ibid.

[3]Joseph P. Guiltinan, "The Price Bundling of Services: A Normative Framework," *Journal of Marketing* 51, April 1987), 74–85.

The Influence of Store Environment on Quality Inferences and Store Image

JULIE BAKER
University of Texas at Arlington

DHRUV GREWAL
A. PARASURAMAN
University of Miami

The study reported here examines how combinations of specific elements in the retail store environment influence consumers' inferences about merchandise and service quality and discusses the extent to which these inferences mediate the influence of the store environment on store image. Results show that ambient and social elements in the store environment provide cues that consumers use for their quality inferences. In addition, store environment, merchandise quality, and service quality were posited to be antecedents of store image—with the latter two serving as mediators—rather than components of store image (as they are typically treated in the store image literature). Theoretical and managerial implications of the findings are discussed, and future research directions are proposed.

Retailers facing an increasingly competitive marketplace are finding it more difficult to differentiate their stores solely on the basis of merchandise, price. promotion, or location. The store itself, however, can offer a unique atmosphere, or environment, that may influence the consumer's patronage decision (Kotler 1973). Consumers interact with retailing environments during virtually all household purchases they make (Sarel 1981), and many consumers make decisions at the point of purchase (Keller 1987). Thus, in-store elements such as color, lighting, style, or music may have more immediate effects on decision making than other marketing inputs that are not present at the point of purchase (e.g., advertising). A key role store environment plays is to provide informational cues to customers about merchandise and service quality (Gardner and Siomkos 1985; Olson 1977; Zeithaml 1988).

Store environment has also been found to be one of several inputs into the consumer's global store image, or overall attitude toward the store (e.g., Lindquist 1974, Darden, Erdem, and Darden 1983; Zimmer and Golden 1988). Furthermore, store image is an important part of the store choice decision (e.g., Stanley and Sewall 1976; Nevin and Houston 1980; Malhotra 1993), Darden, Ordem, and Darden (1983) found that consumers' beliefs about the physical

Julie Baker is an assistant professor of marketing at the University of Texas at Arlington. She received her Ph.D. from Texas A&M University. Her areas of interest include store environment, consumer behavior, and product/service quality. She has published articles in the *International Journal of Research in Marketing* and the *Journal of Retailing*.

Dhruv Grewal is an assistant professor of marketing at the University of Miami. He received his Ph.D. from Virginia Polytechnic Institute and State University. His areas of interest include pricing, consumer behavior, product/service quality, and customer satisfaction. He has published articles in a number of journals, including the *Journal of the Academy of Marketing Science, Journal of Marketing Research, Journal of Consumer Research, Journal of Public Policy and Marketing,* and *Journal of Retailing*.

A. Parasuraman holds the James W. McLamore Chair in Marketing, University of Miami. He received his D.B.A. from Indiana University in 1975. His research interests focus on the measurement and improvement of service quality and on services marketing strategy. He is the recipient of several teaching and research awards. In 1989, he was selected as one of the ten most influential figures in quality by the editorial board of *The Quality Review*. His articles have appeared in the *Journal of Marketing, Journal of Marketing Research, Journal of Services Marketing,* and *Business Horizons,* among other publications. He is the author of *Marketing Research,* a college textbook, as well as coauthor of *Marketing Services: Competing through Quality* and *Delivering Quality Service: Balancing Customer Perceptions and Expectations.* He is also an active consultant to a number of major corporations.

Journal of the Academy of Marketing Science. *Volume 22, No. 4, pages 328–339. Copyright © 1994 by Academy of Marketing Science.*

attractiveness of a store had a higher correlation with patronage intentions than did merchandise quality, general price level, or selection.

The store image literature also treats merchandise quality and service quality as key variables influencing store image (e.g., Hildebrandt 1988; Mazursky and Jacoby 1986). Additionally, merchandise and service quality evaluations are critical inputs to the consumers' decision-making process (Dodds, Monroe, and Grewal 1991; Zeithaml 1988). Thus the literature suggests that there are linkages between store environment, merchandise and service quality, and store image. We propose that these linkages are established through the process of inference making. In particular, we posit that consumers make inferences about merchandise and service quality based on store environment factors and that these inferences, in turn, influence store image. The inference-making perspective is consistent with Mazursky and Jacoby's (1986, p. 147) definition of store image that has been adopted for this study: "a cognition and/or affect (or a set of cognitions and/or affects), which is (are) inferred, either from a set of ongoing perceptions and/or memory inputs attaching to a phenomenon (i.e., either an object or event such as a store, a product, a "sale," etc.), and which represent(s) what that phenomenon signifies to an individual."

In the store image literature, store environment and store image are viewed as different constructs, in that the former has been treated as one of several (e.g., price, quality, selection, location) components of the latter (e.g., Lindquist 1974; Zimmer and Golden 1988). We are proposing, however, that store environment, merchandise quality, and service quality are antecedents of store image rather than components of store image. We are also proposing that rather than having a direct influence on store image, store environment indirectly influences store image through merchandise and service quality inferences. That is, merchandise and service quality inferences mediate the relationship between store environment and store image.

Past research has focused on a general construct called "store atmosphere" rather than on understanding how specific store elements may be combined to create a particular environment. For example, Mazursky and Jacoby (1986) provided pictures of a store's interior as cues for consumers to use in judging merchandise and service quality but did not describe the characteristics of this store. The term "physical attractiveness" used in the Darden, Erdem, and Darden (1983) study was similarly undefined in terms of specific environmental elements. The purpose of the research reported here, therefore, was to examine how combinations of specific elements in the store environment influence inferences about merchandise and service quality as well as the extent to which these inferences mediate the influence of store environment on store image.

The next section reviews the relevant literature on store environment and presents the hypotheses investigated in this study. A $2 \times 2 \times 2$ between-subjects design is then described. We manipulated the store ambient factor (prestige-image vs. discount-image), the store design factor (prestige-image vs. discount-image), and the store social factor (prestige-image vs. discount-image) through videotapes. This experimental approach enabled us to enhance the study's internal validity and complemented past research that primarily manipulated store environment using verbal descriptions (e.g., Gardner and Siomkos 1985). Analysis of variance procedures used to test the hypotheses are discussed next. Finally, the theoretical and managerial implications of the study are presented, along with limitations and avenues for future research.

Literature Review and Research Hypotheses

Inference Making Based on Environmental Cues

Evidence from environmental psychology supports the notion that people form inferences about a focal object or person based on environmental cues. Sadalla, Vershure, and Burroughs (1987) found that subjects were able to correctly infer a homeowner's self-concept from looking at pictures of that person's dwelling. Contemporary judges were able to discriminate appropriately among the nineteenth-century homes of different socioeconomic groups, identifying the status of the original owners from photographs of their houses (Cherulnik and Wilderman 1986).

Similar results have been reported in the marketing literature. Bitner (1990), for example, found that subjects formed attributions about service failures based on the physical environment of a travel agency. In another study, customers' inferences about the prototypicality of restaurants were strongly influenced by environmental cues (Ward, Barnes, and Bitner 1992). Likewise, a study of bank customers showed that expensive-looking facilities would prompt customers to infer that the bank was inappropriately spending their money (Baker, Berry, and Parasuraman 1988).

Consumers with incomplete information about merchandise or service quality tend to base purchase decisions on inferences they make from various information cues (Bloom and Reve 1990; Nisbett and Ross 1980; Zeithaml 1988). The retail store environment offers a multitude of stimuli that can serve as cues to consumers looking for this information-processing shortcut or heuristic. For example, a store with thick carpeting, low-level lighting, and muted, but fashionable, colors may lead customers to infer that the store sells high quality merchandise, or offers high quality service.

The inferences of interest in the present study pertained to merchandise and service quality. Merchandise quality and service quality have been identified as critical components in the consumer's decision-making process (Dodds, Monroe, and Grewal 1991; Kerin, Howard, and Jain 1992; Zeithaml 1988). Additionally, quality is a determinant of store image (Lindquist 1974; Mazursky and Jacoby 1986; Zimmer and Golden 1988). The marketing literature contains limited empirical research on the linkages between specific environmental elements, or combinations of elements, and inferences about merchandise and service quality. The following sections review the extant literature and develop the hypotheses tested in the study.

Effects of Store Environment on Merchandise and Service Quality Inferences

The retail store environment has a major influence on consumers' inferences about merchandise quality (Darden and Schwinghammer 1985; Olshavsky 1985). Mazursky and Jacoby (1986) found that pictures of a store's interior were second only to brand name in being the most heavily accessed of several cues from which consumers could choose to evaluate merchandise quality. Research on the effects of color in retail environments has shown that subjects inferred merchandise in a warm-colored environment to be more up-to-date (arguably one dimension of merchandise quality) than merchandise in a cool-colored environment (Bellizzi, Crowley, and Hasty 1983; Crowley 1993). In a study using verbal descriptions of store environments, Gardner and Siomkos (1985) found that subjects evaluated perfume more favorably when it was sold in an environment with a prestige image (e.g., soft lighting, "mood" music, carpeting, clean and large dressing rooms, wide aisles, nicely dressed salespeople) than when it was sold in an environment with a discount image (e.g., harsh lighting, no music, linoleum floors, dirty and small dressing rooms, narrow aisles, sloppily dressed salespeople).

Consumer inferences about service quality can also be influenced by the retail store environment. This assertion is consistent with work by Parasuraman, Zeithaml, and Berry (1988) that identified elements of the physical environment (e.g., up-to-date equipment, visually appealing facilities, well-dressed and neat employees) as important "tangibles," a key component of service quality. Rys, Fredericks, and Luery (1987)

concluded that environmental factors were the most important cues to consumers judging restaurant quality. In a study by Crane and Clarke (1988), respondents who were asked to list the cues they used to assess the nature and scope of four service providers (doctor, bank, hairstylist, and dentist) indicated that the physical facilities were one type of cue they relied upon. In yet another study, patients who did not have prior knowledge of a physician's reputation appeared to depend on tangible attributes (e.g., the physician's office) to evaluate the physician's competence—one aspect of quality (Baumgarten and Hensel 1987).

A number of environmental elements can affect consumer inferences of merchandise and service quality. Baker (1986) has developed a typology categorizing the elements into three broad groups: ambient factors, design factors, and social factors. The first column of Table 1 presents illustrative elements for the three groups of factors. The remainder of Table 1 demonstrates that specific characteristics associated with prestige-image and discount-image stores in past studies, and those suggested in retailing textbooks and trade publications, can be fit into Baker's (1986) three-category framework.

Based on the framework illustrated in Table 1, this study developed and tested hypotheses addressing the effects of specific store environmental factors on quality inferences. Because the store environment is an entity consisting of multiple elements, consumers' inferences are likely to be based on combinations of these elements, rather than based on only one or two. To provide a realistic store setting, multiple elements representing each factor (ambient, design, and social) were manipulated to create the prestige-image and discount-image conditions. The nature of the factors, and the experimental manipulations and hypotheses pertaining to them, are discussed next.

Store Ambient Factor

Ambient factors are nonvisual, background conditions in the environment, including elements such as temperature, lighting, music, and scent (e.g., Milliman 1982, 1986; Ward and Russell 1981; Wineman 1982; Yalch and Spangenberg 1990). Based on studies already reviewed, environmental effects were hypothesized for both merchandise-quality and service-quality inferences. Lighting levels and music were the elements chosen to operationalize the ambient factor in this study because they were identified in the literature as contributing to store image and because they can be controlled easily by retailers. The prestige-image ambient environment had soft, low-level lighting and played classical music, whereas the discount-image ambient environment used bright

TABLE 1
Characteristics of Prestige-Image and Discount-Image Store Environments

Characteristic	Prestige-Image	Discount-Image	Authors
Ambient factors			
Music	Classical	Top 20	Golden and Zimmerman, 1986 Gardner and Siomkos, 1985
Lighting	Soft/dim	Bright/harsh	Golden and Zimmerman, 1986 Morris, 1985 Gardner and Siomkos, 1985
	Incandescent	Fluorescent	Golden and Zimmerman, 1986
Smell	Not available	Popcorn	Gallager and Cornwall, 1985
Design factors			
Floor covering	Pile carpeting	Linoleum/cement	Berman and Evans, 1989 Gallager and Cornwall, 1985 Gardner and Siomkos. 1985
	Hardwood	Vinyl	"Flooring Choices'" 1987
Wall Covering	Textured/flocked	Paint	Berman and Evans, 1989
Displays/fixtures	Not available Disguised/decorated	Bins Exposed	Golden and Zimmerman, 1986 Berman and Evans, 1989
Color	Gold, silver, black Up-to-date Classifier Neutral/monochromatic	Not available Dated Declassifier Vivid	Golden and Zimmerman, 1986 Birren, 1945 McFarland, 1989 Foote, 1983
Cleanliness	Clean	Dirty	Gardner and Siomkos, 1985
Ceilings	Sheetrock and decorative	Not available and painted	"Chains Respond" 1985
Dressing rooms	Private Large	Semi-private or none Small	Berman and Evans, 1989 Golden and Zimmerman. 1986
Aisles	Wide	Narrow	Berman and Evans, 1989 Golden and Zimmerman, 1986 Gardner and Siomkos, 1985
Layout	Free-form	Grid	Burstiner, 1986
Signs	Discreet	Apparent	"Big Y" 1987
Social factors			
Salespeople	Nicely dressed Cooperative	Sloppily dressed Uncooperative	Gardner and Siomkos, 1985 Berman and Evans, 1989

lighting and Top 40 music (Gardner and Siomkos 1985; Golden and Zimmerman 1986; Morris 1985). A pretest was conducted confirming that the music types were perceived as representing prestige- and discount-image stores for the student subjects used in the study. Both the music selections chosen had a slow tempo, to avoid any possible tempo effect. It was hypothesized that

H1: Consumers will infer higher merchandise quality in a prestige-image ambient environment than in a discount-image ambient environment.

H2: Consumers will infer higher service quality in a prestige-image ambient environment than in a discount-image ambient environment.

Store Functional/Aesthetic Design Factors

Design factors are store environmental elements that are more visual in nature than are ambient factors. These elements may be functional and/or aesthetic in nature (Marans and Spreckelmeyer 1982). Functional store elements include layout, comfort, and privacy.

Aesthetic elements include factors such as architecture, color, materials, and style. In addition to evidence reviewed previously, studies have shown that design elements in the environment influenced individuals' evaluations of people and objects (e.g., Campbell 1979; Morrow and McElroy 1981; Zweigenhaft 1976) and that service-setting design affected consumer perceptions and attitudes about that service (McElroy, Marrow, and Eroglu 1990). For example, the color used within a store was found to affect consumer evaluations of the store and the merchandise it carried (Bellizzi, Crowley, and Hasty 1983). Wheatley and Chiu (1977) demonstrated that consumers evaluating carpet samples perceived a darker shade of carpeting to be of higher quality than a lighter shade of carpeting.

The aesthetics of the prestige-image design environment were operationalized in this study with the use of gold metallic accents on displays (Golden and Zimmerman 1986). Moreover, this environment employed a peach and green color scheme that was popular at the time of the study. A manipulation check confirmed peach and green to be currently fashionable colors (see the appendix for the item pertaining to this attribute). A free-form layout (Burstiner 1986) in the front area of the store operationalized the functional aspect of the prestige-mage design environment. Dated colors (neutral beige and white), lack of gold accent trim, and a grid layout were used in the discount-image design environment. It was hypothesized that

> **H3:** Consumers will infer higher merchandise quality in a prestige-image design environment than in a discount-image design environment.

> **H4:** Consumers will infer higher service quality in a prestige-image design environment than in a discount-image design environment.

Store Social Factor

The social factor involves the people who are within a store's environment. Russell and Snodgrass (1987) noted that the physical presence of another person is an important part of any environment. The number, type, and behavior of other customers and sales personnel in the environment are elements of the social factor.

Several studies have shown that crowded conditions that involved other customers in a retail store negatively affected their inferences (e.g., Eroglu and Harrell 1986; Harrell, Hutt, and Anderson 1980; Hui and Bateson 1991). Sociological theory regarding understaffing sug-

gests that the number of employees influences consumer inferences (Wicker 1973). Understaffing is a condition that occurs when the number of people in a facility is less than the setting requires, resulting in an environment that does not function as it should. According to the understaffing perspective, more sales personnel will be present in a prestige-image social environment than in a discount-image social environment. Mazursky and Jacoby (1986) found that the number of salespeople per department was a critical cue in evaluating service quality.

Furthermore, a prestige-image store is likely to have nicely dressed salespeople, whereas a discount-image store is likely to have sloppily dressed salespeople (Gardner and Siomkos 1995). Berman and Evans (1989) suggested that a prestige-image store would have cooperative salespeople and a discount-image store would have uncooperative salespeople. These social characteristics are consistent with research that defined tangibles (e.g., employee dress), responsiveness (e.g., cooperative employees), and empathy (e.g., employees willing to give customers personal attention) as being important components of service quality evaluation (Parasuraman, Zeithaml, and Berry 1988).

The literature also suggests a linkage between the social factor and merchandise quality. Gardner and Siomkos (1985) found salesperson dress (as a component of high-image vs. low-image store) influenced quality evaluations of perfume. Similarly, Hildebrandt (1988) showed that "good staff," as a component of store atmosphere, was associated with product quality. More directly, the number of salespeople and cashiers per department were used as cues in judging merchandise quality (Mazursky and Jacoby 1986).

The study reported here used store personnel to represent the social factor. The prestige-image social environment had three salespeople on the floor, whereas the discount-image social environment had only one. To incorporate a request to the researchers from a regional sales manager for the store chain used in the study, sales personnel wearing professional-looking aprons were used to operationalize the dress component in the prestige-image condition, whereas no aprons were worn in the discount-image condition. As a cue to salesperson cooperativeness and willingness to give personal attention, a salesperson at the entrance to the store greeted customers in the prestige-image condition, whereas no greeting occurred in the discount-image condition. It was hypothesized that

> **H5:** Consumers will infer higher merchandise quality in a prestige-image social environment than in a discount-image social environment.

H6: Consumers will infer higher service quality in a prestige-image social environment than in a discount-image social environment.

The Mediating Effect of Merchandise and Service Quality on Store Image

Olshavsky (1995) suggested that store image may serve as a cue to the quality of a brand and vice versa. Merchandise quality, styling, price, assortment, locational convenience, sales clerk service, general service, store environment, and pleasantness of shopping have been identified as components of store image (e.g., Lindquist 1974; Mazursky and Jacoby 1986). These studies have examined the effects of merchandise quality, service quality, and store environment as components of store image. Our model refines and extends the literature by proposing that merchandise and service quality are antecedents of rather than components of store image and that they mediate the relationship between store environment and store image. This view is consistent with the study's definition of store image as a cognition/affect that is inferred from a set of perceptions (Mazursky and Jacoby 1986) and with the suggestion of Greenberg, Sherman, and Schiffman (1983) that the relationship between store environment and store image is mediated by consumer inferences. Therefore, it was hypothesized that

H7: The relationships between store environment factors (ambient, design, social) and store image are mediated by merchandise quality and service quality inferences.

Figure 1 provides a pictorial summary of the hypotheses proposed and tested in this study. It also depicts store image as a cognition/affect that is influenced by inferences stemming from store environment cues, as suggested by the store image definition adopted for this study.

Research Method

Overview of Experimental Design

The hypotheses were tested in an experiment in which ambient, design, and social factors were manipulated in a card and gift store to achieve the prestige-image and discount-image conditions. Thus the study employed a 2 (Prestige vs. Discount Ambient) × 2 (Prestige vs. Discount Design) × 2 (Prestige vs. Discount Social) between-subjects factorial design.[1] Each factor was

FIGURE 1

The Influence of Store Atmospherics on Store Image

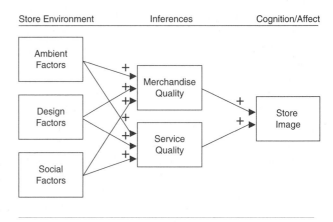

operationalized with more than one environmental element (the specific elements used are summarized in Table 2). The selection of these characteristics was determined by the retailing and store-image literature, two focus groups (one student and one nonstudent), and the remodeling effort of the store participating in the study. In addition, two pretests confirmed the effectiveness of the manipulations.

Five types of music—classical, Top 40, country-western, oldies, and easy listening were pretested for their associations with prestige-image and discount-image stores. The respondents (157 students) each listened to all five selections and used 7-point scales to rate how likely it was that each selection would be heard at prestige-image and discount-image stores. The five selections were rank-ordered. The classical selection ranked as the music most associated with prestige-image stores. The discount-image selection (Top 40) was actually the second lowest-ranked music but was chosen because this music was deemed more likely to be used by a card and gift store than was country-western, which was the lowest prestige-image music. A second pretest (64 students) was conducted to ensure that the operationalizations of the store environment factors were perceived by the subjects as intended. Results of this preliminary investigation indicated that the attributes used to manipulate the ambient, design, and social factors were appropriate.

Experimental Procedures Used

A laboratory experiment was conducted with 297 undergraduate students (35 to 39 students per treatment) enrolled in marketing courses at a large state

TABLE 2

Experimental Treatments

Characteristic	Prestige-Image Store Environment	Discount-Image Store Environment
Ambient factors		
Music	Classical	Top 40
Lighting	Soft	Bright
Design factors		
Color	Green/peach	Brown/white
Brass trim on displays	Yes	No
Layout	Open	Grid
Organization of merchandise	Neat	Messy
Social factors		
Number of salespeople	3	1
Greeting by salesperson	Yes	No
Salesperson dress	Apron	No apron

university. Shopping in a card and gift store, the context used in this study, is within the realm of consumer experience for these students (98% of the subjects indicated that they had shopped in a card and gift store).

The store shopping experience was simulated using videotapes. This protocol has been found to be effective for examining the effects of the environment on customer perceptions (e.g., Bateson and Hui 1992; Carpman, Grant, and Simmons 1985; Hershberger and Cass 1974). The store that was shown on the videotape was a card and gift store located in a large mall. This store underwent extensive remodeling, offering a unique opportunity to study different environmental effects within the same store setting. Familiarity effects were avoided as the store was located in a different city than were the subjects. Eight experimental versions of the store were created to represent all combinations of the prestige- and discount-image levels of the three environmental factors. For example, the treatment that represented the prestige-level operationalization of each factor (ambient, design, social) included classical background music, soft lighting, a green/peach color scheme, an open layout, brass trim on display units, and three salespeople with aprons who greeted the "customer." An example of a treatment that combined prestige and discount levels of the factors was one that included classical background music, soft lighting, a green/peach color scheme, an open layout, brass trim on display units, and one salesperson without an apron who ignored the "customer."

Small groups of subjects viewed the videotape, which visually "walked" them through the store environment. All eight videotapes were the same length (about 5 minutes), and they were equivalent in terms of the path taken through the store. This path differed slightly between the videotapes shot before and after the store was remodeled. Specifically, the remodeling changed the location of the checkout counter and the arrangement of the displays in the front part of the store. After viewing the videotape, subjects were asked to complete a self-administered questionnaire that contained the study measures.

Measures

A questionnaire was developed to measure merchandise quality and service quality inferences as well as store image. A systematic review of the quality and store-image literatures provided a basis for developing scale items for each construct (e.g., Gutman and Alden 1985; Mazursky and Jacoby 1986; Morgan 1985; Parasuraman, Zeithaml, and Berry 1988; Sherry and McGrath 1989). The questionnaire was pretested on several groups of undergraduate students, and refinements were made based on the results of the pretests.

Because the card and gift store carries several types of products (e.g., cards, gifts, party items, gift wrap) that may elicit different quality inferences, it was decided to instruct the study respondents to focus only on the gift category when completing the questionnaire. This decision was made based on pretest respondents' comments that a more general term such as "merchandise" denoting all products in the store was confusing. Cards were viewed by these respondents as a commodity item with little variability in quality, whereas gifts were perceived to have more quality variation. Thus to ensure sufficient variation in the measured constructs, gifts were chosen as the focal merchandise in testing the hypothesized relationships.

Respondents were instructed to think about gift items such as figurines, brass items, and decorative accessories for the home as a category when answering questions. Overall quality inferences for the gift category were measured rather than quality inferences for any specific gift item.

The reliabilities of the three multiple-item scales used to measure the model constructs were evaluated by calculating coefficient alphas (merchandise quality = .72, service quality = .84, and store image = .81). The specific items are provided in Table 3. The results of a principal components factor analysis with varimax rotation supported a three-factor solution (see Table 3). The three factors had eigenvalues greater than 1.00 and accounted for 66.9 percent of the variance in the items.

TABLE 3
Factor Analysis Results

	Item	Principal Component Loadings		
		Factor 1	Factor 2	Factor 3
	Merchandise quality inferences			
1.	Gifts purchased from this store would be high in quality.	.12	.23	*.82*
2.	The workmanship of gift purchased in this store would be high.	.21	.16	*.84*
	Service quality inferences			
3.	Customers could expect to be treated well in this store.	*.66*	.22	.32
4.	Employees of this store could be expected to give customers personal attention.	*.70*	.23	.36
5.	This store's employees would be willing to help customers.	*.83*	.15	.14
6.	This store would offer high-quality service.	*.74*	.31	.21
7.	Employees of this store would not be too busy to respond to customers' requests promptly.	*.71*	.14	−.09
	Store image			
8.	This store would be a pleasant place to shop.	.18	*.73*	.27
9.	The store has a pleasant atmosphere.	.38	*.70*	.11
10.	This store is clean.	.19	*.77*	.05
11.	The store is attractive.	.15	*.81*	.23
	Eigenvalue	5.00	1.29	1.08
	Percentage of variance explained	45.4	11.7	9.8

NOTE: A 7-point scale (1 = *strongly disagree* to 7 = *strongly agree*) was used to assess each of the items.

Analysis and Results

Manipulation Checks

Subjects evaluated the ambient factor using a three-item scale (alpha = .90), the store design factor using a four-item scale (alpha = .78), and the store social factor using a four-item scale (alpha = .83). The scales used to conduct the manipulation checks are provided in the appendix. The results of a principal components factor analysis supported a three-factor solution. The three factors accounted for 70 percent of the variance. Thus these results support the three store-environment factor typology suggested by Baker (1986).

The results indicated that the prestige-image and discount-image manipulations are effective for all three environmental factors: ambient ($\bar{X}_{discount} = 3.83$ vs. $\bar{X}_{prestige} = 5.42$, $F(1, 249) = 73.71$, $p < .001$), design ($\bar{X}_{discount} = 5.35$ vs. $\bar{X}_{prestige} = 5.61$, $F(1, 295) = 5.56$, $p < .05$), and social ($\bar{X}_{discount} = 3.76$ vs. $\bar{X}_{prestige} = 5.07$, $F(1, 293) = 89.55$, $p < .001$).

Hypothesis Tests

The hypotheses were tested using ANOVA, ANCOVA, and regression procedures. The results, summarized in Table 4, are discussed next.

Ambient Factor The results indicate that the prestige ambient environment enhances subjects' inferences of merchandise quality ($\bar{X}_{discount} = 9.42$ vs. $\bar{X}_{prestige} = 10.16$, $F(1, 286) = 10.18$, $p < .01$) and service quality ($\bar{X}_{discount} = 23.61$ vs. $\bar{X}_{prestige} = 26.12$, $F(1, 286) = 17.86$, $p < .01$). Thus the ambient effect on merchandise and service quality inferences proposed in H1 and H2 is supported.

Design Factor The results indicate that the design factor does not influence either merchandise quality or service quality inferences. Thus support is not found for H3 and H4.

Social Factor The results indicate that the prestige social environment enhances subjects' inferences of merchandise quality ($\bar{X}_{discount} = 9.53$ vs. $\bar{X}_{prestige} = 10.05$, $F(1, 286) = 4.78$, $p < .05$) and service quality ($\bar{X}_{discount} = 24.31$ vs. $\bar{X}_{prestige} = 25.40$, $F(1, 286) = 3.32$, $p = .07$). Thus H5 is supported and H6 is marginally supported.

Mediation Tests Procedures suggested by Baron and Kenny (1986) and Hastak and Olson (1989) were followed to assess whether merchandise quality and service quality inferences mediate the effects of the environmental stimuli (ambience, social, and design) on store image. Baron and Kenny (1986)

TABLE 4
ANOVA and Mediation Analysis

	ANOVA: Merchandise Quality (F values)	ANOVA: Service Quality (F values)	ANOVA: Store Image(F values)	ANCOVA: Store Image(F values)
Ambient factor (A)	10.18***	17.86***	9.66***	.32
Design factor (D)	.00	.27	.24	.73
Social factor (S)	4.78**	3.31*	5.08**	1.23
A × S	.07	.65	1.33	1.14
A × D	.06	1.95	3.21*	1.91
S × D	.11	.55	1.79	1.31
A × S × D	.59	.02	.87	.68
Covariates:				
Merchandise quality				24.03***
Service quality				71.28**

NOTE: The ANOVA and ANCOVA analyses each had one degree of freedom. The error had 286 degrees of freedom for ANOVA analyses and 284 degrees of freedom for ANCOVA analysis.

*$p < .10$; **$p < .05$; ***$p < .01$.

recommended that three conditions need to be satisfied between the independent variables (environmental factors), mediators (merchandise and service quality inferences), and the dependent variable (store image) to establish mediation.

First, the independent variables (environment factors) need to affect the mediators (merchandise and service quality inferences). The previous results provide evidence that the ambient and social environment factors significantly affect merchandise and service quality inferences. The results, however, do not support the hypothesized direct effect of the design factor on merchandise and service quality inferences. Thus we could not assess the mediation hypothesis for the design factor.

Second, the independent variables (environmental factors) need to affect the dependent variable (store image). As shown in Table 4, ambient and social factors do affect store image, $p < .01$.

Third, the mediators (merchandise and store quality inferences) need to affect the dependent variable (store image), while the effects of the independent variables (store environment factors—ambient, social, and design) are reduced. The analysis of covariance results indicate that when the two mediators (i.e., merchandise and service quality inferences) are treated as covariates, the effects of the ambient and social factors on store image are virtually eliminated. Furthermore, the effect of these two mediators (covariates in the ANCOVA results) are significant, $p < .01$.

The effects of merchandise and service quality inferences on subjects' store image were also examined using regression analysis, $F(2, 291) = 82.88, p < .001$, adjusted $R^2 = .36$. The results show that as subjects' merchandise quality inferences and service quality inferences increase, their store image perceptions are enhanced (merchandise quality: beta = 0.44, $t = 8.44$, $p < .001$; service quality: beta = 0.26, $t = 4.90, p < .001$).

The above results clearly support the notion that merchandise and service quality inferences mediate the effect of two store environmental factors (ambient and social) on subjects' store image. Thus H7 is supported for the ambient and social factors.

Discussion

This study integrated concepts from marketing and environmental psychology to develop and test a theoretically based model of the cognitive influence of the store environment on inferences of merchandise and service quality and of store image. The findings suggest several theoretical and managerial implications. The potential limitations of the study also offer an agenda for further research.

Theoretical and Managerial Implications

From a theoretical perspective, this study makes two important contributions to the marketing literature on store environment. First, it is one of the few that examines how a combination of specific atmospheric elements influences consumers' inferences about merrchandise and service quality. Managers and researchers alike have recognized that store environment is an important marketing tool and that quality inferences influence consumers' purchase decisions (Sherowski 1983). The extant literature, however, offered little insight into the linkages between specific environmental elements and quality inferences. This study constitutes a modest beginning in terms of filling this void in the literature.

The second theoretical contribution is the refinement of the relationships between store environment, merchandise and service quality, and store image. Conceptual and empirical research to date has identified merchandise quality, service quality, and store environment as components of store image (Lindquist 1974; Mazursky and Jacoby 1986; Zimmer and Golden 1988). The results of this study add to the extant literature by suggesting that the relationship between store environment and store image is mediated by merchandise- and service-quality inferences (i.e., store environment, merchandise quality, and service quality are antecedents of store image, with the latter two serving as mediators rather than components of store image).

For store managers, the study results suggest that ambient and social elements in the store environment provide cues upon which consumers base their quality inferences. Classical music and soft lighting (the ambient elements used in this study) led to inferences that the merchandise and service quality would be higher than did Top 40 music and bright lighting. The store with the prestige-image social factor (more sales personnel on the floor, wearing aprons, and greeting customers) resulted in inferences of higher service quality than did the store with the discount-image social factor (one salesperson on the floor, wearing no apron, and not offering a greeting). Although the generalizability of these findings to other types of store settings has yet to be established, these elements are relatively easy and inexpensive for managers to test and change within their own stores. Moreover, the finding that design factors—the most permanent of the three sets of environment factors—do not have a significant effect on quality inferences has an important message for managers: regardless of design features such as store layout and architecture, managers can improve customers' quality inferences by upgrading the ambient and social factors.

The lack of significant findings regarding the design factor needs to be verified in other store settings because it is possible that for the card and gift category, consumers do not perceive enough difference in physical characteristics across stores. Thus the context may not have been robust enough to test all the relationships in the model. It is also possible that the original (discount-image) store environment was seen as acceptable and/or that the new design did not provide a noticeable difference (the design manipulation was weaker than the ambient and social manipulations). In any case, the lesson for store managers is that if they are planning to spend large amounts of money remodeling their stores, they need to determine in advance if the design changes will contribute to their marketing objectives. Managers could use techniques such as prototypes, videotaping, renderings, and computer-aided design to ascertain the potential impact of alternative store designs.

Finally, the finding that merchandise- and service-quality inferences mediate the relationship between store environment and store image seems to offer additional support for the suggestion above pertaining to the need for aligning decisions about store atmospheric elements with the retailer's marketing and store image objectives. All ambient, design, and social elements need to be orchestrated so that consumers make the appropriate quality inferences. For example, the use of thick pile carpeting or classical music in a discount store is likely to send a wrong, or confusing, message to consumers about the quality of merchandise or service they might expect.

Limitations and Future Research

There are several potential limitations to the study. These limitations, along with the study's findings, also suggest directions for future research.

Although the study results generally support the proposed model, the results are necessarily limited to the study's context. For instance, as already acknowledged, the card and gift store context may not have been robust enough to test the impact of design factors on quality inferences. Future research is needed to explore the effects of store environment on quality inferences in other store types (e.g., discount, department, other types of specialty stores) and for other product categories (e.g., luxury items, durable goods, pure services). Additional store elements also need to be examined. For example, scent would be an interesting element to investigate, given that many stores have distinctive odors (e.g., the smell of popcorn in a discount store or the potpourri used in a bath shop). The effects of store environment on subjects other than students should be studied. Individual characteristics such as age, income, gender, and culture may be critical determinants of how people associate atmospheric elements and quality.

Limitations on the design manipulation were imposed by the remodeling plan of the store used in the study. Although design changes in a real store are expensive to make and are subject to a particular retailer's needs, other methodologies may prove helpful in looking at the effects of alternative design elements. A small-scale, simulated store environment constructed as a laboratory would allow researchers almost unlimited options in testing different design effects on consumers. A less expensive (but also less realistic) alternative may be a computer-aided design system to test many design options. Methods other than using videotape to represent store environments are needed to expand and enrich our understanding of the linkages between store environment and quality. Field studies conducted in actual store settings, participant observation, and in-store verbal protocols are several methods that could achieve this objective.

The model should be expanded to include other store image components such as price, advertising, or selection. Do consumers also make inferences about the price image of a store based on its environment? Does store layout engender inferences about merchandise selection?

It should be pointed out that there was a marginally significant ambient-by-design interaction effect on subjects' assessment of store image (see Table 4). The interaction results suggest that the effect of the ambient factor is more pronounced when the store design factor portrayed a prestige image rather than a discount image, These findings suggest the need for future research to examine the potential interactive effects of store environmental factors on consumers' inferences and assessment of a store's image.

Finally. the findings that store environment and merchandise and service quality are antecedents rather than components of store image implies a need and an opportunity to develop a multiple-item scale to measure store image that is independent of the antecedent constructs and more comprehensive than the scale used in this study. Research is also needed to identify and study the relative impact of other potential antecedents of store image (e.g., advertising, price, word-of-mouth communications).

Conclusion

Characteristics of a store's environment influence the inferences that customers make about the store's merchandise and service quality. Such an influence is likely to be especially pronounced for ambient and social characteristics—factors that retail store managers can alter relatively easily, at least more easily than they can change design factors, which, interestingly, seem to have a weaker influence. Because the study's findings suggest that customers' merchandise- and service-quality inferences have a significant impact on overall store image, managers can strive to achieve a desired store image by changing the store's ambient and social characteristics appropriately. Moreover, the apparently weak impact of design factors on customers' quality inferences suggests that managers can shape store image regardless of a store's current layout and architecture. Finally, the study's findings support the notion that both store environment factors and merchandise and service quality inferences are antecedents of store image rather than components of store image, as typically portrayed in past research. This revised conceptualization of store image and its determinants, in addition to offering managerial guidelines for changing customers' store image perceptions, has implications for modeling and measuring the store image construct in future research attempts to enhance our understanding of this area.

APPENDIX
Manipulation Check Measures and Their Reliability Estimates

Store Ambient Factor Manipulation Check (alpha = .90)

1. The background music (in the video) would make shopping in this store pleasant.

2. If I shopped at this store, the background music that I heard on the video would bother me (R).

3. The background music was appropriate.

Store Design Factor Manipulation Check (alpha = .78)

1. The color scheme was pleasing.

2. The colors used in the store appeared to be currently fashionable.

3. The physical facilities were attractive.

4. The merchandise in the store appeared organized.

Store Social Factor Manipulation Check (alpha = .83)

1. There were enough employees in the store to service customers.

2. The employees were well dressed and appeared neat.

3. The employees seemed like they would be friendly.

4. The employees seemed like they would be helpful.

NOTE: A 7-point scale (1 = *strongly disagree* to 7 = *strongly agree*) was used to assess each of the items. The item denoted with an (R) was reverse scored.

Acknowledgments

Thanks are extended to Diana Grewal, Chuck Lamb, Bob Peterson, and anonymous reviewers for their constructive comments on previous versions of this article. Julie Baker would like to acknowledge the support of a School of Business summer research grant. Dhruv Grewal would also like to acknowledge the support of a James McLamore Summer Award in Business and Social Sciences and a University of Miami General Support Award.

Note

1. One reviewer was concerned about the external validity of the experimental design in that retailers would normally want consistency across the three factors (i.e., all three "high" or all three "low"). We agree that a retailer would want such consistency. In reality, however,

retailing environments do not always show consistency among the three factors. For example, such a lack of consistency was evident in a card and gift store in the same chain as the study store but in a different location. The design and social factors at this store could be classified as prestige-image, but the store was playing Top 40 music, probably because it was located in an area with a large student population. Our pretest showed that students associated Top 40 music with a discount-image store.

References

Baker, Julie. 1986, "The Role of the Environment in Marketing Services: The Consumer Perspective." In *The Services Challenge: Integrating for Competitive Advantage.* Eds. John A. Cepeil et al. Chicago, IL: American Marketing Association, 79–84.

Baker, Julie, Leonard Berry, and A. Parasuraman. 1988. "The Marketing Impact of Branch Facility Design." *Journal of Retail Banking* 10 (July); 33–42.

Baron, Reuben M. and David A. Kenny. 1986. "The Moderator-Mediator Variable Distinction in Social Psychological Research: Conceptual, Strategic, and Statistical Considerations." *Journal of Personality and Social Psychology* 51 (6); 1173–1182.

Bateson, John E. G. and Michael Hui. 1992. "The Ecological Validity of Photographic Slides and Videotapes in Simulating the Service Setting." *Journal of Consumer Research* 19 (September): 271–281.

Baumgarten, Steven A. and James S. Hensel. 1987. "Enhancing the Perceived Quality of Medical Service Delivery Systems." In *Add Value to Your Service.* Ed. Carol Suprenant. Chicago, IL: American Marketing Association, 105–110.

Bellizzi, Joseph A., Ayn E. Crowley, and Ronald W. Hasty. 1983. "The Effects of Color in Store Design." *Journal of Retailing* 59 (Spring): 21–45.

Berman, Barry and Joel R. Evans. 1989. *Retail Management, A Strategic Approach.* New York: MacMillan.

"Big Y Redesigns Its Selling Machine." 1987. *Chain Store Age Executive* 63 (October): 76–78.

Birren, Faber. 1945. *Selling with Color.* New York: McGraw-Hill.

Bitner, Mary Jo. 1990. "Evaluating Service Encounters: The Effects of Physical Surroundings and Employee Responses." *Journal of Marketing* 54 (April): 69–82.

Bloom, Paul N. and Torger Reve. 1990. "Transmitting Signals to Consumers for Competitive Advantage." *Business Horizons* 33 (July-August): 58–66.

Burstiner, Irving. 1986. *Basic Retailing.* Homewood, IL: Irwin.

Campbell, David. 1979. "Interior Office Design and Visitor Response." *Journal of Applied Psychology* 64 (6): 648–653.

Carpman, Janet R., Myron A. Grant, and Deborah A. Simmons. 1985. "Hospital Design and Wayfinding: A Simulation Study." *Environment & Behavior* 17 (May): 296–314.

"Chains Respond to Demands for Upscale Environment." 1985. *Chain Store Age Executive* 61 (July): 28.

Cherulnik, Paul D. and Scott K. Wilderman. 1986. "Symbols of Status in Urban Neighborhoods: Contemporary Perceptions of Nineteenth-Century Boston." *Environment & Behavior* 18 (September): 604–622.

Crane, F. G. and T. K. Clarke. 1988. "The Identification of Evaluative Criteria and Cues Used in Selecting Services." *Journal of Service Marketing* 2 (Spring): 53–59.

Crowley, Ayn E. 1993. "The Two-Dimensional Impact of Color on Shopping," *Marketing Letters* 4 (January): 59–70.

Darden, WIlliam R., Orhan Erdem, and Donna K. Darden. 1983. "A Comparison and Test of Three Causal Models of Patronage Intentions." In *Patronage Behavior and Retail Management.* Eds. William R. Darden and Robert F. Lusch. New York: North-Holland, 29–43.

Darden, William R. and JoAnn K. L. Schwinghammer. 1985. "The Influence of Social Characteristics on Perceived Quality in Patronage Choice Behavior." In *Perceived Quality: How Consumers View Stores and Merchandise.* Eds. Jacob Jacoby and Jerry Olson. Lexington, MA: Lexington Books, 161–172.

Dodds, William B., Kent B. Monroe, and Dhruv Grewal. 1991. "Effects of Price, Brand, and Store Information on Buyers' Product Evaluations." *Journal of Marketing Research* 29 (August): 307–319.

Eroglu, Sevgin and Gilbert D. Harrell. 1986. "Retail Crowding: Theoretical and Strategic Implications." *Journal of Retailing* 62 (Winter): 346–363.

"Flooring Choices Make an Image Statement." 1987. *Chain Store Age Executive* 63 (July): 52, 54, 56.

Foote, Kenneth E. 1983. "Color in Public Spaces." Department of Geography Research Paper No. 205. University of Chicago.

Gallager, Peggy and. Brad Cornwall. 1985. "Visual Merchandising . . . A New Science." *Texas Retailer* (Fall): 21–22.

Gardner, Meryl R. and George J. Siomkos. 1985. "Toward a Methodology for Assessing Effects of In-Store Atmosphere." In *Advances in Consumer Research.* Ed. Richard Lutz. Chicago, IL: Association for Consumer Research, 27–31.

Golden, Lawrence G. and Donald A. Zimmerman. 1986. *Effective Retailing.* Boston, MA: Houghton Mifflin.

Greenberg, C. Jerome, Elaine Sherman, and Leon O. Schiffman. 1983. "The Measurement of Fashion Image as a Determinant of Store Patronage." In *Patronage Behavior and Retail Management.* Eds. William R. Darden and Robert F Lusch. New York: North-Holland, 151–163.

Gutman, Jonathan and Scott D. Alden. 1985. "Adolescents' Cognitive Structures of Retail Stores and Fashion Consumption: A Means-End Chain Analysis of Quality." In *Perceived Quality, How Consumers View Stores and Merchandise.* Eds. Jacob Jacoby and Jerry Olson. Lexington, MA: Lexington Books, 99–114.

Harrell, Gilbert D., Michael D. Hutt, and James C. Anderson. 1980. "Path Analysis of Buyer Behavior under Crowding." *Journal of Marketing Research* 17 (February): 45–51.

Hastak, Maroj and Jerry C. Olson. 1989. "Assessing the Role of Brand-Related Cognitive Responses as Mediators of Communication Effects on Cognitive Structures." *Journal of Consumer Research* 15 (March): 444–456.

Hershberger, R. G. and R. C. Cass. 1974. "Predicting User Responses to Buildings." In *Man-Environment Interactions: Evaluations and Applications.* Ed. D. H. Carson. Stroudsbury, PA: Dowden, Hutchinson & Ross.

Hildebrandt, Lorz. 1988. "Store Image and the Prediction of Performance on Retailing." *Journal of Business Research* 17:91–100.

Hui, Michael K. and John E. G. Bateson. 1991. "Perceived Control and the Effects of Crowding and Consumer Choice on the Service Experience." *Journal of Consumer Research* 18 (September), 174–184.

Keller, Kevin Lane. 1987. "Memory Factors in Advertising; The Effect of Advertising Retrieval Cues on Brand Evaluations." *Journal of Consumer Research* 14 (December): 316–333.

Kerin, Roger, Daniel J. Howard, and Ambuj Jain. 1992. "Store Shopping Experience and Consumer Price-Quality-Value Perceptions." *Journal of Retailing* 68 (4): 376–397.

Kotler, Phillip. 1973. "Atmospherics as a Marketing Tool." *Journal of Retailing* 49 (Winter): 48–64.

Lindquist, Jay D. 1974. "Meaning of Image." *Journal of Retailing* 50 (Winter): 29–38.

Malhoura, Narcsh K. 1983. "A Threshold Model of Store Choice." *Journal of Retailing* 59 (Summer): 3–21.

Marans, Robert W. and Kent F. Spreckelmeyer. 1982. "Measuring Overall Architectural Quality." *Environment & Behavior* 14 (November): 652–670.

Mazursky, David and Jacob Jacoby. 1986. "Exploring the Development of Store Images." *Journal of Retailing* 62 (Summer): 145–165.

McElroy, James C., Paula C. Morrow, and Sevo Eroglu. 1990. "The Atmosphere of Personal Selling." *Journal of Personal Selling and Sales Management* 10 (Fall): 31–41.

McFarland, Gay Elliot. 1989. "The Psychology of Colors." *The Houston Post* (May 13): E1, E4.

Millman, Ronald E. 1982. "Using Background Music to Affect the Behavior of Supermarket Shoppers." *Journal of Marketing* 46 (Summer): 86–91.

———. 1986. "The Influence of Background Music on the Behavior of Restaurant Patrons." *Journal of Consumer Research* 13 (September): 286–289.

Morgan, Leonard A. 1985. "The Importance of Quality." In *Perceived Quality: How Consumers View Stores and Merchandise*. Eds. Jacob Jacoby and Jerry Olson. Lexington, MA: Lexington Books, 61–64.

Morris, Betsy. 1985. "Romanced by the Produce: How Design Sells Groceries." *The Wall Street Journal* (August 26): 1.

Morrow, Paula C. and James C. McElroy. 1981. "Interior Office Design and Visitor Response: A Constructive Replication." *Journal of Applied Psychology* 66 (5): 646–650.

Nevin, John R. and Michael Houston. 1980. "Images as a Component: of Attractiveness to Intra-Urban Shopping Areas." *Journal of Retailing* 56 (Spring): 77–93.

Nisbeu, Richard E. and Lee Ross. 1980. *Human Inference: Strategies and Shortcomings of Social Judgment*. Englewood Cliffs, NJ: Prentice-Hall.

Olshavsky, Richard. 1985. "Perceived Quality in Consumer Decision-Making: An Integrated Theoretical Perspective." In *Perceived Quality: How Consumers View Stores and Merchandise*. Eds. Jacob Jacoby and Jerry Olsen. Lexington, MA: Lexington Books, 3–29.

Olson, Jerry. 1977. "Price as an Informational Cue: Effects on Product Evaluations." In *Consumer and Industrial Buyer Behavior*. Ed. Arch G. Woodside. New York: North-Holland, 267–296.

Parasuraman, A., Valarie Zeithaml, and Leonard Berry. 1998. "SERVQUAL: A Multiple-Item Scale for Measuring Consumer Perceptions of Service Quality." *Journal of Retailing* 64 (Spring): 12–40.

Russell, James A. and Jacalyn Snodgrass. 1987. "Emotion and the Environment." in *Handbook of Environment Psychology*. Eds. Daniel Stokols and Irwin Altman. New York: Wiley, 245–281.

Rys, Melanie E., Joan O. Fredericks, and David Inery. 1987. "Value = Quality: Are Service Value and Service Quality Synonymous: A Decompositional Approach." In *Add Value to Your Service*. Ed. Carol Suprenant. Chicago, IL: American Marketing Association, 25–28.

Sadalla, Edward K., Beth Vershure, and Jeffrey Burroughs. 1987. "Identity Symbolism in Housing." *Environment & Behavior* 19 (September): 569–587.

Sarel, Dan. 1981. "Advances in Environmental Psychology—A New Perspective on Consumer Behavior." In *The Changing Marketing Environment: New Theories and Applications*. Eds. Kenneth Bernhardt et al. Chicago, IL: American Marketing Association. 135–138.

Sherowski, Hank. 1983. "Marketing through Facilities Design." In *Emerging Perspectives in Services Marketing*. Eds. Leonard L. Berry et al. Chicago, IL: American Marketing Association. 134–136.

Sherry. John F., Jr. and Mary Ann McGrath. 1989. "Unpacking the Holiday Presence: A Comparative Ethnography of Two Gift Stores," In *Interpretive Consumer Behavior*. Ed. Elizabeth Hirschman. Provo, UT: Association for Consumer Research. 148–167.

Stanley, T. and M. Sewall. 1976. "Image Inputs to a Probabilistic Model: Predicting Retail Potential." *Journal of Marketing* 39 (July): 48–53.

Ward, James C., John Barnes, and Mary Jo Bitner. 1992. "Measuring the Prototypicality and Meaning of Retail Environments." *Journal of Retailing* 68 (Summer): 194–220.

Ward, Lawrence M. and James A. Russell. 1981. "Cognitive Set and the Perception of Place." *Environment & Behavior* 13 (September): 610–632.

Wheatley, John J. and John S. Y. Chiu. 1977. "The Effect of Price, Store Image and Product and Respondent Characteristics on Perceptions of Quality." *Journal of Marketing Research* 14 (May): 181–186.

Wicker, A. 1973. "Undermanning Theory and Research: Implications for the Study of Psychological Behavioral Effects of Excess Human Populations." *Representative Research in Social Psychology* 4: 185–206.

Wineman, Jean D. 1982. "Office Design and Evaluation: An Overview." *Environment & Behavior* 14 (May): 271–298.

Yalch, Richard and Eric Spangenberg. 1990. "Effects of Store Music on Shopping Behavior." *Journal of Consumer Marketing* 7 (Spring): 55–63.

Zeithaml, Valarie. 1988. "Consumer Perceptions of Price, Quality, and Value: A Means-End Model and Synthesis of Evidence." *Journal of Marketing* 52 (July): 2–22.

Zimmer, Mary R. and Linda L. Golden. 1988. "Impressions of Retail Stores: A Content Analysis of Consumer Images." *Journal of Retailing* 64 (Fall): 265–293.

Zweigenhaft, Richard L. 1976. "Personal Space in the Faculty Office: Desk Placement and the Student-Faculty Interaction." *Journal of Applied Psychology* 61 (4): 529–532.

What to Tell Consumers in Waits of Different Lengths: An Integrative Model of Service Evaluation

MICHAEL K. HUI
DAVID K. TSE

The authors conduct an experimental study to examine the impact of two types of waiting information—waiting-duration information and queuing information—on consumers' reactions to waits of different lengths. The authors test a model that includes three different constructs—perceived waiting duration, acceptability of the wait, and affective response to the wait—as mediators between waiting information and service evaluation. Results show that though acceptability of the wait and affective response to the wait have a significant mediating effect on the relationship between waiting information and service evaluation, perceived waiting duration does not. Moreover, neither type of information has significant impact in the short-wait condition, whereas waiting-duration information has greater impact than queuing information in the intermediate-wait condition and a smaller impact in the long-wait condition. The authors conclude with a discussion of research and managerial implications.

Waiting time is a pivotal factor in consumers' evaluation of many services. Ample evidence has shown that waiting has negative effects on service evaluation (Katz, Larson, and Larson 1991; Taylor 1994). To reduce these negative effects, service organizations can either provide faster service by modifying their service delivery system (Shostack 1987) or take actions designed to reduce the negative effects without changing the real waiting duration. Among other strategies, providing *waiting-duration information*, that is, information about the expected length of a wait, or *queuing information*, that is, a consumer's position in the queue with continuous updates, have been used widely to reduce consumer dissatisfaction with waiting (Larson 1987; Maister 1985).

We address three critical issues pertaining to the impact of waiting-duration information and queuing information on consumers' reactions to waiting. The first is the identification of underlying behavioral mechanisms through which the two types of waiting

information affect service evaluation. There is some evidence supporting a resource-allocation model (Zakay and Hornik 1991), which postulates that waiting information distracts consumers' attention from the passage of time; hence, they perceive the length of the wait as short. However, existing literature suggests that other effects, such as uncertainty reduction and cognitive reappraisal, may also explain the impact of the information on service evaluation. According to the uncertainty reduction explanation, information ameliorates affective response by reducing the uncertainty of the wait, and according to the cognitive reappraisal explanation, information facilitates the reinterpretation of the wait as "not too long."

The second is assessing the effectiveness of the two types of waiting information in waits of different lengths. For example, when a delay is short, does it matter if no waiting information is provided? Are the two types of waiting information equally effective in stimulating the various behavioral mechanisms in waits of different lengths? The key question to service marketers is, What waiting information should be given to customers in waits of different lengths?

The third is concerned with constructs that are implied by the three behavioral mechanisms as being key mediators between the two types of waiting information and service evaluation. These constructs include perceived waiting duration (how long consumers believe they have waited), affective response to the wait, and acceptability of the wait. Testing a model that integrates these constructs provides both researchers and service managers with insights regarding the impact of waiting information on service evaluation.

Michael K. Hui is Lecturer in Marketing, Hong Kong University of Science and Technology, and Associate Professor of Marketing, Concordia University, Canada. David K. Tse is a professor, Department of Business and Management, City University of Hong Kong. The authors thank the editor, three anonymous *JM* reviewers, and seminar participants at Queen's, Victoria, Hong Kong University of Science and Technology, and City University of Hong Kong, for their constructive comments on an earlier version of this article. Their study was supported by a research grant from the Social Sciences and Humanities Research Council of Canada, which was awarded to the first author.

Conceptual Background

We discuss three behavioral mechanisms that explain the positive impact of waiting-duration information and queuing information on service evaluation.

Resource-Allocation Model

From the customer's perspective, one key negative outcome of waiting is time lost. Drawing heavily from time-judgment literature, researchers have employed perceived waiting duration as the key construct in explaining consumers' reaction to a wait (Chebat, Gelinas-Chebat, and Filiatrault 1993; Hornik 1984). The longer a person believes he or she has waited, the more negatively he or she evaluates the service.

How information can affect perceived waiting duration is described comprehensively in Zakay's (1989) resource-allocation model. According to the model, a *time estimate* is a function of the number of *time units* recorded by a cognitive timer, which is activated when a person pays attention to the passage of time. A given time period is often perceived as longer when a person becomes more conscious of the passage of time. Zakay and Hornik (1991) argue that a person naturally is occupied with the passage of time and actively engages in time estimation during the whole waiting period. They also argue that any stimuli that can distract the person's conscious attention from the passage of time reduces the perceived waiting duration and hence enhances his or her service evaluation (e.g., Chebat, Gelinas-Chebat, and Filiatrault 1993). Similarly, the existence of waiting-duration information or queuing information reduces the need for the person to pay attention to the passage of time him- or herself. The result is a shorter perceived waiting duration and, hence, a service evaluation that is more positive.

Previous findings support the resource-allocation model. When subjects were informed of the expected length of a time period, they reported significantly shorter estimates of the period than subjects without the information (Ahmadi 1984). In a field study, Katz, Larson, and Larson (1991) find that providing customers with information about how long they must wait inside a bank reduces customers' perceived wait estimates.

Uncertainty Reduction

Waiting entails both economic and psychological costs (Osuna 1985). Not only do consumers lose some of their valuable asset—time—they also experience a considerable amount of stress. A key factor behind consumers' stress is the uncertainty of how long they must wait. Any information on waiting duration can reduce the uncertainty of the wait and lower the overall level of stress experienced by consumers (Osuna 1985). Findings from Taylor's (1994) study suggest that uncertainty influences service evaluation through consumers' affective responses to the wait. Accordingly, the consumers' affective response (e.g., being irritated, annoyed, dissatisfied) is posited as a key mediator of the impact of waiting information on service evaluation.

Cognitive Reappraisal

Previous research shows that a sense of control significantly affects human physical and psychological reactions to stressful situations, such as crowding and waiting (Hui and Bateson 1991; Langer 1983). *Personal control* refers to a person's need to demonstrate his or her competence, superiority, and mastery over the environment. Averill (1973) suggests that there are at least three different ways that a person can gain and maintain control over a situation: behavioral control, decisional control, and cognitive control.

Behavioral control is the availability of "a response which may directly influence or modify the objective characteristics of an event" (Averill 1973, p. 293). An example of behavioral control is anything consumers can do to shorten the real length of the wait. *Decisional control* is the extent of "choice in the selection of outcomes or goal" (Averill 1973, p. 289). This refers to whether consumers can choose to remain, leave, or come back later in the hopes that the line will be shorter. In contrast, *cognitive control* does not involve any physical change of or withdrawal from the stressful situation. Cognitive control can be subdivided into two mechanisms: information gain and reappraisal of the stressful situation. Both information gain and reappraisal are cognitive efforts that a person can use to cope with the situation. Information increases the predictability of a situation (Averill 1973). When given any information about the wait, consumers perceive the wait as more predictable and controllable and, as a result, exhibit affective responses to the wait that are more positive than those when no information is provided. This is largely in accordance with the uncertainty reduction explanation previously discussed.

Information also facilitates consumers reinterpretation of the wait, that is, the cognitive-reappraisal effect. According to Folkman (1984), cognitive reappraisal is an effective coping strategy when there is no good physical means to change or escape from the situation. For example, consumers not only reported affective responses that were more positive, but also considered the setting less crowded when they knew in

FIGURE 1

An Integrative Model of Waiting Information and Service Evaluation

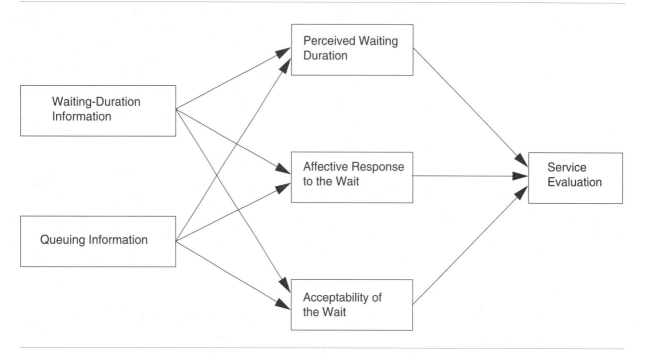

advance that the store might get crowded during their visit (Langer and Saegart 1977). When consumers are *captive to the wait* (i.e., they are not allowed to quit or leave until the service is over), any information regarding it is likely to stimulate cognitive reappraisal and result in consumers perceiving the wait to be more acceptable. This reappraisal effect can be illustrated by the following description from Maister's (1985, p. 118) work: "If a patient in a waiting room is told that the doctor will be delayed thirty minutes, he experiences an initial annoyance but then relaxes into an acceptance of the inevitability of the wait."

In short, the resource allocation explanation focuses on consumers' cognitive activity, namely, the time estimate, during the wait. Such time estimates affect service evaluation. The uncertainty reduction explanation focuses on consumers' affective response to the wait. It conceptualizes how consumers' feelings of annoyance, irritation, and so on color their evaluation of the service. And finally, the cognitive reappraisal explanation centers on consumers' evaluation of the wait as being acceptable or not. Although each of the explanations implies a different mediator, they are not competing explanations, because multiple, not singular, behavioral processes can be stimulated by the two types of waiting information. As shown in Figure 1, each mechanism concentrates on one of the three components—perceived waiting duration, affective

response to the wait, and acceptability of the wait—of consumers' evaluative process.

Length of the Wait

The previous discussion suggests that both waiting-duration information and queuing information favorably affect customers' evaluation of the service. The next question is, Are the two types of information equally effective in different wait durations?

When the wait is short, with or without either type of information, consumers are likely to experience little stress and consider the wait acceptable. They may not be motivated to search for or process any information regarding the wait (Langer and Saegart 1977). The distraction effect, uncertainty-reduction effect, and cognitive-reappraisal effect are not stimulated by either information type. Thus, all mediating effects due to perceived waiting duration, affective response, and acceptability are nonsignificant. Hence, we hypothesize,

H_1: In the short-wait condition, both waiting-duration information and queuing information do not stimulate significant mediating effects of perceived waiting duration, affective response to the wait, and acceptability of the wait on service evaluation.

When the wait is intermediate, the effects due to both types of information begin to become significant. First, both types of information help distract consumers from conscious awareness of the passage of time and improve service evaluation through effects on perceived waiting duration. Second, the information reduces uncertainty, which suggests a significant mediating effect of affective response to the wait on service evaluation. Third, the information facilitates cognitive coping, and consumers reappraise the wait as being more acceptable and hence give a better service evaluation. We therefore hypothesize,

H_2: In the intermediate-wait condition, both waiting-duration information and queuing information stimulate a significant mediating effect of perceived waiting duration on service evaluation.

H_3: In the intermediate-wait condition, both waiting-duration information and queuing information stimulate a significant mediating effect of affective response to the wait on service evaluation.

H_4: In the intermediate-wait condition, both waiting-duration information and queuing information stimulate a significant mediating effect of acceptability of the wait on service evaluation.

The situation becomes interesting when the wait is long. As far as waiting-duration information is concerned, it is logical to expect that both the distraction effect (perceived waiting duration as the mediator) and the uncertainty-reduction effect (affective response to the wait as the mediator) continue to operate. However, when consumers are told the wait is extremely long (e.g., one hour for a dinner table), the anticipation of substantial time lost may reduce the positive effects of waiting-duration information on their reaction to the wait (Osuna 1985). It is hard for consumers to reinterpret an extended wait as acceptable. This implies that acceptability may not be a significant mediator in service evaluation.

On the other hand, with queuing information, consumers do not have a precise estimate of the waiting duration. The statement, "You are twelfth in line," may raise less concern over time lost than the statement, "You must wait one hour." Queuing information may also direct consumers' attributions of the wait from the service firm by indirectly informing them that there are a large number of concurrent users of the service. Without queuing information, consumers may tend to blame the service firm when they experience a long wait (Bitner 1990). This implies that the cognitive reappraisal effect of queuing information may remain significant when the wait is long. This discussion can be summarized by the following research hypotheses:

H_5: In the long-wait condition, both waiting-duration information and queuing information stimulate a significant mediating effect of perceived waiting duration on service evaluation.

H_6: In the long-wait condition, both waiting-duration information and queuing information stimulate a significant mediating effect of affective response to the wait on service evaluation.

H_7: In the long-wait condition, queuing information stimulates a significant mediating effect of acceptability of the wait on service evaluation.

H_8: In the long-wait condition, waiting-duration information does not stimulate a significant mediating effect of acceptability of the wait on service evaluation.

An Experimental Study

The study employed a 3 (no-information control, waiting duration information, and queuing information) × 3 (short wait, intermediate wait, and long wait) factorial design.

Pilot Study

To determine the lengths of wait to use in the main study, a pilot study was conducted. When subjects in the pilot study were asked to try the service (used in the main study), they rarely objected when the wait was 5 minutes or less. On the other hand, most subjects expressed strong signs of disapproval (e.g., complaints to the experimenter) when the wait was as long as 15 minutes. We therefore decided to use 5 minutes as a short delay and 15 minutes as a long delay. According to the results obtained from the pilot study, the two types of information were not expected to create any significant positive effect on subjects' reactions to a wait of 5 minutes. In contrast, informing subjects that they must wait 15 minutes was expected to raise their stress level, as Osuna (1985) suggests. The midpoint between the short wait and the long wait (i.e., 10 minutes) was selected as the intermediate wait.

Procedure

A total of 135 students (15 in each experimental cell) recruited at a Canadian university participated in the study. The sample was equally distributed between women (68) and men (67). The majority (68.9% or 93) of the subjects were 21 to 24 years of age, and they came from 19 different departments of the university.

The subjects were told that they would be participating in a study testing "a new computerized course registration service that the university was considering to offer in the near future." After reading a page of instructions on how to use this new service, each subject proceeded to register for four different courses for the upcoming semester with this new service. The subject was provided with a standard keyboard and a monochrome monitor that was connected to an IBM-compatible personal computer.

There was an initial screen with a message thanking the subject for his or her participation. Based on the respondent number that the subject then entered, the computer put him or her into one of the nine experimental conditions. The second screen marked the beginning of the course-registration process, in which the subject was asked to give his or her personal details, including name, student number major, and program of study. In the third screen, the subject typed in the code numbers of four different courses that he or she wanted to take. The fourth screen carried a message that "the registration of the courses has been successful," and it also presented a tentative timetable for the semester. The final screen informed the subject that the process was ended and that he or she could leave.

A delay of 5, 10, or 15 minutes was introduced in between the third and the fourth screens, that is, after the subject typed in the course codes and before he or she was told that the course registration process was successful. During the wait, for subjects assigned to the no-information control group, the computer advised the subject that "the computer is checking for course prerequisites and any time conflict." For the remaining subjects, the message continued with the statement, "There will be a delay of about X minutes" (waiting-duration information), or "You are the Yth user in line" (queuing information). For the experimental condition for waiting-duration information, the computer gave X a value exactly equal to the length of the delay imposed (i.e., 5, 10, or 15 minutes). For the condition for queuing information, the initial value of Y was the same as X (e.g., for subjects who had a delay of 5 minutes, they were told initially, "You are the fifth user in line"). The computer also reduced the value of Y by one after every minute of delay. For example, during a 5-minute delay, the computer changed the message to, "You are the fourth (and then third, second, and first) user in line" after 1 (2, 3, and 4) minutes of delay. The update of a consumer's posi-

tion in the queue is readily available in most real-life situations (e.g., by moving along a queue or the take-a-number-and-wait system).

The software was reasonably user-friendly, and none of the subjects had difficulty following the instructions provided by the computer. Once the course registration was completed, the subject filled out a questionnaire that requested "his or her opinions about this new service." Before being dismissed, the subject was debriefed and asked not to mention the study to anybody.

By asking the subjects to interact with a computerized registration system, we were able to avoid the extraneous sources of variation associated with the otherwise high-people content (e.g., the mood of the server) of the service-delivery process (Bateson and Hui 1992). The software also greatly improved the realism of the whole study setting (Lynch 1982). In general, our subjects showed a high level of enthusiasm and involvement in the new computerized course registration service because of its value to them. During debriefing sessions, none of the subjects were able to guess the true objective of the study, and a few of them even asked the experimenter when the new service would become available to students.

Measures

The questionnaire included two different measures of the subjects' evaluation of the new service. The first measure (EVAL1) was a question asking the respondent to express the extent of his or her preference for this new service on an eight-point scale ranging from "not at all" to "extremely so." The second measure (EVAL2) consisted of two seven-point semantic differential items (unfavorable/favorable and bad/good; $\alpha = .95$) that are commonly used to measure the subjects' attitudes toward the new service (Ajzen and Fishbein 1980).

Two measures were concerned with the subjects' affective response to the wait. The first measure (AFF1) required the respondent to use an eight-point scale (from "not at all" to "extremely so") to express how much the wait made them feel irritated and annoyed ($\alpha = .88$). The second measure (AFF2) consisted of four semantic differential items extracted from Mehrabian and Russell's (1974) scale of pleasure (satisfied/unsatisfied, pleased/annoyed, happy/unhappy, and bored/relaxed; $\alpha = .87$). This followed Taylor and Claxton's (1994) suggestion that researchers should use a well-established scale to measure consumers' affective responses to the wait. Each subject was asked to estimate the length of his or her wait in terms of minutes and seconds (PTIME). The questionnaire also

FIGURE 2
The Structural Equation Model

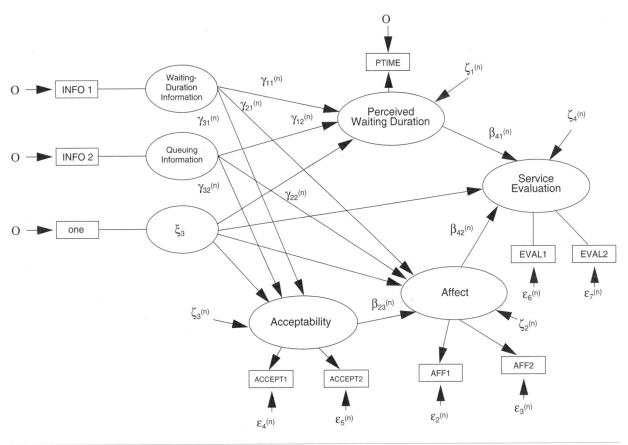

Short-wait condition: n = 1.
Intermediate-wait condition: n = 2.
Long-wait condition: n = 3.

included two measures concerning the acceptability of the wait to the respondent: to what extent the reported waiting duration was acceptable to the respondent (ACCEPT1) (an eight-point scale ranging from "not at all" to "extremely so") and the extent to which the respondent agreed or disagreed that the reported waiting time was too long (ACCEPT2) (a seven-point scale from "strongly agree" to "strongly disagree").

Results

We followed Jöreskog and Sörbom's (1989, Chapter 9) work and used a three-group (divided according to the real length of the wait experienced by subjects; i.e., short, intermediate, or long) structural-equation model to test comprehensively the mediating effects of perceived waiting duration, affective response to the wait, and acceptability of the wait. Initial results indicated that acceptability had no significant direct effect

on service evaluation. Instead, we found that acceptability affects service evaluation indirectly through affective response (Figure 2). This indirect effect is not totally unexpected, because ample evidence obtained from previous satisfaction studies (e.g., Tse and Wilton 1988; Westbrook 1980) show that consumers' evaluative response toward an experience is an important antecedent of their affective state.

As shown in Figure 2, the model includes two dummy variables that represented the three information groups: The first group, INFO1, was coded as a value of 1 when waiting-duration information was available, whereas the second group, INFO2, was coded as a value of 1 when queuing information was available. Because both INFO1 and INFO2 were categorical variables, we added a pseudovariable (i.e., "one") to the model and used the augmented moment matrix in LISREL analysis (for a detailed explanation of this procedure, see Bagozzi and Yi 1989).

TABLE 1
Summary of LISREL Analysis Results[a]

Models	Description	χ^2	d.f.	p
M-1	All parameters are allowed to vary across three groups of different wait durations	71.07	69	.409
M-2	$\gamma_{ij}^{(1)} = \gamma_{ij}^{(2)} = \gamma_{ij}^{(3)}$; i = 1, 2, and 3; and j = 1 and 2	92.10	81	.187
M-3	$\gamma_{ij}^{(1)} = \gamma_{ij}^{(2)} = \gamma_{ij}^{(3)} = 0$; i = 1, 2, and 3; and j = 1 and 2	116.90	87	.018

χ^2 difference tests

Interaction effect: $\chi^2 = 21.03$, d.f. = 12, $p < .05$ (M-1 versus M-2)
Information main effect: $\chi^2 = 24.80$, d.f. = 6, $p < .001$ (M-2 versus M-3)

[a]According to the model shown in Figure 2.

TABLE 2
LISREL Estimates of M-1[a]

Parameters	Short Wait (n = 1)		Intermediate Wait (n = 2)		Long Wait (n = 3)	
$\gamma_{11}^{(n)}$	.160	(.29)[b]	1.102	(1.05)	1.853	(1.85)
$\gamma_{12}^{(n)}$	.333	(.59)	−.617	(−.59)	.507	(.51)
$\gamma_{21}^{(n)}$	.043	(.17)	.985	(2.36)	.876	(2.08)
$\gamma_{22}^{(n)}$	−.027	(−.10)	.422	(1.09)	.342	(.61)
$\gamma_{31}^{(n)}$	.042	(.08)	1.766	(2.83)	.650	(1.41)
$\gamma_{32}^{(n)}$	.487	(.91)	1.192	(1.91)	2.111	(4.50)
$\beta_{23}^{(n)}$	.289	(3.00)	.456	(4.01)	.670	(3.49)
$\beta_{41}^{(n)}$	−.024	(−.38)	−.050	(−.99)	−.105	(−1.65)
$\beta_{42}^{(n)}$	.710	(4.08)	.776	(5.41)	.621	(4.19)

[a]For the sake of simplicity, only the estimated values of the key parameters are presented.
[b]Numbers inside the parentheses are t-values of the estimates. | t-value | > 1.64, $p < .05$ (two-tailed test).

When all parameters were allowed to vary across the three groups, the model (M-1) produced a chi-square value of 71.07 with 69 degrees of freedom ($p = .409$), which indicates a good fit. Two alternative models were used to examine the significance of the information main effect, as well as the interaction effect between the time and information treatments (cf. Bagozzi and Yi 1989). The first alternative model (M-2) constrained all the direct causal effects of INFO1 and INFO2 to be identical across the three groups (i.e., $\gamma_{ij}^{(1)} = \gamma_{ij}^{(2)} = \gamma_{ij}^{(3)}$, for i = 1, 2, and 3; j = 1 and 2). This model registers a chi-square value of 92.10 with 81 degrees of freedom ($p = .187$). The chi-square difference test between M-1 and M-2 reveals a significant interaction effect between information and waiting duration on the dependent constructs. The overall fit of M-1, as indicated by the chi-square value, is significantly better than M-2 ($\chi^2 = 21.03$, d.f. = 12, $p < .05$) and therefore rejects the statistical hypothesis that all the γ_{ij}'s are identical across the three duration groups. In other words, the two types of information tend to have different magnitudes of impact on perceived waiting duration for, affective response to, and acceptability of waits of different lengths.

The second alternative model (M-3) tests the significance of the information main effect by specifying all the direct causal effects of INFO1 and INFO2 as 0 (i.e., $\gamma_{ij}^{(1)} = \gamma_{ij}^{(2)} = \gamma_{ij}^{(3)} = 0$, for i = 1, 2, and 3; j = 1 and 2). This model gave a chi-square value of 116.90 with 87 degrees of freedom ($p = .018$). The chi-square difference test between M-2 and M-3 was significant ($\chi^2 = 24.80$, d.f. = 6, $p < .001$), which implies that the information main effect was significant (Bagozzi and Yi 1989).

A summary of the analysis is presented in Table 1 and the parameter estimates of M-1 (the best of the three models tested) are reported in Table 2.

Short-Wait Condition (H_1)

The short-wait condition was designed to assess potential threshold effects of waiting information. In this condition, when n = 1 (see Table 2), all γs are nonsignificant. This confirms that none of the three mechanisms were operating under the short-wait condition (H_1). The significant $\beta_{23}^{(1)}$ (.289, t-value = 3.00) and $\beta_{42}^{(1)}$ (.710, t-value = 4.08) merely suggest that acceptability and affective response had either a direct or indirect positive effect on service evaluation.

Intermediate-Wait Condition ($H_2 - H_4$)

In the intermediate-wait condition (i.e., when n = 2; see Table 2), $\gamma_{11}^{(2)}$, $\gamma_{12}^{(2)}$, and $\beta_{41}^{(2)}$ are all nonsignificant. The results do not support H_2 that perceived waiting duration is a key mediator between the two types of information and service evaluation.

Regarding the influence of waiting-duration information on the other mediating constructs in the model, the parameters $\gamma_{21}^{(2)}$ (.985, t-value = 2.36), $\gamma_{31}^{(2)}$ (1.766, t-value = 2.83), $\beta_{23}^{(2)}$ (.456, t-value 4.01), and $\beta_{42}^{(n)}$ (.776, t-value = .541) are all significant. For queuing information, the analysis obtained significant estimates with $\gamma_{32}^{(2)}$ (1.192, t-value = 1.91) and $\beta_{23}^{(n)}$ (1.766, t-value = 2.83), but a nonsignificant estimate with $\gamma_{22}^{(2)}$ (.422, t-value = 1.09). The results support H_3 that affective response is a key mediating variable between the two types of waiting information and service evaluation. In addition, a more positive affective response could be partly attributed to subjects perceiving a more acceptable wait ($\gamma_{31}^{(2)}$, $\gamma_{32}^{(2)}$, and $\beta_{32}^{(2)}$ are positively significant) with either type of information. Acceptability is another key variable mediating the effects of the two types of waiting information on service evaluation. This confirms H_4.

Long-Wait Condition ($H_5 - H_8$)

In the long-wait condition (i.e., when n = 3; see Table 2), both $\gamma_{11}^{(3)}$ (1.853, t-value = 1.85) and $\beta_{41}^{(3)}$ (−.105, t-value = −1.65) are significant, but the sign of $\gamma_{11}^{(3)}$ is contrary to that hypothesized by the resource-allocation model, namely, that waiting information reduces perceived waiting duration. According to the model, subjects given waiting-duration information perceive a shorter waiting duration (hence $\gamma_{11}^{(3)}$ should be negative). As in the intermediate-wait condition, queuing information had no significant effect on perceived waiting duration ($\gamma_{12}^{(3)}$ = .507, t-value = .51). The LISREL results again do not support the hypothesis that the perceived waiting duration is a key mediator between the two types of information and service evaluation (H_5).

For affective response and acceptability, analysis showed that $\gamma_{21}^{(3)}$ (.876, t-value = 2.08), $\gamma_{32}^{(3)}$ (2.111, t-value = 4.50), $\beta_{23}^{(3)}$ (.670, t-value = 3.49), and $\beta_{42}^{(3)}$ (.621, t-value = 4.19) were significant, but $\gamma_{22}^{(3)}$ (.342, t-value = .61) was not. These results, similar to those in the intermediate-wait condition, lend support to H_6; namely, affective response mediates the effects of the two types of waiting information on service evaluation. The effect of queuing information on affective response could be attributed primarily to subjects perceiving the wait as more acceptable (H_7). On the other hand, $\gamma_{31}^{(3)}$ (.650, t-value = 1.41) was nonsignificant, and this supported our hypothesis that subjects might find it difficult to reappraise the long wait as acceptable when they are given waiting-duration information (H_8).

Discussion

The LISREL results show that the two types of waiting information had a significant impact on affective response and acceptability in the intermediate- and long-wait conditions only. Moreover, in the long-wait condition, waiting-duration information did not have a significant effect on the acceptability of the wait. This resulted in a significant drop in the effects of waiting-duration information on acceptability and affective response (the latter was partly determined by acceptability) in the long-wait condition, to a level below that produced by queuing information (see Tables 3 and 4). These results also are captured by a significant interaction of the two experimental treatments (waiting durations and information types) on affective response (Hotelling's T^2 = .131, $p < .05$) and acceptability (Hotelling's T^2 = .148, $p < .05$). In Tables 3 and 4, the residual means (Rosnow and Rosenthal 1989; Ross and Creyer 1993) reveal that the significant interaction effects originate from two sources. First, for both dependent constructs, the two information groups registered higher residual means in the intermediate- and long-wait conditions than in the no-information condition, whereas the opposite was true in the short-wait condition. Second, there were higher residual means for the waiting-duration information group than for the queuing-information group in the intermediate-wait condition, but the effects were reversed in the long-wait condition. The same pattern of variation in cell means also applied to the two measures of service evaluation (EVAL1 and EVAL2, see Table 5), though the interaction effect was not significant (Hotelling's T^2 = .095, $p > .1$).

Conclusions and Implications

According to Hornik (1984), perceived waiting duration conventionally is recognized as a powerful construct for capturing the economic cost of waiting, that is, the outcome of variation in objective waiting duration. The salience of perceived waiting duration

TABLE 3
Acceptability as a Function of Information and Wait: Mean Scores

	No Information	Waiting-duration Information	Queuing Information	Row Mean
ACCEPT1[a]				
Short wait	5.00 (+.83)[b]	4.87 (−.14)	4.73 (−.68)	4.87
Intermediate wait	2.53 (−.64)	4.73 (+.72)	4.33 (−.08)	3.87
Long wait	2.07 (−.19)	2.53 (−.57)	4.27 (+.77)	2.96
Column mean	3.20	4.04	4.44	3.90[c]
ACCEPT2[d]				
Short wait	4.73 (+.38)[b]	4.80 (−.29)	5.33 (−.11)	4.96
Intermediate wait	3.47 (−.05)	4.87 (+.61)	4.07 (−.54)	4.13
Long wait	2.07 (−.32)	2.80 (−.33)	4.13 (+.65)	3.00
Column mean	3.42	4.16	4.51	4.03[c]

[a]1-8 rating. Higher score indicates the wait is more acceptable.
[b]Numbers in the parentheses are the residual means.
[c]Grand mean.
[d]1-7 rating. Higher score indicates the wait is more acceptable.

MANOVA Results
Waiting-duration main effect: Hotelling's $T^2 = .271, p, .001$.
Information main effect: Hotelling's $T^2 = .098, p < .05$.
Interaction effect: Hotelling's $T^2 = .148, p, .05$.

TABLE 4
Mean Scores of the Two Measures of Affective Response as a Function of Information and Wait

	No Information	Waiting-duration Information	Queuing Information	Row Mean
AFF1[a]				
Short wait	6.37 (+.77)[b]	6.63 (−.39)	6.57 (−.36)	6.52
Intermediate wait	4.13 (−.54)	6.60 (+.51)	6.03 (+.03)	5.59
Long wait	3.57 (−.22)	5.10 (−.11)	5.47 (+.35)	4.71
Column mean	4.69	6.11	6.02	5.61[c]
AFF2[d]				
Short wait	5.00 (+.54)[b]	5.03 (−.38)	5.15 (−.16)	5.06
Intermediate wait	3.45 (−.16)	5.03 (+.47)	4.13 (−.33)	4.21
Long wait	2.63 (−.38)	3.85 (−.11)	4.33 (+.47)	3.61
Column mean	3.69	4.64	4.54	4.29[c]

[a]1-8 rating. Higher score indicates more positive affective response.
[b]Numbers in the parentheses are the residual means.
[c]Grand mean.
[d]1-7 rating. Higher score indicates more positive affective response.

MANOVA Results
Waiting-duration main effect: Hotelling's $T^2 = .302, p < .001$.
Information main effect: Hotelling's $T^2 = .196, p < .001$.
Interaction effect: Hotelling's $T^2 = .131, p < .05$.

TABLE 5

Service Evaluation as a Function of Information and Wait: Mean Score

	No Information	Waiting-duration Information	Queuing Information	Row Mean
EVAL1[a]				
Short wait	6.40 (+.54)[b]	6.73 (−.15)	6.27 (−.39)	6.47
Intermediate wait	4.87 (−.23)	6.47 (+.35)	5.80 (−.10)	5.71
Long wait	4.00 (−.30)	5.13 (−.19)	5.60 (+.50)	4.91
Column mean	5.09	6.11	5.89	5.70[c]
EVAL2[d]				
Short wait	5.83 (+.44)[b]	5.87 (−.31)	5.80 (−.13)	5.83
Intermediate wait	4.77 (−.07)	5.97 (+.34)	5.10 (−.28)	5.28
Long wait	3.70 (−.38)	4.83 (−.04)	5.03 (+.41)	4.52
Column mean	4.77	5.56	5.31	5.21[c]

[a]1-8 rating. Higher score indicates more positive evaluation.
[b]Numbers in the parentheses are the residual means.
[c]Grand mean.
[d]1-7 rating. Higher score indicates more positive evaluation.

MANOVA Results
Waiting-duration main effect: Hotelling's $T^2 = .237$, $p < .001$.
Information main effect: Hotelling's $T^2 = .110$, $p < .01$.
Interaction effect: Hotelling's $T^2 = .095$, $p < .1$.

TABLE 6

Mean Scores of Perceived Waiting Duration[a] as a Function of Information and Wait

Wait	No Information	Waiting-duration Information	Queuing Information
Short	4.87	5.03	5.20
Intermediate	9.13	10.23	8.51
Long	12.18	14.03	12.69

[a]In minutes.

ANOVA Results
Waiting duration main effect: $F_{(2,126)} = 111.81$, $p < .001$.
Information main effect: $F_{(2,126)} = 2.38$, $p < .1$.
Interaction effect: $F_{(4,126)} = .83$, $p > .1$.

may be related partly to the embryonic link to time-judgment literature. However, our findings suggest that perceived waiting duration is not a salient mediator between the two types of waiting information and service evaluation.

A closer examination of the mean scores of perceived waiting duration (Table 6) suggests the existence of an assimilation effect on time perception (Ahmadi 1984). Subjects with waiting-duration information (see Table 6) appeared to use the given time as an anchor; and their mean time estimate, when compared with those obtained from the other two information groups, was the closest to the real waiting duration. On the other hand, the no-information subjects tended to underestimate the length of the wait for all three durations of wait. The tendency to underestimate waiting duration was also found with subjects who had queuing information (in the intermediate- and long-wait conditions). These results indicate that subjects with either waiting-duration information or queuing information did not perceive a shorter waiting duration than subjects without the information. In contrast, subjects with waiting duration information appeared to report a longer perceived waiting duration than subjects without the information. Although waiting-duration information leads to a significantly longer perceived waiting duration, the information has a positive effect on service evaluation through a more-positive affective response to the wait.

The effects of waiting information are mediated by the psychological cost of waiting (Osuna 1985). The results indicate that affect and acceptability are the key mediators operating between the two types of waiting information and service evaluation. The column means in Tables 3 and 4 show that subjects reported affective responses that are more positive and considered the wait more acceptable when either type of information was available than when no information was available. These findings suggest that researchers may need to look beyond perceived waiting duration to include such variables as affective response and acceptability when examining the impact of waiting on service evaluation (Katz, Larson, and Larson 1991).

The salience of affective response in overall service evaluation has received some support in recent studies of environmental distractions. For example, Kellaris and Kent (1992) suggest that pleasant music reduces consumer dissatisfaction with waiting because of its impact on consumers' emotional feelings during the wait. In addition to the valence (pleasure) dimension, researchers may also want to examine the impact of the arousal dimension (Mehrabian and Russell 1974) on service evaluation by contrasting the effects of stimulating versus nonstimulating music on consumers' reaction to waiting.

Our findings also provide empirical support for Osuna's (1985) conjecture that waiting-duration information may not be the most effective tool to minimize consumer dissatisfaction with extended waits. This is important to service managers when they consider what kind of information they should give their waiting customers. In short waits, no information is needed. When the wait is intermediate, waiting-duration information appears to be a better choice than queuing information. However, when the wait is long, waiting-duration information may be less effective than queuing information in assuaging consumer dissatisfaction with the wait. Our findings indicate that knowing in advance that there will be an extended wait may substantially weaken the cognitive reappraisal effect of waiting-duration information.

An alternative solution suggested by our findings is to replace waiting-duration information with queuing information. For example, in a bank, a continuous update of the queue so that consumers can have a better idea about their position in the line may result in a more positive reaction to the wait than a device that displays the expected length of the delay. This strategy is particularly important when the service organization has difficulty in accurately estimating the length of the wait or when the line is not visible to customers (e.g., waiting for a table in a restaurant or waiting to see a physician at a clinic). An alternative strategy is the installation of a take-a-number-and-wait system at the reception area.

Limitations

It is important to note that our study only examines the effects of queuing information with continuous updates. If there is no update of a person's position in the queue, would the information be equally effective in ameliorating consumers' reaction to the wait? Can our results be attributed to the greater amount of information given in the queuing-information condition than in the waiting-duration information condition? Can consumers' reactions to the wait be improved further when both types of waiting information are available? Furthermore, the controlled laboratory setting in which this study was conducted may not reflect the complexity of many service situations in which consumers are asked to wait. For example, our subjects are captive to the wait, which may not be the case in many real-life situations. A high-balking rate is possible, because consumers may choose to suspend the service encounter when waiting-duration information suggests that there will be a long wait (Katz, Larson, and Larson 1991).

References

Ahmadi, Kate S. (1984), "Effects of Social Influences and Waiting on Time Judgment," *Perceptual and Motor Skills*, 59, 771–76.

Ajzen, Icek and Martin Fishbein (1980), *Understanding Attitudes and Predicting Social Behavior*. Englewood Cliffs, NJ: Prentice-Hall.

Averill, James R. (1973), "Personal Control Over Aversive Stimuli and Its Relationship to Stress," *Psychological Bulletin*, 80 (4), 286–303.

Bagozzi, Richard and Youjae Yi (1989), "On the Use of Structural Equation Models in Experimental Designs," *Journal of Marketing Research*, 26 (August), 271–84.

Bateson, John E. G. and Michael K. Hui (1992), "The Ecological Validity of Photographic Slides and Videotapes in Simulating the Service Setting," *Journal of Consumer Research*, 19 (2), 271–81.

Bitner, Mary Jo (1990), "Evaluating Service Encounters: The Effects of Physical Surroundings and Employee Responses," *Journal of Marketing*, 54 (April), 69–82.

Chebat, Jean-Charles, Claire Gelinas-Chebat, and Pierre Filiatrault (1993), "Interactive Effects of Musical and Visual Cues on Time Perception: An Application to Waiting Lines in Banks," *Perceptual and Motor Skills*, 77, 995–1020.

Folkman, Susan (1984), "Personal Control and Stress and Coping Processes: A Theoretical Analysis," *Journal of Personality and Social Psychology*, 46 (4), 839–52.

Hornik, Jacob (1984), "Subjective vs. Objective Time Measures: A Note on the Perception of Time in Consumer Behavior," *Journal of Consumer Research*, 11 (June), 615–18.

—— (1993), "The Role of Affect in Consumers' Temporal Judgments," *Psychology and Marketing*, 10 (3), 239–55.

Hui, Michael K. and John E. G. Bateson (1991), "Perceived Control and the Effects of Crowding and Consumer Choice on the Service Experience," *Journal of Consumer Research*, 18 (2), 174–84.

Jöreskog, Karl G. and Dag Sörbom (1989), *LISREL 7 User's Reference Guide*. Mooresville, IN: Scientific Software.

Katz, Karen L., Blaire M. Larson, and Richard C. Larson (1991), "Prescription for the Waiting-in-Line Blues: Entertain, Enlighten, and Engage," *Sloan Management Review*, 32 (Winter), 44–53.

Kellaris, James J. and Robert J. Kent (1992), "The Influence of Music on Consumers' Temporal Perceptions: Does Time Fly When You're Having Fun," *Journal of Consumer Psychology*, 1 (4), 365–76.

Langer, Ellen J. (1983), *The Psychology of Control*. Beverly Hills, CA: Sage Publications.

—— and Susan Saegart (1977), "Crowding and Cognitive Control," *Journal of Personality and Social Psychology*, 35 (3), 175–82.

Larson, Richard C. (1987), "Perspectives on Queues: Social Justice and the Psychology of Queuing," *Operations Research*, 35 (November-December), 895–904.

Lynch, John G., Jr. (1982), "On the External Validity of Experiments; in Consumer Research," *Journal of Consumer Research*, 9 (December), 225–39.

Maister, David H. (1985), "The Psychology of Waiting Lines," in *The Service Encounter: Managing Employee/ Customer Interaction in Service Businesses*, John A. Czepiel, Michael R. Solomon, and Carol F. Surprenant, eds. Lexington, MA: Lexington Books, 113–23.

Mehrabian, Albert and James A. Russell (1974), *An Approach to Environmental Psychology*. Cambridge, MA: MIT Press.

Osuna, Edgar Elias (1985), "The Psychological Cost of Waiting." *Journal of Mathematical Psychology*, 29 (1), 82–105.

Rosnow, Ralph L. and Robert Rosenthal (1989), "Definition and Interpretation of Interaction Effects," *Psychological Bulletin*, 105 (1), 143–46.

Ross, William T., Jr. and Elizabeth H. Creyer (1993), "Interpreting Interactions: Raw Means or Residual Means?" *Journal of Consumer Research*, 20 (September), 330–38.

Shostack, G. Lynn (1987), "Service Positioning Through Structural Change," *Journal of Marketing*, 51 (January), 34–43.

Taylor, Shirley (1994), "Waiting for Service: The Relationship Between Delays and Evaluations of Service," *Journal of Marketing*, 58 (2), 56–69.

—— and John Claxton (1994), "Delays and the Dynamics of Service Evaluations," *Journal of the Academy of Marketing Science*, 22 (3), 254–64.

Tse, David K. and Peter C. Wilton (1988), "Models of Consumer Satisfaction Formation: An Extension," *Journal of Marketing Research*, 25 (May), 204–12.

Westbrook, Robert A. (1980), "Intra Personal Affective Influences upon Consumer Satisfaction with Products," *Journal of Consumer Research*, 7 (June), 49–54.

Zakay, Dan (1989), "An Integrated Model of Time Estimation," in *Time and Human Cognition: A Life Span Perspective*, Iris Levin and Dan Zakay, eds. Amsterdam: North Holland.

—— and Jacob Hornik (1991), "How Much Time Did You Wait in Line? A Time Perception Perspective," in *Time and Consumer Behavior*, Jean-Charles Chebat and V. Venkatesan, eds. Montreal: Université du Québec à Montréal.

The Effects of Filled Waiting Time and Service Provider Control over the Delay on Evaluations of Service

SHIRLEY TAYLOR

Queen's University

This article reports on an experiment that investigated the effects of a delay, perceived control over a delay, and the extent to which time was filled during the delay on various performance evaluations in a service encounter. It was determined that delays lower customers' overall evaluations of service and of the tangible and reliability attributes of the service in particular. When delayed, performance evaluations were affected by whether the service provider was perceived to have control over the delay and whether the customer's waiting time was filled. Overall performance evaluations and performance evaluations of tangibility, reliability, and responsiveness were highest when perceived service provider control was low and the waiting customer's time was filled. These evaluations were lowest when perceived service provider control was high and waiting time was not filled.

Delays in service are a common phenomenon. Because of fluctuating demand for many services, service providers often have limited control over the occurrence and length of delays. Moreover, as organizations become leaner, pressures on service providers become more acute, adding to the delay problems. Yet delays are seen by customers as a key source of service dissatisfaction (Bitner, Booms, and Tetreault 1990). As a result, service delays are beginning to draw increased attention from researchers, who strive to better understand the waiting experience and the impact of delays on customer evaluations of service. This study extends this research by examining, in an experimental setting, the main and interactive effects of filled time and service provider control over the delay on performance evaluations in one service encounter.

Although there are exceptions, in North America, waiting for service is generally perceived to be a negative experience (Clemmer and Schneider 1989; Davis and Vollman 1990; Haynes 1990; Katz, Larson, and Larson 1991; Larson 1987; Maister 1985; Osuna 1985; Taylor 1994). Service providers worry about the transfer of negative reactions to delays onto evaluations of service. These concerns are real, because there is evidence to suggest that waiting for service is negatively correlated with service evaluations (Clemmer and Schneider 1989; Davis 1986; Fisk 1980; Katz, Larson, and Larson 1991; Taylor 1994; Taylor and Claxton 1994).

Recently, attention has been focused on the factors that moderate or mediate the impact of waiting on service evaluations. These factors include (1) affective reactions to the wait (Folkes, Koletsky, and Graham 1987; Katz, Larson, and Larson 1991; Larson 1987; Maister 1985; Osuna 1985; Taylor 1994); (2) perceived inequities in the wait (Larson 1987; Maister 1985); (3) the timing of the wait (Dube-Rioux, Schmidt, and LeClerc 1989; Maister 1985); (4) the degree to which time is filled during the wait (Haynes 1990; Katz, Larson, and Larson 1991; Larson 1987; Maister 1985; Taylor 1994); and (5) the perceived level of service provider control over the wait (Folkes, Koletsky, and Graham 1987; Taylor 1994). Filled time and service provider control are the variables of interest in this study. They represent elements of two constructs identified as important in Bitner's (1990, 1991) model of service encounter evaluation—attribution and the extended services marketing mix. Here we focus on one element of attribution—service provider control—and one element of the process environment of the extended services mix—filled waiting time (also called "contextual cues" [Bitner 1991])—and examine their main and interactive effects on performance evaluations in a service encounter.

Attribution has been examined previously in a number of service-failure settings (e.g., Bitner 1990; Folkes 1984, 1988), although its application to service delays is limited (Folkes, Koletsky, and Graham 1987; Taylor 1994). Whereas filled time has been proposed as an important variable in delay contexts (Davis and Vollman 1990; Haynes 1990; Larson 1987; Maister 1985), empirical tests of its effects are also limited (Taylor 1994). Because customers have a tendency to blame the service provider for service failure (Folkes

Journal of the Academy of Marketing Science.
Volume 23, No. 1, pages 38–48.
Copyright © 1995 by Academy of Marketing Science.

and Kotsos 1986; Richins 1985), it is important to understand how different levels of perceived service provider control over a delay can affect service evaluations. Assessing the impact of filled time on service evaluations is also important because this variable can be easily manipulated and controlled by service providers. Taylor (1994) found correlations between these two variables and service evaluations. This study attempted to replicate these findings in an experimental setting and to further that research by examining their interactive effects on service evaluations by answering the following questions:

1. Are performance evaluations of a service encounter different for delayed customers than for non-delayed customers?

2. Does perceived service provider control over the delay affect performance evaluations in a service encounter?

3. Does filling time during the delay affect performance evaluations in a service encounter?

4. Do perceived service provider control and filled time interact in influencing performance evaluations in a service encounter?

These research questions were addressed using an experiment involving preservice delays for a career counseling service. Delayed and nondelayed treatments were established and performance evaluations of various service dimensions by delayed customers were then compared to the evaluations of nondelayed customers to address research question 1. Within the group of delayed customers, perceived service provider control over the delay and how time was filled during the delay were manipulated. The resulting impact on service evaluations was then assessed to answer research questions 2, 3, and 4.

First, the literature on delays and service evaluations is presented, followed by brief summaries of prior research involving service provider control and filled time. Hypotheses relating to the research questions are derived from each of these discussions. The empirical setting used to test these hypotheses is subsequently described and the results presented. The findings are then discussed and concluding comments provided.

Waiting for Service

Waiting and Service Evaluations

The relationship between waiting for service and service evaluations is intuitively straightforward: the longer one has to wait, the lower the evaluation of service. Evidence supporting a negative relationship between preservice waiting and service evaluations in a number of settings is growing (Clemmer and Schneider 1989; Davis 1986; Dube-Rioux, Schmidt, and LeClerc 1989; Fisk 1980; Katz, Larson, and Larson 1991; Roslow, Nicholls, and Tsalikis 1992; see also Taylor [1994] for a review). A recent quasi-experiment also found that delayed and nondelayed customers differed in their overall evaluations of service (Taylor and Claxton 1994). Therefore, it is hypothesized:

H1: Delayed customers will evaluate service performance lower than nondelayed customers.

Service Provider Control over the Delay

The fact that customers' attributions affect evaluations of a service encounter is well recognized (see, e.g., Bitner 1990). Three attribution dimensions, locus, controllability, and stability, are likely to affect a customer's reaction to service failure (Bitner 1990, 1991; Folkes 1984, 1988). The focus of this article is on one loci of attribution, the service provider, and on varying levels of controllability. A service provider locus was selected for study because consumers have a strong tendency to blame the seller for product or service failures (Folkes 1988; Folkes and Kitsos 1986; Richins 1985). Yet even when the service provider is blamed for the delay, customers may perceive varying degrees of service provider control over the delay. For example, in Folkes, Koletsky, and Graham's (1987) study of airline delays, although passengers blamed the airline for both mechanical failures and personnel problems, they perceived the airline to have more control over the latter. These researchers found that the more control the service provider was perceived to have over the delay, the less likely customers were to repurchase. In this research, we ask a related question: do higher levels of perceived service provider control over a delay result in lower performance evaluations?

Evidence suggests that service provider control does influence a customers' reaction to a delay. In related research, customers have been found to be more angry and less inclined to repurchase when they perceived the service provider had control over a product failure (Folkes 1984). Bitner (1990) found that perceived control over service failures resulted in lower evaluations of service. Two other studies obtained similar results when specifically examining reactions to delays in airline flights. Folkes, Koletsky, and Graham (1987) and Taylor (1994) found correlational evidence that the more the airline was perceived to have control over the delay, the more anger the passenger felt and consequently the lower the resulting service evaluation or repurchase intention. These results are consistent with a long history of research finding that the causal attributions made by individuals affect how they react to a situation (Folkes 1988; Weiner 1986). Thus we can hypothesize that:

H2: Performance evaluations of the service encounter will be lower when the service provider is perceived to have a high degree of control over a delay than when a service provider is perceived to have low control over the delay.

The Degree to Which Time Is Filled during the Wait

Filling waiting time during a delay may counteract the delay's negative impact by increasing customers' cognitive activity during the wait because this distracts them from focusing on the wait itself (Kellaris and Kent 1992). Filling preservice waiting time is a common practice. For example, many restaurants fill time by providing waiting customers with menus or inviting them to have a drink at the bar while they wait to be seated for dinner. Medical offices often supply patients with reading materials to fill their time while they wait to see the doctor (Lovelock 1991), and music is often piped across telephone lines when customers are put on hold.

A long tradition of time perception research in psychophysics finds that by filling time (i.e., by increasing people's mental activity), less attention can be paid to the passage of time (e.g., Allan 1979; Gilliland, Hofeld, and Eckstrand 1946; Hicks, Miller, and Kinsbourne 1976). With less attention being paid to the passage of time, the wait seems shorter. In addition, the customer's attention is focused on other activities so the wait is less salient. As a result, the wait's impact on service evaluations is lessened. There is limited empirical evidence in a service setting to support this assertion. Katz, Larson, and Larson (1991) found that increasing the amount of distractions available to queuing bank customers resulted in increased customer satisfaction. Taylor (1994) found that when passengers reported that their time was filled during a delay, they were less angry and consequently gave higher service evaluations than delayed airline passengers who did not fill their time. Here it is expected that even without the mediating effect of anger, filled time will influence service performance evaluations.

How time is filled during the wait may affect service evaluations. Maister (1985) and Haynes (1990)

have argued that service providers should attempt to integrate the waiting experience into the total service experience by relating the "filler" to the service itself. For example, this would mean that waiting medical patients should be provided with health magazines to read as opposed to unrelated magazines. Maister (1985) argues that related fillers act to enhance the service and that unrelated fillers may be annoying to customers simply because they are unrelated to the service. Related fillers not only distract the waiting customer, but they also make him or her feel like the service has already begun, thus making the delay seem shorter or nonexistent. This would suggest that fillers related to the service would result in more positive service evaluations than unrelated fillers or no fillers at all. This leads to the following hypothesis:

H3: Performance evaluations of the service encounter will be higher for waiting customers whose time is filled with an activity related to the service than for customers whose time is filled with an activity that is unrelated to the service, or for customers whose time is not filled.

Interactions between Service Provider Control and Filled Time

The possibility for service provider control and filled time to interact in their impact on service evaluations follows from Bitner (1991), who suggests that the impact on service evaluations of process components of the services marketing mix can be influenced by attribution.[1] In this case, whether or not the waiting customer's time is filled could be considered an element of the process component of the extended services marketing mix. It is expected that service evaluations will be lowest when the service provider is perceived to have a high degree of control over the delay and the delayed customer's time is not filled while waiting. Service evaluations are expected to be highest when the waiting customer's time is filled and the service provider is perceived to have low control over the delay.

Unfilled time allows the waiting customer to focus on the delay and its impact on evaluations; it also allows the customer time to think about how much control the service provider has over the delay. As such, the negative effects of high service provider control over the delay are exacerbated. However, when the waiting customer's time is filled, he or she is distracted from thinking about the high service provider control over the delay. In this case, we would expect that the filled-time customer's service evaluations will be higher than those whose time is unfilled. Low-control/filled conditions should result in the highest evaluations because the customer should be occupied during the wait and not focused on the service provider's control. Because related fillers are expected to result in higher evaluations than unrelated fillers, we would expect that those in a related filler/low-control condition would evaluate service higher than all other conditions. Thus it can be hypothesized:

H4: Performance evaluations of the service encounter will be highest for waiting customers who perceive that the service provider has low control over the delay and whose time is filled with a related activity. Overall performance evaluations of the service encounter will be lowest for waiting customers who perceive that the service provider has high control over the delay and whose time is unfilled.

The Role of Affect in Evaluations of Service

There has been some recent research investigating the role of negative affect on evaluations (Gorn, Goldberg, and Basu 1993). An argument has been made by some researchers that the negative affect generated by the delay can influence evaluations of service (Folkes, Koletsky, and Graham 1987; Katz, Larson, and Larson 1991; Larson 1987; Taylor 1994; Taylor and Claxton 1994). In the present study, the roles of delay, service provider control, and filled time on evaluations of service over and above the role played by negative affect are investigated. As such, negative affect is included as a covariate in the analyses reported below.

Method

Overview

The impact of filled time and service provider control on service evaluations was examined with a two by three (service provider control by filled) factorial between subjects design with a control group. Customers of a student career counseling service called "Career Path" were randomly assigned to one of the experimental or control conditions. Experimental group subjects were each delayed 10 minutes, the reason for the delay differing depending on the assigned service provider control treatment condition. After the delay, each subject worked on an interactive computerized career counseling program called "Career Match." After each subject finished working with

the program, he or she met with the counselor to discuss the program output and then completed a self-administered questionnaire evaluating the "Career Path" service.

Subjects

Two hundred sixty-one undergraduate business school students from a mid-sized university made appointments to use the Career Path service. Twenty-nine of these subjects were not used in the analysis due to various problems (such as the subject being late, or being delayed by a previous subject). The resulting sample size was 232 subjects; 68 of these subjects made up the control (nondelayed) group. Cell sizes for each of the experimental groups ranged between 24 and 31 subjects.

Stimuli and Pretests

The Career Path service was established jointly for the purposes of this study and for the business school's career development office. The service used an expert system, Career Match, to help guide students' career choice decisions. Based on the student's responses to a series of questions, the program developed a personalized profile of that student's skills and career preferences and then matched these against a large number of different career profiles to establish the student's suitability for that career. Students worked through the program on their own; however, the counselor sat with them at the end of the session to interpret and discuss the output. The Career Path counselor was the system developer and also the research assistant for this study; she administered all of the manipulations.

To determine the most appropriate delay duration for the study, four scenarios were developed for pretesting, each describing a service setting in which a customer is delayed. The scenarios differed only in terms of the length of the delay. The delays were either 5 minutes, 10 minutes, 15 minutes, or 20 minutes. A pretest with 23 respondents similar to Career Path customers revealed that the 10-minute wait was adequate for the study; it was rated at the midpoint on 7-point Likert-type scales assessing whether the wait was "a long time" and whether the delay was "an unreasonable amount of time to have to wait for this service." Respondents also neither strongly agreed nor disagreed that a 10-minute wait would be expected in a service such as the one described.

Four different service provider control manipulations were also pretested. In a pretest with 60 respondents similar to the Career Path customers, two manipulations that represented "low control" and "high control" were selected for the final study. According to both of the scenario conditions selected, the counselor left the service setting prior to starting the Career Match program saying that she had to photocopy some materials necessary for the service. In the low-control condition, her rationale for not doing the copying earlier was that the photocopier was broken. In the high-control situation, her rationale was that she had not been organized enough to photocopy the materials prior to the customer's appointment. On a 7-point scale of perceived service provider control, the low-control condition averaged 1.33, whereas the high-control condition averaged 3.69 in the pretests ($F[1,29] = 21.35$, $p < .001$).

Because it was important that only control was being manipulated and not locus or stability of attribution, two other measures were also taken. It was found that the two conditions did not differ in terms of *who* was perceived to have caused the delay (attribution locus $-\chi^2_8 = .0047$, $p > .95$). In addition, the two conditions did not differ in the perceived stability of the delay ($F[1,29] = 1.009$, $p > .30$). As a further precaution, respondents were asked if the delay was necessary in order for the customer to have a meaningful session with the career counselor; subjects in the two selected treatment conditions did not differ in their responses to this question ($F[1,29] = .036$, $p > .85$).

Four potential "fillers" were also pretested. It was important to ensure that two fillers that were selected differed only in terms of their relationship to the service and not in terms of other variables such as involvement. The fillers consisted of magazines, which are commonly used in the waiting areas of many service settings. The "related filler" that was selected consisted of a career counseling magazine; the selected "unrelated filler" was a copy of a national news magazine. In a pretest involving 39 respondents similar to the customers of Career Path, these two magazines did not differ in terms of perceived involvement (Zaichowsky's (1985) PII Scale; ($F[1,20] = .001$, $p > .95$).

The resulting manipulations consisted of either no delay (control group) or a 10-minute delay (experimental groups). For the experimental groups, there were two service provider control conditions—high and low. In both "control" conditions, subjects were told by the counselor that she would be right back; she had to go and photocopy some materials needed for the session. In the low-control condition, subjects were informed that the copies had not been made earlier because the photocopier was broken. In the high-control condition, subjects were told that the copies had not been made earlier because the counselor had

not been organized enough to make them. There were three levels of the "filled" conditions: (1) subjects were not provided with any fillers (unfilled); (2) subjects were provided with a career counseling magazine to read during their delay (related filler); or (3) subjects were provided with a news magazine to read during their delay (unrelated filler).

Measures

Dependent Measures Overall measures and the performance measures of SERVQUAL (Zeithaml, Parasuraman, and Berry 1990) were used to assess service performance evaluations. Overall service evaluation was assessed with two 7-point Likert-type (*agree/disagree*) items: "Overall, I would rate my service experience with Career Path as good" and "I would recommend Career Path to other students" ($\alpha = .83$). Composite scores for each of the five SERVQUAL dimensions were derived by averaging responses to the items for each dimension. The resulting reliabilities were as follows: responsiveness ($\alpha = .80$), assurance ($\alpha = .81$), empathy ($\alpha = .84$), tangibles ($\alpha = .68$), and reliability ($\alpha = .86$) (see Appendix).

Manipulation Checks A number of single-item measures were used as manipulation checks. To assess service provider control and filled manipulations, subjects were asked to respond on two 7-point scales: "How much control did (the counselor)[2] have over the delay?" (*had no control/had complete control*) and "Was your time filled while you were waiting?" (*not at all filled/completely filled*). For interest's sake, both control group and experimental subjects were asked, "Did you have to wait before you could start the Career Match program?" (*yes/no*). It should be noted, however, that subjects' responses to this question could be influenced by the manipulations. For example, if a respondent's time was filled, he or she may not have perceived the delay. Thus the manipulation of concern in this study was the actual delay, not the perceived delay.

Other Questionnaire Items In addition to the SERVQUAL measures and manipulation checks, the questionnaire also included eight affect items, because negative affect was used as a covariate in the analysis. Based on an exploratory factor analysis with principal components extraction (varimax rotation), two affect scales were derived from eight items; these consisted of a positive affect scale (made up subjects' ratings of the extent to which they felt *good, happy,* and *satisfied;* $\alpha = .79$), and a negative affect scale (made up of *uneasy, frustrated, angry,* and *uncertain* items; $\alpha = .65$) Because

TABLE 1

Evaluation Differences between Delayed and Nondelayed Subjects

Independent Variable	Dependent Variable	MANCOVA Results			ANCOVA Results		
		F	df	p<	F	df	p<
Delay	Overall service evaluation				10.29	(1,229)	.001
Covariate					0.07	(1,229)	n.s.[a]
Delay	Service attributes	2.33	(5, 225)	.05			
Covariate		2.15	(5, 225)	.10			
Delay	Tangibles				5.24	(1,229)	.02
Covariate					4.37	(1,229)	.05
Delay	Reliability				5.10	(1,229)	.03
Covariate					6.17	(1,229)	.02
Delay	Responsiveness				0.62	(1,229)	n.s.
Covariate					5.78	(1,229)	.02
Delay	Assurance				0.47	(1,229)	n.s.
Covariate					4.35	(1,229)	.02
Delay	Empathy				0.43	(1,229)	n.s.
Covariate					6.75	(1,229)	.01

[a] n.s. = not significant

negative affect has been found to influence service evaluations (Folkes, Koletsky, and Graham 1987; Taylor 1994), negative affect was used as a covariate in the analyses.

Results

Manipulation Checks

The manipulation checks conducted at the end of the service confirmed that the manipulations worked as intended. Those in high- and low-control conditions differed in their perceptions of service provider control ($F[1,115] = 16.12$, $p < .001$). Subjects in both of the filled conditions (either related or unrelated fillers) differed from those in the unfilled condition in their perceptions of filled waiting time ($F[1,125] = 176.70$, $p < .001$). In general, experimental subjects and control subjects differed in whether or not they perceived that they had to wait ($\chi^2_1 = 61.97$, $p < .001$), although there were some respondents in the delay condition who reported that they were not delayed.

In addition to these manipulation checks, a two by three ANOVA was performed to assess whether or not the manipulations had any impact on the negative affect reported by subjects. Negative affect did not differ between subjects in each of the experimental conditions ($F_{CONTROL}[1,158] = 1.94$, $p > .10$; ($F_{FILLED}[2,158] = .787$, $p > .40$; ($F_{INTERACTION}[2,158] = .26$, $p > .70$);

nor did it differ between delayed and nondelayed subjects ($T[230] = -1.13$, $p > .25$), suggesting that any differences found in service evaluations between experimental groups or between experimental and control groups do not correspond to differences in negative affect.

Service Evaluations

Evaluation Differences Between Delayed and Nondelayed Subjects (H1) H1 proposed a difference in service performance evaluations between delayed and nondelayed customers. To assess this, differences in overall service evaluations and evaluations of each of the five service dimensions were investigated.

The results of an analysis of covariance (ANCOVA)[3] showed that there was a significant difference in overall service evaluations between delayed and nondelayed customers, with delayed customers evaluating service more negatively than nondelayed customers (see Table 1). The negative affect covariate was not significantly related to the overall evaluation. A multivariate analysis of covariance (MANCOVA) on the five service dimensions also revealed a difference between delayed and nondelayed customers. Univariate analysis of this result revealed that delayed subjects had lower ratings of the tangible and reliability

Overview of Variance Analyses

Independent Variables	Dependent Variables	MANCOVA Results			ANCOVA Results		
		F	df	p<	F	df	p<
Service provider control	Overall service				16.85	(1,157)	.001
	Service attributes	5.30	(5,153)	.001			
	Tangibles				0.55	(1,157)	n.s.[a]
	Reliability				17.48	(1,157)	.001
	Responsiveness				11.58	(1,157)	.001
	Assurance				4.04	(1,157)	.05
	Empathy				0.12	(1,157)	n.s.
Filled time	Overall service				9.89	(2,157)	.001
	Service attributes	1.96	(10,306)	.05			
	Tangibles				3.03	(2,157)	.05
	Reliability				2.98	(2,157)	.06
	Responsiveness				3.44	(2,157)	.04
	Assurance				0.21	(2,157)	n.s.
	Empathy				0.04	(2,157)	n.s.
Interaction of control × filled	Overall service				5.12	(2,157)	.007
	Service attributes	2.70	(10,306)	.003			
	Tangibles				3.95	(2,157)	.02
	Reliability				6.56	(2,157)	.002
	Responsiveness				2.88	(2,157)	.06
	Assurance				1.38	(2,157)	n.s.
	Empathy				0.03	(2,157)	n.s.
Negative affect covariate	Overall service				0.50	(1,157)	n.s
	Service attributes	4.165	(5,153)	.001			
	Tangibles				7.38	(1,157)	.007
	Reliability				13.82	(1,157)	.001
	Responsiveness				13.01	(1,157)	.001
	Assurance				13.16	(1,157)	.001
	Empathy				10.17	(1,157)	.001

[a]n.s. = not significant.

attributes (see Table 1). All of these effects were significant over and above the effects of the negative affect covariate, which was also significantly related to each of these service dimensions.

The Impact of Service Provider Control and Filled Time on Evaluations (H2–H4)   A two-by-three 3 ANCOVA was used to assess the impact of perceived service provider control and filled waiting time on overall evaluations of service. Table 2 shows the results of this analysis.

The data were consistent with H2—perceived service provider control over the delay lowered overall service evaluations. Whether and how time was filled also affected the overall service evaluation. Scheffé tests revealed that evaluations from both filled conditions were significantly different from the unfilled condition ($p < .05$) but not from each other; thus H3 was only partially supported because there were no differences in evaluations between related and unrelated filler conditions.

In addition, the interaction between service provider control and filled time was significant. Simple main effects analysis revealed that this interaction was caused primarily by a large decrease in the overall evaluation when a waiting customer's time was not filled and the service provider was perceived to have high control ($F[1,50] = 13.94, p < .0005$) (see *a* in Figure 1). When the waiting customer's time was

FIGURE 1

FIGURE 1

Interactive Effects of Service Provider Control and Filled Time on Evaluations

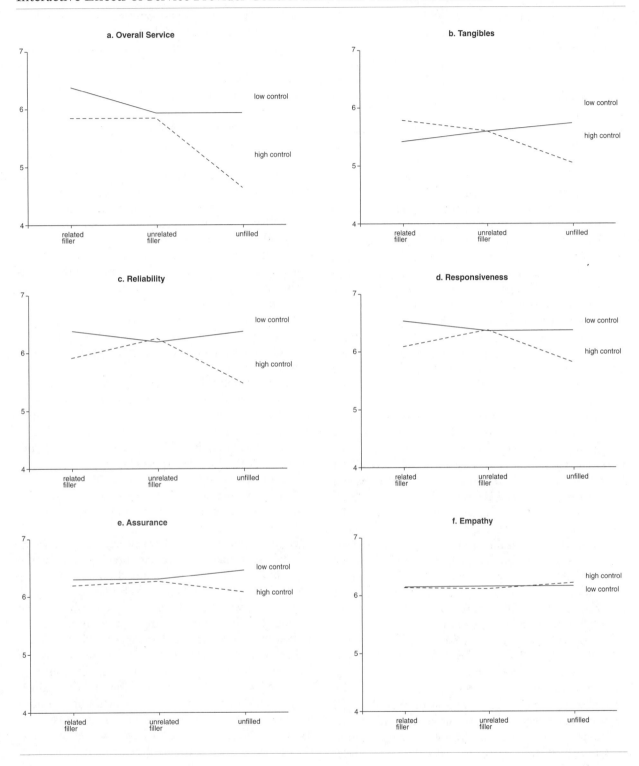

filled with a related filler, the perceived degree of service provider control also affected the overall evaluation ($F[1,51] = 5.91$, $p < .02$), with lower evaluations for those in the high service provider control condition. For subjects in the unrelated filler condition, perceived service provider control did not affect the overall evaluation ($F[1,54] = .12$, $p > .70$). The covariate, negative affect, was not significantly related to the overall evaluation.

Similar results were obtained for evaluations of the specific service dimensions. A two by three MANCOVA was performed to assess the impact of service provider control and filled time on the five SERVQUAL dimensions. Again, both main effects and the interaction were significant. Those in the low service provider control condition evaluated the service dimensions more favorably than those in the high service provider control condition. Looking at the univariate results (see Table 2), it appears that three of the service dimensions, reliability, responsiveness, and assurance, account for the significant differences.

Evaluations of the service dimensions also differed depending on if and how the waiting time was filled. These differences are due primarily to differences in evaluations of tangibles, reliability, and responsiveness. A Scheffé test of these relationships shows that for all of these attributes, the two filled conditions differ from the unfilled conditions ($p < .10$), but not from each other. Thus H3 is again only partially supported; although filled and unfilled time resulted in different service evaluations, how the time was filled had no impact.

The interaction between filled time and service provider control was also significant in its impact on evaluations of service dimensions. According to the univariate tests, these results were driven by significant interactions in evaluations of tangibles, reliability, and responsiveness (see *b, c, d, e,* and *f* in Figure 1). In all three of these cases, the biggest difference between the high- and low-control groups is in the "unfilled" condition; service evaluations are lowest when the service provider is perceived to have a high degree of control over the delay and the customer has nothing to do while waiting. Simple main effects analysis shows that for those in the unfilled condition, evaluations were higher for those who perceived the service provider to have low control over the delay ($F_{TAN}[1,50] = 4.70$, $p < .05$; ($F_{REL}[1,50] = 16.99$, $p < .001$; ($F_{RESP}[1,50] = 9.74$, $p < .003$). The results are similar when one examines the simple main effects for those in the related filler condition. Evaluations of reliability and responsiveness were lower for those in the high control condition than those in the low control condition ($F_{REL}[1,51] = 5.93$, $p < .02$; ($F_{RESP}[1,51] = 5.94$, $p < .02$). These two control conditions had no impact on evaluations in the unrelated filler condition ($F_{REL}[1,54] = .001$, $p > .90$; ($F_{RESP}[1,54] = .11$, $p > .70$; ($F_{RESP}[1,54] = .001$, $p > .90$). The negative affect covariate was significant in the analysis.

Discussion

This study sought to investigate the effects of a delay on service performance evaluations. It also examined the impact on these evaluations of perceived service provider control over the delay and the degree to which waiting time is filled.

The results of this experiment lend further support to earlier correlational research that found that delays are negatively related to overall service evaluations (Clemmer and Schneider 1989; Katz, Larson, and Larson 1991; Taylor 1994). It also replicates the work of Taylor and Claxton (1994), who found that delayed subjects gave significantly lower overall evaluations than did nondelayed subjects. Subjects who were delayed were less likely than nondelayed subjects to feel that the service provider could offer reliable, dependable service. Surprisingly, delayed and nondelayed subjects did not differ significantly in their evaluations of responsiveness. Responsiveness deals with the willingness of the service provider to help customers and provide prompt service. From these results, it appears that subjects treated the delay as a sign of undependable service but not as a sign of unwillingness to help customers.

Interestingly, there was a significant difference between delayed and nondelayed subjects on the tangibles dimension. *Tangibility* refers to the "appearance of physical facilities, equipment, personnel and communication materials" (Zeithaml, Parasuraman, and Berry 1990, p. 26) (see Appendix, items 1–4). Why this dimension, and not the other dimensions of assurance and empathy, should be biased by the delay is not clear. Because delayed and nondelayed subjects did not differ significantly in their reported negative affect, it appears that there were no "carryover effects" (such that a negative mood generated by the delay biased evaluations in a mood-congruent direction). It is quite possible, however, that these evaluations are lower because the delayed subjects had 10 minutes in which to sit in the service room and evaluate the tangible elements of their surroundings. The room that Career Path was using was not physically appealing; it was a very small room in a very old building. It had no windows and contained only a desk, computer, and chair. Although nondelayed subjects may not have had time to attend to this, delayed subjects did, resulting in lower evaluations. It is possible that if the service provider had been present in the room during the delay that customers would have evaluated assurance and empathy lower as well.

For those subjects that were delayed, the perceived level of service provider control over the delay affected their evaluations of service; the more control the service provider was perceived to have over the delay, the lower the overall and specific service attribute evaluations. This result is consistent with the work of Folkes (1984) and Bitner (1990), who found that higher levels of perceived control over product and service failures led to lower evaluations of service. It also corroborates the correlational results of Folkes, Koletsky, and Graham (1987) and Taylor (1994), who found perceived service provider control over a delay to have a negative impact on service evaluations. Evaluations of reliability, responsiveness, and assurance were lower for those who felt that the service provider had a high degree of control over the delay. These results follow logically from how these dimensions are defined; the more control the service provider has over the delay, the more the customer will perceive that the service is not being performed reliably or promptly and the less trust the customer will have in the service provider.

When customers' time was filled during the delay, evaluations of service were higher, supporting the correlational results of Katz, Larson, and Larson (1991) and Taylor (1994). However, contrary to the hypothesis concerning related fillers (H3), both related and unrelated fillers resulted in higher overall evaluations than were achieved for unfilled time. As expected, the same attributes that were lowered as a result of the delay would be further lowered when waiting time is not filled. The evaluations of tangibles, reliability, and responsiveness were lower for those subjects whose waiting time was not filled than for those subjects whose waiting time was filled. As seen, however, the interaction between filled time and perceived service provider control was also significant.

The significant interactions found for both overall evaluations and specific service evaluations point out the importance of considering both perceived control and filled time together. Clearly, in all of the significant cases (the overall evaluation, and evaluations of tangibles, responsiveness, and reliability), the lowest service evaluations resulted when the customer was in the unfilled/high service provider control condition, whereas the highest evaluations occurred when the customer was in either of the filled conditions with low service provider control. In fact, the average overall quality rating for delayed customers in a filled, low control condition is comparable to the service evaluations of nondelayed customers (6.14 vs. 6.26 for nondelayed; $p > .30$). The results are similar for reliability ($p > .30$) and responsiveness ($p > .60$). As long as the customer perceives that the service provider has little control over the delay, and

that customer's time is filled while he or she waits, the negative impact of the delay on service evaluations is mitigated. However, if the customer perceives a high degree of control on the part of the service provider, and if he or she is given ample opportunity to think about the delay (by not having his or her time filled), then service evaluations will be significantly lowered.

Although negative affect was related to many of the evaluations (as a significant covariate), it appears that the conditions of the delay (service provider control and filled time) did not influence reported levels of negative affect; customers' feelings of anger and frustration did not differ depending on the perceived service provider control or the degree to which waiting time was filled. These results are in conflict with Folkes, Koletsky, and Graham (1987) and Taylor (1994), who found that negative affect mediated the relationship between delays and reactions to these delays. This difference may be due to the length of the delay studied and the resulting intensity of the negative affect. Negative affect for the delayed subjects averaged only 2.26 (on a scale in which 7 is very negative). Because longer delays generate more negative affect (Folkes, Koletsky, and Graham 1987; Taylor 1994), it is possible that the 10-minute delay studied here was not long enough to generate intense negative affect. As such, negative affect does not act as a significant mediator between the delay and service evaluations in this study.

It is also interesting to note that some subjects in the delay conditions answered no when asked if they had been delayed. These subjects may not have perceived 10 minutes to be long enough to constitute a delay. As it turns out, these subjects were predominantly those in the filled conditions, suggesting that as long as waiting time is filled, customers may not even perceive that they are experiencing a delay.

The results have implications for Bitner's (1990, 1991) model of service encounter evaluation. According to her model, attribution (which encompasses service provider control) and process components of the marketing mix (which encompasses filled time) are capable of influencing service evaluations; however, in Bitner's model, although process components are modeled to affect service performance evaluations, attribution is not (as is implicit in this study). Instead, attribution is modeled to mediate the relationship between disconfirmation (the discrepancy between service performance and expectations) and satisfaction. The results of the present study suggest that attribution should be considered earlier in Bitner's model because it directly affects performance evaluations.

Limitations and Directions for Future Research

This study furthers our understanding of the relationship between delays and evaluations of service; however, it is not without some limitations. First, this study only examined one type of wait—a preservice delay—and one delay duration—10 minutes. Although it is expected that the results would be similar for waits in queues, one cannot generalize based on these results alone. Longer delays may also affect the waiting customers differently than the 10-minute wait used here. For example, longer delays may generate more negative affect and, as such, the affect may bias evaluations of service. Also, with longer delays there may be a limit to how much you can distract the customer from focusing on the wait; thus even when the customer's time is filled and he or she perceives the service provider to have low control over the delay, the customer may evaluate the service in a very negative fashion. Future studies are needed to assess this.

The service used in this study was a new service with which customers had no prior experience. It is possible that a delay may have affected evaluations differently for services that customers had previously experienced. Future research could be conducted to address how delays affect not only service encounter performance evaluations, but also service satisfaction (performance minus expectations) and longer-term service quality assessments. In addition, the service setting studied involved customers waiting alone, whereas in many service settings customers wait with others. It is possible that solo waiting generates different reactions to a delay than waiting in groups (Maister 1985). For example, interacting with others during the delay may fill time, resulting in higher service evaluations.

A potential limiting factor in this study is the lower than desired reliability on the negative affect construct and the SERVQUAL dimension of tangibles. The low reliability for the negative affect scale could have been increased by adding in the positive affect items; however, these did not load on the same factor in the exploratory factor analysis, suggesting that they are two separate constructs. The negative affect items were drawn from a variety of different scales with an eye to achieving reliability and face validity with the respondents. Perhaps an established mood scale such as Mehrabian and Russell's (1974) PAD scale would have resulted in higher reliability; however, a trade-off in face validity would have had to have been made. Although the lower than desired reliability for the SERVQUAL construct of tangibles is not unusual (see Babakus and Boller 1992), a more reliable measure would have been desirable.

Despite these limitations, the results of this research further our insight into the impact of delays on evalua-

tions of service. The results of this experiment not only provide replication of prior field research results, but they also extend our knowledge of the interactive effects of wait experience variables on service performance evaluation. They provide a better understanding of the service encounter evaluation process (e.g., Bitner 1990, 1991) as well as useful managerial guidelines to act on in minimizing the negative effects of a delay.

APPENDIX
Service Evaluation Survey Items

Overall service evaluation:

1. Overall, I would rate my service experience with Career Path as good.

2. I would recommend Career Path to other students.

Tangibles:

3. Career Path has modern-looking equipment.

4. Career Path's physical facilities are visually appealing.

5. Career Path's employee, XX[*], is neat-appearing.

6. Materials associated with Career Path (such as pamphlets or statements) are visually appealing.

Reliability:

7. When XX at Career Path promises to do something by a certain time, she does so.

8. If I had a problem, XX at Career Path showed a sincere interest in solving it.

9. XX at Career Path performed the service right the first time.

10. XX at Career Path provided me service at the time she promised to do so.

11. XX at Career Path would insist on error-free records.

Responsiveness:

12. XX at Career Path could tell me exactly when services would be performed.

13. XX at Career Path gave me prompt service.

14. XX at Career Path was willing to help me.

15. XX at Career Path was never too busy to respond to my requests.

Assurance:

16. XX's behavior instilled confidence in me.

17. I felt safe in my transactions with Career Path.

18. XX at Career Path was consistently courteous with me.

19. XX had the knowledge to answer my questions.

Empathy:

20. XX at Career Path gave me individual attention.

21. Career Path has operating hours convenient to all students.

22. XX, at Career Path, gave me personal attention.

23. Career Path has your best interests at heart.

24. XX at Career Path understood my specific needs.

* The counselor's actual name was used in the survey.

Acknowledgments

This research was supported by grants from the Social Sciences and Humanities Research Council of Canada (Grant No. 410-91-1646) and the Research Office, School of Business, Queen's University. The author is grateful to Peter Todd and four anonymous reviewers for their helpful comments, and to Barbara Wong and Meredith Laurence for their assistance with data collection and coding.

The Management of Customer-Contact Service Employees:
An Empirical Investigation

MICHAEL D. HARTLINE & O. C. FERRELL

The authors develop and test a model of service employee management that examines constructs simultaneously across three interfaces of the service delivery process: manager-employee, employee-role, and employee-customer. The authors examine the attitudinal and behavioral responses of customer-contact employees that can influence customers' perceptions of service quality, the relationships among these responses, and three formal managerial control mechanisms (empowerment, behavior-based employee evaluation, and management commitment to service quality). The findings indicate that managers who are committed to service quality are more likely to empower their employees and use behavior-based evaluation. However, the use of empowerment has both positive and negative consequences in the management of contact employees. Some of the negative consequences are mitigated by the positive effects of behavior-based employee evaluation. To increase customers' perceptions of service quality, managers must increase employees' self-efficacy and job satisfaction, and reduce employees' role conflict and ambiguity. Implications for the management of customer-contact service employees and directions for further research are discussed.

Many service firms are subject to failures in service delivery because they must depend on customer-contact employees to deliver service to their customers. Because the delivery of service occurs during the interaction between contact employees and customers (the service encounter), the attitudes and behaviors of contact employees can influence customers' perceptions of the service (Bowen and Schneider 1985). Because of the importance of the service encounter, service firms must find ways to effectively manage their customer-contact employees to help ensure that their attitudes and behaviors are conducive to the delivery of quality service.

The management of customer-contact employees has been extensively discussed in the services marketing literature. However, previous research examines the employee management process from one of three perspectives: the manager-employee interface, the employee-role interface, and the employee-customer interface. The manager-employee interface deals with human resource management issues and the activities involved in managing the responses of customer-contact employees. Previous research in this area has examined issues such as management commitment to service quality (cf. Ahmed and Parasuraman 1994), empowerment (cf. Bowen and Lawler 1992), employee socialization (cf. Hartline and Ferrell 1993), traditional managerial functions (cf. Bowen and Schneider 1985), employee reward policies (cf. Bush et al. 1990), and internal marketing (cf. George 1990). The employee-role interface deals with the relationships *among* contact employee behaviors, responses, and attitudes. Research in this area has investigated the effects of role conflict and role ambiguity (cf. Singh 1993); the relationships among job satisfaction, self-efficacy, adaptability, and employee effort (cf. Glisson and Durick 1988; Spiro and Weitz 1990); and the use of cognitive scripts in the delivery of service (cf. Humphrey and Ashforth 1994). The employee-customer interface deals with employee-customer interaction during the service encounter. Previous research in this area has examined the relationship between customer perceptions of the service encounter and contact employees' attitudinal and behavioral responses (cf. Bitner 1990; Bitner, Booms, and Mohr 1994). Specific employee responses that have been investigated include role stress (cf. Singh 1993); ability, competence, and adaptability (cf. Bitner, Booms, and Tetreault 1990); and job satisfaction (cf. Bowen and Schneider 1985).

The findings from previous research lead to two major conclusions: (1) managers can influence

Michael D. Hartline is Assistant Professor, Department of Marketing, College of Business Administration, Louisiana State University. O. C. Ferrell is Visiting Distinguished Professor of Marketing, University of Tampa, and Distinguished Professor of Marketing and Business Ethics, University of Memphis. The authors gratefully acknowledge the financial support of the Marketing Science Institute, as well as the guidance of Emin Babakus, Pat Schul, and Tom Ingram in planning and conducting this study. They also thank Richard Netermeyer, Dan Sherrell, the editor, and three anonymous JM reviewers for their valuable suggestions in preparing and revising this article.

customer-contact employees' responses so as to enhance service quality and (2) the responses of customercontact employees heavily influence customers' perceptions of service quality and the service encounter. Drawing from these conclusions, we attempt to gain a better understanding of contact employee management by simultaneously examining all three interfaces. Within the employee-customer interface, we examine the attitudinal and behavioral responses of customer-contact employees that can influence customers' perceptions of service quality. We also examine the relationships among these responses within the employee-role interface. Within the manager-employee interface, we examine managerial control mechanisms that can be used to manage the responses of customer-contact employees. Consistent with a call from Rust and Oliver (1994), we also capture perceptions and judgments across all three participants in the service quality delivery process: managers, employees, and customers. This approach enables us to examine the relationships between constructs across all three interfaces and determine the relative importance of these relationships within the overall employee management process.

Service Employee Management

Although employee management has been addressed in marketing (primarily in sales research) (cf. Basu et al. 1985; Churchill et al. 1985; Singh 1993; Spiro and Weitz 1990), few attempts have been made to explicate a composite description of the employee management process in service organizations. In one of the first studies to address service employee management, Bowen and Schneider (1985) argue that traditional managerial functions should be altered because of the unique characteristics of services. Some of their recommendations include (1) involving employees in the planning and organizing of service activities, (2) recognizing that the work environment of service employees has a strong influence on how customers experience the service, and (3) understanding that the firm's human resource practices can ultimately influence customers' service experiences. The underlying premise of these recommendations is that if managers treat their employees well, the employees will treat customers well (Bowen and Schneider 1985; Grönroos 1983).

Zeithaml, Berry, and Parasuraman (1988) identify several communication and control processes that managers could implement to manage service employees. These processes include managerial activities and employee responses that are hypothesized to affect ser-

vice quality. Parasuraman, Berry, and Zeithaml (1990) test these relationships, but many of their hypotheses are not supported. Subsequent research suggests that the lack of empirical support is due to the use of gap analysis and problems with the measurement of service quality (cf. Babakus and Boller 1992; Cronin and Taylor 1992). In a later study, Singh (1993) examines several managerial determinants and employee response outcomes of the role ambiguity experienced by boundary-spanning employees. Although his study does not focus exclusively on service employees, it provides empirical evidence that managerial actions do influence boundary-spanning employee responses. Still, Singh's study does not examine service quality as an outcome or the interaction between boundary-spanning employees and the firm's customers.

In the vein of previous attempts to embody the service employee management process, we propose the conceptual model in Figure 1. Drawing from research in a variety of disciplines, this model explores important components of service employee management simultaneously across all three interfaces. Rather than adapt previous models to a services framework, we attempt to develop a model that captures relationships that are unique to service employee management or are understudied within the context of services marketing. In the following discussion, we examine how the attitudinal and behavioral responses of contact employees affect customers' perceptions of service quality (the employee-customer interface). Next, we discuss the relationships among these employee responses (the employee-role interface). Finally, we examine the managerial control mechanisms that can be used to manage employee responses (the manager-employee interface).

The Employee-Customer Interface

The attitudinal and behavioral responses of customer-contact employees are important because of the interactive nature of service delivery (how the service is delivered) (Grönroos 1983). Research has shown that employees' attitudinal and behavioral responses can positively and negatively affect customers' perceptions of the service encounter and their judgments of service quality (Bitner 1990). On the negative side, early studies by Schneider (1980) and Shamir (1980) reveal that employees' role stress (conflict and ambiguity) and dissatisfaction are major contributors to their inability to deliver good service. Singh (1993) provides empirical evidence that the role ambiguity experienced by boundary-spanning employees greatly reduces their job satisfaction and performance. Contact employees who experience ambiguous or conflicting role

FIGURE 1
The Management of Customer-Contact Service Employees: A Conceptual Model[a]

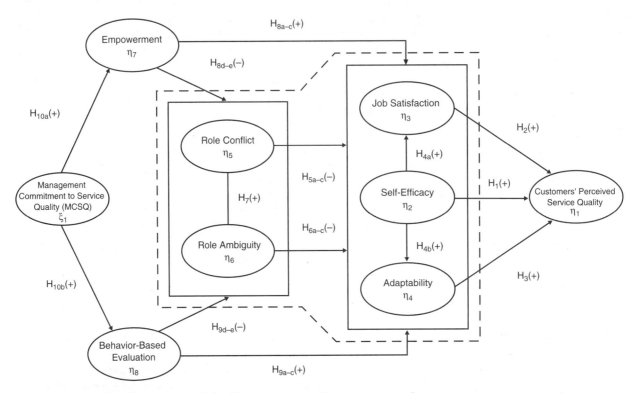

[a]Constructs within the dashed line are the attitudinal and behavioral responses of customer-contact employees.

expectations are likely to exhibit decreased job satisfaction and performance, which leads to a decrease in customers' perceived service quality (Schneider 1980).

Other attitudinal and behavioral responses have been shown to positively affect customer perceptions of quality. Bateson (1985) argues that contact employees are better able to satisfy customers when the employee has some control over the service encounter. Similarly, Bitner (1990) and Bitner, Booms, and Tetreault (1990) show through qualitative studies that customers are more satisfied with the service encounter when employees possess the ability, willingness, and competence to solve their problems. Bitner, Booms, and Tetreault (1990) also find that an employee's ability to adapt to special needs and requests enhances customers' perceptions of the service encounter. Finally, several studies have shown that the friendliness, enthusiasm, and attentiveness of contact employees positively affect customers' perceptions of service quality (cf. Bowen and Schneider 1985; Rafaeli 1993).

Based on a review of the literature, we chose to examine five attitudinal and behavioral responses of customer-contact employees that are hypothesized to

positively (self-efficacy, job satisfaction, and adaptability) and negatively (role conflict and role ambiguity) affect the ability of contact employees to serve customers in a manner that enhances service quality. These responses were chosen for two reasons. First, though self-efficacy, job satisfaction, and adaptability are familiar constructs in other literature, the services marketing literature has yet to empirically link these responses to customers' perceptions of service quality. Second, these five responses have been conceptually linked with all three interfaces. Including these responses enables us to connect the interfaces to examine them simultaneously within the same study. Other constructs that we might have chosen (e.g., effort, persistence, ability) were either too focused within a single interface or too broad for the scope of our study.

Employee Self-Efficacy As a key part of Bandura's (1977) social learning theory, self-efficacy refers to an employee's belief in his or her ability to perform job-related tasks. The importance of self-efficacy lies in its ability to increase employee performance.

Self-efficacy grows stronger over time as the employee successfully performs tasks and builds the confidence necessary to fulfill his or her role in the organization (Gist and Mitchell 1992). As self-efficacy increases, employees exert more effort, become more persistent, and learn to cope with task-related obstacles (cf. Bandura 1977; Gist 1987). Empirical studies confirm that self-efficacy has a strong, positive relationship with employee performance (cf. Earley 1994). It is therefore reasonable to expect that contact employees who possess strong self-efficacy beliefs are more likely to create favorable service encounters than those who do not. Employee performance during a service encounter typically involves responding to customer needs, handling special requests, and performing under adverse circumstances (Bitner, Booms, and Tetreault 1990). Because of the increased effort that accompanies self-efficacy, highly self-efficacious contact employees should perform better in these service activities, thereby increasing customers' perceptions of service quality. Likewise, self-efficacious contact employees should be able to cope with demanding situations that arise during the service encounter.

In summary, the self-efficacy of contact employees should play an important role in shaping customers' perceptions of the service encounter. When customers are served by employees who believe strongly in their own abilities, they are likely to receive higher-quality service. Accordingly, we propose the following hypothesis:

H₁: Higher customer-contact employee self-efficacy leads to a higher level of service quality as perceived by customers.

Employee Job Satisfaction Locke (1969, p. 316) defines job satisfaction as "the pleasurable emotional state resulting from the appraisal of one's job as achieving or facilitating the achievement of one's job values." The conceptual domain of job satisfaction is broad, because it includes "all characteristics of the job itself and the work environment which salesmen [sic] find rewarding, fulfilling, and satisfying, or frustrating and unsatisfying" (Churchill, Ford, and Walker 1974, p. 255). Operationally, job satisfaction consists of several facets, including satisfaction with the supervisor, work, pay, advancement opportunities, coworkers, and customers (Brown and Peterson 1993). Although some studies examine the effects of these facets separately, others average across facets to create a global measure of job satisfaction. We take the latter approach because research indicates that averaging across facets better captures the domain of the job satisfaction construct (Brown and Peterson 1993).

Despite the intuitive connection between job satisfaction and employee performance, meta-analytic research reports a modest correlation of only .15 between employee satisfaction and performance across many studies (Brown and Peterson 1993). However, this weak relationship may be partly due to the fact that most studies measure employee performance in terms of outcomes (i.e., sales volume or quota) rather than in terms of behaviors (i.e., effort, teamwork, friendliness). Churchill and colleagues (1985) argue that job satisfaction is closely related to employees' behavioral performance in a sales context. A similar relationship is likely to occur with respect to service employees. During the service encounter, employee behavioral performance often *is* the service, as it is perceived by customers (Bitner 1990). This relationship lies in the interaction between contact employees and customers, in which satisfied employees are more likely to engage in behaviors that assist customers (Locke and Latham 1990; Weatherly and Tansik 1993). Schneider (1980) finds evidence that job satisfaction is a primary reason that employees deliver good service. Although many other researchers have argued that customers' perceptions of a service are influenced by employee job satisfaction (cf. Bowen and Schneider 1985; Grönroos 1983), the connection between employee job satisfaction and customers' perceptions of service quality has not been empirically examined. Accordingly, we propose the following hypothesis:

H₂: Higher customer-contact employee job satisfaction leads to a higher level of service quality as perceived by customers.

Employee Adaptability We define *adaptability* as the ability of contact employees to adjust their behavior to the interpersonal demands of the service encounter. This definition is consistent with that of *functional flexibility* and *innovativeness* in the organizational behavior literature (cf. Paulhus and Martin 1988), and that of *adaptive selling* in the sales management literature (Spiro and Weitz 1990). All four terms are functionally equivalent, because their definitions include two common components: (1) the ability to adjust behavior and (2) interpersonal situations. Adaptability can be described as a continuum ranging from conformity to an established script, in which employees approach each customer the same way, to service personalization, in which employees must adapt to serve individual customers (Solomon et al. 1985).

Previous research has linked adaptability with employee performance. For example, Spiro and Weitz

(1990) show that salesperson performance is positively correlated with the practice of adaptive selling. Employee adaptability also has been linked with customers' perceptions of the service encounter. Humphrey and Ashforth (1994) provide evidence that employees who "mindlessly" follow a service script are more likely to make mistakes and less likely to meet the individual needs of their customers. Bitner (1990) and Bitner, Booms, and Tetreault (1990) show that customers evaluate the service encounter more favorably when employees are able to adapt to meet their special needs and requests. This finding is further supported in a qualitative study by Bitner, Booms, and Mohr (1994, p. 99), in which they report that "almost half of particularly satisfying customer encounters reported by employees resulted from their ability to adjust the system to accommodate customer needs and requests. Success is attributed in these cases to the employee's own ability and willingness to adjust." Based on previous research, it is reasonable to expect that contact employees who adapt their behaviors during customer interactions are more likely to fulfill the needs and requests of their customers, thereby increasing customers' perceptions of service quality. On the basis of this reasoning, we propose the following hypothesis:

H₃: Higher customer-contact employee adaptability leads to a higher level of service quality as perceived by customers.

The Employee-Role Interface

Effects of Self-Efficacy Previous research suggests that self-efficacy has a positive influence on job satisfaction and adaptability. McDonald and Siegall (1992), who found a significant positive correlation between self-efficacy and job satisfaction, argue that job satisfaction increases, because the feelings of competence and confidence that accompany self-efficacy make the job more enjoyable. Increased competence and confidence also should increase employee adaptability, because employees become more able and willing to adapt to customer requests (cf. Jones 1986). On the basis of these findings, we propose the following hypotheses:

H₄: Higher customer-contact employee self-efficacy leads to higher levels of customer-contact employee (a) job satisfaction and (b) adaptability.

Effects of Role Conflict and Role Ambiguity Role conflict is defined as the incompatibility between one or more roles within an employee's role set, such that fulfilling one role would make fulfilling the others more difficult (cf. Weatherly and Tansik 1993). Role ambiguity occurs when an employee "lacks salient information needed to effectively enact his or her role" (Singh 1993, p. 12). Role conflict or ambiguity have been shown to reduce employees' job satisfaction (cf. Brown and Peterson 1993), self-efficacy beliefs (cf. Jex and Gudanowski 1992), and adaptability (Scott and Bruce 1994). We expect these findings to hold in a services context, because contact employees act as "boundary spanners" between the firm and its customers (Bowen and Schneider 1985). This places the contact employee in the unique position of acquiescing to the demands of the firm (i.e., managers, policy, rules) and its customers (Bateson 1985).

As is indicated in Figure 1, we do not hypothesize a direct relationship between role conflict or ambiguity and service quality. Our placement of conflict and ambiguity within the model is based on Schneider's (1980) argument that conflict and ambiguity *precede* other employee responses. In an empirical test of this relationship, Parasuraman, Berry, and Zeithaml (1990) find no support for a direct relationship between role conflict or ambiguity and service quality. These findings suggest that the effects of role conflict and ambiguity on service quality are mediated by employee responses. As a result, we expect that role conflict and ambiguity will negatively affect the self-efficacy, job satisfaction, and adaptability of customer-contact employees. Hence, we propose the following hypotheses:

H₅: Higher customer-contact employee role conflict leads to lower levels of customer-contact employee (a) self-efficacy, (b) job satisfaction, and (c) adaptability.

H₆: Higher customer-contact employee role ambiguity leads to lower levels of customer-contact employee (a) self-efficacy, (b) job satisfaction, and (c) adaptability.

Previous research also indicates that role conflict exerts a strong influence on role ambiguity (cf. Behrman and Perreault 1984). The conflicting role expectations of the firm, manager, and customers can increase employees' uncertainty about the best way to perform their jobs and the importance of job activities. Hence, we propose the following hypothesis:

H₇: Higher customer-contact employee role conflict leads to a higher level of customer-contact employee role ambiguity.

The Manager-Employee Interface

Many managerial activities have the potential to effectively manage employee behaviors and responses in ways that improve service quality. The problem lies in identifying the most effective activities. Jaworski (1988, p. 26) calls these activities *formal controls* and defines them as "management-initiated mechanisms that influence the probability that employees or groups will behave in ways that support the stated marketing objectives." According to Jaworski, there are three types of formal controls: *input controls* (actions taken prior to the implementation of a marketing activity), *process controls* (attempts to influence behaviors and/or activities during implementation), and *output controls* (setting performance standards and monitoring or evaluating results). Examples of input controls include the recruitment, selection, and training of employees; strategic planning; and resource allocations. Process controls include any mechanism that attempts to influence employee behaviors and responses during implementation (e.g., organizational structure, operating procedures, rewards). Finally, output controls include both performance standards that are stated in terms of quality outcomes (i.e., complaints, service quality, customer satisfaction) and the evaluation of those outcomes.

To make our study manageable, we focus on formal process control mechanisms. This focus seemed appropriate given our study's emphasis on the managerial controls that can be used to make employee behaviors and responses more conducive to the delivery of service quality. Previous service research has addressed the importance of process controls. For example, researchers have argued that to effectively manage boundary-spanning service employees, managers should maintain flexible work climates (Schneider 1980), place greater emphasis on the firm's human resource practices (Bowen and Schneider 1985), reward employees for their contributions to customer satisfaction (Bowen and Schneider 1985; Reardon and Enis 1990), increase their own commitment to service (George 1990; Zeithaml, Berry, and Parasuraman 1988), and increase employees' discretion (empowerment) in serving customers (Bowen and Lawler 1992; Kelley 1993). After reviewing previous research, we selected three service-related process control mechanisms that matched Jaworski's (1988) definition of formal process controls (i.e., mechanisms associated with the *means* to achieving desired employee responses): empowerment, behavior-based evaluation, and management commitment to service quality (MCSQ). Empowerment and behavior-based evaluation are mechanisms that can be used to control employees' behaviors and activities. Management commitment to service quality is a precursor to the use of other process control mechanisms, which makes it one of the most important factors in the successful implementation of service strategy (George 1990).

Empowerment Empowerment refers to a situation in which the manager gives employees the discretion to make day-to-day decisions about job-related activities (Bowen and Lawler 1992; Conger and Kanungo 1988). By allowing contact employees to make these decisions, the manager relinquishes control over many aspects of the service delivery process. Empowerment is thought to be necessary because contact employees need the flexibility to make on-the-spot decisions to completely satisfy customers. Allowing contact employees to use their discretion in serving customers has many positive influences on their responses and the service encounter. Bowen and Lawler (1992) suggest that empowered employees feel better about their jobs and more enthusiastic about serving customers, with an end result of quicker response to customer needs and increased customer satisfaction. Although the effects of empowerment have not been empirically verified, studies that have examined similar constructs provide some evidence of empowerment's positive influence. For example, increases in employee job satisfaction and decreases in employee role stress have been associated with employees' decision-making influence (Niehoff, Enz, and Grover 1990), task autonomy (Brown and Peterson 1993), and decision-making latitude (Westman 1992). Likewise, Singh (1993) reports that boundary-spanning employees who are given job autonomy experience significantly less role ambiguity.

One of the primary outcomes of empowerment is increased employee self-efficacy (Conger and Kanungo 1988). As employees gain more discretion over how their jobs are performed, their levels of self-efficacy increase because *they* decide the best way to perform a given task (Gist and Mitchell 1992). Empowered employees also are likely to be more adaptive because of the increased flexibility that accompanies empowerment (Scott and Bruce 1994). Empowerment removes the constraints imposed on customer-contact employees, which gives them room to maneuver as they attempt to serve customers' needs (Reardon and Enis 1990). The empowerment/adaptability relationship has received tentative empirical support, because adaptability has been associated with autonomy and decision-making influence (Niehoff, Enz, and Grover 1990; Scott and Bruce 1994), as well as with freedom of employee action (Spiro and Weitz 1990).

In summary, empowerment should have a positive influence on the attitudinal and behavioral responses of contact employees. The increased discretion and flexibility experienced by empowered contact employees make them feel better about their jobs, reduce the stress they feel in performing their jobs, increase their confidence in performing job-related tasks, and increase their ability to adapt to changing conditions within the service encounter. On the basis of this reasoning, we propose the following hypothesis:

H₈: An increase in the manager's use of empowerment leads to higher levels of customer-contact employee (a) self-efficacy, (b) job satisfaction, and (c) adaptability, and lower levels of customer-contact employee (d) role conflict and (e) role ambiguity.

Behavior-Based Evaluation As one facet of a behavior-based control system, behavior-based evaluation involves evaluating employees on the basis of how they behave or act rather than on the basis of the measurable outcomes they achieve (Anderson and Oliver 1987). Under a behavior-based system, contact employees are evaluated and compensated on the basis of criteria such as effort, commitment, teamwork, customer orientation, friendliness, the ability to solve customer problems, and/or other behaviors that are directed toward improved service quality (Bowen and Schneider 1985; Reardon and Enis 1990). Linking evaluations to service-related behavioral criteria gives employees the incentive to engage in behaviors that are conducive to improved service quality (George 1990; Grönroos 1983). It also gives employees more control over the conditions that affect their performance evaluations (Anderson and Oliver 1987; Cravens et al. 1993). Although outcomes such as sales and profit can be influenced by several factors, contact employees are solely responsible for their behavioral responses.

Previous research supports the positive relationship between behavior-based evaluation and employee responses. For example, an emphasis on behavioral criteria has been shown to increase employees' competence (Cravens et al. 1993), self-efficacy (Gist and Mitchell 1992), and job satisfaction (Oliver and Anderson 1994). Researchers have also found that employee adaptability increases when employees perceive that rewards are the result of their own behaviors or when rewards are tied to innovative behavioral performance (Scott and Bruce 1994; Spiro and Weitz 1990). Behavior-based evaluation also reduces employees' role conflict and ambiguity because it gives employees more control over the conditions that affect their evaluations (Basu et al. 1985) and frees them from the pressures to produce measurable outcomes (Anderson and Oliver 1987).

In summary, the use of behavior-based evaluation should have a positive influence on the attitudinal and behavioral responses of customer-contact employees. By emphasizing behavioral criteria during employee performance appraisals, managers make employees responsible for their behaviors and give them more

control over the conditions that affect their evaluations. These employees respond by feeling more satisfied, more competent, and more adaptive, while simultaneously experiencing less role stress. Accordingly, we propose the following hypotheses:

H₉: An increase in the manager's use of behavior-based employee evaluation leads to higher levels of customer-contact employee (a) self-efficacy, (b) job satisfaction, and (c) adaptability, and lower levels of customer-contact employee (d) role conflict and (e) role ambiguity.

Management Commitment to Service Quality
Management commitment to service quality is defined as "encompassing the conscious choice of quality initiatives as operational and strategic options for the firm, and engaging in activities such as providing visible quality leadership and resources for the adoption and implementation of quality initiatives" (Ahmed and Parasuraman 1994, p. 85). It involves two components: (1) a strong, personal commitment to quality improvement and (2) a visible and active involvement in the quality-improvement process (Mohr-Jackson 1993). Although some theorists have argued that MCSQ is the single most important determinant of whether good service is delivered to customers (George 1990; Grönroos 1983), it has generated little empirical research. In perhaps the only test of the MCSQ construct, Parasuraman, Berry, and Zeithaml (1990) fail to find a direct relationship between MCSQ and service quality. A probable reason for this finding is that the relationship between MCSQ and service quality is indirect. Theory suggests that managers must first possess a personal, affective commitment to improve the firm's service quality (Mohr-Jackson 1993). Managers who exhibit this commitment are more likely to take initiatives that help the firm and its employees deliver superior quality (George 1990). Examples of these initiatives include creating more flexible processes, dedicating resources to the improvement effort, promulgating a quality-oriented vision throughout the firm, and rewarding employees for their efforts and commitment to the process (Ahmed and Parasuraman 1994; Wall and Zeynel 1991).

We postulate that empowerment and behavior-based evaluation are MCSQ-type initiatives that managers can use to influence contact employee responses during their delivery of service quality. This reasoning is consistent with Jaworski's (1988) definition of process controls (i.e., managerial attempts to influence employee behaviors and activities during implementation). Thus, we hypothesize that managers who are committed to service quality are more likely to empower their employees and emphasize behavioral criteria in employee evaluations. Hence, we propose our final hypotheses:

H_{10}: An increase in the manager's commitment to service quality leads to an increase in the manager's use of (a) empowerment and (b) behavior-based employee evaluation.

Research Method

Sample

We chose hotels as our sampling frame because the delivery of hotel services requires considerable customer contact. To initiate a sample, we contacted the marketing managers of nine hotel chains. Three chains, each offering services in the middle to high price and quality range, agreed to participate by providing a complete mailing list of general managers' names and hotel addresses. This procedure resulted in a pool of 444 hotel units, all of which were sampled. The corporate marketing managers of the three chains mailed a letter to each general manager that explained the research and asked for their support. Approximately two weeks later, questionnaire packets were mailed to each general manager. Each packet contained one manager survey, five employee surveys, forty guest surveys, one page of instructions, and postage-paid return envelopes. Each respondent group was surveyed regarding the issues for which they would be most knowledgeable. Hotel managers were asked about their commitment to quality, their use of empowerment, and their emphasis on behavioral criteria in employee evaluations. Customer-contact employees were asked about their levels of role stress, self-efficacy, satisfaction, and adaptability. Service quality was assessed by questioning hotel guests.

Constraints imposed by the participating hotel chains prohibited us from directly contacting employees or guests. As a result, we relied on the general managers to distribute the employee and guest surveys. The general managers were instructed to distribute the employee surveys across a broad range of customer-contact positions (e.g., front desk, food service, housekeeping, bellstaff) and to distribute the guest surveys during checkout. Approximately two months after the initial mailing, a second wave of materials was mailed. All questionnaires were returned directly to the researchers.

Of the total sample, 279 different hotel units responded by returning at least one questionnaire from a manager, employee, or customer (a total of 2389 questionnaires). Of these, only 24 employee and 35 customer surveys were unusable. Usable questionnaires were returned by 236 hotel managers (53.2% response rate), 743 employees (33.5% response rate), and 1351 customers (5.1% response rate). Because 165 hotels failed to return any type of questionnaire, we tested for nonresponse bias using a time-trend extrapolation test (Armstrong and Overton 1977). We found no differences in perceived service quality between early and late customer respondents and no differences in demographic characteristics between early and late employee or manager respondents. The demographic characteristics of employees and general managers are reported in Table 1. Employee respondents were screened to ensure that their jobs involved customer contact by asking them to report their job position on the questionnaire. Customer-contact positions were confirmed through discussions with corporate managers. The 182 employees who did not meet this criterion were dropped before we tested the measures and the hypothesized model.

Measures

To remain consistent with previous research, the measures were taken or adapted from previous studies in marketing, management, and psychology. A list of the measures is provided in Appendix B.

Management Commitment to Service Quality We operationalized MCSQ as the manager's affective desire to improve his or her unit's service quality. Although Parasuraman, Berry, and Zeithaml (1990) developed a four-item scale to measure MCSQ, we did not use their scale because it exhibited low reliability (average of .54) and the items measure MCSQ initiatives rather than affective commitment. Because our goal was to tap affective MCSQ, we adapted nine items from Mowday, Steers, and Porter's (1979) organizational commitment scale. Because this scale was originally designed to measure affective commitment to an organization, we reworded the items to reflect the manager's affective commitment to service quality. Managers were asked to indicate their agreement with each item through a five-point scale ranging from "strongly disagree" to "strongly agree." Higher scores reflect a stronger commitment to service quality. We were concerned that our measure might be negatively skewed, with managers reporting high MCSQ. A highly skewed distribution could attenuate the correlations between MCSQ and other variables, thus underestimating the "true" relationship. Although our measure is slightly skewed (skewness = −1.11), it is not sufficiently skewed to cause a bias in the responses.

Empowerment Empowerment was operationalized as the extent to which managers allow employees to use their own initiative and judgment in performing their jobs. Because no measure of empowerment existed at the time of our study, we used the eight-item tolerance-of-freedom scale from the LBDQ XII, which measures the degree to which managers encourage initiative, give employees freedom, and trust employees to use their judgment (Cook et al. 1981). Hotel managers rated each item on a five-point scale ranging from "strongly disagree" to "strongly agree." Higher scores indicate that the manager uses a greater degree of empowerment in managing their employees.

Behavior-Based Evaluation Behavior-based evaluation was operationalized as the extent to which managers emphasize behavioral criteria in evaluating employees. The scale we employed uses five items from the behavior-based performance scale of Bush and colleagues' (1990) study, which assess the importance of several behavioral criteria (courtesy, innovativeness, commitment to the firm and customers, and ability to resolve customer problems) in the manager's evaluation of contact employees. Managers rated this importance on a five-point scale ranging from "not at all important" to "extremely important." Higher scores indicate that managers emphasize behavioral criteria when conducting employee evaluations.

Role Conflict and Ambiguity Although the scales developed by Rizzo, House, and Lirtzman (1970) are the most commonly used measures of role conflict and ambiguity, we chose not to use them because research casts doubt on their validity (cf. McGee, Ferguson, and Seers 1989). Instead, we used the role conflict and role ambiguity scales developed by Chonko, Howell,

TABLE 1

Demographic Characteristics of Customer-Contact Employees and Managers

	Customer-Contact Employees n = 561		Managers n = 236	
	Frequency	%	Frequency	%
Sex				
Male	176	32.0	158	67.2
Female	379	68.0	77	32.8
Age (years)				
Under 20	32	5.8	0.0	0.0
20 to 30	354	63.8	65	27.8
31 to 40	83	14.9	109	46.6
41 to 50	55	9.9	44	18.8
51 to 60	22	4.0	13	5.5
Over 60	9	1.6	3	1.3
Education				
Some high school	42	7.6	1	.4
High school graduate	128	23.1	17	7.2
Some college	240	43.3	82	34.9
College graduate	119	21.5	109	46.4
Some graduate work	14	2.5	9	3.8
Graduate degree	11	2.0	17	7.2
Position				
Front desk/customer service	301	53.7		
Housekeeping	116	20.7		
Food/room service	53	9.4		
Reservations/sales	41	7.3		
Bellstaff	30	5.3		
Assistant manager	20	3.6		
Industry Experience (years)				
0 to 5			36	15.3
5 to 10			71	30.2
10 to 15			52	22.1
15 to 20			49	20.9
Over 20			27	11.5

and Bellenger (1986). The original 30-item role conflict and 36-item role ambiguity scales were designed for use in a sales context. To adapt the scales for our use, we selected scale items that could apply to any boundary-spanning employee (i.e., items pertaining to expense accounts, extending credit, and/or sales commissions were deleted). The final 12-item role conflict asks employees to indicate the agreement between themselves and their job expectations, supervisors, and customers on a scale ranging from "no agreement" to "complete agreement." The final 17-item role ambiguity scale asks employees to indicate how certain they are about performing job tasks on a scale ranging from "not at all certain" to "completely certain." After reversing the scale responses, higher scores reflect higher role conflict and role ambiguity.

Self-Efficacy Self-efficacy was operationalized as the extent to which employees feel confident about their job skills and abilities. The measure we used is an eight-item scale developed by Jones (1986), which is designed to measure employees' perceptions about their job skills, abilities, qualifications, and confidence. Employees rated each item on a seven-point scale ranging from "strongly disagree" to "strongly agree." Higher scores reflect higher perceived self-efficacy.

Job Satisfaction Consistent with the work of Brown and Peterson (1993), employee job satisfaction was operationalized as an eight-item measure that assesses satisfaction with eight facets of the overall job (e.g., pay, coworkers, supervisor). The measure asks employees to indicate how satisfied they are with each facet, using a five-point scale ranging from "extremely dissatisfied" to "extremely satisfied." After averaging across facets, higher scores reflect higher overall job satisfaction. Research by Peterson and Wilson (1992) suggests that many satisfaction measures are negatively skewed, with most respondents reporting high satisfaction. Our satisfaction measure is negatively skewed to a small degree (skewness = − .600), which indicates that the responses are not significantly biased.

Adaptability Employee adaptability was operationalized as the ability of customer-contact employees to adjust their behavior to the interpersonal demands of the service encounter. To measure adaptability, we modified the 16-item adaptive selling scale developed by Spiro and Weitz (1990) by dropping 6 redundant items and changing the wording of the remaining items to eliminate the personal selling aspects within each statement. The final 10-item scale assesses contact employees' ability to adapt to changing service encounters by altering their approach toward cus-

tomers. Employees indicated their agreement with each item, using a seven-point scale ranging from "strongly disagree" to "strongly agree." Higher scores reflect a greater degree of employee adaptability.

Perceived Service Quality Parasuraman, Berry, and Zeithaml (1990) define service quality as the difference between customer expectations and perceptions of service. Their SERVQUAL scale has been criticized for the use of gap scores, positively and negatively worded items, the generalizability of SERVQUAL dimensions, and the defining of a baseline standard for "good" quality (cf. Brown, Churchill, and Peter 1993; Oliver 1993a). To help alleviate these problems, researchers have shown that combining expectations and perceptions into a single measure outperforms the SERVQUAL scale in terms of both reliability and validity (cf. Babakus and Boller 1992; Brown, Churchill, and Peter 1993). Cronin and Taylor (1992) argue for the superiority of a performance-only measure of service quality on the basis that it is more efficient and generalizable than SERVQUAL. After evaluating the criticisms leveled against their approach, Parasuraman, Zeithaml, and Berry (1994, pp. 120–21) state: "Because the cumulative empirical evidence . . . has not established conclusively the superiority of one measure over the other, additional research in this area is warranted." Because of these unresolved issues, choosing the "correct" measure of service quality has become somewhat problematic.

We chose to use items from the original SERVQUAL scale with two major modifications. First, research indicates that customers judge quality on the basis of specific quality-related attributes (Oliver 1993a; Taylor and Baker 1994). Because our intent is to measure only one attribute (i.e., the quality of service delivered by customer-contact employees), we restricted our measure to ten items that specifically assess employee-related aspects of service quality. Second, we combined expectations and perceptions into a single measure, as was suggested by Brown, Churchill, and Peter (1993). This modification is consistent with Silverman and Grover's (1995) findings that customers do use expectancy disconfirmation in their assessments of quality. Our measure asks hotel guests to rate each item, using a five-point scale ranging from "much worse than I expected" to "much better than I expected." Higher scores reflect higher perceived service quality.

Measure Validation

We subjected all measures to confirmatory factor analysis to assess their psychometric properties and unidimensionality. Because of sample size restrictions associated with the large number of measures used in the study, we performed separate analyses for each sample group by using three complete (nonaggregated) data sets. After we accounted for missing data, the sample sizes were 236 responses for managers, 561 responses for employees, and 1238 responses for customers. To assess discriminant validity across all three samples, the employee and customer responses were aggregated (averaged) and matched with the manager responses to create a single data set in which the cases represent hotel units rather than persons. Hotel units that did not provide at least three responses from both employees and customers were dropped. These procedures resulted in a final sample of 97 hotel units, with each unit consisting of the matched responses from one general manager, an average of 3.37 employees, and an average of 9.38 customers. The details and results of our measure validation procedures are in Appendices A and B.

Analysis and Results

We tested our hypotheses with structural equation modeling. The procedures associated with estimating the hypothesized model and the statistical results are reported in Appendix A. Within the employee-customer interface, employee self-efficacy and job satisfaction have a positive effect on customers' perceived service quality, which supports H_1 and H_2. These effects are fairly strong, with self-efficacy having a stronger influence on perceived quality than job satisfaction. Contrary to H_3, employee adaptability does not have a significant effect on perceived service quality.

Within the employee-role interface, the effect of employee self-efficacy on job satisfaction is significant and negative (contrary to H_{4a}), which indicates that highly self-efficacious contact employees tend to be less satisfied with their jobs. H_{4b} also is not supported, because self-efficacy does not have a significant effect on employee adaptability. Role ambiguity appears to be the most influential construct within the employee-role interface. In accord with H_6, role ambiguity has a significant negative effect on employee self-efficacy, job satisfaction, and adaptability. These results differ from those of H_5, in which role conflict does not reduce employee self-efficacy, job satisfaction, or adaptability. In fact, contrary to H_{5a}, role conflict has a significant positive effect on self-efficacy. Role conflict also has a significant positive effect on role ambiguity, which supports H_7. Overall, the results indicate that role ambiguity has a direct influence on contact employees' responses and mediates most of the effects of role conflict.

Within the manager-employee interface, overall support for H_8 and H_9 is somewhat limited. In accord

with H_{8a}, empowerment increases employee self-efficacy. Contrary to H_{8d}, empowerment increases role conflict. The remaining parts of H_8 are not supported. However, the results indicate that empowerment has an indirect negative effect on employees' job satisfaction ($-.358$, $p < .001$) and adaptability ($-.100$, $p < .001$), and an indirect positive effect on role ambiguity ($.245$, $p < .001$). Overall, the results suggest that though empowered employees are more confident in their job skills, they experience increased conflict and ambiguity in their attempts to balance role demands.

In support of H_{9c} and H_{9d}, behavior-based evaluation increases employee adaptability and decreases employee role conflict. The remaining parts of H_9 are not supported. However, the results indicate that behavior-based evaluation has an indirect positive effect on job satisfaction ($.117$, $p < .01$), and an indirect negative effect on self-efficacy ($-.03$, $p < .05$) and role ambiguity ($-.198$, $p < .001$). Finally, the use of empowerment and behavior-based evaluation are dependent on MCSQ, which supports both parts of H_{10}. Although not hypothesized, the results also indicate that MCSQ increases employee job satisfaction. This relationship was indicated by a large modification index in the LISREL analysis.

Discussion

Few studies have approached the management of service employees by examining the process simultaneously from three perspectives. By capturing perceptions and judgments across managers, employees, and customers, our study is among the first to empirically link the perceptions of all three groups in a single study. This combination of perspectives sheds light on the practical and theoretical issues involved in managing customer-contact employee responses in order to enhance the delivery of service quality. Our study also helps lay the groundwork for additional research into the complex issues associated with the management of customer-contact employees.

The Employee-Customer Interface

The importance of customer-contact employees to the delivery of service quality is underscored by the results of our study. Specifically, we found that employee self-efficacy and job satisfaction increase customers' perceived service quality. Because many services (e.g., hotels) are produced and consumed "in the factory," confident and satisfied employees are likely to perform better than apprehensive and dissatisfied employees during the service encounter, which leads to an increase in customers' perceptions of service quality.

Although both responses are important, self-efficacy has a stronger effect on service quality than job satisfaction. This finding may be due to the boundary-spanning nature of the employees' positions. As contact employees become more confident in their ability to serve customers, they become more proactive and persistent, and they put forth greater effort. As a result, highly self-efficacious contact employees may be better able to handle the difficulties inherent in their jobs, which leads to better performance and higher perceived service quality.

We found no evidence of a relationship between employee adaptability and customers' perceived service quality. There are two plausible reasons for this finding. First, service encounters are situation specific, which means that the degree of adaptation that customers expect or receive varies from one service encounter to another. In encounters in which customers expect little or no adaptation, their judgments of service quality may be based on getting what they expect with no "surprises" (Solomon et al. 1985). Thus, for a hotel-based encounter, employee adaptability may not affect service quality, because customers do not expect or receive adapted service from employees. Second, the conceptualization and measurement of adaptability may not match the way customers perceive employee adaptability. As was conceptualized and measured in the literature and our study, employee adaptability occurs across service encounters (i.e., from one customer to another). However, customer perceptions of employee adaptability occur *within* the service encounter that they experience; therefore, customers are unlikely to notice adaptive employee responses as they occur across employee-customer encounters. As a result, adaptation across service encounters is likely to have no effect on service quality within a single encounter.

The Employee-Role Interface

Role ambiguity appears to have the most prominent effect within the employee-role interface, because it maintains a negative relationship with employees' self-efficacy, job satisfaction, and adaptability. Role ambiguity also is exacerbated by role conflict. Although these findings are not new, they underscore the difficulties inherent in fulfilling a customer-contact position. As contact employees span the boundary between the firm and its customers, they can become frustrated and confused in their search for the best way to fulfill their multiple roles. Role ambiguity is especially menacing because of its negative relationship with employee self-efficacy and job satisfaction. As its negative effects extend into the employee-customer interface, role ambiguity can diminish employees' ability to

serve customers and indirectly decrease customers' perceptions of service quality. Reducing the ambiguity associated with the customer-contact position could be one of the biggest challenges in the management of service employees.

Our finding that role conflict increases self-efficacy was not expected. However, research indicates that the emotional or physiological arousal caused by role conflict may increase employees' self-efficacy beliefs (cf. Bandura 1986). Employees who experience role conflict become emotionally aroused in their efforts to cope with conflicting role demands. As employees learn to cope with these difficulties, their self-efficacy increases. Because role conflict is an unavoidable aspect of the contact employee's job (Shamir 1980), coping with role conflict may be a prerequisite for successful role performance (Behrman and Perreault 1984). This could lead to a symbiotic relationship: role conflict increases self-efficacy, which enables the employee to better cope with conflicting role expectations (cf. Gist 1987).

Although previous research indicates that self-efficacy increases job satisfaction and adaptability, our results do not support these contentions. The lack of a self-efficacy/adaptability relationship is most likely due to the ability of other constructs in the model (i.e., role ambiguity and behavior-based evaluation) to predict adaptability better than self-efficacy. In particular, the level of role ambiguity inherent in customer-contact positions may suppress the effects of self-efficacy. Self-efficacy may lead to an increase in adaptability only when contact employees are certain about how to fulfill their role requirements. This relationship deserves further empirical investigation.

The negative relationship between self-efficacy and job satisfaction may lie in the nature of the customer-contact position, in which employees are typically underpaid, undertrained, overworked, and highly stressed (cf. Weatherly and Tansik 1993). The employees in our study also are typical of many retail service employees in that they are young, well-educated, and likely to be holding the job while attending school (see Table 1). Considering the characteristics of a customer-contact position and that most of these jobs do not require specialized skills, these employees are not likely to consider their current job as a permanent career choice. The young, college-educated employees that fill many customer-contact positions are likely to have goals of upward mobility that simply do not match the characteristics of most boundary-spanning retail positions.

The higher-level goals to which these employees aspire may be the cause of the negative self-efficacy/job satisfaction relationship. Research has shown that self-efficacious people set higher goals for themselves, which creates a situation in which the person must accomplish more to be satisfied (Locke and Latham 1990). The relationship between goals and satisfaction creates a unique situation: "[I]f goals are set at a low level, the individual will be satisfied but unproductive, and if they are set at a high level, the individual will be productive but dissatisfied" (Locke and Latham, 1990, p. 243). The job characteristics theory of Hackman and Oldham (1980) also argues that employees experience greater job satisfaction when the job has personal significance for them. As a contact employee's goals and self-efficacy increase, it is likely that the job takes on less personal significance. Thus, highly self-efficacious employees could be dissatisfied with their jobs because they aspire to higher goals. This could cause the personal significance attached to the job to decrease and further lower the level of job satisfaction.

The Manager-Employee Interface

The most striking finding within the manager-employee interface is that the use of empowerment leads to both positive and negative employee outcomes. Our findings suggest that though empowered employees gain confidence in their abilities, they also experience increased frustration (conflict) in their attempt to fulfill multiple roles at the organization's boundary. In addition to fulfilling the demands of their managers and customers, empowered employees take on added job responsibilities (Conger and Kanungo 1988). For some employees, this situation could prove to be frustrating. Although this conflict leads to an increase in self-efficacy as employees learn to cope with conflicting role demands, it also increases role ambiguity and indirectly reduces job satisfaction and adaptability. These complex relationships create a challenge for service managers to find ways to alleviate the role conflict associated with the empowerment of their contact employees.

One way to alleviate employees' role conflict may be to emphasize behavioral criteria in employee evaluations. Because employees can control their own behaviors more easily than work-related outcomes, behavior-based evaluation gives employees more control over their evaluations, thereby reducing conflict (Basu et al. 1985). Emphasizing behavioral criteria also gives contact employees the incentive to adapt to changing customer needs. Furthermore, behavior-based evaluation leads indirectly to reduced role ambiguity and increased job satisfaction. These findings suggest that the use of behavior-based evaluation complements the use of empowerment by mitigating some of its negative consequences.

Finally, our results strengthen the argument that managers must be committed to improving service quality before engaging in activities that have the potential to improve service quality (i.e., empowerment and behavior-based evaluation). Previous research also has argued that MCSQ is the most important determinant of exceptional service quality (cf. George 1990; Grönroos 1983; Wall and Zeynel 1991). Our results lend some empirical support to these theorists, because MCSQ has an *indirect* positive effect on service quality (.105, p < .01). Although this connection is important, our results show it to be entirely mediated by managerial controls and employee responses, particularly employee job satisfaction. Thus, though we concur that MCSQ is vital to the delivery of good service, our findings suggest that the attitudinal and behavioral responses of customer-contact employees are the primary determinants of customers' perceptions of service quality.

Implications and Suggestions for Further Research

Before discussing managerial implications and future research suggestions, the limitations of our study should be noted. First, a cross-sectional study incorporating multiple sample groups is extremely difficult to execute. Because we were not allowed to contact employees or customers directly, we relied on the hotel managers to distribute the surveys. If the managers did not randomly distribute the surveys as instructed, an increased potential for bias exists. Despite this risk, we did not note any bias as we coded the questionnaires. We did, however, observe one consequence that could have resulted from our reliance on general managers: Most (68%) of the employee respondents were female, whereas most (67.2%) of the general managers were male. We feel that this outcome may be a reflection of the distribution of employees within the sampled chains and is not likely to bias the results of our study.

Second, though it would have been desirable to measure many of the same constructs across managers and employees as a form of cross-validation, real concerns over questionnaire length precluded our doing so. However, by assessing the model's constructs across three separate samples, we were able to examine all three interfaces simultaneously. Such an approach would seem preferable to asking a single sample (e.g., managers) to assess every construct in the model. The major drawback of our approach is that aggregating and matching sample groups limited the overall sample size to 97 hotel units. In addition, the limited sample size required that we create summed-scale indicators for each construct and fix the measurement portion of the model to account for measurement error. Using single rather than multiple indicators makes it somewhat easier to confirm each hypothesis. Likewise, the use of multiple indicators would have made the results more reliable.

Third, though the total variance explained by the model is fairly high, the model's explanatory power is limited to its included constructs. Obviously, many other constructs could affect service employee management. For example, Parasuraman, Berry, and Zeithaml (1990) discuss how employee-job fit, horizontal communication, and task standardization affect contact employees and their delivery of service quality. Likewise, we did not examine the effects of formal input controls (i.e., employee recruitment, selection, and training) or formal output controls (i.e., performance standards). Furthermore, our measure of service quality does not include an assessment of the affective reactions of customers (Oliver 1993b).

Fourth, our focus on a single service industry may raise concerns about limited generalizability. However, constraining the study to a single industry eliminates problems associated with the effects of industry differences. Additionally, neither the high end (e.g., Ritz-Carlton) nor the low end (e.g., Motel 6) of the hotel services spectrum is represented in the sample. Notwithstanding these limitations, the constructs examined in our study could be applied to any industry, service, or otherwise.

Managerial Implications

Issues concerning the three interfaces of service employee management were addressed in our study. Based on our findings, we maintain that the employee-customer interface is the most important determinant of customers' perceptions of service quality. As a result, managers must find ways to increase the self-efficacy and job satisfaction of contact employees. However, these two goals may be incompatible given the characteristics of the typical customer-contact position. Self-efficacious contact employees are likely to serve customers more effectively; however, these employees may be less satisfied with the job because their goals of upward mobility do not match the characteristics of the customer-contact position. The challenges for the service manager are to (1) recruit and retain self-efficacious employees who also can be satisfied in a customer-contact position and (2) manage these employees in ways that maintain or increase their levels of self-efficacy and job satisfaction.

To meet these challenges, our results highlight the importance of four issues. First, managers must be committed to improving the firm's service quality. Put simply, managers who are personally committed to service quality are more likely to engage in activities that improve service quality. In our study, MCSQ translates into an increased use of empowerment and behavior-based evaluation and to an increase in employee job satisfaction. Although we did not hypothesize the relationship between MCSQ and job satisfaction, previous research has alluded to a possible connection (cf. Niehoff, Enz, and Grover 1990). Management commitment to service quality is important because it helps align the firm toward a common goal of superior service quality (cf. Reardon and Enis 1990). In this sense, MCSQ can become the manager's "vision" for the firm. This vision is likely to be noticed and modeled by employees, which ultimately increases employee satisfaction and service quality (cf. Niehoff, Enz, and Grover 1990).

Second, managers must recognize that the use of empowerment has both positive and negative consequences for contact employees and the firm's service quality. Because of the importance of self-efficacy in the employee customer interface, the use of empowerment has positive outcomes for both employees and the firm's service quality. However, empowered employees can become frustrated in their attempts to balance role demands, which can lead to an increase in role conflict and many negative consequences for employees and service quality. For this reason, we caution managers to use empowerment under the appropriate conditions. Previous research suggests that empowerment works best when the firm's culture supports its use by guiding and limiting employee actions (Bowen and Lawler 1992). If the firm's culture does not support employees for exercising discretion, empowerment is likely to be counterproductive (Kelley 1993). To support empowerment, managers should focus on behavioral criteria in evaluating contact employees. By evaluating contact employees on the basis of their behaviors (i.e., use of discretion) rather than outcomes (i.e., mistakes), behavior-based evaluation can help reduce employees' role conflict. In addition to behavioral evaluation, managers also should train employees on how to use their decision-making authority wisely. Training can help ensure that empowered employee decisions are in the best interests of the organization (Conger and Kanungo 1988).

Third, the use of behavior-based evaluation also increases employee adaptability. Although employee adaptability does not have an effect on service quality in our study, it is likely to be an important component of the service encounter for other services. One of the best ways to ensure that employees behave in certain ways is to reward them for doing so. To enhance adaptability, or other customer-oriented behaviors, managers should tie the behavior to the employee evaluation system.

Fourth, managers must find ways to reduce contact employees' role conflict and ambiguity. Although both exert a considerable negative influence on employee responses, role ambiguity appears to have the most prominent effect, particularly on self-efficacy and job satisfaction. When contact employees are unsure about how to perform their jobs, their confidence and job satisfaction decline. This translates into a decrease in customers' perceived service quality. Role ambiguity also reduces employees' ability to adapt to changes in the service encounter. Managers should make every effort to ensure that contact employees fully understand their role requirements and expectations. Although good socialization and training program can help alleviate employees' role ambiguity (Hartline and Ferrell 1993), reducing role conflict may depend on the manager's ability to communicate with his or her employees (Reardon and Enis 1990).

Suggestions for Further Research

Our findings suggest several directions for further research. First, our study could be replicated within other services (e.g., banking, insurance, hospitals) to further examine our hypothesized relationships. For example, the relationship between employee adaptability and customers' perceived service quality may vary from one service to another. To examine this relationship, qualitative research methods may be more useful than a cross-sectional approach (cf. Bitner 1990; Kelley 1993). Additional research also is needed on the relationship between employee self-efficacy and job satisfaction. In professional services (e.g., nurses, lawyers, accountants) in which employees have chosen the service position as a career, self-efficacy may lead to an increase in job satisfaction. Likewise, the relationship between employee self-efficacy and adaptability may depend on the level of role stress experienced by employees.

Second, the mixed effects of empowerment raise an interesting question for further research: What are the conditions under which empowerment is beneficial and/or detrimental to employee management and service delivery? Conger and Kanungo (1988) argue that managers who use empowerment expect greater effort and performance from their employees. Thus, additional research could address the impact of empowerment on employee motivation, effort, and performance. The relationship between empowerment and its outcomes also may be moderated by other employee responses. For example, empowered employees may exhibit increased effort and performance when they are committed to the firm and/or share the firm's value system. Likewise, further research could investigate the importance of employee socialization and training in the effective use of empowerment (cf. Hartline and Ferrell 1993).

Third, methodological issues in aggregating and matching responses across multiple samples warrant further empirical research. Cross-validation of responses, though difficult to obtain in lengthy surveys, also could offer insights into the differences between manager and employee perceptions of the employee management process. In addition, researchers could explore whether the problems associated with the use of positively and negatively worded items (such as those in the SERVQUAL scale) extend to other constructs. In situations in which data are aggregated and matched across samples, the use of positive and negative scale items might lead to problems in estimating measurement models. Furthermore, though the "best" measure of service quality is open to debate, researchers could consider adapting the service quality measure to the service context. This would allow for more precise measurement of the employee and nonemployee elements of service quality.

Fourth, additional research is needed on the internal aspects of service quality, service implementation, and service employee management. The debate over measurement issues in service quality research ignores the important strategic and managerial problems associated with the people involved in service delivery. Further research could examine issues such as communication processes, organizational structure, management styles, employee socialization and training, or the use of internal marketing strategies. Likewise, the roles of "other" people in service delivery, such as noncontact employees and nonfocal customers, could be investigated. Studying these issues could give academicians and practitioners a stronger basis for making prescriptive statements about the management of service employees and service quality.

APPENDIX A
Measure Validation and Model Estimation

Measurement Model We analyzed the data by using PRELIS to create covariance matrices with pairwise deletion. These matrices were used as input to LISREL 8, in which the "completely standardized solution" was requested (Jöreskog and Sörbom 1993). In the initial stage of the analysis, several items were deleted from the scales because of nonsignificant

TABLE A1
Measure Correlations, Means, and Standard Deviations

Measure	Mean	SD	1	2	3	4	5	6	7	8
1. MCSQ	4.61	.429								
2. EMPOWER	4.07	.529	.43							
3. BEHAVIOR	4.41	.532	.63	.31						
4. CONFLICT	1.95	.330	−.13	.26	−.13					
5. AMBIG	1.94	.360	−.09	.25	−.16	.70				
6. SELFEFF	4.88	.743	.23	.24	.19	.16	−.07			
7. SATIS	3.83	.517	.14	−.27	.01	−.56	−.42	−.64		
8. ADAPT	5.95	.455	.38	−.02	.41	−.39	−.46	.19	.23	
9. QUALITY	3.95	.401	.07	.04	.04	−.18	−.22	.21	.09	0.0

Correlation coefficients are ϕ estimates from LISREL. Coefficients of .21 or greater are significant at the $p < .10$ level, coefficients of .31 or greater are significant at the $p < .05$ level, and coefficients of .38 or greater are significant at the $p < .01$ level.

t-values. This item-deletion procedure has been suggested as a method for respecifying indicators that do not "work out" (Anderson and Gerbing 1988). For the remaining items, all t-values exceed 2.00, thus meeting this criterion for convergent validity (Anderson and Gerbing 1988). These results, and the construct reliabilities of each scale (Jöreskog 1971), are provided in Appendix B.

Discriminant validity was assessed in two phases. First, we performed one-at-a-time chi-square difference tests for the largest cross-construct correlations within the manager and employee samples (the ϕ coefficient was constrained to 1.00). We also examined the 95% confidence interval (CI) to ensure that the correlation plus or minus two standard errors did not include the value 1.00 (Anderson and Gerbing 1988). Within the manager data, the largest correlation occurred between MCSQ/BEHAVIOR[1] ($\phi = .461$; $\chi^2_{diff} = 143.35$, 2 df; CI = .329 to .593). Within the employee data, the largest correlations were between CONFLICT/AMBIG ($\phi = .691$; $\chi^2_{diff} = 514.43$, 4 df; CI = .635 to .747), CONFLICT/ADAPT ($\phi = -.539$; $\chi^2_{diff} = 391.53$, 4 df; CI = −.619 to −.459), and AMBIG/SATIS ($\phi = -.451$; $\chi^2_{diff} = 760.46$, 4 df; CI = −.531 to −.371). In each case, the increase in the value of chi-square exceeded the critical value by a wide margin ($\propto < .001$), and no confidence interval contained the value 1.00.

Second, we assessed discriminant validity across all three samples by aggregating and matching responses. Because the final sample size (97 units) was small in relation to the number of scale items, we averaged the items in each scale to create a summed-scale indicator for each construct. Each indicator was standardized (mean = 0, standard deviation = 1) to account for scale differences. To account for measurement error, each λ coefficient was fixed at the square root of its construct reliability, and each θ_δ coefficient

was fixed at one minus the construct reliability (cf. Anderson and Gerbing 1988). The cross-construct correlations (ϕ coefficients) resulting from this analysis are reported in Table A1.

As before, we assessed discriminant validity for the largest cross-construct correlations: CONFLICT/AMBIG ($\phi = .700$; $\chi^2_{diff} = 89.86$, 8 df; CI = .426 to .974), SATIS/SELFEFF ($\phi = -.641$; $\chi^2_{diff} = 64.79$, 8 df; CI = −.939 to −.343), MCSQ/BEHAVIOR ($\phi = .632$; $\chi^2_{diff} = 54.94$, 8 df; CI = .346 to .918), and CONFLICT/SATIS ($\phi = -.556$; $\chi^2_{diff} = 114.84$, 8 df; CI = −.828 to −.284). In each case, the increase in the value of chi-square exceeds the critical value and no confidence interval contains the value 1.00. These results provide evidence for the discriminant validity of the measures.

Structural Model Estimation and Fit Before estimating the hypothesized conceptual model, we computed the variance inflation factor (VIF) for each variable in order to assess multicollinearity. In this test, each variable becomes a dependent variable and is regressed on the remaining independent variables. The VIF, the inverse of $(1 - R^2)$, should be close to 1.00, which indicates little or no multicollinearity. Hair and colleagues (1995) suggest a cutoff value of 10.00 as an acceptable VIF. Among the variables in our study, the highest VIF occurs for SATIS (VIF = 1.97, $R^2 = .492$), which indicates that the effect of multicollinearity among the variables is negligible.

We tested the hypothesized model by using LISREL 8 (Jöreskog and Sörbom 1993). Hypothesis testing was accomplished by examining the completely standardized parameter estimates and their t-values. Estimating the hypothesized model produced the following statistics: $\chi^2_{12} = 10.68$ ($p = .557$), goodness-

---

[1]For definitions of terms, see Appendix B.

TABLE A2

Hypothesized and Final Path Models of Service Employee Management:
Structural Parameter Estimates (n = 97)

Path	Hypothesis	Hypothesized Model			Final Model		
		Coeff.	t-value	R^2	Coeff.	t-value	R^2
SELFEFF→QUALITY	H_1 (+)	.598	2.93	.194	.448	2.54	.117
SATIS→QUALITY	H_2 (+)	.530	2.74	.	.383	2.28	
ADAPT→QUALITY	H_3 (+)	−.198	−1.45				
CONFLICT→SELFEFF	H_{5a} (−)	.383	1.92	.170	.436	2.21	.215
AMBIG→SELFEFF	H_{6a} (−)	−.381	−1.97		−.461	−2.44	
EMPOWER→SELFEFF	H_{8a} (+)	.214	1.34		.287	2.10	
BEHAVIOR→SELFEFF	H_{9a} (+)	.139	0.93				
SELFEFF→SATIS	H_{4a} (+)	−.662	−5.51	.695	−.744	−6.92	.722
CONFLICT→SATIS	H_{5b} (−)	−.255	−1.65				
AMBIG→SATIS	H_{6b} (−)	−.293	−1.97		−.474	−5.19	
EMPOWER→SATIS	H_{8b} (+)	.035	0.29				
BEHAVIOR→SATIS	H_{9b} (+)	.098	0.90				
MCSQ→SATIS	a				.212	2.37	
SELFEFF→ADAPT	H_{4b} (+)	.086	0.64	.368			.353
CONFLICT→ADAPT	H_{5c} (−)	−.138	−0.73				
AMBIG→ADAPT	H_{6c} (−)	−.282	−1.55		−.410	−3.80	
EMPOWER→ADAPT	H_{8c} (+)	−.037	−0.26				
BEHAVIOR→ADAPT	H_{9c} (+)	.372	2.77		.380	3.21	
EMPOWER→CONFLICT	H_{8d} (−)	.321	2.32	.123	.343	2.51	.141
BEHAVIOR→CONFLICT	H_{9d} (−)	−.259	−1.94		−.276	−2.11	
CONFLICT→AMBIG	H_7 (+)	.654	6.29	.505	.714	7.61	.510
EMPOWER→AMBIG	H_{8e} (−)	.115	0.99				
BEHAVIOR→AMBIG	H_{9e} (−)	−.102	−0.94				
MCSQ→EMPOWER	H_{10a} (+)	.421	3.43	.177	.429	3.50	.184
MCSQ→BEHAVIOR	H_{10b} (+)	.667	6.17	.445	.655	6.02	.429

Goodness-of-fit statistics:							
		$\chi^2_{12} = 10.68$, $p = .557$			$\chi^2_{21} = 13.72$, $p = .881$		
		GFI = .974			GFI = .968		
		AGFI = .904			AGFI = .931		
		CFI = 1.00			CFI = 1.00		
		PNFI = .316			PNFI = .544		
		RMSR = .032			RMSR = .045		
		Overall R^2 = .504			Overall R^2 = .532		

aNot hypothesized.

of-fit index (GFI) = .974, adjusted goodness-of-fit index (AGFI) = .904, comparative fit index (CFI) = 1.00, and parsimonious normed fit index (PNFI) = .316. The structural parameter estimates from the hypothesized model are reported in Table A2. Because many of the paths were not significant, we dropped these paths to create a more parsimonious model. Model trimming is appropriate in exploratory research if it is not used as a substitute for a priori hypothesis development (Anderson and Gerbing 1988). Although ADAPT did not have a significant effect on QUALITY, we retained ADAPT in the trimmed model because of its theoretical importance to service delivery.

After reestimating the model, the modification indices revealed that one new path (MCSQ→SATIS) and two original paths (AMBIG→ADAPT, EMPOWER→SELFEFF) should be set free. Estimating the final, trimmed model produced the following statistics: χ^2_{21} = 13.72 (p = .881), GFI = .968, AGFI = .93 1, CFI = 1.00, and PNFI = .544. The structural estimates from the trimmed model are reported in Table A2. A comparison of the AGFIs and PNFIs from both models indicates that the final model is more parsimonious and fits somewhat better than the hypothesized model. In addition, the overall R^2 for the trimmed model is good at .532. The final path model is shown in Figure Al.

Service Employee Management: A Path Diagram of Structural Relationships

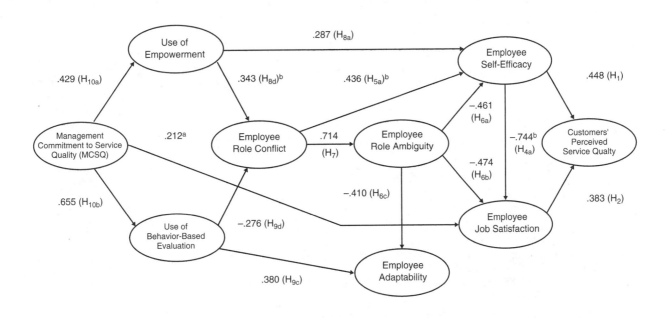

Confirmatory Factor Analysis Results

Manager Data (n = 236)

Fit Statistics: χ^2_{74} = 156.80, p = .000; GFI = .912; AGFI = .876; CFI = .919; RMSR (root mean square residual) = .025

		Factor Loading	t-value
Management Commitment to Service Quality (MCSQ)[a]			
(Cronbach's α = .86; Construct reliability = .86)			
MQ1	I feel strongly about improving the quality of my organization's services	.675	11.09
MQ2	I enjoy discussing quality-related issues with people in my organization	.809	14.24
MQ3	I gain a sense of personal accomplishment in providing quality services to my customers	.658	10.74
MQ4	I explain to all of my employees the importance of providing high quality services to our customers	b	
MQ5	I often discuss quality-related issues with people outside of my organization	b	
MQ6	Providing high quality services to our customers should be the number one priority of my organization	b	
MQ7	I am willing to put in a great deal of effort beyond that normally expected in order to help my organization deliver high quality services to our customers	.694	11.51
MQ8	The way I feel about quality is very similar to the way my organization feels about quality	.660	10.79
MQ9	I really care about the quality of my organization's services	.774	13.36
Empowerment (EMPOWER)[c] (Cronbach's α =.71; Construct reliability = .71)			
EM1	I allow employees complete freedom in their work	b	
EM2	I permit employees to use their own judgment in solving problems	.592	8.27
EM3	I encourage initiative in my employees	.668	9.37
EM4	I let employees do their work the way they think best	b	
EM5	I assign tasks, then let employees handle them	b	
EM6	I turn employees loose on a job, and let them go to it	b	
EM7	I allow employees a high degree of initiative	.651	9.14
EM8	I trust employees to exercise good judgment	.533	7.37

	Factor Loading	t-value

Behavior-Based Evaluation (BEHAVIOR)[d] (Cronbach's α = .74; Construct reliability = .75)

How important is each of the following factors when you evaluate the performance of customer-contact employees?

BB1	A track record of courteous service to customers	b	
BB2	The ability to resolve customer complaints or service problems in an efficient manner	.808	12.50
BB3	The ability to innovatively deal with unique situations and/or meet customer needs	.616	9.21
BB4	The employee's commitment to the organization	.545	8.00
BB5	The employee's commitment to customers	.622	9.31

Employee Data (n = 561)
Fit Statistics: χ^2_{892} = 3673.47, p = .000; GFI = .730; AGFI = .700; CFI = .722; RMSR = .100

Employee Role Conflict (CONFLICT)[e]
(Cronbach's α = .83; Construct reliability = .83)

How much agreement is there between you and your job on

RC1	The amount of work you are expected to do and the amount of work you actually do (−)[f]	.461	10.79
RC2	The number of customers you are expected to serve and the number of customers you actually serve (−)	.491	11.58
RC3	The number of non-work tasks you are expected to perform and the number of non-work tasks you actually perform (−)	.436	10.13
RC4	The amount of leisure time you expect to have and the amount of leisure time you actually have (−)	.361	8.26

How much agreement is there between you and your supervisor on

RC5	How often you should report to your supervisor (−)	.568	13.76
RC6	How far you should bend the rules to satisfy customers (−)	.502	11.90
RC7	How much service you should provide to customers (−)	.615	15.16
RC8	How much authority you have in making decisions (−)	.537	12.87

How much agreement is there between you and your customers on

RC9	Your performance in serving customer needs (−)	.677	17.15
RC10	How much service you should provide to customers (−)	.672	16.97
RC11	How you resolve customer complaints (−)	.637	15.84
RC12	How far you should bend the rules to satisfy customers (−)	.487	11.47

Employee Role Ambiguity (AMBIG)[g] (Cronbach's α =.91; Construct reliability =.91)

How certain are you about

RA1	How best to serve customers (−)	.578	14.48
RA2	How much time you should spend on various aspects of your job (−)	.631	16.13
RA3	How to resolve customer complaints (−)	.567	14.13
RA4	How to fill out required paperwork (−)	.483	11.72
RA5	How to plan and organize your daily work activities (−)	.604	15.28
RA6	How to handle unusual problems or situations (−)	.669	17.39
RA7	Where to get assistance in doing your job (−)	.514	12.58
RA8	The extent to which you can bend the rules to satisfy customers (−)	.527	12.97
RA9	The extent to which you can make decisions without your supervisor's approval (−)	.579	14.49
RA10	Your company's rules and regulations (−)	.616	15.64
RA11	How your supervisor will evaluate your performance (−)	.697	18.35
RA12	How satisfied your supervisor is with your performance (−)	.685	17.92
RA13	The aspects of your work-related training (−)	.686	17.97
RA14	The factors that determine your promotion and advancement (−)	.610	15.45
RA15	How your supervisor expects you to allocate your time (−)	.709	18.79
RA16	How satisfied your customers are with your performance (−)	.624	15.91
RA17	What your customers expect of you in performing your job (−)	.645	16.59

Employee Self-Efficacy (SELFEFF)[h] (Cronbach's α =.67; Construct reliability =.71)

SE1	My job is well within the scope of my abilities	b	
SE2	I did not experience any problems in adjusting to work at this organization	b	
SE3	I feel that I am overqualified for the job I am doing	.766	18.04
SE4	I have all the technical knowledge I need to deal with my job, all I need now is practical experience	b	

		Factor Loading	t-value
SE5	I feel confident that my skills and abilities equal or exceed those of my colleagues	.455	10.15
SE6	My past experiences and accomplishments increase my confidence that I will be able to perform successfully in this organization	b	
SE7	I could have handled a more challenging job than the one I am doing	.799	18.86
SE8	Professionally speaking, my job exactly satisfies my expectations of myself (−)	.399	8.80

Employee Job Satisfaction (SATIS)[i] (Cronbach's α = .82; Construct reliability = .82)

JS1	Your overall job	.632	15.55
JS2	Your fellow workers	b	
JS3	Your supervisor(s)	.615	15.04
JS4	Your organization's policies	.753	19.58
JS5	The support provided by your organization	.825	22.21
JS6	Your salary or wages	b	
JS7	Your opportunities for advancement with this organization	.638	15.74
JS8	Your organization's customers	b	

Employee Adaptability (ADAPT)[j] (Cronbach's α = .77; Construct reliability = .77)

AD1	Every customer requires a unique approach	b	
AD2	When I feel that my approach is not working, I can easily change to another approach	.589	13.75
AD3	I like to experiment with different approaches	.503	11.45
AD4	I don't change my approach from one customer to another (−)	b	
AD5	I am very sensitive to the needs of my customers	.586	13.68
AD6	I find it difficult to adapt my style to certain customers (−)	b	
AD7	I vary my approach from situation to situation	.572	13.28
AD8	I try to understand how one customer differs from another	.547	12.62
AD9	I feel confident that I can effectively change my approach when necessary	.764	18.99
AD10	I treat all customers pretty much the same (−)	b	

Customer Data (n = 1238)
Fit Statistics: χ^2_{35} = 450.29, p = .000; GFI = .931; AGFI = .892; CFI = .969; RMSR = .015

Customers' Perceived Service Quality (QUALITY)[k]
(Cronbach's α = .97; Construct reliability = .97)

Please rate the quality of service you received in each of the following areas:

SQ1	Receiving prompt service from our employees	.831	35.80
SQ2	Never being too busy to respond to your requests	.853	37.36
SQ3	Employee behaviors that instill confidence in you	.882	39.41
SQ4	The safety you feel in transactions with our employees	.856	37.50
SQ5	The courteousness of our employees	.840	36.44
SQ6	The ability of our employees to answer your questions	.846	36.87
SQ7	The individual attention you received from us	.890	40.03
SQ8	The personal attention you received from our employees	.906	41.21
SQ9	Having your best interests at heart	.910	41.55
SQ10	The ability of our employees to understand your specific needs	.851	37.15

[a]A nine-item scale adapted from the organizational commitment scale developed by Mowday, Steers, and Porter (1979). Items from the original scale were reworded to reflect the manager's affective commitment to service quality.

[b]Item was dropped during confirmatory factor analysis because of a nonsignificant t-value.

[c]The eight-item Tolerance of Freedom scale from the LBDO XII (Cook et al. 1981).

[d]A five-item scale adapted from the behavior-based performance scale of Bush and colleagues (1990).

[e]A 12-item scale adapted from the role conflict scale of Chonko, Howell, and Bellenger (1986).

[f]Negative signs (−) indicate reverse scoring.

[g]A 17-item scale adapted from the role ambiguity scale of Chonko, Howell, and Bellenger (1986).

[h]The eight-item self-efficacy scale developed by Jones (1986).

[i]An eight-item measure designed to assess employee job satisfaction across eight facets of the overall job. The selection of facets for the scale was based primarily on the research of Brown and Peterson (1993) and Churchill, Ford, and Walker (1974).

[j]A ten-item scale adapted from the adaptive selling scale developed by Spiro and Weitz (1990).

[k]A ten-item scale based on the original SERVQUAL scale (Parasuraman, Berry, and Zeithaml 1990). We restricted our measure to those items that pertained specifically to employee-related aspects of service quality. The scale was also modified to combine expectations and perceptions into a single measure, as per the suggestion of Brown, Churchill, and Peter (1993).

References

Ahmed, Irfan and A. Parasuraman (1994), "Environmental and Positional Antecedents of Management Commitment to Service Quality: A Conceptual Framework," in *Advances in Services Marketing and Management*, Vol. 3, Teresa A. Swartz, David E. Bowen, and Stephen W. Brown, eds. Greenwich, CT: JAI Press, 69–93.

Anderson, Erin and Richard L. Oliver (1987), "Perspectives on Behavior-Based versus Outcome-Based Salesforce Control Systems," *Journal of Marketing*, 51 (October), 76–88.

Anderson, James C. and David W. Gerbing (1988), "Structural Equation Modeling in Practice: A Review and Recommended Two-Step Approach," *Psychological Bulletin*, 103 (May), 411–23.

Armstrong, J. Scott and Terry S. Overton (1977), "Estimating Nonresponse Bias in Mail Surveys," *Journal of Marketing Research*, 14 (August), 396–402.

Babakus, Emin and Gregory W. Boller (1992), "An Empirical Assessment of the SERVQUAL Scale," *Journal of Business Research*, 24 (May), 253–68.

Bandura, Albert (1977), *Social Learning Theory*. Englewood Cliffs, NJ: Prentice-Hall.

——— (1986), *Social Foundations of Thought and Action: A Social Cognitive Theory*. Englewood Cliffs, NJ: Prentice-Hall.

Basu, Amiya K., Rajiv Lai, V. Srinivasan, and Richard Staelin (1985), "Sales Compensation Plans: An Agency Theoretic Perspective," *Marketing Science*, 4 (Fall), 267–91.

Bateson, John E. G. (1985), "Perceived Control and the Service Encounter," in *The Service Encounter: Managing Employee/Customer Interaction in Service Businesses*, John A. Czepiel, Michael R. Solomon, and Carol F. Surprenant, eds. Lexington, MA: D. C. Heath and Company, 67–82.

Behrman, Douglas N. and William D. Perreault, Jr. (1984), "A Role Stress Model of the Performance and Satisfaction of Industrial Salespersons," *Journal of Marketing*, 48 (Fall), 9–21.

Bitner, Mary Jo (1990), "Evaluating Service Encounters: The Effects of Physical Surroundings and Employee Responses:" *Journal of Marketing*, 54 (April), 69–82.

———, Bernard H. Booms, and Lois A. Mohr (1994), "Critical Service Encounters: The Employee's Viewpoint," *Journal of Marketing*, 58 (October), 95–106.

———, ———, and Mary Stanfield Tetreault (1990), "The Service Encounter: Diagnosing Favorable and Unfavorable Incidents," *Journal of Marketing*, 54 (January), 71–84.

Bowen, David E. and Edward E. Lawler III (1992), "The Empowerment of Service Workers: What, Why, How, and When," *Sloan Management Review*, 33 (Spring), 31–39.

——— and Benjamin Schneider (1985), "Boundary-Spanning Role Employees and the Service Encounter: Some Guidelines for Management and Research," in *The Service Encounter. Managing Employee/Customer Interaction in Service Businesses*, John A. Czepiel, Michael R. Solomon, and Carol F. Surprenant, eds. Lexington, MA: D. C. Heath and Company, 127–47.

Brown, Steven P. and Robert A. Peterson (1993). "Antecedents and Consequences of Salesperson Job Satisfaction: Meta-Analysis and Assessment of Causal Effects," *Journal of Marketing Research*, 30 (February), 63–77.

Brown, Tom J., Gilbert A. Churchill, Jr., and J. Paul Peter (1993), "Improving the Measurement of Service Quality," *Journal of Retailing*, 69 (Spring), 127–39.

Bush, Robert P., Alan J. Bush, David J. Ortinau, and Joseph F. Hair, Jr. (1990), "Developing a Behavior-Based Scale to Assess Retail Salesperson Performance," *Journal of Retailing*, 66 (Spring), 119–36.

Chonko, Lawrence B., Roy D. Howell, and Danny N. Bellenger (1986), "Congruence in Sales Force Evaluations: Relation to Sales Force Perceptions of Conflict and Ambiguity," *Journal of Personal Selling and Sales Management*, 6 (May), 35–48.

Churchill, Gilbert A., Jr., Neil M. Ford, Steven W. Hartley, and Orville C. Walker, Jr. (1985), "The Determinants of Salesperson Performance: A Meta-Analysis," *Journal of Marketing Research*, 22 (May), 103–18.

———, ———, and Orville C. Walker, Jr. (1974), "Measuring the Job Satisfaction of Industrial Salesmen," *Journal of Marketing Research*, 11 (August), 254–60.

Conger, Jay A. and Rabindra N. Kanungo (1988), "The Empowerment Process: Integrating Theory and Practice," *Academy of Management Review*, 13 (July), 471–82.

Cook, John D., Sue J. Hepworth, Toby D. Wall, and Peter B. Warr (1981), *The Experience of Work*. New York: Academic Press.

Cravens, David W., Thomas N. Ingram, Raymond W. LaForge, and Clifford E. Young (1993), "Behavior-Based and Outcome-Based Salesforce Control Systems," *Journal of Marketing*, 57 (October), 47–59.

Cronin, J. Joseph, Jr. and Steven A. Taylor (1992), "Measuring Service Quality: A Reexamination and Extension," *Journal of Marketing*, 56 (July), 55–68.

Earley, P. Christopher (1994), "Self or Group? Cultural Effects of Training on Self-Efficacy and Performance," *Administrative Science Quarterly*, 39 (March), 89–117.

George, William R. (1990), "Internal Marketing and Organizational Behavior: A Partnership in Developing Customer-Conscious Employees at Every Level," *Journal of Business Research*, 20 (January), 63–70.

Gist, Marilyn E. (1987), "Self-Efficacy: Implications for Organizational Behavior and Human Resource Management," *Academy of Management Review*, 12 (July), 472–85.

——— and Terence R. Mitchell (1992), "Self-Efficacy: A Theoretical Analysis of Its Determinants and Malleability," *Academy of Management Review*, 17 (April), 183–211.

Glisson, Charles and Mark Durick (1988), "Predictors of Job Satisfaction and Organizational Commitment in Human Service Organizations," *Administrative Science Quarterly*, 33 (March), 61–81.

Grönroos, Christian (1983), *Strategic Management and Marketing in the Service Sector*, Marketing Science Institute Working Paper Series, Report No. 83–104. Cambridge, MA: Marketing Science Institute.

Hackman, Richard J. and Greg R. Oldham (1980), *Work Redesign*. Reading, MA: Addison-Wesley.

Hair, Joseph F., Jr., Rolph E. Anderson, Ronald L. Tatham, and William C. Black (1995), *Multivariate Data Analysis*, 4th ed. New York: Macmillan Publishing Company.

Hartline, Michael D. and O. C. Ferrell (1993), *Service Quality Implementation: The Effects of Organizational Socialization and Managerial Actions on Customer-Contact Employee Behaviors*, Marketing Science Institute Working

Paper Series, Report No. 93–122. Cambridge, MA: Marketing Science Institute.

Humphrey, Ronald H. and Blake E. Ashforth (1994), "Cognitive Scripts and Prototypes in Service Encounters," in *Advances in Services Marketing and Management*, Vol. 3, Teresa A. Swartz, David E. Bowen, and Stephen W. Brown, eds. Greenwich, CT: JAI Press, 175–99.

Jaworski, Bernard J. (1988), "Toward a Theory of Marketing Control: Environmental Context, Control Types, and Consequences," *Journal of Marketing*, 52 (July), 23–39.

Jex, Steve M. and David M. Gudanowski (1992), "Efficacy Beliefs and Work Stress: An Exploratory Study," *Journal of Organizational Behavior*, 13 (September), 509–17.

Jones, Gareth R. (1986), "Socialization Tactics, Self-Efficacy, and Newcomers' Adjustments to Organizations," *Academy of Management Journal*, 29 (June), 262–79.

Jöreskog, Karl (1971), "Statistical Analysis of Sets of Congeneric Tests," *Psychometrika*, 36 (June), 109–33.

———— and Dag Sörbom (1993), *LISREL 8: A Guide to the Program and Applications*. Chicago, IL: SPSS.

Kelley, Scott W. (1993), "Discretion and the Service Employee," *Journal of Retailing*, 69 (Spring), 104–26.

Locke, Edwin A. (1969), "What Is Job Satisfaction?" *Organizational Behavior and Human Performance*, 4 (April), 309–36.

———— and Gary P. Latham (1990), "Work Motivation and Satisfaction: Light at the End of the Tunnel," *Psychological Science*, 1 (July), 240–46.

McDonald, Tracy and Marc Siegall (1992), "The Effects of Technological Self-Efficacy and Job Focus on Job Performance, Attitudes, and Withdrawal Behaviors," *Journal of Psychology*, 126 (September), 465–75.

McGee, Gail W., Carl E. Ferguson, Jr., and Anson Seers (1989), "Role Conflict and Role Ambiguity: Do the Scales Measure These Two Constructs?" *Journal of Applied Psychology*, 74 (October), 815–18.

Mohr-Jackson, Iris (1993), "Comparing Total Quality with Market Orientation: An In-Depth Interview Approach," in *AMA Winter Educators' Conference Proceedings*, Rajan Varadarajan and Bernard Jaworski, eds. Chicago: American Marketing Association, 427–32.

Mowday, Richard T., Richard M. Steers, and Lyman W. Porter (1979), "The Measurement of Organizational Commitment," *Journal of Vocational Behavior*, 14 (April), 224–47.

Niehoff, Brian P, Cathy A. Enz, and Richard A. Grover (1990), "The Impact of Top-Management Actions on Employee Attitudes and Perceptions," *Group & Organization Studies*, 15 (September), 337–52.

Oliver, Richard L. (1993a), "A Conceptual Model of Service Quality and Service Satisfaction: Compatible Goals, Different Concepts," in *Advances in Services Marketing and Management*, Vol. 2, Teresa A. Swartz, David E. Bowen, and Stephen W. Brown, eds. Greenwich, CT: JAI Press, 65–85.

———— (1993b), "Cognitive, Affective, and Attribute Bases of the Satisfaction Response," *Journal of Consumer Research*, 20 (December), 418–30.

———— and Erin Anderson (1994), "An Empirical Test of the Consequences of Behavior- and Outcome-Based Sales Control Systems," *Journal of Marketing*, 58 (October), 53–67.

Parasuraman, A., Leonard L. Berry, and Valarie A. Zeithaml (1990), *An Empirical Examination of Relationships in an Extended Service Quality Model*, Marketing Science Institute Working Paper Series, Report No. 90–122. Cambridge, MA: Marketing Science Institute.

————, Valarie A. Zeithaml, and Leonard L. Berry (1994), "Reassessment of Expectations as a Comparison Standard in Measuring Service Quality: Implications for Future Research," *Journal of Marketing*, 58 (January), 111–24.

Paulhus, Delroy L. and Carol Lynn Martin (1988), "Functional Flexibility: A New Conception of Interpersonal Flexibility," *Journal of Personality and Social Psychology*, 55 (July), 88–101.

Peterson, Robert A. and William R. Wilson (1992), "Measuring Customer Satisfaction: Fact and Artifact," *Journal of the Academy of Marketing Science*, 20 (Winter), 61–71.

Rafaeli, Anat (1993), "Dress and Behavior of Customer Contact Employees: A Framework for Analysis," in *Advances in Services Marketing and Management*, Vol. 2, Teresa A. Swartz, David E. Bowen, and Stephen W. Brown, eds. Greenwich, CT: JAI Press, 175–211.

Reardon, Kathleen K. and Ben Enis (1990), "Establishing a Company-Wide Customer Orientation Through Persuasive Internal Marketing," *Management Communication Quarterly*, 3 (February), 376–87.

Rizzo, John R., Robert J. House, and Sidney I. Lirtzman (1970), "Role Conflict and Ambiguity in Complex Organizations," *Administrative Science Quarterly*, 15 (June), 150–63.

Rust, Roland T. and Richard L. Oliver (1994), "Service Quality: Insights and Managerial Implications From the Frontier," in *Service Quality: New Directions in Theory and Practice*, Roland T. Rust and Richard L. Oliver, eds. Thousand Oaks, CA: Sage Publications, 1–19.

Schneider, Benjamin (1980), "The Service Organization: Climate Is Crucial," *Organizational Dynamics*, 9 (Autumn), 52–65.

Scott, Susanne G. and Reginald A. Bruce (1994), "Determinants of Innovative Behavior: A Path Model of Individual Innovation in the Workplace," *Academy of Management Journal*, 37 (June), 580–607.

Shamir, Boas (1980), "Between Service and Servility: Role Conflict in Subordinate Service Roles," *Human Relations*, 33 (October), 741–56.

Silverman, Steven N. and Rajiv Grover (1995), *Forming Perceptions of Overall Quality in Consumer Products: A Process of Quality Element Integration*, Marketing Science Institute Working Paper Series, Report No. 95–103. Cambridge, MA: Marketing Science Institute.

Singh, Jagdip (1993), "Boundary Role Ambiguity: Facets, Determinants, and Impacts," *Journal of Marketing*, 57 (April), 11–31.

Solomon, Michael R., Carol Surprenant, John A. Czepiel, and Evelyn G. Gutman (1985), "A Role Theory Perspective on Dyadic Interactions: The Service Encounter," *Journal of Marketing*, 49 (Winter), 99–111.

Spiro, Rosann L. and Barton A. Weitz (1990), "Adaptive Selling: Conceptualization, Measurement, and Nomological Validity," *Journal of Marketing Research*, 27 (February), 61–69.

Taylor, Steven A. and Thomas L. Baker (1994), "An Assessment of the Relationship Between Service Quality and Customer Satisfaction in the Formation of Consumers' Purchase Intentions," *Journal of Retailing*, 70 (Summer), 163–78.

Wall, Stephen J. and S. Charles Zeynel (199 1), "The Senior Manager's Role in Quality Improvement," *Quality Progress*, 24 (January), 66–68.

Weatherly, Kristopher A. and David A. Tansik (1993), "Managing Multiple Demands: A Role-Theory Examination of the Behaviors of Customer Contact Service Workers," in *Advances in Services Marketing and Management*, Vol. 2, Teresa A. Swartz, David E. Bowen, and Stephen W. Brown, eds. Greenwich, CT: JAI Press, 279–300.

Westman, Mina (1992), "Moderating Effect of Decision Latitude on Stress-Strain Relationship: Does Organizational Level Matter?" *Journal of Organizational Behavior*, 13 (December), 713–22.

Zeithaml, Valarie A., Leonard L. Berry, and A. Parasuraman (1988), "Communication and Control Processes in the Delivery of Service Quality," *Journal of Marketing*, 52 (April), 35–48.

Going to Extremes:

Managing Service Encounters and Assessing Provider Performance

LINDA L. PRICE
ERIC J. ARNOULD
PATRICK TIERNEY

The authors advance a framework for analysis and comparison of service encounters using three neglected dimensions—duration, affective content, and spatial proximity. They focus on service encounters that fall at the extreme of these three dimensions, termed extended, affectively charged, intimate (EAI) encounters. Employing qualitative and quantitative data, they develop measures of service provider performance and test a structural model of the relationships among service provider performance, affective response, and service satisfaction for EAI encounters.

A dramatic shift in focus from transactions to relationships is underway in services marketing (Berry 1983; Gummeson 1993). Although many firms recognize the importance of developing good relationships with customers, it is not always clear how to create and sustain good relationships. Nor is it self-evident what kinds of relationships service firms should seek with customers and what kinds customers want from service firms (Barnes 1994). We extend understanding of service relationships, specifically, considering three neglected dimensions of the "moment of truth" when the customer interacts with the service provider: (1) temporal duration; (2) affective or emotional content; and (3) the spatial proximity of service provider and customer. These dimensions of the service encounter shape service provider performance and the links among provider performance, affective response, and satisfaction but have received no systematic attention in the marketing literature. Nevertheless, they have been shown to frame the contour and content of interpersonal relationships (Derlaga 1984; Goffman 1961; Hall 1974; McCroskey, Richmond, and Stewart 1986). A major contribution of our study is to show that understanding encounters in terms of these relationship dimensions provides useful analytic tools for successful service encounter management.

In the first section, we identify three neglected dimensions of the service encounter. Using previous literature, the second section explores the characteristics of temporally extended, affectively charged, spatially (i.e., proxemically) intimate service encounters (EAI). We then describe an exploratory field study of service provider-customer relationships in an EAI context. Using extensive qualitative data, we provide empirical grounding for service provider performance characteristics. We develop measures of service provider performance and conclude with a test of a structural model linking service provider performance, affective responses, and service satisfaction.

Linda L. Price is an Associate Professor of Marketing and Eric J. Arnould is an Associate Professor of Marketing, College of Business, University of South Florida. Patrick Tierney is an Associate Professor, Department of Recreation and Leisure Studies, San Francisco State University. The authors thank the editor and four reviewers for their helpful comments. They benefited from responses to earlier versions of this article presented at the 1993 AMA Faculty Consortium and 1992 AMA Frontiers in Services Conference. They are grateful to the organizers of these symposia for the opportunity to present their work. Five Colorado River Basin outfitters and the U.S. Forest Service, Dinosaur National Monument made this research both possible and delightful.

Service Encounter Dimensions, Provider Performance, and Service Outcomes

Numerous typologies describe important differences between services, but little attention has focused specifically on dimensions of service encounters (Gronroos 1990; Lovelock 1983). Because a service encounter is an interpersonal relationship, we would expect that duration, affective content, and spatial proximity play basic roles in how the service relationship develops and the outcomes of the encounter. In Figure 1, we provide illustrative examples of service

FIGURE 1
Examples of Service Encounters by Service Encounter Dimensions

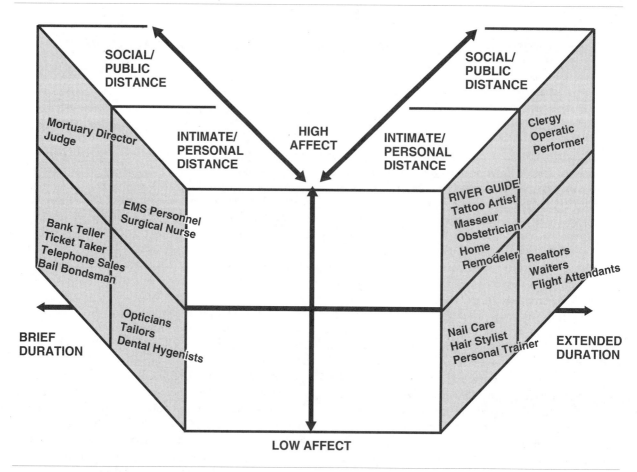

encounters judgmentally grouped by variation on these three service encounter dimensions.[1]

In Figure 2, we posit that variation in these three dimensions of the service encounter will affect service provider performance and service outcomes. "Service

provider performance" refers to service delivery skills and competencies as revealed in the service encounter, including those customers take for granted, those they can articulate (i.e., expectations) and those that they do not articulate but that can lead to delight when used skillfully (Bitner, Booms, and Mohr 1994). Building on prior research, in Figure 2, we posit that service provider performance directly affects both affective responses and satisfaction and indirectly affects satisfaction through its impact on affective response.

Figure 2 includes both positive (pleasure), and negative (anger, sadness) affective responses and satisfaction. Because of their complexity, service encounters are likely to evoke both negative and positive affective reactions (Derbaix and Pham 1991), with positive and negative affect making independent contributions to consumer satisfaction (Rust, Zahorik, and Keiningham 1995). The relationship between affective response and service satisfaction represented in Figure 2 extends prior, product-based research to the service context (Mano and Oliver 1993; Oliver 1993; Westbrook 1987).

---

[1]We thank the editor for suggesting the format for this figure. Examples on the left side of the figure are encounters typically of brief duration (under 10 minutes); those on the right extend over longer periods of time (often more than 30 minutes). Examples in the lower half of the figure are encounters with low levels of associated affect. Those in the upper half involve higher levels of affect. Examples close to the center of the figure take place in intimate or personal spatial distance (less than 36 inches); examples on the outer edge of the figure take place in social or public space (greater than 36 inches). Examples in the figure are illustrative and should be interpreted cautiously. Some classifications may be unproblematic, as context is key. Service providers may engage in encounters that vary on these encounter dimensions. For example, clergy may spend hours at hospital bedsides in high-affect, intimate encounters, or may solicit donations to a church rummage sale in short, low-affect phone calls. We have learned that both real estate agents and home remodelers sometimes must provide significant emotional benefits to customers. In the first case, selling a home, especially one long lived in, may be highly stressful because of the nostalgic significance of the home. In the second, homes partake of the extended self, and people feel that the inside of their home is a very intimate place.

FIGURE 2

A General Model of Service Encounter Dimensions, Provider Performance, and Service Satisfaction

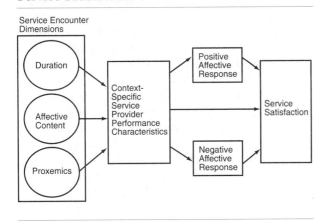

TABLE 1

Summary Characteristics of EAI Encounters

Duration

C1. Extended encounters are likely to develop into boundary open transactions.

C2. Extended encounters are likely to require service providers to expend significant emotional labor.
   A. Extended encounters create significant opportunities for service providers to experience emotional dissonance.
   B. Service provider self-identity and role congruence is very important to the success of extended encounters.

C3. Significant opportunities for service script interference emerge during extended encounters.
   A. Script interference can impede mutual understanding and hence service satisfaction.
   B. When scripts are noncongruent, service providers must orchestrate mutual understanding to manage the interaction and ensure service satisfaction.
   C. Service satisfaction is highly dependent on service provider performance.

Affect

C4. Affective content contributes to the development of boundary open relationships between service providers and customers.

C5. Affective content requires sustained emotional labor likely to lead to emotional dissonance, role stress, and role conflict.

C6. In delivering affective services content, service providers interpret and explain events to crystallize customer expectations and provide evidence that expectations are being met.

Proxemics

C7. Close proxemics motivate self-revelation, and interactions are likely to develop into boundary open transactions.

C8. Close proxemics positively affect the overall evaluation of the service encounter.

Extended, Affective, Intimate (EAI) Service Encounters

Temporally extended service encounters with high affective content, in which service provider and customer are in personal or intimate (touching) spatial proximity (see Figure 1 for examples) provides the context for this research. Examining exceptional EAI encounters provides insight for managing the growing number of service businesses that involve encounters that last longer, are more intricate and variant between use episodes, and involve more relationship work (Shugan 1992). Examples of these types of services include personal financial planning (e.g., IDS, a division of American Express), interactive information services (e.g., New Order Media), and long-term medical care and diagnostic services (e.g., University of South Florida's Moffit Cancer Center). We next turn to a discussion of the three dimensions and their impact on service provider performance and service outcomes.

Duration

Previous research has ignored the temporal duration of service encounters. By default, it has examined brief transactions, the majority lasting only a few minutes. However, a defining characteristic of relationships is that they unfold in time; they have a history, however brief. To "unpack" service relationships, we must understand the dynamics of how customer and service provider relate to each other over time (Bakeman and Gottman 1986).

We posit three characteristics of temporally extended service encounters summarized in Table 1. All else being equal, we would anticipate that brief encounters would be less likely to exhibit these characteristics than extended ones. First, we propose that *extended encounters are likely to develop into boundary open transactions.* In a study of waiters, Mars and Nicod (1984) distinguish "boundary open" from "boundary closed" transactions, describing the former as resembling a meeting between friends. The service provider is expected to be actively involved and share feelings with customers. A boundary open exchange is associated with customers' beliefs that the service provider is interested in them as persons. The service encounter has a feeling of a relationship rather than merely a transaction (see Siehl, Bowen, and Pearson 1992, p. 541). In this way, it transcends commercial transaction boundaries. By contrast, boundary closed transactions impose transaction-specific boundaries around the service relationship, such that the service provider may be expected to perform in a certain prescribed way in the interests of service delivery (Mohr and Bitner 1991) but not necessarily to exhibit friendship.

Extended encounters are likely to become boundary open for a variety of reasons. In American contexts, extended interpersonal encounters elicit interpersonal exchange and displays of positive and esteem-enhancing emotions. During an extended service encounter, there is more time for customer and employee display of these emotions (Nisbett and Ross 1980; Sutton and Rafaeli 1988). Relatedly, extended interpersonal encounters often provoke self-revelation, which is the key to feelings of intimacy (McCroskey, Richhmond, and Stewart 1986). Thus, we expect that service provider communication of responsiveness, empathy, and assurance is relatively more important to customers' satisfaction in extended encounters than in brief ones. Partial corroboration of these claims is provided in a variety of studies across service contexts (Korsch, Gozzi, and Francis 1968; Spradley and Mann 1975; Todd 1989). Hence, extended encounters, albeit commercially motivated, are likely to become boundary open (Mills and Morris 1986; Siehl, Bowen, and Pearson 1992; Trice and Beyer 1991).

Second, *extended encounters are likely to require service providers to expend significant emotional labor.* Emotional labor is defined as the management of feelings and the expenditure of imagistic-emotional energy to produce an observable emotional state in others (Hochschild 1983). The display of emotions and self-revelation expected in an extended service encounter suggests that emotional labor becomes an important aspect of the service provider's performance.

This characteristic has two associated consequences. First, extended encounters create significant opportunities for service providers to experience emotional dissonance, that is, a disparity between inner feelings and prescribed emotions. In temporally extended commercial encounters, the individual service provider and the customer must sustain role performances over a long period of time. For Americans, inner feelings are difficult to disguise or displace in prolonged encounters (Rafaeli and Sutton 1987). Hence, extended role performance increases the likelihood that service providers will experience and express emotional dissonance. Moreover, sustained performance reduces opportunities for expressing emotional dissonance in ways that do not affect the quality of provider-client interactions (Sutton 1991).

A second consequence of the premium placed on the expenditure of emotional energy in extended encounters is that service provider self-identity and role congruence become especially important to the success of extended encounters. Although it may be possible to initiate service scripts at odds with provider self-concepts for brief interactions, it is more problematic for managers to ask providers (or clients) to perform roles (which may well be discrepant from their self-identities) for long intervals (Hochschild 1983; Van Maanen and Kunda 1989).

Third, *significant opportunities for service script interference emerge during extended encounters.* Service roles are interdependent; hence mutual understanding and service satisfaction are likely to be greater when both customers and employees hold similar scripts (i.e. cognitive structures that describe appropriate sequences of behavior) for interaction (Bitner, Booms, and Mohr 1994; Mohr and Bitner 1991; Shank and Abelson 1977). Enactment of shared scripts is impeded by script interference, which occurs because of obstacles and errors (Shank and Abelson 1977). All else being equal, as encounter duration increases, opportunities for script interference from uncontrollable, and sometimes unpredictable, environmental intra- and interpersonal causes increase. Script interference reduces the likelihood of congruence between customers' and employees' scripts. Noncongruence between patient and doctor scripts, for example, is an important problem during prolonged labor and delivery. The resultant perceived lack of mutual understanding becomes an important source of patient dissatisfaction with birthing services (Graham and Oakley 1981).[2]

Mounting evidence confirms a relationship between service provider performance and service satisfaction even for relatively brief, well-scripted encounters (Patterson, Powell, and Lenihan 1986; Sutton and Rafaeli 1988). But when encounters become long and outcomes less predictable, service providers must do more. They must orchestrate mutual understanding to produce service satisfaction. By orchestrating mutual understanding, we mean the service provider must oversee the emergence of shared customer-provider scripts. Providers must interpret service episodes, explain unexpected events to crystallize customer expectations, and then provide evidence

---

[2]The opportunities for script interference—errors in and obstacles to service delivery—in this context are almost endless. For example, the practice's scheduling may mean that a doctor unknown to the patient attends the birth. Many physical contingencies can interfere with the birth plan, resulting in the presence of unknown personnel, the introduction of unplanned and unwanted medical procedures, or an unexpected hospital stay. Support personnel vary in terms of the degree of control they seek to impose on patients, amount of information they are willing to share, and emotion work in which they engage. And patients and their coaches can hardly anticipate how they will respond even if they have been through labor and delivery before.

that expectations are being met. Service providers' scripts in temporally extended encounters are likely to be much more elaborate than customers'. Providers cannot share all the details with every customer; some parts may be understood to be unpredictable. In extended encounters, ongoing communication and nurturing of mutual understanding regarding service outcomes becomes especially important.

Affective Content

Most previous research in services marketing ignores the emotional content of service delivery. By "affective content," we refer to emotional arousal associated with the encounter. Most previous services marketing research focuses on the provision not only of predominantly functional benefits (Czepiel, Solomon, and Surprenant 1985; Parasuraman, Zeithaml, and Berry 1988), but also low-affect contexts such as bank transactions, making airline reservations, or hotel check-ins. We distinguish two service encounter contexts likely to have high affective content.

In the first type, the consumer is motivated by the expected functional benefits of service encounters, but emotional content is nonetheless an important part of interaction and service satisfaction. In this case, emotions may be part of the encounter because of psychological reactance (e.g., criminal lawyers, parole officers, bill collectors); invasive procedures on the self (e.g., plastic surgery, tattooing, hair styling, even home redecorating); or risks associated with credence goods (e.g., financial advising). In the second type, the consumer is motivated by the affective benefits offered by the service. Examples include services valued for their multisensory, emotive content or narrative and ritualistic meanings, such as multi-day white water river rafting, art lessons and artistic performances, martial arts training, encounter groups, health spas, funeral services, and adventure recreations (Arnould and Price 1993; Donohue 1991; Hirschman and Holbrook 1982).

Table 1 summarizes three exploratory characteristics associated with service encounters with high affective content. We anticipate that (all else being equal) low-affect service encounters would be less likely to exhibit these characteristics than high-affect encounters. First, we propose that *affective content contributes to the development of boundary open relationships between service providers and customers.* Emotional content motivates self-revelation, contributing to intimacy and the development of boundary open relationships (Mars and Nicod 1984; Siehl, Bowen, and Pearson 1992).

Second, *affective content requires sustained emotional labor likely to lead to emotional dissonance, role stress, and*

role conflict. To deal with the customer's emotional intensity regularly requires that the service provider expend significant imagistic-emotional energy (Hirschman and Holbrook 1982; Hochschild 1983). Encounters that are routine for the service provider are often exceptional or even extraordinary for the customer. This creates asymmetry in feelings and expectations, as the following example from medical services illustrates (Todd 1989, p. 16):

> An important factor in the doctor-patient relationship is that patients are usually sick and doctors are usually healthy. Illness is always anxiety-provoking and emotionally difficult. The patient is a stranger in a strange land, where only a small minority understand the gadgets, procedures, and options; for doctors the territory is familiar.

A disparity between the emotional state of the customer and the service provider places a premium on the emotion work of the service provider, as in service encounters related to death (Gentry et al. 1995). To provide authentic emotional outcomes, the provider may attempt to displace or "backstage" commercial intentions, because "synthetic compassion can be more offensive than none at all" (Thompson 1976, p. 115). Provider emotions must be perceived by the consumer as authentic (Ashforth and Humphrey 1993; Hochschild 1983; Rafaeli and Sutton 1987; Romm 1989)—spontaneous responses to environment, activities, and social interaction (Abrahams 1986)—rather than directed process.

As noted previously, emotional performances, especially if they are at odds with self-identity, can lead to role stress, role conflict, and burnout (Singh, Goolsby, and Rhoades 1994). The masking or reworking of authentic emotions to make them conform to emotion norms has been linked to psychological and physical dysfunctions, as well as to overall stress and job dissatisfaction (King and Emmons 1990; Parkinson 1991; Rutter and Fielding 1988). Thus, emotional dissonance, role stress, and role conflict that arise in affectively charged service encounters pose serious managerial challenges.

The third characteristic is that *in delivering affective services content, service providers both orchestrate the encounter to define customized service benefits and deliver them.* In service encounters with high affective content, the provider, like an artistic performer, is an important conduit of benefits contributing to service satisfaction (Holbrook 1987). Service providers convey the affective content of events through their own engagement, emotions, sense of drama, and skills

(Deighton 1992; Grove and Fisk 1992). Competence and efficiency still will be expected of service providers, but emotional labor and the engineering of emotion will have expanded roles (Arnould and Price 1993).

The virtual impossibility of standardizing the delivery of emotional content poses special burdens for service providers. In emotionally charged encounters, customers want recognition of the uniqueness of their personal experience. They want providers to interact with them on the basis of their emotional state, rather than according to a standardized script. For example, grieving relatives do not want to be told, "I know just how you feel," or to compare their loss to others' losses (Gentry et al. 1995). Because customers often see their emotional state as unique, each expects to be treated by the provider in what they perceive to be a unique way.

Proxemics

Most previous research has ignored the proxemic dimension of contact between service provider and customer, although proxemic relationships vary markedly (for an exception, see Goodwin and Frame 1989). Service providers and customers may be remote, as in telephone contacts, or they may be separated by desks or counters, as in retail settings. Other encounters may be quite intimate, as in therapeutic massage. The omission of the proxemic dimension in the services marketing literature is significant because research demonstrates that proxemics has a strong impact on perceptions of interpersonal encounters (Hall 1974; Willis and Hamm 1980).

Table 1 summarizes two exploratory characteristics associated with intimate service encounters. "Intimate service encounters" refer to those in which provider and customer are spatially proximate—in American culture, within 36 inches. Intimate service encounters are more likely to exhibit these characteristics than encounters in social or public space, or outside 36 inches (Hall 1974). First, we posit that *intimate proxemics heighten involvement and feelings of attachment, and interactions are more likely to develop into boundary open transactions.* Spatial proximity produces feelings of attachment and personal involvement while facilitating perceptions of service providers' trustworthiness and warmth (Mehrabian 1981). Moreover, intimate nonverbal signals, especially touching, are perceived as more genuine (Hornik 1992). One study found that legal counselors who touched clients were liked better and were viewed as more empathic (Pattison 1973). Intimacy, feelings of attachment, personal involvement, and empathy contribute to the development of boundary open relationships (Mars and Nicod 1984; Siehl, Bowen, and Pearson 1992).[3]

We also propose that *close proxemics positively affect the overall evaluation of the service encounter.* This point also follows from research findings on nonverbal communication. Close proxemics heighten positive feelings and mood and increase attentional arousal, subsequently affecting overall evaluation of associated stimuli (Patterson, Powell, and Lenihan 1986). Moreover, research suggests that spatial proximity positively influences evaluations of encounters (Hornik 1992).

Implications for the EAI Service Provider Role

To summarize, we anticipate that EAI encounters demand a service provider role that incorporates empathic sharing, communication of caring, evolving intimacy, and exchange more characteristic of friendship than commercial service provision. Service providers engage in substantial emotion work, work that must appear authentic. Successful service providers expend sustained emotional energy to orchestrate service encounter goals while still delivering functional outcomes. Providers must orchestrate service encounter goals and manage script interference that constrains mutual understanding and threatens satisfaction. Because customer expectations must be both crystallized and delivered in EAI encounters, service provider performance is critical to affective response and service satisfaction. The emotion work required in each EAI encounter can lead to emotional fatigue and role stress. Role conflict can arise from negotiating boundaries between transactional and relational exchanges.

Description of Research Activity

We now describe an exploratory field study of service provider-customer relationships on commercial, multi-day river rafting trips in the Colorado River Basin. Findings are based on a two-year, multi-method study of commercial rafting that incorporates data reflecting outfitter (management), guide (service provider), and customer perspectives (Arnould and Price 1993).

In Figure 2, we posit that service provider performance characteristics and the relationship between these characteristics and customer responses vary with the duration, affective content, and proxemic intimacy of the service encounter. The approach taken here con-

---

[3]Of course, as one reviewer points out, some people in some encounters will reject proxemic intimacy because they find it inappropriate or unattractive, and providers must be responsive to customer cues. Failing to provide a level of intimacy keyed to the nature, duration, and affective content of the encounter can produce negative evaluations of the service encounter.

trols service encounter dimensions and explores service provider performance characteristics and customer responses, consistent with the influential recommendations of Glaser and Strauss (1967) for the development of grounded theory. Multi-day commercial river rafting trips are extended in time, have high affective content, and take place in personal and intimate proxemic space—in other words, an EAI encounter (Arnould and Price 1993).

We employed an emergent research design fully detailed in Arnould and Price (1993). Emergent design is the standard in ethnography, in which succeeding methodological steps are based on the results of steps already taken and imply the presence of a continuously interacting and interpreting investigator (Arnould and Wallendorf 1994). We used case-based descriptive data focused on the meanings of the service encounter to extend conventional measures of customers' perceptions of service provider performance and reported customer satisfaction appropriate for EAI encounters. Therefore, we did not begin with existing measures or a priori conceptualizations of service provider performance (Brown and Swartz 1989; Parasuraman, Zeithaml, and Berry 1988); instead, it was our goal to trace the evolution of one particular shared service encounter script.

As detailed in Arnould and Price (1993), we used a variety of data-gathering procedures to incorporate multiple perspectives and sample across the temporal frame of the encounter. To understand the temporal moments of the encounter, data were gathered repeatedly from outfitters and guides. For the same reason, data were gathered from customers before, during, immediately after, and well after their river trips. Dates of data collection are noted in the text, along with the data collection technique and general type of sample. For more complete descriptions of the samples and techniques, the reader is referred to Arnould and Price (1993). Data collection proceeded according to well-established guidelines for each of the three data gathering techniques: systematic interviewing, participant observation, and survey research (Denzin and Lincoln 1994; Dillman 1978; Fowler 1988; McCracken 1988). Interpretation proceeded iteratively according to established guidelines, combining and integrating convergent and divergent data into a trustworthy representation of the encounter (Arnould and Wallendorf 1994; Denzin and Lincoln 1994; Wallendorf and Belk 1989).

Findings

We first use extensive qualitative data to examine an EAI encounter, providing a textured account of salient features of these encounters and how the service provider role is constituted. Then, using quantitative measures consistent with previous research and faithful to the qualitative data, we test an overall model of the relationships among service provider performance, affective response, and service satisfaction for the case of an EAI service encounter.

EAI Encounter Characteristics

Table 1 illustrates characteristics we anticipate to be associated with extended, affective, intimate encounters. These characteristics in turn have important implications for how the service provider role is constituted and how performance relates to affective response and service satisfaction. Specifically, the service provider is charged with conveying authentic understanding, provision of extras, and orchestration of service encounter goals in addition to functional performance. In this section, we depict one EAI encounter to illustrate these characteristics.

Movement Toward Boundary Open Relationships
As we might predict from our conceptual framework, both sides of an EAI exchange gravitate toward boundary open relationships. Often a process of personal revelation contributes. For example, participant observation field notes from the last night of one trip reveal emotional intimacy and sharing consistent with an exchange of confidences between close friends:

> And I stayed up and spent a lot of time talking with . . . the few people who were still up. And the few people who were still up included Dan and Jeff and Stan and Rich [all guides], . . . plus Bill . . . and then lots of the girls [sic] . . . What was interesting . . . this evening there was a lot of candid conversation and self-revelation. At least amongst the people who were still hanging out.

In effective EAI encounters, both sides work to establish authentic understanding and empathic connections. One river outfitter instructs his guides not to let clients know that he is the owner, because if they know, it becomes difficult to get "close" to the guests. In guide focus group data, one comment focused on the delicacy with which boatpersons must handle interaction with guides they know who work for other outfitters so as to maintain their fragile connections with customers:

> Yeah, just have to make sure people [i.e., clients] don't feel unimportant. Have to keep in mind they don't really care about Joe [the other boatperson] and make sure they don't feel unimportant because Joe [is] . . . "really

my friend" and not paying to be on my boat (5/90).

The attempt of clients to establish a boundary open relationship with the guides was evident across data sets. For example, participant observation field notes from one trip record several people encouraging one of the guides to interview for a teaching job in their community (7/91). Field notes from another trip record an exchange of addresses and phone numbers between several of the teenage boys and one of the male guides on the trip (5/90).

In contrast to sparse remarks about expected guide qualities recorded in pre-trip surveys that emphasize functional skills, post-trip surveys are filled with affectively charged remarks that indicate the boundary open quality of the relationship that often develops between guide and client. In response to the open-ended query, "The guide on my raft was . . . ," people said things that conveyed authentic understanding and developing friendships:

Like a true friend after only a couple of hours.

Excellent! Let us in on her personal life . . . the type of person I would like for a sister

Some respondents imputed sharing and empathetic motives to guides, saying:

[The guides were] Extremely nice . . . they were very connected with our group. They did not build a little group of guides.

All of the guides were so friendly and fun . . . They made the trip most enjoyable. They were cooperative and *wanted to do what we wanted to do* (emphasis added; 6–8/91).

The impression that guides go out of their way, provide special attention, and give extras to clients is also communicated in post-trip customer survey responses:

In my case, he went out of his way to make sure I was comfortable and he gave me a lot of time being captain . . .

. . . always willing to lend a hand . . . They were very patient with me and always said something to encourage me. (6–8/91)

Guides also report evidence of clients' making efforts to transcend commercial relationships. In the focus group, one guide noted customers' desire to solidify friendship through gift giving:

I've had a lot of conversations with people where . . . they want to help you get moving

with a real job. They want to give you something (5/90).

Evolving Proxemic Intimacy and Display of Authentic Understanding

Proxemic intimacy in EAI service encounters elicits the communication of increasingly empathic feelings. Photographic evidence recorded during participant observation documents changing proxemic relationships between guide and clients from public to intimate over the course of the trip. Photos from the beginning of the trips show guides wearing distinctively equipped and colored life jackets, lecturing to rings of clients who stand 7–12 feet from them (Hall's [1974] public distance) about safety procedures and rafting techniques. Then, groups of clients and guides are thrown together on rafts with little elbow room for the first day's journey. As the trip progresses, forced spatial proximity necessitated by the "servicescape" predictably changes the affective quality of their relationships—creating the appearance of authentic exchanges of feelings and connection. Photos from the final days show group activities in which it is difficult to distinguish guides from clients: a group back rub, water fights in the river, group play in a waterfall, or groups of rafters clacking paddles overhead after successfully running a rapid. On the last day, photos show groups of people, virtually indistinguishable in clothing or demeanor as guide or client, hugging, smiling, standing together, and waving at the camera. In these photos, clients and guides display personal and intimate proxemic distances by choice (Hall 1974).

Emotional Labor and Fatigue

Although emotional labor is a component of most service encounters (Bitner, Booms, and Mohr 1994; Paules 1991; Spradley and Mann 1975), it may be exaggerated in EAI service encounters in which the service provider is not just expected to deliver a functional benefit but is often expected to communicate emotional benefits and be a "friend."

Arnould and Price (1993) illustrate that service providers offer clients emotional benefits: in this case, personal challenges, harmony with nature, and feelings of community. A client recollection illustrates the desire for emotional benefits that permeates this service encounter:

The fear of falling pumps up your adrenaline, making you feel alive, and you suddenly find yourself wanting to become more and more afraid.

To orchestrate these emotional outcomes, service providers expend emotional energy. The following verbatims from post-trip surveys illustrate how emotion work figures into client evaluations of service providers' functional performance. Guides become both a focus of positive affect:

> [The guide was] . . . delightful, competent without being authoritarian, good sense of humor and fun. Relaxing to be around (6–8/91).

and a conduit of positive affect for participants:

> He was willing to do anything to make sure we knew what we were doing and why we were doing it (6–8/91).

In the focus group data, one guide mentions the edge between safety and excitement that the guide must walk to "make things fun for the customers"—in his words, "Running the rapids well, but close to the edge." Participant observation shows how guides orchestrate clients' desires for excitement and danger "close to the edge" in a variety of ways. Some guides steer the boats through the rapids backwards to enhance clients' excitement without necessarily increasing danger. They will allow some customers they believe are competent to negotiate rapids alone in one of the rubber kayaks or "duckies" that are carried along. Clients are invited to pilot the raft, an experience that most clients find both exhilarating and humility inducing. After going through a rapid uneventfully, boatpersons will sometimes relate that it was nonetheless a "close call," and explain how disaster has occurred in other cases. Water fights and "trust me" games are often initiated by guides at the end of a series of rapids. For some city-dwelling clients, merely being initiated into life in the outdoors—bathing, sleeping, defecating—can represent a major life challenge.

Of course, the flip side of emotion work outcomes also shows up in post-trip reports. One retrospective report that mentioned the guide notes, "My guides were too lame to allow anyone to have fun" (1/90). The quote indicates that "lame" guides do not always successfully orchestrate customers' evolving desires for emotional highs.

In commercial rafting, the provider and customers are in intimate contact for extended periods on a small raft. Dealing with clients in an emotionally charged and expectant state and facilitating hedonic experience creates emotional fatigue for guides. Some focus group comments of commercial river guide trainees just after they have completed training, and even before they have started taking clients down the river, anticipate this fatigue:

> It's really a lot of work . . . I anticipated mostly frolicking down white water. Packing

for a day trip takes 2–3 hours, there's sending out brochures, lots of details . . .

> Lots of the romanticism goes out of it. If you still like it after the romance is gone, then it's still worth doing (5/90).

In a post-season survey, one river guide commented incisively on the emotional fatigue he experiences as a result of repeated episodes of temporally extended, emotionally demanding service encounters:

> Very little personal time living out of your dry bag, . . . once begun, a trip is often inescapable. That can be a real headache with some groups. Burnout, fatigue . . . but you need to maintain the same quality of experience (1/91).

Seasonal turnover in river guides is quite high—very few go more than two or three seasons, and end-of-season burnout is a commonly recognized problem.

Script Interference and Orchestrating Outcomes
Arnould and Price (1993) illustrate ways in which service providers orchestrate client outcomes (e.g., create team spirit, provide connections to nature, present clients with personal challenges). Guides' recognition of their primary responsibility for orchestrating outcomes is reflected clearly in the following verbatim from a focus group guide comment:

> On a river like that, you [the guide] have to make it happen, do it yourself. If there's a problem you have to solve it (5/90).

The complexity of orchestrating appropriate outcomes is illustrated in the following record of a guide's comments from participant observation field notes:

> A lot of factors played into whether or not it was a good trip. And he [the guide] talked about how important it was: the kind of people you're on the trip with; the crew that you're on the trip with, both whether you get along with them and whether they're competent and do good stuff, good work. And . . . the river makes a big difference. Because when it's low water, it's still hard work and you still have to finesse around rocks and things. But it's not as exciting for anybody. . . . that's a frustration . . . It also depends upon . . . how many trips he's gone on lately, and how worn out he feels (7/91).

As this excerpt indicates, the personalities and dynamics of the individuals involved become critical in successfully orchestrating EAI encounters.

The social environment in which the encounter takes place, "people you're on the trip with," varies uncontrollably between trips. An example of the diversity in social environments with which guides must contend comes from the guide focus group data. A guide said,

> [We] Get all sorts of people. . . . A client tells you he's a high official for the Ku Klux Klan . . . You're thinking, "How am I going to drown this person?" but you have to say, "Great! That must be a complicated organization. . . ."(5/90).

In spite of this diversity, the guides are charged to deliver an extended, positive affective experience to each group of customers in an intimate setting regardless of their affective orientation toward the clients.

The extension of the encounter in time dramatically increases opportunities for "things to go wrong." A good example of the script interference that may intrude on the extended service encounter is depicted in a verbatim from a guide focus group illustrating how the commercial construction of guide-client relations may intrude on the relational, affective construction of the "trip":

> There is a boat[person] culture. All these boat[persons] know each other and they work together. . . . [Sometimes we'll] pull in and talk for a while. Clients just become faceless blobs, [we boatpersons] just focus on each other, talk quietly and all [about] gear. "Moment out of trip." Breaks up the flow of the trip for a few minutes, . . . brings up the concept of other outfitters and other trips. [Clients] realize that they are not the only experience. [We are] trying to communicate [the uniqueness of] "just our trip" but this [encounter] reminds them they are just "this week's group of clients" . . . they are just "my load" when I run into another outfitter.

In this example, contact with other boats pushes the commercial nature of the trip from the "backstage" arena of commercial management into the foreground arena of service performance, exposing it to client perception, and interrupting the flow of the trip and the careful orchestration of the "uniqueness" of "our trip." Successful guides know they must backstage the commercial aspect of the trip after such an encounter between boatpersons.

Role Stress and Role Conflict   The emotion work just described can lead to role stress and role conflict. One kind of guide role conflict derives from the delivery of emotional benefits. As illustrated in comments from the guide focus group (5/90), the employers, the river outfitters, evaluate guides' performance more heavily in terms of safety, and clients may evaluate guides' performance more in terms of thrills and excitement:

> The religion of [commercial] boating is "smooth run." [But] the people [clients] who have the best time are the people who fall out. . . . To us it's bad boating and to them [the customers] it's radical and they love it. [Clients develop] unrealistic expectations.

Attempts by service providers and clients to move toward a boundary open relationship also create role conflicts for both parties. Evidence of this role conflict between inner feelings and expressed emotions abounds in the focus group and participant observation notes. For example, in a guide focus group, a boatperson asked a rhetorical question that reflected the dissonance he sometimes experiences: "How much does the boat[person] have to suspend his [or her] own personality and beliefs?" More evidence of role conflict associated with the move toward a boundary open relationship in a commercial context showed up in the comments of a client in a focus group:

> We wondered if they [the guides] felt kind of in conflict because, they're getting paid for doing a certain amount of things. You know, for doing the camp stuff and doing the raft trip. And they have to do that. But they're interacting with us like we are friends. But at the same time we're in the position to have to tip them at the end [of the trip], or decide if we want to tip them, and how much. And that's kind of a weird . . . position to be in, with people you associate with on a friends level (9/90).

This woman expresses her contradictory feelings about the transactional versus relational construction of service encounter between client and guide. She also provides evidence that the guides on her trip felt this conflict, too:

> I think that I got the impression that maybe they had the conflict or felt that way because, after the trip was done, they asked if we were going to stay around, and if we wanted to go to . . . some sort of dance or event in town, you know, with them.

She suggests that the guides offered them the option of extending and confirming the noncommercial nature of their relationship by together entering a different context in which neither guide nor client would stand in a commercial relationship. The conflict between transactional and relational exchanges is a real one for client and guide alike. Role conflicts affect not only guides' decisions to deliver affectively charged experiences (e.g., flipped boats), which may also negatively affect customer safety and protection of capital equipment, but also the feelings that guides and clients develop for one another.

Service Provider Performance

In contrast to clients' pre-trip expectations of provider performance, which are neither elaborate nor focused on emotion work, we show that in EAI encounters the successful service provider orchestrates mutually acceptable goals for the service encounter in the face of social diversity, evolving desires for emotional content, and script interference. In the case of river rafting, the guide orchestrates the goals of fun, community and personal challenge while not neglecting the functional tasks of safety, boatspersonship, and customer caretaking that management stresses (Arnould and Price 1993). Moreover, the service provider role must seem authentic; he or she must behave, "like a friend." In the case of river rafting, in which the affective content is positive, the guide must appear to enjoy the job and the customers. The service provider role incorporates aspects of self-revelation—"let us in on her personal life," empathic connection—"they wanted to do what we wanted to do," and mutual giving—"in my case, he went out of his way" that are more characteristic of friendship than commercial service provision. In the context of an EAI encounter, authentic understanding and mutual giving facilitate the service provider's orchestration of primary goals by promoting a relational exchange between customers and service providers.

Relationships among Provider Performance, Affective Response, and Customer Satisfaction

Analysis of the qualitative data reveals the salient characteristics of service provider performance in this EAI context. Using quantitative measures, we now test a theory-driven model of relationships among provider performance, affective response, and customer satisfaction. That is, the service encounter dimensions represented as exogenous constructs in Figure 2 —duration, affective content, and proxemic intimacy—are held constant (extended, affective, intimate) to focus on the relationships among service provider performance characteristics, affective responses, and service satisfaction. This approach, building general theory (i.e., of service encounters) by beginning in a particular substantive domain (i.e., EAI encounters), conforms to Glaser and Strauss's (1967) recommendations.

Measurement

Service Provider Performance   Three dimensions measure the service provider performance construct: Overall Performance; Authentic Understanding, and Extras. Most research evaluating service providers does so as part of more global measures of service quality and service satisfaction and often uses simplistic indicators (Westbrook 1980). Measures of the emotional performance or relational aspects of service provider roles are especially superficial. Typical examples include "perceive employees as polite," and "perceive hospitals to have the patients' best interests at heart" (Mangold and Babakus 1991; for a review see Frazer-Winsted 1993). Some of the measures we used are hinted at in the literature (Brown and Swartz 1989). We drew directly on Bitner, Booms, and Tetrault (1990) to develop measures of emotional performance and the relational aspects of service provider performance. The latter's research suggests that connecting with customers' lives, inviting and sharing personal exchanges, and being genuine contribute to customers' perceptions of providers' empathy and mutual understanding. They also report that customers frequently indicate provision of special attentions and little extras in their memorable encounters. Rust, Zahorik, and Keiningham (1995, p. 6) posit that "adding unexpected extras" moves customers from satisfaction to delight even with functional services, such as the hotel experience. Other measures were inspired by our qualitative data and refined and validated through quantitative methods employed during the first season of research.

Descriptions and summary statistics for the service provider dimensions are included in Appendix A. An unconstrained principal components factor analysis of 17 service provider characteristics yielded three separate factors with eigenvalues > 1. Together these three factors explain 68% of the variance in the service provider's role.

The *overall performance* factor, which includes eight items, is a global construct that deals with guides' overall effectiveness (α = .91). Loading on this performance dimension are measures of guide orchestration of the affectively charged themes of developing community ("created team spirit") and providing "personal challenge," while "making things fun." The latter element also captures the idea of the guide as a conduit for service encounter benefits. These elements emerged in the first research season as key determinants of satisfaction (Arnould and Price 1993). In addition, core functional items such as "making things safe," "boat handling skills," and "taking care of details" loaded on this factor. Outfitters were correct to identify these functional items as components of the guide role, but they are only part of the overall construction of performance in this EAI context.

The second factor that emerged from analysis we have labeled *authentic understanding*. Some specific items in other marketing research hint at the importance of this dimension, but without additional development (e.g., Brown and Swartz 1989, p. 95). The authentic understanding construct (α = .90) measures extent of agreement with six items, such as the guide "understood me," "connected to my life and experience," and "revealed personal things." This construct suggests that the service provider and client engage in self-revelation, expend emotional energy, and connect as individuals rather than simply performing their respective roles. It seems to capture both the perceived authenticity of the provider role, and some aspects of the boundary open (friendship) quality of relationships that develop in EAI service encounters.

The third factor, *extras*, included measures of three items: The service provider "paid me special attention," "gave me something extra," and "went out of his/her way" (α = .86). Extras transcend a standard transactional exchange, including benefits neither expected nor purchased (i.e., gifts). The provision of extras implies that a boundary open relationship, characterized by more generalized reciprocity, develops between service provider and client.[4]

Affective Response   The two affective dimensions measured are Pleasure and Negative and were adapted from Edell and Burke (1987) and Holbrook and Batra (1987). Summary statistics for the two measures of affect are reported in Appendix A. Consistent with our conceptual framework, mean response is quite high on the positive affect dimension and low on the negative dimension. To provide a comparison, mean response on the pleasure dimension scale in this database was 4.3 (s.d. = .67) as compared with a mean response of only 2.9 in a database consisting of 917 service

encounters of all types (Price, Arnould, and Deibler forthcoming).

Satisfaction   Service satisfaction is measured using a six-item scale (α = .93); (Arnould and Price 1993; Fisher and Price 1991; MacInnis and Price 1990). Consistent with recent thinking on satisfaction measures in general (Oliver 1993; Westbrook and Oliver 1991) and customer outcomes associated with this EAI encounter (Arnould and Price 1993), this measure taps affective and narrative characteristics of the experience with items such as "This trip had many unique or special moments" and "this river trip stands out as one of my best experiences." The satisfaction scale mean was 5.9 (s.d. = 1.1). Summary statistics for overall satisfaction for the second research season are reported in Appendix A.

Structural Relationships

We used LISREL 7 with maximum likelihood estimation to examine the relationships between satisfaction and affective responses (Pleasure and Negative), overall service provider performance, authentic understanding between service provider and client, and providers' provision of extras (Jöreskog and Sörbom 1989). The constructs in the model were represented with single indicators using summated scales. Utilization of single-item constructs parallels several past efforts, yields an acceptable variable/sample size ratio, and reduces the model's complexity (Homer and Yoon 1992, p. 25). In Figure 3, we show the model tested and the estimated parameters for the structural equations.

With covariance matrix as input, the model has an acceptable fit with an overall χ^2 = 4.73 (d.f. = 7, p = .692), an adjusted GFI = .986, and a root mean square residual = .034. The total coefficient of determination for the structural equations is .701. The results, including the t-values on the parameter estimates, the very small normalized residuals, and the acceptable range of values (i.e., no negative variances) suggest that the model fits the data well.

Figure 3 shows, first, that overall service provider performance contributes directly and significantly to positive affective response, which contributes directly and significantly to customer satisfaction. This is consistent with our conceptual model. Second, the overall service provider performance construct can be partially understood as an articulation of two other dimensions of the service provider role: authentic understanding and provision of extras. These two dimensions signify that successful service provider performance for an EAI encounter turns on key elements in boundary open relationships. Thus, consistent with

---

[4]This use of extras is very different than the use of extras in service recovery to compensate for some other service deficiency. In such cases, extras are not really extra, but part of attempts to adjust perceptions of equity or fairness (Oliver and Swan 1989). Our use of extras recalls the case of the Tattered Cover Bookstore in Denver, Colorado. When this popular retailer changed locations some years ago, several hundred loyal customer volunteers turned out to help (Len Berry, personal communication). Indeed, one might argue that the provision of extras in a context of generalized reciprocity is a good way to demarcate the existence of boundary open relationships in business.

FIGURE 3

LISREL Model of Service Provider Performance Characteristics, Affect and Satisfaction for an EAI Encounter

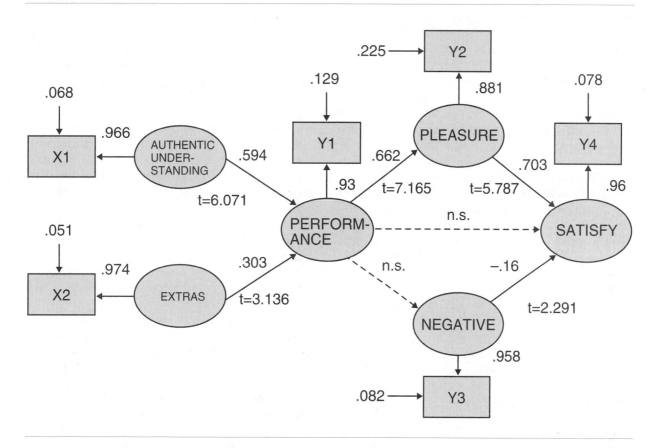

our conceptual model of EAI encounters, relational elements of the role are critical to performance, whereas functional effectiveness is important to the service provider role. Third, contrary to expectations, the data do not support a significant path between performance and satisfaction, suggesting that the effect of performance on satisfaction is fully mediated through positive affective response. Finally, negative affective response has a small but significant negative effect on satisfaction. Interestingly, the path between overall performance and negative affective response is not significant. This may suggest that factors not under the service providers' control may produce negative affect in EAI encounters, consistent with our conceptual model, which posits numerous opportunities for script interference.

Readers might still question whether the two dimensions of guide performance (Authentic Understanding and Extras) are fully mediated through the overall performance construct or have separate significant effects on Pleasure, Negative, and Satisfaction. A

test of this model reveals that none of the direct paths between these constructs and Pleasure, Negative, and Satisfaction approach significance, and the model fit is not significantly improved by adding these paths. T values for these added paths ranged from .07 to 1. 15 (all nonsignificant).

Discussion and Conclusion

We began by identifying three neglected dimensions of service encounters that emerge from an examination of basic research on interpersonal relations. Figure 1 illustrates that service encounters vary on these three dimensions. Figure 2 indicates that the service provider role and customer response depend on dimensions of the service encounter. Table 1 summarizes characteristics of service encounters and service provider performance that fall at the extreme of these three dimensions, termed EAI encounters. Using extensive qualitative data, we provide empirical grounding for

EAI encounter characteristics and the service provider role. Finally, we develop measures of service provider performance and test an overall model of the relationships among service provider performance, affective response, and service satisfaction for the case of an EAI service encounter. We now discuss practical and theoretical consequences of our research.

A major achievement of rethinking service encounters is demonstrating that the way in which service provider performance is constituted depends in part on the characteristics of the service encounter context: its duration, affective content, and proxemic intimacy. Our research suggests that a general theory of service encounters should be based in broad social science theory of human relationships and grounded in substantive understanding of varied service encounter contexts. We show how the service provider role is constituted for an EAI encounter and how provider performance plays a central role in customer outcomes in such encounters. Provider performance involves developing authentic understanding, provision of extras, and orchestration of primary goals in addition to functional performance. Further theoretical development may grow out of systematic studies of encounters that vary across key relationship dimensions, including duration, affective content, and proxemic intimacy. Managers should then be able to identify the key dimensions of encounter contexts and the requisite performance characteristics for satisfaction.

Two affective constructs are highly related to perceptions of overall provider performance in EAI encounters. The first, authentic understanding, is achieved when the provider's performance connects with the client's life experiences and both engage in self-disclosure. This construct is qualitatively different from the SERVQUAL definition of empathy or measures of courtesy employed in the service quality literature. The qualitative data presented underscore how much more is involved than merely "providing personal attention to customers." Authentic understanding involves something more than a pecuniary transaction; it involves a relational exchange that requires emotion work, real giving on the part of the provider. To be successful, this relationship work must appear to the client to be genuine—not that the provider is merely playing his or her role well, but that he or she is not playing a role at all.

Extras, the second factor that relates highly to overall provider performance, is achieved by giving something more to the customer than expected within the norms of a commercial transaction. But what is especially important about these extras is that they are *not* a standardized part of the service delivery package,

not merely part of a transaction mediated by money, but instead convey a relationship of generalized reciprocity between provider and customer (Sahlins 1972; Sherry 1983). Emergence of generalized reciprocity is evident in the qualitative results in the desire of clients to *give something other than money back* to the guides (e.g., advice, job offers, invitations) and the role conflicts experienced by both parties over the boundaries of the relationship (e.g., to tip or not to tip, to socialize or not after the trip).

Any time the service encounter context involves greater temporal duration, is more proxemically intimate, and is more affectively charged, provider performance is likely to be a critical determinant of customer outcomes. It is likely to involve relational performance dimensions such as mutual understanding and extras in addition to functional performance. In general, in complex, extended encounters, managers should assist service providers in developing tactics to develop authentic relational links with customers and provide extras appropriate to the service judiciously, at the same time, without compromising providers' self-identity.

In the EAI service context, provider and client do not necessarily share a definition of service provision. For the guide, the trip is relatively routinized; for the client, the trip is dramatic and unique. The client relies on the guide to orchestrate this drama and adventure in a context that is less highly charged for the guide. Other service encounters may also feature these differing orientations between provider and customer. What is routine for lawyers, trauma center staff, funeral home directors, and maternity ward nurses, for example, is often unique, dramatic, and bewildering for clients. Provider training for high-affect encounters such as these should emphasize effective management of this asymmetry, that is, acknowledge perceived singularity and intensity of client feelings.

As a result of the weakness in script strength and congruence in EAI encounters, goal orchestration is likely to be a recurrent challenge for providers. Although the specific definition of functional role performance and primary goals orchestrated by a personal trainer, obstetrician, doctoral adviser, parole officer, lawyer, and psychiatrist, for example, will vary, successful orchestration will become part of the provider's role and central in client evaluation of service outcomes. Arguments are often made in favor of standardizing service delivery to meet customer expectations. However, the presence of weak scripts and script interference suggests the need for service providers to negotiate shared goals instead of standardizing service delivery.

Our results show that emotional fatigue, role stress, role conflict, and the problem of negotiating relationship boundaries pose important managerial challenges for EAI services. The role stresses inherent in transcending the commercial relationship and meeting customers' demands for emotional outcomes inconsistent with the provider's inner feelings and managerial responsibilities are challenges potentially faced by numerous providers operating in contexts sharing one or more dimensions with EAI encounters, ranging from extended care nurses and psychological therapists to interior decorators and hair stylists. Further research is needed to identify aspects and implications (including the ethical implications) of role stress for service provision. Similarly, the burnout and fatigue associated with EAI service encounters deserve research attention. Without further research, it is hard to predict which managerial strategies will effectively combat these problems.

Several implications stemming specifically from the quantitative results presented here merit discussion. Our results support the view that in EAI encounters provider performance strongly influences positive affect, and affect, both negative and positive, in turn influences encounter satisfaction. Two aspects of these results are of special interest. First, research generally supports the idea that the influence of performance on satisfaction is mediated through affective response (consistent with our results; Mano and Oliver 1993). But some research also supports a modest, direct path between performance and satisfaction (inconsistent with our results; Oliver 1993). Our findings may stem from looking at an affectively charged service context rather than a more affectively neutral product context

(Mano and Oliver 1993). Overall, these results suggest that more careful consideration of the relationship between service encounter type, service type, affect, and satisfaction is needed.

Second, our results support research proposing that positive and negative affect have independent effects on satisfaction (Oliver 1993). Interestingly, although provider performance strongly affects positive affect, it is not related to negative feelings. Again, this is at odds with results in product-based studies. Consistent with an encounter context fraught with uncontrollables (less likely to be the case in product evaluations), it is possible that customers believe providers in EAI encounters have little control over the factors that produce negative affect. With the increased liking attached to the provider in a boundary open relationship, it is also possible that the provider is not held responsible for negative aspects of the trip. An interesting extension of the present research would be to look at the attribution process associated with positive and negative feelings in an EAI service context.

A final implication stemming from the quantitative results has to do with the relationships among authentic understanding, provision of extras, overall provider performance, and satisfaction. As indicated in Appendix A, authentic understanding and provision of extras are strongly correlated with satisfaction. However, the relationship of these dimensions of service provider performance to satisfaction is fully mediated through their impact on overall provider performance. In EAI encounters, the impact of these variables comes from understanding how they contribute to the orchestration of primary service encounter goals and functional provider performance.

APPENDIX

Measure	Scale Mean/ Standard Deviation	Cronbach's Alpha	Factor Loading	Correlation with Satisfaction
Provider Performance	6.3/.88	.91		.514
Provide challenges		.	.641	($p < .001$)
Made things fun			.636	
Created team spirit			.430	
Enjoys his/her job			.726	
Performed as expected			.647	
Made me feel safe			.907	
Took care of details			.877	
Was skilled boat handier			.754	
Authentic Understanding	5.6/1.19	.90		.491
Connected to my life			.856	($p < .001$)
Revealed something personal			.795	
Invited me to reveal myself			.872	
Understood me			.729	
Seems like own person			.585	
Out of ordinary			.614	

Measure	Scale Mean/ Standard Deviation	Cronbach's Alpha	Factor Loading	Correlation with Satisfaction
Provision of Extras	5.4/1.38	.86		.470
Gave me something extra			.902	(p < .001)
Went out of his/her way			.762	
Paid me special attention			.591	
Pleasure	4.3/.067	.82		.66
Happy			.773	(p < .001)
Elated			.618	
Pleased			.757	
Warm-hearted			.740	
Negative	1.9/1.1	.87		−.076
Sad			.818	
Sorry			.884	
Regretful			.857	
Angry			.755	
Satisfaction	5.9/1.1	.93		1.00
Had some unique or special moments			.881	
Has special meaning to me			.882	
Was as good as I expected			.805	
Was satisfying to me			.848	
Stands out in my mind as one of my best experiences			.864	
Was worth the price I paid for it			.620	

References

Abrahams, Roger D. (1986) "Ordinary and Extraordinary Experience," in *The Anthropology of Experience*, Victor W. Turner and Edward M. Bruner, eds. Urbana, IL: University of Illinois Press, 45–73.

Arnould, Eric J. and Linda Price (1993), "River Magic: Extraordinary Experience and the Extended Service Encounter," *Journal of Consumer Research*, 20 (June), 24–45.

——— and Melanie Wallendorf (1994), "Market-Oriented Ethnography: Interpretation Building and Marketing Strategy Formulation," *Journal of Marketing Research*, 31 (November), 484–504.

Ashforth, Blake E. and Ronald H. Humphrey (1993), "Emotional Labor in Service Roles: The Influence of Identity, " *Academy of Management Review*, 18 (1), 88–115.

Bakeman, Roger and John M. Gottman (1986). *Observing Interaction: An Introduction to Sequential Analysis*. Cambridge: Cambridge University Press.

Barnes, James G. (1994), "The Issue of Establishing Relationships with Customers in Service Companies: When Are Relationships Feasible and What Form Should They Take?" paper presented at Frontiers in Services Conference, Nashville, TN.

Berry, Leonard (1983), "Relationship Marketing," in *Emerging Perspectives on Services Marketing*, Leonard L. Berry, Lynn G. Shostack and Gregory D. Upah, eds. Chicago: American Marketing Association, 25–28.

Bitner, Mary Jo, Bernard H. Booms, and Lois A. Mohr (1994), "Critical Service Encounters: The Employee's View," *Journal of Marketing*, 58 (October), 95–106.

———, Bernard H. Booms, and Mary Stanfield Tetreault (1990), "'The Service Encounter: Diagnosing Favorable and Unfavorable Incidents," *Journal of Marketing*, 54 (January), 71–84.

Brown, Stephen W. and Teresa A. Swartz (1989), "A Gap Analysis of Professional Service Quality," *Journal of Marketing*, 53 (April), 92–98.

Czepiel, John A. Michael R. Solomon, and Carol Surprenant (1985), *The Service Encounter. Managing Employee/ Customer Interaction in Service Businesses*. Lexington, MA: Lexington Books.

Deighton, John (1992), "The Consumption of Performance," *Journal of Consumer Research*, 19 (December), 362–72.

Denzin, Norman K. and Yyonna S. Lincoln, eds. (1994), *Handbook of Qualitative Research*. Thousand Oaks, CA: Sage Publications.

Derbaix, Christian, and Michel T. Pham (1991), "Affective Reactions to Consumption Situations: A Pilot Investigation," *Journal of Economic Psychology*, 12 (June), 325–55.

Derlaga, Valerian J. (1984), *Communication, Intimacy, and Close Relationships*. Orlando, FL: Academic Press.

Diamond, Timothy (1992), *Making Gray Gold. Narratives of Nursing Home Care*. Chicago: University of Chicago Press.

Dillman, D. A. (1978), *Mail and Telephone Surveys: The Total Design Method*. New York: John Wiley & Sons, Inc.

Donohue, John (1991), "Dancing in the Danger Zone: The Martial Arts in America," paper presented at the annual meeting of the Association for Consumer Research, Chicago.

Edell, Julie and Marian C. Burke (1987), "The Power of Feelings in Understanding Advertising Effects," *Journal of Consumer Research*, 14 (December), 421–33.

Fisher, Robert J. and Linda L. Price (1991), "The Relationship Between International Travel Motivations and Cultural Receptivity," *Journal of Leisure Research*, 23 (3), 193–208.

Fowler, Floyd, J., Jr. (1988), *Survey Research Methods*. Newbury Park, CA: Sage Publications.

Frazer-Winsted, Kathy (1993), "A Cross-Cultural Investigation of Service Encounter Satisfaction," doctoral dissertation, University of Colorado.

Gentry, James, Patricia F. Kennedy, Catherine Paul, and Ronald Paul Hill (1995), "'The Vulnerability of Those in Grief: Implications for Public Policy," *Journal of Public Policy & Marketing*, 14 (1), forthcoming.

Glaser, Barney G. and Anselm L. Strauss (1967), *The Discovery of Grounded Theory*. Chicago: Aldine.

Goffman, Erving (1961). *Encounters: Two Studies In the Sociology of Interaction*. Indianapolis: Bobbs-Merrill.

Goodwin, Cathy and Charles D. Frame (1987), "Social Distance within the Service Encounter: Does the Customer Want to Be Your Friend?" in *Advances in Consumer Research*, Vol. 16, Thomas K. Srull, ed. Provo, UT: Association for Consumer Research, 64–71.

Graham, H. and A. Oakley (1981), "Competing Ideologies of Reproduction: Medical and Maternal Perspectives in Pregnancy," in *Women, Health, and Reproduction*, H. Roberts, ed. London: Routledge & Kegan Paul.

Gronroos, Christian (1990). *Service Management and Marketing: Managing the Moments of Truth in Service Competition*. Lexington, MA: Lexington Books.

Grove, Stephen J. and Raymond P. Fisk (1992), "The Service Experience as Theater," in *Advances in Consumer Research*, Vol. 19, John F. Sherry, Jr. and Brian Sternthal eds. Provo, UT. Association for Consumer Research, 455–61.

Gummesson, Evert (1993), *Relationship Marketing: From 4Ps to 30Rs*. Stockholm: Stockholm University.

Hall, Edward T. (1974), *Handbook for Proxemic Research*. Washington, DC: Society for the Anthropology of Visual Communication.

Hirschman, Elizabeth and Morris B. Holbrook (1982), "Hedonic Consumption: Emerging Concepts, Methods, and Propositions," *Journal of Marketing*, 46 (Summer), 92–101.

Hochschild, Arlie R. (1983), *The Managed Heart*. Berkeley, CA: University of California Press.

Holbrook, Morris B. (1987), "O, Consumer, How You've Changed: Some Radical Reflections on the Roots of Consumption," *Philosophical and Radical Thought in Marketing*, A. Fuat Firat, Nikhilesh Dholakia, and Richard P. Bagozzi, eds. Lexington, MA: Lexington Books, 137–77.

——— and Rajeev Batra (1987), "Assessing the Role of Emotions as Mediators of Consumer Responses to Advertising," *Journal of Consumer Research*, 14 (December), 404–20.

Homer, Pamela M. and Sun-Gil Yoon (1992), "Message Framing and the Interrelationships among Ad-Based Feelings, Affect and Cognition," *Journal of Advertising*, 21 (March), 19–33.

Hornik, Jacob (1992), "Tactile Stimulation and Consumer Response," *Journal of Consumer Research*, 19 (December), 449–58.

Jöreskog, Karl G. and Dag Sörbom (1989), *LISREL 7: A Guide to the Program and Applications*, 2nd ed. Chicago: SPSS.

King, W. A. and R. A. Emmons (1990), "Conflict over Emotional Expression: Psychological and Physical Correlates," *Journal of Personality and Social Psychology*, 58, 864–77.

Korsch, B. M., E. Gozzi, and V. Francis (1968), "Gaps in Doctor-Patient Communications," *Pediatrics*, 42, 846.

Lovelock, Christopher H. (1983), "Classifying Services to Gain Strategic Marketing Insights," *Journal of Marketing*, 47 (Summer), 9–20.

MacInnis, Deborah J. and Linda L. Price (1990), "An Exploratory Study of the Effect of Imagery Processing and Consumer Experience on Expectations and Satisfaction," in *Advances in Consumer Research*, Vol. 17, Marvin E. Goldberg, Gerald Gorn, and Richard W. Pollay, eds. Provo, UT: Association for Consumer Research, 41–47.

Mangold, W. Glynn and Emin Babakus (1991), "Service Quality: The Front-Stage vs. the Back-Stage Perspective," *Journal of Services Marketing*, 5 (Fall), 59–70.

Mano, Haim and Richard L. Oliver (1993), "Assessing the Dimensionality and Structure of the Consumption Experience: Evaluation, Feelings, and Satisfaction," *Journal of Consumer Research*, 20 (December), 451–66.

Mars, G. and M. Nicod (1984), *The World of Waiters*. London: George Allen & Unwin.

McCracken, Grant (1988), *The Long Interview*. Newbury Park, CA: Sage Publications.

McCroskey, James C., Virginia P. Richmond, and Robert A. Stewart (1986), *One on One: The Foundations of Interpersonal Communication*. Englewood Cliffs, NJ: Prentice-Hall.

Mehrabian, Albert (1981), *Silent Messages*. Belmont, CA: Wadsworth.

Mills, Peter K. and James H. Morris (1986), "Clients as 'Partial' Employees of Service Organizations: Role Development in Client Participation," *Academy of Management Review*, 11 (4), 726–35.

Mohr, Lois A. and Mary Jo Bitner (1991), "Mutual Understanding between Customers and Employees in Service Encounters," in *Advances in Consumer Research*, Vol. 18, Michael Solomon and Rebecca Holman, eds. Provo, UT: Association for Consumer Research, 611–17.

Nisbett, R. and L. Ross (1980), *Human Inference: Strategies and Shortcomings of Social Judgment*. Englewood Cliffs, NJ: Prentice Hall.

Oliver, Richard L. (1993), "Cognitive, Affective, and Attribute Bases of the Satisfaction Response," *Journal of Consumer Research*, 20 (December), 418–30.

——— and John E. Swan (1989), "Equity and Dis-confirmation Perceptions as Influences on Merchant and Product Satisfaction," *Journal of Consumer Research*, 16 (December), 372–83.

Parasuraman, A., Valarie A. Zeithaml, and Leonard L. Berry (1988), "SERVQUAL: A Multiple-Item Scale for Measuring Consumer Perceptions of Service Quality," *Journal of Retailing*, 64 (1), 12–40.

Parkinson, B. (1991), "Emotional Stylists: Strategies of Expressive Management among Trainee Hairdressers," *Cognition and Emotion*, 5, 419–34.

Patterson, Miles L., Jack L. Powell, and Mary G. Lenihan (1986), "Touch Compliance and Interpersonal Affects," *Journal of Nonverbal Behavior*, 10 (1), 41–50.

Pattison, John (1973), "Effects of Touching on Self-Exploration and the Thereapeutic Relationship," *Journal of Consulting and Clinical Psychology*, 40 (2), 170–75.

Paules, Greta Foff (1991), *Dishing It Out: Power and Resistance among Waitresses In a New Jersey Restaurant.* Philadelphia: Temple University Press.

Price, Linda L., Eric J. Arnould, and Sheila L. Deibler (forthcoming), "Service Provider Influence on Consumers' Emotional Responses to Service Encounters," *International Journal of Service Industry Management,* 6 (3).

Rafaeli, Anat and Robert I. Sutton (1987), "Expression of Emotion as Part of the Work Role," *Academy of Management Review,* 12 (1), 23–37.

Romm, David (1989), "'Restauration' Theater: Giving Direction to Service," *The Cornell Hotel and Restaurant Association Quarterly* (February), 31–39.

Rust, Roland T., Anthony J. Zahorik, and Timothy L. Keiningham (1995), "Return on Quality (ROQ): Making Service Quality Financially Accountable," *Journal of Marketing,* 59 (2), 58–70.

Rutter, D. R. and Fielding, P. J. (1988), "Sources of Occupational Stress: An Examination of British Prison Officers," *Work and Stress,* 2, 291–99.

Sahlins, Marshall (1972), *Stone Age Economics.* Chicago: Aldine.

Shank, R. C. and Robert P. Abelson (1977), *Scripts, Plans, Goals and Understanding.* Hillsdale, NJ: Lawrence Erlbaum Associates.

Sherry, John F., Jr. (1983), "Gift Giving in Anthropological Perspective," *Journal of Consumer Research,* 10 (September), 157–68.

Shott, Susan (1979), "Emotion and Social Life: A Symbolic Interactionist Analysis," *American Journal of Sociology,* 84 (May), 1317–34.

Shugan, Steven M. (1992), "Explanations for Services Growth," *Frontiers in Services Marketing* (September 24–26).

Siehl, Caren, David E. Bowen, and Christine M. Pearson (1992), "Service Encounters as Rites of Integration: An Information Processing Model," *Organization Science,* 3 (November), 537–55.

Singh, Jagdip, Jerry R. Goolsby, and Gary K. Rhoades (1994), "Behavioral and Psychological Consequences of Boundary Spanning Burnout for Customer Service Representatives," *Journal of Marketing Research,* 31 (November), 558–69.

Spradley, James P. and Brenda J. Mann (1975), *The Cocktail Waitress: Woman's Work In a Man's World.* New York: Alfred A. Knopf.

Sutton, Robert (1991), "Maintaining Norms about Expressed Emotions: The Case of Bill Collectors," *Administrative Science Quarterly,* 38, 245–68.

——— and Anat Rafaeli (1988), "Untangling the Relationship between Displayed Emotions and Organizational Sales: The Case of Convenience Stores," *Academy of Management Journal,* 31 (3), 461–87.

Thompson, V. A. (1976), *Bureaucracy and the Modern World.* Morristown, NJ: General Learning Press.

Todd, Alexandra Dundas (1989), *Intimate Adversaries: Cultural Conflict between Doctors and Women Patients.* Philadelphia: University of Pennsylvania Press.

Trice, H. M. and J. M. Beyer (1991), "Cultural Leadership in Organizations," *Organization Science,* 2, 149–69.

Van Maanen, John and Gideon Kunda (1989), "Real Feelings: Emotional Expression and Organizational Culture," in *Research in Organizational Behavior,* L. L. Cummings and Barry M. Staw, eds. Greenwich, CT: JAI Press, 11, 43–104.

Wallendorf, Melanie and Russell W. Belk (1989), "Assessing Trustworthiness in Naturalistic Consumer Research" in *Interpretive Consumer Research,* Elizabeth C. Hirschman: ed. Provo, UT Association for Consumer Research, 69–84.

Westbrook, Robert (1980), "A Rating Scale for Measuring Product/Service Satisfaction," *Journal of Marketing,* 44 (Fall), 68–72.

——— (1987), "Product/Consumption-Based Affective Responses and Postpurchase Processes," *Journal of Marketing Research,* 24 (August), 258–70.

——— and Richard L. Oliver (1991), "The Dimensionality of Consumption Emotion Patterns and Consumer Satisfaction," *Journal of Consumer Research,* 18 (June), 84–91.

Willis, Frank N. and Helen K. Hamm (1980), "The Value of Interpersonal Touch in Securing Compliance," *Journal of Nonverbal Behavior,* 5 (1), 49–55.

A Comparison of Advertising Content:

Business to Business versus Consumer Services

L. W. TURLEY

SCOTT W. KELLEY

Several studies have investigated differences between goods and services advertisements, but no research has examined differences between business-to-business services advertising and consumer services advertising. The authors use the content analysis method to investigate differences in several message elements in the context of the two types of services advertisements. In their sample of 186 advertisements, 91 ads were for business-to-business services and 95 were for consumer services. The specific message elements evaluated were message appeal, headline usage, price information, quality claims, and the inclusion of an Internet address. The findings indicate significant differences between business-to-business and consumer services advertisements in the types of message appeals used.

Several studies have investigated differences between goods and services advertisements, but no research has examined differences between business-to-business services advertising and consumer services advertising. The authors use the content analysis method to investigate differences in several message elements in the context of the two types of services advertisements. In their sample of 186 advertisements, 91 ads were for business-to-business services and 95 were for consumer services. The specific message elements evaluated were message appeal, headline usage, price information, quality claims, and the inclusion of an Internet address. The findings indicate significant differences between business-to-business and consumer services advertisements in the types of message appeals used.

According to industry reports, business and consumer service organizations spent nearly $6.5 billion on advertising in 1993, and services advertising trailed only automotive and retail advertising as a category (*Advertising Age* 1995). Other sources indicate that business services comprise 23.9% of all service establishments in the United States (Census of Service Industries 1995), and total advertising spending in the business-to-business market increased 22.2% in 1994 to $2.39 billion (Kosek 1995). Specific data on adver-

tising expenditures for business-to-business services are not available, but on a list of the top 100 business marketing firms, a service firm (AT&T) ranks first in ad spending and service-oriented firms account for five of the top 10 firms (*Business Marketing* 1995).

Services researchers have long recognized that services are likely to have different advertising needs than more tangible products (Cutler and Javalgi 1993; George and Berry 1981; Legg and Baker 1987; Stern 1988; Zeithaml 1981). Fewer studies, however, have explicitly acknowledged that different types of services are likely to require different advertising strategies (Zeithaml, Parasuraman, and Berry 1985). A review of the pertinent literature indicates that the advertising differences between consumer services and business-to-business services have not been examined empirically.

We conducted a study to compare the content of magazine ads for business-to-business and consumer services on a variety of advertising execution variables (Stewart and Furse 1985). Such empirical research can benefit both researchers and practitioners. Initially, a theory-based assessment of industry practices provides a view of how advertising is being used by consumer and business-to-business service organizations. Ultimately, the findings will give managers and researchers a standard of comparison that can be used to assess industry practices. Academic researchers can build on the findings to further our knowledge of services advertising. Practitioners can use the findings as constructive criticism about and normative recommendations for services advertising managers.

The unique characteristics that distinguish services from goods (i.e., intangibility, heterogeneity, inseparability, and perishability) and their strategic implications have been well documented in the literature (e.g., Zeithaml, Parasuraman, and Berry 1985).

L. W. Turley (D.B.A., University of Kentucky) is Associate Professor for the Department of Marketing, Bowling Green College of Business Administration, Western Kentucky University.

Scott W. Kelley (D.B.A., University of Kentucky) is Associate Professor for the Marketing Area, School of Management, Carol Martin Gatton College of Business and Economics, University of Kentucky.

Journal of Advertising, *Volume XXVI, Number 4, Winter 1997*

Further, early research in services marketing by Lovelock (1983) suggested strategic distinctions across services. For example, business-to-business services have several distinctive characteristics that may differentiate them from consumer services (Cooper and Jackson 1988), such as a more rational buying process, longer term relationships, greater product complexity, larger amounts of money exchanged, greater use of group decision making, and the design of customized service mixes unique to particular organizations. Although the unique characteristics of business-to-business services appear to be readily accepted by marketing and advertising researchers, differences in advertising content between business-to-business and consumer services ads arising from those characteristics are not documented in the literature.

The lack of research examining the content of business-to-business services advertising is surprising because the selection of effective message content strategies is critical to advertising's success. A survey of advertising professionals indicates the content of the message is the single most important influence on the success of a service advertising campaign (Korgaonkar, Bernhardt, and Bellenger 1986).

Content analysis, a research approach used to study message content, has flourished in a variety of advertising contexts since Kassarjian (1977) introduced the method into consumer research. For example, recent content analysis studies have explored international advertisements (Frith and Wesson 1991; Graham, Kamins, and Oetomo 1993; Roberts and Hart 1994), environmental advertising (Banerjee, Gulas, and Iyer 1995; Carlson, Grove, and Kangun 1993), teleshopping (Auter and Moore 1993), and the use of print advertising visuals (Moriarty 1987).

Relatively few content analyses have been performed in a services advertising context, and all have examined the content differences between services ads and tangible goods ads. In some cases, the study findings have been contradictory. Cutler and Javalgi (1993) found that more emotional appeals and headlines were used in services ads than were used in ads for tangible goods. Abernethy and Butler (1992) found that services ads contained fewer informational cues. Zinkhan, Johnson, and Zinkhan (1992) reported that although services ads used more informational than transformational appeals, informational appeals were used less in services ads than they were in ads for goods. Finally, LaBand, Pickett, and Grove (1992) found that services advertisements were more likely to contain informational appeals than ads for goods.

In the following section we develop hypotheses pertaining to differences in advertising content between business-to-business and consumer services ads.

Hypothesis Development

Content analysis can be used at a variety of levels to examine such variables as words, themes, characters, items, and space-and-time measures (Kassarjian 1977). The specific message elements evaluated in our study were the appeal, headline usage, price information, quality information, and the inclusion of an Internet address.

Appeal

One of the most basic elements associated with an advertising strategy is the choice of an appeal. Advertising appeals are commonly categorized into two broad types, rational and emotional. Stafford and Day (1995) note that the traditional view in advertising has been that the effectiveness of a particular message appeal is contingent on the type of product being advertised.

Interestingly, research on the advertising of services is contradictory on appeal usage. Several researchers have argued on a variety of conceptual grounds that services advertising lends itself to use of emotional appeals. For example, Young (1981) contended that services have a different hierarchy of effects than goods (feel→do→learn, rather than learn→feel→do), which makes emotional appeals more effective for services advertising. Firestone (1983) noted the importance of developing a service personality through services advertising. Again, emotional appeals seemingly would be most effective in conveying a service personality to consumers. Upah (1983) noted the importance of services advertising to communicate the emotional end-benefit the firm is providing. Finally, Legg and Baker (1987) and Stern (1988) cited the need for dramatizing abstract offerings through service advertising.

Stafford and Day (1995) reported findings contradictory to previous ones. They conducted an experiment exploring the effectiveness of services advertising, using message appeal as an independent variable. The findings indicated that rational appeals were more effective than emotional appeals in generating favorable levels of attitude toward services advertisements. On the basis of their results, Stafford and Day argued that informational appeals should be used regardless of service type.

Previous research on the message appeals of services advertising has not considered the possibility that different types of services might require different types of message appeals. Generally accepted distinctions between business-to-business services and consumer services suggest that different message appeals should be used in advertising the two types of services. For example, a more rational decision-making process, greater product complexity, and greater reliance on group decision making are associated with business-to-business services (Cooper and Jackson 1988). The need for rational justifications therefore seems likely to be greater in the context of organizational buying, which involves a continual search for alternatives that yield the best combinations of quality, service, and price (Dobler and Burt 1996), than in consumer buying.

> **H1:** Rational appeals are used more frequently in business-to-business services ads than in consumer services ads.

Headline

Headlines in print ads are closely connected to the message appeal. Some researchers consider the headline to be of central importance to the effectiveness of an ad because the headline is sometimes the only part of an ad that is read (Hitchon 1991). In addition, the headline of a print ad may strongly influence the reading of the ad copy (Hitchon 1991).

Headlines can be written in many styles. Bovee and Arens (1992) classify headlines into five basic styles or categories: benefit, provocative, news/information, question, and command. A benefit headline makes a direct promise to the reader. A provocative headline attempts to stimulate the reader's curiosity. News/information headlines provide news, promise information, or include how-to information that seeks recognition for ad sponsors. Question headlines ask the reader a question, which generally is answered in the body copy. Finally, a command headline orders the reader to do something.

Like advertising message appeals, advertising headline styles seem apt to differ between business-to-business and consumer services ads. Specifically, news and information and benefit headlines seem likely to be used more frequently in business-to-business services ads than in consumer services ads because of the rational nature of those two types of headlines. Provocative, question, and command headlines seem likely to be used widely in both business-to-business and consumer services ads because those types of headlines can be readily adapted to for both rational and emotional appeals.

> **H2:** News and information headlines and benefit headlines are used more frequently in business-to-business services ads than in consumer services ads.

Quality Claims

Service quality has been a dominant research stream during the last decade. Theorists have developed several models to explain how service quality perceptions are formed, which have sparked wide discussion in the academic community (e.g., Gronroos 1983; Parasuraman, Zeithaml, and Berry 1985). In several of the models, external communications with consumers play a central role in the formulation of customer perceptions of service quality (e.g., Parasuraman, Zeithaml, and Berry 1985). One of the strategic uses of external communications (e.g., advertising) with the consumer is to communicate special efforts to achieve quality that may not be apparent or visible because of the intangible nature of services. As a result, quality claims are often an important and vital message element in services advertising.

Quality claims are important in both business-to-business and consumer services advertising; however, Dobler and Burt (1996) suggest that quality is a particularly strong influence in organizational buying. In a study of perceptions of business-to-business service quality, Westbrook (1995) concurred and found the top three quality attributes to be responsiveness, competence, and reliability.

Quality claims can give potential buyers strong rational criteria for decision making. Because rational appeals are expected to be more widely used in business-to-business than in consumer services advertising (H1), business-to-business services ads seem more likely to include quality claims, as such claims provide rational criteria on which business-to-business buyers can base their decisions.

> **H3:** Quality claims are used more frequently in business-to-business services ads than in consumer services ads.

Price Information

Price information is another part of the advertising message that may differentiate business-to-business services advertising from consumer services advertising. Researchers have not compared the frequency of occurrence of price information in the context of the two types of services advertising; however, LaBand, Pickett, and Grove (1992) found that services ads were more likely than tangible product ads to contain information about price. In contrast, Abernethy and Butler (1992) reported that only 19.4% of the services ads in their sample made price-value claims, a significantly smaller proportion than the 78.7% they found for tangible product advertisements.

The conflicting evidence about the frequency of use of price information in services and tangible product advertising does not provide even indirect insight about the relative frequency of use of price information in business-to-business and consumer services advertising. However, price information gives buyers a rational criterion on which to base their purchase decisions. Further, price is generally viewed as a strong influence on organizational buying decisions (Dobler and Burt 1996). The rationality of the organizational buying process suggests that business-to-business services ads are likely to include price information in their message content more frequently than consumer services ads.

> **H4:** Price information is provided more frequently in business-to-business services ads than in consumer services ads.

Internet Address

The World Wide Web has given advertisers a new and efficient means of advertising and marketing their products (Hoffman and Novak 1996). As a result, World Wide Web Internet addresses have recently emerged in print ads as an advertising content element. Placing an Internet address in an ad enables a reader to acquire additional information about the product or sponsor in a timely and efficient way at his or her own convenience. Moreover, use of the World Wide Web and Internet addresses in advertisements has reportedly resulted in marketing and advertising cost savings associated with direct marketing, increased efficiency, and customer service (Hoffman and Novak 1996).

Because Internet addresses are a relatively new execution element for advertisers, little research is available on which to base a hypothesis about the relative usage of the World Wide Web for business-to-business and consumer service print ads. For both business-to-business buyers and consumers, the World Wide Web provides an efficient channel for acquiring information on which to base buying decisions (Hoffman and Novak 1996). However, Internet addresses seem most likely to be included in services advertisements targeted to the business-to-business market because organizational buyers are more likely than consumers to approach the buying decision-making process as rational decision makers (Cooper and Jackson 1988).

> **H5:** Internet addresses are provided more frequently in business-to-business services ads than in consumer services ads.

Method

We examined magazine ads for services by using content analysis methods. Although a content analysis does not investigate the effectiveness of a particular advertising strategy, it enables researchers to identify approaches most commonly used by advertisers.

Sample

As the objective of the study was to examine magazine ads for both business-to-business and consumer services, we decided to draw a sample of ads from widely circulated news/business magazines that are targeted toward business people and/or final consumers and hence contain both business-to-business and consumer services ads. We surveyed two recent issues of each of the following magazines: *Business Week, Forbes, Fortune, Newsweek, Time,* and *U.S. News & World Report.* All six magazines are widely circulated and are widely read by individuals who are business people and/or final consumers. Each of the magazines individually appeared to meet the criteria for our sample and as a group they seemed to provide a fair level of generalizability.

Full-page or two-page display ads for services were used as the sample. We each classified the ads independently as either business-to-business or consumer services ads, and were in 100% agreement about the classification. Services ads that explicitly mentioned businesses as a target market or were explicitly oriented toward business audiences were classified as business-to-business ads. All other services ads were classified as consumer ads. The sampling procedure generated a total of 186 services advertisements, 91 for business-to-business services and 95 for consumer services.

Content Classification

The contents of the service ads were classified according to the five variables (message appeal, type of headline, price claims, quality claims, and Internet address). We independently evaluated each of the 186 ads on the five message dimensions.

The message appeal was categorized by the approach described by Cutler and Javalgi (1993), which was revised slightly to accommodate service appeals. Appeals were classified as emotional appeals if the theme of the ad emphasized adventure, fear, humor, romance, sensuousness/sex, status, care for loved ones, guilt, play/contest, or affiliation. They were classified as rational if the theme emphasized comfort, convenience, ease of use, economy, health, profitability, quality, reliability, time-saving, efficiency,

Reliability Data

Variable[a]	Number of Categories	Number of Ads Agreed On	Percentage of Ads Agreed On	I_r
Appeal	2	160	86	.849
Headline	6	112	60	.723
Price	3	164	88	.907
Quality	2	134	72	.664

[a] As agreement was 100% on the Internet address variable, that variable is not included in the table.

variety/diversity, or environmental friendliness, or if they were comparative.

Headlines were classified according to the typology described by Bovee and Arens (1992) as either benefit, news/informational, provocative, question, or command headlines, or as no headline if one was not used.

As noted by Mazumdar and Monroe (1990), price information can be encoded in two ways. An ad was classified as having an absolute price if an actual price was mentioned (e.g., $39.99). An ad was classified as having relative pricing information if it contained non-numerical pricing information (e.g., indicating lower price than competitors, percentage discounts, or a promise of value). Ads that did not mention price in any form were classified as containing no price information.

Quality appeals were classified by recording whether ads made direct quality claims or made no mention of quality. Ads that referred to generally accepted dimensions of service quality such as tangible aspects, reliability, responsiveness, assurance, or empathy (Parasuraman, Zeithaml, and Berry 1988) were also classified as mentioning quality. Finally, ads were coded for the presence or absence of an Internet address.

Reliability

We each evaluated all of the ads independently. As noted by Kassarjian (1977, p. 14) interjudge reliability is "the degree of consistency between coders applying the same set of categories to the same content." When discrepancies occurred, we discussed them and reached a consensus decision on an appropriate classification. Table 1 reports the number of categories for each variable, the number of advertisements whose classification was initially agreed on for each variable, the percentage of advertisements initially agreed on, and the reliability index I_r recommended by Perreault

and Leigh (1989). The percentage of advertisements initially agreed on ranges from 60% to 88%. The I_r value exceeds .70, the value suggested as a guideline by Perreault and Leigh (1989) for research such as ours, for all variables but quality claims (I_r = .664).

Results

The principal classificatory variable we considered was the type of advertisement (business-to-business services vs. consumer services). Frequency counts and percentages for each variable are reported in Table 2.

In the sample of 91 business-to-business ads, the most common type of service was information management (13), followed by insurance (11), lodging (11), consulting (11), financial (9), transportation/delivery (9), airlines (8), communications (6), corporate credit cards (4), benefits administration (3), food (2), staffing (2), seminars (1), and legal (1). For the consumer services, ad categories were financial services (42), insurance (13), airlines (10), credit cards (7), lodging (7), communications (4), health care (4), education (3), amusement services (2), delivery (1), utilities (1), and car rental (1).

Hypothesis testing results are reported in Table 3. H1, that rational advertising appeals are more frequent in business-to-business services ads than in consumer services ads, is supported (x^2 = 55.92; d.f. = 1; p = .000).

H2, that business-to-business services ads are more likely than consumer services ads to include news and information headlines and benefit headlines, was tested directly by including only the advertisements containing those two types of headlines in the analysis. The sample size for the analysis was 77. The hypothesis is not supported (x^z = .894; d.f. = 1; p = .345).

H3, that quality claims are used more frequently in business-to-business service ads than in consumer service ads, is not supported (x^2 = .194; d.f. = 1;

TABLE 2
Frequency Data

Variable/Category	Frequency Count	Frequency Percentage
Ad Type		
B to B	91	48.9
Consumer	95	51.1
Appeal		
Emotional	52	28.0
Rational	134	72.0
Headline		
Benefit	36	19.4
News	41	22.0
Provocative	75	40.3
Question	19	10.2
Command	5	2.7
None	10	5.4
Price Info		
Absolute	14	7.5
Relative	27	14.5
None	145	78.0
Quality Claims		
Yes	93	50.0
No	93	50.0
Internet Address		
Yes	57	30.6
No	129	69.4

TABLE 3
Hypothesis Testing Results

Variable/Category	Type of Advertisement		χ^2 (d.f.)
	B-to-B	Consumer	
Appeal			55.92 (1)*
Emotional	4	48	phi = .514*
Rational	87	47	
Headline			.894 (1)[a]
Benefit	17	19	
News	15	26	
Provocative	4	29	
Question	9	10	
Command	1	4	
None	3	7	
Quality Claims			.194 (1)
Yes	47	46	
No	44	49	
Price Info			2.61 (2)
Absolute	4	10	
Relative	14	13	
None	73	72	
Internet Address			1.72 (1)
Yes	32	25	
No	59	70	

[a] Only ads containing benefit headlines or news and information headlines were included in the analysis. The sample size for this test was n = 77.
* $p < .05$.

$p = .660$). The frequency of usage of quality claims was essentially the same for the two types of services in the advertisements sampled.

H4, that price information is provided more frequently in business-to-business services ads than in consumer services ads, also is not supported ($\chi^2 = 2.61$; d.f. $= 2$; $p = .271$).

Finally, H5, that business-to-business services ads are more likely to include an Internet address than consumer services ads, is not supported ($\chi^2 = 1.72$; d.f. $= 1$; $p = .190$).

Discussion

We proposed and tested five hypotheses related to expected differences between business-to-business and consumer services advertising. In comparison with consumer buying decisions, the business-to-business buying process is generally acknowledged to (1) be more rational, (2) involve longer term relationships, (3) address products of greater complexity, (4) involve the exchange of larger amounts of money, (5) depend more on group decision making, and (6) often involve service mixes that are customized in some way for a particular organization (Cooper and Jackson 1988). The notion that business-to-business buyers are more rational decision makers provided a common underlying basis for the development of the five hypotheses.

Only one of the five proposed hypotheses is supported. The finding of significant differences for message appeals (H1) indicates that the general tone of business-to-business services ads differs from that of consumer services ads. Table 3 suggests that emotional appeals are rare in the business-to-business context, being present in only four of the 91 ads sampled (4.4%). In contrast, emotional appeals were present in slightly more than half of the consumer services ads sampled (50.5%). Hence, as expected, emotional appeals seem to be used more widely in ads to final consumers than in ads to business-to-business segments.

In a normative sense, the fact that the other four hypotheses are not supported gives services advertisers potentially valuable information. Apparently services advertisers use essentially the same advertising content to appeal to both business-to-business service customers and final consumers, not recognizing the distinctions between the buying process used by business-to-business buyers and that used by final consumers.

The notion that business-to-business decision makers are more likely than consumers to rely on a rational buying process implies that business-to-business services ads are more likely than consumer services ads to contain news and information headlines and benefit headlines (H2). However, use of those two "rational" headline types did not differ significantly between the two types of services advertisements sampled.

That notion also implies that business-to-business services ads are likely to make greater use of quality claims (H3). Exactly one half of the services ads in our sample made quality claims, and the use of quality claims was not significantly different across the types of services ads investigated. The relative scarcity of quality information is somewhat surprising given the emphasis placed on service quality in both the business and academic literature during the last decade. Why more services are not including information about quality in their magazine ads is unknown and warrants research attention in the future. In related research, both LaBand, Pickett, and Grove (1992) and Abernethy and Butler (1992) found that services ads were more likely than goods ads to include quality claims. Future research might explore whether the frequency of usage of quality claims is associated with media choice, and whether other types of service classifications (e.g., professional vs. nonprofessional) yield significant differences in the use of quality claims.

Quality claims may be difficult to identify and classify in ads for services. Table 1 shows that of all the variables considered in the study, the quality claims variable had the lowest I_r coefficient ($I_r = .664$). Just as service quality may be difficult for consumers to judge (Zeithaml 1981), it may be difficult to communicate effectively as it tends to be somewhat abstract and multidimensional (Parasuraman, Zeithaml, and Berry 1985). Future service ad content analysis studies might explore the development of alternative methods for the classification of quality claims in service advertisements. For example, researchers might include the multidimensionality of the service quality construct (e.g., reliability, responsiveness, assurance, empathy, and tangibles aspects) in their classification scheme.

Price information is noticeably absent in our sample of advertisements. We expected business-to-business services ads to contain price information more frequently than consumer services ads (H4), as price gives the business decision maker information that seemingly would be invaluable in a rational decision-making process. The results of our hypothesis testing indicate that the inclusion of price information does not differ significantly between the business-to-business and consumer services advertisements sampled.

In addition, Table 2 indicates that only 7.5% of all the advertisements considered contained absolute price information and only 14.5% included relative price information. Traditionally, services researchers have suggested that because price is one of only a limited number of search properties available to purchasers of services, it may be relied on heavily (e.g., Zeithaml 1982). The limited number of ads in our sample containing price information is therefore somewhat surprising. Several plausible explanations can be offered. First, the lack of price information in the services print ads sampled may be a function of the advertising medium being investigated. Specifically, characteristics of magazines such as relative durability, potential for pass-around readership, and lag time between ad submission and publication may make the extensive use of price information difficult. In addition, the nonstandardized nature of many services may lead to cost variations that limit the use of price information in services advertisements.

Finally, although Internet addresses were used more frequently in business-to-business services ads than in consumer services ads as hypothesized (H5), the difference between the service types is not significant. Only 30.6% of the ads in the sample contained Internet addresses, but the proportion is likely to increase dramatically in the future. Internet addresses are an advertising message factor that should be tracked closely by researchers because the marketing value of the Internet is still developing rapidly (Hoffman and Novak 1996). Also, it will be interesting to note whether future ads provide information about what can be found on home pages rather than just referring to them. The Internet is likely to be a major advertising medium at some point in the future.

Limitations

Several limitations were inherent in our research. First, we sampled ads from only one advertising medium. In the future, researchers might use other advertising media to consider similar research questions. Second, we judged the ad content ourselves. Although we content analyzed the ads independently, some bias may have affected the process. Ideally, independent judges should be used in content analysis procedures. Finally, the content analysis resulted in relatively low reliability results for two of the measures used in the study. Specifically, the content analysis of the ad headlines resulted in a 60% agreement rate and an I_r coefficient of .723; the content analysis of ad quality claims resulted in a 72% agreement rate and an I_r coefficient of .664.

Conclusion

We found only limited differences in message content between ads for business-to-business services and ads for consumer services. Because organizational buyers are believed to use a more rational decision-making process than final consumers, we expected business-to-business and consumer services advertisements to differ in several message elements. However, only the type of message appeal used differed significantly between the two types of services advertisements. The fact that other advertising content variables did not differ raises interesting questions for services advertising practitioners. Should advertisers continue to use essentially the same content to appeal for both business-to-business and consumer service customers? Or should advertisers recognize differences between the buying processes used by the two groups and design their ads accordingly?

Content analysis is a method that should be used increasingly to study the promotion of services. Future studies might explore alternative advertising media (e.g., outdoor, newspapers, radio, or television) and service classifications (e.g., professional vs. nonprofessional, local vs. national) to examine other potential differences in the strategies used to advertise services.

References

Abernethy, Avery M. and Daniel D. Butler (1992), "Advertising Information: Services versus Products," *Journal of Retailing*, 68(4), 398–419.

Advertising Age (1995), "Total Measured U.S. Ad Spending by Category and Media," (September 27), 62.

Auter, Philip J. and Roy L. Moore (1993), "Buying from a Friend: A Content Analysis of Two Teleshopping Programs," *Journalism Quarterly*, 70(2), 425–426.

Banerjee, Subhabrata, Charles S. Gulas, and Easwar Iyer (1995), "Shades of Green: A Multidimensional Analysis of Environmental Advertising," *Journal of Advertising*, 24(2), 21–31.

Bovee, Courtland L. and William F. Arens (1992), *Contemporary Advertising*, 4th ed., Homewood, IL: Richard D. Irwin.

Business Marketing (1995), "The Business Marketing 100," (October), 12.

Carlson, Les, Stephen J. Grove, and Norman Kangun (1993), "A Content Analysis of Environmental Advertising Claims: A Matrix Method Approach," *Journal of Advertising*, 22(3), 27–39.

Census of Service Industries (1995), *Summary-Nonemployer Statistics Series: 1992*, Washington, DC: U.S. Government Printing Office.

Cooper, Philip D. and Ralph W. Jackson (1988), "Applying a Services Marketing Orientation to the Industrial Services Sector," *Journal of Services Marketing*, 2(4), 67–70.

Cutler, Bob D. and Rajshekhar G. Javalgi (1993), "Analysis of Print Ad Features: Services versus Products," *Journal of Advertising Research*, 33 (March/April), 62–69.

Dobler, Donald W. and David N. Burt (1996), *Purchasing Supply and Management: Text and Cases*, New York: The McGraw-Hill Companies.

Firestone, Sidney H. (1983), "Why Advertising a Service Is Different," in *Emerging Perspectives on Services Marketing*, Leonard L. Berry, G. Lynn Shostack, and Gregory D. Upah, eds., Chicago: American Marketing Association, 86–89.

Frith, Katherine Toland and David Wesson (1991), "A Comparison of Cultural Values in British and American Print Advertising: A Study of Magazines," *Journalism Quarterly*, 68 (1/2), 216–223.

George, William R. and Leonard L. Berry (1981), "Guidelines for the Advertising of Services," *Business Horizons*, 24 (July/August), 52–56.

Graham, John L., Michael A. Kamins, and Djoko S. Octoma (1993), "Content Analysis of German and Japanese Advertising in Print Media from Indonesia, Spain, and the United States," *Journal of Advertising*, 22(2), 5–15.

Gronroos, Christian (1983), *Strategic Management and Marketing in the Service Sector*, Cambridge, MA: Marketing Science Institute.

Hitchon, Jacquelin (1991), "Headlines Make Ads Work (Caples 1979): New Evidence Highlights of the Special Topic Session," in *Advances in Consumer Research*, Vol. 18, Rebecca H. Holman and Michael R. Solomon, eds., Provo, UT: Association for Consumer Research, 752–754.

Hoffman, Donna L. and Thomas P. Novak (1996), "Marketing in Hypermedia Computer-Mediated Environments: Conceptual Foundations," *Journal of Marketing*, 60 (July), 50–68.

Kassarjian, Harold H. (1977), "Content Analysis in Consumer Research," *Journal of Consumer Research*, 4 (June), 8–18.

Korgaonkar, Pradeep, Kenneth L. Bernhardt, and Danny N. Bellenger (1986), "Correlates of Successful Advertising Campaigns of Services: A Survey of Advertising Professionals," in *Creativity in Services Marketing: What's New, What Works, What's Developing*, M. Venkatesan, Dianne M. Schmalensee, and Claudia Marshall, eds., Chicago: American Marketing Association, 108–110.

Kosek, Char (1995), "Spending Vaults 22.2%: Top Business-to-Business Advertisers Tune In TV," *Business Marketing* (October), 11.

LaBand, David N., Gregory M. Pickett, and Stephen J. Grove (1992), "An Empirical Examination of the Informational Content of Services Advertisements," in *Enhancing Knowledge Development in Marketing*, Robert P. Leone and V. Kumar, eds., Chicago: American Marketing Association, 166–167

Legg, Donna and Julie Baker (1987), "Advertising Strategies for Service Firms," in *Add Value to Your Service Firm*, Carol Suprenant, ed., Chicago: American Marketing Association, 163–168.

Lovelock, Christopher H. (1983), "Classifying Service to Gain Strategic Marketing Insights," *Journal of Marketing*, 47 (Summer), 9–20.

Mazumdar, Tridib and Kent B. Monroe (1990), "The Effects of Buyers' Intentions to Learn Price Information on Price Encoding," *Journal of Retailing*, 66(1), 15–32.

Moriarty, Sandra E. (1987), "A Content Analysis of Visuals Used in Print Media Advertising," *Journalism Quarterly*, 64 (1/2), 550–554.

Parasuraman, A., Valerie A. Zeithaml, and Leonard L. Berry (1985), "A Conceptual Model of Service Quality and Its Implications for Future Research," *Journal of Marketing*, 49 (Fall), 41–50.

———, ———, and ———(1988), "SERVQUAL: A Multi-Item Scale for Measuring Consumer Perceptions of Service Quality," *Journal of Retailing*, 64(1), 12–40.

Perreault, William D., Jr. and Laurence E. Leigh (1989), "Reliability of Nominal Data Based on Qualitative Judgments," *Journal of Marketing Research*, 26 (May), 135–148.

Roberts, Scott D. and H. Stanley Hart (1995), "A Comparison of Cultural Value Orientations as Reflected by Advertisements Directed at the General U.S. Market, the U.S. Hispanic Market, and the Mexican Market," in *Enhancing Knowledge Development in Marketing*, Barbara B. Stern and George M. Zinkhan, eds., Chicago: American Marketing Association, 153–154.

Stafford, Marla Royne and Ellen Day (1995), "Retail Services Advertising: The Effects of Appeal, Medium, and Service," *Journal of Advertising*, 24 (1), 57–71.

Stern, Barbara B. (1988), "How Does and Ad Mean? Language in Services Advertising," *Journal of Advertising*, 17(2), 3–14.

Stewart, David A. and David H. Furse (1985), "Analysis of the Impact of Executional Factors on Advertising Performance," *Journal of Advertising Research*, 24(6), 23–26.

Upah, Gregory D. (1983), "Impression Management in Services Marketing: Key Research Issues," in *Emerging Perspectives on Services Marketing*, Leonard L. Berry, G. Lynn Shostack, and Gregory D. Upah, eds., Chicago: American Marketing Association, 105–107.

Westbrook, Kevin W. (1995), "Business-to-business Service Encounters: An Empirical Assessment of the Underlying Determinants for Industrial Service Quality," in *Enhancing Knowledge Development in Marketing*, Barbara B. Stern and George M. Zinkhan, eds., Chicago: American Marketing Association, 10–11.

Young, Robert F. (1981), "The Advertising of Consumer Services and the Hierarchy of Effects," in *Marketing of Services*, James H. Donnelly and William R. George, eds., Chicago: American Marketing Association, 196–199.

Zeithaml, Valerie A. (1981), "How Consumer Evaluation Processes Differ between Goods and Services," in *Marketing of Services*, James H. Donnelly and William R. George, eds., Chicago: American Marketing Association, 186–190.

———. (1982), "The Acquisition, Meaning, and Use of Price Information by Consumers of Professional Services," in *Marketing Theory: Philosophy of Science Perspectives*, R. Bush and S. Hunt eds., Chicago: American Marketing Association, 237–241.

———, A. Parasuraman, and Leonard L. Berry (1985), "Problems and Strategies in Services Marketing," *Journal of Marketing*, 49 (Spring), 33–46.

Zinkhan, George M., Madeline Johnson, and F. Christian Zinkhan (1992), "Difference between Product and Services Television Commercials," *Journal of Services Marketing*, 6(3), 59–66.

III

Competing as a Service Firm

art I of this book provided the basic building blocks necessary to understand the problems of marketing in a service firm. Part II showed how these building blocks relate to the configuration of the service firm in terms of operations, physical setting, people, communications, and pricing. Unfortunately, firms do not exist in isolation from competition. Part III therefore looks at how the firm can compete using the configuration it has created.

Chapter 10, "Competing as a Service Firm: Generic Competitive Strategies," provides the theatrical framework for much of the rest of the book. It suggests a firm must first configure a viable economic formula on which to build. Once that formula has been perfected, depending on the nature of the firm, it can choose to compete in one or more of the following ways:

- Attempt a broader range customer (reach)

- Expand geographically to dominate the market (geography)

- Increase market share (share)

Competition for reach and geography tends to happen first. Once a stable market has been established, competition then revolves around share. This in turn involves three different systems. The organization must attempt to satisfy existing customers in order to retain them (the satisfaction system). If the system does fail, it must be still attempt to keep the customer (the recovery system). If all else fails, then it must create barriers to switching the customer (the retention system).

Article 3.1 by Lovelock and Yip deals with one aspect of competition from reach and geography—global strategy for service firms—and should be read in conjunction with Chapter 10. The article discusses the drivers of globalization and classifies services into people-processing, possession-processing and information-based. Potential globalization strategies for each category are then developed.

Chapter 11, on customer satisfaction, should be read in conjunction with Articles 3.2 and 3.3. The chapter first provides a justification for customer satisfaction based on the cost of new versus old customers, and especially the value to service firms of old or retained customers. Finally, it describes the creation of a satisfaction information system which, by using multiple measures and approaches, can overcome many of these problems.

Article 3.2 attempts to take some of the fervor out of the current fascination with "exceeding customer expectations." While not denying the value of the concept, it points out that customer satisfaction is simply part of good marketing. It also suggests that the balance between cost and customer satisfaction is a real one, and shareholders will not welcome an excessively large investment in the customer.

Article 3.3 introduces the important topic of the American Customer Satisfaction Index. This index uses measures of customer expectations, perceived quality, and perceived value, as well as an overall satisfaction index. In addition, measures of customer complaints and loyalty are taken. The power of this index is not just in the measures but in the ability to use the same measures across many different sectors. The index measures 250 respondents from each firm's customer base, and uses this data to derive scores for a particular sector. The results enable different industry sectors to compare their satisfaction measures with each other. Moreover, it is possible to compare the impact of expectations, for example, overall satisfaction by sector.

Chapter 12 considers service recovery: how to capture failed service experiences and put them right. This chapter should be read with Article 3.4. The chapter first discusses the sources of service failure, which are usually much broader than simple core failure and can include unrealistic customer requests and spontaneous actions by service providers. This leads into a discussion of why customers complain, and how to get them to complain more if things go wrong. Finally, the chapter discusses how to set up and implement service recovery strategies.

Article 3.4 introduces the idea of justice theory, in the form of the complaint-handling argument. The authors argue that a customer's evaluation of a complaint-handling experience will be determined by the outcomes they receive (distributive justice), the procedures used to arrive at the outcomes (procedural justice), and the nature of the interpersonal experience (interactional justice). One can argue that a complaint experience is like any other service experience and will be evaluated in the same way. The authors go on to show that even a bad recovery experience can be mitigated to some extent by prior positive experiences with the firm.

Chapter 13, on customer retention systems, should be read in conjunction with both Articles 3.5 and 3.6. The chapter first shows why loyal customers can be more profitable to service firms. It then goes on to discuss the creation of a safety net, which will help to retain customers even after a failed service recovery. One earlier approach was to price for loyalty, but the chapter shows the pitfalls of such an approach. It suggests instead that the key is the creation of individual franchises and of a defection management system including unconditional guarantees.

Article 3.5 attacks the premise of customer loyalty in general. Its main argument is based on the work of Ehrenberg. It is important to understand that this research, and much of its data, comes from the consumer packaged goods sectors where loyalty is probably lower than in service sectors. The article goes on to suggest criteria for building a successful loyalty program.

Article 3.6, by comparison, provides the results of a critical incident study that shows why people switch between service providers. As well as basic issues such as price, convenience, and moving out of the locale, it shows the importance of three things: core service failure, service encounters, and response to failure (or recovery). The nature of the data brings a relative perspective to the three systems discussed in the chapter: the satisfaction system, the recovery system, and the retention system.

Chapter 14 provides a broader focus and looks at the area of service quality as an all-embracing model for competing. The chapter introduces the "Gap Model," which breaks down any potential customer service quality failure into its component parts. It also introduces the SERVQUAL measurement tool, which is an attempt to create a generic measure for service quality, irrespective of the industry or firm being measured.

Articles 3.7 and 3.8 are both discussions of the potential pitfalls to be encountered using the SERVQUAL scale, along with suggestions for change. Article 3.7 focuses on the measurement problem created by the fact that the scale uses the difference between expectation and perception as the measure. Article 3.8, by comparison, is broader in scope. It too worries about the value of measuring expectations, and suggests instead a simple measure of performance. However, it goes on to investigate the relationship between customer satisfaction, service quality, and purchase intentions. The results conflict somewhat with the conceptualization of quality, since they suggest it is an antecedent of satisfaction and not the other way around.

The final chapter, Chapter 15, discusses the organizational implications of many of the topics in this section. Its emphasis is on the role of marketing in creating the kind of customer focus needed to execute the ideas found in many of the other chapters. It discusses the evolving role of the marketing department within service firms, and alternative ways of creating a customer-oriented organization.

10

Competing as a Service Firm: Generic Competitive Strategies

Chapter Overview

This chapter provides the framework for the whole of this section of the book, which deals with competition. It suggests that when competing in the marketplace, a service firm has a broad range of alternatives available to it. Fundamentally, however, it must first create an economically viable service formula on which to build.

Once the formula exists, depending on the restrictions imposed by the nature of the service, the firm can use any of the following strategies separately or together.

Competing for reach is the major thrust for those firms that succeed by attracting customers to travel to their fixed sites. Hotels and tourist attractions compete by extending their reach into as many markets as possible.

Competing for geography is based on the twin premises that service formulas are often easy to copy and that being second into a market is a disadvantage. Success therefore comes from rapid geographic expansion using multiple sites.

Competing for share can take place in one or many markets at the same time and can involve expansion of both the service offered and the segments targeted.

The major constraint on the use of multiple strategies is the potential loss of focus. Complexity increases as the number of sites, segments, services, and countries increases. Unless carefully managed, this increase can mean that the firm becomes uncompetitive in each area.

The end game for all service firms is competition for share and loyalty. After expansion for reach and geography, the arrival of competition switches the emphasis to share. Given the high cost of acquiring customers from the competition, the most cost-effective way of gaining share is to maintain existing customers. These customers are doubly valuable because the nature of services means that long-term customers are inherently more profitable.

Competing for a Basic Formula

A successful service firm should operate on the KISS principle—*Keep It Simple, Stupid!* It should have a highly focused strategy built on a tightly defined target segment, a clearly defined benefit concept, a highly focused servuction system, and a clear service image (Figure 10.1).[1]

From the arguments developed in the rest of this book, it is clear why such a strategy might be appropriate. The whole concept of segmentation takes on a different meaning within different services. Mixing segments in the same servuction system means that two groups will influence each other's experience and can also be the cause of role stress for service providers. A tightly defined target segment can therefore lead to many service benefits.

The benefit concept is the encapsulation in the consumer's mind of the bundle of benefits received from the service firm. A clearly defined benefit concept allows the correct amount of focus to be directed to the servuction system. The complexity of that servuction system means that the more clearly objectives can be established for its design, the simpler and more elegant that design will be. Simplicity is likely to lead to efficiency.

The complexity of the product purchased by consumers means that a clearly defined image can be difficult to achieve. That image comes not only from advertising and communications, but also from the whole part of the organization that is visible to the consumer.

A clearly defined formula can also simplify the nature of the task for the service providers. If they know what the organization is supposed to be delivering, to whom it is to be delivered, and what image is to be defined, then the possibility of role conflict is reduced. If a firm possesses a "strategic service vision," that vision will guide the behavior of both the service provider and the consumers.[2]

FIGURE 10.1   BASIC FORMULA FOR SUCCESS

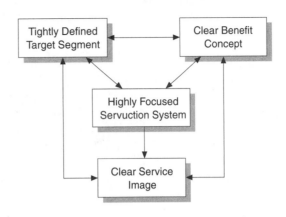

Finding a successful formula is by definition the first level of competition for service firms. One of the characteristics of service firms that is seldom discussed is the lack of patent protection. The formula for a particular brand of detergent or drug can be patented and will provide a competitive advantage for as long as the patent protection lasts. Unfortunately, not only is this not possible for a service formula, but the formula itself is often totally transparent to competition. The United States recently witnessed the office supply wars, with firms such as Office Depot and Staples competing with start-ups all over the country. Once the first site was operating successfully, many people visited it and immediately tried to copy it. Indeed, start-ups and competition are one of the key sources of new formulas for any service organization.

Basic Competitive Choices

Once a successful formula has been created, the firm is faced with an array of alternative competitive strategies, which it can choose to implement individually or in combination. Although the alternatives are generic, there are basic choices that have to be made. These can best be explained by considering the matrix shown in Figure 10.2, which was first formulated by Riddle when discussing international services.[3]

Firms in different cells of the matrix have greater or less degrees of freedom in developing competitive strategies.

The inseparability of customers from the servuction process means that it is relevant to consider the mobility of both the customers and the rest of the servuction system. Cell A, in which both customer and system are static, consists of two basic types of services. The first types are those that have made a strategic choice to remain in one geographic location and to serve one geographic market. They can only *compete for market share* through new client acquisition or loyalty. The second type of firm in this cell is those whose servuction system is based on the telephone and/or the mail system. They are truly place-independent firms, such as the telecommunications networks, the global commodity trading businesses, many nonretail banking firms, and mail-order businesses such as L. L. Bean. These too can only *compete for market share*, but often do so in a global market.

A firm can decide to remain in one geographic location but serve many geographic markets. To do this, they require the customers to be mobile (cell B). Firms in this category include all those based on tourism or travel. Such firms *compete for reach*, and hotel chains will create complete competitive programs to market their services throughout the globe. They can also compete for market share of the local market.

FIGURE 10.2   **COMPETITIVE CHOICE MATRIX**

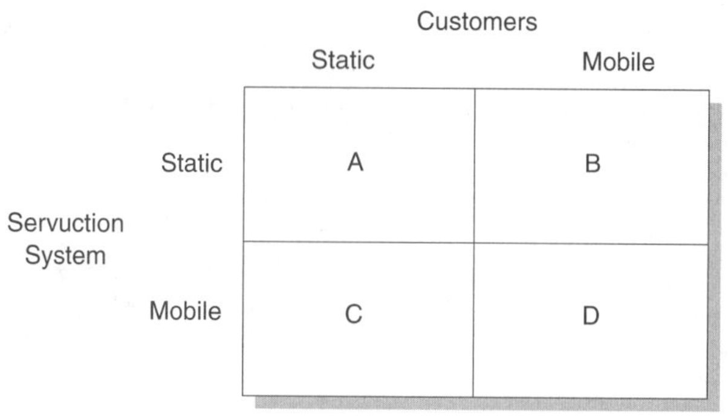

	Customers	
Servuction System	**Static**	**Mobile**
Static	A	B
Mobile	C	D

If customers are to remain in their geographic location but the servuction system is mobile, then they must *compete for geography* (cell C). This is the area of the multi-site firms that spread "factories in the field" across geography and countries. In the absence of patent protection, preemptively occupying geography is one of the few competitive barriers that can be built. To be second supplier into the market can be economically impossible because the volume of customers is potentially low and the cost of taking customers from existing suppliers is high. If competition does arrive or the firm is second into the market, then competition will clearly be either for share or to increase the size of the catchment area (reach).

Cell D combines the characteristics of both cell B and cell C. It is perhaps best typified by a Club Méditerranée in, for example, Kuantan, Malaysia. This club has been built on a beautiful beach in the middle of nowhere. It is surrounded by guards and was built by a French company. It is clearly therefore part of competition-for-geography strategy, but in this case the site has not been built where the customers were. Instead, the customers themselves are mobile, coming predominantly in this case from France, Australia, and Japan. The ability to handle older, affluent French couples, Australian singles from Perth, and Japanese honeymoon couples in the same servuction system is only part of the competitive advantage. The other part is the ability to attract these groups to the operation in the first place.

After competing for reach and geography, the "end-game" for all service firms is the competition for share. As geographic expansion for markets becomes more competitive, service firms must compete for share (see Services in Action 10.1). This is the day-to-day blocking-and-tackling job of the service marketing management team. Within that, there is a growing awareness of the need to *compete for loyalty*. Given the high cost of winning new customers away from competitors, the best way of gaining share is to maintain your existing customer base. At the same time, the nature of services means that customers who are loyal to a firm over time show increasing levels of profitability for the firm.

Competing for Reach

If the service firm is to remain static and the service requires the physical presence of the customer, then the customer must come to the service. This competition focuses on the size of the catchment area. The firm needs to know how large the area is on which it can draw and how far customers will travel to use the service. This is clearly a function of the distinctiveness and uniqueness of the firm. Customers will travel from

The Club Mediterannée of the Ski Slopes

In the 1990s, a lean time for the ski resort industry in general, Intrawest has been bucking the trend. At Blackcomb Mountain, some 90 miles north of Vancouver, British Columbia, more than one million skiers visited the slopes in 1996, three times the number using the site 10 years earlier. As important, during the same period Blackcomb's revenues increased eightfold to $42 million.

Intrawest is now seeking to replicate the Blackcomb formula elsewhere. A rapid expansion program saw Intrawest acquire five more resorts, including Tremblant in Quebec, Snowshoe in West Virginia, and a one-third stake in Mammoth Mountain in California. The aim is to acquire still more resorts and to increase the customer base of the chain from its present 2.8 million to 5 million.

This would make Intrawest the largest ski resort operator in North America. More important, says CEO Joe Houssian, it would help to establish Intrawest as the leading brand name in skiing. Intrawest wants to acquire the same cachet among skiers that the Walt Disney Co. has among theme park visitors or that Club Med has among beach holidaymakers.

Intrawest's North American strategy could give it an edge in luring the most desirable skiers, those who vacation at "destination" resorts such as Blackcomb. At the latter, Japanese- and Chinese-speaking instructors are now being hired to cater for the nearly one-third of visitors each year who come from Asia. These "destination skiers" spend nearly four times as much on goods other than tickets and lodging than do local visitors.

In trying to brand ski resorts, Intrawest faces considerable challenges. The main problem is to enhance uniqueness while at the same time trying to ensure uniform excellence, and this in an industry in which equipment costs for service facilities such as chairlifts are very high. However, through growth the company now has more resources to devote to quality improvement.

What really sets Intrawest apart is its real estate expertise. Intrawest creates not just ski resorts but "total mountain villages" with all services on offer. Here again, the parallels between the all-inclusive holidays of Club Med and the full facilities available at Walt Disney sites can be seen.

all over the world to shop at Harrods in London because it is a unique experience. They will not travel more than a block to McDonald's because that is how far it is to Burger King. Clearly, this strategy requires distinctiveness and an understanding of the multisite strategy.

To create a large catchment area, the firm's marketing department must create a "destination" (see Services in Action 10.2). This does not necessarily mean providing beautiful and/or unique characteristics, such as in the example of Club Mediterannée. Large groups of shoppers now travel hundreds of miles to visit factory outlet malls in out-of-the-way places all over the United States. The barrier to entry protecting firms using this strategy is not location but the cost of marketing to such broad geographic areas. The identical problem is faced by luxury destination hotels. Consider the Royal Scotsman, a luxury hotel built on a train that "cruises" through Scotland. With a six-month season each year and capacity for only 28 passengers per trip, occupancy is the key. The major problem is to find an economical way to reach a tiny segment that is spread worldwide. It is precisely for this reason that the "channel of distribution" represented by travel agencies emerged. Although the physical service can never use channels of distribution, tickets that purchase that service can. It is in the area of target marketing and channels of distribution that marketing adds value in the competition for reach.

Competing for Geography

If the service formula cannot be defended with a patent, the only alternative is to spread out geographically and to do so quickly. This is the essence of the multisite strategy. This strategy involves the replication of the same basic formula in multiple sites. It is perhaps best represented by the fast-food chains and certain large motel

Never Mind the Ugly Americans

Laden with overstuffed shopping bags from Ferragamo, an up-market shoe shop, Yumi Yamada, 27, stands surveying her purchases near Rome's ritzy Via Condotti. A Tokyo-based stewardess, Yamada headed straight to Rome this summer after hearing about how the sinking lira has made Italy a shopper's dream. "Things are cheaper now. My favorite thing about Italy is the shopping," Yamada says.

Currency is just one reason for Europe's tourist boom. Another is new wealth in emerging economies in Asia and eastern Europe. As disposable incomes rise in countries ranging from South Korea and Taiwan to Russia, travelers are heading west. Rich Russians are plunking down cash to buy houses on the Costa del Sol. Tour groups from Indonesia, Korea, Taiwan, and Malaysia hustle to catch a glimpse of Big Ben and Versailles.

Europe needs to attract travelers from Asia and the former Soviet bloc to keep its industry growing. As tourists from the United States, Japan, and other developed countries head for more exotic destinations in Asia and Latin America, Europe's share of the world tourism business is shrinking. Its $150 billion in tourism last year was 47 percent of the world total, down from 53 percent five years ago.

Most of Europe's growth will come from Asia, industry sources believe. More than 80,000 non-Japanese Asians came to Europe last year. Although the numbers do not yet rival the crowds from Japan, which dispatched 1.6 million visitors to Europe in 1994, they are growing in the double digits. With airline departures worldwide from Asia already increasing at a rate of 15 percent per year, "the growth potential is enormous," says Linda Tuttiett, head of the Asia Pacific Department at the British Tourist Authority.

The number of Koreans visiting Europe this year will grow by some 30 percent, to 320,000, according to Korean Airlines. The Chinese will be close behind. China sent 40,000 visitors to Europe last year. Their numbers are expected to rise by 18 percent per year until at least 2000, as the Chinese middle class grows and the government further eases travel restrictions.

To lure more Asians to their countries, European airlines and tourist agencies are stepping up their marketing in the region. The British Tourist Authority now spends the largest chunk of its marketing budget in Asia. The Dorchester Hotel in London's fashionable Mayfair district has boosted its promotional trips to Jakarta, Hong Kong, and Singapore. France's tourist board has recently opened a new office in Taipei.

The goal is to attract more tourists such as South Korean Mi Ji Lee, 32. Soaking up the ambience near Rome's Trevi Fountain, she says, "This is my first trip to Europe. For all the beautiful paintings and sculptures I've seen, it's worth the price." The airlines, hotels, and tour operators hope she will come back for more.

Adapted from *Business Week*, September 4, 1995, 23.

---

chains. A simple formula is established in one or two locations and perfected. It is then replicated in a large number of sites, with everything other than location remaining constant. The complexities involved concern only the selection of locations and the management of the ever-increasing infrastructure.

From a marketing perspective, the decisions that need to be made can be divided into capital decisions and tactical decisions. The creation of the successful formula will have involved much research input from marketing. Once the formula is fixed, however, the critical marketing decision is location—the capital decision. The organization needs to answer the question, "Will it work here?" After the facility is built, all that remains are the tactical marketing problems of optimizing the number of customers and their spending. This tactical marketing for share is very much a street fight in a war among local competitors to acquire new consumers or retain old ones.

Franchising and the Competition for Geography

Franchising involves the sale of the basic formula to an outsider who establishes a new site. Such an arrangement can be viewed from the perspective of either the franchiser or the franchisee.

Why would a company with a successful formula wish to sell franchises? There are many reasons cited for such an approach. Franchising provides outside capital to fund growth that might not otherwise be available, and perhaps more important, it provides management in the form of the franchisee. The Domino's Pizza chain, for example, opened more than 800 outlets in 1987. To have found suitable management to run those sites would have been extremely difficult without franchising.

There are many negatives to franchising, however. Obviously, there is a financial cost because a franchise has to be profitable for the franchisee and that profit is lost to the franchisor. The problem of quality control is also very real. Under a franchising agreement, the franchisee buys the franchise name and the formula. Failure to maintain the franchising firm's standards—operate by the franchise manual—will result in lost image not only for the single site but for the entire chain because of the shared franchise name.

From the franchisee's perspective, it is helpful to view the franchisor as being in a separate service business, that of selling franchises. Using the perspective of this book, the franchisee must then ask, What is the benefit and what is the servuction system? The implied benefit is guaranteed profit. Buying a franchise is supposed to be a less risky way of going into business than setting up on one's own.

The servuction system for the franchising business is complex, however, and the development of the prototype is crucial. A prototype is a demonstration site in which the formula has been perfected and in which the franchisee can see the complete system to be provided. The profit track record of that site and of any existing franchises becomes part of the product offering. So too does the equipment layout, and so does training. Overlaying this is the marketing support that the franchisor provides for the franchisees. Only if all these parts of the servuction system provide an assurance of guaranteed profit will the purchase be made.

If the balance between the value added by the franchisor and the fee paid is not correct, then the firm faces the prospect of franchisee breakout—in which franchisees merely change their name and then set up in competition—or franchisee rebellion. The troubles faced by McDonald's in 1997 are a classic example of this problem.

Known as the "Campaign 55" wars, the problem arose because of increasing levels of competition faced by McDonald's from the likes of Wendy's and Burger King. McDonald's responded by rapidly expanding numbers of store openings in the United States. Sales for McDonald's increased as a result. However, some of the company's owner-operators, who account for 85 percent of North American sales, resented the drop in their profits caused by new outlets opening close to existing ones. McDonald's reduced the pace of store openings, but clearly the damage to the relationship between McDonald's and franchisees had already been done.

Then came Campaign 55, designed to win back customers with 55 cent burger promotions. Unfortunately, many customers were confused by the promotion and did not realize that they had to buy fries and a drink at full price to get the discount. Moreover, the franchisees complained that they lost money if customers bought just a small drink and fries. McDonald's had once again spoiled their benefit concept and reduced the profitability of franchisees. Within a week, McDonald's had to withdraw the promotion.

Internationalization

The internationalization of a service firm often develops from the same profit pressures that drive domestic expansion. It is too easy to view such strategies as purely multisite strategies. The interactive nature of the service experience means that the consumer is an integral part of the process. For internationalization to be viewed as purely a multisite strategy, it is clear that the consumers must be identical in both domestic markets and in foreign countries (see Services in Action 10.3). In certain cases this is feasible, and the fast-food chains have succeeded to a large extent in finding the same "occasion segment" in many countries. However, a McDonald's in the center of Beijing is unlikely to be drawing on the same segment as one in the heart of New York.

SERVICES IN ACTION 10.3

BanPonce Corp

BanPonce is a 102-year-old financial services conglomerate that dominates Puerto Rico's banking sector. With assets of $16 billion and a market cap of nearly $1.3 billion, it is a virtual proxy for the island's economy, writing 40 percent of commercial and personal loans and holding more than 30 percent of all deposits.

But BanPonce's most impressive performance of late has been on the mainland of the United States, where deposits, currently at $2 billion, are 10 times the amount of only six years ago. With Latinos a growing presence in the U.S. economy, BanPonce has simply followed its customers northward. The bank operates 30 branches in New York City and ten more in New Jersey, Illinois, and California.

Operating in working-class barrios, the bank makes customers feel at home with bilingual tellers and hours custom-tailored for individuals who often work late shifts. BanPonce also taps small niches. At East Tremont Avenue, in New York's Bronx, ATM screens are open until 10 P.M., whereas nearby Chemical Bank, its only competition for blocks around, shutters its screens at 3 P.M. At just this one branch, more than 10,000 ATM transactions are recorded each month, 60 percent by noncustomers, who each pay 75 cents per transaction. The expansion strategy is simple: target an emerging Hispanic neighborhood and move in fast, often by acquiring a branch from a troubled bank and retooling it.

Adapted from *Forbes*, February 26, 1996, 97.

Multisite retail chains have had less success. Often, the foreign consumer attracted by the retail formula is different from the one in the domestic market. This raises all the problems of a multisegment approach. Also, management may not realize that it is actually dealing with a different segment. At the most prosaic level, McDonald's has found it difficult to persuade customers in the United Kingdom to clear their own tables after eating. This simple difference in cultural norms can have major operational impacts.

All these problems are compounded by the simple logistics of managing multiple sites some distances apart and by managers who may themselves have different cultural backgrounds.

Competing for Market Share

With a fixed market or catchment area, a service firm still has many strategies it can use. Without modifying the range of service it offers or the segments it tries to attract, it can still look to compete for the loyalty of its existing customers or to acquire new ones from the competition. Conversely, it can expand both the services offered and the segments targeted.

Multiservice Strategy

Service firms can also compete for market share by broadening the range of services that they offer. In this strategy, the service organization capitalizes on its reputation and on its knowledge of its customers to sell other services. A good model for this strategy is the professional service firm. The large accounting firms, for example, have broadened the range of services they offer their clients to include tax advice, management consulting, executive recruitment, and compensation consulting. A firm that follows a pure multiservice strategy restricts itself to a single site and to a single segment of customers.

The basic marketing challenge for such an approach is the development of new services. Such development must be rooted not only in a knowledge of the segment but also in a firm understanding of exactly what the servuction system is capable of delivering (see Chapter 3). Langeard and Eiglier suggest distinguishing between core and peripheral services.[4] The latter are added to the basic formula to increase profitability as, for example, boutiques or a bar in a hotel lobby. Such peripheral services add considerable complexity to an operation. La Quinta Inns, for example, has chosen to avoid this problem and offers a very simple service—a bedroom.[5]

Langeard and Eiglier point out that the complexity can multiply if one of the peripheral services becomes a second core. For example, the restaurant in a hotel can be established as a profit center. At that point, strategy may broaden to multiservice/multisegment as the manager searches for a profitable business beyond the hotel-guest restriction. Worse still, the restaurant may lose its focus, and guests may find that it is packed in the evening and they are unable to get a meal. This can reflect badly on the hotel.

Multisegment Strategy

Service firms can also increase their share of the market by broadening the range of segments that they serve. This strategy often emerges from a fixed-cost/spare-capacity argument. Site costs are generally fixed, so if there is spare capacity during operating hours, why not fill it with a different segment? In the mass transit field, for example, spare daytime capacity outside of commuter hours is often met with a demand to fill the trains and buses with shoppers.

The marketing problem is, of course, to find new consumer segments that want to buy the existing bundle of services. This is almost an antimarketing argument, because in its purest form it implies finding customers to fit the service rather than fitting the service to the customer's needs. The temptation is always to deviate from the pure strategy and drift into a single-site/multiservice/multisegment approach.

Dangers of Loss of Focus

The generic service strategies presented here have been described as the geographic or multisite, the multiservice, and the multisegment strategies. Implicitly, we have assumed that a firm will use only one of these approaches. Each carries with it a set of management challenges and requires a unique set of skills. However, many firms adopt multiple strategies at the same time. Whether driven by a competitive threat or a need for growth, the complexity produced by multiple strategies can lead to a loss of focus and control.

The example of major European retail banks shows the operating and marketing complexity of such multiple strategies. With 3,000 branches selling 285 different services, complexity exists at all levels. The services are difficult for service providers to understand, and indeed many bank tellers are incapable of selling or delivering even a small percentage of them. It is also difficult for consumers to comprehend the range of banking services, because the banks offer everything from check cashing to sophisticated financial advice, from foreign exchange to will preparation. Often, these services are offered to the customer from a single site or branch of the bank.

Each of these banking services can have a different script for the consumer and the service provider to follow. Service providers have a tendency to become bureaucratically oriented simply to cope with the range of scripts they have to deliver. Finally, the banks are making matters worse by broadening their target markets to encompass multiple segments. A single branch will attempt to service regular and high net-worth individuals as well as large and small firms.

Multiservice/Multisegment Firms

These firms operate on a single site but offer multiple core and peripheral services to multiple segments (see Services in Action 10.4). The problems of operating with multiple segments within the same site are compounded if the firm also wishes to provide multiple services and cannot keep the segments separated from one another.

S E R V I C E S   I N   A C T I O N   1 0 . 4

Delta Express, or "Delta Distress"?

The airline industry has its own version of the Edsel, and it is called Continental Lite. After less than two years of operation and more than $100 million in losses, in early 1995 Continental Airlines grounded its shuttle operation as a hopeless exercise that confused customers, cannibalized its full-fare operations, and distressed employees.

That is why, as Delta Airlines prepares its own shuttle, Delta Express, for an October 1 launch, industry wags have already christened the enterprise "Delta Distress." Rivals and industry experts alike say the plan to launch a low-cost shuttle could tarnish the airline's image, even as it fails to deliver on hoped-for savings and profitability targets. "A separate entity with a separate brand name confuses the public and takes management attention away from the main product," says Michael Boyd, president of the consulting firm Aviation Systems Research Corp.

Delta is determined to make its shuttle work. W. E. "Skip" Barnette, managing director of Delta's low-fare initiative, says Delta can run at a low enough cost with enough daily flights to make its shuttle profitable from day one.

On paper, at least, Delta's plan appears to have promise. First, pilots flying the Express agreed in April to a 32 percent pay cut in a deal to return 532 furloughed Delta pilots to work. The planes will fly an average of 12 hours per day, up from Delta's average of 7.4 for 737s. And with first-class sections removed, Delta will be able to board more customers, who will pay only about one-third of what they would pay for a same-day, one-way coach fare on a regular Delta flight.

The airline is turning its operations inside out in a bid to save time and money. To encourage passengers to arrive early, Delta Express agents will assign seats only after passengers appear at the gates. Magazines and blankets will be stowed in the back of the plane so that customers do not dawdle.

Still, along with the savings and efficiencies, Delta has built in serious potential for trouble. For example, to limit the customer confusion that was Continental Lite's biggest problem, the airline is eliminating full-fare flights on all Express routes. But that means it is sacrificing several lucrative routes. Also, Delta Express managers can expect morale problems as the pilots who took the 32 percent pay cut work alongside other employees still drawing full pay.

Adapted from *Business Week*, August 16, 1996, 33.

Perhaps the classic example of a multiservice/multisegment firm is a large luxury hotel. At any one time, the hotel may be serving various segments: the standard-rate hotel guest, the package tour guest, the conference/seminar guest, the large-banquet guest, the restaurant-only guest, and the bar-only guest. All of these different guests can be using the hotel on business or for pleasure. They may have similar demographic profiles, but they are segmented by occasion and by the benefits they are seeking.

Each of the segments is being offered a benefit concept of varying complexity and involving different mixes of the services provided. The ultimate might be the conference guest who is allowed to use all the hotel's services as part of the package deal set up by the conference sponsor.

The marketing problems in such situations are wide-ranging. The price bundling of different services becomes very complex. Appealing to the different segments selectively without detracting from the overall image of the hotel is very difficult.

The problems of quality maintenance are also profound. Each guest can approach the same servuction system but with a different script. The standard-rate guest expects a very different level of service than a conference guest, who can be paying as little as 30 percent of the full rate. Even the perceived restaurant dress code may be different, with standard-rate guests wearing tie and jacket and conference guests arriving in the informal wear customary during conferences.

Multisite/Multisegment Firms

These firms offer a restricted number of services out of any given site but try to attract multiple segments. In one sense, McDonald's operates this way, although the range of menu items that it is now offering might preclude the company from this category. Clearly, such firms are forced to mix different groups of segments closely together.

Because of the focused nature of each site, it is impossible to segregate different segments.

The need for the multiple segments comes from a desire to use excess capacity. The segments must be different; otherwise their demands are likely to coincide and fail to alleviate the capacity problem. Unfortunately, unless great care is taken, the segments do interfere with one another. Consider the steak house chain that wants to attract families in the early evening to soak up spare capacity. To this end, it offers a children's meal. However, unless the project is carefully managed, the children will occupy empty seats that otherwise could have been taken by adults, who offer a greater profit opportunity.

Refocusing the Service Firm

An emerging phenomenon among mature service networks has been the attempt to refocus. If we return to our European bank networks, there is a trend now for fragmentation and specialization. Networks of branches are being broken up, and traditional geographic operating units are being replaced with segmented approaches. Designated "high net-worth individual" branches are appearing all over the world. These branches have a much simplified formula because their target segment has been much simplified. Similarly, small business bank branches are now appearing, and large business accounts are being withdrawn from branches and are becoming "national or multinational" accounts.

On the service side, refocusing is also taking place. Cash shops are being created in branches that can only provide cash either from tellers or machines. Mortgage offices are being created to provide expert advice to customers who are prepared to travel much farther to get a mortgage than to get cash. Banking by telephone is moving banks to cell A and dispensing with the need for multiple branches.

Geographic retrenchment, particularly withdrawing from international operations, has also been forced on the banks by the complexity of maintaining quality standards at thousands of miles distance from the headquarters. The specialization of outlets implies the removal of customers and services from other branches, reversing the original shared-cost logic. This, in turn, is leading to branch closure programs by banks all over the world.

Competing for Loyalty

Cost of New versus Old Customers

Figure 10.3 portrays two companies. Each company is working hard to generate new customers each year and has managed to generate 10 percent more new customers per year, perhaps using new services or targeting new segments. However, not all of the customers acquired by the firm in a given year stay with the firm. The retention rate is not 100 percent; there is a "hole in the bucket." For company A, the "hole" is small, and the company loses only 5 percent of its customers each year. As a result, after 14 years company A has doubled the number of its customers. Company B has a bigger problem, because retention is 90 percent and the "hole in the bucket" is 10 percent. As a result, company B loses and gains customers at the same rate.

The "hole in the bucket" or its converse, the retention rate, is, of course, determined at least in part by customer satisfaction. However, other ways of increasing retention have also been proposed: these include service recovery, client loyalty programs such as frequent-flyer programs, and unconditional guarantees. All these can be lumped together into the "customer loyalty system." This system consists of three parts: the service satisfaction system, the service recovery system, and the customer retention and quality system. These systems can best be understood by focusing on the customer.

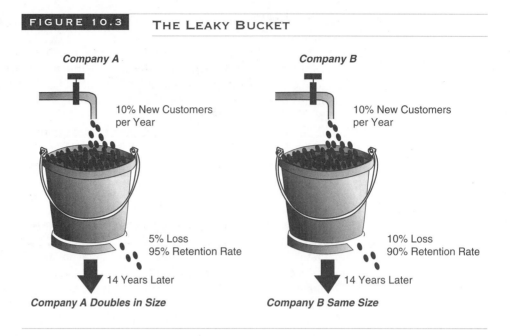

FIGURE 10.3   THE LEAKY BUCKET

Company A
10% New Customers per Year
5% Loss
95% Retention Rate
14 Years Later
Company A Doubles in Size

Company B
10% New Customers per Year
10% Loss
90% Retention Rate
14 Years Later
Company B Same Size

Service Satisfaction System

The service satisfaction system focuses on the creation of a satisfied customer from each and every service experience. Chapter 11 describes such a system, which links together the multiple decisions made in creating the service experience through a tracking system for customer satisfaction. The chapter focuses on the need to "close the loop" but also on the difficulty of measuring customer satisfaction. Chapter 14 extends this idea to look at the broader issue of service quality when the focus is not on an individual service experience but on the cumulative experience of an individual across many service encounters.

If as a result of the service satisfaction system the customer is satisfied, then there is no need for the other parts of the customer loyalty system, as illustrated by Figure 10.4. However, if the satisfaction system has failed to produce a satisfied customer, then the service recovery system must definitely swing into place.

Service Recovery System

Despite the firm's best efforts, service failures are inevitable. If customers are dissatisfied, they can choose to complain. If they do, then the firm has the opportunity to recover the situation. Chapter 12 describes such service recovery systems. A service recovery paradox often exists, wherein customers will often rate performance as higher if a failure occurs and the contact personnel then recover from the failure than if the service had been delivered successfully in the first place. The chapter explains how and why customers complain and how firms should set up their service recovery systems.

Customer Retention and Quality System

A dissatisfied customer does not necessarily defect to another firm. This chapter highlights that the relationship between satisfaction and loyalty is not linear. The firm must do everything in its power to create barriers to defection. The customer retention system focuses on creating these barriers. A flyer with many miles in a frequent-flyer program is less likely to defect to another airline because of an unsatisfactory experience. Chapter 13 focuses on these customer retention systems.

Service quality is an overarching "attitude-like" dimension that is built up from cumulative service experiences. High levels of service quality, as perceived by the con-

FIGURE 10.4   CUSTOMER LOYALTY SYSTEM

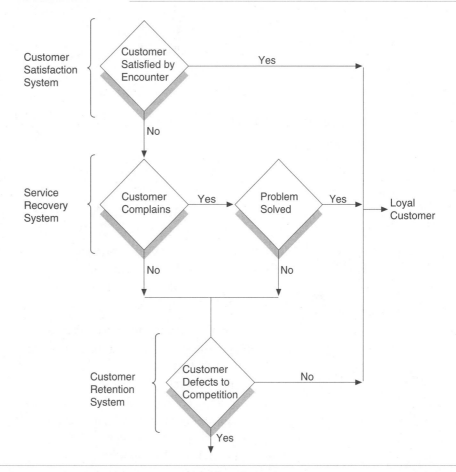

sumer, can encourage consumers to excuse a single unsatisfactory encounter as an aberration and hence remain loyal to the service firm.

Questions

1. Discuss the management problems that might emerge for Delta Express.

2. Give an example, other than those in the chapter, of how combining multiple segments within a service business can cause problems for customers and staff.

3. How would you classify the various competitive strategies used by a chain of department stores? What problems would you expect these stores to have?

Notes

[1]Eric Langeard and Pierre Eiglier, "Strategic Management of Service Development," in Leonard Berry, G. Lynn Shostack, and Greg Upah, eds, *Emerging Perspectives on Services Marketing* (1983), 68–72.

[2]James M. Carman and Eric Langeard, "Growth Strategies for Service Firms," *Strategic Management Journal* 1 (1980): 7–22.

[3]Dorothy L. Riddle, *Service Led Growth* (New York: Praeger Publishing, 1986).

[4]Langeard and Eiglier, "Strategic Management of Service Development."

[5]"La Quinta Inns Faces the Eighties," Harvard Business School Case 9-581-038.

11

Customer Satisfaction System

Chapter Overview

Customer satisfaction is to many companies what motherhood is to many politicians. It is taken for granted that customer satisfaction and motherhood are good. This is almost an act of faith; to question whether a company should increase customer satisfaction is almost heresy.

But at the same time that the chief executive is proclaiming customer satisfaction as the mission of the organization, the finance director is driving through cost-cutting programs and reducing capital expenditure. When the two conflict, often it is customer satisfaction that suffers. The main reason for this is that the economic justification for customer satisfaction is never made explicit in many organizations. When this happens, it is impossible to defend an expensive customer service initiative. At the same time, the measurement of satisfaction is becoming increasingly difficult.

The justification for customer satisfaction comes from three broad sources: the cost of new versus old customers, the competitive demand for satisfaction, and the life-cycle value of customers. After discussing these, this chapter goes on to discuss how to operationalize customer satisfaction and covers the calculation of the return on investment in satisfaction, the measurement of satisfaction, and the use of these measures. Finally, the chapter covers the creation of a satisfaction information system.

Justification for Customer Satisfaction

Cost of New versus Old Customers

Many changes in the marketplace[1] are coming together to make it more and more expensive to acquire new customers, and hence keeping old customers is becoming more attractive. It has been estimated that it now costs three to five times less to keep a customer than to acquire a new one.[2] The first major change within the United States' consumer markets is that they are stagnant. As an example, the U.S. population for the next 50 years is predicted to grow at half the rate of the period spanning from 1965 to 1990. Consequently, there are less new customers to go around. Concurrent with the decrease in population growth, the gross national product also has slowed substantially to an annual growth rate of less than 3 percent. In sum, there are not as many new customers as there used to be, and the customers that are around are spending less.

Another reason customer retention has become important to today's marketers is the increase in competition. Factors contributing to increased competition include:

- The relative parity and lack of differential advantage of goods and services on the market

- Deregulated industries that now must compete for customers in the open market

- Accessible market information that is available to more firms, thereby minimizing informational advantages among competing firms

As a result of the increase in competition, firms are finding that acquiring new customers is becoming increasingly expensive.

A third reason that customer retention is becoming increasingly important can be attributed directly to the rising costs of marketing. In particular, the cost of mass marketing, the primary tool of conquest marketers, has increased substantially. For example, the cost of a 30-second television spot in 1965 was $19,700. By contrast, a 30-second spot in 1991 sold for $105,400.

Coupled with the increased cost of advertising has been the loss of the advertiser's "share of voice." Due to the shorter time period now allotted for individual commercials (the length of commercials has decreased from 60 seconds to 30 seconds to 15 seconds), the sheer number of commercials has increased by approximately 25 percent over the past 10 years. Hence, firms are competing for attention in a medium that is constantly expanding. In addition, new forms of advertising have evolved, and consumer markets have become more fragmented, which further dilutes the chances for the advertiser's message reaching its intended target audience.

Interestingly, the growth of direct mail in the 1980s is attributed directly to the high costs of mass marketing and subsequent heightened importance of customer retention efforts. In the past decade, marketers became more selective regarding how and where their advertising dollars were spent. The databases built for direct marketing were used as a means to identify current customers and to track purchases. Subsequently, advertising to current customers became a much more efficient means than mass marketing to reach the firm's target market.

The typical consumers of the 1990s, compared to their 1960s and 1970s counterparts, are older, are more informed regarding purchasing decisions, command more discretionary income, and are becoming increasingly sceptical about the average firm's concern for the customer's business. Consequently, firms engaged in customer-retention practices are noticed by today's consumers and are rewarded for their efforts via repeat sales.

Chapter 2 highlighted the fact that the purchase of a service carries with it increased consumer risk. One way for the consumer to reduce that risk is to repeat purchase from the same firm. One satisfying experience may be a good predictor of another one. If a bank can give satisfaction with a current account, then it may be a lower risk for the consumer to open a deposit account with the same bank than to start again with a new bank. This is particularly the case when the consumer already knows the script for the bank.

Competitive Demand for Satisfaction

Higher levels of customer satisfaction can be expected to be associated with higher levels of retention. The relationship, however, is not necessarily linear. Figure 11.1, drawn from a study done by Thomas Jones and Earl Sasser,[3] shows the relationship between customer satisfaction and loyalty. Loyalty here is operationalized as a set of surrogate measures such as "intent to repurchase." The data represented by this chart are very powerful, being drawn from satisfaction studies using large samples in each of the represented industries. As the chart shows, the relationship between satisfaction and loyalty is by no means linear.

There are many explanations for the different steps of the curves, but the key one proposed by the authors is the extent of competition in the industry. In noncompetitive marketplaces that exhibit some of the characteristics of a monopoly, a customer who is not satisfied has no choice but to remain loyal. For local telephone service, for example, even if the customer gives the supplier a low score for satisfaction, until very recently there was no alternative supplier to switch to and hence that customer gave a high loyalty score. Conversely, in highly competitive markets small changes in customer satisfaction can be associated with large changes in intended loyalty.

In the figure, hospitals, airlines, and telephone services are in the less competitive areas and automobiles and personal computers in the more competitive areas. However, Jones and Sasser point out that if competition is introduced into apparently monopolistic markets, the relationship very quickly switches back to one with a much higher sensitivity to satisfaction. They cite many reasons for why such a shift might take place.

Deregulation has taken place in many markets that were once monopolies. Telecommunications, airlines, savings and loans, and even electrical power have all been deregulated with the expressed intent of increasing customer choice. Loss of patent protection can dramatically increase the extent of competition, as demonstrated

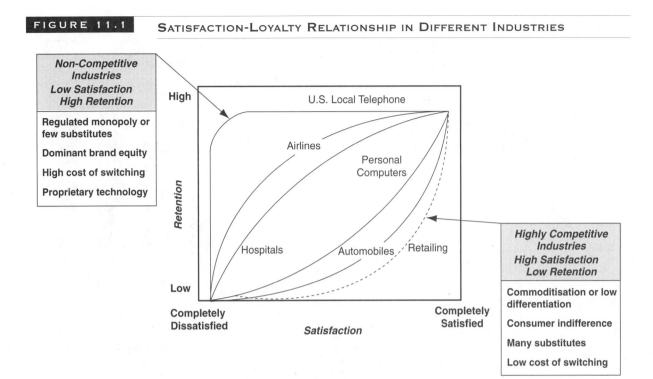

| FIGURE 11.1 | SATISFACTION-LOYALTY RELATIONSHIP IN DIFFERENT INDUSTRIES |

SOURCE: Adapted from T. O. Jones, W. Earl Sasser, Jr., "Why Satisfied Customers Defect," *Harvard Business Review* (November–December 1995).

by the growth in generic products when drug patents expire. New competitors and the decline in the power of brands can all lead to more choice for customers and an increase in the importance of customer satisfaction.

The Life-Cycle Value of Customers

Loyalty is an ill-defined concept in marketing. It can probably best be defined as "intention to repurchase" or some measure of repeat purchase. By focusing on the life cycle of a customer relationship, Reichheld[4] has defined loyalty in terms of those customers who stay with a firm over many years. Based on empirical data, he has looked at the profitability of different groups or classes of customers who have been with a firm for different periods of time. This is a very different way of segmenting a base of customers, and one for which normal accounting systems are ill-equipped to provide the relevant data. Normal financial reporting models do not focus on customers but on transactions. An individual's checking account, deposit account, mortgage, etc., are probably held on different unconnected databases. Moreover, the time-based data for an individual, from when they first become a customer, are probably held on a different database as well.

Figure 11.2 shows just such an analysis for an auto insurance company and an auto service company. The horizontal axis of each chart shows the number of years a particular group of customers had been with the firm, and the vertical axis the profitability of those particular customers. Thus, in the auto service example, customers who are in their first year with the firm are very unprofitable, to the level of $250 per customer. This is due to the high cost of acquiring those customers and the administrative costs of directing computer records and so on. By year 3, however, based on the chart, the firm can expect those customers to be profitable to the extent of $75 each.

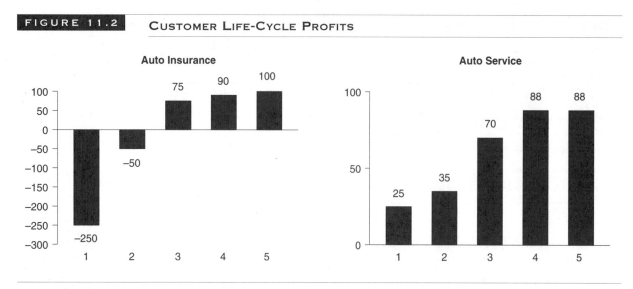

FIGURE 11.2 | CUSTOMER LIFE-CYCLE PROFITS

SOURCE: Frederick F. Reichheld, *The Loyalty Effect* (Boston, MA: Harvard Business School Press, 1996).

For the auto service company, there are lower costs of acquisition in that customers are profitable in their first year. However, as they stay with the firm they become increasingly profitable.

Operationalizing Customer Satisfaction

Given the strong logic for customer satisfaction as a key driver for a service organization, firms would be expected to have adopted customer satisfaction measurement as a key tool. There are two barriers to this: the return or investment calculation and the problems of measuring satisfaction. Unfortunately, like advertising, the returns from increasing investment in satisfaction are obvious in principle but difficult to assess in practice. In organizations driven by hard measurement systems, this can provide sizable problems; when combined with concerns over satisfaction measurement, this can become an insurmountable barrier.

Calculating the Return from an Investment in Customer Satisfaction

Given a reasonable set of assumptions, it is possible to model directly the impact of satisfaction on long-run market share. Pete Babich, the quality arranger for the San Diego division of Hewlett-Packard, was faced with the classic satisfaction question: "If your firm currently boasts a 95 percent customer satisfaction rating, is it worth a $100,000 investment to improve satisfaction to 98 percent?"[5]

Hewlett-Packard defines customer satisfaction as the customer's willingness to refer Hewlett-Packard products to friends. Hewlett-Packard had found that 70 percent of its purchases are made due to previous positive experiences with the product or referrals from others.

Although Babich found an abundance of anecdotal evidence that retaining customers was much cheaper than seeking out new customers, this information failed to answer the original question. Consequently, he proceeded to develop a customer satisfaction model that would predict market share changes over time as they relate to customer satisfaction ratings.

The model is based on an algorithm that can easily be put into a spreadsheet program and is built on a number of assumptions. First, in this particular example, the model assumes a closed market of three firms that begin at period 0 with equal market shares. The three firms offer comparable products and prices and compete for a growing customer base. Next, the model assumes that satisfied consumers will continue to buy from the same firm and dissatisfied customers will defect to other firms in the market. For example, dissatisfied customers of firm A will buy from firm B or firm C during the next time period. The length of the time periods varies depending on the product (e.g., eye exam versus lawn care).

The direction of customer defection is dependent on the firm's market share. In other words, if firm C's market share is higher than firm B's market share, then firm C will obtain a higher share of firm A's dissatisfied customers. This logic is based on the premise that dissatisfied customers are more particular the next time around and will conduct more research and seek out referrals from others. In this case, due to firm C's higher market share, firm C would be the beneficiary of more positive referrals.

Results generated from the customer satisfaction model that depict three different scenarios are presented in Figure 11.3. Figure 11.3A illustrates the scenario of how a firm with a 95 percent customer satisfaction rating would stack up against firms commanding 90 percent and 91 percent customer satisfaction ratings. Clearly, the firm with 95 percent satisfaction dominates the market after 12 time periods. Figure 11.3B illustrates how that same firm with a 95 percent satisfaction rating would compete with firms commanding 98 percent and 99 percent satisfaction ratings. In this scenario, the 95 percent firm controls less than 10 percent of the market in 24 time periods. This scenario dramatically illustrates the impact of the competition's satisfaction ratings.

Finally, Figure 11.3C illustrates the effect of customer satisfaction on market share at lower customer satisfaction levels. In this third scenario, firms A, B, and C command satisfaction ratings of 90 percent, 82 percent, and 80 percent, respectively. In essence, Figure 11.3C illustrates the effect of increasing the dissatisfaction levels of Figure 11.3B by two. In this scenario, firm A once again achieves market dominance but at a much faster rate.

What does Peter Babich's customer satisfaction model tell us? First, firms with higher customer satisfaction ratings make the firm more resistant to competitor's efforts to improve their own market share. Second, if the firm knows what a 1 percent improvement in market share does for the firm's bottom line, then comparing the 1 percent increase in market share to the investment needed to improve customer satisfaction provides the firm the necessary information to make a business decision. Finally, the model points out the necessity of not only knowing your own firm's satisfaction rating, but your competitors' satisfaction ratings as well.

Should a firm invest $100,000 to improve customer satisfaction ratings from 95 percent to 98 percent? It depends on the satisfaction ratings of the firm's competitors, the dollar investment necessary to increase customer satisfaction relative to the impact of increasing the firm's market share, the number of time periods required to recoup the investment, and the opportunity costs associated with other uses of the firm's $100,000.

Measuring Customer Satisfaction

Measures of customer satisfaction are derived via indirect and direct measures. Indirect measures of customer satisfaction include tracking and monitoring sales records, profits, and customer complaints. Firms that solely rely on indirect measures of customer satisfaction are taking a passive approach to determining if customer perceptions are meeting or exceeding their expectations. Moreover, if the average firm does not hear from 96 percent of its unhappy customers, the firm is losing a plethora of customers while waiting for the other 4 percent to speak their minds.

The understatement of the chapter is that direct measures of satisfaction are not standardized among firms. The scales used to collect the data vary (e.g., five-point

FIGURE 11.3   MARKET SHARE MODELS

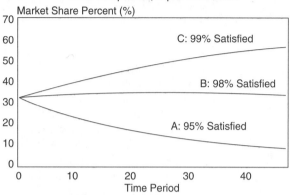

A
Market Share Model
Three Competitors, Equal Initial Share

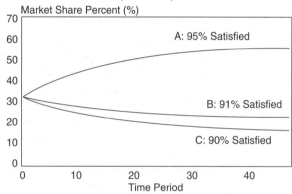

B
Market Share Model
Three Competitors, Equal Initial Share

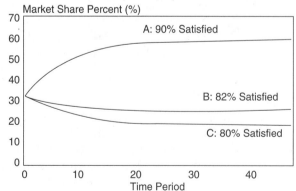

C
Market Share Model
Three Competitors, Equal Initial Share

SOURCE: Peter Babich, "Customer Satisfaction: How Good Is Good Enough?" *Quality Progress* (December 1992), 65–67.

to 100-point scales), questions asked of respondents vary (e.g., general to specific questions), and data collection methods vary (e.g., personal interviews to self-administered questionnaires). The following section primarily focuses on the use of various scales. Issues pertaining to question content and data collection method are discussed later in the chapter.

Scale of 100 Approach   Some firms request customers to rate the firm's performance on a scale of 100. In essence, the firm is asking customers to give the firms a grade. However, the problems with this approach are readily apparent. Let's say that the firm scores an average of 83. What does the 83 mean? The firm got a B-minus? Does an 83 mean the same thing for all customers? Not likely. More important, what should the firm do to improve on its satisfaction rating? The 83 does not provide specific suggestions for improvement within the firm that would lead to an increased customer satisfaction rating.

"Very Dissatisfied/Very Satisfied" Approach   Other firms present customers with a five-point scale, which is typically labeled by using the following format:

1 very dissatisfied

2 somewhat dissatisfied

3 neutral

4 somewhat satisfied

5 very satisfied

Firms using this format generally combine the percentage of "somewhat satisfied" and "very satisfied" responses to arrive at their satisfaction rating. Similarly, firms that use a 10-point scale with anchor points of "very dissatisfied" and "very satisfied" define customer satisfaction as the percentage of customers rating their satisfaction higher than a six. Although this approach provides more meaning to the satisfaction rating itself, it still lacks the diagnostic power to indicate areas of improvement.

Combined Approach   The combined approach uses the quantitative scores obtained by the "very dissatisfied/very satisfied" approach and a qualitative analysis of customer feedback obtained from respondents who indicate that they were less than "very satisfied." Customers indicating that they are less than "very satisfied" are informing the firm that the delivery system is performing at levels less than customer expectations. By prompting customers to make suggestions regarding what the firm could do better, the suggestions can then be categorized and prioritized for continuous improvement efforts.

The combined approach provides two valuable pieces of information. The quantitative satisfaction rating provides a benchmark on which future satisfaction surveys should be compared. In addition, the quantitative rating also provides the means to compare the firm's performance against its competitors. Complementing the quantitative rating, the qualitative data provide diagnostic information to the firm and pinpoint areas for improvement. Combining the qualitative and the quantitative data outperforms either approach when used alone.

Understanding Customer Satisfaction Ratings

After conducting a customer satisfaction survey for a regional engineering firm, the results were revealed to upper management that the firm commanded an 85 percent customer satisfaction rating. Immediately, upper management wanted to know whether 85 percent was a good satisfaction rating. To effectively use customer satisfaction

| FIGURE 11.4 | CONCEPTUAL DISTRIBUTION OF SATISFACTION MEASUREMENTS |

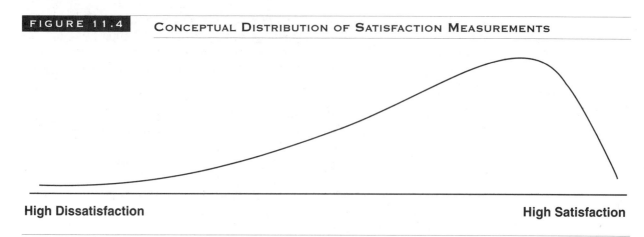

High Dissatisfaction   **High Satisfaction**

SOURCE: Robert A. Peters and William R. Wilson, "Measuring Customer Satisfaction: Fact or Artifact?" *Journal of the Academy of Marketing Science* 20, no. 1 (1992): 61.

ratings, it is necessary to understand the factors that may influence customer responses to satisfaction surveys.

Despite the lack of standardization among satisfaction studies, they share one common characteristic. "Virtually all self-reports of customer satisfaction possess a distribution in which a majority of the responses indicate that customers are satisfied and the distribution itself is negatively skewed."[6] Figure 11.4 depicts the negatively skewed distribution of customer satisfaction results.

Typically, customer satisfaction ratings are fairly high (see Services in Action 11.1). It is not unusual for results to be reported in the 80 percent to 90 percent range. Repeated findings such as these have led some researchers to arrive at the conclusion that "to feel above average is normal."

The truth of the matter is that satisfaction ratings may be influenced by numerous confounding factors that occur during the data collection process. The following section provides a variety of explanations for inflated satisfaction results and reinforces the notion that obtaining accurate measures of customer satisfaction is not a task that is easily accomplished. [7]

Customers Are Genuinely Satisfied   One possible reason for the high satisfaction scores is simply that customers are satisfied with the goods and services they typically purchase and consume; that is why they buy these products in the first place. Intuitively, this makes good sense. If the majority of customers were neutral or dissatisfied, they would most likely defect to the competitor's offering of goods and services. Of course, this explanation assumes that competitors that exist within the market are better at providing goods and services than the original supplier.

Response Bias   Another possible explanation for inflated satisfaction results may be due to response bias. Some experts argue that the reason ratings are so high is that companies only hear from satisfied customers. In contrast, dissatisfied customers do not believe that the firm's survey will do the customer any good; therefore, the questionnaire is thrown away or the customer hangs up on the interviewer.

Other experts discount this explanation. Their argument is that it makes more sense for highly dissatisfied customers to express their opinion than it does for highly satisfied customers. This position is supported based on prior research that indicates that dissatisfaction itself is more action-oriented and emotionally intense than satisfaction.[8] Others argue that it is possible that highly dissatisfied customers and highly satisfied customers are more likely to respond than those who are more neutral.

SERVICES IN ACTION 11.1

Measuring Customer Satisfaction in the United States

Tracking customer satisfaction in the United States is a highly complex task that has recently been undertaken through the joint efforts of the American Society for Quality Control and the University of Michigan's business school. Working together, they have developed the American Customer Satisfaction Index (ACSI), which is based on 3,900 products representing more than two dozen manufacturing and service industries. Companies included in the study are selected based on size and U.S. market share, and together represent about 40 percent of the U.S. gross domestic product. Government services are also included in the index.

The ACSI consists of 17 questions rated on a scale from 1 to 10, concerning issues such as consumer perceptions of service, quality, value, the performance of the product compared with expectations, how the product compares with an ideal product, and how willing consumers would be to pay more for the product.

Consumer responses are gathered by telephone surveys to approximately 30,000 people. The products of each company included in the survey are assessed approximately 250 times.

Results from the latest ACSI survey indicate that, as a whole, customer satisfaction in the United States is headed slightly downward, with the exception of manufactured goods. On a scale of 0 to 100, the national satisfaction average is 73.7, down 1.1 percent from the previous year's national average. Dole Food's canned pineapple topped the satisfaction list with a score of 90, whereas the Internal Revenue Service came last, with 54.

Other notable trends included good news, such as increases in customer satisfaction with domestically produced automobiles, and bad news, such as a large decrease in consumer satisfaction with computers, which fell by 3.8 percent last year. An overview of the results of the ACSI is presented in the table below.

Although these additional explanations are intriguing, they fail to explain the traditional response distribution depicted in Figure 11.4.

Data Collection Method A third possible explanation for inflated satisfaction scores is the data collection method used to obtain results. Prior research suggests that higher levels of satisfaction are obtained via personal interviews and telephone surveys as compared with mail questionnaires and/or self-administered interviews. In fact, studies indicate that as much as a 10 percent difference exists between questionnaires administered orally compared with self-administered questionnaires. The reasoning is that respondents of personal interviews and telephone surveys may feel awkward expressing negative statements to other individuals as opposed to expressing these opinions anonymously on a self-administered questionnaire.

Research regarding the data collection modes' effect on satisfaction ratings has produced some interesting results. The data collection mode does indeed appear to influence the level of reported satisfaction; however, the negatively skewed distribution of the satisfaction ratings remains unchanged regardless of the data collection mode.

Question Form The form of the question on the questionnaire has also been posited as a possible explanation for inflated satisfaction ratings. It does appear that whether the question is formed in positive form—"how satisfied are you?"—as opposed to a negative form—"how dissatisfied are you?"—does have an impact on satisfaction ratings. Stating a question in the positive form appears to lead to greater reported levels of satisfaction than posing the question in a negative form.

Table 11.1 presents results from a study that investigated the effects of stating the same question in two different forms. In one version, the question asked respondents "how satisfied" they were, and the other version asked "how dissatisfied" they were. Results reveal that 91 percent of respondents report feeling "very" or "somewhat satisfied" when the question was stated in its positive form compared with 82 percent when stated in the negative form. Similarly, 9 percent of respondents expressed that they were somewhat or very dissatisfied in the positive form compared with nearly 18 percent in the negative form.

TABLE 11.1	RESPONSES BY QUESTION FORM	
Response Category	**"Satisfied"**	**"Dissatisfied"**
Very satisfied	57.4%	53.4%
Somewhat satisfied	33.6%	28.7%
Somewhat dissatisfied	5.0%	8.5%
Very dissatisfied	4.0%	9.4%

SOURCE: Robert A. Peterson and William J. Wilson, "Measuring Customer Satisfaction: Fact or Artifact?" *Journal of the Academy of Marketing Science* (1992), 65.

Context of the Question   The context of the question may also affect the satisfaction rating. Question-context effects pertain to the ordering of questions and whether questions asked earlier in a questionnaire influence answers to subsequent questions. For example, in a study concerning satisfaction with vehicles, asking a general satisfaction question (e.g., in general, how satisfied are you with the products in your house?) prior to a specific vehicle satisfaction question (e.g., how satisfied are you with your Saturn?) increased the tendency toward a "very satisfied" response. Consequently, the order of the questions appears to have some influence on respondent responses.

Timing of the Question   Satisfaction ratings may also be influenced by the timing of the question relative to the date of purchase. Customer satisfaction appears to be highest immediately after a purchase and then begins to decrease over time. Again, with regard to automobile purchases, researchers have noted a 20 percent decline in satisfaction ratings over a 60-day time period. It's not clear whether the initial ratings are inflated to compensate for feelings of cognitive dissonance or that the latter ratings are deflated. There has been some consideration given that there may be different types of satisfaction measured at different points in time.

Another possible explanation is that satisfaction rates may decay over time as customers reflect on their purchase decision. Prior research indicates that the influence of negative events, which are more memorable than positive events, carries more weight in satisfaction evaluations over time. Consequently, satisfaction surveys distributed during the latter time periods provide the respondent with the opportunity to take retribution as they recall these negative events.

Social Desirability Bias   Social desirability bias describes the respondent's tendency to provide information that the respondent believes is socially appropriate. With regards to satisfaction surveys, some researchers argue that a tendency exists for respondents to withhold critical judgment on satisfaction surveys because to do otherwise would be socially inappropriate. This explanation would explain high satisfaction ratings and the shape of the distribution of results. Although this explanation is intriguing, widespread empirical support is lacking.

Mood   One more factor that could possibly influence customer satisfaction ratings is the mood of the customer while the customer is completing the survey. An abundance of research exists that demonstrates the influence of positive mood states toward prosocial behaviors.[9] More specifically, prior research has shown that respondents in positive mood states make more positive judgments, rate products they own more favorably, tend to see the brighter side of things, and are more likely to rate strangers favorably. Hence, consumers occupying positive mood states should give higher marks to service personnel and service firms than their neutral or negative mood counterparts.

Measuring Service Quality: The Federal Express Approach

We believe that service quality must be mathematically measured.
—Frederick W. Smith, Chairman and CEO, Federal Express

When Federal Express first opened its doors on April 17, 1973, it shipped eight packages, of which seven were trial runs addressed from one Federal Express employee to another. No one had any idea that this event marked the birth of an entire industry: overnight delivery. Particularly inspiring to college students is the fact that Fred Smith, the CEO of Federal Express, had sketched out the early details of the operation in an undergraduate paper at Yale University (the paper was given a C grade!). By 1990, the company was generating $7 billion in annual sales and controlled 43 percent of the air express market.

Federal Express has two ambitious goals: 100 percent customer satisfaction with every interaction and transaction, and 100 percent performance on every package handled. In its early days, Federal Express defined customer satisfaction and service performance as the percentage of packages delivered on time. After cataloging complaints for many years, it had become apparent that percentage of on-time delivery was an internal measure of customer satisfaction and did not necessarily reflect absolute customer satisfaction by customer standards.

The customer's definition of customer satisfaction, which influenced eight service failures to be avoided, became known as the "Hierarchy of Horrors" and included (1) wrong day delivery, (2) right day, late delivery, (3) pick-up not made, (4) lost package, (5) customer misinformed by Federal Express, (6) billing and paperwork mistakes, (7) employee performance failures, and (8) damaged packages. Based on these categories generated by customer complaints, it was readily apparent that on-time delivery was not the only measure important to Federal Express customers.

In addition to categorizing customer complaints, Federal Express measures customer satisfaction by tracking 12 service quality indicators every day, both individually and in total. Moreover, the firm conducts numerous customer satisfaction studies each year within five major categories: (1) customer satisfaction studies conducted quarterly in four market segments, namely, base business that is phoned to Federal Express, U.S. export customers, manned-center customers, and drop-box customers; (2) 10 targeted customer satisfaction studies conducted semiannually, which contact customers who have had an experience with one of 10 specific Federal Express processes such as customer service, billing, and invoice adjustments; (3) Federal Express Center comment cards, which are collected and tabulated twice a year and provided as feedback to the managers of each of the centers; (4) customer automation studies of Federal Express's 7,600 largest customers, representing 30 percent of the company's total package volume, who are equipped with automated systems that permit package tracking, and a variety of other self-service activities; and (5) the Canadian customer study, conducted yearly, which is the single most frequent point of destination for Federal Express packages shipped outside the United States.

How successful is Federal Express? In monetary terms, the success of Federal Express has been history making. Federal Express was the first company in U.S. history to top $1 billion within its first 10 years of existence. Customer satisfaction ratings at Federal Express are also legendary. The highest quarterly rating of customer satisfaction achieved thus far has been a 94 percent "completely satisfied" rating from customers, on a five-point scale ranging from "completely satisfied" to "completely dissatisfied." Most firms combine "somewhat satisfied" and "completely satisfied" responses when calculating customer satisfaction ratings. This is not the case at Federal Express. Due to achievements such as these, Federal Express has been a recipient of the Malcolm Baldrige National Quality Award.

SOURCE: "Blueprints for Service Quality: The Federal Express Approach," AMA Management Briefing, New York: American Management Association, 1991. Reproduced by permission of the publisher. Copyright 1991 American Management Association. All rights reserved.

Are Customer Satisfaction Surveys Worth It?   Customer satisfaction ratings may reflect the Hawthorne effect; that is, in and of themselves, customer satisfaction surveys increase customer satisfaction regardless of the good or service being evaluated. Due to the high levels of customer satisfaction, it may not make sense to attempt to increase satisfaction levels across the board. Two areas of satisfaction that do deserve special attention are (1) company attempts to maintain satisfaction over time due to the decay effect and (2) concentrating on the tail of the satisfaction distribution—those customers that are dissatisfied. In and of themselves, satisfaction ratings cannot be interpreted with much meaning. Consequently, benchmarking with past performance and comparisons with competition provides some norm or standard.

Building a Satisfaction Information System

A satisfaction information system can be defined as an ongoing research process that provides relevant data on a timely basis to managers who use the data for decision-making purposes.[10] (See Services in Action 11.2.) More specifically, a service satisfaction information system would use customer satisfaction measures in conjunction with other measures obtained at various points in time to assess the firm's overall performance. Components of a service satisfaction information system should include (1) solicitation of customer complaints, (2) after-sales surveys, (3) customer focus group interviews, (4) mystery shopping, (5) employees surveys, and (6) total market service satisfaction surveys.

In general, service satisfaction information systems focus on two types of research: customer research and noncustomer research. Customer research examines the customer's perspective of a firm's strengths and weaknesses and includes such measures as customer complaints, after-sales surveys, focus group interviews, and service quality surveys. In contrast, noncustomer research focuses on employee perspectives of the firm's strength and weaknesses and employee performance (e.g., employee surveys and mystery shopping). In addition, noncustomer research examines how competitors perform on service via total market service quality surveys and serves as a basis for comparison.

Solicitation of Customer Complaints   The primary objective of soliciting customer complaints is twofold. First, customer complaints identify unhappy customers. The firm's follow-up efforts may enable the firm to retain many of these customers before they defect to competitors. The second objective of soliciting customer complaints is to identify weaknesses in the firm's service delivery system and to take the corrective actions necessary to minimize future occurrences of the same problem. Hence, customer complaints should be solicited on a continuous basis.

The value of continuous customer feedback cannot be understated. Unfortunately, many firms address one complaint at a time and fail to analyze the content of the complaints as a group. It took the Chicago Marriott 15 years to figure out that 66 percent of its calls to customer service concerned requests for an iron or ironing board. As a result, the hotel redesignated $20,000 that was earmarked for color televisions for guest bathrooms to purchase irons and ironing boards for the hotel. Interestingly, few, if any, customers had ever complained about the black-and-white televisions in the bathrooms. If the color televisions had been installed, this would have been a classic example of the firm defining service quality as opposed to listening to the voice of the customer. Chapter 12 takes an in-depth look at analyzing customer complaints and developing effective recovery strategies for use when service failures do occur.

After-Sales Surveys   As part of the service information system, after-sales surveys should also be conducted on a continuous basis (see Services in Action 11.3). Because after-sale surveys pertain to discrete transactions, after-sale surveys are a type of satisfaction survey and as such are subject to the advantages and disadvantages of all customer satisfaction surveys discussed earlier in the chapter. For example, after-sales surveys address customer satisfaction while the service encounter is still fresh in the customer's mind. Consequently, the information reflects the firm's recent performance but may be biased by the customer's inadvertent attempt to minimize cognitive dissonance.

Although after-sales surveys can also identify areas for improvement, after-sales surveys are a more proactive approach to assessing customer satisfaction than solicit-

SERVICES IN ACTION 11.3

Marriott International, Inc.
Corporate Headquarters

Marriott Drive
Washington, D.C. 20058
800-621-0999

J. Willard Marriott, Jr.
Chairman of the Board
and Chief Executive Officer

Dear Marriott Guest,

I would like to take this opportunity to thank you personally for selecting one of our hotels for your business and personal accommodations.

All of us at Marriott Hotels, Resorts and Suites are dedicated to providing you with the finest service possible. I am asking you, therefore, to evaluate our hospitality – telling us what we do right as well as identifying areas where we must improve. We will share your comments on the attached survey with the General Manager, who will follow-up on your suggestions and recommendations. I, too, will review some of the surveys, as well as the overall results from the responses we receive.

If you have received surveys in the past and provided comments, I want to thank you and encourage you to respond once again so we can be updated on your most recent Marriott experience.

We appreciate your time to assist us. I assure you that your comments will receive our attention. We genuinely want to provide you with the quality service you deserve and have come to expect from Marriott.

Again, thank you for your time.

Best personal regards,

J. W. Marriott, Jr.

Enclosures

ing customer complaints. Many firms wait for customers to complain and then take action based on those complaints. Given the average customer's reluctance to complain, waiting for customer complaints does not provide the firm with a "true" picture of the firm's performance. The after-sale survey attempts to contact every customer and to take corrective action if the customers are less than satisfied with their purchase decision.

Customer Focus Group Interviews Another important component of the service quality information system involves customer focus group interviews.[11] Focus group interviews are informal discussions with eight to twelve customers that are usually

Guest Satisfaction Survey

Marriott.
HOTELS · RESORTS · SUITES

09/830.17 BREADSALL PRIORY MARRIOTT HOTEL

Name: _____

Address: _____

_____

Country: _____

Arrival Date: _____ Departure Date: _____

Please be sure to fill the response circle completely.

Correct Mark
●

Incorrect Marks
⊘ ⊗

Please take a moment and answer the following questions. If a question is not applicable to your stay, please skip to the next question.

How would you rate this hotel on:

1. Quality of Accommodation . . .

	EXCELLENT									POOR
Cleanliness of your guest room upon entering	⑩	⑨	⑧	⑦	⑥	⑤	④	③	②	①
Condition of furniture in guest room	⑩	⑨	⑧	⑦	⑥	⑤	④	③	②	①
Good guest room lighting	⑩	⑨	⑧	⑦	⑥	⑤	④	③	②	①
Guest room work area that meets my needs	⑩	⑨	⑧	⑦	⑥	⑤	④	③	②	①
Peaceful, quiet guest room	⑩	⑨	⑧	⑦	⑥	⑤	④	③	②	①
Spacious feel of guest room	⑩	⑨	⑧	⑦	⑥	⑤	④	③	②	①
Cleanliness of bath and tiled areas	⑩	⑨	⑧	⑦	⑥	⑤	④	③	②	①
Overall cleanliness of guest room	⑩	⑨	⑧	⑦	⑥	⑤	④	③	②	①
Cleanliness and servicing of your room during stay	⑩	⑨	⑧	⑦	⑥	⑤	④	③	②	①
Overall guest room quality	⑩	⑨	⑧	⑦	⑥	⑤	④	③	②	①
Condition of the grounds	⑩	⑨	⑧	⑦	⑥	⑤	④	③	②	①
Condition of the lobby/reception area	⑩	⑨	⑧	⑦	⑥	⑤	④	③	②	①
Lobby/reception decor	⑩	⑨	⑧	⑦	⑥	⑤	④	③	②	①
Condition of the corridors	⑩	⑨	⑧	⑦	⑥	⑤	④	③	②	①
Overall maintenance and upkeep	⑩	⑨	⑧	⑦	⑥	⑤	④	③	②	①

Was everything in your room in working order? .... ○ Yes ○ No

What was your room number? _____

Please share any comments you may have about the quality of our rooms, lobby and outside areas.

_____
_____
_____
_____
_____
_____
_____
_____
_____
_____
_____

2. Quality of Hotel Staff and Services . . .

When you arrived at the hotel, was the information the hotel had concerning your reservation correct? Yes No

How were you reservations made?

Hotel reservation department   Free-phone number
Travel agent   Group reservation card

Other *(please specify)* _____

	EXCELLENT									POOR
Ease of reservations process	⑩	⑨	⑧	⑦	⑥	⑤	④	③	②	①
Check-in speed	⑩	⑨	⑧	⑦	⑥	⑤	④	③	②	①
Staff efficiency	⑩	⑨	⑧	⑦	⑥	⑤	④	③	②	①
Staff attitude	⑩	⑨	⑧	⑦	⑥	⑤	④	③	②	①
Attentiveness of front desk clerk	⑩	⑨	⑧	⑦	⑥	⑤	④	③	②	①
Attentiveness of bell staff	⑩	⑨	⑧	⑦	⑥	⑤	④	③	②	①
Check-out speed	⑩	⑨	⑧	⑦	⑥	⑤	④	③	②	①
Availability and frequency of airport transportation*	⑩	⑨	⑧	⑦	⑥	⑤	④	③	②	①
Overall quality of Service and Staff	⑩	⑨	⑧	⑦	⑥	⑤	④	③	②	①
Providing adequate information about the activities/facilities in and around the hotel	⑩	⑨	⑧	⑦	⑥	⑤	④	③	②	①

Was your bill correct? .... ○ Yes ○ No

Please share any comments about the quality of our hotel staff or their service.

_____
_____
_____
_____
_____
_____
_____
_____

*(*Not available at all hotels)*   **Please continue to next page ▶**

3. Value . . .

	EXCELLENT									POOR
Reasonableness of charges for hotel services (e.g., minibar, parking)	⑩	⑨	⑧	⑦	⑥	⑤	④	③	②	①
Value of room	⑩	⑨	⑧	⑦	⑥	⑤	④	③	②	①
Value of breakfast	⑩	⑨	⑧	⑦	⑥	⑤	④	③	②	①
Value of dinner	⑩	⑨	⑧	⑦	⑥	⑤	④	③	②	①
Price	⑩	⑨	⑧	⑦	⑥	⑤	④	③	②	①
Overall value	⑩	⑨	⑧	⑦	⑥	⑤	④	③	②	①

4. Food and Beverage . . .

	EXCELLENT									POOR
Overall breakfast experience	⑩	⑨	⑧	⑦	⑥	⑤	④	③	②	①
Overall lunch experience	⑩	⑨	⑧	⑦	⑥	⑤	④	③	②	①
Overall dinner experience	⑩	⑨	⑧	⑦	⑥	⑤	④	③	②	①
Room service overall	⑩	⑨	⑧	⑦	⑥	⑤	④	③	②	①
Overall eating/dining experience	⑩	⑨	⑧	⑦	⑥	⑤	④	③	②	①

Restaurant name _____

Please share any additional comments, positive or negative, you may have regarding your recent stay with us.

_____
_____
_____
_____
_____
_____
_____

In General

5. How would you rate THIS hotel on an overall basis compared to other hotels, including other Mariott Hotels with which you may be familiar?

   EXCELLENT   **POOR**
   ⑩ ⑨ ⑧ ⑦ ⑥ ⑤ ④ ③ ② ①

6. During your hotel stay, did you experience any problems?

   ○ Yes   ○ No *(If No, skip to #7.)*

   Did you report your problem(s) during your stay?

   ○ Yes   ○ No

   If YES, were all problems resolved during your stay to your satisfaction?

   ○ Yes   ○ No

   Which of the following statements best describes your feelings about the action taken by the hotel to resolve your problems?

   ○ More than satisfied
   ○ Completely satisfied
   ○ Not completely satisfied, but the action taken was acceptable
   ○ Left feeling dissatisfied
   ○ Left feeling very dissatisfied

   If YES, was your problem resolved with a single phone call or contact?

   ○ Yes   ○ No

7. What was the primary purpose of your visit?

   ○ Business
   ○ Pleasure
   ○ Both business and pleasure combined
   ○ Conference/group meeting/banquet

8. IF IN THIS AREA AGAIN, how likely would you be to stay in this Marriott again?

   ○ Definitely would *(skip to #9)*
   ○ Probably would *(skip to #9)*
   ○ Might or might not *(skip to #9)*
   ○ Probably would not
   ○ Definitely would not

   If "Probably" or "Definitely" would not return, please mark the main reason for not returning.

   ○ Other hotels more convenient
   ○ Quality of guest rooms
   ○ Quality of service
   ○ Quality of restaurants
   ○ Price
   ○ Other *(please specify)*
   _____

9. Based only on your personal preference, if all of the following major hotels were located in the area where you were planning your next stay. which ONE hotel would be your first choice?

For Business:	For Pleasure:
○ Copthorne	○ Copthorne
○ Hilton	○ Hilton
○ Holiday Inn	○ Holiday Inn
○ Marriott	○ Marriott
○ Posthouse	○ Posthouse
○ Stakis	○ Stakis
○ Other (specify)	○ Other (specify)
_____	_____

10. Are you a member of Marriott's Honored Guest Awards programme or the Marriott Miles programme?

    ○ Yes   ○ No

Thank you for taking the time to assist us.

guided by a trained moderator. Participants in the group are encouraged to express their views and to comment on the suggestions made by others in the group. Due to the group interaction, customers tend to feel more comfortable, which motivates them to talk more openly and honestly. Consequently, researchers feel that the information obtained via focus group interviews is richer than data that reflect the opinions of an individual.

Focus groups are probably the most widely used market research method. However, their primary purpose is to identify areas of information to be collected in subsequent survey research. Although the information provided by the group is considered very valuable, other forms of research are generally necessary to confirm that the groups' ideas reflect the feelings of the broader group of customers. Advocates of service information systems believe that customer focus groups should be conducted on a monthly basis.

Mystery Shopping   Mystery shopping is a form of noncustomer research that measures individual employee service behavior. As the name indicates, mystery shoppers are generally trained personnel who pose as customers and who shop at the firm unannounced. The idea is to evaluate the individual employee during an actual service encounter. As such, mystery shoppers evaluate employees on a number of characteristics such as the time it takes for the employee to acknowledge the customer, eye contact, appearance, and numerous other specific customer service and sales techniques that are promoted by the firm.

Mystery shopping is a form of observation research and is recommended to be conducted on a quarterly basis. Results obtained from mystery shoppers are used as constructive employee feedback concerning the employee's strengths and weaknesses demonstrated during the encounter. Consequently, mystery shopping aids the firm in coaching, training, and evaluating and in the formal recognition of its employees.

Employee Surveys   Another vital component of the service quality information system is employee research. When the product is a performance, it is essential that the company listens to the performers. Too often employees are forgotten in the quest for customer satisfaction. However, the reality is that employee satisfaction with the firm directly corresponds with customer satisfaction (see Chapter 4). Hence, the lesson to be learned by service firms is that if the firm wants the needs of the customers to come first, it cannot place the needs of its employees last.

Conducted quarterly, employee surveys provide an internal measure of service quality concerning employee morale, attitudes, and perceived obstacles to the provision of quality services. Often, employees would like to provide a higher level of quality service but feel that their hands are tied by internal regulations and policies. Employee surveys provide the means to uncover these obstacles so that they can be removed when appropriate. Moreover, employees are customers of internal service and assess internal service quality. Due to their direct involvement in the provision of service delivery, employee complaints serve as an early warning system; that is, employees often see the system breaking down before customers do.

Total Market Service Surveys   The total market service quality surveys not only measure the service satisfaction of the firm sponsoring the survey but also assess the perceived service quality of the firm's competitors. When service quality and satisfaction measures are used in conjunction with other measures, the firm can evaluate its own performance as compared with previous time periods and relative to its competitors. Service surveys also provide the firm with information pertaining to needed improvements within the service delivery system plus a measure of progress concerning how improvements previously identified are being corrected over time.

As is the case with all the components of the service quality information system, the recommended frequencies are dependent on the size of the customer base. Too-frequent contact with the same customers can be an annoyance to the customer. The main point to remember is that conducting surveys every five to ten years to save costs may cost the business its existence.

Overall, the service information system provides a comprehensive look at the firm's performance and overcomes many of the shortcomings of the individual measures when used in isolation. As with all measures, their true value lies in the information they provide to managers for decision-making purposes. Hence, the measures should serve as a support system for decisions and should not be used as the only inputs into the decision process. Managerial expertise and intuition remain critical components of every business decision.

Questions

1. Collect a customer feedback card from a local service business. Discuss the relevance of the information requested and how useful you think it would be when fed back to managers.

2. Review the course evaluation forms used in your institution. Do they meet the criteria for a good customer satisfaction measurement system?

Notes

[1] Terry G. Vaura, *Aftermarketing: How to Keep the Customer for Life through Relationship Marketing* (Homewood, IL: Business One Irwin, 1992), 2–6.

[2] Barry Farber and Joyce Wycoff, "Customer Service: Evaluation and Revaluation," *Sales and Marketing Management* (May 1991): 44–51.

[3] Thomas O. Jones and W. Earl Sasser, Jr., "Why Satisfied Customers Defect," *Harvard Business Review* (November–December 1995): 88–99.

[4] Frederick F. Reichheld, *The Loyalty Effect* (Cambridge, MA: Harvard Business School Press, 1996).

[5] Adapted from Pete Babich, "Customer Satisfaction: How Good Is Good Enough?" *Quality Progress* (December 1992): 65–67.

[6] Robert A. Peters and William R. Wilson, "Measuring Customer Satisfaction," *Journal of the Academy of Marketing Science* 20, no. 1 (1992): 61.

[7] Adapted from ibid.

[8] Marshal and Richins, "Negative Word-of-Mouth by Dissatisfied Customers: A Pilot Study," *Journal of Marketing* 47 (Winter 1983): 68–78.

[9] Adapted from Babich, "Customer Satisfaction."

[10] Based on a service quality framework originally proposed by Leonard L. Berry, A. Parasuraman, and Valerie Zeithaml, "Improving Service," 34.

[11] Adapted from Henry Assael, *Marketing Principles and Strategy*, 2nd ed (Fort Worth, TX: The Dryden Press, 1993), 226; and Michael Levy and Barton Weitz, *Retailing Management* (Homewood, IL: Irwin, 1992), 149.

12

Service Recovery

Chapter Overview

The following are some basic facts about service failures:

- For every complaint a corporate headquarters receives, there are 19 other dissatisfied customers who did not take the time to complain.[1]

- It costs five to ten times more in resources to replace a customer than it does to retain one.[2]

- A customer must have 12 positive experiences to overcome one negative one.[3]

- An average customer who has a complaint tells nine or ten individuals about it; however, customers whose complaints are resolved satisfactorily tell only five other persons.[4]

- Most companies spend 95 percent of service time redressing problems and only 5 percent trying to figure out what went wrong to make the customers angry in the first place.[5]

- For those companies that do try to do something about their customers' anger, more than half of all efforts to respond to customer complaints actually reinforce negative reactions, making the customer even more dissatisfied.[6]

These facts capture the essence of the service recovery problem. Customers who complain provide the firm with the opportunity to recover from the service failure. Unfortunately, not all customers complain. If they do complain and service recovery is successful, a service recovery paradox often exists in which the customer will rate performance higher if the failure occurs and the contact personnel recover from the failure than if the service had been delivered successfully in the first place.

Unfortunately, service recovery is not always successful and the consequences are many and disastrous. Customers require many positive experiences to overcome one failure and will often tell many individuals about the complaint. Service firms expend huge amounts of energy dealing with the complaints, often with negative results for the consumer and without learning from the failures themselves.

Although some companies are great at delivering service until something goes wrong, other companies thrive on recovering from service failures and impressing customers in the process. The purpose of this chapter is first to discuss the nature of services failures and customers' responses to them, in particular the reasons why customers complain and the reasons why they do not. It then goes on to explain how the firm can create a service strategy to encourage complaints and respond once a complaint has been received and how to manage such service recovery efforts.

Service Failures

Despite the firm's best efforts, service failures are inevitable. Planes are late, employees are rude or inattentive, and the maintenance of the tangibles surrounding the service is not always perfect. The very nature of services means that failures are bound to occur. Customers perceive a "service failure" when a service is not delivered as originally planned or expected.

A key building block of a recovery strategy is to understand the potential sources of failure in the mind of the consumer. Consider Table 12.1, adapted from an article by Bitner, Booms, and Tetreault.[7] This is the result of an analysis of 352 dissatisfactory incidents collected from customers in the airline, restaurant, and hotel industries. Each incident was described by a respondent and then classified by independent judges

TABLE 12.1	DISSATISFACTORY INCIDENTS					
		Total	Percent of Total	Airline	Restaurant	Hotel
Employee Responses to Service Delivery Failures						
Response to unavailable service		29	8.2			
Response to unreasonable service		53	15.1			
Response to other core service failures		69	19.6			
Subtotal		151	42.6	45.5	39.8	47.6
Employee Responses to Customer Needs and Requests						
Response to "special needs" customers		6	1.7			
Response to customer preferences		37	10.5			
Response to admitted customer error		8	2.3			
Response to potentially disruptive others		4	1.1			
Subtotal		55	15.6	37.3	9.9	17.9
Unprompted and Unsolicited Employee Actions						
Attention paid to customer		48	13.6			
Truly out-of-the-ordinary employee behavior		41	11.6			
Employee behaviors in the context of cultural norms		42	11.9			
Gestalt evaluation		15	4.3			
Performance under adverse circumstances		—	—			
Subtotal		146	41.5	27.3	50.3	34.5

according to its source. Less than half the failures came from *failures in the delivery system*. In general, service delivery system failures consist of employee responses to three types of failure: (1) unavailable service, (2) unreasonably slow service, and (3) other core service failures. Unavailable service refers to services normally available that are lacking or absent. Unreasonably slow service concerns services or employees that customers perceive as being extraordinarily slow in fulfilling their function. Other core service failures encompass all other aspects of core service failure; this category is deliberately broad to reflect the various core services offered by different industries (e.g., food service, cleanliness of the aircraft, and baggage handling). Operations management and design and quality system approaches can try to reduce these failures but perhaps at the expense of the empowerment of the contact personnel, which may be necessary to successfully undertake service recovery.

The second type of service failure, *responses to customer needs and requests*, pertains to employee responses to individual customer needs and special requests. Customer needs can be explicit or implicit. Implicit needs are not requested; if an airline customer becomes ill and faints, his or her needs will be readily apparent. The airline can fail to meet an implicit need when a flight schedule is changed and the airline fails to notify its customers so that alternative connecting flights can be arranged.

By contrast, explicit requests are overtly requested. In general, explicit requests are of four types: (1) special needs, (2) customer preferences, (3) customer errors, and (4) disruptive others. Employee responses to special needs involve complying with requests based on a customer's special medical, dietary, psychological, language, or sociologic difficulties. Preparing a meal for a vegetarian would count as a special request. Employee responses to customer preferences require the employee to modify the service delivery system in some way that meets the preferred needs of the customer. A customer request for the substitution of a menu item at a restaurant is a typical example of a customer preference. An employee response to a customer error involves a scenario in which the failure is initiated by a customer mistake (e.g., lost tickets or a lost hotel key). Finally, employee responses to disruptive others require employees to settle disputes between customers, such as requesting patrons to be quiet in movie theaters or requesting that smoking customers not smoke in the nonsmoking sections of restaurants.

The third type of service failure, *unprompted and unsolicited employee actions*, pertains to events and employee behaviors—both good and bad—that are totally unexpected by the customer. These actions are not initiated by the customer, nor are they part of the service delivery system. Subcategories of this group include (1) level of attention, (2) unusual actions, (3) cultural norms, (4) gestalt, and (5) adverse conditions. Negative levels of attention to customers pertain to employees who have poor attitudes, employees who ignore a customer, and employees who exhibit behaviors consistent with an indifferent attitude.

The unusual behavior subcategory can also reflect positive as well as negative events. For example, a Domino's employee happened to see a family's members searching through the burnt-out remains of their house while making a delivery to another customer in the area. The employee reported the event to his manager, and the two immediately prepared and delivered pizzas for the family free of charge. The family was stunned by the action and never forgot the kindness extended toward them in their time of need. Unfortunately, an unusual action can also be a negative event. Employee actions such as rudeness, abusiveness, and inappropriate touching would qualify as negative actions.

The cultural norms subcategory refers to actions that either positively reinforce cultural norms, such as equality, fairness, and honesty, or violate the cultural norms of society. Violations would include discriminatory behavior, acts of dishonesty such as lying, stealing, and cheating, and other activities considered unfair by customers.

The gestalt subcategory refers to customer evaluations that are made holistically; that is, the customer does not describe the service encounter as discrete events but uses overall terms such as *pleasant* or *terrible*.

Finally, the adverse conditions subcategory covers employee actions under stressful conditions. If an employee takes effective control of a situation when all others around him or her are "losing their heads," customers are impressed by the employee's performance under those adverse conditions. By contrast, if the captain and crew of a sinking ship board the lifeboats before the passengers, this would obviously be remembered as a negative action under adverse conditions.

Customer complaining behavior, however, is not just a result of service failures. Customers consciously choose whether to complain or not when a failure occurs and will often complain even when a failure has not taken place. The firm must understand complaining behavior if it is to successfully create and implement a recovery strategy.

Customer Complaining Behavior

As a striking example regarding the impact of service failures, results from a past study that asked consumers "Have you ever gotten so upset at a store (or manufacturer) that you said 'I'll never go into that store or buy that brand again,' and you haven't?" had to limit respondents to three incidents to keep the interview time reasonable. The oldest incident happened more than 25 years ago, and 86 percent of the incidents were more than five years old.

The consequences of service failures can be dramatic. The vast majority of respondents (87 percent) indicated that they were still somewhat or very emotionally upset and were more upset about the treatment they received from employees than at the store or product performance. More than three-quarters of respondents indicated that they had engaged in negative word-of-mouth communications regarding the incident (46 percent claimed they told "lots of people"). Finally, true to form in what is typical consumer complaint behavior today is that only 53 percent voiced their complaint to the store even though 100 percent defected to other firms.[8]

Generically, customers respond to a service failure in a number of ways:

Attribution. The customer will ask: Who caused the problem? A negative attribution might involve blaming the employee for the failure rather than attributing blame to a factor beyond the firm's control.

Evaluation. Assuming that the problem is attributed to the firm, then the failure will cause a lower satisfaction with the service employee and/or the firm.

Behavior. Consumers have behavioral options both within the encounter and beyond it. Within the encounter, they can complain. After the encounter, they can complain, engage in negative word-of-mouth communication, and, of course, switch service providers.[9]

The same kinds of factors will determine the responses in each category. Clearly, attribution is likely to occur first. This can be caused by something as simple as the physical setting. One study showed that an untidy rather than a tidy office caused respondents to switch the attribution for a mistake involving an air ticket to the travel agent.[10] Factors such as the image of the firm, the complexity of the service, and the service recovery communication are also bound to have an impact.

Evaluation is also likely to be influenced by the image of the firm. However, it is most likely to be influenced by the service recovery and how this is communicated. Attribution and evaluation will clearly drive behavior, particularly complaining behavior.

Value of Complaining Customers

Most companies cringe at the thought of customers who complain, whereas other companies look at complaints as a necessary evil in conducting business. The truth of the matter is that every company should encourage its customers to complain. Complainers are telling the firm that it has some operational or managerial problems that need to be corrected. Hence, complainers are offering a free gift to the company; that is, they act as consultants and diagnose the firm's problems—at no fee.

Moreover, complainers are providing the firm with the chance to reestablish the customer's satisfaction. Complainers are more likely to do business with the firm again than noncomplainers. Consequently, successful firms view complaints as an opportunity to satisfy unhappy customers and prevent defections and unfavorable word-of-mouth communications.[11]

It is not the complainers that the company should worry about; it is the noncomplainers. Customers who do not express their complaints are gone or ready to leave to the competition at any moment. In fact, 63 percent of dissatisfied customers who do not complain and who have purchased goods or services costing $1.00 to $5.00 will defect to a competitor. Even more disturbing is that as purchases exceed $100.00, the defection rate approaches 91 percent.[12]

Types of Complaints   Based on past research in consumer psychology, complaints can be **instrumental** or **noninstrumental**. **Instrumental** complaints are expressed for the purpose of altering an undesirable state of affairs. For example, complaining to a waiter about an undercooked steak is an instrumental complaint. In this case, the complainer fully expects the waiter to correct the situation. Interestingly, research has indicated that instrumental complaints only make up a very small amount of complaints that are voiced everyday.

By contrast, **noninstrumental** complaints are voiced without any expectation that the undesirable state will be altered and are voiced much more often than instrumental complaints. For example, complaints concerning the weather or one's personal physical states such as "It's too hot!" or "I'm so ugly!" are voiced without any real expectation that conditions will change. Another case of an noninstrumental complaint is an instrumental complaint voiced to a secondary party and not to the offending source. For example, complaining to your friends about your roommate being a "slob" is a noninstrumental complaint.

Why Do Customers Complain?   In the case of the instrumental complaint, the answer to why customers complain is pretty clear. The complainer wants the undesirable state to be corrected. However, the answer is not so clear with respect to noninstrumental complaints. Experts believe that there are several reasons noninstrumental complaints occur. First, complaining serves the function of a pressure valve and allows the complainer an emotional release from frustration. Hence, the complaint provides the person with the mechanism to "blow off some steam" and "get it off their chest."

Complaining also serves as a mechanism for the complainer to regain some measure of control. (See Chapter 2 for a discussion of the importance of control.) Control is reestablished if the complainer is able to influence others' evaluation of the source of the complaint. For example, negative word-of-mouth that is spread by the complainer for the purpose of taking revenge on an offending business provides the complainer with some measure of control through indirect retribution.

A third reason that individuals complain to others is to solicit sympathy and to test for consensus of the complaint, thereby validating the complainer's subjective evaluation of events that led to the complaint. In other words, the complainer wants to know if others would feel the same way under similar circumstances. If so, the complainer then feels justified in voicing the complaint.

Finally, a fourth reason complainers may complain is to create an impression. Strange as it may seem, complainers are often considered more intelligent and discerning than noncomplainers.[13] By complaining, it may be implied that the complainer's standards and expectations are higher than those of noncomplainers.

Why Do Customers Not Complain?   "A greater percentage of services' problems than goods' problems are not voiced because potential complainers do not know what to do or think that it would not do any good."[14] This situation can be directly contributed to the intangibility and inseparability characteristics inherent in the provision of services. Due to intangibility, evaluation of the service delivery process is primarily subjective. Consequently, consumers often lack the security of making an objective observation and may doubt their own evaluation.

Due to inseparability, the customer often provides inputs into the process. Hence, given an undesirable outcome, the customer may shift much of the blame on themselves[15] for failing to convey to the service provider a satisfactory description of the level and type of service desired. In addition, the inseparability dimension describes the often face-to-face interaction between the customer and the service provider. The customer may feel uncomfortable about complaining due to the physical presence of the provider.

Finally, many services are technical and specialized. Customers may not feel adequately qualified to voice a complaint for fear that they lack the expertise to evaluate the quality of the service. For example, do you really know if your auto mechanic did everything he billed you for?

Complaining Outcomes   In general, complaining behavior results in three outcomes: **voice, exit,** and **retaliation.**[16] **Voice** refers to the outcome in which the consumer verbally communicates his or her dissatisfaction with the store or the product.

High voice means that the communication is expressed to the manager or someone higher up in the management structure. **Medium voice** occurs when the consumer communicates the problem to the sales clerk. **Low voice** occurs when the consumer does not communicate the problem to anyone associated with the store or product.

Exit means that the consumer stops patronizing the store or using the product. **High exit** occurs when the consumer makes a conscious decision never to purchase from the firm or buy the product again. **Medium exit** reflects the consumer's conscious decision to try not to use the store or product again if at all possible. **Low exit** means that the consumer does not change his or her purchasing behavior and continues to shop as usual.

The third type of complaint behavior is **retaliation.** Retaliation refers to the situation in which the consumer takes action deliberately designed to damage the store or hurt future business. **High retaliation** involves physically damaging the store or going out of the consumer's way to communicate to others negative aspects concerning the business. **Medium retaliation** is caused by the consumer creating minor inconveniences for the store and only telling a few persons about the incident. **Low retaliation** reflects no retaliation against the store at all.

Interestingly, the three complaining behavior outcomes are not mutually exclusive and can be considered as three dimensions that may occur simultaneously. Consumers experiencing high levels of all three outcomes simultaneously can lead to explosive behavior. For example, "in one high-high-high example, the customer shouted his dissatisfaction at the clerk and the store manager, vowed never to buy at the store again, went out of the store, got in his car, and drove it in the front doors of the store through the checkout counter and between two lines of shelving, destroying everything in its path."[17] By contrast, a consumer that is high voice, low exit, and low retaliation would typify the perpetual complainer who continues to shop at the store.

Service Recovery Strategy

If failures are endemic and complaining behavior limited, it is obvious that three broad building blocks are needed for a recovery strategy:

1. The firm must encourage complaining behavior.

2. The firm must develop the capability to listen and to learn from complaints.

3. The firm must develop recovery strategies throughout the organization and create a culture in which these strategies are used.

Actively Encouraging Complaints

Experts refer to actively encouraging complaints as a way to break the silence. Remember that complainers that actually voice their complaint to the source of the problem are the exception; most customers do not speak up. This does not mean that customers do not complain. The problem is that they complain to friends and family. The average unhappy customer voices his or her displeasure with the firm to nine or ten other persons.[18] Strategies to encourage complaints include customer surveys, focus groups, and actively monitoring the service delivery process to ensure customer satisfaction.

Listening to Complaints

Figure 12.1 shows an information processing model of complaint handling.

Although effective handling of customer complaints is obviously in the consumer interest, consumer complaints can also offer benefit far beyond the individual complainant. Fornell and Westbrook[19] define *complaint management* as the dissemination

FIGURE 12.1 **INFORMATION FLOWS WITHIN CONSUMER COMPLAINTS**

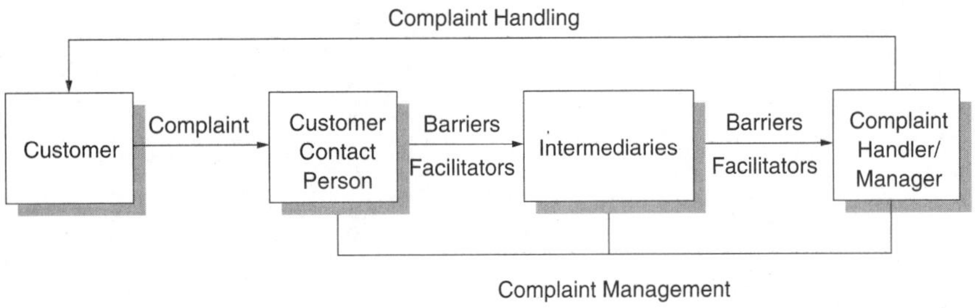

of information for the purpose of finding and correcting the causes of consumer dissatisfaction. An organization thus potentially has to respond to a complaint on two levels. The individual incident must be resolved to create a satisfied customer. Beyond that, the information about the complaint must reach a level within the organization at which steps can be taken to redefine processes, systems, etc., to eradicate the root cause of the problem.

In the next step of the process, customer contact personnel forward the complaint if they think that they cannot solve the problem. In manufacturing firms, this step can take place over a period of time. In services, however, if the incident is to be resolved at all, then this stage has to take place in real time.

Finally, if the system can create spontaneous complaint resolution, then the next step in the process is for the "complaint manager" to change policies and procedures to avoid future failures. Within service firms, even the complaint manager may, in fact, be multiple managers in different sites, with no system existing to consolidate learning.

In one study based in a hospital, the following results were identified:

- Complaints made to managers are more likely to be passed on; hence the organization is more likely to learn from them.

- Formally designated complaint handlers are more likely to pass on complaints to someone who can resolve them.

- Having a personal tie to someone who can resolve the complaint makes it more likely that the complaint will be passed on.

- Managers are more likely to recommend action on complaints than are other service providers, especially if the managers are designated as complaint handlers.

- Complaints concerning the quality of service are rated as more important by employees than are complaints about the attitudes of personnel.

The study highlighted the fact that traditional barriers to communication, such as functional and hierarchical boundaries, are powerful inhibitors of complaint flows.[20]

Implementing Service Recovery Strategies

Customers expect firms to fail to deliver service on occasion, but they also expect them to be able to recover from those failures. This relationship is shown in Figure 12.2. The approach suggested here is that consumers expect higher levels of service recovery from organizations with higher levels of service quality and from organizations to which they have a higher level of commitment. The latter represents a mutual sharing

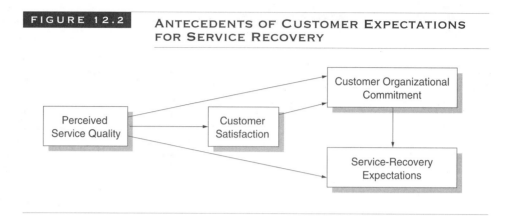

FIGURE 12.2 ANTECEDENTS OF CUSTOMER EXPECTATIONS FOR SERVICE RECOVERY

of roles and expectations between the firm and the individual. In turn, commitment is influenced by customer satisfaction and perceived quality.

A firm wishing to have a high perceived service quality must therefore create recovery strategies. Consumers have high expectations of such strategies and will be doubly dissatisfied if there is a service failure and no recovery strategy in place.

Experts in the area of service recovery recommend that to establish service recovery skills, firms need to consider the following.[21]

Measure the Costs

As discussed in the chapter on customer retention, the costs and benefits associated with keeping existing customers as opposed to chasing new customers are substantial. In short, the costs of obtaining new customers are five to ten times greater than keeping existing customers; current customers are more receptive to the firm's marketing efforts and are therefore an important source of profit for the firm; and existing customers ask less questions, are familiar with the firm's procedures and employees, and are willing to pay more for services.

Anticipate Needs for Recovery

As mentioned previously, every service encounter is made up of a series of critical incidents that reflect the points in the system at which the customer and the firm interact. Firms that are effective in service recovery anticipate in advance the areas within the service delivery process at which failures are most likely to occur. Of course, these firms take every step possible to minimize the occurrence of the failure in the first place, but they are prepared for recovery if delivery goes awry. Experts believe that firms should pay special attention to areas in which employee turnover is high. Many of these positions are low paying customer contact positions, and employees often lack motivation and/or are inexperienced in effective recovery techniques.

Respond Quickly

When a service failure does occur, the faster the company responds, the more likely the recovery effort will result in a successful outcome. In fact, past studies have indicated that if the complaint is handled promptly, the company will retain 95 percent of its unhappy customers. In contrast, if the complaint is not resolved at all, the firm retains just 64 percent of its customers.[22] Time is of the essence. The faster the firm responds to the problem, the better the message the firm sends to customers.

A firm that learned this lesson the hard way is a bank in Spokane, Washington. A customer who had millions of dollars in the bank's checking, investment, and trust

---

TABLE 12.2 **RESTAURANT FAILURE ANALYSIS**

The failures were broken into the three broad categories identified in other studies:

Employee responses to service delivery system failures

Employee responses to customer needs and requests

Unprompted and unsolicited employee actions

The first group, employee responses to system delivery failures, accounted for 44.4 percent of the critical incidents. Core service failures included the following subclass categories:

Product defects: food was described as cold, soggy, raw, burnt, spoiled, or containing inanimate objects such as hair, glass, bandages, bag ties, and cardboard

Slow/unavailable service: waiting for an excessive amount of time and/or not being able to find assistance

Facility problems: cleanliness issues such as bad smells, dirty utensils, and animate objects (e.g., insects) found on the table or in the food

Unclear policies: restaurant policies that were perceived as unfair by the customer, such as coupon redemption or forms of payment

Out-of-stock conditions: an inadequate supply of menu items

The second group, employee responses to customer needs and requests, accounted for 18.4 percent of incidents reported. Customer requests included the following categories:

Food not cooked to order: the customer had asked for the food to be cooked in a specific manner (e.g., medium rare, no mustard) and this request had not been met

Seating problems: involved seating nonsmokers in smoking sections and vice versa, lost or disregarded reservations, denial of requests for special tables, and seating among unruly or disruptive customers

The third group, unprompted and unsolicited employee actions, accounted for 37.2 percent of the total. These actions included the following:

Inappropriate employee behavior: including rudeness, inappropriate verbal exchanges, and poor attitudes

Wrong orders: the delivery of an incorrect food item, either to the table or, in the case of fast food, in packaging so that the mistake was not discovered until the customer had left the premises

Lost orders: situations in which the customer's order was misplaced and never fulfilled

Mischarging: including being charged for items that were never sent, being charged incorrect prices for items that were ordered, and providing incorrect change

---

accounts was denied getting his parking validated because he only cashed a check as opposed to making a deposit. The customer was at a branch bank that was not his normal bank. After explaining the situation to the teller who was unimpressed and more loudly voicing his opinion to the branch manager, the customer drove to his usual bank and demanded a response from the bank's upper management by the end of the day or he would close his accounts. As incredible as it may seem, the call never came, and the customer withdrew $1 million first thing in the morning. This action did get the bank's attention, and the bank has been trying to recover ever since.[23]

Define Recovery Strategies

Not all recovery strategies are equally attractive to customers. One study, written in the context of a restaurant,[24] has explored these issues directly. The study used the critical incident technique and asked respondents to report a failure they had experienced that resulted in a satisfactory recovery and also a failure that resulted in an unsatisfactory recovery. Their descriptions were analyzed to create categories to explain both service

TABLE 12.3	RECOVERY STRATEGIES: PERCEIVED EFFECTIVENESS AND RETENTION RATES	
Recovery Strategy	**Effectiveness**	**Retention Rate (%)**
Free food	8.05	89.0
Discount	7.75	87.5
Coupon	7.00	80.0
Managerial intervention	7.00	88.8
Replacement	6.35	80.2
Correction	5.14	80.0
Apology	3.72	71.4
Nothing	1.71	51.3

SOURCE: K. Douglas Hoffman and John E. G. Bateson, *Essentials of Services Marketing* (Fort Worth, TX: Dryden, 1997), 345.

failures and unsuccessful and successful recoveries. Table 12.2 summarizes the retail failure analysis.

Perhaps of more interest is the rating of the recovery strategies used by stores. Respondents were asked to rate the approach on a scale of 1 (very poor) to 10 (very good). They were also asked whether they still shopped at the store involved in the incident. A retention rate was computed as a percentage of respondents who said yes. The results are shown in Table 12.3.

The customer retention rates revealed in this study suggest that it is possible to recover from failures, regardless of type. Overall, customer retention for the incidents considered was above 75 percent. Even customers experiencing less than acceptable recoveries were still retained at a rate approaching 60 percent. However, in general, the statistical relationship between failure rating and recovery rating does indicate that as the magnitude of the seriousness of the failure increases, so does the difficulty of executing a recovery.

Other studies document the fact that both the service failure complaint-handling procedure and the nature of the compensation affect customer attitudes toward the firm. One study found that consumers who were offered a marginal discount and an apology as compensation perceived greater satisfaction and also considered the firm to be more "fair" than those that were only offered an apology.[25]

The amount of restitution (as a percentage of the initial charge) and prior usage experience have also been shown to have positive impact on customer satisfaction, retention, and intention to return to the same service outlet.[26] Furthermore, providing an opportunity for customers to express their feelings and then listening courteously to customer complaints increased customers' perceptions of fairness and satisfaction.[27]

In general, customers seem to assess the service recovery strategy based on perceived justice. Perceived justice suggests that the recovery process itself, the outcomes connected to the recovery strategy and the interpersonal behaviors enacted during the recovery process, and the delivery of outcomes are all critical in recovery evaluation. Accordingly, perceived justice consists of three components: procedural justice, distributive justice, and interactional justice.

Distributive justice focuses on the specific outcome of the firm's recovery effort. In other words, what specifically did the offending firm offer the customer to recover from the service failure, and did this outcome (output) offset the costs (inputs) of the service failure? Typical distributive outcomes mentioned in the literature include compensation, offers to mend or totally replace/reperform, and apologies.

The second component of perceived justice, *procedural justice*, examines the process that is undertaken to arrive at the final outcome. Hence, even though a customer may be satisfied with the type of recovery strategy offered, recovery evaluation may be poor due to the process endured to obtain the recovery outcome. For example, when implementing identical recovery strategies, those that are implemented "promptly" are much more likely to be associated with higher consumer effectiveness ratings and retention rates than their "delayed" counterparts. Procedural justice has been operationalized as the delay in processing the complaint; and as decision control, accessibility, timing/speed, process control, and flexibility to adapt to the customer's recovery needs.

Interactional justice, the third component of perceived justice, refers to the manner in which the service recovery process is implemented and how recovery outcomes are presented. Examples of interactional justice include the courtesy and politeness exhibited by personnel, empathy, effort observed in resolving the situation, and the firm's willingness to provide an explanation why the failure situation occurred. Based on the components of perceived justice, authors have suggested both good and poor responses to failure.

Good responses to failure attributed by consumers to the firm:

Acknowledge the problem: customers need to know that their complaints are being heard.

Make the customers feel unique or special: convey to them that their opinions are valued and their business is important to the firm.

Apologize when appropriate, when the failure is clearly the fault of the firm: a sincere apology is often one effective form of recovery, although Table 12.3 would suggest that it is not the best.

1. Explain what happened: providing the customer with extra information about events that led to the failure conveys that the firm thinks the customer is of value and that his or her understanding of events is important

Offer to compensate: compensation is often the most desired response by customers, but firms tend to forget the hidden costs associated with the service failure, such as time and frustration

Poor responses to failure attributed by consumers to the firm:

Fail to recognize the seriousness of the problem.

Fail to adequately accommodate the customer.

1. Act as though nothing is wrong.

2. Fail to explain why the problem occurred.

3. Leave the customer to solve the problem on his or her own.

4. Promise to do something and then fail to follow through.

Experts also suggest several good and poor responses to service failures that occur through customer error. Assisting customers in recovering from their own errors is especially memorable from the customer's perspective and is likely to translate into repeat business.

Good responses to failure due to customer error:

Acknowledge the customer's problem: listening and being attentive to customer needs conveys the message that the firm is seriously concerned about the customer's well-being, regardless of who committed the error.

Take responsibility: anticipate the errors customers are likely to make, such as losing room keys or leaving behind personal items, and make provision to accommodate these events when they do occur. Avoiding responsibility means leaving customers to fend for themselves.

Assist in solving the problem without embarrassing the customer: when solving the problem, avoid making flippant statements that refer to the customer's lack of intelligence and/or unique ability to create the current situation. The chances are that the customer is already embarrassed when asking for assistance. Do not further aggravate the situation by laughing or speaking loudly about the predicament in the presence of other customers or employees.

Poor responses to failures due to the customer:

Laugh and embarrass the customer.

Avoid any responsibility.

1. Be unwilling to assist the customer in solving the problem

Train Employees

Expecting employees to be naturals at service recovery is unrealistic. Most employees do not know what to do when a failure occurs, and many others find that making decisions on the spot is a difficult task. Employee training in service recovery should take place on two levels. First, the firm must work at creating an awareness of customer concerns within the employee. Placing the employee in the shoes of the customer is often enlightening for employees who have forgotten what it's like to be a customer of their own firm. For example, hospitals have placed interns and staff in hospital gowns and have had them rolled around on gurneys to experience some of the hospital's processes first hand.

The second level of employee training, beyond developing an appreciation for customer needs, is defining management's expectation toward recovery efforts. What is acceptable behavior from management's perspective? Inquiring employees really want to know. Effective recovery often means that management has to let go and allow employees to take risks. This transition often leads to empowering front-line employees.

Empower the Front Line

Ironically, effective recovery often means that the employee has to bend the firm's rules and regulations—the exact type of activity that employees are trained not to do at any cost. Often, the rules and regulations of the firm tie the hands of the employee when it comes to effective recovery efforts—particularly in the area of prompt response. In many instances, firms require managerial approval before any effort to compensate the customer is undertaken. However, the manager is often engaged in other duties, which delays the response and adds to the frustration for the customer and the employee.

Questions

1. Describe a situation in which you recently complained about a service experience and a similar service falure in which you did not complain. Why did you not complain?

2. Describe a service failure about which you complained. Using the "Complaining Outcome" framework on pages 315 and 316, describe why you complained.

3. Using the framework in Figure 12.2, describe two service firms for which you had very different service recovery expectations.

Notes

[1] Technical Assistance Research Project (TARP), *Customer Complaint Handling in America: An Update Study*, part 2.

[2] TARP, unpublished, industry-specific research data gathered from 1990 to 1993.

[3] Ibid.

[4] TARP, *Measuring the Grapevine, Consumer Response and Word of Mouth* (Atlanta, GA: Coca-Cola USA, 1981).

[5] John Goodman, "The Nature of Customer Satisfaction," *Quality Progress* (February 1989): 37–40.

[6] Christopher W.L. Hart, James L. Heskett, and W. Earl Sasser, Jr, "The Profitable Act of Service Recovery," *Harvard Business Review* (July–August 1990): 148–156.

[7] Mary Jo Bitner, Bernard H. Booms, and Mary Stansfield Tetreault, "The Service Encounter: Diagnosing Failure and Unfavourable Incidents," *Journal of Marketing* 54 (January 1990): 71–84.

[8] N. K. Hunt, N. D. Hunt, and T. C. Hunt, "Consumer Grudgeholding," *Journal of Consumer Satisfaction, Dissatisfaction and Complaining Behavior* 1 (1988): 116–118.

[9] Based on an unpublished paper by Neeli Berdapili and V. Parker Lessing, "Customer Responses to Service Failures."

[10] Mary Jo Bitner, "Evaluating Service Encounters: The Effects of Physical Surroundings and Employee Responses," *Journal of Marketing* 54 (April 1990): 42–50.

[11] See Article 11.3

[12] Oren Novari, "Thank Heaven for Complainers," *Management Review* (January 1992): 60, 21–28.

[13] T.N. Amabile, "Brilliant but Cruel: Perceptions of Negative Evaluators," *Journal of Experimental Social Psychology* 19 (1983): 146–156.

[14] See Article 11.3.

[15] Bitner, "Evaluating Service Encounters."

[16] H. Keith Hunt, "Consumer Satisfaction, Dissatisfaction and Complaining Behavior," *Journal of Social Issues* 47, no. 1 (1991): 107–117.

[17] Ibid., 115.

[18] Donna Partow, "Turn Gripes into Gold," *Home Office Computing* (September 1993): 24.

[19] Claes Fornell and R. A. Westbrook, "The Relationship between Consumer Complaint Magnitude and Organizational States of Complaint Processing in Large Corporations," in Ralph L. Day and H. Keith Hunt, eds, *New Dimensions of Consumer Satisfaction and Complaining Behaviour* (Bloomington, IL: Bureau of Business Research, 1979), 95–98.

[20] Ibid.

[21] Hart et al., "The Profitable Act of Service Recovery."

[22] Karl Albrecht and Ron Zemke, *Service America! Doing Business in the New Economy* (Homewood, IL: Dow Jones Irwin, 1985), 6.

[23] Hart et al., "The Profitable Act of Service Recovery."

[24] Based on Richard C. Oliver, "A Conceptual Model of Service Quality and Service Satisfaction," *Advances in Services Marketing and Management* 2 (1993): 65–85.

[25] K. Douglas Hoffman, Scott W. Kelley, and Holly M. Rotowsky, "Tracking Service Failures and Employee Recovery Efforts," *Journal of Services Marketing* 9, no. 2 (1995): 49–61.

[26] Scott W. Kelley, K. Douglas Hoffman, and Mark A. Davis, "A Typology of Retail Failures and Recoveries," *Journal of Retailing* (Winter 1993), 429–445.

[27] Ibid.

13

The Customer Retention System

FIGURE 13.1   INCREASE IN PROFIT DUE TO CUSTOMER RETENTION

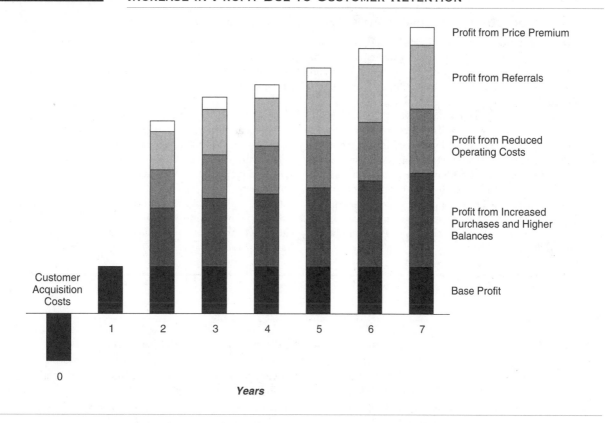

SOURCE: F. Reichheld and W. Earl Sasser, Jr., "Zero Defections: Quality Comes to Services," *Harvard Business Review* (September–October 1990).

Chapter Overview

Businesses commonly lose 15 to 20 percent of their customers each year.[1] In some industries, the rate is much higher. For example, the cable television industry loses in excess of 50 percent each year,[2] the cellular phone industry experiences turnover at a rate of 30 to 45 percent a year,[3] and customer defections in the pager industry range from 40 to 70 percent annually.[4] Reducing customer defections is associated with immediate pay-offs for the firm. Within the credit card industry, a 2 percent decrease in defections has the same net effect on the bottom line as a 10 percent decrease in overhead.[5]

This chapter starts with a discussion of why loyal customers are valuable to service businesses and highlights that it is the intrinsic nature of services, as described in earlier chapters, that provides the logic.

The chapter goes on to discuss strategies for retaining customers, including building on customer franchise, pricing, defection management, and service guarantees.

Figure 13.1 shows a stereotyped breakdown of the profit over time of a single customer and the different sources of increased profit.

Why Are Loyal Customers Valuable to Service Business?

Loyal customers tend to reward their suppliers with increased revenue (see Services in Action 13.1). Due to high levels of perceived risk, loyal customers tend to concentrate their purchases with suppliers that they trust. They even may be prepared to pay a price premium in exchange for the reduced levels of perceived risk.

The Profitability of Customer Retention Efforts at MBNA

MBNA America, a Delaware-based credit card company, recently has improved its industry ranking from 3.8 to 4 and increased its profits sixteenfold. How did they do it? Profitability in the credit card industry is linked directly to customer retention.

In general, credit card companies lose money during the first year of a new account. These companies make money from an individual by collecting fees from the retailer and for each transaction that individual makes. In the first year of the account, the fees obtained from credit card honoring establishments do not offset the costs of advertising, setting up new accounts, and printing statements. Consequently, retaining customers beyond that first year is critical to the profitability of the credit card industry.

MBNA reinforces the importance of customer retention to its employees through the company's reward structure. MBNA's employees earn up to 20 percent of their salaries in bonuses associated with customer retention efforts. MBNA employees talk with every customer that wishes to drop its services and, by doing so, retains 50 percent of these customers.

How do MBNA's customer retention efforts affect the bottom line? MBNA's customer retention rate is 95 percent, and MBNA keeps its customers twice as long as industry averages. In addition, MBNA's credit losses due to bad debt are one-third to one-half lower than those of other companies. Moreover, MBNA customers use their cards more often and maintain higher balances as compared with customers of competing firms.

Cost Savings

In Chapter 9, the cost structure of service firms was discussed in some detail. The very high fixed and semifixed costs incurred by these firms mean that the cost of the marginal or incremental customer is very small indeed. The profitability of retained customers is therefore very high, because marketing effort need not be expended on that individual to create more sales. It is therefore worth investing considerable amounts of money to retain those customers. This is particularly the case for those services that are increasingly dependent on information technology. The shift in banking from people-based operations to computer-based operations has reduced the cost of each transaction dramatically. It has done so, however, at the cost of a much increased fixed-cost base.

Overall, long-term customers tend to have lower maintenance costs. Existing customers become accustomed to the company, employees, and procedures; therefore, they ask fewer questions and have fewer problems. Some of the consequences of the airlines price war that took place in the summer of 1992 presented a few unforeseen problems for the airlines. On the one hand, the lower prices did achieve their desired effect: increased sales. However, many of these sales were to passengers who had never flown before and were unfamiliar with ticketing practices, baggage handling, and typical behavior on an airline. Services such as "complimentary beverages" had to be explained to new passengers who were unfamiliar with the term *complimentary*. In one instance, a flight attendant was requested by a passenger for instructions on how to "roll down her window." The end result of adding new customers to the mix was stressed out and overworked flight attendants and existing customers who were the recipients of lower-than-average service.

Profits from Referrals

Another benefit of customer retention is the positive word-of-mouth advertising generated by satisfied customers. Existing customers are necessary for the firm to develop a reputation that attracts new business. Satisfied customers often refer businesses to their friends and family, which in turn reinforces their own decision. As discussed in Chapter 8, personal sources of information are particularly important to consumers of services due to intangibility and the perception of increased risk associated with the

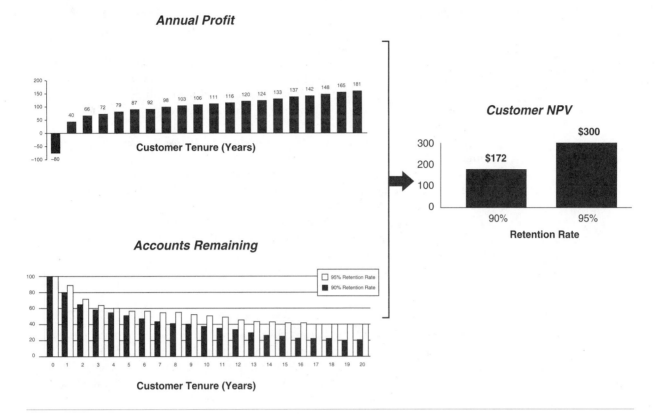

SOURCE: Frederick Reicheld.

purchase. Business attributed to current customer referrals can be dramatic. For example, a leading home builder in the United States has found that 60 percent of its business is based on referrals from past customers.[6]

The relationship between the life-cycle model suggested by Reichheld and the normal customer satisfaction model is clearly retention. A given retention rate is mathematically related to the average customer tenure. An 80 percent retention rate relates to an average tenure of five years, but a 90 percent retention rate relates to an average 10-year tenure. Figure 13.2 shows that it is possible to calculate an expected net present value (NPV) for changes in retention rate.[7]

The top part of Figure 13.2 shows the annual profitability of customers with different tenures. The bottom part shows the percentage of customers of different tenure depending on the retention rate. Combining the two, and allowing for the time value of money, allows the calculation of the NPV of increasing retention rate. The NPV can be compared to the cost of changing that retention rate (e.g., a new computer system) to decide if the investment is worthwhile.

Customer Retention System Components

As described in Chapter 10, the customer retention system can be thought of as a safety net. The system is needed according to this model because the service organization has failed to provide a service encounter that generates customer satisfaction. Worse still, the service recovery strategy has failed. The consumer is therefore likely to be unhappy and at the point of switching firms. The customer retention system is designed to prevent the switch.

In economic theory terms, the objective is to build a barrier to switching that is sufficiently high that the single unacceptable encounter will be overlooked and the customer remains loyal. Clearly, there are factors outside the control of the service firm, such as the availability of a suitable alternative supplier, that can influence switching propensity. There are also naturally occurring barriers to switching. For example, the high perceived risk and the consumer's familiarity with the service script of the particular firm will tend to make switching less likely. However, a retention system is based on action taken by management to retain customers.

Retention strategies tend to fall into four broad categories: pricing, creating a customer franchise, defection management, and guarantees. Loyalty-based pricing mechanisms were partially discussed in Chapter 9. By relating price or reward to multiple usage, they are intended to create loyalty. A firm with a strong customer franchise with individual consumers created through focused marketing and retention programs such as frequent-flyer programs is more likely to be forgiven for a failed encounter. Defection management refocuses the organization on retaining existing customers rather than capturing new ones. Guarantees create an efficient and equitable process for consumers to be compensated for service failures.

Pricing for Loyalty

A frequent-flyer program run by an airline is a classic example of a pricing mechanism designed to reward loyalty. The more the flyer travels with the airline, the more "miles" are accumulated in his or her account. Because the miles are redeemable for free trips, there is every incentive to be loyal to the airline. Even a bad flight is likely to be forgiven if the miles accumulated are high enough.

The more sophisticated programs vary the shape of the reward curve. Simple schemes reward mile for mile (i.e., for every mile traveled the passenger is credited with one frequent-flyer mile). By varying the rewards according to accumulated spending, the incentive to stay with one airline increases. After a threshold of, say, 50,000 miles, if the program gives two frequent-flyer miles for every mile traveled then the incentive is to work toward the different thresholds. The programs arose because of the airlines' interest in business travelers. In 1986, frequent flyers (those who fly 12 or more round trips per year) made up only 3 percent of the flying public but bought 27 percent of the tickets sold. Not only that but these travelers paid more for their flights, accounting for 46 percent of flights but 58 percent of passenger revenues.[8] In 1979, United Airlines had just finished a strike and wanted to rebuild passenger volume as quickly as possible. Because many trips were booked well in advance, they needed a mechanism to switch passengers. To do this, it announced that a discount coupon good for half-off a subsequent flight would be given to passengers flying its aircraft.[9] Those early coupons were transferable, and very quickly a gray market developed with coupons being bought and sold.

Other airlines copied the idea, modifying its appeal to restrict it to business travelers (e.g., Western Airlines "Travel Pass" gave no benefit until six trips had been taken). Finally in 1983, American Airlines instituted a promotion that turned out to be the model for most current frequent-flyer programs. The AAdvantage offered specific rewards for accumulated mileage and related the value of the award to the number of miles accumulated.

Unfortunately, pricing is one of the easiest competitive advantages to copy. In a matter of years, all major airlines were offering similar schemes. Indeed, in 1988 the U.S. airlines made matters worse by engaging in a mileage program war by offering double and triple mileage programs and incentives for joining their schemes. Most airline routes are only serviced by a limited number of airlines, and it did not take travelers long to realize that they could join all the programs. The loyalty effect therefore

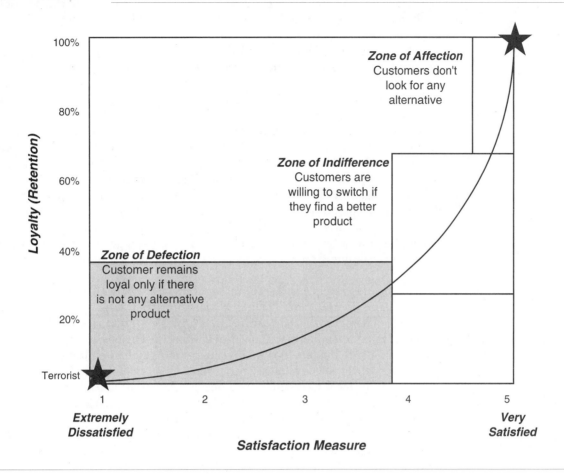

FIGURE 13.3 SATISFACTION/LOYALTY RELATIONSHIP

Zone of Affection
Customers don't look for any alternative

Zone of Indifference
Customers are willing to switch if they find a better product

Zone of Defection
Customer remains loyal only if there is not any alternative product

Terrorist

Loyalty (Retention)

Satisfaction Measure

Extremely Dissatisfied

Very Satisfied

SOURCE: T.O. Jones and W. Earl Sasser, Jr., "Why Satisfied Customers Defect," *Harvard Business Review* (November–December 1995).

only "kicked in" when a passenger approached a particular threshold or was close to accumulating enough miles for a particular incentive on a particular airline.

By the beginning of the 1990s, the total value of the U.S. industries' frequent-flyer programs was estimated to be $1 billion at full ticket price. Clearly, the miles could be redeemed at marginal cost, but the scale of the task of redeeming miles means that full-paying passengers might have to be displaced. On many holiday destinations flights, up to half of first-class seats are full of "free passengers." Other sources have stated that it would take 590,000 Boeing 747's flying one return trip to redeem the outstanding frequent-flyer miles in the United States.

The airline story illustrates well the potential problems of using price to induce loyalty. There are many other emerging problems with the airline schemes, including potential taxation problems, problems with employers who pay for the tickets, and conflicts with travel agents who complain when rental cars and hotels are bundled with schemes and restrict their flexibility. However, as discussed in the next section, such schemes do provide the opportunity to engage in "one-to-one" marketing.

Creating Individual-Level Consumer Franchises

In the discussion of the customer satisfaction system, it was clear that many factors other than customer satisfaction can influence customer defection. Figure 13.3, drawn from Jones and Sasser,[10] expresses this relationship in terms of three zones: the zone of defection; the zone of indifference, and the zone of affection. Clearly, the firm's objective must be to increase the percentage of the firms' customers who do not look for alternatives even if one individual encounter is less than satisfactory and hence are in the "zone of affection."

The most advanced loyalty approach is one-to-one (i.e., to treat each customer as a unique individual). The essence of this approach is that every customer has a long-term value but that value is different by customer. Given individual preference, the service is customized for each customer based on a "collaborative" dialogue. The more a dialogue can be created at the individual level, the more marketing can focus on "segments of one" and truly create a franchise at the individual level.

In industrial marketing, the concept of a "segment of one" has been recognized longer. Ross Contrab, a pneumatic valve supplier, saves in an electronic library all the specific characteristics of those products tailored to customers' needs. When it deals with a client again, it can build on what it has already done.[11] Such a model reflects the two basic principles of one-to-one marketing. This approach suggests that *the true value of a customer depends on future not past purchases*. The authors suggest that a customer who visits a car dealership for the first time has a potential of $300,000 and that during a business career a frequent flyer will generate more than $100,000 in revenue.[12]

The second principle is that *increasing the share of customer expenditure is another way of increasing market share*. Traditional marketing approaches tend to focus on the acquisition of new customers, but share can be increased just as successfully by increasing the share of expenditures of individual customers. The one-to-one focus is therefore very similar to the retention management approach. Customization becomes the key but must obviously be balanced against the efficiency of the service operation.

Some of the most successful one-to-one programs exist in banking. By the nature of the service offered, banks accumulate large amounts of transaction data for each customer. In the past, this was often kept in unrelated files based on the nature of the transaction: current account, deposit account, mortgage, etc. With the advent of large-scale data warehouses and data mining technology, it has become possible to look across all these transactions and better understand the consumer. The result is the creation of individual-level promotions, service offers, and incentives all designed to better satisfy the needs of the consumer.

Ritz-Carlton Hotels, the Atlanta-based luxury hotel corporation, maintains a customer database that allows it to cater to individual guests regardless of where they spend the night within the chain. "If we come to learn you prefer rocks in your pillows, however unlikely that might be, we're going to have rocks in your pillow when you arrive," said Patrick Mene, vice president of quality.[13]

Combining Loyalty Pricing and One-to-One Marketing

The emergence of the data warehouses has provided the opportunity for more pricing-based loyalty schemes to break out of the vicious circle of competition. Airlines such as British Airways have long realized that frequent-flyer programs could be converted into clubs. Loyalty could therefore be created by building a sense of affiliation not just on economic grounds. Dedicated reservation systems, priority check in, lounges, etc., were all designed to reward and to provide a sense of belonging to a club. These programs, of course, can now provide a database on which to base a one-to-one marketing program of special offers, etc. Even customer magazines can serve to lock customers into the service provider.

Tesco supermarkets in the UK has launched a club card that offers a retrospective discount to customers. With every transaction, the card is also registered so that discounts can be calculated. The net effect is to create a complete record of individual's shopping behavior in the store because the card is tied into the EPOS system. The potential now exists to give individual or family level couponing programs and other incentives.

Defection Management

One important way of looking at increasing customer retention rates is by reducing customer defections. The concept of defection management has its roots in the total quality management (TQM) movement. Defection management is a systematic process that actively attempts to retain customers before they defect. Defection management involves tracking the reasons why customers defect and using this information to improve the service delivery system continuously—thereby reducing future defections.

Zero Defects versus Zero Defections

Since the acceptance of total quality management within the manufacturing sector, the guide to follow has been the zero-defects model. Although appropriate within the manufacturing sector, where specifications can be identified well ahead of productions, the zero-defects model does not work very well within the service sector.[14]

Service customers carry specifications around in their heads and can only approximate their desires to the service provider. Each consumer has their own set of expectations and corresponding specifications. For example, customers often show hair stylists a picture of another person's hair style and request a similar style for their own. The picture is an approximation of a desired result. The picture does not specify exact lengths to be cut or specific degree of curve for curls. As one hair stylist bemoaned: "They (some consumers) come in here with two spoonfuls of hair and expect to leave here looking like Diana Ross!" Consequently, specifications that are available within the service sector frequently cannot be standardized for all customers. As a result, the service provider must be able to adapt to each set of expectations on the spot.

Due to the unique properties of the service delivery system, the traditional zero-defects model held by the manufacturing sector is out of touch with the realities of the service sector. A more appropriate philosophy for service firms is to minimize the amount of defections. In contrast to the defect pile for the manufacturing sector that consists of defective goods, the defect pile for services is customers who will not come back.

Importance of Defection Management

Defector Types Customers defect for a variety of reasons.[15] *Price defectors* switch to competitors for lower-priced goods and services and are probably the least loyal of any customer type. Many businesses that pursue a customer retention philosophy are willing to sacrifice price defectors to avoid constantly discounting their own products and services. In particular, firms that differentiate themselves from competitors based on factors such as reliability, responsiveness, empathy, assurance, and the effective management of tangible evidence that surrounds the service are generally able to retain customers without constantly discounting their products.

Product defectors switch to competitors who offer superior goods and services. As such, product defectors are the most difficult to bring back to the fold once they leave. For example, it is difficult to imagine returning to a provider of an inferior service once a superior service is found. The secret to minimizing product defectors is to not become complacent with today's successes and ignore the changing needs of customers. Innovations and continuous improvement are critical in the battle of retaining product defectors.

Service defectors defect due to poor customer service. Unlike other defector types, firms that are plagued by service defectors are actually providing existing customers with reasons to take their business elsewhere. Inadequately informed personnel, unfulfilled promises, and unacceptable employee behavior are typical reasons why customers flee to the competition. Service failures like these combined with inadequate employee responses to those failures can lead to service defections. Although other defector types are primarily externally driven, service defectors leave as a result of problems with the internal operations of the firm.

Market defectors exit the market because of relocation or business failure reasons. Customers, both individuals and businesses, who move out of the market area would be considered market defectors. Similarly, companies that go out of business and are no longer in the market for goods and services are market defectors.

Technological defectors switch to products outside the industry. Typical examples of technological defections include the switch from the oil lamp to electricity and from rail to air transportation. As is the case with product defections, technological defections may occur due to the complacency of the firm. Successful firms are often lulled into a false sense of security and fail to react to technological developments outside their own industry. For example, the manufacturers of vinyl albums were caught off guard by the development and consumer acceptance of the compact disk and lost much of their business through technological defections.

Organizational defectors result from political considerations inside the firm. In some instances, organizational defections will occur due to reciprocal buying arrangements. For example, an engineering firm may switch its paper products purchasing to a firm that sells the brand of paper products marketed by the pulp and paper firm that retains the engineering firm's services. In other instances, organizational defections may occur as a result of friendships that develop through civic clubs, country clubs, and a variety of other social and business gatherings.

Defection Management Process

Although customer defections are frustrating for many firms, defection rates are measurable and manageable.[16] Defections indicate where profits are heading and indicate specific reasons why customers are leaving. Information obtained by analyzing defections can assist firms toward the goal of continuous improvement.

The key to defection management is the creation of a zero-defections culture within the firm. Everyone within the firm must understand that zero defections is a primary goal of the organization. To be established as a primary goal, the first step in the defection management process is that the firm must communicate to its employees not only the importance of retaining current customers, but also the benefits obtained by reducing defections.

The zero-defections goal communicated to employees must have supporters at all levels, starting at the top of the organization. It is critical that upper management leads by example and "walks what they talk." Managers that speak of customer service in employee meetings and then bad mouth customers behind their backs never will successfully implement a zero-defections culture within their firm.

The second step in creating a zero-defections culture is to train employees in defections management. Defections management involves

1. Gathering customer information.

2. Providing specific instructions concerning what to do with the information.

3. Instructing employees on how to react to the information.

4. Encouraging employees to respond to the information.

S E R V I C E S   I N   A C T I O N   1 3 . 2

Southwestern Bell Volunteer Ambassador Program

Southwestern Bell launched this program in the middle of 1995 to build customer retention. Employees volunteer as ambassadors and establish relationships with a number of customers. The ambassadors come from all parts and levels of the company except the sales organization. They work with between five and ten customers. As well as visiting the customers approximately every three months, they give them their office telephone number.

The ambassadors' role is to let each customer know that the company cares about him or her. To do this, the ambassadors answer questions and concerns about service. The program started with 1,300 volunteers but had grown to nearly 3,500 by the middle of 1996. Although being an ambassador involves extra work and keeping up with new services, many employees value the opportunity of getting out from behind their desks.

Southwestern Bell claims a double benefit for the program because as well as encouraging customer loyalty it makes for stronger, smarter, and more involved employees. "The ambassador program cuts to the quick. It gets us through the thicket of technology issues and regulating and legislative issues and it puts two people together—a person representing the company and a person who's a customer of that company—getting together one-to-one and making connections," says Larry Bommarite of Southwestern Bell.

Adapted from "Customer Loyalty, One Customer at a Time," *Marketing News*, February 3, 1997, 8.

Information provided in Chapter 12 regarding identifying service failures and effective recovery strategies provides employees and managers with the specifics of defections management.

The third and perhaps the most critical step within the defection management process is to tie incentives to defection rates. Simply stated, if the firm truly values reducing defections, the reward structure should reinforce customer retention efforts. Firms such as MBNA, as mentioned in the Services in Action 13.1, are dedicated to customer retention and have developed reward systems that are consistent with their customer retention efforts. MBNA's employees earn up to 20 percent of their salaries in bonuses associated with customer retention efforts. As a result of the reward structure and these extra communication efforts with customers, MBNA retains 50 percent of customers who call with the intent to end the relationship.[17] Another example is State Farm Insurance: State Farm agents receive as high a commission for renewals as they do for getting new customers.[18] As a company, State Farm recognizes the value of customer retention and rewards employees for their customer retention efforts.

Overall, the key to defection management is the realization that customer defections are measurable and manageable (see Services in Action 13.2). Too often, firms simply write off customers who no longer request their services. Defection management focuses on retaining customers before they defect and on determining the reasons for defections when defections were not prevented. In sum, defectors are a valuable source of information regarding the firm's operations, its employees, and the firm's future.

Service Guarantees

One of the most innovative and intriguing customer retention strategies to be developed in recent years is the service guarantee. Although guarantees in and of themselves are not particularly new, they are very new with respect to services. Overall, service guarantees appear to facilitate three worthwhile goals: (1) they reinforce customer retention; (2) they build market share; and (3) they force the firm offering the guarantee to improve its overall service quality.

Characteristics of Successful Guarantees

In general, successful guarantees are unrestrictive, stated in specific and clear terms, meaningful, hassle-free when invoked, and quick to pay out. However, issues to avoid when constructing a guarantee include (1) promising something that is trivial and normally expected; (2) specifying an inordinate amount of conditions as part of the guarantee; and (3) making the guarantee so mild that is never invoked.

In general, there are three types of guarantees: an implicit guarantee, a specific-result guarantee, and an unconditional guarantee. The discussion that follows briefly describes each type of guarantee and the trade-offs associated with each type.

Implicit Guarantees An implicit guarantee is essentially an unwritten, unspoken guarantee that establishes an understanding between the firm and its customers. An example might be a department store that automatically provides refunds or exchanges goods for dissatisfied customers even though it is under no obligations to do so. Although the guarantee is not specified, customers of firms that offer implicit guarantees are ensured that the firm is dedicated to complete customer satisfaction. Consequently, a partnership spirit is developed between the firm and its customers, based on mutual trust and respect.

The trade-offs associated with an implicit guarantee strategy are intriguing. On the positive side, because the guarantee is implicit, there are no explicit specifications regarding exactly what the firm will do should the guarantee need to be invoked. Consequently, the service firm can tailor the pay-out of the guarantee to fit the magnitude of the service failure. Hence, an implicit guarantee may not result in an all-or-nothing type of arrangement. Other benefits to the firm associated with the implicit guarantee strategy include avoiding the appearance of a tacky marketing ploy (as compared with an explicit guarantee) and avoiding stating publicly the possibility that the firm, on occasion, may not fulfill its promises. In sum, an implicit guarantee is thought to be the classy way of pursuing a guarantee strategy.

An implicit guarantee also has its drawbacks. Because an implicit guarantee is unspoken and unwritten, "a firm pursuing an implicit-guarantee strategy has to earn its reputation by repeated acts of goodwill communicated to potential clients via word of mouth, a time-consuming process."[19] Hence, an implicit guarantee does little to differentiate a firm early in its business life cycle. In addition, because the guarantee is implicit, new customers may be unaware of the firm's stance on customer satisfaction and may not bring problems to the firm's attention.

Specific-Result Guarantees Another type of guarantee is a specific-result guarantee. This guarantee is considered milder than an explicit unconditional guarantee as "the conditions for triggering the guarantee are narrower and well defined, and the payouts are less traumatic."[20] In contrast to an unconditional guarantee, which covers every aspect of the service delivery process, a specific-result guarantee only applies to specific steps or outputs.

On the positive side, specific-result guarantees are most easily applied to quantitative results. For example, Federal Express guarantees overnight delivery. Moreover, by guaranteeing a specific result as opposed to an overall guarantee, the firm may be able to state its commitment to a particular goal more powerfully. On the negative side, a specific-result guarantee may appear weak compared with an unconditional guarantee, and customers may perceive this as the firm's lack of confidence in its own abilities.

Unconditional Guarantees An unconditional guarantee is the most powerful of the three types of guarantees (see Services in Action 13.3). The unconditional guarantee "in its pure form, promises complete customer satisfaction, and, at a minimum, a full

SERVICES IN ACTION 13.3

The Hampton Inns' Unconditional Service Guarantee

Hampton Inns is a hotel chain based in Memphis, Tennessee, with 240 units across the country. Hampton's rooms are priced in the upper-economy range.

In 1990, Hampton began nationally advertising a "100 Percent Satisfaction Guarantee." This guarantee states that if, for any reason, guests are not entirely satisfied with their stay at a Hampton Inn, they will receive that night's accommodation for free. Hampton is relying on this guarantee to help provide differentiation in the hotel market.

Survey research has found that Hampton's unconditional guarantee of quality has an impact on the perceived value of the hotel by two customer groups: those who were not satisfied with the quality of their stay, and those who were. Further, the guarantee has positively affected employee motivation and attitudes.

Customers who were dissatisfied and who invoked the guarantee pronounced themselves satisfied with the outcome. More than half reported the service at Hampton Inns to be better than that provided by other hotels. When ranking attributes for choosing a hotel, these guests rated the guarantee second among eight possible attributes. Ninety-nine percent of these customers said they would stay at other Hampton Inns, and 90 percent pronounced themselves ready to stay at the same hotel location again. (During the period of the study, nearly 40 percent of these guests actually did use the chain again.)

Customers who were initially satisfied with their stay had less-strong reactions. Fewer found the guarantee to be appealing when making their initial selection of the Hampton Inn, although substantial numbers, particularly leisure travelers, did so. About two-thirds of these guests thought that the guarantee did differentiate Hampton from its competition and that they received more value for money from the chain than from its competitors. Forty-two percent said the guarantee would make them more likely to stay at a Hampton Inn in the future.

Managers and employees clearly believe in the guarantee, stating that it makes them more motivated and more willing to work hard. Ninety-four percent of employees think the guarantee differentiates Hampton from its competitors. Nearly 70 percent said it has improved employee pride in their company.

For Hampton, the guarantee can provide a unifying role. If motivated employees correctly understand the needs of customers attracted by the guarantee and correctly fill them, the guarantee will not be invoked; customers will be satisfied. However, it is worth noting that those customers who did invoke the guarantee were almost more satisfied, in the end, than those who did not.

---

refund or complete, no-cost problem resolution for the payout."[21] In general, offering unconditional guarantees benefits the firm in two ways. First, the firm benefits from the effect that the guarantee has on customers. More specifically, customer-directed benefits associated with unconditional guarantees include:

Customers perceive that they are getting a better value.

The perceived risk associated with the purchase is lower.

The consumer perceives the firm to be more reliable.

The guarantee helps consumers decide when comparing competing choices; consequently, the guarantee serves as a differential advantage.

The guarantee helps in overcoming customer resistance toward making the purchase.

The guarantee reinforces customer loyalty, increases sales, and builds market share.

A good guarantee can overcome negative word-of-mouth advertising.

The guarantee can lead to brand recognition and differentiation; consequently, a higher price can be commanded.

A necessary condition for a firm to offer an unconditional guarantee is that the firm must first have its own operations in order. If not, the payouts associated with an unconditional guarantee eventually will bankrupt the firm. Organization-directed benefits of offering unconditional guarantees include the following:[22]

> The guarantee forces the firm to focus on the customer's definition of good service as opposed to the firm's own definition.
>
> In and of itself, the guarantee states a clear performance goal that is communicated to employees and customers.
>
> Guarantees that are invoked provide a measurable means of tracking poor service.
>
> Offering the guarantee forces the firm to examine its entire service-delivery system for failure points.
>
> The guarantee can be a source of pride and provide a motive for team building within the firm.

As with the other types of guarantees, several risks associated with unconditional guarantees are worth discussing. First, guarantees may send a negative message to some customers, thereby tarnishing the image of the firm that offers the guarantee. Some customers may ponder why the firm needs to offer the guarantee in the first place. For example, customers may consider whether the guarantee is due to failures in the past or whether the firm is desperate for new business. Another drawback to unconditional guarantees involves the actual payout when the guarantee is invoked. Customers may be too embarrassed to invoke the guarantee; consequently, the guarantee actually may motivate customers not to complain. Other potential problems associated with the payout involve the amount of documentation the firm requires to invoke the guarantee, as well as the time it takes for the actual refund to be completed.

Questions

1. Choose a service firm with which you are familiar and which currently has an implicit guarantee. Write a specific results guarantee and an unconditional guarantee for the firm.

2. Using the example of Tesco's UK supermarket mentioned in the chapter, describe how the data collected could be used to create a one-to-one marketing program.

3. For a service firm with which you have had a bad experience, describe the experience and identify how their defection management failed.

Notes

[1] F. Reichheld and W. E. Sasser, Jr., "Zero Defections: Quality Comes to Services," *Harvard Business Review* (September–October 1990), 105–111.

[2] "How Five Companies Targeted Their Best Prospects," *Marketing News*, February 18, 1991, 22.

[3] *The Cellular Telephone Industry: Personal Communicators* (Silver Spring, MD: Herschel Shostack Associates, 1992), 122.

[4] *The Pager Industry: ProNet Annual Report*, 1989.

[5] Reichheld and Sasser, "Zero Defections."

[6] Ibid., 107.

[7] F. Reichheld, *The Loyalty Effect* (Boston: Harvard Business School Press, 1996).

[8] Terrance J. Kearney, "Frequent Flyer Programs: A Failure in Competitive Strategy, with Lessons Learned for Management," *Journal of Consumer Marketing* 7, no. 1 (Winter 1990).

[9]J. Bramcotelli, "Why the Other Share Dropped," *Official Airline Guide: Frequent Flyer* (March 1987): 51–60.

[10]T. O. Jones and W. Earl Sasser, Jr., "Why Satisfied Customers Defect," *Harvard Business Review* (November–December 1995).

[11]J. Pine II, D. Peppers, and M. Rogers, "Do You Want to Keep Your Customer Forever?" *Harvard Business Review* (March–April 1995).

[12]D. Peppers and M. Rogers, *The One to One Future: Building Relationships One Customer at a Time* (New York: Currency/Doubleday, 1993).

[13]"The Perfect Fit," Continental Airlines in-flight magazine *Profiles* (May 1996), 21–26.

[14]Ron Zemke, "The Emerging Art of Service Management," *Training* (January 1992), 37–42.

[15]Glenn De Souza, "Designing a Customer Retention Plan," *The Journal of Business Strategy* (March/April 1992), 24–28.

[16]Reichheld and Sasser, "Zero Defections."

[17]Larry Armstrong, "Beyond May I Help You," *Business Week/Quality* (1991), 100–103.

[18]Patricia Sellers, "Keeping the Buyers," *Fortune* (Autumn/Winter 1993), 56–58.

[19]Christopher W.L. Hart, Leonard Schlesinger, and Dan Mahler, "Guarantees Come to Professional Service Firms," *Sloan Management Review* (Spring 1992), 19, 29.

[20]Ibid., 28.

[21]Ibid., 20.

[22]"Service Guarantees Yield Surprising Results," *The Cornell N.R.A Quarterly* (February 1991), 14–15.

14

Competing as a Service Firm: Service Quality

Chapter Overview

Service quality rightly deserves its place in the capstone section of this book because it closes many service loops. At the same time, service quality is an elusive and indistinct construct. Researchers do, however, make a distinction between the two constructs of customer satisfaction and service quality. Satisfaction, as discussed in Chapter 11, is the outcome of the evaluation a consumer makes of any specific transaction or experience. Quality is more generally conceptualized as an attitude, the customer's global evaluation of a service offering. Quality is built up from a series of evaluated experiences and hence is much less dynamic than satisfaction.

More important, perhaps, quality is generally viewed as an attribute in consumers' choice processes. Quality closes the loop between evaluation and the choice process.

To deliver a consistent set of satisfying experiences that can build into an evaluation of high quality requires the entire organization to be focused on the task. The needs of the consumer must be understood in detail, as must the operational constraints under which the firm operates. The service providers must be focused on quality, and the system must be designed to support that mission. The system must be correctly controlled and deliver to its specification. Finally, customers' expectations must be managed through communications and pricing. To achieve all this, the organization must be consumer-orientated (see Chapter 13). Thus the delivery of quality requires a deep understanding of all the topics covered in this book.

Introduction to Service Quality

Service quality offers a way of achieving success among competing services. Particularly when several firms that offer nearly identical services are competing within a small area, such as banks, establishing service quality may be the only way of differentiating oneself. Such differentiation can yield a higher proportion of consumer choices and hence mean the difference between financial success and failure.

There is ample evidence to suggest that quality can deliver repeat purchases as well as new customers. The value of retaining existing customers is amply illustrated in Chapter 13. Repeat customers confer many benefits on the organization. The cost of marketing to them is lower than to new customers. Once customers have become regulars of the service, they know the script and are very efficient users of the servuction system. As they gain trust in the organization, the level of risk for them is reduced, and they are more likely to consolidate their business with the firm.

This lesson has already been learned over the past decade by goods manufacturers, many of whom have made goods quality a priority issue. Improving the quality of manufactured goods has become a major strategy for both the establishment of efficient, smoothly running operations and to increase consumer market shares in an atmosphere in which customers are consistently demanding higher and higher quality. Goods quality improvement measures have focused largely on the quality of the product itself and specifically on eliminating product failure. Initially, these measures relied on rigorous checking of all finished products before they came into contact with the consumer. More recently, quality control has focused on the principle of ensuring quality during the manufacturing process, on "getting it right the first time," and on reducing end-of-production line failures to zero. The final evolution has been to define quality as delivering the appropriate product to the right customer, thus using external as well as internal benchmarks.

However, service quality cannot be understood in the same way. The servuction system depends on the customer as a participant in the production process, and normal quality control measures, which depend on eliminating defects in the factory before the consumer sees the product, will not suffice. Service quality is not a specific goal or program that can be achieved or completed but needs to be an ongoing part of all management and service production.

What Is Service Quality?

Perhaps the best way to begin a discussion of service quality is to first attempt to distinguish service quality measurement from customer satisfaction measurement. Most experts agree that customer satisfaction is a short-term, transaction-specific measure, whereas service quality is an attitude formed by a long-term overall evaluation of a performance.

Without a doubt, the two concepts of customer satisfaction and service quality are intertwined. However, the relationship between these two concepts is unclear. Some believe that customer satisfaction leads to perceived service quality, whereas others believe that service quality leads to customer satisfaction. In addition to the confusion surrounding the relationship between customer satisfaction and service quality, the way these two concepts relate to purchasing behavior remains largely unexplained.[1]

One plausible explanation is that satisfaction assists customers in revising service quality perceptions.[2] The logic for this position consists of the following:

1. Consumer perceptions of the service quality of a firm with which he or she has no prior experience is based on the consumer's expectations.

2. Subsequent encounters with the firm lead the consumer through the disconfirmation process and further revise perceptions of service quality.

3. Each additional encounter with the firm further revises or reinforces service quality perceptions.

4. Revised service quality perceptions modify future consumer purchase intentions toward the firm.

To deliver a consistent set of satisfying experiences that can build into an evaluation of high quality requires that the entire organization be focused on the task. The needs of the consumer must be understood in detail, as must the operational constraints under which the firm operates. Service providers must be focused on quality, and the system must be designed to support that mission by being controlled directly and delivering as it was assigned to do (see Services in Action 14.1).

Diagnosing Service Quality Failures

There are obviously many difficulties inherent in evaluating service quality. In the first place, perceptions of quality tend to rely on a repeated comparison of the customer's expectation about a particular service, compared with the actual performance of that service. If a service, no matter how good, fails repeatedly to meet a customer's expectations, then the customer will perceive that service to be of poor quality. Second, unlike goods markets in which customers evaluate the finished product alone, in services the customer evaluates the process of the service as well as its outcome. A customer visiting a hairdresser, for example, will evaluate service not only on the basis of whether he or she likes the haircut but also on whether the hairdresser was friendly, competent, and personally clean.

The service quality process can be described in terms of gaps between expectations and perceptions on the part of management, employees, and customers, as shown in Figure 14.1. The most important gap is between customers' expectation of service and their perception of the service actually delivered. The goal of the service firm must be to close that gap or at least narrow it as far as possible. However, it should be

Montgomery County, Ohio

Montgomery County is in the southwest section of the state of Ohio, centered around the city of Dayton. Recently, the area has undergone considerable economic decline. The troubles of the farming economy have been matched by the closure of many small manufacturing plants, formerly the region's chief economic base. As a result, Montgomery County government has had considerable demands made on it, particularly on its Human Services Department.

As well as Dayton, Montgomery County includes 19 municipalities, 12 rural townships, and 16 school districts and is also responsible for operating a number of countywide services. These services include a broad spectrum ranging from welfare and schools through information and economic development. Although it is not a profit-making business, the county government is nonetheless a provider of professional services to a very broad and very diverse group of people. Service quality affects the overall quality of life in the county.

In November 1986, Montgomery County government and its various agencies launched a long-term program to improve services. The first necessary step was customer identification. Each county agency attempted to establish whom it was serving, and customer groups such as homeowners, parents, patients, and employers were created. The second step was to study these groups and learn how the customers perceived the service they were receiving from the county. When customers deemed services to be of poor quality, the county and its agencies attempted to establish why the service failed to meet customer expectations. Two basic problems were identified: delays in service delivery (long waits for service), and lack of courtesy (service by impersonal bureaucrats). The research also attempted to discover customer needs that were not being met by any existing service, ranging from consolidated child support services to better information about employment vacancies.

Once marketing research had determined what customers expected, the next stage was to configure operations to provide services to meet customer demands. Each agency had its own distinct client base and therefore its own distinct needs. Montgomery County's goal was to meet these needs in a way that showed government was fulfilling its prime purpose and serving its constituents. The new "Service Excellence" program required changes to operations, redesigning services and service environments, new policies regarding employees, and a new orientation of the county administration and its agencies toward those whom it perceived to be its customers.

---

remembered that the focus here is on the cumulative attitudes toward the firm, assembled by the consumer from a number of successful or unsuccessful service experiences.

Before the firm can close this gap, however, there are four other gaps that also need to be closed or narrowed.[3] These are

Gap 1: Difference between what consumers expect of a service and what management perceives consumers expect

Gap 2: Difference between what management perceives consumers expect and the quality specifications set for service delivery

Gap 3: Difference between the quality specifications set for service delivery and the actual quality of service delivery

Gap 4: Difference between the actual quality of service delivery and the quality of service delivery described in the firm's external communications

Consumer Expectation versus Management Perception

The most immediate and obvious gap is usually that between what customers want and what managers think customers want. Briefly, many managers think they know what their customers want but are, in fact, mistaken. Banking customers may prefer security to a good rate of interest. Some restaurant customers may prefer quality and taste of food to the arrangement of the tables or the view from the window. A hotel may think that its customers prefer comfortable rooms, when, in fact, the bulk of them spend little time in their rooms and are more interested in on-site amenities.

FIGURE 14.1   CONCEPTUAL MODEL OF SERVICE QUALITY

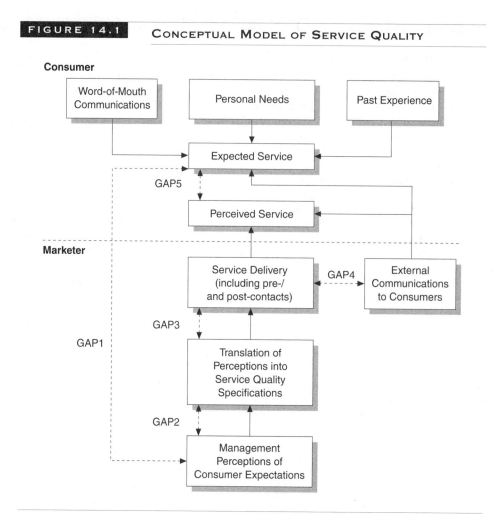

The reasons for this gap are numerous and can be related back to the various issues covered earlier in this book. Chapter 2 suggests that consumer behavior for services may be extremely difficult to understand. The complexity of the service experience may mean that the simplistic multiattribute perspective may not be rich enough to capture all the subtleties.

If such a gap occurs, a variety of other mistakes tends to follow. The wrong facilities may be provided, the wrong staff may be hired, and the wrong training may be given to them. Services may be provided that customers have no use for, whereas the services they do desire remain absent. Closing this gap requires very detailed knowledge of what customers *do* desire and then building a response to that desire into the service operating system.

Management Perception versus Quality Specifications

Even if customer expectations have been accurately determined, another gap then opens, between management's perceptions of customer expectations and the actual specifications set for service delivery. Unfortunately, consumers tend to articulate their needs in terms that are not immediately convertible into operational objectives. Consider the dimensions of the SERVQUAL model: tangibles, responsiveness, empathy, assurance, and reliability. Each dimension was elicited from focus groups and had meaning for the consumers. Such dimensions raise considerable difficulties for management when trying to write a service quality specification. A specification can be set either from the perspective of the consumer or from that of the operating system. The important thing is that the two types of specification are linked together. Thus a specification can be written based on consumers' rating of the responsiveness of the organization. Unfortunately, although this is a tangible measure it does little to guide the behavior of operations managers and contact personnel. Moreover, such a rating may be influenced in the consumer's mind by factors not readily apparent to managers.

Leaving aside for the moment the consumer's idiosyncratic moods and attitudes, several studies have shown the diversity of clues used by consumers when rating services. The "Midas touch" study[4] shows how a single touch can affect many different evaluations. A recent study shows that even if a service firm generates a disconfirmation for a consumer, it may not be judged as delivering a poor level of satisfaction. Being part of the process, the consumers may attribute failures to themselves or to factors outside the control of the firm. Such attributions are shown to depend on the physical characteristics of the service firm. A tidy setting leads to negative attributes being directed away from the firm, whereas an untidy one generates attributes of dissatisfaction directed toward the firm[5].

Conversely, a flowchart analysis, described in Chapter 5, can be performed to identify all points of contact between the firm and its customers. Detailed specifications can then be written for the behavior of the system and contact personnel at each point. Contact personnel can, for example, be instructed to make eye contact and smile. However, it is then important to understand how such a specification will be assimilated into a quality specification that includes responsiveness and empathy.

Because of the difficulties in measuring quality as pointed out above, some managers think that quality measurement is not worth the effort. In still other cases, managers do not believe that customer requirements can be met at all. Some customer expectations are perceived as illogical or impossible, and no attempt is made to meet them. In some cases, especially in financial services, there may be regulatory constraints in the nature of services that are outside the firm's control.

Service Quality Specifications versus Service Delivery

This gap concerns the actual performance of service and can occur even if customer expectations are determined and quality specifications are correctly set. The existence of a service performance gap depends on both the willingness and the ability of employees to provide the service according to specification.

Employees' willingness to provide a service can, as noted in Chapter 4, vary greatly from employee to employee and with individual employees over time. Many employees who start off working at the limit of their potential often become less willing over time because of frustration or dissatisfaction. There is, furthermore, a considerable range between what the employee is actually capable of doing and the minimum the employee must do to avoid being dismissed; it is very difficult to keep employees working at full pitch continuously.

Chapter 4 illustrated that satisfying experiences are often generated because employees respond to consumers over and above their expectations and the system design. Moreover, the data clearly illustrate the power that an organization can gain by recovering from a systems failure. A performance in line with expectations generates minimal levels of satisfaction. It is only by exceeding expectations dramatically that the greatest impact is obtained. An excellent time to generate such an impact comes when the system has failed and the consumers' expectations have been dramatically lowered (see Chapter 12).

Other employees, no matter how willing, may not be able to perform a service according to specifications. They may have been hired into jobs for which they are not qualified or to which they are temperamentally unsuited, and they may not have been given sufficient training for the roles expected of them. An employee who is not capable of performing a service will also, generally, become less willing to keep trying in that particular role.

One common cause of the service gap, as discussed in Chapter 4, is *role conflict*. Whether or not the gap between management perceptions and customer expectations has been closed, service providers may still think that there is an inconsistency between the service management expects them to provide and the service their customers want. A waiter who is expected to promote various items on the menu may alienate some customers who prefer to make their choices undisturbed, and this may reflect badly on the waiter if the customers fail to leave a tip. In other cases, the service provider may be expected to do too many different kinds of work, such as simultaneously answering telephones and dealing with customers face to face in a busy office. If this kind of conflict occurs, employees may become frustrated and gradually lose their commitment to provide the best service they can.

Sometimes, rather than perceiving a role conflict, employees may not understand their role at all. *Role ambiguity* results when employees, whether from incompatibility or inadequate training, do not understand the processes of their job or what the job is intended to do. Sometimes, too, they are unfamiliar with the service firm and its goals. Even when there is a clear service quality specification, there may still arise instances in which employees fail to comprehend or misinterpret that specification.

A further complication for employees is *dispersion of control*, when control over the nature of the service they provide is removed from their hands. When employees may not make independent decisions about individual cases without referring the case to a higher authority, they may feel alienated from the service and less a part of their jobs. When control over certain aspects of service is removed to a different location, such as control over credit being removed from individual bank branches, alienation may increase. Employees may feel unable to respond to customer requests for help.

Both of the above can stem partly from *inadequate support*, when employees do not receive the personal training and/or technological and other resources necessary for them to perform their functions in the best possible manner. Even the best employees can be discouraged if they are forced to work with antiquated or faulty equipment, especially if the employees of competing firms have much superior resources and are able to reach the same level of service with less effort. Failure to properly support employees can lead to wasted effort, poor productivity, and unsatisfied customers.

Service Delivery versus External Communication

As developed in Chapter 8, this is what might be termed the "promises gap," which lies between what the firm promises to deliver in its communications and what it actually does deliver to the customer. If advertising or sales pitches promise one kind of service and the consumer receives a different kind of service, that promise is broken. A diner who sees a bottle of wine on a menu and orders it only to be told it is out of stock and he will have to make do with one of inferior quality may think that the offer held out to him or her on the menu has not been fulfilled. A customer who is promised delivery in three days and then has to wait for a week will perceive service quality to be lower than expected.

It is worth pointing out that price can, under certain circumstances, become an indicator of quality. In the absence of more tangible clues, consumers will use the price that they are paying as a benchmark for the quality of service that they expect through expressions such as "The restaurant was wonderful and the service superb, but given the price it should have been."

One further gap can be added to this original model, based on Chapter 6, which discussed the concept of the servicescape. Gap 6 would be the *perception gap* between the service delivery and the perceived service. Clearly, an organization can deliver to specification and produce, for example, a one-minute queue. Chapter 6 demonstrated that this could be perceived as a longer or shorter time period, depending on the servicescape. The same logic applies to many other dimensions.

Setting and Improving Service Standards

Although the gap model proposed by Berry, Parasuraman, and Zeithaml provides a key diagnostic tool for service quality, to be effective this model needs to be embedded in a service quality process that encompasses the whole firm. They provide a pragmatic list of actions that service organizations can take to improve the quality of the service that they deliver.[6] These lessons also capture the key components that need to be built into any service quality system. They include:

Lesson One: Listening. Quality is defined by the customer. Conformance to company specifications is not quality; conformance to customers' specifications is. Spending wisely to improve service comes from continuous learning about expectations and perceptions of customers and manufacturers.

Lesson Two: Reliability. Reliability is the core of service quality. Little else matters to a customer when the service is unreliable.

Lesson Three: Basic Service. American service customers want the basics: they expect fundamentals, not fancies; performance instead of empty promises.

Lesson Four: Service Design. Reliably delivering the basic service that customers expect depends in part on how well various elements function together in a service system. Design flaws in any part of a service system can reduce quality.

Lesson Five: Recovery. Research shows that companies consistently receive the most unfavorable service quality scores from customers whose problems were not resolved satisfactorily. In effect, companies that do not respond effectively to customer complaints compound the service failure and thus fail the service twice.

Lesson Six: Surprising Customers. Exceeding customers' expectations requires the element of surprise. If service organizations cannot only be reliable in output but can also surprise the customer in the way the service is delivered, then they are truly excellent.

Lesson Seven: Fair Play. Customers expect service companies to treat them fairly and become resentful and mistrustful when they perceive they are being treated otherwise.

Lesson Eight: Teamwork. The presence of service "teammates" is an important dynamic in sustaining servers' motivation to serve. Service team building should not be left to chance.

Lesson Nine: Employee Research. Employee research is as important to service improvement as customer research.

Lesson Ten: Servant Leadership. Delivering excellent service requires a special form of leadership. Leadership must serve the servers, inspiring and enabling them to achieve.

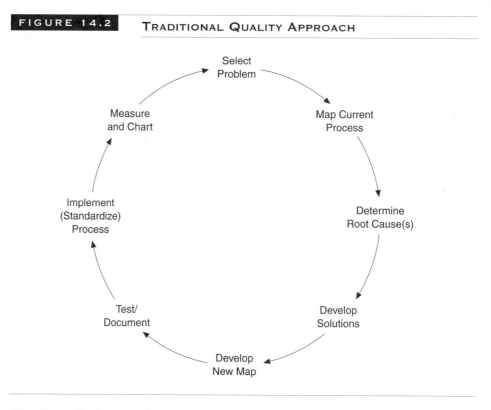

| FIGURE 14.2 | TRADITIONAL QUALITY APPROACH |

SOURCE: Gary K. Johnson and Roland A. Dumas, "How to Improve Quality If You're Not in Manufacturing," reprinted with permission from *Training*, November 1992, 36.

An Appropriate Quality Logic

Such lessons alone do not constitute a systematic approach. To establish such an approach requires three things: an appropriate quality logic, a measurement system, and a quality culture. The problem-solving quality logic systematizes the lessons model but needs to be supported by a measurement system to track results and by a deeply embedded quality culture. The traditional quality approach is shown in Figure 14.2.

Johnson and Dumas suggest that adopting such a manufacturing-oriented approach is a major source of problems for service companies.[7] They argue that most nonmanufacturing or service jobs do not have the clear simplified outcomes—the specifications—of manufactured products. Nor do they have the certainty of preexisting physical measurements that determine whether a product meets those specifications.

In such a situation, starting the improvement cycle with an identified problem can often lead to a wild goose chase because the problem may not be the one that is relevant to the customer. Without specifications of what you have committed to supply the customer, how do you know when it is not being done? A service quality improvement cycle therefore must include a step that establishes customer commitments.

A problem or failure identified in a manufacturing process can be removed from the production line and will never reach the customer. Services production takes place in real time and in the presence of the customer. The failure needs equally to be rectified in real time. Employees need to be empowered to engage in service recovery. These steps need to be built into the service quality cycle. The extended cycle developed by Johnson and Dumas is shown in Figure 14.3.

FIGURE 14.3   NONMANUFACTURING APPROACH

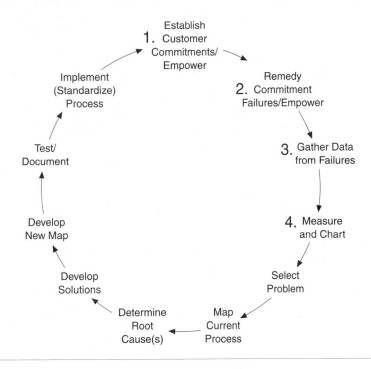

SOURCE: Gary K. Johnson and Roland A. Dumas, "How to Improve Quality If You're Not in Manufacturing," reprinted with permission from *Training*, November 1992, 36.

Measuring Service Quality: The SERVQUAL System

The measurement of service quality was the focus of a systemic research program undertaken by Parasuraman, Berry, and Zeithaml.[8] They started from the position of the consumer and, by using focus groups, tried to elucidate the dimensions of service quality that were independent of the particular firm or industry. As a result, they identified five dimensions: tangibles, reliability, responsiveness, assurance, and empathy.

Based on the satisfaction model, they postulate that quality also is a result of a comparison of expectations and perceptions. They used the dimensions of this logic to develop a generic service instrument. The SERVQUAL instrument consists of two sections: a 22-item section that records customer expectations of excellent firms in the specific service industry, and a second 22-item section that measures consumer perceptions of a particular company in that service industry (e.g., the firm being evaluated). Results from the two sections are then compared to arrive at "gap scores" for each of the five dimensions. The smaller the gap, the higher the service quality expectation. Customer expectations are measured on a seven-point scale, with the anchor labels of "not at all essential" and "absolutely essential." Similarly, customer perceptions are measured on another seven-point scale, with anchor labels of "strongly agree" and "strongly disagree." Hence, SERVQUAL is a 44-item scale that measures customer expectations and perceptions regarding five service quality dimensions.

The Tangibles Dimension   Because of the absence of a physical product, consumers often rely on the tangible evidence that surrounds the service in forming evaluations. The tangibles dimension of SERVQUAL compares consumer expectations and the firm's performance regarding the firm's ability to manage its tangibles. A firm's tangibles consist of a wide variety of objects such as carpeting, desks, lighting, wall colors, brochures, daily correspondence, and the appearance of the firm's personnel. Consequently, the tangibles component in SERVQUAL is two-dimensional—one focusing on equipment and facilities, the other focusing on personnel and communications materials.

The tangibles component of SERVQUAL is obtained through four expectations questions (E1–E4) and four perceptions questions (P1–P4). It must be borne in mind that the expectation questions apply to excellent firms within a particular industry, whereas the perception questions apply only to a particular firm. Comparing the perception scores with the expectations scores provides a numerical variable that indicates the tangibles gap. The smaller the number, the smaller the gap and the closer consumer perceptions are to their expectations. The questions that pertain to the tangibles dimension are as follows[9]:

Tangibles Expectations

E1. Excellent companies will have modern-looking equipment.

E2. The physical facilities at excellent companies will be visually appealing.

E3. Employees of excellent companies will be neat in appearance.

E4. Materials associated with the service (e.g., pamphlets or statements) will be visually appealing in an excellent company.

Tangibles Perceptions

P1. XYZ has modern-looking equipment.

P2. XYZ's physical facilities are visually appealing.

P3. XYZ's employees are neat in appearance.

P4. Materials associated with the service (e.g., pamphlets or statements) are visually appealing at XYZ.

The Reliability Dimension In general, reliability reflects the consistency and dependability of a firm's performance. Does the firm provide the same level of service time after time, or does quality vary dramatically with each encounter? Does the firm keep its promises, bill its customers accurately, keep accurate records, and perform the service correctly the first time? Nothing can be more frustrating for customers than unreliable service providers. A constantly amazing observation is the number of businesses that fail to keep their promises. In many instances, the consumer is ready to spend money if only the service provider would show up and perform the transaction as promised.

Consumers perceive the reliability dimension to be the most important of the five SERVQUAL dimensions. Consequently, failure to provide reliable service generally translates into an unsuccessful firm. The questions used to assess the reliability gap are as follows:

Reliability expectations

E5. When excellent companies promise to do something by a certain time, they will do so.

E6. When customers have a problem, excellent companies will show a sincere interest in solving it.

E7. Excellent companies will perform the service right the first time.

E8. Excellent companies will provide their services at the time they promise to do so.

E9. Excellent companies will insist on error-free records.

Reliability perceptions

P5. When XYZ promises to do something by a certain time, it does so.

P6. When you have a problem, XYZ shows a sincere interest in solving it.

P7. XYZ performs its service right the first time.

P8. XYZ provides the services at the time it promises to do so.

P9. XYZ insists on error-free records.

The Responsiveness Dimension   Responsiveness reflects a service firm's commitment to provide its services in a timely manner. As such, the responsiveness dimension of SERVQUAL concerns the willingness and/or readiness of employees to produce a service. Occasionally, customers may encounter a situation in which employees are engaged in their own conversations with one another while ignoring the needs of the customer. Obviously, this is an example of unresponsiveness.

Responsiveness also reflects the preparedness of the firm to provide the service. Typically, new restaurants do not advertise their opening night, so that the service delivery system can be fine-tuned and prepared to handle larger crowds, thereby minimizing service failures and subsequent customer complaints. The SERVQUAL expectation and perception items that address the responsiveness gap are as follows:

Responsiveness Expectations

E10. Employees of excellent companies will tell customers exactly when services will be performed.

E11. Employees of excellent companies will give prompt service to customers.

E12. Employees of excellent companies will always be willing to help customers.

E13. Employees of excellent companies will never be too busy to respond to customer requests.

Responsiveness Perceptions

P10. Employees of XYZ tell you exactly when the service will be performed.

P11. Employees of XYZ give you prompt service.

P12. Employees of XYZ are always willing to help you.

P13. Employees of XYZ are never too busy to respond to your requests.

The Assurance Dimension   SERVQUAL's assurance dimension addresses the competence of the firm, the courtesy that it extends to its customers, and the security of its operations. Competence pertains to the firm's knowledge and skill in performing its service. Does the firm possess the required skills to complete the service on a professional basis?

Courtesy refers to how the firm's personnel interact with the customer and the customer's possessions. As such, courtesy reflects politeness, friendliness, and consideration for the customer's property (e.g., the car mechanic who places paper floormats in a customer's car in order not to soil the car's carpet).

Security is also an important component of the assurance dimension. Security reflects a customer's feelings that he or she is free from danger, risk, and doubt. Recent robberies at ATM locations provide ample evidence of the possible harm that may arise at service locations. In addition to physical danger, the security component of the assurance dimension also reflects financial risk issues and confidentiality issues. The SERVQUAL items used to address the assurance gap are as follows:

Assurance Expectations

E14. The behavior of employees of excellent companies will instill confidence in customers.

E15. Customers of excellent companies will feel safe in their transactions.

E16. Employees of excellent companies will be consistently courteous with customers.

E17. Employees of excellent companies will have the knowledge to answer customer questions.

Assurance Perceptions

P14. The behavior of employees of XYZ instills confidence in customers.

P15. You feel safe in your transactions with XYZ.

P16. Employees of XYZ are consistently courteous to you.

P17. Employees of XYZ have the knowledge to answer your questions.

The Empathy Dimension Empathy is the ability to experience another's feelings as one's own. Empathetic firms have not lost touch with what it is like to be a customer of their own firm. As such, empathetic firms understand their customers' needs and make their services accessible to their customers. By contrast, firms that do not provide their customers with individualized attention when requested and that offer opening hours convenient to the firm but not to its customers fail to demonstrate empathetic behaviors.

The SERVQUAL empathy dimension addresses the empathy gap as follows:

Empathy Expectations

E18. Excellent companies will give customers individual attention.

E19. Excellent companies will have operating hours convenient to all their customers.

E20. Excellent companies will have employees who give customers personal attention.

E21. Excellent companies will have the customer's best interest at heart.

E22. The employees of excellent customers will understand the specific needs of their customers.

Empathy Perceptions

P18. XYZ gives you individual attention.

P19. XYZ has operating hours convenient to all its customers.

SERVICES IN ACTION 14.2

Parkview Episcopal Medical Center

Parkview Episcopal Medical Center is one of two hospitals serving Pueblo, Colorado. Hospital Corporation of America, which manages the facility, designated it as a "role model" hospital for quality improvement. Strict limitations in revenue prompted Parkview to undertake the cultural changes associated with Deming management. Ninety-five percent of its patient base is made up of Medicare and Medicaid beneficiaries, HMO members, and the medically indigent. "With that amount of fixed payment," says CEO Michael Pugh, "it's clear that we have to do something different to survive."

Pugh was introduced to the Deming quality management philosophy for the first time in the spring of 1988. By autumn, many Parkview senior managers had received quality training. Pugh established a quality improvement council of senior managers to help guide the implementation of Deming's "new philosophy." The hospital jumped on Deming Point 6, "Institute Training," with a vengeance. Quality improvement teams were formed to address hospital problems under the direction of a group of managers trained specifically to lead them. Almost all department managers attended a week-long course on statistics taught by a consultant. All hospital employees were scheduled to attend a quality awareness course.

Pugh estimates that it takes two to three years to integrate Deming quality methods into organizational culture. He advises managers to expect a steep employee learning curve. As Parkview moves further into its new philosophy, Pugh notes definite improvements in employee morale. The hospital turnover rate was less than 12 percent in 1990, compared with rates of 15 to 18 percent in previous years. Cost savings are more difficult to quantify, but quality improvement teams in operating room (OR) scheduling and food service delivery provided the hospital with more than $10,000 in annual savings in each department during 1990.

Parkview's approach to surgery scheduling provides an example of its utilization of the Deming approach to quality. The hospital had a history of not meeting early morning surgery schedules; 48 percent of morning surgical schedules began late, affecting operating times for the rest of the day. Therefore, an OR quality improvement team was formed that included nurses, technicians, and physicians. The group tracked actual causes for delays, finding two common system causes: either the surgeon was late or the OR was not ready. The team tried to encourage surgeons to arrive on time by (1) reminding physicians that they were expected to be on time for surgeries; (2) not permitting any surgeon who was late to surgery two times in one month to schedule the first case of the day; and (3) posting the names of late surgeons in the physicians' lounge.

When the team examined instances when the OR was not ready to begin surgery at the scheduled 7:30 A.M. starting time, it discovered that extensive surgeries, such as total hip or knee replacements, were most likely to start late. The OR staff, coming in at 7:00 A.M., were unable to prepare instrumentation for extensive operations in 30 minutes. The team suggested moving start times for major surgeries to 8:00 A.M. Changing the rules meant that operations still started on time; morale improved because staff had more time to prepare and surgeons were not kept waiting. As a result of the team's efforts, the number of late surgeries dropped from 48 to 8 percent.

P20. XYZ has employees who give you personal attention.

P21. XYZ has your best interests at heart.

P22. Employees of XYZ understand your specific needs.

Creating a Quality Culture

Such mechanistic approaches to quality can add value, but exponents of total quality management will argue that the problem-solving logic must be embedded in the current quality culture if it is to survive. Edward Deming, the father of American and Japanese quality management, argues that a charge of management philosophy is necessary.[10] He articulates 14 points in his philosophy, summarized in Table 14.1

Clearly, this is not the norm for most organizations, which might be typified by the "management by numbers" style: "Do it. I don't care how, just do it."

To make such a radical shift in the organization requires companywide commitment at all levels. Upper management must act to improve corporate business systems, often at the rest of lower levels of the organization. They must create the corporate culture consistent with the 14 points (see Services in Action 14.2).

TABLE 14.1   THE FOURTEEN POINTS FOR MANAGEMENT

1. Create Constancy of Purpose for Improvement of Product and Service
Continuation of a business requires a core set of values and a purpose that do not change with time. Constancy of purpose means accepting obligations that include innovation, research, education, and continuous improvement of product and service design.

2. Adopt the New Philosophy
The new philosophy seeks to optimize holistic systems rather than suboptimize components. It eschews management practices that rob people of pride of workmanship, and seeks profound knowledge as the basis for plans and decisions.

3. Cease Dependence on Mass Inspection
Inspection to improve quality is too late, ineffective, and costly. Quality does not come from inspection, but rather from improvements in the process. No amount of inspection affects process quality.

4. End the Practice of Awarding Business on the Basis of Price Tag Alone
Price has no meaning without a measure of the quality being purchased. Reliance on price must be replaced by evaluations of the effects of purchased goods and services on the operation of all processes involved in their use. Purchasers and suppliers should move from adversarial positions to cooperative ones.

5. Improve Constantly and Forever the System of Production and Service
Quality should be built in at the design stage, and systems should be redesigned continually for improved quality. Variation should be minimized as systems draw nearer and nearer to operating at optimum points. Statistical tools and operational definitions (definitions determined by use in practice) can be extremely useful in implementing this point. They can provide the means with which to measure improvement.

6. Institute Training
Training should be based on system optimization and customer satisfaction. It should be a springboard from which workers can develop pride of workmanship. Training should provide managers and workers with the tools they will need to evaluate processes and improve systems. Deming recommends at least some training in statistical thinking so workers can appreciate variation.

7. Adopt and Institute Leadership
Real leadership requires profound knowledge. Deming states that leaders must know the work they supervise. They must be empowered and directed to inform higher-level management about conditions that need correction. Higher-level management must act on that information. Leadership is the engine that drives systems toward optimization.

8. Drive Out Fear
Deming claims that workers cannot put in their best performance unless they feel secure. Fear begets misinformation, hidden agendas, and padded numbers. It may induce workers to satisfy a rule or a quota at the expense of the best interests of the company. All these consequences make system optimization very difficult.

9. Break Down Barriers between Staff Areas
This point is a direct result of an integrated, systemic view of business processes. Optimization of systems is impossible unless all components recognize their systemic function and have some feedback concerning the way their activities are affecting system performance. Interstaff teams provide the best means to break down barriers between staff areas and enhance communication.

10. Eliminate Slogans, Exhortations, and Targets for the Work Force
Deming claims that posters and exhortations are directed at the wrong people. Posters represent the hope that workers could, by some additional effort, accomplish the goals set by management. Managers must learn that the responsibility for improving the business system is theirs, not the workers'. If posters and exhortations ask people to do what the system will not allow them to do, the only result will be disillusionment and frustration.

11A. Eliminate Numerical Quotas for the Work Force
Deming views quotas as "fortresses" against improving quality and productivity. Quotas do not consider quality. They cannot provide data valuable in improving the system: they destroy pride in workmanship.

11B. Eliminate Numerical Goals for People in Management
Numerical goals are set when managers do not know the capabilities of the systems they are managing. They are generally set in ignorance or, at best, on the basis of what seems reasonable by experience. Stable systems do not need numerical goals. Output will be determined by system capability. Unstable systems have no capability. There can be no basis for setting a numerical goal in an unpredictable system.

12. Remove Barriers that Rob People of Pride of Workmanship
This point recommends that all workers be given the tools and training they need to do a job in which they can take pride. It requires managers to listen to workers and act upon their suggestions and requests. Listening and follow-up action, which are hard work, need to be reinforced by high-level management. Some organizations seem more interested in bureaucratic procedures than their own employees.

13. Encourage Education and Self-Improvement for Everyone
Systems will improve as a result of applied knowledge, which is linked to education. Deming recommends lifelong learning, whether in formal or informal settings. Committed, knowledgeable people have the best chance of optimizing systems in which they work.

14. Take Action to Accomplish the Transformation
If business systems are to be optimized, everyone must be involved. The leadership for this involvement rests clearly with management. Managers must show the work force that they are serious about adopting a systems view of their business. They must demonstrate their concern for worker interests, provide adequate training to measure system performance, and measure attempts to improve it.

SOURCE: Thomas F. Rienzo, "Planning Deming Management for Service Organizations," *Business Horizons* (May–June 1993): 20–23.

Middle managers must understand the systems for which they are responsible and target the contributors to performance. Adopting the new philosophy, they will take a systems perspective and improve business processes, often at the request or recommendation of lower-level management.

Lower-level management and nonmanagerial workers must be instructed and trained so that they can measure systems performance, recognize variations, and do root-cause analysis of the problems. Their role is to fix what they can and communicate the rest to the next level of management.

Questions

1. Choose an example of a service firm that you believe delivers low quality. Explain your choices by using the gaps model.

2. What is the difference between the enthusiast orientation advocated by Schneider in Article 4.2 and a quality orientation?

3. Would you advocate the appointment of a quality vice president for a service firm? Explain your reasoning.

Notes

[1] Thomas A. Stewart, "After All You've Done for Your Customers, Why Are They Still NOT HAPPY," *Fortune*, December 11, 1995, 178–182.

[2] J. Joseph Cronin, Jr., and Steven A. Taylor, "Measuring Service Quality: A Reexamination and Extension," *Journal of Marketing* 56 (July 1992): 60–63.

[3] Ibid.

[4] Jeffrey Fisher, Martin Rytting, and Richard Neslin, "Hands Touching Hands: Affective and Evaluative Effects on Interpersonal Touch," *Sociometry* 39, no. 4 (1976): 416–421.

[5] Mary Jo Bitner, "Evaluating Service Encounters: The Effects of Physical Surroundings and Employees Responses," *Journal of Marketing* 54 (April 1990): 42–50.

[6] Leonard A. Berry, A. Parasuraman, and Valerie A. Zeithaml, "Diagnosing Service Quality in America," *Academy of Management Executive* 8, no. 2 (1994): 32–52.

[7] Gary K. Johnson and Roland A. Dumas, "How to Improve Quality If You're Not in Manufacturing," *Training* (November 1992): 36.

[8] A. Parasuraman, Leonard A. Berry, and Valerie A. Zeithaml, "Refinement and Reassessment of the SERVQUAL Scale," *Journal of Retailing* 67 (Winter 1991): 420–450.

[9] Ibid.

[10] Thomas F. Rienzo, "Planning Deming Management for Service Organizations," *Business Horizons* (May–June 1993): 19–29.

15

Competing as a Service Firm: Building a Customer-Focused Service Organization

Chapter Overview

Chapter 3 developed the idea that the decisions made by the operating and marketing functions are interlinked. Almost everything operations decides to do has an impact on the servuction system and hence on the consumer; likewise, many of the decisions made by marketing affect the expectations or behavior of the consumer and hence also the servuction system.

Because of the interactive nature of that system, any department or function that influences all or part of it will find itself interrelating with all the other functions that have influence. For example, a service business that does not delegate its personnel function to operations, as many do, will find itself with a three-cornered fight:

Somehow, marketing always seems to lose in this fight. The purpose of this chapter is first to describe why marketing may often have less influence in service companies than in goods companies. Second, the chapter goes on to describe alternative ways of increasing customer orientation in the culture of service firms.

The Historical Weakness of Marketing in Service Firms

It is necessary to draw an important distinction between marketing orientation, the marketing function, and the marketing department. Gronroos defines the marketing orientation as follows:

> Marketing orientation means that a firm or organization plans its operations according to market needs. The objectives of the firm should be to satisfy customer needs rather than merely to use existing production facilities or raw materials.[1]

An orientation is thus clearly an attitude of mind that puts the customer's needs first in any trade-off. Such an orientation does not require a formally designated marketing department.

The functions of marketing in services encompass such tasks as the design of the product, pricing, and promotion. Decisions in these areas must be made for the organization to operate, but they need not necessarily be made by persons with a marketing title nor by individuals in a marketing department. In a typical goods company, these distinctions are not necessary, but they are in service firms in which a formal marketing department may not necessarily exist. Because the product is an interactive process, it may be more appropriate to leave the different functional "decisions" to different departments.

The Technology Matrix

Figure 15.1 shows a matrix originally suggested some years ago by Maister and Lovelock.[2] One axis of the matrix relates directly to the work of Chase[3] and represents the degree of customer contact. According to Chase's ideas, the higher the level of customer contact, the higher the level of inefficiency that will be produced because of the uncertainty introduced by those consumers. This idea is based largely on the concept

FIGURE 15.1   CUSTOMIZATION/CUSTOMER-CONTACT MATRIX

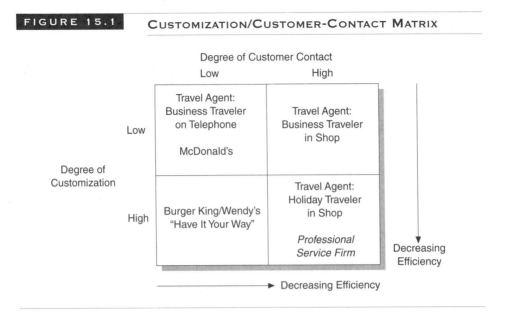

of an interactive system and the participation of the consumers in the process. The second axis relates to the amount of customization of the service available to the consumers. Once again, we would expect the "low" state to be preferable, because it would allow the system to operate close to the ideal "production line." Several sample systems have been introduced into the cells to illustrate how the matrix is used.

For example, a travel agency can simultaneously operate in a number of cells. Booking an airline ticket by telephone for a business traveler fits into the low/low cell. But the same organization could well operate in a different cell if it also maintained a shop. From within that system, both high and low customization are possible, depending on whether the customer is a business traveler wanting a ticket or a vacationer planning a multistop European trip.

The matrix has an ideal cell from an operations perspective—the low/low state. In that cell, the degree of customer contact is minimized so that large parts of the organization can be isolated and run like any other manufacturing plant.[4] In that cell, also, the level of customization is minimized so that the operating system can be focused on a limited range of output and its efficiency can thus be increased.[5] However, a move into this cell can have major implications for marketing. Customers may actually be seeking contact and customization and be willing to pay a premium for them.

A top-quality French restaurant might fit into the high/high category. Compared with McDonald's, this is a different business with a different formula (but interestingly, the target segment may be the same person on a very different occasion). The loss of efficiency implied by the high/high cell is compensated for by the price that can be charged.

More important for the purposes of this discussion, the different cells suggest alternative roles and places for the marketing departments of firms operating within them. Two contrasting examples are the provision of legal services by a traditional law firm and by Hyatt Legal Services.

Operationally, the traditional firm will fit into the high/high cell in the matrix, and we might expect little scope for operational efficiency. The firm's lawyers will be in intensive contact with the clients and will be customizing the service, client by client. Except for routine cases, there will be little scope for economies of scale.

From a marketing point of view, the product in the high/high cell is often created in the client's offices, away from the home firm of the lawyer. In such situations, it is clear that a central marketing department could have little influence over the product and that most of the marketing needs to be delegated to the field if not to the individual level. Selling is done by the consultants or professionals, so that too must be delegated.

The alternative is Hyatt Legal Services. Operationally, this firm represents a clear attempt to move the technology away from the inefficiency of the high/high cell toward the low/low or at least the high contact/low customization cell. By reducing the types of problems tackled, operations can be simplified and economies of scale generated. These economies can, in turn, be passed on to the customer through lower fees.

The marketing implications of such a change of technology are relatively straightforward. The service is branded to add value to the consumer in a market that is traditionally not heavily branded. The system depends on standardization and, from an operations point of view, implies centralization. We would therefore expect to find a strong centralized marketing department as well. Clearly, many service firms do not operate in the low/low cell of the matrix, even though they might wish to. For many service firms, therefore, the traditional combination of marketing functions in a marketing department breaks down. The result is that there is not a strong marketing group to drive a marketing orientation within the organization. The weakness of the marketing function is compounded by the strength of the operations group and the interlinkages between them.

The Evolutionary Place of Marketing

All service businesses start with the kind of service formula described in Chapter 10. The up-front work necessary to create the formula requires a strong marketing unit. Once the prototype is built, however, the next problems are operational ones. Without the appropriate level of operational efficiency, the formula simply will not work.

If the firm then chooses to compete for geography (see Chapter 10) and adopt a multisite strategy, the formula is frozen. The role of marketing becomes one of site selection and advertising, but if loss of focus is to be avoided, then the "product" must be fixed (see Services in Action 15.1).

By the end of the multisite phase, the operations group is huge, whereas the marketing group is small and often fragmented. Only when the service firm decided it needs to begin to compete for share with multiple services or multiple segments is marketing needed again. Before that happens, however, a lowly branch manager in such a network might receive these three memoranda on the same day:

From the Marketing Department
We will shortly be launching a new advertising campaign based on the friendliness of our staff. This is in direct response to the increasingly competitive marketplace we face. Please ensure your staff members deliver the promises we are making.

From the Operations Department
As you are aware, we are facing an increasingly competitive marketplace, and as a result, our profits have come under pressure. It is crucial, therefore, that we minimize waste to keep our costs under control. From today, therefore, no recruitment whatsoever will be allowed.

From the Personnel Department
Our staff members have become increasingly militant. This is due in large part to the availability of alternative employment with our new competitors. We are currently involved in a particularly delicate set of negotiations and would be grateful if you could minimize any conflicts at the local level.

These instructions obviously conflict with one another. To obey the operations department means no recruitment and therefore an increase in the workload of the contact personnel. Such an increased workload will undoubtedly spill over into the labor negotiations and could be disastrous for the personnel function. Finally, the increased

---

SERVICES IN ACTION 15.1

La Quinta Motor Inns

La Quinta Motor Inns was founded in 1968 with the establishment of two hotels in San Antonio, Texas. In the following decade, the company experienced rapid growth, and by 1980, La Quinta had 95 units in 23 states, with a total of more than 11,000 rooms. La Quinta, by offering a quality product priced consistently below the competition, achieved one of the highest occupancy rates of any hotel chain in the country.

The firm was very much led from the top. La Quinta's president took an active role in the running of the company, particularly when it came to selecting sites for new inns, a task that he regarded as a key part of the firm's marketing strategy. Each site was chosen personally by the president, and the factors that went into each site-selection decision were determined by him on the basis of experience and "gut feeling." The other important officer of the firm was the senior vice president of operations, who was personally responsible for quality and frequently made impromptu personal inspections of sites.

La Quinta employed a vice president of marketing, who was responsible to the vice president of operations. Under the vice president of marketing were three more officers: the vice president of advertising, the publicity director, and the editor of the firm's internal magazine.

The major role of the marketing department was to handle the firm's communications. Advertising and publicity were aimed at creating public awareness of the chain in a cost-effective manner. Marketing had no role in the site-selection process, which was handled by the president, or in selling; the sales director reported separately to the vice president of operations. Nor did the marketing department play any role in developing new services or making pricing decisions.

Senior management believed that marketing was, in fact, an integral function of many departments: finance (in setting prices), sales, and operations. The existence of a specific marketing department was necessary only to fulfill the communications and public relations functions that other departments could not handle. The concept of marketing as a separate function was considered unnecessary in a firm of LaQuinta's type.

The personnel of the marketing department, however, thought that they were being underused and that they could, in particular, provide greater inputs to operations and pricing decisions. They complained that they frequently did not know what specific services would be offered until after the service decision had been made. Marketing also considered personal opinions on the part of management to be an inadequate substitute for market research, particularly when coping with change.

---

workload will in all probability have a negative effect on staff morale. Given the transparency of the service organization, this low morale will be visible to customers and will adversely affect their satisfaction levels.

When the firm is marketing oriented, the site manager will trade off the three sets of instructions, giving added weight to marketing. It should be stressed that within service firms it is nearly impossible to be totally marketing oriented. Customers cannot be given everything they want because of the very real constraints imposed by the operating system. Unfortunately, by now our service firm is operations dominated and oriented toward operational efficiency, and operations has line responsibility for branches. As a result, the manager throws away all but the operations department memo. The final result may be an abusive memo from the operations vice president to his or her counterpart in marketing. The memo would ask why marketing was sending a memorandum to the branches at all and suggest that in future all memos be cleared with operations. This would not be personal but a manifestation of the different cultures in marketing and operations. Different departments have a tendency in all organizations to develop different cultures and to move away from each other. This is a naturally occurring phenomenon, which organizational theorists call "differentiation."[6]

Organizational theorists define differentiation as the difference between departments in terms of goals, time behaviors, reward structures, and tasks. The original work by Lawrence and Lorsch[7] suggested that marketing had longer time horizons than manufacturing, was less rigidly and hierarchically organized, and tended to reward innovation and creativity, which were less valued in manufacturing. These findings were reviewed in the study by Langeard et al.,[8] which found differences in revenue versus cost orientation, time horizons, and motivations for change between service operations and marketing departments.

Within goods companies, such differences do not become pathologic. Fortunately, in goods-producing companies, the availability of inventory allows the two departments to operate semiautonomously, at least in the short term. Manufacturing needs to know the likely demand that marketing will create and the particular products that are needed, but once these targets are agreed on, the two departments can operate independently. Production can then be scheduled to create inventory as it is needed. Marketing does not need to know when or how production takes place. Once inventory is available, it can be formally transferred; indeed, it is often "sold" by manufacturing to marketing. Coordination may be achieved by a planning manager or coordinator who interfaces between the two departments. Conflicts, when they arise, can be resolved only by the general manager in such organizations who oversees the different functions.

In a service firm, the technology is different. There is very little opportunity to inventory anything, and the system itself contains no inventories; it is a real-time experience. The impact of this is that the coordination of the different functions takes place at two points in the organization—at the very top and at the very bottom. Branch managers at the bottom of an organization take a very different perspective on interfunctional trade-offs than do their general management counterparts at the top.

The Need for More Customer Orientation

The service firm has reached the limits of the multisite strategy and now needs to become marketing oriented again. Alternatively, or sometimes simultaneously, the firm starts to feel threatened by serious competition. Unfortunately, most service operations find it difficult to defend against competition. Because service systems and concepts cannot be shielded from infringement, there are few barriers other than location to protect a service firm.

The traditional goods marketing logic would argue that the implications for marketing are twofold. First, an increasing need for effective marketing may require closer coordination of the various marketing decisions. That coordination may, in turn, require the creation of a marketing function, either at the site level or at the head office, to collect all relevant information and generally improve the quality of marketing decision making.

The second implication is the need to give added weight to the marketing orientation. Particularly if the organization has been operations-dominated in the past, a strong marketing department may be necessary to keep the natural search for operational efficiency from predominating. Unfortunately, this denies the interrelatedness of the different functions implied by the servuction system. Marketing effectiveness can generally be bought only at the expense of operational efficiency. Moreover, neither operational nor marketing objectives can be allowed to predominate. A compromise between the two must be reached. A marketing department may not be the answer.[9] Indeed, the creation of a marketing department might produce nothing more than interdepartmental warfare that refocuses the organization inward, precisely when it should be focusing outward. More important is the need to generate increased levels of marketing orientation. To do this requires a change in the dominant culture of the organization, away from operations and toward marketing.

Building Customer Orientation in Service Firms

Figure 15.2 presents a simple framework for considering culture change. It suggests that culture is integrally linked and partly an outcome of three organizational components:

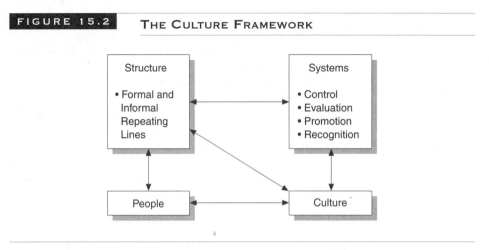

FIGURE 15.2   THE CULTURE FRAMEWORK

SOURCE: Richard B. Chase and Robert H. Hayes, "Beefing Up Operations in Service Firms," *Sloan Management Review* (Fall 1991); 15–26.

structure, systems, and people. Structure is self-explanatory and relates to the formal reporting structures normally represented in an organization chart. Systems are a more complex area in this context because they deal not with information technology systems but with people management systems for control, evaluation, promotion, and recognition. Each has both an informal and a formal component. Control systems provide individuals and groups with a score, and the informal system tells them which item matters to their boss at the moment. Evaluation and promotion systems cover all the formal paraphernalia of management by objectives but also by the informal "What do I have to do to be a hero?" criteria. Recognition systems focus on formal and informal rewards from company trips to lunch with the chief executive.

An attempt to change to a more customer-oriented culture can therefore use any of four levers—structure, systems, people, or culture, separately or together.

Changing Culture through Structure

Structure can change culture. However, it is a blunt weapon because it takes years to successfully implement an organizational change, and only when implementation is successful will culture start to change. Two different approaches to using the cultural lever have been tried: a marketing department as a change agent and restructuring around the servuction system model.

Marketing Departments as Change Agents   Marketing departments can be created in environments in which one might not expect them to be, for their role can be merely to change the orientation of the organization by creating an advocate for the consumer.

But, as Gronroos points out, there is a real danger in this approach. Gronroos suggests that once such a department has been created, operations personnel will merely transfer responsibility for consumers to the marketing department.[10] Even worse, Lovelock and colleagues showed that in such a situation, there is also the likelihood that open warfare will break out between the two departments.[11]

Many of the conflicts implied by this approach have been suggested by organizational behavior theorists. Conflicts emerge in the first place because of differences in orientation between the marketing and operations departments. Operations departments, by their very nature, tend to be cost-driven; their focus is on evaluating the operation to find costs to save and procedures to simplify. This outlook tends to have a short time horizon. Marketing, by comparison, is looking for enhancements that can

Dunfey Hotels

The Dunfey Hotel Corporation is not so much a hotel chain as it is four separate hotel chains managed by one group. In 1980, the company owned, leased, or managed 22 hotels in the following divisions:

- Dunfey Classic and Luxury Hotels, four properties in the luxury/executive end of the market, including the Ambassador East in Chicago and the Berkshire Place in New York City.

- Dunfey Major Meeting and Convention Hotels, seven properties in the eastern states and Texas.

- Dunfey Inns and Airport Hotels, nine lower-priced hotels for travelers, located in New England and Pennsylvania.

- International Hotels, two properties, one each in London and Paris.

Dunfey managed these diverse properties through a single management system known as the Dunfey Planning Process. A key figure in this process was the managing director, and ex-marketing employee. Under the Dunfey Planning Process, the directors of operations from each of the four groups annually submitted their proposed plans and broad strategy documents for the forthcoming year. These plans and strategies then were reviewed by the corporate planning committee, a group that included the chairman, managing director, senior controller, operations directors, and marketing director.

Rather than working in individual departmental teams, Dunfey combined the various departments into one team at the highest level. If the plans submitted by the groups were approved, the marketing director and the group of directors of operations then wrote mission statements for each group. Each mission statement set forth the desired market position for each hotel and defined the "ideal business mix," which, in turn, defined the desired customer base, room rate, and time of use. This mission statement, if approved by the planning committee, then was translated into a marketing plan for each hotel.

The role of the marketing department was to provide an interface between the central planning committee and the four hotel groups during the planning process. Marketing was charged first with providing input into the planning process at the top and then with managing the planning process as it was implemented by the individual groups. No direct advertising or selling was done by the Dunfey marketing department; each hotel was responsible for its own promotion and selling.

be made to the product to create a competitive advantage. The creation of such an advantage is not something that firms can expect to achieve in the short term.

Coordination of such highly differentiated functions usually requires the use of nonconventional integrating mechanisms. To mesh these different perspectives and to allow the two groups to understand each other, several strategies have been suggested by organizational behavior theory. Interfunctional taskforces provide a classic way of forcing disparate individuals to work together and to develop a better understanding of each other's perspective. In the same way, interfunctional transfers can create informal networks of individuals from different departments who understand and trust each other.

For example, operations managers promoted to run a marketing department will face certain initial problems. Their orientation is toward operations, but their new role requires a marketing perspective. If such a transfer can be successfully achieved, the result is usually a general manager who makes rational and clear trade-offs between operations and marketing. Moreover, it also creates a marketing person who has direct contacts in the operations group and can overcome many of the traditional barriers to change (see Services in Action 15.2).

Once the orientation of the organization has become one of general management with a strong consumer orientation, the marketing department can shrink. For example, in the early 1980s many professional service firms created marketing departments in this way. The departments focused on advertising but also on research and customer satisfaction surveys. The result was a shift in the culture of the firm and the reassertion of the primacy of the client.

Restructuring around the Model   Several service firms have explicitly or implicitly restructured around the servuction model. For example, one major airline has all departments that have direct customer contact report to the head of marketing. Only engineering and flight crew (pilots) report to the head of operations. Combining all customer-facing departments with the marketing group has reversed the argument from "it will cost too much; it is inefficient" to "the customer needs this; how can we make it happen?"

Changing Culture through Systems

Several different approaches have been used. Some firms, for example, have started to give bonuses to managers at all levels based on the firm's score in terms of customer satisfaction. Research can be tailored to measure satisfaction, if necessary, down to the branch level and managers can be rewarded for improved scores. Unfortunately, as Chapter 2 pointed out, only part of customer satisfaction is under the control of management. Expectations can be raised by competitive offerings, and the satisfaction score can drop as a consequence.

An alternative approach has been to introduce revenue into branch manager targets. A major New York bank wished to change the retail branch manager orientation from costs and security to customers. They introduced a revenue-based performance evaluation system. For the first time, managers had to worry about where the customers come from and to stop thinking of the customers as "people who made a mess of my branch." Early successes by a few managers produced interesting results. Up to 20 percent of managers left the company, claiming that this was not what they had been hired for. The balance woke up the moribund central marketing group to demand help with getting more customers. The long-run result of the change in systems was an increase in customer orientation and bad debt. The managers had discovered that money is an easy product to sell, and the bank had discovered it needed to revamp its credit control function.

Planning systems can also be used to change the orientation of companies. Formal marketing planning can drive organizations through the logic of marketing and force them to develop an understanding of consumers needs. Such planning exercises can become "mind-numbing bureaucratic exercises," but for the first two or three cycles, the process can become educational. This is all the more powerful if combined with training and/or direct attacks on the culture.

Changing Culture through People

Outsiders are increasingly being brought into the marketing department of service firms to try to change the orientation. What a package goods marketing person discovers in a service firm was described in Chapter 1. In essence, they discover the complexity of the marketing task, assuming they stay long enough.

Such an approach must be supplemented with development programs inside the firm. Cross-functional transfers and taskforces were discussed earlier in the context of structure. The result of such activities is, however, a cadre of persons who understand both marketing and operations. Operations people need to be trained in marketing, and marketing people need to understand all the areas described in this text.

Changing Culture Directly

Culture change programs are becoming increasingly popular, especially when combined with the other levers described here. The programs range from broad-scale educational activities to highly empowered process reengineering around the consumer. Figure 15.3 provides a simple way of categorizing such activities. Along one axis are the natures of groups used. Mixed groups are cross-sectional; family groups can be a

FIGURE 15.3	CATEGORIZING CULTURE CHANGE INITIATIVES

Group

		Mixed	Family
Empowerment	Low	"Putting the Customer First"	"Orientation Change"
	High	"Change the Way You Work"	"Change the Way We Work"

department or a natural-occurring group based on a process (e.g., all individuals involved with loading a particular flight with passengers). The second axis deals with the level of empowerment envisaged. Low levels of empowerment imply that individuals will change their behavior, but the group will have no authority to change the processes and systems of the organization. High-level empowerment implies the ability to change the organization during the event or series of events.

The slogans in the cells represent the hypothetical titles of such change programs, which often involve one or more meetings.

"Putting the Customer First" programs take place in mixed groups within the organization. Drawn together in sessions, they are lectured to and motivated to put the customer first. Through role playing, they are encouraged to recognize the importance of the customer and change their behavior accordingly.

These programs can be very successful, particularly when rolled through the organization quickly. This overcomes the "major problems on the return to work" syndrome. To be successful, the new behavior needs to be reinforced on the job. If managers and colleagues are not aligned, the value of the program can be wiped out within hours. New behaviors created in the sessions will be focused on by colleagues, and old habits will be quickly reinstated.

"Orientation Change" overcomes these problems by processing individuals in family groups that can reinforce each other on the job. Both cells, however, focus on changing attitudes and individual behaviors. Changing organizational processes and systems is not part of this type of initiative. This potentially produces role conflict as desired behaviors are stopped by the physical environment or the operating system.

"Change the Way You Work" draws on the empowerment ideas described in detail in Chapter 7. It implies active empowerment of persons attending the session. They are allowed to break the rules in the context of serving their customer. However, because of the mixed group, this type of initiative is focused on the individual rather the process level empowerment.

"Change the Way We Work" initiatives draw on many of the ideas in this book. Groups are in families and can be asked to flowchart their activities. They can then be asked to reengineer the process to better serve the customer. The level of excitement in such groups is matched only by the anxiety of their bosses. Empowerment at this level really does place the boss in the role of coach and enabler.

Summary

Many factors mean that focused strong marketing departments exist only in certain special types of service firms. Moreover, in certain phases of the competitive strategy of the firm, the role of marketing is a narrow one. The result is often a large and politically strong operations group that dominates the culture.

Marketing is needed because of strategy or competitive environment changes that result in a culture change. The marketing orientation must increase above everything else. Tools do exist to change culture, and marketing has an active role to play in that process.

Questions

1. Complete the culture instrument for a firm you are familiar with. What does it tell you? Do they need to change? Why?

2. On a recent flight on Scandinavian Airlines, a passenger asked for a *London Times*. He was informed that unfortunately all copies were gone, and he settled for a *Wall Street Journal* instead. A few moments later, the stewardess returned with a *Times* that was slightly crumpled. When queried, she answered that she had noticed the captain was carrying a *Times* when he came on board and that she had borrowed it for the passenger!
   a. Would such behavior be a competitive weapon in the U.S. airline business?
   b. What stops that behavior today?
   c. How would you develop an initiative in a U.S. airline to induce this kind of behavior?

3. How would you describe the role of the marketing departments in Holiday Inns; the U.S. Postal Service; Morgan Stanley?

4. What is it in the environment of the three companies in Question 3 that dictates the nature and role of their marketing departments?

Notes

[1]C. Gronroos, "Designing a Long Range Marketing Strategy for Services," *Long Range Planning* 13 (April 1980): 36; and C. Gronroos, "Innovative Marketing Strategies and Organizational Structures for Service Firms," in L. Berry, G. L. Shostack, and G. D. Upah, eds, *Emerging Perspectives in Services Marketing* (Chicago: American Marketing Association, 1985): 9–21.

[2]D. H. Maister and C. H. Lovelock, "Managing Facilitator Services," *Sloan Management Review* (Summer 1982): 19–31.

[3]R. B. Chase, "Where Does the Consumer Fit in a Service Operation?" *Harvard Business Review* 56, no. 6 (November–December 1978): 137–142.

[4]Ibid.

[5]W. Skinner, "The Focused Factory," *Harvard Business Review* 52, no. 3 (May–June 1974): 113–121.

[6]P. R. Lawrence and J. Lorsch, "Differentiation and Integration in Complex Organizations," *Administrative Science Quarterly* 12 (1967): 1–47.

[7]Ibid.

[8]E. Langeard, J. Bateson, C. Lovelock, and P. Eiglier, *Marketing of Services: New Insights from Consumers and Managers*, report 81-104 (Cambridge, MA: Marketing Science Institute, 1981).

[9]Gronroos, "Innovative Marketing Strategies," 16.

[10]Gronroos, "Designing a Long Range Marketing Strategy"; Gronroos, "Innovative Marketing Strategies."

[11]C. H. Lovelock, E. Langeard, J. E. G. Bateson, and P. Eigler, "Some Organizational Problems Facing Marketing in the Service Sector," in J. Donnelly and W. George, eds, *Marketing of Services* (Chicago: American Marketing Association, 1981), 148–153.

Developing Global Strategies for Service Businesses

CHRISTOPHER H. LOVELOCK
GEORGE S. YIP

How do the distinctive characteristics of service businesses affect globalization and the use of global strategy? This is a crucial question for managers in numerous industries. Not only are services continuing to grow rapidly in domestic economies, but international trade in services is increasing, too. The United States, like some other developed countries, has a trade surplus in services that helps offset the deficit in merchandise trade. In contrast, Japan has been much less successful in internationalizing its service businesses.[1] So it is essential to national competitiveness that governments, as well as companies, achieve a better understanding of how to develop effective global strategies for different types of service businesses.

Most research to date has focused either on why and how service firms internationalize or on different modes of internationalization.[2] In contrast, we examine how globalization drivers and the use of global strategy might apply to various types of services, and what differences might exist relative to manufacturing businesses. In doing so, we combine two different frameworks, one developed to analyze global strategy[3] and one for service businesses.[4]

Overview

A major theme in international business is the increasing use of global strategies. These involve the worldwide integration of strategy formulation and implementation, in contrast to a multidomestic (or multilocal) approach that provides for independent development and implementation of strategies by country or regional units.[5] One key theme is that globalization potential depends on industry characteristics,[6] and on specific industry globalization drivers—market, cost, government, and competitive.[7] A second key theme is that the use of global strategy should differ by dimension of strategy and for different elements of the value-adding chain.[8] The linkage between industry globalization drivers and global strategy—as well as the relationship of these drivers to organization structure and management processes and to consequent effects on performance—have been empirically tested for manufacturing businesses in major American and Japanese multinational

corporations (MNCs).[9] But research into global strategy for service businesses is still in an evolutionary stage.[10]

Defining Globalization

The terms "global" and "globalization" are often used rather loosely. Many writers use them interchangeably with words such as international (and internationalization), transnational,[11] and multinational. We believe that some clarification is in order. Strictly speaking, any service firm doing business across national frontiers can claim to be international. When passengers ride a scheduled bus line from Buffalo, New York, to Toronto, Ontario, they are using an international transportation service. A retail chain that operates in both the United Kingdom and Ireland can claim to be an international business. Moving up a notch, a bank with offices in several European countries could even claim to be multinational. None of these services, however, is global in scope. Nor, for that matter, is an insurance company doing business throughout Europe and North America.

In our view, a truly global company is one that not only does business in both the eastern and western hemispheres, but also in both the northern and southern ones. In the process, geographic distances and time zone variations are maximized. With the rise of non-Japan Asia, Latin America, and Eastern Europe, operating in just the "Triad" of North America, Western Europe and Japan is no longer sufficient. Other differences also tend to be sharpened, such as the variety of languages, currencies, cultures, legal and political systems, government policies and regulations, educational backgrounds of managers and employees, levels of national economic development, and climates. In this article, we will emphasize companies that meet our criterion of being truly global, although not all our examples will do so. Furthermore, we shall stress that simply operating globally does not mean that a company possesses a global strategy.

Defining Service Businesses

We will examine the ways in which global strategy for service businesses, given their distinctive characteristics, should be significantly different from manufacturing businesses. Furthermore, a fundamental premise underlying our analysis is that not all services are the same. So we will use three "lenses" with which to examine the global strategies of service-based businesses:

- A set of characteristics by which service-based businesses differ from goods-based businesses.

- A categorization of three fundamental types of service businesses.

- A set of eight supplementary services surrounding the core product or offering.

An Overall Global Strategy Framework for Service Businesses

Our overall global strategy framework is illustrated in Figure 1. In this framework, industry globalization drivers give rise to industry globalization potential, but this effect is filtered by the special characteristics of service businesses. In turn, industry globalization potential should result in four types of global strategy response: in terms of market participation, the service offering, the location and configuration of the value-adding chain, and in the nature of the marketing strategy. Here, the global strategy response is filtered by the three distinct types of service businesses. Lastly, supplementary services, which augment the core product like petals around the center of a flower, play a direct role in the make up of each aspect of global strategy.

Understanding the Nature of Services

"Services versus Goods" Distinctions

Early research into services sought to differentiate them from goods, focusing particularly on four generic differences—intangibility, heterogeneity (variability), perishability of output, and simultaneity of production and consumption.[12] Although these characteristics are still commonly cited, they. have been criticized as too generic[13] and there is growing recognition that they are not universally applicable to all services. A better sense of the processes underlying service delivery is provided in an alternative set of eight characteristics.[14] These characteristics begin with the nature of the output—a performance rather than an object—and also include customer involvement in production, people as part of the service experience, greater likelihood of quality control problems, harder for customers to evaluate, lack of inventories for services, greater impor-

tance of the time factor, and availability of electronic channels of distribution. Although these characteristics provide a useful starting point for thinking about the distinctive aspects of service management, not every service is equally affected by all of them.

Three Categories of Services

The previous list helps distinguish service-based businesses from goods-based ones. But service businesses also differ from each other, All products—both goods and services—consist of a core element that is surrounded by a variety of sometimes optional supplementary elements. Whether one is looking at service strategy locally or globally, it is unwise to talk in broad brush terms about the service sector or service industries as though all organizations faced more or less the same strategic problems. At the same time, it is also a mistake to fall into the trap of examining services only on an industry-by-industry basis. Probably the most useful and relevant classification concerns differences and commonalities in operational processes, since the way in which inputs are transformed into outputs has a significant effect on strategy.[15]

By looking at core services from an operational perspective, we can assign them to one of three broad categories, depending on the nature of the process (whether it is primarily tangible or intangible) and the extent to which customers need to be physically present during service production.

People-processing services involve tangible actions to customers in person. These services require that customers themselves become part of the production process, which tends to be simultaneous with consumption. In businesses such as passenger transportation, health care, food service, and lodging services, the customer needs to enter the "service factory" (although. we know it by such names as an airliner and air terminal, a hospital, a restaurant, or a hotel) and remain there during service delivery. Either customers must travel to the factory or service providers and equipment must come to the customer. In both instances, the firm needs to maintain a local geographic presence, stationing the necessary personnel, buildings, equipment, vehicles, and supplies within reach of target customers. If the customers are themselves mobile—as in the case of business travelers and tourists—then they may patronize a company's offerings in many different locations and make comparisons between them.

Possession-processing services involve tangible actions to physical objects to improve their value to customers. Examples include freight transport, warehousing, equipment installation and maintenance, car repair, laundry, and disposal. The object needs to be involved

FIGURE 1
Globalization Framework for Service Businesses

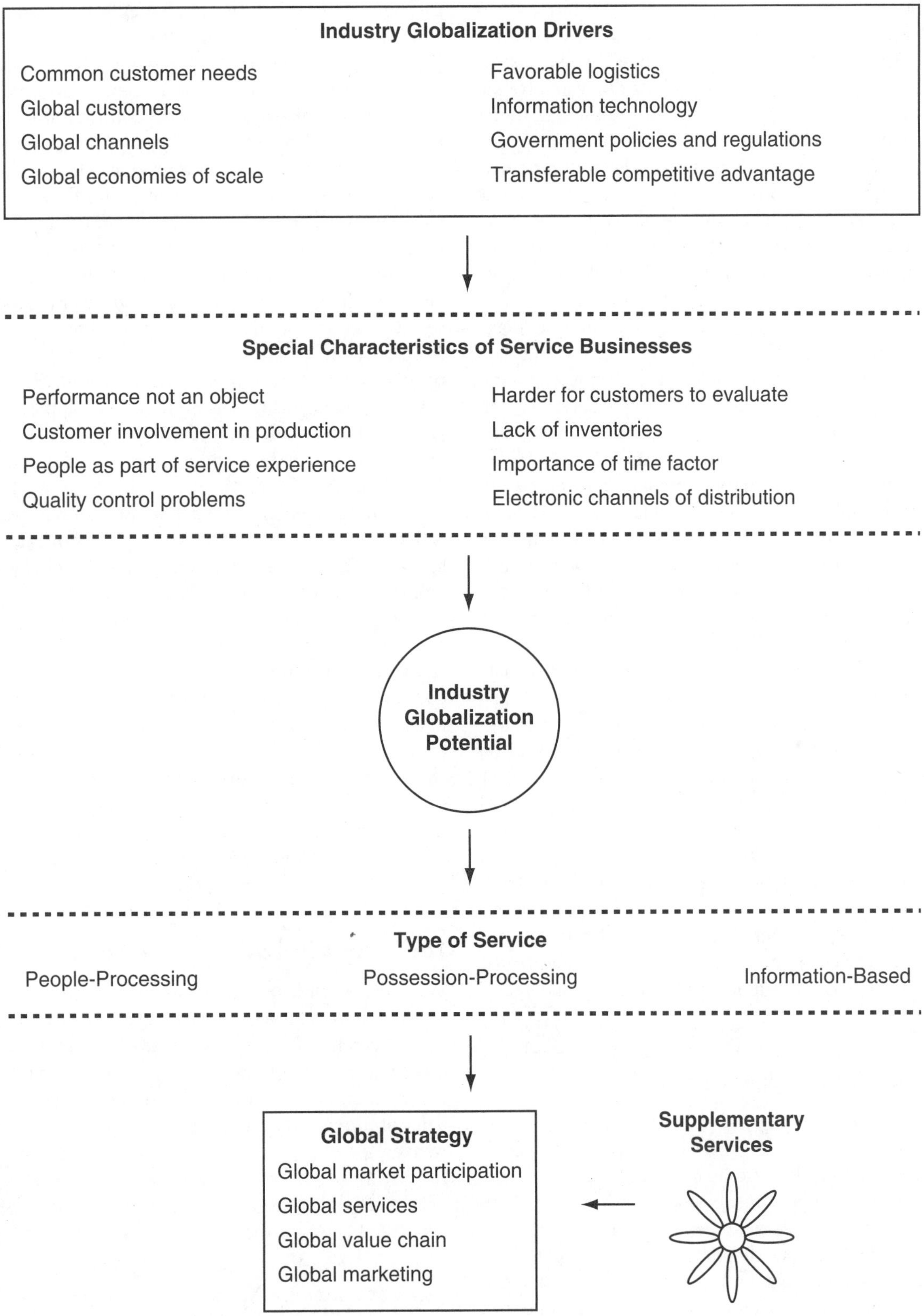

Industry Globalization Drivers

Common customer needs   Favorable logistics

Global customers   Information technology

Global channels   Government policies and regulations

Global economies of scale   Transferable competitive advantage

↓

Special Characteristics of Service Businesses

Performance not an object   Harder for customers to evaluate

Customer involvement in production   Lack of inventories

People as part of service experience   Importance of time factor

Quality control problems   Electronic channels of distribution

↓

Industry Globalization Potential

↓

Type of Service

People-Processing   Possession-Processing   Information-Based

↓

Global Strategy
Global market participation

Global services

Global value chain

Global marketing

Supplementary Services

←

in the production process, but the customer does not, since consumption of the output tends to follow production. Again, the service "factory" may be fixed or mobile. A local geographic presence is required when the supplier needs to provide service to physical objects in a specific location on a repeated basis. In the case of smaller, transportable items, the vendor can provide remote service centers for servicing—although transportation costs, customs duties, and government regulations may constrain shipment across large distances or national frontiers. Modern technology now allows a few service processes to be administered from a distance, using electronic diagnostics to pinpoint the problem.

Information-based services are, perhaps, the most interesting category from the standpoint of global strategy development because they depend on collecting, manipulating, interpreting, and transmitting data to create value. Examples include accounting, banking, consulting, education, insurance, legal services, and news. Customer involvement in production of such services is often minimal. The advent of modern global telecommunications, linking intelligent machines to powerful databases, makes it possible to use electronic channels to deliver information-based services from a single "hub" to almost any location. Local presence requirements may be limited to a terminal—ranging from a telephone or fax machine to a computer or more specialized equipment like a bank ATM—connected to a reliable telecommunications infrastructure. If the latter is inadequate, then use of mobile or satellite communications may solve the problem in some instances.

Service production and delivery systems can be divided into "back office" and "front office," the latter being the portion of the "service factory" encountered by customers.[16] People-processing services necessarily involve a high degree of contact with service personnel and facilities; possession-processing and information-based services, by contrast, have the potential to be much lower contact in nature. Retail banking, for instance, can take place either through traditional branch banks or through such channels as mail, telephone, and Internet.

The Role of Supplementary Services

The core service product—a bed for the night, restoring a defective computer to good working order, or a bank account—is typically accompanied by a variety of supplementary elements. Most businesses, whether they are classified in government statistics as manufacturing or service, offer their customers a package that includes a variety of service-related activities, too. Increasingly, these supplementary elements not only add value, but also provide the differentiation that separates successful firms from the also-rans; they also offer opportunities

for firms to develop effective globalization strategies. Writers and managers alike often use the terms "augmented product,"[17] "extended product," or "product package" to describe the supplementary elements that add value to the core product.[18]

There are potentially dozens of different supplementary services, although they can be grouped into eight categories (information, consultation, order-taking, hospitality, caretaking, exceptions, billing, and payment) encircling the core product like a corona of petals: collectively, they comprise "the flower of service" (Figure 2 and Table 1).[19] Many of these petals are based on informational processes that can be located in one part of the world and delivered electronically to another. Not every core product—whether a good or a service—is surrounded by supplementary elements from all eight clusters. In practice, the nature of the product, customer requirements, and competitive practices help managers to determine which supplementary service must be offered and which might usefully be added to enhance value and make it easy to do business with the organization.

One determinant of what supplementary services to include is the market positioning strategy that management has selected. A strategy of adding benefits to gain a competitive edge will probably require more supplementary services (and also a higher level of performance on all such elements). In developing a global strategy, management must decide which, if any, supplementary elements should be consistent across all markets and which might be tailored to meet local needs, expectations, and competitive dynamics. This is the essence of standardization and customization, but services offer much more flexibility in this respect than do physical goods, lending themselves in many contexts to what is known as "mass customization."[20]

Industry Globalization Drivers

What drives globalization of service businesses? Many types of drivers have been suggested for the analysis of manufacturing firms.[21] We identify here the eight most relevant ones (listed in Figure 1) for service businesses, then systematically evaluate how the characteristics of different types of services might strengthen or weaken the effects of these drivers. We will also examine how these effects differ among the three categories of service business—people-processing, possession-processing, and information-based services.

Common Customer Needs

Industries with customer needs and tastes that are common across countries offer more potential for globaliza-

FIGURE 2
The Manufacturing Strategy Paradigm Applied to Service

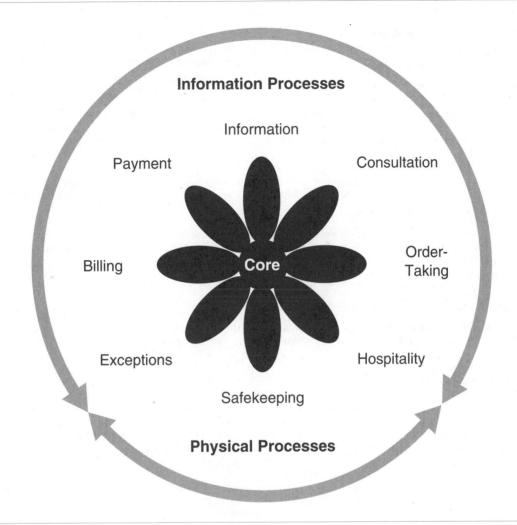

tion. Product categories such as consumer electronic devices, cigarettes, soft drinks, and computer hardware provide many instances of successful global standardization. (The simultaneous presence of successful local strategies in these categories in no way undermines the global opportunity for multinational companies. Similarly, less than total standardization, as in Coca-Cola's local adaptation of its syrup, does not void the benefits of pursuing global standardization as much possible in the appropriate industries and categories.) The service characteristic of "customer involvement in production" reduces the degree to which many services can be standardized and still meet the needs of a broad cross section of customers around the world. In general, the less the involvement, whether physical or psychological, the better the opportunity for a global approach. So we are more likely to see global standardization in fast food and airlines, where customer involvement is tightly controlled, than in medical care or education, where customer involvement is both stronger and more prolonged. Note that our observations apply to the broad "middle market" rather than to the relatively small market segment composed of affluent, highly educated, cosmopolitan customers.

The service characteristic of "people as part of the service experience" also limits the potential commonality of customer needs and tastes. Differences can arise even within the same industry. In banking, the service provided by human tellers is far less standardized and standardizable than that provided by automated teller machines. Accounting services depend heavily on people. The higher status of accountants in Britain than in the United States means that British accountants provide more general business advice than do their American counterparts. And U.S.-style

TABLE 1

Eight Categories of Supplementary Services

Information

To obtain full value from any good or service, customers need relevant information about it, ranging from schedules to operating instructions, and from user warnings to prices. Globalization affects the nature of that information (including the languages and format in which it is provided). New customers and prospects are especially information hungry and may need training in how to use an unfamiliar service.

Consultation and Advice

Consultation and advice involve a dialogue to probe customer requirements and then develop a tailored solution. Customers' need for advice may vary widely around the world, reflecting such factors as level of economic development, nature of the local infrastructure, topography and climate, technical standards, and educational levels.

Order-Taking

Once customers are ready to buy, suppliers need to make it easy for them to place orders or reservations in the language of their choice, through telecommunications and other channels, at times and in locations that are convenient to them.

Hospitality: Taking Care of the Customer

Well-managed businesses try, at least in small ways, to treat customers as guests when they have to visit the supplier's facilities (especially when, as is true for many people-processing operations, the period extends over several hours or more). Cultural definitions of appropriate hospitality may differ widely from one country to another, such as the tolerable length of waiting time (much longer in Brazil than in Germany) and the degree of personal service expected (not much in Scandinavia but lavish in Indonesia).

Safekeeping: Looking After the Customer's Possessions

When visiting a service site, customers often want assistance with their personal possessions, ranging from car parking to packaging and delivery of new purchases. Expectations may vary by country, reflecting culture and levels of affluence.

Exceptions

Exceptions fall outside the routine of normal service delivery. They include special requests, problem solving, handling of complaints/suggestions/compliments, and restitution (compensating customers for performance failures). Special requests are particularly common in people-processing services, as in the travel and lodging industries and may be complicated by differing cultural norms. International airlines, for example, find it necessary to respond to an array of medical and dietary needs, sometimes reflecting religious and cultural values. Problem solving is often more difficult for people who are traveling overseas than it would be in the familiar environment of their native country.

Billing

Customers need clear, timely bills that explain how charges are computed. With abolition of currency exchange restrictions in many countries, bills can be converted to the customer's home currency. Hence, currencies and conversion rates need to be clarified on billing statements. In some instances. prices may be displayed in several currencies even though this policy may require frequent adjustments in the light of currency fluctuations.

Payment

Ease and convenience of payment (including credit) are increasingly expected by customers when purchasing a broad array of services. Major credit cards and travelers' checks solve the problem of paying in foreign funds for many retail purchases, but corporate purchasers may prefer to use electronic fund transfers in the currency of their choice.

---

psychotherapy is unlikely to yield a global "McShrink" franchise.

One of the greatest dilemmas in global strategy for manufacturing businesses is the need to balance global standardization with local customization. Designing, then manufacturing, a global product with a degree of local customization requires major trade-offs. In contrast, the nature of service delivery—at the point of consumption in many cases—makes both standardization and customization equally feasible. Local elements (e.g., Balinese dancing in Indonesia) can be easily added to a global formula (Club Med vacations); using local nationals as service providers may overcome the foreignness of a standardized service (e.g., use of local cabin crews by international airlines). The practice of augmenting a core service with many supplementary elements makes it relatively easy to provide a globally standardized core service augmented (and differentiated) by nationally customized supplementary service elements. This tends to be easier than for manufacturing businesses.[22]

Global Customers

As large corporate customers become global, they often seek to standardize and simplify the array of services they consume. For instance, firms may seek to minimize the number of auditors they use around the world, using "Big Six" accounting firms that can apply a consistent worldwide approach (within the context of national rules within each country of operation). Global management of telecommunications is provided by the "Concert" service offered by British Telecom and its American partner MCI, allowing a multinational company to outsource all responsibility for management of its purchase and use of telecommunications. Corporate banking, insurance, business logistics, and management consulting are further examples. Individuals act as global customers when they purchase goods and services on their travels. The service characteristics of "a performance rather than an object" and "greater importance of the time factor" create special opportunities for travel-related services, a very large and growing segment that starts with transportation but extends to credit, communication, and emergency support.

Global customers for possession-processing services prefer common procedures and standards. For example, airlines absolutely depend on their aircraft being maintained in the same way everywhere—and, increasingly, so do customers of factory and machinery maintenance services. Global customers for people-processing services may care particularly about ubiquity, especially when traveling. The New Zealander who breaks her leg in Pamplona needs medical treatment on the spot. Global customers for information-based services may have a more diffuse set of needs, but these certainly include comprehensiveness, accuracy, and accessibility. The American executive who has lost his traveler's checks in Shanghai needs reimbursement there, now, not back home in Indiana, later.

Global Channels

Distributors of physical goods have globalized relatively slowly. Few distributors in any category have adequate worldwide coverage. National giants like Wal-Mart and Toys R Us from the United States, Carrefour and IKEA from Europe, and Watson's and Dairy Farm from Asia, are beginning to establish regional networks, but all are far from being able to distribute worldwide. In contrast, the "availability of electronic channels of distribution" for services provides nearly total global coverage for more and more service offerings—notably travel services, banking. customer support services, entertainment, and most forms of information products themselves. Furthermore, these electronic global channels support not just information-based services but augment people-processing (e.g., health care) and possession-processing (e.g., delivery of time-sensitive materials) services. The latest electronic channel, the World Wide Web, now offers global outreach to even the smallest of companies. The Web can help sell any type of core product through information-based supplementary services and can actually deliver many information-based services directly to customers.

Global Economies of Scale

Global scale economics apply when single-country markets are not large enough to allow competitors to achieve optimum scale. Scale can then be increased through participation in multiple markets, combined with product standardization and/or concentration of selected value activities. But "lack of inventories," "customer involvement in production," and "people as part of the service experience" all work against being able to concentrate production to achieve scale. So service companies typically have to find global scale economies by standardizing production processes rather than through physical concentration, as well as by concentrating the upstream, rather than the downstream, stages of the value chain.

The effect of cost globalization drivers, like global scale economies, varies sharply according to the level of fixed costs required to enter an industry (although equipment leasing schemes, or awarding franchises to local investors, provide a way to minimize such entry barriers). So cost globalization drivers may be less favorable for services that are primarily people-based and face lesser scale economies and flatter experience curves. One common solution for the would-be global company is to do as McDonald's does—substitute equipment for labor in order to achieve lower costs and better performance than local companies using traditional business systems.

Favorable Logistics

Low transportation costs allow concentration of production for physical goods. For services, "customer involvement in production" raises the logistical stakes in globalization. In most people-processing services, the need for convenience prevents concentration. But in some possession-processing services, customers are willing to transport their possessions to another location for better service. Thus, many airlines bring their aircraft to Singapore. Some people-processing services have achieved similar success in having customers come to them. London hospitals maintain a flourishing business among wealthy Middle Eastern patients, as do Miami hospitals for patients from Latin America.

Companies have to balance the tradeoffs between logistics and appeal. Disney favored logistics over appeal in selecting northern France rather than southern Spain for the location of Euro Disney. More people can get more easily to the Euro Disney site outside Paris, but once there they often face cold weather and colder service. Service businesses can also create their own favorable logistics. Club Med organizes charter flights from urban centers to its off-the-beaten-path locations. British Airways and Air France provide limousine ground transport to and from their Concorde flights.

Lastly, logistics is seldom a barrier to globalization for information-based services. Using electronic channels to deliver such services allows providers to concentrate production in locations that have specific expertise and to offer cost savings or other meaningful advantages. For instance, banks in the Cayman Islands are not conveniently located from a purely geographic standpoint, but money can be shipped there electronically to take advantage of the tax benefits conferred by offshore funds status.

Information Technology

For information-based services, the growing availability of broad-band telecommunication channels, capable of moving vast amounts of data at great speed, is playing a major role in opening up new markets. Access to the Internet or World Wide Web is accelerating around the world. But there may be no need to duplicate all informational elements in each new location. Significant economics may be gained by centralizing "information hubs" on a global basis, as Federal Express does in Memphis. For all three types of services, the use of information technology may allow companies to benefit from favorable labor costs or exchange rates by consolidating operations of supplementary services (such as reservations) or back office functions (such as accounting) in just one or a few countries. While a globalization driver in its own right, information technology also interacts with all of the other drivers.

Government Policies and Regulations

Host governments affect globalization potential through import tariffs and quotas, non-tariff barriers, export subsidies, local content requirements, currency and capital flow restrictions, technical and other standards, ownership restrictions and requirements on technology transfer. Governments' exercise of these policies and regulations can make it difficult for com-

panies to globalize. For services, "customer involvement in production" may mitigate many government barriers to global strategy. Government drivers are often favorable for people-processing and possession-processing services that require a significant local presence, since they create local employment opportunities. On the other hand, governments often impose regulations to protect home carriers in the case of mobile services, such as passenger and freight transportation. For instance, restricting foreign airlines' landing rights or ability to pick up passengers at an intermediate stop ("third freedom" rights) provides a way to protect home-based airlines on international routes.

Nations may perceive both an economic and a cultural threat in unrestricted imports of information-based services through electronic channels. Government regulations range from controls on international banking to bans on private ownership of satellite dishes (as in countries such as China, Singapore, and Saudi Arabia). Some nations are now trying to manage citizen access to the Worldwide Web.

For people-processing services, government barriers to global strategy include country differences in social policies (e.g., health) affecting labor costs, the role of women in front line jobs, and the hours or days on which work can be performed. For possession-processing services, tax laws, environmental regulations, and technical standards may decrease/increase costs and encourage/discourage certain types of activity. For information-based services, special policies on education, censorship, public ownership of communications, and infrastructure quality may apply; technical standards may vary; and government policies may distort pricing.

Transferable Competitive Advantage

The single most important competitive globalization driver arises from transferability of competitive advantage. If one industry participant can leverage its competitive position in one country to build an advantage in other countries, all its competitors need to develop a global strategy too.[23] For services, "customer involvement in production," and "lack of inventories" limit the leverage of competitive advantage based on foreign factors of production such as labor productivity (e.g., no "Toyota" exports), although advantage in management systems can be a basis for globalization (e.g., Hilton). So Hong Kong hotel chains, such as Mandarin, Peninsula and Regent, that have set world class standards for service, find such excellence far harder to reproduce as they expand overseas. Similarly, Disney has suffered from not being able to transfer to Paris Disneyland the highly motivated and pliant staff of its U.S. parks.

Overall Assessment of Drivers

As we look at the three categories of services identified earlier, it seems that most industry globalization drivers do apply to services, but their impact varies by service type and even by industry. For example, government drivers (expressed in terms of economic policy, regulation, and protectionism) are often industry specific (as evidenced by the recent Uruguay Round of negotiations on GATT and bilateral British-American negotiations on commercial air travel). This conclusion highlights the importance of conducting a systematic evaluation of globalization drivers for individual industries, rather than taking generalized views that service businesses can be more (or less) easily globalized than can manufacturing businesses.

Service Effects in Global Strategy

To complete our analysis, we now present a more detailed view of how each dimension of global strategy might differ for service businesses. We use four dimensions ("global strategy levers") that determine whether international strategy is more multilocal or more global.[24] The global end of each dimension consists of the following:

- *Global Market Participation*—countries are selected not just on the basis of stand-alone attractiveness, but also in terms of their potential contribution to globalization benefits.

- *Global Products and Services*—a standardized core product or service that requires a minimum of local adaptation.

- *Global Location of Value-Adding Activities*—the value chain is broken up; each activity may be conducted in a different country rather than many activities being duplicated around the world.

- *Global Marketing*—a uniform marketing approach is applied around the world, although not all elements of the marketing mix need be identical.

Services and Global Market Participation

A global strategy approach to market participation involves building significant share in globally strategic markets. Such countries are important beyond their stand-alone attractiveness and may be a source of volume to meet economies of scale, the home or significant market of global customers or global competitors, or a major source of industry innovation. Failure to participate in strategic markets can undermine global competitiveness. Many American and European manufacturing companies have suffered from not building significant positions in Japan, thereby limiting their potential economies of scale in manufacturing, lacking exposure to the innovation and high customer standards in Japan, and being unable to create a hostage for good behavior on the part of Japanese rivals.

A few Western service companies have built successful businesses in Japan, either because their western orientation (such as American-style fast food) appealed to Japanese consumers or because they were creating an international network that could not afford to be absent from such a major market. For network firms, such as airlines, financial services, and logistics firms, highly specific geographic locations may be seen as essential. No financial service firm with global ambitions, for instance, can afford not to have a presence in New York, London, and Tokyo. With the exception of such network organizations, it is hard to see how presence or absence in Japan (or any other individual country) significantly affects a service firm's global strategic position, other than contributing revenues and profits.

Travel-related services pose an exception. Inherently, wider global market participation makes a brand of service more valuable to a customer. Thus, American Express traveler's checks and credit cards are useful precisely because they are widely accepted in most countries. Similarly, international airlines enhance their appeal as they fly to more destinations.

Designing and Delivering Globally Standardized Services

Globally standardized products or "global products" are, perhaps, the one feature most commonly identified with global strategy. As mentioned earlier, the fact that services comprise a bundle of core and supplementary services makes them particularly easy to both globalize and localize. In perhaps the most extreme example, McDonald's now plans to open restaurants in India that, in deference to Hindu reverence for cows, will not serve hamburgers at all. Were McDonald's a goods-based business, that would be equivalent to selling a car without an engine. But as a service-based business, the other core and supplementary elements can make up for the lack of beef. McDonald's also adds items, such as Veggie Burgers, to menus to meet local tastes. In Britain, McDonald's includes both tea and coffee in its menus, while in France and Germany it also serves beer. Interestingly, these local variations are in the food itself, the product element, rather than in the service elements.

Hewlett-Packard is a global leader in computer-based customer support services for its customers. It maintains a globally standardized set of services that range from site design to systems integration and remote diagnostics. This global standardization includes seamless service at any hour of the day or night from anywhere in the world.

Professional service firms vary in their ability to provide a globally standardized service. Some firms, such as those in the accounting industry, face significant international differences in technical standards, making uniformity more difficult. But it is also a matter of strategy. Arthur Andersen has chosen to lead in offering globally standardized services. Its competitors now have to play catch-up. Similarly, advertising agencies face international differences in culture and consumer behavior, but some have chosen to overcome these differences.

Global Location of Value-Adding Service Activities

Where to locate a business's activities and how to coordinate them constitute critical choices in global strategy. Every functional or value-adding activity—from research to manufacturing to customer service—is a candidate for globalization.[25] Traditionally, multinational companies (MNCs) have faced two choices in activity location. The classic MNC strategy has been to reproduce activities in many countries. Alternatively, an MNC can concentrate activities in its home country.

The trend in global strategy is to concentrate each activity as much as possible, although not necessarily all activities in the same country.[26] As discussed earlier, many service businesses need local presence for their downstream activities. But at the same time, they can take advantage of differences in national comparative advantage to build more efficient and effective value chains. Some service-based businesses conduct key activities that can be conducted in a different country from their customers. For example, some U.S. banks and insurance companies now send checks and claims to be processed in East Asia or in Ireland. McKinsey & Company, the management consulting firm, now sends some of its work for clients from high-cost countries to its offices in low-cost countries like India.

To provide its global customer support service, Hewlett-Packard maintains a global chain of activity locations—its more than 30 Response Centers around the world are integrated into a global network headed by four major centers: Bracknell (United Kingdom), Atlanta (Georgia) and Mountain View (California) in the United States, and Melbourne (Australia). Each center is staffed during extended daytime hours, seven days a week, by between 12 and 200 engineers. Problems that cannot be resolved in a smaller center may be transferred to one of the major centers. Because of time-zone differentials, at least one of the major centers is always in full operation at any time.

Citibank, one of the world's largest banks, has positioned itself as a "uniquely global consumer bank."[27] The company's objective is to allow its customers to do their banking "any way, any where, any time." To provide this service it has expanded its Citicard Banking Centers with their automated teller machines to 28 countries. These centers are globally linked, allowing 24 hour, seven days a week access. And, of course, non-cash transactions can be conducted by phone.

Global Marketing of Services

A worldwide business uses global marketing when it takes the same or similar approach or content for one or more elements of the marketing mix, i.e., the same or similar brand names, advertising, and other marketing elements in different countries. The uncertainty engendered by intangibility requires strong branding to offset it. So the primary task of the brand name or trademark for a service is to offer recognition and reassurance, rather than performing other functions such as positioning or local adaptation. McDonald's, for instance, has to be the same name around the world, so that both locals and travelers know that they will get the genuine McDonald's experience. (We doubt, however, that the Spago and Planet Saigon restaurants in Ho Chi Minh City will provide the same experiences as the Hollywood originals after which they are named.) Travel-related services virtually require the same brand name globally. What use would an American Express card be if the brand were Russian Express in Moscow? One solution is to be both global and local. Federal Express combines global and local brand names. In France the company uses partly localized names like FedEx Priorité, FedEx Rapide, and FedEx Fret.

Global positioning is also important. McDonald's has a globally consistent positioning and image, but this is not a globally neutral image. It is clearly American, so it stands for "us" in the United States, and "them" elsewhere. Similarly, Chili's, a U.S.-based restaurant chain offering Mexican food, has its largest store in Monterrey, Mexico. But customers there go for an "American experience," not a Mexican one. In contrast, Benetton, both a goods-based (clothes) and a service-based (stores) company, strives for a universalistic, non-national image.

Global advertising works equally for goods-based and service-based businesses. Whether to use it depends on such industry globalization drivers as common customer needs and the salience of global customers or global channels. Travel-related services can obviously benefit from global advertising, although the communications task may vary by country. A solution is the dual campaign, one for global themes and one for local messages. For many years, British Airways has used a succession of dramatic global advertising campaigns to establish its position as "The World's Favourite Airline" (backed up by significant improvements in service quality since privatization). At the same time, British Airways provides a smaller budget for local campaigns that focus on schedules, prices, and promotion of special tour packages. Singapore Airlines has achieved significant advertising impact with its temporally and globally consistent theme of the "Singapore Girl," a highly successful way of personalizing and differentiating a commodity service.

While most services are not physically packaged, staff uniforms and the layout and decor of facilities can be considered part of the package. Global consistency can bring significant benefits. Singapore Airlines has maintained the same uniform for its stewardesses for over 25 years. The "sarong kebaya," designed by Paris couturier, Pierre Balmain, makes the Singapore Airlines stewardess globally recognizable, unlike those of most other airlines. And like McDonald's, Citibank designs its new retail branches to look and operate in the same way around the world.

In contrast, "lack of inventories" in many service businesses means that such firms need worry less about using global pricing, Manufacturing businesses increasingly need to charge globally uniform prices to provide consistency with global customers and distribution channels, and to avoid "gray market" parallel importation or "trans-shipment." It is relatively difficult to buy a service in one country and to re-sell it in another.

McDonald's prices certainly vary, so much so that *The Economist* magazine uses a "McDonald's Big Mac Price Index" to compare the cost of living in major business cities around the world. In the case of multinational customers as opposed to individuals, however, even service businesses need to avoid charging different prices in different countries to the same customer without good justification. Increasingly, multinational companies are beginning to behave as global rather than multilocal customers. Hewlett-Packard, for example, now provides worldwide contracts to its major global accounts for both products and services.

Implications for Types of Service Businesses

While there are always exceptions, some overall conclusions can be made about the three types of service business and how easily they can use each of the four dimensions of global strategy.

Global Market Participation Some types of service business seem very easy to spread around the world,

and others very difficult. In the easy category fall simple service concepts that are easily replicable (and therefore franchisable). All three types of services have such simple examples (e.g., fast food in the people-processing category, package delivery in the possession-processing category, and English-language news in the information-based category). In contrast, some "essential" services—such as banking, telecommunications, hospitals, and airlines—operate in heavily regulated environments, making it difficult to get rapid penetration of foreign markets.

Historically, businesses that rely on trust and the reputation of their personnel—such as law firms and other professional service providers—have found it difficult to demonstrate quality to potential foreign customers and to adopt a professional style that fits the local culture. Ways to overcome such hurdles include extensive advertising and public relations as well as hiring host country nationals who have obtained education and work experience in other countries.

Globally Standardized Service Possession-processing businesses can probably provide the most globally standardized offerings. These services need not cope with cultural and taste differences, only with those technical specifications that vary geographically, such as differences in electrical voltages or measurement systems. For people-processing services some deviation from standardization is almost always needed. For information-based services, such deviation will vary widely, from none at all (e.g., information on international flight schedules) to near total (e.g., local weather forecasts or tax advice).

Global Location of Value Chain By their "virtual" nature, most information-based services should find it the easiest to locate globally. In many cases, such as pure information services, no local physical presence may be needed at all. In other cases, information services that also have a physical component (e.g., the provision of currency or traveler's checks) or require specialized delivery equipment (e.g., pay-per-view entertainment) will need some local physical presence, provided by the company itself or by local partners, The ease of global value chain location for people-processing and possession-processing services will depend on the extent of local presence needed. In general, more local sites will be needed for people-processing, making that type of service probably the most difficult to operate globally.

Globally Uniform Marketing All three types of services should be able to make use of globally uniform marketing, although the extent will differ for each element of the marketing mix. Uniform pricing will be least possible for people-processing services, given the wide international variations in both costs and per capita income. Conversely, people-processing services probably have the most to gain from uniform branding as a way to build recognition with both local and foreign (visiting) customers. Possession-processing services often attract multinational customers (e.g., aircraft maintenance and package delivery), making it necessary to coordinate global marketing strategy and offer uniform terms of service.

Discussion: Implications for Theory and Practice

What are the implications of our framework for both theory building and management practice? A key point is that making broad generalizations about "services" cannot be expected to provide useful insights into opportunities for globalization. Instead, researchers and managers alike have to understand the components of a service and the processes by which its different elements are created and delivered. First, they need to distinguish between the core product (which may be either a service or a physical object) and supplementary service elements. Second, they must recognize that there are three broad categories of core product, reflecting differences in the underlying processes, degree of customer involvement, and potential for delivery through electronic channels. Third, the Flower of Service model offers both researchers and practitioners a means of understanding and disaggregating the package of "supplementary services" that augments and adds value to the core product.

Locating the Service Facility

In the future, we shall see a greater distinction between services that require an on-site "factory" in each country and those that require only a delivery system. By definition, all people-processing services that do not require customers to travel outside their home country for service delivery will require on-site operations in each country. The same will be true of any possession-processing service that cannot readily transport the object in question to another location for servicing. In these instances, managers may find that the best way to achieve global consistency in the core product is to create easily replicable service concepts, backed by clear standards, that allow for either franchises or country managers to clone the original core product in a new setting.

Information-based services offer management greater flexibility to split the back office and front office, with opportunities to centralize the former on a global or regional basis. Production can thus take place in one location (or just a few), yielding economies of scale and access to global expertise, while delivery remains local. Banking, insurance, and other financial service products lend themselves well to delivery through electronic channels. Many forms of news, information, and entertainment can also be delivered worldwide through public or private networks. Key issues in globalization include the constraints imposed by language, culture, and government regulations.

Customizing Global Services through Supplementary Service Elements

Increasingly, core service products that are sold globally are more likely to be standardized than customized (McDonald's Veggie Burgers should be seen as an exception rather than a trend). Managers should, however, be looking for supplementary service elements that can be customized in ways that tailor the overall service package to meet local requirements. Each of the eight petals in the Flower of Service lends itself to adaptation on three dimensions: the level of service provided can be adapted to reflect local preferences and ability to pay; the style of delivery can be adapted to cultural norms; and information transfers can be adapted to local idioms and offered in local languages.

Global Location of Value Chain

Different service elements can be sourced from different locations. The physical supplies needed for certain types of service delivery (such as food for hotels, fuel for transport vehicles, or spare parts for repair jobs) are often shipped from one country for consumption in another. The same is sometimes true for imported labor. But some companies, like McDonald's, are choosing to build up a network of local suppliers and to train host country nationals for local jobs as quickly as possible.[28]

As noted earlier, information-based services can be produced in one part of the world and delivered through electronic channels for consumption elsewhere. Indeed, information technology is emerging as a key globalization driver for such services. In mutual funds, for instance, offerings are now being pieced together from elements created in many different countries. Unlike physical goods, the logistics of service "assembly" and delivery tend to be much simpler once the necessary infrastructure and network are in place. Further, as shown in Table 1 earlier, a majority of the petals of the Flower of Service are information-dependent and can potentially be delivered from remote locations. In theory, a global company could centralize its billing on a global basis, using postal or telecommunication distribution channels to deliver the bills to customers, suitably converted to the relevant currency.

Similarly, information, consultation, order-taking/reservations, and many aspects of problem solving and payment could all be handled through telecommunications channels, ranging from voice telephone to the World Wide Web. So long as service personnel speaking the appropriate languages are available, many such service elements could be delivered from almost anywhere. Recent patterns of immigration in a country may create a comparative advantage in multilingual capabilities. By contrast, hospitality and safekeeping will always have to be provided locally because they are responsive to the physical presence of customers and their possessions.

Like manufacturers, service firms should be looking for opportunities to exploit differences in national comparative advantages as they seek to build more efficient value chains. Significant economies may be gained by centralizing "information hubs" on a global basis, as Federal Express does in Memphis. Through outsourcing, firms can also reduce the need for large fixed cost investments. Taking advantage of favorable labor costs and exchange rates, a growing number of service-based businesses have identified key back-office activities that can be conducted more cheaply but without loss of quality in a different country from where their customers are located. This is happening with front-office elements, too, as companies build global reservation and customer service systems that are networked around the world.

Global Marketing of Services

Difficulties in evaluating services lead to uncertainty, but this problem can be offset by strong branding and a globally consistent use of corporate design elements. Hence, the primary task of the brand name or trademark for a service may be to offer recognition and reassurance, rather than performing other functions such as positioning or local adaptation. Global branding should be supported by global advertising and globally-consistent corporate design, featuring recognizable color schemes (yellow for Hertz, bright green for BP service stations), an easily identified logo and trademark, and even consistency in retail office design. One of the challenges when creating global campaigns is to create visual themes that will travel well across different cultures (it is relatively simple to add voice-overs in the local language). This requirement may pose a need to retain a global advertising agency.

In contrast, simultaneity of production and consumption in many service businesses means that firms have less need to worry about globally consistent pricing. Except for those information-based services that can be captured in printed or electronic hard copies, it is still relatively difficult to buy a service created in one country for resale in another. On the other hand, there are sometimes wide disparities between prices for international telephone calls, depending on the country in which it originates. For instance, a call from Rome to New York is far more expensive than from New York to Rome. (This anomaly has been exploited by companies such as AT&T, which offers customers traveling abroad the opportunity to dial a local number to place the call and charge it at American rates to the customer's home account.) In the case of multinational customers, service businesses need to consider the use of global account management as a means of achieving coordination and consistency.[29]

Conclusion

More and more service businesses are now operating across national borders. Globalization and global strategy concepts developed for manufacturing businesses can also be applied to service businesses. Some significant differences may exist, particularly among people-processing, possession-processing, and information-based services. Companies can develop effective global strategies by systematically analyzing the specific globalization drivers affecting their industries and the distinctive characteristics of their service businesses.

Notes

1. Johny K. Johansson, "Japanese Service Industries and Their Overseas Potential," *The Service Industries Journal*, 10/1 (January 1990): 85–109.
2. See John H. Dunning, "Transnational Corporations and the Growth of Services: Some Conceptual and Theoretical Issues," *United Nations Centre on Transnational Corporations*, Series A, No. 9 (March 1989); Hervé Mathe and Cynthia Perras, "Successful Global Strategies for Service Companies," *Long Range Planning*, 7/1 (1994), 36–49; Sandra Vandermerwe and Michael Chadwick, "The Internationalization of Services," *The Services Industry Journal* (January 1989), pp. 79–93.
3. George S. Yip, *Total Global Strategy; Managing for Worldwide Competitive Advantage* (Englewood Cliffs, NJ: Prentice Hall, 1992).
4. Christopher H. Lovelock, *Services Marketing* (Englewood Cliffs, NJ: Prentice Hall, 1991); Christopher H. Lovelock, *Product Plus: How Product + Service = Competitive Advantage* (New York, NY: McGraw-Hill, 1994).
5. See Thomas Hout, Michael E. Porter, and Eileen Rudden, "How Global Companies Win Out," *Harvard*

Business Review (September/October 1982), pp. 98–108; C. K. Prahalad and Yves L. Doz, *The Multinational Mission: Balancing Local Demands and Global Vision* (New York, NY: Free Press, 1987); George S. Yip, "Global Strategy . . . In a World of Nations?" *Sloan Management Review*, 31/1 (Fall 1989): 29–41.

6. Michael E. Porter, "Changing Patterns of International Competition," *California Management Review*, 28/2 (Winter 1996): 9–40.

7. Yip (1989), op. cit.; Yip (1992), op. cit.

8. See, for example, Bruce Kogut, "Designing Global Strategies: Comparative and Competitive Value-Added Chains," *Sloan Management Review* (Summer 1985), pp. 27–38; Prahalad and Doz, op. cit.

9. Johny K. Johansson and George S. Yip, "Exploiting Globalization Potential: U.S. and Japanese Strategies," *Strategic Management Journal* (October 1994), pp. 579–601.

10. See Susan Segal-Horn, "Strategic Issues in the Globalization of Service Industries: A discussion paper," in P. Jones, ed., *The Management of Service Industries* (London: Pittman, 1988/89); Ram Kesavan and Eric Panitz, "Standardizing Services for Global Competitiveness: Literature Review and Hypotheses Generation," in Ben L. Kedia and Lars Larson, eds., *U.S. Competitiveness in the Global Marketplace: A Special Focus on the Service Sector*, Conference Proceedings, CIBER, Memphis State University, Memphis, TN, 1991; Alexandra Campbell and Alain Verbeke, "The Globalization of Service Multinationals," *Long Range Planning*, 2 (1994): 95–102; and Mathe and Perras, op. cit.

11. Christopher A. Bartlett and Sumantra Ghoshal, *Managing Across Borders: The Transnational Solution* (Boston, MA: Harvard Business School Press, 1989).

12. W, Earl Sasser, R. Paul Olsen, and D. Daryl Wyckoff, *Management of Service Operations: Text, Cases, and Readings* (Boston, MA: Allyn & Bacon, 1978).

13. Christopher H. Lovelock, "Think Before You Leap in Services Marketing," in L. L. Berry, G. Lynn Shostack, and G. D. Upah, Proceedings of Conference on *Emerging Perspectives in Services Marketing*, American Marketing Association, Chicago, 1983, pp. 115–119.

14. Lovelock (1991), op. cit.

15. Christopher J. Lovelock, "Classifying Services to Gain Strategic Marketing Insights," *Journal of Marketing*, 47

(Summer 1983): 9–20; Lovelock (1991), op. cit.; Lovelock (1994), op. cit.

16. Richard B. Chase, "Where Does the Customer Fit in a Service Operation?" *Harvard Business Review* (November/December 1978), pp. 137–142.

17. See Theodore Levitt, *Marketing for Business Growth* (New York, NY: McGraw-Hill, 1974), p. 47.

18. Several theorists have attempted to develop frameworks for understanding the structure of service products. G. Lynn Shostack, "Breaking Free from Product Marketing" *Journal of Marketing*, 41 (April 1977): 73–80, developed a molecular model, applicable to either goods or services, to help marketers visualize and manage what she termed a "total market entity." At the centre is the core benefit, addressing the basic customer need, which is then linked to a series of other service elements. She argues that, as in chemical formulations, a change in one element may completely alter the nature of the entity. Surrounding the molecules are a series of bands representing price, distribution, and market positioning (communication messages).

19. Lovelock (1994), op. cit.

20. B. Joseph Pine, *Mass Customization: a New Frontier in Business Competition* (Boston, MA: ABS Press, 1993).

21. See review in Yip (1989), op. cit.; Yip (1992), op. cit.

22. Kesavan and Panitz (1991), op. cit.

23. Gary Hamel and C. K. Prahalad. "Do You Really Have a Global Strategy?" *Harvard Business Review* (July/August 1985), pp. 139–148.

24. Yip (1992), op. cit.

25. For an in-depth discussion of the role of value-adding activities in competitive strategy, see Michael E. Porter, *Competitive Advantage* (New York, NY: The Free Press, 1985).

26. Johansson and Yip (1994), op. cit.

27. Pei-yuan Chia, "Citibanking the World," *Bank Management* (July/August 1995).

28. Andrew E. Serwer, "McDonald's Conquers the World," *Fortune*, October 17, 1994, pp. 103–116.

29. See George S. Yip and Tammy L. Madsen, "Global Account Management: The New Frontier in Relationship Marketing," *International Marketing Review* (Forthcoming 1996).

Customer Satisfaction Fables

DAWN IACOBUCCI

KENT GRAYSON

AMY OSTROM

Can a company constantly strive to exceed customers' expectations by providing service that "delights" or "amazes" them? Or is this just another marketing trend that really doesn't ensure that the customer will purchase the service again? Are customers always right, or are there some who may not be profitably worth satisfying? Do customers judge service on the core offering (e.g., the plane flight) or on the supplemental "frills" (e.g., the movie and meal during the flight)? The authors point out that the concept of customer satisfaction is nothing more than good marketing, something companies should have been striving for all along. They poke holes in a number of marketing trends and suggest that, rather than embracing every new fad that comes along, managers should think creatively and choose their own paths to successful marketing.

In the 1980s, U.S. manufacturers turned to quality as a way to create competitive advantage and sustain customer loyalty. The 1990s are emerging as the era for customer satisfaction in service industries. Service quality and customer satisfaction are important to marketers because a customer's evaluation of a purchase is thought to determine the likelihood of repurchase and, ultimately, to affect bottom-line measures of business success. Customer satisfaction is important to all marketers, but especially to service marketers, because, unlike their manufacturing counterparts, they have fewer objective measures of quality for judging their production.

In particular, service marketers have embraced the "gap model," which suggests that consumers will judge a service encounter as high quality if the experience exceeds his or her expectations. This concept is simple and intuitively appealing; it is consistent with our own experiences as consumers who have been frustrated by service that did not meet our expectations or pleasantly surprised by the service provider who "went the extra mile" for us and performed "above and beyond the call of duty."

Simple ideas are often those that "catch on" fastest, and, true to form, the gap concept is popular in industry and academia. Books on customer service feature examples of service providers who made extra efforts to please their customers. Furthermore, it is currently in vogue for managers in many industries to make statements such as, "We don't want to just meet our cus-

tomers' expectations; we want to exceed them," or "We don't want to simply satisfy our customers (by meeting expectations); we want to "delight" them (or "amaze" them) by exceeding their expectations."

Despite the pervasiveness of managers striving to "exceed their customers' expectations," this point of view has its limitations. The strength of the concept—its simplicity—is simultaneously its weakness; it is too simple to provide a thorough understanding of customer evaluations. We recognize that these ideas have taken the industry by storm and, indeed, seem so well accepted that they are beyond questioning. However, we feel compelled to discuss the shortcomings in order to put a brake on the current unquestioned use of the "exceeding expectations" ideology.

The Emperor's New Clothes— There's Nothing New Going on Here

"Customer satisfaction" may be a new buzzword, but the concept is not new. Striving for customer satisfaction is no different than good marketing. By "marketing," we do not mean the "Four Ps" (product, price, promotion, and place) but, rather, marketing in the classic sense of being customer oriented and market driven. Attempting to find out what customers want and then trying to deliver may be seen as striving for customer satisfaction or simply doing good marketing.

Attention to customers is what distinguishes marketers from engineers and operations and other personnel. The goal of the satisfied customer, like good marketing, must permeate the entire service delivery process, from planning through execution; if customer satisfaction is used only for post-purchase assessment,

Dawn Iacobucci is an associate professor and Kent Grayson and Amy Ostrom are doctoral candidates, Department of Marketing, Kellogg Graduate School of Management, Northwestern University.

then it is no more advanced than a salesforce counting its receipts.

We are not saying that a focus on customer satisfaction is not necessary or is a bad thing. Indeed, that would be like saying marketing is not necessary or is bad. If it takes a new buzzword to refresh an attention to the consumer, so be it.

A new industry of consultants has appeared who offer their experience and advice in measuring and achieving customer satisfaction. They, too, offer nothing new. Do we begrudge them their careers? Of course not, but, in hiring them, one should realize that they are simply doing marketing and marketing research. Asking customers whether they are satisfied is no different from asking for their other opinions, e.g., "How does this ad make you feel?" "Which package design do you prefer?" "How far would you drive for this discount?"

Consistent with the gap model, recent customer surveys ask a particular question that addresses the extent to which the firm has "exceeded," "met," or "fallen short of" your expectations. This type of question has no more inherent value than questions that ask whether the service experience was "good," "average," or "poor." The former question may provide more information only if other questions are also posed to explicate the customer's expectations, but this argument is true only because more information is always better. Asking questions about whether customers' expectations have been exceeded is trendy. While this trend is not harmful, neither is it helpful.

Chicken Little Proclaims, "The Sky Is Falling"—Gross Exaggerations

Managers are running around proclaiming "The Customer Is King" and sketching organizational charts with customers positioned where CEOs used to sit. Achieving customer satisfaction is an admirable goal, but a firm must answer to multiple sets of "customers" (e.g., consumers, boards, shareholders), many of whose goals may be in conflict. For example, while a consumer may wish for a wide variety of products and customization to his or her needs, this flexibility and personalization may not be supportable financially. From a shareholder's point of view, businesses are not in business to satisfy customers; businesses are in business to make money. In many situations, the customer need not be satisfied at all; monopolies (and most oligopolies) are extreme examples, but consider also industries in which a customer makes a purchase from a competitor known for good quality in its core product (goods or services), but whose supplemental services are spartan. There is repeat purchasing with minimal customer satisfaction.

Similarly, the claim, "The Customer Is Always Right," is utter nonsense. Studies of product liability constantly attribute at least half of product failures to consumer misuse. In addition, the briefest inquiry to any salesforce will confirm that some customers are uninformed, unrealistic, and demanding. Most businesses have certain segments of customers who are not profitably worth satisfying.

Little Red Riding Hood and the Wolf—Customer Satisfaction and Price

Customers evaluate purchases as an aggregate function of a number of factors. Value, or the tradeoff between the quality of the item and its costs, is a primary consideration. In essence, this judgment is one of equity—how do the outcomes rate (e.g., the quality of what I receive) relative to the inputs (e.g., the price I paid or efforts and costs I incurred). Learning the price after finding suitable merchandise or service provision is like discovering granny is a wolf—costs too have teeth.

Notice too that a simple derivation of the desire to "exceed expectations" would be to sell products at costs low enough to be unprofitable to businesses, e.g., giving away a Mercedes would no doubt satisfy (and even "delight") a customer. While many businesses are seeking high levels of customer satisfaction, none would do so rationally if it meant jeopardizing their long-term existence. The "exceed expectations" perspective would be more thoughtful and useful if such constraints were also explicitly considered.

Goldilocks and the Three Bears— Segmentation

Aside from the rare "Coca-Colas," most firms cannot be all things to all people. Most businesses know this and typically offer a variety of products in an attempt to please multiple segments of consumers. Thus, for a given consumer making a given purchase, some of a firm's offerings may be "too hot" or "too cold," but the company hopes there is a product that is "just right."

The question then is, what drives customer satisfaction? A company may modify the goods and services it offers, and it needs guidance to know which alterations are most desirable and profitable. An important distinction that has developed in discussions of services, but is equally applicable to goods, is the difference between one's "core" product offering and one's "supplemental" (or sometimes, "value-added") services. Examples of core products are: safe transport from one city to another via airplane, a physician's proper diagnosis and treatment, an attorney's sound legal advice, a hotel room with a comfortable bed and clean bath, the car to be purchased from an auto dealer, etc. Examples of supplementals are: a movie and meal on board the airplane, the physician's friendly bedside manner, the trustworthiness of the attorney, bathroom amenities and minibars in the hotel room, and the car dealership's financing.

In studies of customer satisfaction in these and other industries, managers are frequently surprised to find their customers are judging them "on the little things" (i.e., on the "supplementals"). There are good reasons for this phenomenon. First, customers assume the core offering will be of high quality—it is a given. And while a poor "core" will result in customer dissatisfaction, a good "core" execution is not sufficient for customer satisfaction.

A supporting reason is that, within and across competitors, there is typically little variability in the core product offerings—planes usually do arrive safely, medical treatment is fairly accurate, hotel rooms usually do have decent bedding, etc. With so few differences among competitors on the core product (or within a competitor across different purchases), this information is not distinctive and therefore not useful to a customer forming an evaluation. Furthermore, most consumers find the core of some services hard to judge (e.g., most do not have the expertise to judge an attorney's contracts and suggestions). What varies more, and is easier to evaluate, are the supplementals. Interpersonal skills differ greatly from physician to physician and attorney to attorney, and hotel room and lobby accoutrements also vary widely; all these things are easy to judge. Thus, in an evaluation of a service experience or in a choice between service providers, supplemental services provide greater information to consumers and become those features of the product offering that drive satisfaction and choice.

Snow White and the Seven Dwarfs— Empowerment and Service Guarantees

Just as customers differ in their wants and needs, so too do employees differ in their abilities. Even with rigorous selection and hiring, and education and training procedures, front-line (and other) personnel differ in their abilities to deal with customers and prevent or recover from service failures. No matter what the cor-

porate culture, those front-line people can occasionally be sleepy, grumpy, and dopey!

Due to innate individual differences in ability and/or personality, a blanket policy of empowerment may be optimistic and naive. Is it good business practice for a firm to adopt a policy of giving every employee some discretion in resolving customer conflicts? Some employees are more capable than others in using that discretion wisely.

Is it wise for a firm to offer customer service guarantees? Not only do service providers' abilities vary, but even a "good" employee has mood fluctuations. It is not clear that some portion of a firm's profits should be tied to a component in the service delivery system that is not entirely in the firm's control.

Tortoise and Hare, Fox and "Sour" Grapes, and Pied Piper—In Summary

Just as in the tale of the tortoise and the hare, those firms that have been customer focused all along will show stronger performances than those firms that have only recently turned their attention to satisfying their customers, perhaps in reaction to increased competition. Continual efforts toward improvement, even if slow, are superior to mad-dash redefinitions of one's business priorities.

In the fable about the fox who could not jump high enough to reach a bunch of grapes, he finally walked away, rationalizing that the grapes were probably sour anyway. During the past ten to fifteen years, many "quality" and related efforts have been proposed as "the answer," and, as each new adaptation yields little in the way of immediate results, managers are left feeling wary of the next trend. Their experiences do not necessarily lead to the conclusion that these various programs are not useful, but rather, in all likelihood, that none of the programs had been truly integrated into the firm. Thus, while much is said about managing customers' expectations, management also needs to set reasonable expectations.

For example, industry spokespersons are currently trying to encourage firms to "delight" their customers or have them get "emotional" about their purchases. This advice is not realistic; it ignores the fact that many, many purchases are low involvement. Seeking "delight" or "emotions" for such items will prove fruitless and lead to much frustration.

Similarly, service industries may be attracted to the manufacturing-based TQM- and "six sigma"- like philosophies but may be thwarted in their specific attempts to apply them. For example, in many services (e.g., personal, professional), a standardized service encounter tends to be less satisfying than a personalized service, but the former is easier to measure and control than the latter. The contrast between routinized and tailored encounters suggests that a blanket goal of "minimized variance" needs to be rethought. Furthermore, it is not clear whether a target such as "six sigma" or "99.5 percent" is meaningful for subjective rating scales of customer satisfaction or perceptions of service quality.

Finally, rather than follow the "Pied Piper" like everyone else who is seeking to "exceed expectations,"

managers should be more creative and wary of mindless trends. Businesses need to find their own way in striving for excellence; choosing a different route may be more appropriate for each business's needs and lead to surer successes.

We are especially grateful to Sidney Levy and Louis Stern for their encouraging and amused reactions to this article.

The American Customer Satisfaction Index:
Nature, Purpose, and Findings

CLAES FORNELL

MICHAEL D. JOHNSON

EUGENE W. ANDERSON

JAESUNG CHA

BARBARA EVERITT BRYANT

The American Customer Satisfaction Index (ACSI) is a new type of market-based performance measure for firms, industries, economic sectors, and national economies. The authors discuss the nature and purpose of ACSI and explain the theory underlying the ACSI model, the nation-wide survey methodology used to collect the data, and the econometric approach employed to estimate the indices. They also illustrate the use of ACSI in conducting benchmarking studies, both cross-sectionally and over time. The authors find customer satisfaction to be greater for goods than for services and, in turn, greater for services than for government agencies, as well as find cause for concern in the observation that customer satisfaction in the United States is declining, primarily because of decreasing satisfaction with services. The authors estimate the model for the seven major economic sectors for which data are collected. Highlights of the findings include that (1) customization is more important than reliability in determining customer satisfaction, (2) customer expectations play a greater role in sectors in which variance in production and consumption is relatively low, and (3) customer satisfaction is more quality-driven than value- or price-driven. The authors conclude with a discussion of the implications of ACSI for public policymakers, managers, consumers, and marketing in general.

The economy—the economy is changing. The central feature of the old economy was the mass production and consumption of commodities. The modern economy is based on production and consumption of increasingly differentiated goods and services.

How should we measure economic performance in this new world? As the economy changes, theories and measures must change, too. In particular, it seems clear that conventional "output," or "quantity," mea-

Claes Fornell is the Donald C. Cook Professor of Business Administration and Director of the National Quality Research Center, University of Michigan Business School. Michael D. Johnson is Professor of Marketing and a core faculty member of the National Quality Research Center, University of Michigan Business School. Eugene W. Anderson is Associate Professor of Marketing and a core faculty member of the National Quality Research Center, University of Michigan Business School. Barbara Everitt Bryant and Jaesung Cha are Research Scientists at the National Quality Research Center, University of Michigan Business School. The authors gratefully acknowledge the financial support of the University of Michigan Business School, the American Society for Quality Control (ASQC), and the ACSI's corporate sponsors. The authors also thank Jack West of ASQC for his contributions in spearheading the development and deployment of the ACSI. This research has benefited from the constructive contributions of the Editor and three anonymous *JM* reviewers.

sures of economic performance, such as productivity, are not only extremely difficult to compute in a differentiated marketplace, but also that they probably tell us less than they used to. For example, the United States leads the world in productivity, but incomes have stagnated. Italy has had one of the most dramatic productivity increases of any country, but it has not translated into strong economic growth. The current trend toward downsizing in U.S. firms may increase productivity in the short term, but the downsized firms' future financial performance will suffer if repeat business is dependent on labor-intensive customized service (Anderson, Fornell, and Rust 1996).

Hence, in the new economy, producing more—however efficiently—is not necessarily better. There is a pressing need to augment current approaches to evaluating the financial health of individual firms, let alone the wealth of nations. Moreover, as the economy continues to evolve, "the gap between the two economies—the one that government measures and the one businesses and economists are struggling to understand—is widening" (*Fortune* 1993, p. 108). To understand more fully the modern economy, and the firms that compete in it, we must measure the quality of economic output, as well as its quantity.

We introduce the American Customer Satisfaction Index (ACSI), which represents a new type of customer-based measurement system for evaluating—

and enhancing—the performance of firms, industries, economic sectors, and national economies. It is designed to be representative of the economy as a whole and covers more than 200 firms, with 1994 sales in excess of $2.7 trillion competing in over 40 industries in the seven major consumer sectors of the economy. On an annual basis, the ACSI system estimates a firm-level customer satisfaction index for each company in the sample and weights these firm-level indices to calculate industry, sector, and national indices.

The American Customer Satisfaction Index measures the quality of the goods and services as experienced by the customers that consume them. An individual firm's ACSI represents its served market's—its customers'—overall evaluation of total purchase and consumption experience, both actual and anticipated (Anderson, Fornell, and Lehmann 1994; Fornell 1992; Johnson and Fornell 1991). Analogously, an industry ACSI represents an industry's customers' overall evaluation of its market offering, a sector ACSI is an overall evaluation of that sector, and the national ACSI gauges the nation's total consumption experience. Hence, ACSI represents a cumulative evaluation of a firm's market offering, rather than a person's evaluation of a specific transaction. Although transaction-specific satisfaction measures may provide specific diagnostic information about a particular product or service encounter, overall customer satisfaction is a more fundamental indicator of the firm's past, current, and future performance (Anderson, Fornell, and Lehmann 1994).

The balance of this article is structured into five sections. First, we explain the nature of ACSI: the theory underlying the ACSI, the nation-wide survey methodology used to collect the data, and the econometric approach employed to estimate ACSI. Second, we discuss the use of ACSI in conducting benchmarking studies, both cross-sectionally and over time. Third, to demonstrate the model's general applicability and usefulness, we estimate the model for the seven major economic sectors for which data are collected. Fourth, we discuss systematic cross-sector variation in each of these areas. Fifth, we conclude with a discussion of the implications of ACSI for public policymakers, managers, and individual consumers, as well as for marketing in general.

The ACSI Model and Methodology

The concept behind ACSI, namely, a measure of overall customer satisfaction that is uniform and comparable, requires a methodology with two fundamental properties.[1] First, the methodology must recognize that ACSI and the other constructs in the model represent different types of customer evaluations that can-

not be measured directly. Accordingly ACSI uses a multiple indicator approach to measure overall customer satisfaction as a latent variable. The result is a latent variable score or index that is general enough to be comparable across firms, industries, sectors, and nations.

Second, as an overall measure of customer satisfaction, ACSI must be measured in a way that not only accounts for consumption experience, but also is forward-looking. To this end, ACSI is embedded in the system of cause and effect relationships shown in Figure 1, which makes it the centerpiece in a chain of relationships running from the antecedents of overall customer satisfaction—expectations, perceived quality, and value—to the consequences of overall customer satisfaction—voice and loyalty. As was indicated, the primary objective in estimating this system or model is to explain customer loyalty. It is through this design that ACSI captures the served market's evaluation of the firm's offering in a manner that is both backward- and forward-looking. Moreover, modeling ACSI as part of such a system serves to validate the index from a nomological standpoint. Nomological validity, a form of construct validity, is the degree to which a construct behaves as predicted within a system of related constructs called a nomological net (Cronbach and Meehl 1955). To the extent that the model predictions are supported, the validity of the ACSI is supported.

ACSI Antecedents

As is shown in Figure 1, overall customer satisfaction (ACSI) has three antecedents: perceived quality, perceived value, and customer expectations. The first determinant of overall customer satisfaction is perceived quality or performance, which is the served market's evaluation of recent consumption experience, and is expected to have a direct and positive effect on overall customer satisfaction. This prediction is intuitive and fundamental to all economic activity. To operationalize the perceived quality construct, we draw on the quality literature to delineate two primary components of consumption experience: (1) customization, that is, the degree to which the firm's offering is customized to meet heterogeneous customer needs, and (2) reliability, that is, the degree to which the firm's offering is reliable, standardized, and free from deficiencies.

The second determinant of overall customer satisfaction is perceived value, or the perceived level of product quality relative to the price paid. Adding perceived value incorporates price information into the

---

[1]For a more extensive and detailed description of the ACSI methodology, please see American Society for Quality Control (1995).

FIGURE 1

The American Customer Satisfaction Index (ACSI) Model

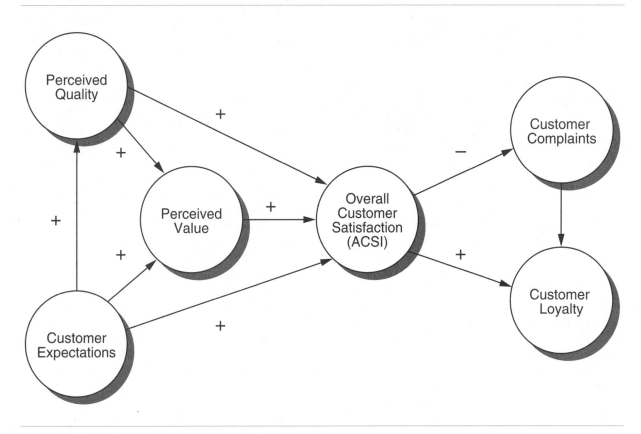

model and increases the comparability of the results across firms, industries, and sectors. Using value judgments to measure performance also controls for differences in income and budget constraints across respondents (Lancaster 1971), which enables us to compare high- and low-priced products and services. For perceived quality, we expect a positive association between perceived value increases and customer satisfaction.

The third determinant of overall customer satisfaction is the served market's expectations. The served market's expectations represent both the served market's prior consumption experience with the firm's offering—including nonexperiential information available through sources such as advertising and word-of-mouth—and a forecast of the supplier's ability to deliver quality in the future. As such, the expectations construct is both backward- and forward-looking. It captures all previous quality experiences and information from $t - 1, t - 2, \ldots, t - m$. Hence, it naturally has a direct and positive association with a cumulative evaluation of the firm's performance, such as overall customer satisfaction. At the same time, the served market's expectations at time t forecast a firm's ability to satisfy its market in future periods $t + 1, t + 2, \ldots, t + n$.

This role of expectations is important because the nature of the ongoing relationship between a firm and its customer base is such that expected future quality is critical to overall customer satisfaction. This predictive role of expectations also suggests that it should have a positive effect on overall customer satisfaction (Anderson, Fornell, and Lehmann 1994).

Finally, customer expectations should be positively related to perceived quality and, consequently, to perceived value. Customer knowledge should be such that expectations accurately mirror current quality. Hence, we expect the served market to have expectations that are largely rational and that reflect customers' ability to learn from experience and predict the levels of quality and value they receive (Howard 1977).

ACSI Consequences

Following Hirschman's (1970) exit-voice theory, the immediate consequences of increased customer satisfaction are decreased customer complaints and increased customer loyalty (Fornell and Wernerfelt 1987). When dissatisfied, customers have the option of exiting (e.g., going to a competitor) or voicing their complaints in an attempt to receive retribution. An increase in overall customer satisfaction should decrease the incidence of complaints. Increased overall customer satisfaction should also increase customer loyalty. Loyalty is the ultimate dependent variable in the model because of its value as a proxy for profitability (Reichheld and Sasser 1990).

The final relationship in the model is between customer complaints and customer loyalty. Although there are no direct measures of the efficacy of a firm's customer service and complaint-handling systems, the direction and size of this relationship reflect on these systems (Fornell 1992). When the relationship is positive, the implication is that the firm is successful in turning complaining customers into loyal customers. When negative, the firm's complaint handling has managed to make a bad situation even worse—it has contributed further to customer defection.

ACSI Methodology

The American Customer Satisfaction Index is designed to be representative of the nation's economy as a whole. Accordingly, in selecting the companies to measure, each of the seven major economic sectors (one-digit standard industrial classification [SIC] code level) with reachable end-users were included in the design: (1) Manufacturing/Nondurables, (2) Manufacturing/Durables, (3) Transportation/Communications/ Utilities, (4) Retail, (5) Finance/Insurance, (6) Services, and (7) Public Administration/Government. Within each sector, the major industry groups (two-digit SIC codes) were included on the basis of relative contribution to the gross domestic product. Within each industry group, several representative industries (four-digit SIC codes) were included on the basis of total sales. Finally, within each industry the largest companies were selected, such that coverage included the majority of each selected industry's sales.

For each firm, approximately 250 interviews were conducted with the firm's current customers. Interviews came from 48 replicate national probability samples of households in the continental United States with telephones (95% of households). Prospective respondents (selected without substitution from the household by the "nearest birthday" method) were screened to identify purchasers of specific goods or services within defined purchase and consumption time periods. These periods vary from three years for the purchase of a major durable, to "within the past month" for frequently purchased consumer goods and services, to currently having a bank account or insurance policy in the person's own name.

Once a respondent was identified as a customer, the interviewer proceeded with the customer satisfaction questionnaire. Each questionnaire contains the same 17 structured questions and 8 demographic questions. Lead-in wording and examples were tailored to specific goods and services. In Table 1, we describe the 15 measurement variables from the ACSI survey that are used in the model estimation and identify the associated latent variable.

Customer expectations were measured by asking respondents to think back and remember the level of quality they expected on the basis of their knowledge and experience with a good or service.[2] Three expectation measures were collected: (1) overall expectations, (2) expectations regarding customization, and (3) expectations regarding reliability. Customers then rated their recent experience with the good or service by using three measures: (1) overall perceived quality, (2) perceived customization, and (3) perceived reliability. Two questions then tapped perceived value, quality relative to price, and price relative to quality.

Overall customer satisfaction (ACSI) was operationalized through three survey measures: (1) an overall rating of satisfaction, (2) the degree to which performance falls short of or exceeds expectations, and (3) a rating of performance relative to the customer's ideal good or service in the category. Whereas the latter are commonly used as antecedents in models of transaction-specific satisfaction (Oliver 1980; Yi 1991), their use as reflective indicators of overall customer satisfaction is consistent with the cumulative nature of ACSI, because each measure represents a qualitatively different benchmark customers use in making cumulative evaluations, such as overall customer satisfaction (ACSI). Moreover, the latent variable methodology employed to estimate overall customer satisfaction only extracts shared variance, or that portion of each measure that is common to all three questions and related to the ACSI construct's position in the model's chain of cause and effect. Thus, satisfaction is not confounded by either disconfirmation or comparison to an ideal. Only the psychological distance between performance and expectations, and between performance and the customer's ideal point, was used to estimate overall customer satisfaction (ACSI).

Customer complaints were measured by whether a customer had complained either formally (as in writing or by phone to a manufacturer) or informally (as to service personnel or a retailer). In addition, there were two measures of customer loyalty. The first was repurchase likelihood. The second measure was constructed from two survey variables: the degree to which a firm

---

[2]Although such post hoc measures of expectations are imperfect, the cost of obtaining expectations prior to purchase is prohibitive in a study of this magnitude.

TABLE 1
Measurement Variables Used in the ASCI Model

Measurement Variable	Latent Variable
1. Overall expectation of quality (prepurchase)	Customer expectations
2. Expectation regarding customization, or how well the product fits the customer's personal requirements (prepurchase)	Customer expectations
3. Expectation regarding reliability, or how often things would go wrong (prepurchase)	Customer expectations
4. Overall evaluation of quality experience (postpurchase)	Perceived quality
5. Evaluation of customization experience, or how well the product fit the customer's personal requirements (postpurchase)	Perceived quality
6. Evaluation of reliability experience, or how often things have gone wrong (postpurchase)	Perceived quality
7. Rating of quality given price	Perceived value
8. Rating of price given quality	Perceived value
9. Overall satisfaction	ACSI
10. Expectancy disconfirmation (performance that falls short of or exceeds expectations)	ACSI
11. Performance versus the customer's ideal product or service in the category	ACSI
12. Has the customer complained either formally or informally about the product or service?	Customer complaints
13. Repurchase likelihood rating	Customer loyalty
14. Price tolerance (increase) given repurchase	Customer loyalty
15. Price tolerance (decrease) to induce repurchase	Customer loyalty

could raise its prices as a percentage before the customer would definitely not choose to buy from that firm again the next time (given that the customer has indicated he or she is likely to repurchase) and the degree to which a firm could lower its prices as a percentage before the customer would definitely choose again from that firm the next time (given that the customer has indicated he or she is unlikely to repurchase).

Scales and Model Estimation

The frequency distribution of satisfaction and quality ratings is always negatively skewed in competitive markets (Fornell 1995). To reduce the statistical problems of extreme skewness, the ACSI uses 10-point (versus 5- or 7-point) rating scales to enable customers to make better discriminations (Andrews 1984). The use of multiple indicators also reduces skewness (Fornell 1992). A version of partial least squares (PLS) is used to estimate the model (Wold 1989). Partial least squares is an iterative procedure for estimating causal models, which does not impose distributional assumptions on the data, and accommodates continuous as well as categorical variables. Because of the model structure, PLS estimates weights for the survey measures that maximize their ability to explain customer

loyalty as the ultimate endogenous or dependent variable. The estimated weights are used to construct index values (transformed to a 0- to 100-point scale) for ACSI and the other model constructs.

The ACSI values for individual industries and sectors, as well as the overall economy, are computed by aggregating firm-level results. An industry-level ACSI is an aggregate of firm results weighted by firm sales (such as Philip Morris sales for Miller Beer in the beverages and beer industry and excluding other corporate Philip Morris sales). A sector ACSI is an aggregate of industry results weighted by industry sales. The overall ACSI is an average of the sector results weighted by each sector's contribution to the gross domestic product. A formal statement of the ACSI model and its measurement is provided in the Appendix.

The Evolution of National Indices

The first truly national customer satisfaction index was the Swedish Customer Satisfaction Barometer, or SCSB (Fornell 1992). Developed in 1989, the SCSB includes 31 major Swedish industries. In Germany, the Deutsche Kundenbarometer, or DK, was introduced in 1992 and as of 1994 also includes 31 industries (Meyer 1994). The American Customer Satisfaction Index was first introduced in the fall of 1994, with information on 40 industries and seven major sectors of the U.S. economy (National Quality Research Center 1995). Recently, New Zealand and Taiwan also have started indices for customer satisfaction. The European Union also has recommended that it be done in its member countries.

The original Swedish Barometer used perceived value (quality given price and price given quality) and a single measure of customer expectations. It has since been respecified to conform to the ACSI. By drawing on the quality literature and its distinction between customization and reliability, the ACSI approach introduces a perceived quality index to go with the original value index. The addition of this quality construct has two advantages. Distinguishing between quality and value provides information regarding the degree to which satisfaction is price- versus quality-driven. The quality construct also provides information regarding the relative importance of customization and reliability in determining quality.

Other improvements incorporated into the ACSI focus on the measurement properties of the model. The three measures of perceived quality (see Table 1) furnish the ACSI model with three corresponding measures for operationalizing customer expectations (compared to the single expectations measure used in the original SCSB model). An additional question is asked in the ACSI to improve the measurement of price tolerance. In the original Swedish model, customers were only asked how much more they would pay, given that they were likely to repurchase. In the ACSI model, customers are also asked how much the price would need to be reduced for them to repurchase, given that they are unlikely to repurchase. This provides a more complete price tolerance measure that improves the measurement properties of the loyalty construct.

Finally, the ACSI requires a different approach to survey sampling because of the complexity of the U.S. economy. In the SCSB, a firm is surveyed for customer satisfaction with a single representative brand. This is impractical in the United States, where manufacturers such as the domestic "big three" automobile companies and General Electric offer a wide range of popular models under more than one brand name. As was described, customers in the ACSI are surveyed at the brand or model level, and the various brand or model observations are combined to estimate a firm-level model.

ACSI as a Benchmark Cross-Sectionally and Over Time

In Figure 2, we provide a breakdown of the industry, sector, and overall ACSI results for the baseline ACSI released October 1994. The overall ACSI for the 1994 baseline was 74.5. What do the numbers shown in Figure 2 mean? As latent variables, the ACSI measures are comparable (albeit not blindly) across firms, industries, sectors, and nations. For example, the ACSI averages approximately 80 for goods, 75 for services and retailers, and 64 for public and government agencies. This implies that customers are generally more satisfied with goods than with services and are least satisfied with public administration and government agencies.

The American Customer Satisfaction Index measures lend themselves well to benchmarking over both time and context. For example, the 1994 ACSI indices provide a baseline for determining whether the marketplace is becoming more or less satisfied with the goods and services provided by individual firms, entire industries, and different sectors of the economy, as well as with the economic life of the nation as a whole. With regard to the last item, it is interesting to observe the decline in ACSI at the national level, which is shown in Figure 3. The American Customer Satisfaction Index falls from the baseline level of 74.5 in 1994 to a low of 73.0 in the first quarter of 1996. The decline is driven primarily by decreasing customer satisfaction with services. To the extent that long-term profitability depends on customer loyalty and the efficiencies gained from long-term buyer-seller relationships, this drop in satisfaction with services should be seen as a warning signal about the long-term financial prospects for the firms affected. More important, because services are a large and growing portion of the economy, such a decline may reflect a weakening of the economy in general and a lowering of living standards with regard to consumption quality.

Tracking ACSI over time can also yield interesting insights at the firm level. One of the biggest winners in the first release of the firm-level results of the index was the U.S. Postal Service, which rose 13.0% to 69 in 1995 (*Fortune* 1995). The postal service is engaged in a massive effort to improve the quality of their services, and it posted record profits last year. Large declines in the index were seen at companies that recently engaged in substantial downsizing, such as GTE (down 5.3% to 72) and Kmart (down 5.4% to 70).

Firm, industry, sector, and national ACSI scores also can be compared cross-sectionally within a given time period. For example, we can determine how well a particular firm is doing relative to the best firms in its own industry, the best firms in other industries in that sector, or the best in nation as a whole. Industries and sectors can be compared with one another in a similar fashion.

The American Customer Satisfaction Index also can be compared to the findings of Sweden's SCSB and Germany's DK. For example, the pattern of sector differences found in the ACSI is consistent with that

FIGURE 2
1994 Baseline ACSI Results

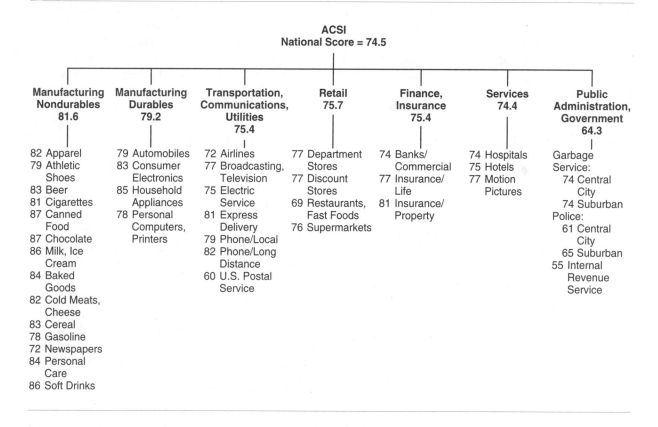

ACSI
National Score = 74.5

Manufacturing Nondurables 81.6	Manufacturing Durables 79.2	Transportation, Communications, Utilities 75.4	Retail 75.7	Finance, Insurance 75.4	Services 74.4	Public Administration, Government 64.3
82 Apparel	79 Automobiles	72 Airlines	77 Department Stores	74 Banks/ Commercial	74 Hospitals	Garbage Service:
79 Athletic Shoes	83 Consumer Electronics	77 Broadcasting, Television	77 Discount Stores	77 Insurance/ Life	75 Hotels	74 Central City
83 Beer	85 Household Appliances	75 Electric Service	69 Restaurants, Fast Foods	81 Insurance/ Property	77 Motion Pictures	74 Suburban
81 Cigarettes	78 Personal Computers, Printers	81 Express Delivery	76 Supermarkets			Police:
87 Canned Food		79 Phone/Local				61 Central City
87 Chocolate		82 Phone/Long Distance				65 Suburban
86 Milk, Ice Cream		60 U.S. Postal Service				55 Internal Revenue Service
84 Baked Goods						
82 Cold Meats, Cheese						
83 Cereal						
78 Gasoline						
72 Newspapers						
84 Personal Care						
86 Soft Drinks						

FIGURE 3
National ACSI Over Time

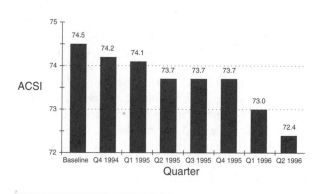

and/or services, it is a different question to ask whether a particular firm, industry, sector, or nation is "performing well." To do so, it is necessary to put the ACSI index numbers in context. From research conducted using SCSB data, it is known that certain factors make it more or less difficult to achieve high customer satisfaction and are likely to lead to higher or lower customer satisfaction for different types of industries. Fornell and Johnson (1993) find customer satisfaction higher in industries with a significant level of competition and differentiation. Anderson (1994) finds satisfaction higher when competition, differentiation, involvement, or experience is high or when switching costs, difficulty of standardization, or ease of evaluating quality is low. Both studies find satisfaction higher for goods than for services or retailers. This research enables us to conjecture that the observed higher satisfaction in the United States is due to the greater degree of competition found in most U.S. industries.

The question remains, however, once structural differences are taken into account, is a particular ACSI score "good" or "bad"? This question pertains to differences in the ACSI that are attributable to conduct as opposed to structure. Such benchmarking judgments are relatively straightforward within a particular industry, in

observed in the SCSB and the DK. That is, goods score higher than services, and public administration is always the lowest scoring sector. However, viewed against the SCSB and DK, the ACSI scores are relatively high, especially in the goods and services sectors.

Although it is relatively straightforward to ask which firms, industries, sectors, and nations are relatively more effective at providing satisfying goods which firms can be compared against one another. In such cases, industry structure is held constant, such that differences in firm performance may be attributed to the firm's conduct.

Firms that do particularly well relative to their competition include Southwest Airlines, with an ACSI of 76 relative to an industry average of 69, and Wal-Mart, with a score of 80 relative to an industry average of 74. Both firms have developed difficult-to-imitate strategies and resources that have put them far ahead of the competition in their respective industries. Firms that trail the competition in their industry include Hyundai, with an ACSI of 68 relative to the automobile industry average of 80, and A&P, with a score of 69 relative to the supermarket industry's average of 74, and are each increasingly vulnerable to aggressive competitors.

Within a sector, though different industries are likely to share similar characteristics, benchmarking should be done with deference to differences in industry structure, such as the degree of competition. As is shown in Figure 2, the ACSI for long-distance telephone service (82) is greater than local telephone service (79). Consequently, it is possible to say that customer satisfaction with long-distance service is higher. However, it is not possible to say whether industry performance is good or bad without first taking into account differences in satisfaction due to structural characteristics. In other words, greater competition is likely driving the ACSI higher in long-distance service, but it is not appropriate to evaluate the conduct of the industry without first taking this structural difference into account. For example, long-distance service's score of 82 may be weak, given the industry's structural characteristics, whereas the local telephone industry's score of 79 may be high, given its situation. If so, then though long-distance service would be providing higher customer satisfaction, it might be encouraged to do better. At the same time, local telephone's performance would be "better," because the served market is more satisfied than would be expected on the basis of its industry characteristics. Hence, benchmarking requires further "handicapping" to account for differences in both. Development of a deeper understanding of how to handicap ACSI scores for benchmarking purposes is a promising avenue for further research.

General Applicability and Usefulness of ACSI

Using individual respondents as observations, we here describe the results of estimating the ACSI model for the seven measured sectors of the economy.[3] In contrast to the baseline results, in which the model is estimated for each firm and the results are aggregated to industry and sector indices and to an overall national ACSI, here each sector is treated as a subsegment of the overall ACSI population of respondents. In particular, we discuss the general applicability of the model and several key findings regarding (1) the relative importance of customization and reliability, (2) the predictive nature of expectations, and (3) the relative importance of price and quality. Throughout, we use standardized variables (correlations) to evaluate the measurement portion of the model and fit measures, whereas we use unstandardized variables (covariances) as input to estimate effect sizes. Jackknifing is used to obtain standard errors for each of the model parameters. Wherever model estimates (loadings and effects) are compared or contrasted across sectors in the discussion of results, the differences are significant ($p < .05$).

General Applicability of the Model Overall, we expect the ACSI model to be generally applicable to multiple sectors. The model and measures are designed to provide this generality. This prediction is examined through several indicators. The first is whether the estimated path coefficients are significant in the predicted directions. We find the model's path coefficients to be significant and in the predicted direction for 54 of 56 possible cases.[4]

The second indicator of the model's performance is its ability to explain important latent variables in the model, especially overall customer satisfaction (ACSI) and loyalty. We find that the estimated model explains a substantial proportion of the variance in both constructs. For overall customer satisfaction (ACSI), R^2 measures range from .70 for sector 1 to .80 for sector 5 (average of .75). For customer loyalty, R^2 ranges from .26 for sector 6 to .47 for sector 5 (average of .36).

The third and fourth indicators capture the fit of the measurement variable (MV) and latent variable (LV) portions of the model: the proportion of available covariance in the MVs explained, and the proportion of available covariance in the LVs explained. The measurement variable loadings for the ACSI model (not shown) are all relatively large and positive. The percent of MV covariance explained ranges from 84% for sector 1 to 89% for sectors 3 and 5 (average of .87).

---

[3] The samples were as follows: (1) Manufacturing/Nondurables (n = 12,075, 26.8% of sample), (2) Manufacturing/Durables (n = 7,828; 17.4%), (3) Transportation/Communications/Utilities (n = 10,101; 22.4%), (4) Retail (n = 7,243; 16.1%), (5) Finance/insurance (n = 3,236; 7.2%), (6) Other Services (n = 3,328; 7.4%), and (7) Public Administration/Government (n = 1,183; 2.6%).

[4] The two relationships that were not correctly predicted were for sector 5 (Finance/Insurance), in which there is a negative, albeit not significant, effect of expectations on overall customer satisfaction, and sector 7 (Public Administration/Government), in which the effect of expectations on value is positive but not significant (.035).

The percent of LV covariance explained ranges from 92% for sector 2 to 95% for sector 5 (average of 94%). Each model, therefore, explains well over 90% of the LV covariance available in a model that specifies 9 of 15 possible LV relationships. This suggests that there are no major relationships in our data that the ACSI model fails to capture.

Customization versus Reliability The measurement loadings suggest that customization is more central to customers' expectations and perceptions of quality than reliability. The average loadings for the expectations construct were .81, .85, and .68 for expected quality, customization, and reliability, respectively. The average loadings for the perceived quality construct were .907, .906, and .77 for quality, customization and reliability, respectively. Consistent with the nature of production and consumption in service-oriented sectors, customization is more central to quality for sectors 3, 5, 6, and 7 (average of .909) than for the manufactured goods sectors, 1 and 2 (average of .899). For all sectors, the loadings for the customization measures are significantly higher than the loadings for the reliability measures (for both the expectations and perceived quality constructs). This implies that squeezing more variance out of a manufacturing or service delivery process may not increase perceived quality and customer satisfaction as much as tailoring goods and services to meet customer or market segment needs.

The Predictive Nature of Customer Expectations
As was expected, we find that customer expectations are largely rational in that expectations predict quality, value, and customer satisfaction. This is consistent with previous research using the SCSB, which shows that the served market's expectations are relatively stable and accurate, especially in the aggregate (Anderson, Fornell, and Lehmann 1994; Johnson, Anderson, and Fornell 1995).

With regard to the impact of expectations on quality and value, it is useful to look at the sum of the two effects ([expectations on quality] + [expectations on value]). This joint effect is greatest in four sectors: Manufacturing/Nondurables = .68; Transportation/Communications/Utilities = .71; Retail = .81; and Public Administration/Government = .67. The joint effect is smaller in Manufacturing/Durables, Finance/Insurance, and Services (.45, .58, and .59, respectively). These findings are compatible with the argument that expectations are less predictive when variance in consumption and production factors are high (Anderson 1994). On the production side, if a particular good or service is difficult to standardize or quality is relatively unambiguous, variance in consumption experience is greater and expectations should have less influence.

The Direct Effect of Expectations on
Customer Satisfaction

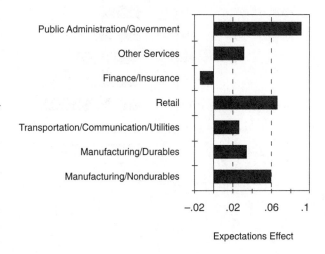

Similarly, on the consumption side, if customers are more likely to perceive variance in production—perhaps because of involvement or expertise gained through experience—then expectations should, again, have less influence. For example, customer expectations should be better predictors of quality, value, and satisfaction in those sectors in which customers make frequent and relatively routine purchase and consumption decisions (Howard 1977). When such interactions are less frequent, customers have less direct knowledge and their expectations should be weaker predictors of perceived quality and value.

The findings for the direct association between expectations and satisfaction are similar (see Figure 4). The impact of expectations is larger in two sectors (sector 1: Manufacturing/Nondurables = .06, and sector 4: Retail = .07), in which variance in production and consumption factors is relatively low. The effect is not as high in the other four competitive market sectors. The largest effect of expectations on satisfaction is for sector 7: Public Administration/Government at .09. This may reveal the impact that a negative image can have on satisfaction because of the halo surrounding certain publicly provided services (such as the Internal Revenue Service). This interpretation is consistent with research in which negative factors and framing effects have a larger impact on evaluations than do their positive counterparts (Kahneman and Tversky 1979). The observed negative effect for Finance/Insurance (− .01) is not significant.

An examination of the total effect of expectations on satisfaction—the direct effect of expectations on satisfaction plus the effect of expectations on overall customer

Price- versus Quality-Driven Satisfaction Ratio

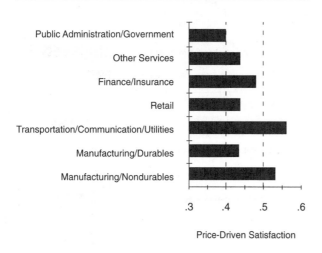

Price-Driven Satisfaction

quality-driven satisfaction ratio is calculated as the impact of a one-point change in perceived value on overall customer satisfaction divided by the total effect of a one-point change in perceived quality on overall customer satisfaction (the direct effect of quality on satisfaction plus the indirect effect of quality on satisfaction through value).

As is shown in Figure 5, relative price-driven satisfaction is greatest in sectors 1 and 3, in which the ratio of effects equals .53 and .56, respectively, compared to an overall average of .47 across sectors. For sector 1 (Manufacturing/Nondurables) the result is consistent with the shift toward price-based competition in this industry, which was observed throughout the 1980s (Buzzell, Quelch, and Salmon 1990), in which price competition is fostered by the availability of low-priced house and generic brands and discount retailing. Price-driven satisfaction is highest for sector 3 (Transportation/Communications/Utilities), in which competition is relatively commodity-based and price plays a correspondingly important role.

Relative price-driven satisfaction is lowest for Manufacturing/Durables (.43), Services (.43), Retail (.44), and Government Agencies (.40), which implies that quality is relatively more central to market behavior in these sectors. For the first two, this finding is consistent with the high involvement and customized nature of the products involved. For Retail, the effects on both quality and value are relatively low. This may be due to the location-driven nature of this sector. The ratio for Public Administration/Government most likely reflects the "take it or leave it" nature of pricing in this sector.

Although our observations are based on aggregation over the wide variety of segments, firms, and industries within a given sector, overall it appears that a ratio of the impact of value to the impact of quality on satisfaction provides a useful measure of price-versus quality-driven satisfaction with strong face validity. In further research, the efficacy of the price-driven satisfaction ratio also should be demonstrated through association with other constructs in the database, as well as through the relationships between those constructs. For example, in industries in which overall customer satisfaction is relatively price-driven we might expect the effect of overall customer satisfaction on loyalty to be relatively low. At the sector level, we find this to be the case for Manufacturing/Nondurables, yet the Transportation/ Communications/Utility sector is average in terms of how sensitive loyalty is to overall customer satisfaction. Thus, the price-driven satisfaction ratio also should be associated with degree of loyalty.

With the notable exception of Manufacturing/ Nondurables, we find loyalty to be lower in sectors in

satisfaction through quality and value—yields similar results. Expectations have the greatest impact in the Public Administration/Government (.59) and Retail (.59) sectors, followed by Transportation/Communications/Utilities (.53), Manufacturing/Nondurables (.49), and Services (.47). The total effect of expectations is lowest for the Manufacturing/Durables (.36) and Finance (.41) sectors. For the latter, current quality experiences may be relatively more salient such as the performance of an automobile or a mutual fund—and may take precedence over previous quality experiences in determining overall customer satisfaction, whereas long-term reputation effects may play a greater role in sectors in which expectations have a greater impact.

Price- versus Quality-Driven Satisfaction The impact of quality on overall customer satisfaction is greater than that of value in each of the seven sectors. The average direct effect of quality on overall customer satisfaction is .55, whereas the direct effect of value on overall customer satisfaction is .36. The total effect of quality on satisfaction—the direct effect plus the effect through value—averages .76. This difference is consistent with the notion that though value may be more central to the formation of customers' initial preferences and choice, quality, in contrast, is more central to the consumption experience itself.

An important question is how does the relative importance of price versus quality vary across sectors? If price, rather than quality, is driving overall customer satisfaction, the effect of a one-point change in value on overall customer satisfaction should be high relative to the total effect of a one-point change in quality on overall customer satisfaction. A price- versus which overall customer satisfaction is relatively price-driven. In part, this is driven by relatively high price tolerance because of the low-priced nature of goods sold in that sector. However, repurchase likelihood also is highest in this sector, as well as in the Transportation/Communications/Utilities sector. Clearly, the mixed nature of these findings suggests that additional research on these subjects must carefully control for category characteristics and industrial organization factors, such as switching costs and concentration, that can affect loyalty and the overall customer satisfaction-loyalty relationship.

Discussion and Implications

The American Customer Satisfaction Index represents a significant step forward in the evolution of national satisfaction indicators. It provides an independent and uniform means of assessing the quality of what is consumed and produced in the economy. It is a much needed missing link in what we need to understand about the health of the economy and the individual firms that compete in it. For example, if quality in the United States is declining as a consequence of declining overall customer satisfaction with the service sector, this should be cause for concern.

For public policymakers, ACSI has the potential to be a useful tool for evaluating and enhancing the health of the nation's economy, both in terms of national competitiveness and the welfare of its citizens. In assessing the health of the economy, it can provide an important complement to conventional measures of the quantity of goods and services produced—such as productivity and price indices—and can balance these measures against the quality of goods and services produced. For legislative efforts, ACSI can be useful in predicting and monitoring the effects of public policy decisions on issues as diverse as deregulation, taxes, interest rates, price ceilings, and subsidies. In terms of balance of trade, ACSI can provide an early warning as to whether an industry is vulnerable to competitive encroachment under conditions of free trade.

For managers and investors, ACSI provides an important measure of the firm's past and current performance, as well as future financial health. The ACSI provides a means of measuring one of a firm's most fundamental revenue-generating assets: its customers. Higher customer satisfaction should increase loyalty, reduce price elasticities, insulate current market share from competitors, lower transaction costs, reduce failure costs and the costs of attracting new customers, and help build a firm's reputation in the marketplace (Anderson, Fornell, and Lehmann 1994). As such,

ACSI provides a leading indicator of the firm's future financial health. By establishing a standard measure of quality with clear links to long-term performance, ACSI may even help instill more of a long-term perspective in both management and investors.

The empirical evidence that ACSI is a leading indicator of financial performance is becoming increasingly persuasive. This is true for accounting profits, as well as for shareholder value. Specifically, it has been shown that both the ACSI (Ittner and Larcker 1996) and its Swedish counterpart (Anderson, Fornell, and Lehmann 1994) have a positive association with return on investment. In terms of market value, Ittner and Larcker (1996) estimate that a one-unit change in ACSI is associated with a $654 million increase in the market value of equity above and beyond the accounting-book value of assets and liabilities. Stock trading strategies based on either the ACSI or SCSB have delivered portfolio returns well above market returns (Fornell, Ittner, and Larcker 1995, 1996). Also, recent results suggest that the public release of ACSI scores causes a significant stock market reaction—positive market adjusted returns for high-scoring firms and negative adjusted returns for low-scoring firms (Fornell, Ittner, and Larcker 1996).

The American Customer Satisfaction Index also has implications for managers formulating competitive strategy. One of its key benefits is that ACSI represents a uniform and comparable system of measurement that allows for systematic benchmarking over time and across firms. In addition, it can be useful in analyzing the strengths and weaknesses of the firm or its competitors. For example, declining overall customer satisfaction is likely to be symptomatic of deeper problems facing a firm. Because ACSI provides a measure of the effectiveness with which a firm is defending current customers, firms with low ACSI scores are particularly vulnerable and provide expansion opportunities for more competent organizations.

For customers, ACSI provides information that is not only useful in making purchase decisions, but also likely to lead to improvements in the quality of the goods and services they consume, as well as in their overall standard of living. The independence, uniformity, and methodology underlying ACSI mean that it provides information to buyers not found in ad hoc methodologies employed in product ratings by popular magazines and commercial market research. Moreover, the mere existence of such a measure would likely lead to improvements in the quality of goods and services. In a monopoly situation, ACSI may help police the market. In addition, ACSI should have particularly important implications for both the quality of these services and the prices customers pay for them. In competitive situations, too, ACSI should encourage quality competition and lead to greater customer satisfaction over time. The ultimate outcome should be an improvement in the quality of economic life.

To summarize, ACSI represents a new means of evaluating and enhancing performance for the modern firm and the modern economy. It provides a complement to conventional measures, such as productivity and price indices, that treat quality as a residual. In doing so, it has the potential to move to center stage the quality goods and services—as experienced by the customers of those goods and services—of firms, industries, and nations seeking to maintain and/or strengthen their positions in the increasingly competitive economic environment that is unfolding as we move into the twenty-first century. Because marketing scholars and practitioners have long recognized that customer satisfaction is an important and central concept, as well as an important goal of all business activity, the role of marketing in this new world should be self-evident.

APPENDIX

The formal expression of the model depicted in Figure 1 can be written as a series of equations such that the systematic part of the predictor relationships is the conditional expectation of the dependent variables for given values of predictors. The general equation is thus specified as stochastic:

$$E[\eta \mid \eta, \xi] = B\eta + \Gamma\xi,$$

where $\eta' = (\eta_1, \eta_2, \ldots, \eta_m)$ and $\xi' = (\xi_1, \xi_2, \ldots, \xi_n)$ are vectors of unobserved (latent) endogenous and exogenous variables, respectively, B $(m \times m)$ is a matrix of coefficient parameters for η, and Γ $(m \times n)$ is a matrix of coefficient parameters for ξ. This implies that $E[\eta \zeta'] = E[\xi\zeta'] = E[\zeta] = 0$, where $\zeta = \eta - E[\eta|\eta, \xi]$.

The corresponding equation that relates the latent variables in the model is

$$\begin{bmatrix} \eta_1 \\ \eta_2 \\ \eta_3 \\ \eta_4 \\ \eta_5 \end{bmatrix} = \begin{bmatrix} 0 & 0 & 0 & 0 & 0 \\ \beta_{21} & 0 & 0 & 0 & 0 \\ \beta_{31} & \beta_{32} & 0 & 0 & 0 \\ 0 & 0 & \beta_{43} & 0 & 0 \\ 0 & 0 & \beta_{53} & \beta_{54} & 0 \end{bmatrix} \begin{bmatrix} \eta_1 \\ \eta_2 \\ \eta_3 \\ \eta_4 \\ \eta_5 \end{bmatrix} + \begin{bmatrix} \gamma_{11} \\ \gamma_{21} \\ \gamma_{31} \\ 0 \\ 0 \end{bmatrix} \xi + \begin{bmatrix} \zeta_1 \\ \zeta_2 \\ \zeta_3 \\ \zeta_4 \\ \zeta_5 \end{bmatrix}$$

where

ξ = customer expectations,
η_1 = perceived quality,
η_2 = perceived value,
η_3 = ACSI,

η_4 = customer complaints, and
η_5 = customer loyalty.

The general equations relating the latent variables to the measurement variables are

$$y = \Lambda_y\eta + \epsilon,$$

and

$$x = \Lambda_x\xi + \delta,$$

where $y' = (y_1, y_2, \ldots, y_p)$ and $x' = (x_1, x_2, \ldots, x_q)$ are the measured endogenous and exogenous variables, respectively. Λ_y $(p \times m)$ and Λ_x $(q \times n)$ are the corresponding regression matrices. By implication from PLS estimation (Fornell and Bookstein 1982), we have $E[\epsilon] = E[\delta] = E[\eta\epsilon'] = E[\xi\delta'] = 0$. The corresponding equations in ACSI are

$$\begin{bmatrix} x_1 \\ x_2 \\ x_3 \end{bmatrix} = \begin{bmatrix} w_{11} \\ w_{21} \\ w_{31} \end{bmatrix} \xi + \begin{bmatrix} \delta_1 \\ \delta_2 \\ \delta_3 \end{bmatrix}$$

and

$$\begin{bmatrix} y_1 \\ y_2 \\ y_3 \\ y_4 \\ y_5 \\ y_6 \\ y_7 \\ y_8 \\ y_9 \\ y_{10} \\ y_{11} \end{bmatrix} = \begin{bmatrix} w_{11} & 0 & 0 & 0 & 0 \\ w_{21} & 0 & 0 & 0 & 0 \\ w_{31} & 0 & 0 & 0 & 0 \\ 0 & w_{12} & 0 & 0 & 0 \\ 0 & w_{22} & 0 & 0 & 0 \\ 0 & 0 & w_{13} & 0 & 0 \\ 0 & 0 & w_{23} & 0 & 0 \\ 0 & 0 & w_{33} & 0 & 0 \\ 0 & 0 & 0 & w_{14} & 0 \\ 0 & 0 & 0 & 0 & w_{15} \\ 0 & 0 & 0 & 0 & w_{25} \end{bmatrix} \begin{bmatrix} \eta_1 \\ \eta_2 \\ \eta_3 \\ \eta_4 \\ \eta_5 \end{bmatrix} + \begin{bmatrix} \epsilon_1 \\ \epsilon_2 \\ \epsilon_3 \\ \epsilon_4 \\ \epsilon_5 \\ \epsilon_6 \\ \epsilon_7 \\ \epsilon_8 \\ \epsilon_9 \\ \epsilon_{10} \\ \epsilon_{11} \end{bmatrix}$$

where

x_1 = customer expectations about overall quality,
x_2 = customer expectations about reliability,
x_3 = customer expectations about customization,
y_1 = overall quality,
y_2 = reliability,
y_3 = customization,
y_4 = price given quality,
y_5 = quality given price,
y_6 = overall customer satisfaction,
y_7 = confirmation of expectations,
y_8 = distance to ideal product (service),
y_9 = formal or informal complaint behavior,
y_{10} = repurchase intention, and
y_{11} = price tolerance (reservation price).

The general form of the ACSI is as follows:

$$\text{ACSI} = \frac{E[\xi] - \text{Min}[\xi]}{\text{Max}[\xi] - \text{Min}[\xi]} \times 100.$$

where ξ is the latent variable for overall customer satisfaction, and $E[\,.\,]$, $Min[\,.\,]$, and $Max[\,.\,]$ denote the expected, the minimum, and the maximum value of the variable, respectively. The minimum and the maximum values are determined by those of the corresponding measurement variables:

$$\text{Min}[\xi] = \sum_{i=1}^{n} w_i \, \text{Min}[x_i],$$

and

$$\text{Max}[\xi] = \sum_{i=1}^{n} w_i \, \text{Max}[x_i],$$

where x_i's are the measurement variables of the latent overall customer satisfaction, w_i's are the weights, and n is the number of measurement variables. In calculating the ACSI, unstandardized weights must be used if unstandardized measurement variables are used.

In ACSI, there are three indicators for overall customer satisfaction, which range from 1 to 10. Then, the calculation is simplified to

$$\text{ACSI} = \frac{\sum_{i=1}^{3} w_i \bar{x}_i - \sum_{i=1}^{3} w_i}{9 \sum_{i=1}^{3} w_i} \times 100,$$

where the w_i's are the unstandardized weights.

References

American Society for Quality Control (1995), *American Customer Satisfaction Index: Methodology Report*. Milwaukee, WI: American Society of Quality Control.

Anderson, Eugene W. (1994), "Cross-Category Variation in Customer Satisfaction and Retention," *Marketing Letters*, 5 (January), 19–30.

———, Claes Fornell, and Donald R. Lehmann (1994), "Customer Satisfaction, Market Share, and Profitability: Findings From Sweden," *Journal of Marketing*, 58 (January), 53–66.

———, ———, and Roland T. Rust (1996), "Customer Satisfaction, Productivity, and Profitability: Differences Between Goods and Services," working paper, National Quality Research Center, Ann Arbor, MI.

Andrews, Frank M. (1984), "Construct Validity and Error Components of Survey Measures: A Structural Modeling Approach," *Public Opinion Quarterly*, 48, 409–42.

Buzzell, Robert D., John A. Quelch, and Walter J. Salmon (1990), "The Costly Bargain of Trade Promotion," *Harvard Business Review*, Reprint No. 90201, 68 (October/November), 33–45.

Cronbach, Lee J. and Paul E. Meehl (1955), "Construct Validity in Psychological Tests," *Psychological Bulletin*, 52 (4), 291–302.

Fornell, Claes (1992), "A National Customer Satisfaction Barometer: The Swedish Experience," *Journal of Marketing*, 56 (January), 6–21.

——— (1995), "The Quality of Economic Output: Empirical Generalizations about Its Distribution and Association to Market Share," *Marketing Science*, 14 (3), G203–11.

——— and Fred L. Bookstein (1982), "Two Structural Equation Models: LISREL and PLS Applied to Consumer Exit-Voice Theory," *Journal of Marketing Research*, 14 (November), 440–52.

———, Christopher D. Ittner, and David F. Larcker (1995), "Understanding and Using the American Customer Satisfaction Index (ACSI): Assessing the Financial Impact of Quality Initiatives," *Proceedings of the Juran Institute's Conference on Managing for Total Quality*, forthcoming.

———, ———, and ——— (1996), "The Valuation Consequences of Customer Satisfaction," National Quality Research Center Working Paper, National Quality Research Center, Ann Arbor, MI.

——— and Michael D. Johnson (1993), "Differentiation as a Basis for Explaining Customer Satisfaction across Industries," *Journal of Economic Psychology*, 14 (4), 681–96.

——— and Birger Wernerfelt (1987), "Defensive Marketing Strategy by Customer Complaint Management," *Journal of Marketing Research*, 24 (November), 337–46.

Fortune (1993), "Why the Economic Data Mislead Us," (March 8), 108–14.

——— (1995), "Americans Can't Get No Satisfaction," (December 11), 178–94.

Hirschman, Albert O. (1970), *Exit, Voice, and Loyalty—Responses to Decline in Firms, Organizations, and States*. Cambridge, MA: Harvard University Press.

Howard, John A. (1977), *Consumer Behavior: Application of Theory*. New York: McGraw-Hill.

Ittner, Christopher D. and David F Larcker (1996), "Measuring the Impact of Quality Initiatives on Firm Financial Performance," in *Advances in the Management of Organizational Quality*, Vol. 1, Soumeh Ghosh and Donald Fedor, eds. Greenwich, CT: JAI Press, 1–37.

Johnson, Michael D., Eugene W. Anderson, and Claes Fornell (1995), "Rational and Adaptive Performance Expectations in a Customer Satisfaction Framework," *Journal of Consumer Research*, 21 (March), 128–40.

——— and Claes Fornell (1991), "A Framework for Comparing Customer Satisfaction across Individuals and Product Categories," *Journal of Economic Psychology*, 12 (2), 267–86.

Kahneman, Daniel and Amos Tversky (1979), "Prospect Theory: An Analysis of Decision under Risk," *Econometrica*, 47 (2), 263–91.

Lancaster, Kelvin (1971), *Consumer Demand: A New Approach*. New York: Columbia University Press.

Meyer, Anton (1994), *Das Deutsche Kundenbarometer 1994*. München, Germany: Ludwig-Maximilians-Universität München.

National Quality Research Center (1995), *American Customer Satisfaction Index: Methodology Report*, University of Michigan Business School, Milwaukee, WI: American Society for Quality Control.

Oliver, Richard L. (1980), "A Cognitive Model of the Antecedents and Consequences of Satisfaction Decisions," *Journal of Marketing Research*, 17 (November), 460–69.

Reichheld, Fredrick F. and W. Earl Sasser (1990), "Zero Defections: Quality Comes to Services," *Harvard Business Review*, 68 (September/October), 105–11.

Wold, Herman (1989), *Theoretical Empiricism: A General Rationale for Scientific Model Building*. New York: Paragon House.

Yi, Youjae (1991), "A Critical Review of Customer Satisfaction," in *Review of Marketing 1990*, Valerie Zeithaml ed. Chicago: American Marketing Association, 68–123.

Customer Evaluations of Service Complaint Experiences:
Implications for Relationship Marketing

STEPHEN S. TAX
STEPHEN W. BROWN
MURALI CHANDRASHEKARAN

Many companies consider investments in complaint handling as means of increasing customer commitment and building customer loyalty. Firms are not well informed, however, on how to deal successfully with service failures or the impact of complaint handling strategies. In this study, the authors find that a majority of complaining customers were dissatisfied with recent complaint handling experiences. Using justice theory, the authors also demonstrate that customers evaluate complaint incidents in terms of the outcomes they receive, the procedures used to arrive at the outcomes, and the nature of the interpersonal treatment during the process. In turn, the authors develop and test competing hypotheses regarding the interplay between satisfaction with complaint handling and prior experience in shaping customer trust and commitment. The results support a quasi "brand equity" perspective—whereas satisfaction with complaint handling has a direct impact on trust and commitment, prior positive experiences mitigate, to a limited extent, the effects of poor complaint handling. Implications for managers and scholars are discussed.

Considerable evidence indicates that recovering effectively from service failures contributes to customer evaluations of firms. Effective complaint handling can have a dramatic impact on customer retention rates, deflect the spread of damaging word of mouth, and improve bottom-line performance (e.g., Fornell and Wernerfelt 1987; Kelley, Hoffman, and Davis 1993; McCollough and Bharadwaj 1992; Reichheld 1993). The Hampton Inn hotel chain, for example, recently realized $11 million in additional annual revenue and achieved the highest customer retention rate in the industry from the implementation of its service guarantee, part of a strategy to ensure that customer problems would be dealt with effectively (Ettorre 1994).

Effective resolution of customer problems and relationship marketing are linked closely in terms of

their mutual interest in customer satisfaction, trust, and commitment (Achrol 1991; Morgan and Hunt 1994). Complaint handling strategies are important particularly in managing customer relationships in service businesses. Challenges in managing quality, combined with the important role played by customers in the service production process and evidence that customer loyalty drives profitability, make complaint handling a critical "moment of truth" in maintaining and developing these relationships (Berry and Parasuraman 1991; Dwyer, Schurr, and Oh 1987).

One theme evident in the complaint management approaches of many service quality leaders (e.g., Ritz Carlton, Federal Express, Xerox) is the desire to provide "just" resolutions. This fairness ethic is reflected in these companies' internal specifications for the speed and convenience of the complaint procedure, as well as in their concern for appropriate customer compensation delivered by caring employees. Nevertheless, these kinds of positive initiatives are tempered by startling evidence that more than half of customers feel more negative about a company after they have gone through the service complaint process (Hart, Heskett, and Sasser 1990).

Despite calls for increasing investments in complaint handling, little is known about how customers evaluate a company's response to their complaints or how those efforts influence subsequent customer relationships with the firm (Goodwin and Ross 1992). Kelley and Davis (1994, p. 52) observe that "a dearth of empirical research confines any theoretical discussion

Stephen S. Tax is Associate Professor of Marketing, Faculty of Business, University of Victoria. Stephen W. Brown is First Interstate Chair of Services Marketing and Professor of Marketing, College of Business, Arizona State University. Murali Chandrashekaran is The Ronald J. Dornoff Fellow of Teaching Excellence and Associate Professor of Marketing, College of Business Administration, University of Cincinnati. The authors thank the Center for Services Marketing & Management at Arizona State University for providing support for the project and Lance Bettencourt, Mary Jo Bitner, and Ajith Kumar, all of Arizona State University; Bob Dwyer of the University of Cincinnati; and the three anonymous *JM* reviewers for their constructive comments on earlier drafts of the manuscript.

[of complaint handling] to anecdotal reports." Our purpose here is to provide a comprehensive understanding of service complaint handling evaluations and help managers develop effective complaint handling programs. The results of the empirical study also will clarify the importance of complaint resolution management to relationship management, providing insights into investment decisions. More specifically, we focus on the following questions:

1. How do customers evaluate an organization's efforts to resolve their service problems?

2. How do complaint handling evaluations affect customer satisfaction and how does satisfaction then influence the important relationship variables, trust and commitment?

3. How does prior experience with an organization affect the influence of complaint handling satisfaction on trust and commitment?

We address the first research question through content analysis of customer descriptions of specific complaint incidents. We examine the other two questions through the analysis of customer survey data about actual complaint experiences.

The balance of the article is organized as follows: First, a framework integrating complaint handling with relationship marketing variables is presented. Second, justice literature is reviewed and integrated into the framework. Using this foundation, a com-

plaint is viewed as a conflict between the customer and the organization in which the fairness of (1) the resolution procedures, (2) the interpersonal communications and behaviors, and (3) the outcome are the principal evaluative criteria of the customer. Given this base, key elements of relationship marketing (trust and commitment) are examined and incorporated into the framework. Third, the methodology is presented, including a description of the respondents' self-reports of complaint incidents and a delineation of the structured questions used to test the hypothesized relationships among the justice, satisfaction, and relationship variables. Following an examination of the results, we conclude with key managerial and research implications.

Complaint Handling Framework

Complaint handling refers to the strategies firms use to resolve and learn from service failures in order to (re)establish the organization's reliability in the eyes of the customer (Hart, Heskett, and Sasser 1990). Complaint data are key in quality management efforts because they can be used to correct problems with service design and delivery, which makes it more likely that performance will be done right the first time (Lovelock 1994).

Figure 1 displays the framework guiding the study. We focus on complaints lodged directly with the firm because they are the only responses that provide the

FIGURE 1

A Framework for Examining Complaint Handling Relationships

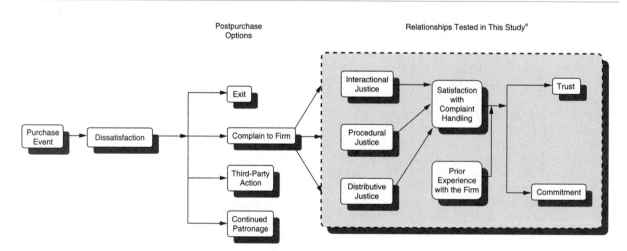

[a]In addition to the direct effects of the three justice concepts on satisfaction with complaint handling, we hypothesize all two-way interactions. They are omitted from the figure for purpose of clarity.

organization with an opportunity to recover effectively from the service failure. The shaded area describes the relationships tested in this study. The factors that link satisfaction with complaint handling include both the direct effects and two-way interactions between the three justice concepts. Satisfaction with complaint handling is positioned as the mediator between the perceived justice evaluations and the relationship variables. Prior experience with the firm is proposed to moderate the influence of satisfaction with complaint handling on both trust and commitment. A review of the literature supporting the relationships posited in Figure 1 follows.

Justice and Complaint Handling Evaluations

Research across several contexts (e.g., legal, organizational, buyer-seller, marriage) has found the concept of justice valuable in explaining people's reactions to conflict situations (e.g., Gilliland 1993; Goodwin and Ross 1992; Lind and Tyler 1988). Justice has been linked to complaint handling in a limited way through use of global fairness measures (Blodgett, Granbois, and Walters 1993) and the experimental manipulation of a narrow set of "justice elements" (Conlon and Murray 1996; Goodwin and Ross 1992).

From a process perspective, complaint handling can be viewed as a sequence of events in which a procedure, beginning with communicating the complaint, generates a process of interaction through which a decision and outcome occurs. Justice literature suggests that each part of the sequence is subject to fairness considerations and that each aspect of a complaint resolution creates a justice episode (Bies 1987). The service encounter and quality literature also stress the influence of interpersonal treatment, process elements, and benefits/outcomes as core components of service evaluations (e.g., Parasuraman, Zeithaml, and Berry 1985; Taylor 1994). Justice offers a comprehensive framework for understanding the complaint process from initiation to completion—hence its value in studying the phenomenon.

Dimensions of Justice and Satisfaction with Complaint Handling

Justice involves the propriety of decisions. A three-dimensional view of the concept has evolved over time to include *distributive justice* (dealing with decision outcomes), *procedural justice* (dealing with decision-making procedures), and *interactional justice* (dealing with interpersonal behavior in the enactment of procedures and delivery of outcomes). This is clari-

fied by Austin (1979, p. 24), who observes, "Justice pertains not merely to outcome distributions, but also to how the distribution is arrived at and the manner by which it is implemented."

Distributive Justice Theories of distributive justice focus on the allocation of benefits and costs (Deutsch 1985). Social exchange theory emphasizes the role of distributive or exchange considerations in shaping interpersonal relations. As many as 17 standards and/or rules of distributive justice have been identified in the literature (Reis 1986). Notable among these are the principles of equity, equality, and need (for an overview of relevant literature, see Table 1).

Marketing literature focuses almost exclusively on the equity principle. Several studies support equity evaluations affecting consumer satisfaction (e.g., Oliver and DeSarbo 1988; Oliver and Swan 1989), repurchase intention, and word-of-mouth decisions (e.g., Blodgett, Hill and Tax 1997). Research settings include stockbrokers, airlines, and retail, providing support for equity having a robust impact on postpurchase judgments.

There is some evidence of the use of the equity principle in complaint handling practices. For example, Domino's Pizza's decision to change its service guarantee from "Delivery within 30 minutes or receive a free pizza" to "Delivery within 30 minutes or $3.00 off the purchase price" was explained as an equity decision. The firm found that customers believed that providing a free pizza for just missing a delivery deadline was too generous. In complaint handling, distributions and outcomes can take the form of corrections of charges, refunds, repairs, credit, replacements, and apologies (Kelley, Hoffman, and Davis 1993).

Although support has been found for customers making equity judgments with respect to outcomes, equality and/or need also are relevant to a complainant's evaluation of distributive justice. Firms that promise to take care of customer needs and tout that they will provide "110% satisfaction" create expectations that complaints will be dealt with in a manner most closely reflecting the needs rule. People who enter a complaint situation knowing how fellow customers have been treated in similar circumstances are likely to expect similar treatment. Therefore, the customer might assess the fairness of compensation differently on the basis of his or her (1) prior experience with the firm in question and other firms, (2) awareness of other customers' resolutions, and (3) perceptions of his or her own loss. This suggests that distributive justice in complaint handling is operationalized best in more general terms, such as whether the outcome was perceived to be deserved, met one's needs, or was fair. We hypothesize that:

H1: Distributive justice is related positively to satisfaction with complaint handling.

Procedural Justice Although previous studies of justice concentrated on the perceived fairness of outcomes, more recent interest has focused on procedural justice—defined as the perceived fairness of the means by which the ends are accomplished (Lind and Tyler 1988). Procedural justice is meaningful because it aims to resolve conflicts in ways that encourage the continuation of a productive relationship between the disputants, even when outcomes are unsatisfactory to one or both parties (Folger 1987; Greenberg 1990a).

In Table 1, we describe five elements of procedural justice identified in the legal, marketing, psychology, and organizational literature that appear relevant particularly to complaint evaluations. The elements collectively suggest that a fair complaint procedure is easy to access, provides the complainant with some control over the disposition, is flexible, and is concluded in a convenient and timely manner.

Organizational research has found relationships between procedural justice and satisfaction with variables such as pay, performance appraisals, layoff policies, and selection procedures (summarized by Greenberg 1990a). Although the few marketing studies that have examined procedural justice directly support its impact on customer attitudes (e.g., Clemmer 1988; Goodwin and Ross 1992), considerable research indirectly supports the influence of procedural issues on customer satisfaction (e.g., Bitner, Booms, and Tetreault 1990; Taylor 1994). This leads to our second hypothesis:

H2: Procedural justice is related positively to satisfaction with complaint handling.

Interactional Justice This third justice dimension refers broadly to the fairness of the interpersonal treatment people receive during the enactment of procedures (Bies and Shapiro 1987; Gilliland 1993). The inclusion of interactional factors helps explain why some people might feel unfairly treated even though they would characterize the decision-making procedure and outcome as fair (Bies and Shapiro 1987). Research indicates that aspects of communication between customers and employees/managers (Clemmer 1988; Goodwin and Ross 1992), as well as the effort expended to resolve a conflict (Mohr and Bitner 1995), affect customer satisfaction. Additional studies in service quality (e.g., Parasuraman, Zeithaml,

and Berry 1988) and complaint handling (e.g., Blodgett, Hill, and Tax 1997; Goodwin and Ross 1992) support the central role of interactional justice in customer decision making.

Research in marketing organizational behavior and social psychology provides insight into five potentially important interactional elements (see Table 1). Fair interpersonal treatment reflects aspects of politeness, concern, and honesty in the complaint process, as well as the provision of an explanation and meaningful effort in resolving a conflict. The cited studies support the influence of interactional justice on complaint handling evaluations. We consequently hypothesize that

H3: Interactional justice is related positively to satisfaction with complaint handling.

Interactions between Justice Dimensions Although it has been argued that people evaluate the justice variables independently (Greenberg 1990b), there is theoretical and considerable empirical support for two-way interactions significantly affecting the relationship between the justice components and satisfaction and attitude variables.

Procedural-Interactional McCabe (1990) suggests that when employees are responsible for enacting procedures, there is an opportunity for interpersonal behavior to influence procedural justice evaluations. When customers attribute employees' behavior to the organization, interpersonal treatment will influence assessments of procedural justice (Tyler and Bies 1989). Because frontline employees are frequently the focus of service customers' interaction with the firm, it is likely that such attributions are prevalent. The positive impact of procedural justice on complaint handling satisfaction can be compromised when employees behave unfairly (Goodwin and Ross 1992). Procedural justice evaluations also can be affected by an explanation that justifies the process used to allocate outcomes (e.g., Conlon and Murray 1996). An adequate explanation for the complaint procedure enhances evaluations, whereas a poor explanation (excuse) for the process lowers evaluations of procedural justice and overall satisfaction with the process. Furthermore, research indicates that the value of acceptable explanations can be suppressed if companies are perceived as slow in responding to complaints (Conlon and Murray 1996).

Procedural-Distributive Referent cognitions theory predicts that perceived procedural injustice will exacerbate feelings of distributive injustice when people believe a better outcome could have been achieved with

TABLE 1
Definition of Justice Elements and Associated Research

Justice Concept	Definition	Dependent Variable(s)	Representative Research
Distributive Justice			
Equity	Provision of outcomes proportional to inputs to an exchange	Satisfaction, repurchase intention, word of mouth	Goodwin and Ross (1992) Oliver and Desarbo (1988) Oliver and Swan (1989)
Equality	Equal outcomes regardless of contributions to an exchange	Satisfaction, social harmony	Greenberg (1990a) Deutsch (1985)
Need	Outcome based on requirements regardless of contributions	Satisfaction	Deutsch (1985)
Procedural Justice			
Process Control	Freedom to communicate views on a decision process	Satisfaction, commitment	Goodwin and Ross (1992) Kanfer et al. (1987) Lind and Tyler (1988)
Decision Control	Extent to which a person is free to accept or reject a decision outcome	Satisfaction, relationship investment	Brett (1986) Heide and John (1992)
Accessibility	Ease of engaging a process	Satisfaction	Bitner, Booms, and Tetreault (1990) Bowen and Lawler (1995)
Timing/Speed	Perceived amount of time taken to complete a procedure	Anger, uncertainty, satisfaction, service quality	Fisk and Coney (1982) Maister (1985) Taylor (1994)
Flexibility	Adaptability of procedures to reflect individual circumstances	Market orientation, satisfaction	Bitner, Booms, and Tetreault (1990) Narver and Slater (1990)
Interactional Justice			
Explanation/Causal Account	Provision of reason for a failure	Attributions for failure, satisfaction, fairness	Bies and Shapiro (1987) Bitner, Booms, and Tetreault (1990)
Honesty	Perceived veracity of information provided	Satisfaction (complaint handling)	Goodwin and Ross (1989)
Politeness	Well-mannered, courteous behavior	Complaint evaluation, repurchase intention, satisfaction	Blodgett, Hill, and Tax (1997) Clemmer (1988) Goodwin and Ross (1989)
Effort	Amount of positive energy put into resolving a problem	Anger, satisfaction, trust	Folkes (1984) Mohr and Bitner (1995)
Empathy	Provision of caring, individual attention	Service quality, satisfaction	Parasuraman, Zeithaml, and Berry (1988)

a fairer procedure (Folger 1984). Studies considering pay cuts and increases and wage freezes have found that procedural justice might overcome some of the disappointment associated with unfair outcomes and increase both the perceived fairness of those outcomes and overall satisfaction with the institution (e.g., Lind and Tyler 1988; McFarlin and Sweeney 1992). In a complaint context, unfair procedures, especially ones that cause inconvenience for the customer (e.g., having to return for a third time to receive a refund because no one in the store had the authority to authorize the check), can be expected to contribute to the customer's cost and lower evaluations of the fairness of the outcome.

Distributive-Interactional Although few studies have considered distributive and interactional justice jointly, the extant research supports an interactive effect. Causal account literature suggests that making excuses or delivering outcomes in a rude or insincere manner affects the value of the outcome (e.g., Bies and Shapiro 1987), whereas performance appraisal research indicates that the manner in which the review is communicated influences the perceived fairness of its outcome (Greenberg and McCarty 1990). The impact of providing explanations for product failures on customer satisfaction is enhanced if the explanation is accompanied by a coupon or other reimbursement (Conlon and Murray 1996). This leads to our fourth hypothesis:

H_4: Two-way interactions among the three justice components will affect satisfaction with complaint handling.

Complaint Handling Satisfaction and Relationship Marketing

Westbrook (1987, p. 28) observes that satisfaction "usually is regarded as the central mediator of postpurchase behavior, linking prechoice product beliefs to postchoice cognitive structure, consumer communications, and repurchase behavior." Similarly, satisfaction with complaint handling could be the central mediator that links perceptions of the fairness dimensions to postcomplaint attitudes and behaviors.

Extant research supports this connection. As we show in Table 1, most of the studies find a relationship between justice evaluations and satisfaction with variables such as pay, work, performance appraisals, trial verdicts, salespeople, and, most important, consumer services. For example, Bitner, Booms, and Tetreault (1990) find that customers were likely to have positive reactions to encounters in which initial service failures were followed by effective recoveries, such as being upgraded to a better room, compensated with a free meal or drink, provided with an explanation as to why the service was unavailable, or assisted in solving the problem. In contrast, failure to apologize, compensate, or explain the problem led to an unfavorable recollection encounter.

The attitudinal and behavioral consequences of customer satisfaction play a central role in driving long-term customer relationships. However, the extant satisfaction research focuses mainly on behavioral intentions toward a product or organization and not on variables highlighting the potential for long-term customer relationships. Behavioral intention measures might not reflect fully the underlying attitudes that contribute to fostering long-term relationships. Repurchase intentions, for example, influenced strongly by structural factors such as switching costs, availability of alternatives, or contractual arrangements. In this study, we focus on two variables that have been pervasive in discussions of relationship development: commitment and trust.

Commitment

Definitions of commitment focus on the enduring desire of parties to maintain a relationship (Morgan and Hunt 1994). Kelley, Donnelly, and Skinner (1990, p. 322) state that "the organizational commitment of service customers is indicative of the organization's likelihood of developing or maintaining customer identification with organizational goals and values and retaining the service customer as an active participant in the service encounter." The need for customer participation in the delivery process makes the concept of commitment especially relevant to services (Kelley and Davis 1994).

One variable frequently associated with affecting both customer and employee commitment is satisfaction (e.g., Kelley and Davis 1994; Kelley, Hoffman, and Davis 1993). Satisfaction reinforces the customer's decision to participate in the service process, leading over time to commitment (see Fornell 1992). Satisfaction with complaint handling can enhance the evaluation of service experiences (Bitner, Booms, and Tetreault 1990) and contribute to customer retention (Technical Assistance Research Program 1986). McCollough and Bharadwaj (1992) refer to the situation in which effective recovery leads to a customer rating an encounter more favorably than if no problem had occurred in the first place as the "paradox of service recovery." This is consistent with the view that customer satisfaction with complaint handling leads to an updating of customer commitment (Kelley and Davis 1994). This leads to our fifth hypothesis:

H_5: Satisfaction with complaint handling is related positively to customer commitment.

Trust

Trust is an important factor in the development of marketing relationships and exists "when one party has confidence in an exchange partner's reliability and integrity" (Morgan and Hunt 1994, p. 23). Holmes and Rempel (1989, p. 199) observe that "trust is strengthened if partners are responsive in ways that acknowledge an individual's particular needs and affirm their sense of worth." Trust in a person or organization is acquired by observing the party or learning of previous interactions, such as conflicts, the partner has had with others in similar situations (Holmes 1991). Because it is directly linked to meeting expectations, satisfaction over time reinforces the perceived reliability of the firm and contributes to trust (Ganesan 1994). Achrol (1991) stresses the central role of conflict management in fostering interfirm trust. In the framework described in Figure 1, the impact of effective conflict resolution is captured by the "Satisfaction with Complaint Handling" variable. Accordingly, we hypothesize that

> **H₆**: Satisfaction with complaint handling is related positively to trust.

Role of Prior Experience

Although support for the positive impact of a well-handled complaint on the relationship variables appears consistent, the consequences of poorly handled complaints are more controversial. We adopt a belief-updating perspective to analyze the role of prior experience when customers are dissatisfied with complaint handling. In this perspective, decision processes unfold over time, and each new piece is integrated with existing knowledge about the service. Evaluations are updated and subsequent purchase decisions are based on this revised information. To derive the impact of prior experience, however, we specify what aspect of prior incidents is used to update evaluations. Two alternative perspectives offer competing hypotheses.

Perspective 1: Accumulated Goodwill and Brand Equity Effects Brand equity literature (Aaker 1991) implicitly follows a belief-updating perspective in predicting the effect of prior experience on the relation-

ship variables. Here, similar to an anchor-and-adjusting process, prior experience serves as the basis for updating an evaluation. This, along with the insights from the catastrophe model (Oliva, Oliver, and MacMillan 1992), supports the position that the accumulation of equity (goodwill) through satisfying experiences will mitigate the negative effects of a poorly handled complaint. For customers whose experiences have been very positive, one poor recovery should have no effect on commitment or trust. Conversely, low satisfaction with complaint handling should have the most damaging impact on trust and commitment among customers who have had poor prior encounters. The interaction between prior experience and dissatisfaction that emerges from this perspective is presented in Figure 2 (line 1) and can be stated as follows:

> **H₇A**: The effect of dissatisfaction with complaint handling on trust and commitment will become *smaller* as the prior experience becomes more positive and approach zero when prior experience is highly positive.

Perspective 2: Service Quality, Expectations, and the Double-Deviation Effect Unlike the brand equity perspective, in which the basis of updating is satisfaction with prior encounters, this perspective

FIGURE 2

Interaction between Complaint Handling Dissatisfaction and Prior Experience: Competing Predictions[a]

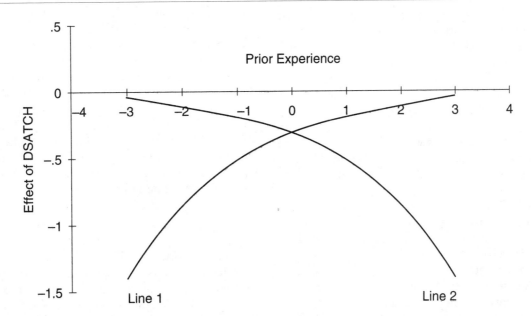

[a]The y-axis "Effect of DSATCH" represents the effect of dissatisfaction with the complaint handling on each of the dependent variables of COMMIT and TRUST as a function of prior experience.

Note: Line 1 represents the brand equity prediction for the effect of dissatisfaction with the complaint handling hypothesized in H₇A, and Line 2 represents the service quality prediction for the effect of dissatisfaction with the complaint handling expected in H₇B.

perceives the expectations fashioned by experience as the basis of updating. Service quality literature perceives a failed complaint incident as a "double deviation" in that both the initial event and the recovery attempt are failures (Bitner, Booms, and Tetreault 1990). Because of the initial failure, expectations for recovery tend to be high, particularly for loyal customers, which makes the process of complaint handling highly significant to commitment and trust (Kelley and Davis 1994). Organizational research supports this view and finds that unfair treatment has the greatest negative influence on those employees previously most committed to the organization (Brockner, Tyler, and Cooper-Schneider 1992).

Thus, service quality literature predicts that poor complaint handling will damage the relationship most when prior experience is positive and expectations for recovery are high and damage it least when prior experiences are poor and expectations are low. This line of reasoning is presented graphically in Figure 2 (line 2) and leads to the following competing hypothesis to H_{7A}:

H_{7B}: The effect of dissatisfaction with complaint handling on trust and commitment will start from zero and become *larger* as prior experience becomes more positive.

Empirical Study

Design

A cross-sectional survey design was used to assess respondents' evaluations of their most recent service-related complaint, with the stipulation that it was lodged within the past six months. This approach is consistent with that used in much of the service encounter and complaint research (e.g., Bitner, Booms, and Tetreault 1990; Kelley, Hoffman, and Davis 1993). The survey instrument included two distinct parts. In the first part, respondents were asked to describe the details of the complaint process. This was used both to explore pertinent aspects of justice in complaint handling and to examine the relevance of the elements identified in the literature and presented in Table 1. This portion of the survey addresses the first research question: How do customers evaluate an organization's efforts to resolve their service problems?

In the second part, structured questions measuring the variables of justice, satisfaction with complaint handling, trust, commitment, and prior experience were used to test the hypothesized relationships. This section addresses the study's second and third research questions regarding how complaint handling satisfaction affects the key relationship variables and how prior experience moderates that impact.

Sample

Employees from the local or national office of four medium- to large-sized firms, located in a large western city, constituted the sampling frame. The firms included a telecommunications company, a health care insurer, a bank, and a provider of ambulatory and emergency services. The employees in these firms participated as "everyday consumers," not in their role as employees of their respective organizations. This sampling procedure was used to acquire a reasonably large, motivated, and able sample. The length and relative complexity of the instrument indicated that a low response rate would be achieved from a random probability sample. A cover letter from a senior executive in each firm encouraged employees to respond conscientiously. A post hoc evaluation of the thoroughness of the vast majority of responses suggests that this approach enhanced both the rate and the quality of the responses.

Procedure

The same questionnaire was administered to the four sample groups. Three firms used internal mail systems for delivery and return, whereas the fourth firm sent questionnaires directly to potential respondents' homes. The data-gathering procedure was designed to obtain high return rates efficiently. A total of 1167 questionnaires was distributed with 257 returned, which yielded a 23% return rate. This percentage underestimates the actual response rate, because many potential respondents had not complained in the stated time frame and therefore were not considered part of the population of interest. Eighteen of the questionnaires had to be excluded from the first phase of the analysis, either because they did not involve services or the details of the complaint experience were too vague. Three of the firms' return rates were in excess of 25% (26%, 27%, and 32%), whereas the fourth firm's rate was only 7%. We attribute the low response rate of the one firm to the home mailing procedure. In the other cases, employees were allowed to use work time to complete the questionnaire.

Measures

Service Encounter The initial portion of the instrument contained questions that required subjects to report the details of a recent service experience leading to their lodging a complaint. Details included the type of service receiving the complaint, the media used to lodge the complaint (e.g., telephone, mail, in person), the persons complained to (e.g., waiter, service representative, manager), and the number of people involved in resolving the dispute. These questions provided useful information that contributed to understanding complaint-handling evaluations and helped the respondents focus on the encounter.

Two principal questions were included to discover how respondents, through personal experience and in their own terms, viewed fairness in complaint resolution situations. The phrasing and content were based on prior service encounter research (e.g., Bitner, Booms, and Tetreault 1990; Kelley, Hoffman, and Davis 1993). The following questions were placed immediately after a scaled item that asked how the respondent felt the complaint had been handled (seven scale anchored by Fairly and Unfairly):

- "Why do you feel this way? That is, exactly what happened?"

- "What, if anything, could the firm have done to handle the complaint more fairly?"

Scaled Questions Each of the five interactional and procedural elements (see Table 1) was measured with multi-item scales. Many of the measures were adapted from previous studies (e.g., Bitner, Booms, and Tetreault 1990, Clemmer 1988; Mohr and Bitner 1995; Parasuraman, Zeithaml, and Berry 1988), whereas others were constructed. Scores for interactional and procedural justice were developed in a two-step procedure. First, items measuring each of the formative indicators (e.g., honesty, empathy, politeness in the case of interactional justice) were summed. Second, the scores for the indicators were summed to obtain a score for interactional and procedural justice for use in the regression analysis.[1]

Because of the multiple distributive rules that might be relevant to complaint evaluations, items used to measure distributive justice reflected broad evaluations of the fairness of the outcomes. These included questions about whether the results of the complaint met the complainant's needs, and were equitable, fair, or right. These items built on measures used in other marketing studies (e.g., Clemmer 1988; Oliver and Swan 1989).

Satisfaction with complaint handling, commitment, trust, and prior experience were measured with items adapted specifically for this research context (e.g., Crosby, Evans, and Cowles 1990; Mowday, Porter, and Steers 1982). Pretest findings (n = 80) indicated a few problematic items, and revisions were made to the final instrument. Examples of items and reliability assessments appear in Appendix A.

Results

The results of the study are organized as follows: We present the results from the descriptive questions. Next, we assess content analysis of the open-ended, complaint handling questions. Finally, we perform extensive model testing to assess the hypothesized relationships.

Descriptive Results

The respondents' average age was 36 years (standard deviation = 10.77), and 63% were women. Most of the complaints were lodged either in person (45%) or by telephone (45%), with only 10% using the mail. In most cases, complaint handling involved more than one member of the firm (mean = 2.12, standard deviation = 1.26). More than 30 different types of services were the subject of respondent complaints. The most frequently identified were restaurants (37), auto repair (32), banks (26), doctors and dentists (18), airlines (15), and hotels/motels (13). The score for complaint handling fairness (mean = 4.37, standard deviation = 1.45, seven-point scale where 1 = Fairly) indicates that, overall, respondents believed that these complaints were not being handled fairly. Finally, most complaints were lodged in reference to problems judged to be highly important by the complainant. Direct evidence of this was provided in the responses to the question, "How important to you was the problem which led to your complaint?" The mean response was 1.57 (standard deviation = 0.993) on a seven-point scale (1 = Very Important).

The Service Encounter: Content Analysis of Open-Ended Complaint Questions

Content analysis, using a coding approach consistent with other service encounter research (e.g., Bitner, Booms, and Tetreault 1990; Kelley, Hoffman, and Davis 1993), was employed to examine the two

---

[1]We first performed factor analysis and found strong evidence for the unidimensionality of each of the subdimensions of the formative indicators of interactional and procedural justice. Specifically, factor analysis revealed that (1) in all cases only one factor had an eigenvalue exceeding 1.0, (2) the factor loadings were well over .90 in a majority of the cases, and (3) the standardized regression scoring coefficients were similar for each element of each subdimension. (Thus weighting each element in each subdimension would be equivalent to an averaging procedure that we used.) Next, factor analysis uncovered unidimensionality for each of the justice components (the first and second largest eigenvalues in the case of interactional, procedural, and distributive justice were 3.72 and .70, 3.24 and .75, and 4.37 and .21, respectively). Again, in all cases, the loadings were high, and the standardized regression scoring coefficients were similar for each element of the justice components. On the basis of this evidence, we are confident in the applicability of the two-step summation approach to compute the justice components. In addition, both confirmatory factor analysis and the Bagozzi and Warshaw (1990) test provide support for discriminant validity among all the variables in the study.

questions that reflected what respondents believed was (un)fair about their complaint experience. Two coders, working independently, first coded responses into one of the three justice components. For example, if a respondent stated that the employee was polite (interactional), the process took too long (procedural), and the compensation was not sufficient (distributive), three items were coded. Next, the interactional and procedural items were categorized into one of the specific formative elements identified in Table 1. If references were made to an interactional or procedural fairness issue that did not fit with any of the predetermined categories, a new category was created. The distributive justice items were placed into categories on the basis of the outcome groupings from the classification method developed by Kelley, Hoffman, and Davis (1993). Disagreements in classifying statements were resolved by the coders and the principal researcher. To assess reliability a third coder categorized the initial statements. The overall agreement, determined by comparing the final independent coding with the results of the initial two coders, was 86%.

We present the results in Table 2, organized around the three justice concepts. Although most respondent comments refer to multiple justice issues, the sample quotes were selected to highlight specific aspects of each justice concept.

Distributive Justice   A few distinct distributive categories emerged in this analysis. Issues involving evaluations of the compensation provided by the service provider were most prevalent. Many commented on the fairness of the refund, repair, or replacement they received as restitution for the service failure.

The provision or absence of an apology was the next most frequently mentioned issue. Many commented that they deserved an apology as compensation for being treated unfairly. Therefore, the decision was made to include apologies as a distributive rather than an interactional justice element as it has appeared in other research (e.g., Goodwin and Ross 1992). Viewing apologies as outcomes is consistent with the concept of restoring "psychological equity" (Walster, Berscheid, and Walster 1973) to people who have been treated poorly. Many respondents commented on the sincerity or insincerity of the apology, which infers that apologies can be perceived as outcomes that can be delivered in a fair or unfair manner. In each case with no resolution, respondents believed that they were dealt with unfairly. This suggests that just getting dissatisfied customers to complain will not have positive effects if the complaint is not resolved, contrary to other findings (e.g., Technical Assistance Research Program 1986).

Most interesting was the apparent relationship between the assessment of outcomes and procedural and interactional matters. For example, in several cases, respondents indicated that outcomes provided in a rude, indifferent manner were less valuable than if the same compensation had been delivered by a more concerned person. Another important cause of (dis)satisfaction was related to "compensation for the hassle." Several customers cited the compensation as not being worth the trouble, especially when the complaint process was inefficient.

Procedural Justice   Although each of the literature-based procedural elements was mentioned a minimum of three times, frequency of reference varied considerably (see Table 2). The most often mentioned issue was the organization's taking responsibility for the problem. Many respondents suggested that the "struggle" to get the process moving forward often was thwarted by the organization's attempts to shift responsibility for the failure to the customer, which prompted one respondent to comment that the organization to which she complained operated on the principle that the "customer is always wrong."

Procedural elements associated with the perceived speed (tardiness) and (in)convenience of the process also were prominent themes. A different issue related to the organization "following up" to ensure that the complaint was resolved effectively. Respondents appeared particularly delighted to hear back from the organization inquiring whether the complaint had been handled to their satisfaction. Comments about follow-up also tended to be linked with comments about empathy and concern, which suggests a possible association between these interactional and procedural issues.

Interactional Justice   Although each of the five interactional elements identified in the literature was mentioned, basic expectations of courtesy and empathy were most pervasive (see Table 2). Experiences related to these elements were split roughly 40% positive and 60% negative.

The provision of information about the service problem created a split among respondents. On the one hand, respondents expressed favorable feelings about information provided to assist them in understanding the service failure and help them obtain a quick and fair resolution. On the other hand, when information was provided in the form of an excuse to mitigate the organization's accountability, it was perceived negatively and associated with failure to take responsibility. This suggests an association between interactional and procedural evaluations. Further evidence of this relates to comments about effort. If

TABLE 2
Results of Qualitative Questions

Justice Dimensions	Number of Times Mentioned	% Positive	Sample Comments
Distributive justice			"They were very thorough with my complaint. One week later I received a coupon for a free oil change and an extensive apology."
Compensation Issues:			
Reimbursement/ Refund	38	44	
Replacement	35	40	"Their refusal to refund money or make up for the inconvenience and cold food was inexcusable."
Repair	25	38	
Credit	12	50	"The situation was never remedied. Once they had my money, they disappeared when I had problems."
Correction Plus	8	85	
Apology	47	47	"If I wanted a refund, I had to go back to the store the next day. It's a 20-minute drive. The refund was barely worth the trouble."
No Resolution	20	0	
			"The waitress immediately noticed there was a problem and quickly got the manager. The sandwiches were taken back to the kitchen and recooked."
Procedural Issues			"The representative was pleasant and quick to resolve the problem."
Assuming Responsibility	45	40	
Timing/Speed	42	33	"They should have assisted me with the problem instead of giving me a phone number. No one ever returned my call and I never had a chance to speak to a real person."
Convenience (number of people/times)	30	40	
Follow-up	23	43	"I appreciated the server following up to make sure that the problem was corrected."
Process Control	19	36	
Flexibility	10	50	"I had to tell my story to too many people. I had to become an irate, dissatisfied customer in order to talk to the manager, who apparently was the only one who could provide a solution."
Knowledge of Process	9	33	
			"I was spoken to very rudely; was accused of causing the problem myself. I was not given any options of what could be done."
Interactional Justice			"The loan officer was very courteous, knowledgeable and considerate—kept me informed about the complaint."
Politeness	33	48	
Empathy	32	44	"The person who handled my complaint wasn't going to do anything about it and didn't seem to care."
Effort	20	50	
Explanation/Information	20	35	"The manager took the stance that it was not his problem and made no effort to help resolve it."
Honesty	11	27	
Attitude	8	25	"They lied to me about the free Pepsi, and they wouldn't give me a clear explanation as to why my pizza was late to begin with."
			"The manager had a good attitude. She wanted to make sure that I left satisfied."

frontline employees took it upon themselves to investigate the complaint and promptly resolve the problem, the effort was linked with process convenience and organization responsiveness. In other cases, poor effort contributed to negative comments about the process and the organization.

In summary, this part of the study provides evidence that elements identified with each of the three justice dimensions are relevant to customers' assessments of fair recoveries. The results also imply that each of the justice components is quite complex in its makeup, consistent with both the literature review and the elements measured in this study. Finally, the responses provide initial insights into the nature of interactions among the justice concepts.

Testing the Hypothesized Relationships

In this section we examine the relationships proposed in Figure 1 and specified in the hypotheses. The antecedents of satisfaction with complaint handling are examined; then the antecedents of trust and commitment are considered.

Antecedents of Satisfaction with Complaint Handling To test H_1–H_4, we estimated a regression model for satisfaction with complaint handling (SATCH) using ordinary least squares that included the main effects of interactional (INTJUST), procedural (PROJUST), and distributive justice (DISJUST), and the two-way interactions among the constructs. The results provide strong support for H_1–H_4.

The overall model was significant ($R^2 = .881$, $F_{6,214} = 264.1$, $p < .0001$), as were the interactions between DISJUST and INTJUST and DISJUST and PROJUST (both significant at $\alpha = .05$ level). We then computed the overall direct impacts of the three justice components.[2] These were .390 ($p < .0001$), .368 ($p < .0001$), and .457 ($p < .0001$) for DISJUST, PROJUST, and INTJUST, respectively.

To illuminate the pattern of the interactions, we computed predicted values of SATCH for various levels of the justice variables. These are presented in Figure 3. The predicted scores indicate that to achieve even a modest satisfaction with complaint handling, a firm must attain a relatively high score on all three justice components. Although improving any particular element has an impact, it is difficult to achieve a high score (five-point scale) if one or both of the other elements are poor. For example, going from a relatively low (2) to a relatively high (4) score on DISJUST has little impact on SATCH if INTJUST and PROJUST remain low (2). Overall, satisfaction would change

from 1.37 to 1.80. The same improvement in DISJUST has a much more dramatic impact when INTJUST and PROJUST are relatively high (4). In this case satisfaction would move from 2.63 to 3.83.

Antecedents of Commitment and Trust The next set of analyses centers on the antecedents of commitment (COMMIT) and trust (TRUST), which tests H_5 and H_6, and a non-linear interaction between dissatisfaction with complaint handling and prior experience, which tests competing hypotheses H_{7A} and H_{7B}. Appendix B provides the regression framework and the specific statistical tests that were used to assess the hypotheses. The regression results are presented in Table 3.

Segment of First-time Customers Among customers in this segment, COMMIT and TRUST were predicted to be shaped by the complaint handling. As was expected, as dissatisfaction with the compliant handling (DSATCH) increases, COMMIT and TRUST decrease (note in Table 3 that the estimate of γ_1 is significantly negative for both relationship variables; see issue [a] in Appendix B). These results provide support for H_5 and H_6.

Segment of Existing Customers Customers in this segment integrate aspects of prior and current experience to determine their commitment and trust. We were particularly interested in how prior experience (PE) moderated the effects of dissatisfaction with complaint handling (DSATCH). As was anticipated, we obtain a significant interaction of DSATCH and PE. The results support the brand equity perspective (H_{7A}) as opposed to the service quality perspective (H_{7B})—the estimate of γ_3 is significantly negative for both TRUST and COMMIT (see issue [b-iii] in Appendix B).

We now turn to the cumulative effect of dissatisfying complaint handling in the segment of existing customers. Two considerations directed our analysis. First, there is a significant interaction between the independent variables of DSATCH and PE. Second, PE is a continuous variable (ranging from -3 to $+3$). Therefore, as outlined in Appendix B, we took partial derivatives and assessed the effect of DSATCH on TRUST and COMMIT at various levels of PE. Table 4 presents the results. Observe in the table that across all levels of PE, DSATCH is associated with a decrease in TRUST and COMMIT. These results again support H_5 and H_6.

Next, note that as PE becomes more positive, the effect of DSATCH on the relationship variables decreases as predicted in the equity-driven hypothesis H_{7A}. Contrary to H_{7A}, however, even at very positive

---

[2]Owing to the significant interactions, the overall direct effects of the justice components must be interpreted in the light of the interactions. Therefore, we took partial derivatives with respect to each justice component in the following equation: SATCH $= \beta_0 + \beta_1$ INTJUST $+ \beta_2$ PROJUST $+ \beta_3$ DISJUST $+ \beta_4$ INTJUST $\times$ PROJUST $+ \beta_5$ INTJUST $\times$ DISJUST $+ \beta_6$ PROJUST $\times$ DISJUST. The estimated values of $\beta_0 - \beta_6$ were .23 ($p < .01$), .27 ($p < .01$), .15 ($p < .01$), -17 ($p < .01$), $-.03$ (ns), .094 ($p < .05$), and .10 ($p < .05$), respectively. Because of the significant interactions, we took partial derivatives with respect to each justice component in the estimated regression model to assess the relative magnitude of their impact. For example, the overall impact of INTJUST is given by ∂SATCH$/\partial$INTJUST $= \beta_1 + \beta_4$ PROJUST $+ \beta_5$ DISJUST. Furthermore, we evaluated the relative impact of each justice component at the mean value of the other justice dimensions.

FIGURE 3

Predicted Values for Satisfaction with Complaint Handling (SATCH)[a]

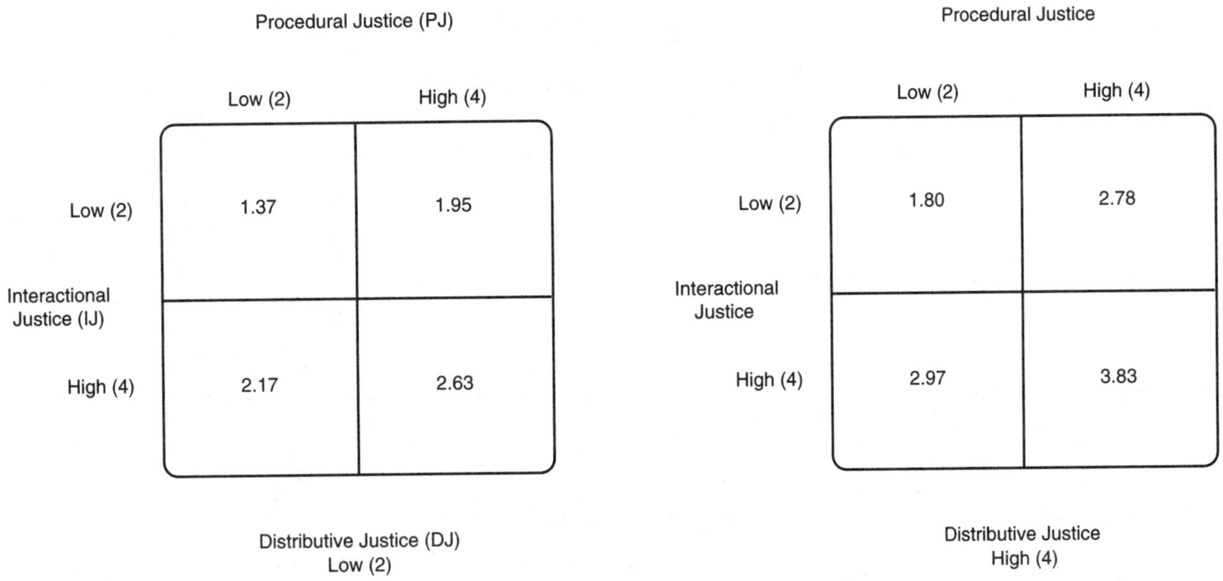

Procedural Justice (PJ)

	Low (2)	High (4)
Low (2)	1.37	1.95
High (4)	2.17	2.63

Interactional Justice (IJ)

Distributive Justice (DJ)
Low (2)

Procedural Justice

	Low (2)	High (4)
Low (2)	1.80	2.78
High (4)	2.97	3.83

Interactional Justice

Distributive Justice
High (4)

[a]SATCH = .23 + .27 IJ − .17 DJ + .15 PJ − .03 IJ × PJ + .1 DJ × PJ + .94 DJ × IJ

TABLE 3

Antecedents[a] of COMMIT and TRUST

			Dependent Variable	
Segment	Analysis focus	Parameter	COMMIT	TRUST
	Constant	γ_0	4.916*** (.134)	5.259*** (.125)
First-time customers	Effect of dissatisfaction with complaint handling	γ_1	− .740*** (.039)	− .733*** (.036)
Existing customers	Effect of dissatisfaction with complaint handling at neutral prior experience	$\gamma_2 - 1$	− .704*** (.038)	− .704*** (.035)
	Moderating effect of prior experience	γ_3	− .031 ** (.010)	− .016* (.009)
Log-likelihood			− 234.92	− 218.99
Log-likelihood under H$_0$: $\gamma_1 = \gamma_2 = \gamma_3 = 0$			− 354.89	− 347.68
Likelihood-ratio (χ^2_3)			239.94***	257.38***

***$p < .0001$; **$p < .01$; *$p < .05$.

[a]Appendix B specifies the functional form of the regression equation. Values in the columns under "Dependent Variable" are parameter estimates (standard errors are in parentheses).

levels of PE, DSATCH still has a negative effect on TRUST and COMMIT.

Following this analysis, we estimated many models to shed light on the relative impacts of the main effect of DSATCH and the moderating effect of PE.

Following Chandrashekaran and colleagues (1995; see footnote 8), we computed the unique contribution of the moderating effect of PE (ω_{PE}) as the reduction in the model log-likelihood value upon adding the moderating effect of PE. We similarly assessed the

TABLE 4

Impact[a] of Dissatisfaction Among Existing Customers on COMMIT and TRUST
at Various Levels of PE

	Relationship Variable				
	COMMIT			TRUST	
Level of PE	Estimate	Different from γ_1?		Estimate	Different from γ_1?
Negative (−3)	−.800* (.053)	No; t = −1.292		−.754* (.048)	No; t = −.513
Neutral (0)	−.704* (.038)	No; t = .973		−.704* (.035)	No; t = −.813
Positive (3)	−.615* (.044)	Yes; t = 2.483*		−.657* (.041)	No; t = 1.617

*$p < .01$.

[a]To test if the impact of dissatisfaction among existing customers is different from that among first-time customers, we use the Wald test to assess the following null hypothesis H_0: $\gamma_2 - \exp(\gamma_3 P) - \gamma_1 = 0$ (see Appendix B).

value (ω_{DSATCH}) of incorporating the direct effect of DSATCH.[3]

Results indicate that though including the moderating role of PE improved model fit, its impact was significantly smaller than the main effect of DSATCH. Specifically, focusing on TRUST, we found that whereas ω_{PE} = 2.01 log-likelihood units, ω_{DSATCH} = 31.67 log-likelihood units (corresponding values in the case of COMMIT were 5.25 and 27.91 log-likelihood units, respectively). These results indicate that though existing customers integrate aspects of prior and current experience to articulate their commitment and trust, current experience is a better diagnostic signal in shaping the relationship variables.

Segment Differences   Finally, we examined differences in the impact of DSATCH among first-time and existing customers. Note from Table 4 that at all levels of PE the impact of DSATCH on TRUST is not different between the two groups. Regardless of prior experience, a poorly handled complaint lowers trust. However, at highly positive levels of PE, the impact of DSATCH among existing customers on COMMIT is significantly smaller than it is for first-time customers, which provides additional support for the brand equity hypothesis (H_{7A}).

---

[3]Specifically, we computed the unique contribution of the moderating effect of PE (ω_{PE}) as follows: $\omega_{PE} = \lambda\ (\gamma_0, \gamma_1, \gamma_2, \gamma_3) - \lambda\ (\gamma_0, \gamma_1, \gamma_2, \gamma_3 = 0)$, where $\lambda\ (\gamma_0, \gamma_1, \gamma_2, \gamma_3)$ denotes the log-likelihood value for the full model, and $\lambda\ (\gamma_0, \gamma_1, \gamma_2, \gamma_3 = 0)$ is the log-likelihood value for the model that restricts the moderating effect of PE to be zero. Similarly, $\omega_{DSATCH} = \lambda\ (\gamma_0, \gamma_1, \gamma_2, \gamma_3) - \lambda\ (\gamma_0, \gamma_1, \gamma_2 = 0, \gamma_3)$. We note that though other approaches are possible (e.g., stepwise regression), the present approach is more conservative and corresponds to the approach that is based on computing Type III sums of squares in a conventional regression model.

Discussion

The major intents of this study were to (1) develop a greater understanding of how customers evaluate complaint handling experiences with firms and (2) examine the relationship between satisfaction with complaint handling, prior experience with the firm, and important relationship variables. The results have significant implications for both practice and scholarship.

Antecedents of Satisfaction with Complaint Handling

Both the open-ended and scaled questions provide considerable insights to the question: "How are complaint handling efforts evaluated?" Whereas previous research identifies complaint handling as central to repurchase decisions, this study reveals the complex criteria customers use to assess complaint handling efforts. Results support the view that justice concepts provide an effective theoretical framework for explaining satisfaction with complaint situations.

The interactional justice results include several aspects of (un)fair communication and behavior, such as honesty, empathy, and politeness. This is consistent with many of the elements of interactive marketing identified in services literature (e.g., Bitner 1995; Parasuraman, Zeithaml, and Berry 1985). The high frequency (greater than 50%) of unfavorable customer experiences associated with most of the interactional dimensions (see Table 2) is noteworthy because it implies that customer expectations regarding interpersonal treatment in the face of a failure are considerably higher than they are in standard service encounter situations, especially for loyal customers (Kelley and Davis 1994). We found that complaints frequently are lodged concurrent with a service failure and typically concern important problems that place customers in heightened states of frustration and anger. The employee or manager acting in a polite and empathetic manner, coupled with a strong effort to resolve the problem, contributed to diffusing customers' anger in many of the complaint incidents, whereas rude, uncaring behavior exacerbated the anger.

Procedural justice findings reflect aspects of customer convenience and firm follow-up and accessibility, which suggests that the adage "justice delayed is justice denied" applies to complaint handling. These findings represent a different emphasis than the focus on process and decision control found in the legal and organizational contexts of procedural justice literature (e.g., Lind and Tyler 1988). In the open-ended questions, respondents shared relatively few references to process and decision control, which implies that giving customers the opportunity to voice their complaint and have some control over its outcome is insufficient to ensure positive perceptions of procedural justice. Expectations that the firm should assume responsibility, respond quickly, and follow up are consistent with findings indicating that customers value responsiveness and reliability and dislike delays (e.g., Kelley, Hoffman, and Davis 1993; Taylor 1994).

Distributive justice results focus on compensation for financial loss and an apology. The importance of the apology suggests that restitution is not just for economic cost, but also for emotional costs. This finding is consistent with the view that distributive justice requires the provision of psychological equity (Walster, Berscheid, and Walster 1973). There is also some evidence that customers include the cost of complaining associated with interactional and procedural issues in their calculation of outcome fairness. Finally, complaints left unresolved universally were considered unfair, which challenges the results of prior research (Technical Assistance Research Program 1986).

The significant distributive-procedural justice and distributive-interactional justice interactions shed further light on customer decision making. The value of outcomes can be compromised or enhanced by interactions and procedures. We found many cases in which the inconvenience of the complaint process (e.g., having to go back to the store twice) made the compensation less appreciated than if it had come immediately. In other cases, firm follow-up to ensure that the problem was resolved appeared to enhance customers' assessments of the outcome. Similarly, outcomes delivered by rude employees or managers appeared less valuable to customers, whereas instances in which employees put considerable effort into resolving the problem strengthened customer outcome assessments.

The hypothesized interaction between procedural and interactional justice was not statistically significant. One possible explanation for this is that we did not measure "assuming responsibility" as a procedural indicator. This variable could be particularly associated with the interactional indicators of empathy and effort. The open-ended responses provide some evidence of this interactive effect.

Consequences of Satisfaction with Complaint Handling

Complaint handling satisfaction is significantly and strongly associated with both trust and commitment, which provides empirical support for the proposition that complaint handling is tied closely to relationship marketing. This result implies that customers who choose to complain are offering firms the opportunity to demonstrate their trustworthiness and that the resolution process drives customers' subsequent attitudes and behavior.

The findings on the role of prior experience are interesting, though its effects clearly were smaller than the main effect of satisfaction with complaint handling. Prior positive service experiences mitigated to a greater extent the effects of a poorly handled complaint on commitment but not on trust. Indeed, a poorly handled complaint hurt trust among existing customers just as much as it did among first-time customers. This implies that customers who have poor complaint handling experiences still might want to deal with the organization on the basis of expectations of future benefits grounded on past encounters (brand equity perspective).

Implications for Practice

The results indicate that a firm's favorable actions during episodes of conflict demonstrate its reliability and trustworthiness and imply that investments in complaint handling can improve evaluations of service quality, strengthen customer relationships, and build customer commitment. Given this finding, firms should reassess the fairness and appropriateness of existing processes (procedural justice), outcomes (distributive justice), and employee-customer communications (interactional justice). This is especially important because the results indicate that more than half of customers are dissatisfied with their complaint-handling experiences.

Early in their self-evaluation, firms should determine who is interacting with the complainant. Frontline employees frequently receive complaints (65% of the complaints in this study were initiated at this level). Establishing complaint handling as an important part of contact employees' job description is critical to ensuring fair treatment. Furthermore, training these employees is required in a variety of skill areas. For example, Ford employees with primary responsibility for complaint handling receive training on topics involving company policies, warranties, listening skills, diffusion of anger, and interpersonal communications. The training includes simulation exercises that focus on an irate customer meeting and a meeting with dealers.

Managers have several options in developing fair complaint handling procedures. Much discussion has surrounded the policy of empowering frontline service personnel to make decisions, including resolving complaints (Bowen and Lawler 1995). Empowerment addresses the critical issues of speed, convenience, accessibility, and flexibility of complaint procedures. Procedural fairness in complaint handling also might be facilitated through the adoption of call centers staffed by specialists in resolving customer problems, which contributes to accessible, fast, and consistent recovery. Service guarantees can be used to assist the consistent and efficient processing of complaints.

Providing fair outcomes requires that firms understand the full costs incurred by customers as a result of both the service failure and the complaint process. Firms that focus on providing dissatisfied customers with generous dispute settlements are unlikely to reap the desired effects on satisfaction, commitment, and trust if the remuneration is delivered through unfair procedures or by uncaring employees. Fair interactions and procedures can lower the cost of complaining and thereby reduce the compensation required to achieve distributive justice.

Limitations and Implications for Scholarship

Despite the interesting findings and implications that emerge from this study, it is important to recognize its limitations and the need for additional research. This research used a cross-sectional design based on retrospective reports; therefore, recall bias could have influenced the results. Furthermore, understanding the dynamics between complaint handling efforts and postcomplaint behaviors would be enhanced by tracing the relationship between the customer and the organization over time. This longitudinal research could go beyond the complaint handling and examine how organizations win back lost trust and commitment. Customer behaviors, such as exploring alternative service providers, also should be examined. Panel research designs that periodically survey complainants about their subsequent experiences with the firm and their assessments about trust and commitment can be developed.

One procedural element, assuming responsibility, was discovered first in the open-ended questions but was not included in the scaled questions. This might have reduced the magnitude of procedural influences on satisfaction. Assuming responsibility might signal to customers that the organization cares and wants to resolve the problem fairly. Additional research that directly includes this variable might uncover interactions between procedural and interactional justice not found in this study.

We also observed that respondents appreciated information that helped them understand the service failure and obtain a quick resolution, but when information was provided in the form of an excuse it was perceived negatively and associated with failure to take responsibility. More research is needed on the effect of different types of explanations on complaint handling satisfaction. Furthermore, research incorporating the impact of justice variables with traditional predictors (i.e., expectations, disconfirmation, and attributions) would contribute to our understanding of the determinants of complaint handling satisfaction.

The following questions about distributive justice warrant further examination: Do customers perceive differences in the fairness of the various distributive justice rules (equity, equality, need, and others)? Which rules do customers most frequently apply? What factors influence the rule customers choose to assess a particular complaint episode? These questions might be addressed best in controlled experimental designs (Deutsch 1985).

The role of justice in influencing trust and commitment in business conflicts is another interesting avenue for research. Several questions are worthy of investigation: Do the three justice concepts have the same magnitude on satisfaction with the conflict resolution? Do the same elements form interactional and procedural justice concerns? Is satisfaction with the conflict resolution more or less important than prior experience in forming trust and commitment in business relationships?

APPENDIX A
Construct Measures

One questionnaire item from each of the variables measured in the study is presented. All items except for the respondent's prior experience with the firm were measured on five-point scales anchored by Strongly Agree and Strongly Disagree. In the case of prior experience, respondents first were asked if they had made a purchase from the firm previously (yes or no). If they answered yes, they were asked to rate their experiences on three seven-point scales (anchored by Very Good and Very Poor). The total number of items measuring the construct and Cronbach's Alpha (CA) for the construct are as follows:

Interactional Justice (CA = .91)
Honesty (4 items, CA = .91): They did not appear to be telling me the truth.
Explanation (4 items, CA = .84): I was given a reasonable account as to why the original problem occurred.
Empathy (4 items, CA = .94): They seemed very concerned about my problem.
Politeness (4 items, CA = .94): I felt I was treated rudely.
Effort (4 items, CA = .93): They put a lot of positive energy into handling my problem.

Procedural Justice (CA = .86)
Decision Control (4 items, CA =.83): I had no say in the outcome of the complaint.
Accessibility (4 items, CA = .86): It was hard to figure who to complain to in this organization.
Timing/Speed (4 items, CA = .91): They responded quickly to my complaint.
Process Control (4 items, CA = .89): I was not given an opportunity to tell my side of the story.
Flexibility (4 items, CA = .89): They were willing to adapt their complaint handling procedures to satisfy my needs.

Distributive Justice (5 items, CA = .97): I got what I deserved from the complaint.

Satisfaction with Complaint Handling (4 items, CA = .96): I was not happy with how the organization handled my complaint.

Trust (4 items, CA = .96): I believed the organization could not be relied upon to keep its promises.

Commitment (4 items, CA = .92): I wanted to continue dealing with this organization.

Prior Experience (3 items, CA = .93): How would you rate your experiences with this organization prior to the incident which [led] to the complaint? (seven-point scale anchored by Very Negative and Very Positive).

APPENDIX B
Regression Framework for the Antecedents of COMMIT and TRUST

H_5, H_6, H_{7A}, and H_{7B} focus on the antecedents of the relationship variables. Because we examine the role of prior experience valence when customers are dissatisfied with the service recovery, we first defined DSATCH = 6 − SATCH. Next, because we have competing hypotheses regarding the role of prior experience, it is important that we specify one regression model that under different values of parameters will correspond to one or the other competing hypothesis. In turn, the estimation will produce estimates whose values will offer support for one over the other competing hypothesis. Accordingly, the following nonlinear regression equation was specified (identical specifications were used for COMMIT and TRUST):

$$\text{COMMIT} = \gamma_0 + \gamma_1 \text{ DSATCH} \times (1 - D_p) + (\gamma_2 - e^{\gamma_3 PE}) \times \text{DSATCH} \times D_p,$$

where $D_p = 1$ if a consumer had any prior experience with the firm and zero otherwise. The effect of DSATCH on COMMIT is given by

$$\partial\text{COMMIT}/\partial\text{DSATCH} = \gamma_1 \times (1 - D_p) + (\gamma_2 - e^{\gamma_3 PE}) \times D_p.$$

The various parameters are estimated using the standard nonlinear least squares procedure (Greene 1993). In turn, the various hypotheses can be examined as follows:

(a) In the segment of *first-time consumers* (substitute $D_p = 0$ in the previous equations), the direct effect of DSATCH on commitment is given by γ_1 (similarly for trust). H_5 and H_6 reason that γ_1 will be significantly negative.

(b) Among *existing consumers* (substitute $D_p = 1$ in the previous equations), the effect of DSATCH on commitment is given by $[\gamma_2 - \exp(\gamma_3 PE)]$; we anticipate a nonlinear moderating effect of prior experience. We now note the following:
(i) When PE = 0 (neutral prior experience), the impact of DSATCH on COMMIT, among existing consumers, is given by $(\gamma_2 - 1)$, which we have hypothesized (H_5 and H_6) to be negative; we therefore expect $\gamma_2 < 1$,
(ii) At any specific value of PE, say *p*, the impact of DSATCH on COMMIT will be given by $[\gamma_2 - \exp(\gamma_3 p)]$; testing this against any

hypothesized value is accomplished by using the Wald-test (Greene 1993),

(iii) If the brand equity perspective (H_{7A}) governs the interplay of DSATCH and PE as they shape COMMIT, γ_3 will be significant and negative, whereas the service quality perspective (H_{7B}) will be supported if $\gamma_e 3$ is significant and positive.

(c) Finally, the previous regression framework also can enable us to examine whether the impact of DSATCH among first-time consumers is different from that among existing consumers. At a specific value of PE, say p, the Wald test can be employed to test H_0: $\gamma_2 - \exp(\gamma_3 p) - \gamma_1 = 0$.

References

Aaker, David A. (1991), *Managing Brand Equity*. New York: The Free Press.

Achrol, Ravi S. (1991), "Evolution of the Marketing Organization: New Forms for Turbulent Environments," *Journal of Marketing*, 55 (October), 77–93.

Austin, William G. (1979), "Justice, Freedom and Self-Interest in Intergroup Relations," in *The Social Psychology of Intergroup Relations*, William G. Austin and S. Worchel, eds. Belmont, CA: Brooks/Cole, 20–37.

Bagozzi, Richard P. and Paul R. Warshaw (1990), "Trying to Consume," *Journal of Consumer Research*, 17 (September) 127–40.

Berry, Leonard L. and A. Parasuraman (1991), *Marketing Services: Competing through Quality*. New York: The Free Press.

Bies, Robert J. (1987), "The Predicament of Injustice: The Management of Moral Outrage," *Research in Organizational Behavior*, 9, 289–319.

——— and Debra L. Shapiro (1987), "Interactional Fairness Judgments: The Influence of Causal Accounts," *Social Justice Research*, 1, 199–218.

Bitner, Mary Jo (1995), "Building Service Relationships: It's All about Promises," *Journal of the Academy of Marketing Science*, 23 (Fall), 246–51.

———, Bernard M. Booms, and Mary Stanfield Tetreault (1990), "The Service Encounter: Diagnosing Favorable and Unfavorable Incidents," *Journal of Marketing*, 54 (January), 71–85.

Blodgett, Jeffrey G., Donald H. Granbois, and Rockney G. Walters (1993), "The Effects of Perceived Justice on Complainants' Negative Word of Mouth Behavior and Repatronage Intentions," *Journal of Retailing*, 69 (4), 399–428.

———, Donna J. Hill, and Stephen S. Tax (1997), "The Effects of Distributive, Procedural, and Interactional Justice on Postcomplaint Behavior," *Journal of Retailing*, 73 (2), 185–210.

Bowen, David E. and Edward E. Lawler (1995), "Empowering Service Employees," *Sloan Management Review*, 36 (Summer), 73–84.

Brett, Jeanne M. (1986), "Commentary on Procedural Justice Papers," in *Research on Negotiation in Organizations*, Vol. 1, Roy Lewicki, Max Bazerman, and Blair Sheppard, eds. Greenwich, CT: JAI Press, 81–90.

Brockner, Joel, Tom R. Tyler, and Rochelle Cooper-Schneider (1992), "The Influence of Prior Commitment to an Institution on Reactions to Perceived Unfairness: The Higher They Are, the Harder They Fall," *Administrative Science Quarterly*, 37 (June), 241–61.

Chandrashekaran, Murali, Beth A. Walker, James C. Ward, and Peter H. Reingen (1995), "Modeling Individual Preference Evolution and Choice in a Dynamic Group Setting," *Journal of Marketing Research*, 33 (May), 211–23.

Clemmer, Elizabeth C. (1988), "The Role of Fairness in Customer Satisfaction with Services," doctoral dissertation, Psychology Department, University of Maryland.

Conlon, Donald E. and Noel M. Murray (1996), "Customer Perceptions of Corporate Responses to Product Complaints: The Role of Expectations," *Academy of Management Journal*, 39 (4), 1040–56.

Crosby, Lawrence A., Kenneth R. Evans, and Deborah Cowles (1990), "Relationship Quality in Service Selling: An Interpersonal Influence Perspective," *Journal of Marketing*, 54 (July), 68–81.

Deutsch, Morten (1985), *Distributive Justice*. New Haven, CT: Yale University Press.

Dwyer, F. Robert, Paul H. Schurr, and Sejo Oh (1987), "Developing Buyer–Seller Relationships," *Journal of Marketing*, 51 (April), 11–27.

Ettorre, Barbara (1994), "Phenomenal Promises That Mean Business," *Management Review*, (March), 18–23.

Fisk, Raymond P. and Kenneth A. Coney (1982), "Postchoice Evaluation: An Equity Theory Analysis of Consumer Satisfaction/Dissatisfaction with Service Choices," in *Conceptual and Empirical Contributions to Consumer Satisfaction and Complaining Behavior*, Keith Hunt and Ralph L. Day, eds. Bloomington: Indiana University, 9–16.

Folger, Robert (1984), "Emerging Issues in the Social Psychology of Justice," in *The Sense of Injustice: Social Psychology Perspectives*, Robert Folger, ed. New York: Plenum Press, 4–23.

——— (1987), "Distributive and Procedural Justice in the Workplace," *Social Justice Research*, 1, 143–60.

Folkes, Valerie S. (1984), "Consumer Reactions to Product Failures: An Attributional Approach," *Journal of Consumer Research*, 10 (March), 398–409.

Fornell, Claes (1992), "A National Customer Satisfaction Barometer: The Swedish Experience," *Journal of Marketing*, 56 (January), 6–21.

——— and Birger Wernerfelt (1987), "Defensive Marketing Strategy by Customer Complaint Management: A Theoretical Analysis," *Journal of Marketing Research*, 24 (November), 337–46.

Ganesan, Shankar (1994), "Determinants of Long-Term Orientation in Buyer-Seller Relationships," *Journal of Marketing*, 58 (April), 1–19.

Gilliland, Stephen W. (1993), "The Perceived Fairness of Selection Systems: An Organizational Justice Perspective," *Academy of Management Review*, 18 (4), 694–734.

Goodwin, Cathy and Ivan Ross (1989), "Salient Dimensions of Perceived Fairness in Resolution of Service Complaints," *Journal of Consumer Satisfaction/Dissatisfaction and Complaining Behavior*, 2, 87–92.

——— and ——— (1992), "Consumer Responses to Service Failures: Influence of Procedural and Interactional Fairness Perceptions," *Journal of Business Research*, 25 (2), 149–63.

Greenberg, Jerald (1990a), "Looking Fair versus Being Fair: Managing Impressions of Organizational Justice," *Research in Organizational Behavior*, 12, 11–157.

——— (1990b), "Organizational Justice: Yesterday, Today, and Tomorrow," *Journal of Management*, 16 (2), 399–432.

——— and Claire McCarty (1990), "The Interpersonal Aspects of Procedural Justice: A New Perspective in Pay Fairness," *Labor Law Journal*, 41 (August), 580–85.

Greene, William H. (1993), *Econometric Analysis*. New York: McMillan.

Hart, Christopher W. L., James L. Heskett, and W. Earl Sasser Jr. (1990), "The Profitable Art of Service Recovery," *Harvard Business Review*, 68 (July/August), 148–56.

Heide, Jan B. and George John (1992), "Do Norms Matter in Marketing Relationships?" *Journal of Marketing*, 56 (April), 32–44.

Holmes, John G. (1991), "Trust and the Appraisal Process in Close Relationships," *Advances in Personal Relationships*, 2, 57–104.

——— and John K. Rempel (1989), "Trust in Close Relation ships," in *Review of Personality and Social Psychology: Close Relationships*, Vol. 10, Clyde Hendrick, ed. Beverly Hills, CA: Sage Publications, 187–220.

Kanfer, Ruth, John Sawyer, P. Christopher Early, and E. Allan Lind (1987), "Fairness and Participation in Evaluation Procedures: Effects on Task Attitudes and Performance," *Social Justice Research*, 1, 235–49.

Kelley, Scott W. and Mark A. Davis (1994), "Antecedents to Customer Expectations for Service Recovery," *Journal of the Academy of Marketing Science*, 22 (1), 52–61.

———, James H. Donnelly, and Steven J. Skinner Jr. (1990), "Customer Participation in Service Production and Delivery," *Journal of Retailing*, 66 (3), 315–35.

———, K. Douglas Hoffman, and Mark A. Davis (1993), "A Typology of Retail Failures and Recoveries," *Journal of Retailing*, 69 (4), 429–52.

Lind, E. Allen and Tom R. Tyler (1988), *The Social Psychology of Procedural Justice*. New York: Plenum Press.

Lovelock, Christopher H. (1994), *Product Plus*. New York: McGraw-Hill.

Maister, David H. (1985), "The Psychology of Waiting Lines," in *The Service Encounter*, John D. Czeipel, Michael R. Solomon, and Carol F. Surprenant, eds. Lexington, MA: Lexington Books, 113–23.

McCabe, Douglas M. (1990), "Corporate Nonunion Grievance Procedures: Open Door Policies—A Procedural Analysis," *Labor Law Journal*, 41 (August), 551–56.

McCollough, M. A. and S. G. Bharadwaj (1992), "The Recovery Paradox: An Examination of Consumer Satisfaction in Relation to Disconfirmation, Service Quality and Attribution-Based Theories," in *Marketing Theory and Application*, Chris T. Allen et al. eds. Chicago: American Marketing Association.

McFarlin, Dean B. and Paul D. Sweeney (1992), "Distributive and Procedural Justice as Predictors of Satisfaction with Personal and Organizational Out-

comes," *Academy of Management Journal*, 35 (March), 626–37.

Mohr, Lois A. and Mary Jo Bitner (1995), "The Role of Employee Effort in Satisfaction with Service Trans-actions," *Journal of Business Research*, 32 (3), 239–52.

Morgan, Robert M. and Shelby D. Hunt (1994), "The Commitment-Trust Theory of Marketing Relation-ships," *Journal of Marketing*, 58 (July) 20–38.

Mowday, Richard T., Lyman W. Porter, and Richard M. Steers (1982), *Employee-Organization Linkages*. New York: Academic Press.

Narver, John C. and Stanley F. Slater (1990), "The Effect of Market Orientation on Business Profitability," *Journal of Marketing*, 54 (October), 20–35.

Oliva, Terence A., Richard L. Oliver, and Ian C. MacMillan (1992), "A Catastrophe Model for Developing Service Satisfaction Strategies," *Journal of Marketing*, 56 (July), 83–95.

Oliver, Richard L. and Wayne S. DeSarbo (1988), "Response Determinants in Satisfaction Judgments," *Journal of Consumer Research*, 14 (March), 495–507.

——— and John E. Swan (1989), "Consumer Perceptions of Interpersonal Equity and Satisfaction in Transactions: A Field Survey Approach," *Journal of Marketing*, 53 (April), 21–35.

Parasuraman, A., Valerie A. Zeithaml, and Leonard L. Berry (1985), "A Conceptual Model of Service Quality and Its Implications for Future Research," *Journal of Marketing*, 49 (Fall), 41–50.

———, ——— and ——— (1988), "SERVQUAL: A Multiple-Item Scale for Measuring Consumer Percep-tions of Service Quality," *Journal of Retailing*, 64 (Spring), 12–40.

Reichheld, Frederick F. (1993), "Loyalty-Based Manage-ment," *Harvard Business Review*, 71 (March/April), 64–74.

Reis, Harry T. (1986), "Levels of Interest in the Study of Interpersonal Justice," in *Justice in Social Relations*, Hans W. Bierhoff, Ronald L. Cohen, and Jerald Greenberg, eds. New York: Plenum Press, 187–210.

Technical Assistance Research Program (1986), "Consumer Complaint Handling in America: An Update Study," Washington, DC: Department of Consumer Affairs.

Taylor, Shirley (1994), "Waiting for Service: The Relationship between Delays and Evaluations of Service," *Journal of Marketing*, 58 (April), 56–69.

Tyler, Tom R. and Robert 1. Bies (1989), "Beyond Formal Procedures: The Interpersonal Context of Procedural Justice," in *Applied Social Psychology in Organizational Settings*, J. S. Carroll, ed. Hillsdale, NJ: Lawrence Erlbaum and Associates, 77–98.

Walster, Eileen, E. Bersheid, and G. W. Walster (1973), "New Directions in Equity Research," *Journal of Personality and Social Psychology*, 29 (February), 151–76.

Westbrook, Robert A. (1987), "Product/Consumption-Based Affective Responses and Postpurchase Processes," *Journal of Marketing Research*, 24 (August), 258–70.

Do Customer Loyalty Programs Really Work?

GRAHAME R. DOWLING
MARK UNCLES

Given the popularity of loyalty programs, they are surprisingly ineffective. To stand the best chance of success in tough market conditions, programs must enhance the overall value of the product or service and motivate loyal buyers to make their next purchase.

Customer loyalty schemes have attracted considerable interest as companies practice one of marketing's most familiar strategies—"If you see a good idea, copy it." Some banks have offered regular customers credit cards with a range of valuable benefits. In business-to-business markets, loyal customers have traditionally been treated better than those who buy on the spot market. Other well-known customer loyalty schemes are the frequent-flyer programs of the major airlines. These and other well-patronized programs were originally hailed as imaginative ways to instill and maintain loyalty, but, over the years, more and more doubt has been cast on them. Both the academic and trade press have criticized the programs with headlines such as: "A Failure in Competitive Strategy," "War in the Air: The Scramble for Points Hits Turbulence," "Frequent Flyer Offers Fail to Boost Loyalty."[1]

Loyalty programs that seek to bond customers to a company or its products and services by offering an additional incentive pose an interesting dilemma. Although these schemes often attract widespread customer interest, they are difficult to support, using our current knowledge of competition and buyer behavior. This research suggests that most schemes do not fundamentally alter market structure. They *might* help to protect incumbents and *might* be regarded as a legitimate part of the marketer's armory, but at the cost of increasing marketing expenditures.

Many senior managers now ask their marketing departments to measure the potential contribution of any program developed to implement loyalty marketing. Do these programs really create extra loyalty beyond that which is derived from the relative value of the product or service? Do they encourage customers to spend more? Or do they merely bribe a customer to buy again? In a competitive market, is it really feasible for every organization to increase customer loyalty by implementing a loyalty marketing program?

Underlying the increasing interest in these program are some marketing managers' widely held beliefs about customer loyalty:

- Many customers want an involving relationship with the brands they buy.

- A proportion of these buyers are loyal to the core and buy only one brand.

- The hard-core, loyal buyers are a profitable group because there are many of them and they are heavy or frequent buyers.

- It should be possible to reinforce these buyers' loyalty and encourage them to be even more loyal.

- With database technology, marketers can establish personalized dialogues with customers, resulting in more loyalty.

We encountered such beliefs in the rhetoric of relationship marketing, direct marketing, database marketing, and so-called "1:1 marketing."[2] However, in this paper, we compare these beliefs with growing research that challenges their accuracy. First, we describe the origins and aims of loyalty marketing. We then review research that examines empirical patterns of behavioral loyalty. We also consider psychological research on rewards, a major component of most loyalty programs. These two sections provide the context for our comments on frequent-buyer loyalty programs such as those of the major airlines. Finally, we suggest how to design a customer loyalty program that avoids the common traps undermining the effectiveness of many existing schemes.

Grahame R. Dowling is an associate professor, Australian Graduate School of Management, University of New South Wales. Mark Uncles is a professor, School of Marketing, University of New South Wales.

Why Companies Introduce Customer Loyalty Programs

In the 1970s, European researchers studying business-to-business marketing discovered that suppliers who form close working relationships with their customers tend to have "better" customers.[3] That is, the customers are more loyal to their suppliers and often give them a greater share of their business. The customers also reported having "better" suppliers. In short, it is a win-win arrangement.

Subsequent research claimed that loyal customers are more profitable to a firm.[4] This profitability was thought to be generated by reduced servicing costs, less price sensitivity, increased spending, and favorable recommendations passed on to other potential customers by loyal buyers. Add to this the claim that it costs much more to entice a new customer to do business with a company than to get a current one to purchase again, and the strategy of gaining and maintaining loyalty seems like the source of sustainable competitive advantage.[5]

For a company to practice loyalty marketing, however, it must first know who its loyal customers are, which is a lot easier for many business-to-business marketers than for most consumer good marketers. As the number of customers increases, companies have to use database marketing and market research in the absence of personal knowledge. As computerized database technology becomes more sophisticated, so does a firm's ability to monitor its customers' behavior. Retailers and packaged-goods manufacturers use these techniques to efficiently target products and services and allocate marketing resources to achieve the maximum return.[6] In business markets, companies conduct customer profitability analyses and calculate the lifetime value of their customers. However, the processes are complex and costly.

What began as a strategy for small businesses, business marketing, and catalogue selling has evolved into a new industry. Direct marketing practitioners are creating loyalty programs that tie the buyers of a wide range of consumer goods and services to a particular brand or supplier. But do customers for these products want a relationship with the supplying company? In a small business deal or for a risky purchase, the answer may be yes. For low-involvement products and the types of brands sold by, say, Nestlé, Procter & Gamble, Shell, or Unilever, it is unclear whether customers really want a relationship.

Press releases about launches of frequent-buyer or customer loyalty programs suggest that companies expect these schemes to achieve various objectives or practical measures of success. The most common objective is to retain existing customers and in so doing: (1) maintain sales levels, margins, and profits (a defensive outcome to protect the existing customer base), (2) increase the loyalty and potential value of existing customers (an offensive outcome to provide incremental increases in sales, margins, and profits), and (3) induce cross-product buying by existing customers (defensive or offensive). Usually these desired outcomes refer to specific target segments, for instance, heavy buyers or high-net-worth customers. The underlying belief is that a small percentage of customers generate most of a company's sales and that these customers can be locked in forever. Companies often invoke the "80/20 law" in support of this viewpoint.

The 80/20 law states that about 80 percent of revenue typically comes from only 20 percent of customers. With such a skewed distribution of customers, it makes sense to concentrate most marketing resources on the 20 percent. The problem for loyalty programs is that the "best" 20 percent are not necessarily loyal buyers, especially in the sense of exclusive loyalty. As we describe in the next section, there is reliable empirical evidence to suggest that many or most heavy users are multibrand loyal for a wide range of products and services. That is, a company's most profitable customers will probably be the competitors' most profitable customers as well.

For companies with poor data about their customers, an additional benefit of customer loyalty programs is that members can identify themselves at the point of purchase or service delivery. Membership cards are a quick, efficient way for customers to signal that they deserve special attention. As a by-product, the company gains market research information—another espoused benefit of loyalty schemes. However, such a self-selected group is unlikely to represent all a company's potential customers. Hence, it is only one source of market research information.

Companies openly discuss all these espoused benefits in public announcements. In practice, however, their decision to launch a program is often motivated as much by fears of competitive parity as anything else, which companies rarely state publicly. Therefore we add the following tactical motives to the previous list: (4) attempting to differentiate a parity brand, (5) preempting the entry of a new (parity) brand, and (6) preempting a competitor from introducing a similar loyalty scheme.

Most airlines and many leading companies, such as American Express, General Motors, Holiday Inn, Toyota/Lexus, John Deere, and Shell, have found enough merit in customer loyalty programs to implement such schemes. While they do not seek all the above benefits from each program, at least some benefits must occur for the scheme to pay off when the full cost is compared to other marketing alternatives. But, does a customer loyalty program offer a better return than an alternative such as a price cut, a move to everyday low pricing, increased advertising, or increasing distribution coverage? For many programs, the answer to this question lies in some interesting academic research that we review in the next two sections.

The Leaky Bucket Theory versus Polygamous Loyalty

Ehrenberg, in what he dubbed the "leaky bucket theory," observes that many marketing strategies seem to be designed to replace "disloyal" customers who leak away with new ones in order to keep the sales level steady.[7] But, while the marketing strategies of customer loyalty programs appear to be designed this way, is the underlying leaky bucket theory true?

To address this question and to establish norms of consumer behavior for different markets, Ehrenberg and his colleagues gathered data from various markets in Britain, continental Europe, Japan, and the United States over more than twenty years. Their research describes people's purchase habits of products like coffee ready-to-eat breakfast cereals, newspapers, aviation fuel, toothpaste, laundry detergents, gasoline, television programs, airline tickets, ethical drugs, and even repeat purchases of management development programs at business schools. Their focus was on people's observed behavior, not their needs, motivations, personalities, or attitudes toward a brand.[8] Gordon's subsequent research provided qualitative support for the emergence of these behavioral norms.[9]

Typically, the researchers measured five types of behavior over certain time periods: (1) the percentage of consumers buying a brand, (2) the number of purchases per buyer, (3) the percentage who continue to buy the brand (repeat buyers), (4) the percentage who are 100 percent loyal, and (5) the percentage who also buy other specific brands (duplicate buyers). From these data, a company can determine how much of a buyer's requirement for the category is met by a specific brand. Using statistical analysis, it can predict norms for each type of behavior in a competitive market.[10]

The empirical facts make it difficult to be enthusiastic about using a loyalty marketing program to create a large group of 100 percent loyal customers. The empirical record and the predictive norms show that only about 10 percent of buyers for many types of frequently purchased consumer goods are 100 percent loyal to a particular brand over a one-year period.[11] Even in service situations, exclusive loyalty is confined to a small number of buyers. Moreover, 100 percent loyal buyers tend to be light buyers of the product or service.

The research of Ehrenberg and his colleagues indicates that in stationary markets, customer loyalty is divided among a number of brands, as if there were long-run propensities to buy brands A, B, and C, say, some 70 percent, 20 percent, and 10 percent of the time.[12] Hence, invariably, customers do not buy only one brand. "Polygamous loyalty" better describes actual consumer behavior than either brand switching (a conscious once-and-for-all change of allegiance to another brand, as if propensities were 100 percent or zero) or promiscuity (the butterfly tendency to flit from brand to brand without any fixed allegiance, when there are no long-run propensities, only next-purchase probabilities).

Polygamous loyalty is readily apparent, for instance, in the soft drink and breakfast cereal markets but extends well beyond to car rentals, fast-food outlets, and business airline travel. It is also evident in customers' multiple memberships in loyalty schemes. For example, surveys of European business airline travelers show that more than 80 percent are members of more than one airline loyalty scheme. In 1993, the average membership of airline loyalty clubs was 3.1 per traveler, and the figure seems to be rising.[13]

Many reasons for the generalized patterns of divided loyalty or polygamy are straightforward. For example, people buy different brands for different occasions or for variety. Or the brand may have been the only one in stock or may have offered better value because of a special deal. Most buyers who change brands are not lost forever or disloyal; usually, they prefer to buy a number of brands rather than one particular brand.

Given the amount of research that supports these patterns of buyer behavior, it seems unlikely that a loyalty program could *fundamentally* alter this behavior, especially in established, competitive markets (where copycat responses are most likely). Even a path-breaking scheme may alter only short-run probabilities. Once the market has settled down again, or a competitor has launched a similar scheme, patterns of divided loyalty reemerge. Then the issue is whether the longer-run propensities settle at old or new levels.

In a market in which competitive response occurs quickly, the market is expected to settle at its old levels. For example, at the beginning of 1995, there were no national loyalty schemes in the British grocery market, but once one retailer broke rank, all others followed

FIGURE 1
Double Jeopardy and Brand Loyalty

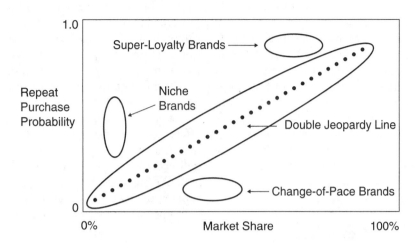

within months. Despite the amount of loyalty building, market shares have been reasonably steady. Much the same had happened ten years earlier when American Airlines launched the first frequent-flyer scheme; within weeks, other carriers began to follow suit.[14]

When aggregated across many product and service markets, these research results suggest that the marketing mix of a brand (its product or service formulation, price, promotion, and distribution) determines its market share, and, once this settles down, the level of brand loyalty is strongly correlated with market share. Consequently, although marketers might give brands some fancy names, it is better to think about them as either big or small, rather than strong or weak in terms of loyalty (see Figure 1).[15]

A secondary effect is that big brands tend to have more buyers, and somewhat more of these buy slightly more frequently. Equally, small brands suffer "double jeopardy" in that there tend to be fewer buyers who buy the brand less frequently.[16] If a loyal buyer is one who again purchases the brand frequently, the bigger the brand, the larger the number of more, loyal buyers. Add to this the empirical fact that some large-share brands may have a slightly higher proportion of heavy users and loyal buyers than predicted by the double jeopardy phenomenon, and there is more bad news for loyalty marketing programs designed to rescue small brands.

Most brands lie along the double jeopardy line (see Figure 1).[17] However, there may also be big brands that exhibit some signs of super loyalty; i.e., they have more frequent buyers than double jeopardy would predict. At the other end of the scale, a niche brand is small, with a relatively higher proportion of buyers who are more loyal than predicted by double jeopardy. In its early days, the ecological Body Shop was a good example of a niche brand, but as it increased its distribution and appeal, it became a "normal" brand. As with most so-called niche brands, those that survive and prosper end up along the double jeopardy line, and they cease to be a niche.

The change-of-pace brand is one with a higher than expected market share but a less than expected proportion of loyal buyers. Many low-alcohol beers fit this description; people may buy them only when they are in a special situation such as before driving a car. Or they may have a premium beer as a predinner drink in a restaurant. The significant point is that super-loyalty, niche, and change-of-pace brands are much less common than big or small double jeopardy brands. Any of these brands can be profitable, because profit is determined by margin, not by the type or size of the brand.

A more effective way to grow a brand's market share or become big is to get more people to buy the brand rather than try to get current customers to buy it more often. Fader and Schmittlein's research suggests that one of the most effective ways to get more buyers is to gain more distribution outlets. It's as simple as that.[18] Leading global players like British Airways, Coca-Cola, and Ford are only too aware of this, which is why they strive so hard to protect their air routes, distribution channels, and dealerships. Loyalty programs and other marketing tactics such as price cuts and promotions are effective only in the long term, to the extent that they entice more distributors to stock the brand or build presence in the marketplace.

In summary, research implies that, in many established, competitive markets, purchasing of products and services is characterized by a number of empirical regularities. Given that these regularities are so widespread, it is difficult to increase brand loyalty above the market norms with an easy-to-replicate "add on" like a customer loyalty program. We do not deny that companies can have a short-term lucky break, or that they may be forced to act because of competition. But, for any customer loyalty program to be as effective as possible, given the prevailing competitive conditions, it must leverage the brand's value proposition in the eyes of customers (that is, the balance of benefits relative to price).

Linking Customer Rewards to Loyalty Programs

Products and services provide functional, economic, and psychological benefits or solutions to buyers. These are the prime sources of customer value. As research suggests, the relative amount of customer value and distribution coverage drives market share and the number of loyal customers that a brand will acquire. The rewards that many customer loyalty programs offer are designed to alter this relationship.

To explore loyalty programs' potential to alter normal patterns of behavior, we need to examine three psychological effects: (1) the extent to which loyalty is to the brand (a direct effect) or to the program (an indirect effect), (2) how buyers value the rewards offered, and (3) the effect of timing. We consider each in turn.

Direct or Indirect Effect

Rothschild and Gaidis have used behavioral learning theory to suggest that the type of incentives that many customer loyalty schemes offer may induce loyalty to the program (deal loyalty) rather than to the core product or service (brand loyalty).[19] The extent to which this is desirable depends on the buyer's level of involvement with the product. For many low-involvement products, the incentive and not the product can become the primary reward, especially if the incentive is exotic and out of proportion to the money spent. This might create a point of product differentiation, but once the incentive is taken away, the prime reason for purchase disappears. Many gasoline company loyalty schemes are caught in this trap, locking them onto a treadmill of continuous promotions.

However, for high-involvement products and services, which are typically accompanied by a small incentive, the product and not the incentive is the primary reward. For example, in the General Motors rebate scheme (the GM card), which allows participants to build up savings toward the cost of a new GM car, the car and not the accumulation of a discount is paramount. This seems to be more desirable because the creation of a point of difference reinforces the longer-term value proposition of the product itself.

In this way, we can classify customer loyalty programs by whether their explicit rewards directly support the value proposition of the product or service offered to customers (e.g., the GM card), or whether the rewards are designed to motivate loyalty by a more indirect route (e.g., free air travel from gasoline retailers). We suggest that loyalty programs that directly support the value proposition and positioning of the target product better fit the goals of loyalty marketing.

How Buyers Value Rewards

Psychologists have long been interested in the role of rewards in behavior modification and learning. They have developed numerous cognitive-learning theories that give insight into how the rewards of customer loyalty programs might help to achieve loyalty to the product rather than the program. O'Brien and Jones suggest five elements that combine to determine a program's value: (1) the cash value of the redemption rewards (e.g., the ratio of the cost of an airline ticket to the dollar purchases necessary to accumulate frequent-flyer points), (2) the range of choice of these rewards (e.g., choice of flight destinations), (3) the aspirational value of the rewards (e.g., exotic free travel is more desirable than a cash-back offer), (4) the perceived likelihood of achieving the rewards (e.g., how many points are required to qualify for a flight), and (5) the scheme's ease of use.[20] To this, we add the psychological benefits of belonging to the program and accumulating points.

Timing

The potential of a loyalty program to attract members depends not only on the value of its rewards but also on when the rewards are available. Research in psychology suggests that when a loyalty program's redemption rewards are delayed, they are less powerful.[21] Many accumulating benefit programs, such as frequent-flyer schemes, try to alleviate this problem by regularly sending their members a statement of accumulated points. Typically, the statements are accompanied by promotional material about the aspirational value and ease of achieving various rewards.

We suggest that more immediate rewards are preferable to delayed rewards, and that direct support

FIGURE 2
Types of Reward Schemes

	Timing of Reward	
	Immediate	Delayed
Directly Supports the Product's Value Proposition	1 Retailer/Brand Manufacturer Promotions (Price Promotions)	2 Airline Frequent-Flyer Clubs Coupons, and Tokens (GM card)
Type of Reward Other Indirect Types of Reward	3 Competitions and Lotteries (Instant Scratches)	4 Multiproduct Frequent-Buyer Clubs (Fly Buys)

of the target product's value proposition increases the chance that the program will build loyalty for the product and not just the program. We classify different types of loyalty schemes according to the reward's support of the product or service value proposition and the reward's timing (see Figure 2). From the customers' perspective, the instant gratification programs (in sections one and three of the figure) should be preferable to those with delayed gratification (in sections two and four). However, from the sponsor's perspective, programs that make an explicit link between product and program and have a bearing on long-term behavior (in sections one and two) should be preferable to those with indirect rewards (in sections three and four). From either perspective, those in section four appear to be least preferable, yet many current loyalty schemes fall into this category, for example, the Australian "Fly Buys" frequent-buyer program.

Sponsors offer membership in the Fly Buys program at no cost. Members accumulate points toward free air travel and hotel accommodation by using a bank credit card and/or a magnetic-strip membership card with the scheme's sponsors—a major retailer, a car rental company, and a gasoline company. Within a year of launch, 1.7 million Australians had taken this free option, which represented 10 percent of the Australian population, with one member in every four households.[22] The customers' immediate rewards are psychological, namely, a feeling of participation, the anticipation of future rewards, and a sense of belonging. The delayed rewards are a bimonthly summary of accumulated points and sometimes the qualification for a reward.

A customer cost-benefit analysis helps explain why the least desirable loyalty program (according to Figure 2) has attracted so many members. On the cost side of the equation, joining the program is free, and each transaction is handled with an easy-to-use magnetic strip card. Many people perceive rewards, however, as very difficult to achieve, so the sponsors have run a TV ad campaign to counter the perception.[23] On the reward-benefit side, many people value the aspirational aspect of air travel, and others just like being part of a program.

With such a huge market penetration, this program would seem to be a runaway success. But, while the sponsors had hoped that rewards would be sufficient to increase sales volumes, in practice, they have been fairly elusive.[24] Also, with so many members, the scheme is expensive to maintain.

Both the Fly Buys case and the research on rewards suggest that designing a loyalty program to disrupt established patterns of behavioral loyalty is difficult. Despite these difficulties, many schemes have recently been launched. In the next section, we review some claimed benefits.

The Claimed Benefits of Loyalty Programs

Advocates of loyalty programs contend that they are profitable because:

- The costs of serving loyal customers are less.

- Loyal customers are less price sensitive.

- Loyal customers spend more with the company.

- Loyal customers pass on positive recommendations about their favorite brands or suppliers.

These alluring benefits go far to explain the interest in customer loyalty programs. But, with one notable exception,[25] there is little well-documented empirical research to substantiate these claims. As we have outlined, evidence from behavioral loyalty and reward research suggests the opposite. Hence, before willingly accepting that customers in loyalty programs are always more profitable, let's examine each source of increased profitability,

When there are specific start-up costs involved in serving a new customer, such as prospecting, credit checks, and entering the customer's account details in a database, the costs exceed those of serving a repeat customer. However, it is not at all clear why the costs of serving a very regular, loyal, repeat customer should in principle be different from those of serving any other type of repeat customer. Why some transactions will differ in cost has more to do with the type of transaction, not the loyalty of the customer or his or her membership in a loyalty program. The key variables driving cost are first purchase versus repeat purchase, size and type of order, special versus standard order, and so on, not loyal versus divided-loyal customers.

Why would loyal customers be less price sensitive? They may be, but then again, they may not. It depends on how important they think price is and on the value proposition that the brand offers. Although one frequent claim of brand-equity researchers is that brand loyalty and higher prices are positively correlated, this does not automatically mean that more loyal buyers are less price sensitive.[26] It may simply mean that these people buy a brand at a higher price because they perceive it to be better. For example, usually a brand is clearly in only one price category. Less price-conscious people then have the opportunity to buy at either the cheaper or higher price depending on whether the brand can offer a good reason (functional or psychological) to justify its higher price. It is perceived brand value, not brand loyalty, that drives price insensitivity.

Alternatively, loyal customers may come to expect a price discount or better service. In other words, what are the rewards to the customer for his or her loyalty? If we consider the double jeopardy relationship, these loyal customers are likely to be slightly more frequent buyers and hence may expect a volume discount.

The next assumption is that loyal customers spend more with the company. This may be simply because they buy more of the product category than less loyal customers (e.g., business air travelers versus holiday travelers). As such, it is the weight of purchase that matters most, not necessarily customer loyalty. And, as we argue in the next section, this is more likely to be a function of the better value offered than of any add-on loyalty program.

The last assumption contends that loyal customers pass on favorable comments. While this seems a sensible assertion, there is little research to indicate what percentage of loyal customers help a company to market its products. The interesting question here is whether only loyal customers, or only those in a loyalty program, are likely to do this, or is it simply that *satisfied* customers are the ones that say nice things about good products and services. If satisfaction is the key driver of positive recommendations, any satisfied customer should provide this benefit. The only way that a loyalty program can give extra leverage to a company's word-of-mouth marketing is if the loyal customers offer substantially more, or more effective, positive comments. We are not aware of research that demonstrates this.

In short, the contention that loyal customers are always more profitable is a gross oversimplification. Each company needs to use its customer data to determine the truth of these assertions. Here is where the behavioral loyalty research has relevance. If a particular brand fits the market conditions under which these research findings hold, there are some interesting implications for the introduction of a customer loyalty program. The market conditions are:

- There is open competition.

- Products and services are functionally equivalent in broad terms (and are therefore substitutable).

- There is little tendency for any brand to uniquely appeal to a particular subgroup of consumers (despite brands within a product category being superficially different).

- There is little dynamic variation over time in competing brands' market shares (despite considerable marketing activity under the surface to maintain these shares).[27]

We can hear your sighs of relief. "This doesn't apply to our brand!" you say. But are you sure? Certainly there are some products and services—those for state monopolies, highly innovative new products, and products whose success depends on fad and fashion—that do not appear to match these market conditions. Moreover, some trivial differences certainly seem to affect choice.[28] However, most airlines, banks, beers, executive education programs, frozen foods, hardware stores, instant coffees, mineral waters, gas stations, plastic pipes, cars, stationery suppliers, TV soap operas, and so on compete directly with each other within their product category. This usually means that when specific products and services are not conveniently available, most people will not hesitate to buy a similar brand or may deliberately seek variety.

Our argument is that these market conditions hold more often than you may think. Given these effects, in the next section, we make some suggestions for designing a loyalty program that offers the best chance of providing a positive return on its investment.

How to Design an Effective Loyalty Program

Here we focus on loyalty programs that attempt to lock in a customer by offering an accumulating benefit, which increases the switching costs to the buyer over time (the programs in section two and four of Figure 2). In economic terminology, they try to change the customer's choice process from operating in a spot market to operating in a multiperiod, contractual relationship market. The programs are potentially dangerous because they require a company's long-term commitment and funding. The programs in section one and three of Figure 2 are short-term promotions; they might well stimulate sales for the duration of the promotion but do not have any long-term behavioral after-effects.[29]

For frequent-buyer loyalty programs, the level of customer involvement is an important consideration. For a high-involvement purchase, the consumer is likely to be involved with both the category purchase decision (Will I fly or go by train from London to Paris?) and the brand choice (Will I fly British Airways or Air France?). For low-involvement decisions, the level of involvement is likely to be low for both decisions, although somewhat higher for the category purchase decision. We suggest that loyalty programs will be more effective for high- than low-involvement products and services, primarily because low-involvement products are often bought by consumers out of habit, while, for high-involvement products, consumers might form a relationship with the supplier (the difference between the habitual purchase of Nescafé, say, and joining ClubMed).

In either case, to maximize the program's chances of success, the following guidelines are helpful:

1. *Design the loyalty program to enhance the value proposition of a product or service.* To the extent that frequent-flyer clubs and the GM card enhance the value of the airline or car, these schemes are more worthwhile than a frequent-buyer scheme, such as Fly Buys, which does not. In this respect, probably the least useful rewards for customer loyalty are free gifts such as lottery tickets; these are nice to receive but tend to be only short-term tactical froth that can devalue the brand.

2. *Fully cost the loyalty program.* There are a number of highly visible costs, such as those associated with program launch, database creation and maintenance, value of rewards claimed, and issue of regular activity statements. The costs of frequent-flyer programs are reportedly between 3 percent and 6 percent of an airline's revenue.[30]

   Many airlines peg their advertising spending at approximately 3 percent of revenue. Many other loyalty costs are less visible, namely, the opportunity cost of managers' time spent on the loyalty program rather than on other marketing activities, and the effectiveness of the loyalty program compared with an alternative use of the funds. It is wise, therefore, to be cautious in allocating the marketing budget to a loyalty program. If competitors make a countermove, resources will be needed for a robust response.

3. *Design a reward scheme that maximizes the buyer's motivation to make the next purchase.* Most existing reward schemes achieve this only indirectly because they don't account for customers' current situations (Are they light or heavy buyers? How many reward points have they accumulated?).

   In many reward schemes, for each dollar spent, a participant gains the same number of points (see Figure 3, section A). In the Fly Buys program, the more a member buys, the more he or she flies. Airlines often use a variation of this scheme; an economy class airfare results in 1 point per mile or dollar spent, business class 1.5 points, and first class 2 points. The incentive is to spend enough to gain access to different reward levels. Some other reward schemes are more transparent to the buyer (see section B). They offer more reward points for each additional dollar spent so that the next purchase is increasingly more valuable to the buyer. The three zones (1, 2, and 3) in the response function are designed to balance the costs to the company of having too many unprofitable participants with the customers' motivation to participate in the scheme.

   In zone 1, light buyers may join but will not gain many rewards. Unless a company can be extremely effective in cross-selling other products and services to these buyers, it doesn't want them in a loyalty program. Maintenance of a database and regular communication with too many of these buyers can be costly; however, it is

FIGURE 3
Loyalty Program Reward Schedules

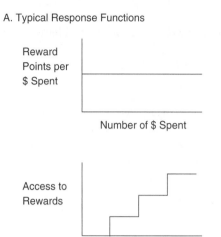

A. Typical Response Functions

Reward Points per $ Spent

Number of $ Spent

Access to Rewards

Accumulated Spending

B. Alternative Response Functions

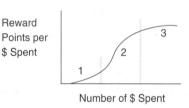

Reward Points per $ Spent

Number of $ Spent

TABLE 1
Can a Customer Loyalty Program Help?

Inhibiting Situation	Comment
• Core customers buy many brands in the category.	• At best only marginally, and not cost effective.
• Brands imitate each other's strategies.	• Unlikely, because any move will be neutralized.
• Large-share, niche, or change-of-pace brand.	• Only as a defensive move that may not be cost effective.
• In-use experience is very important to customers.	• Unlikely, because the experience is the key.
• Technology changes lead to better price or performance.	• Unlikely, because better value is the key.
• Brand is highly differentiated.	• Unlikely, because the difference is the key.
• Brand is highly fashionable.	• Unlikely, because fashion is the key motivator.
• Intrinsic retention of customers is low.	• Unlikely, because they desire change.

Enhancing Situations (if none of the above situations apply)

• Scheme directly supports customer value proposition.	• Yes, if its full cost is less than an equally effective alternative.
• Relationship building adds to perceived value.	• Yes, if it is cost effective relative to other programs.
• Lifetime customer value is high.	• Yes, if it is cost effective relative to other programs.
• Customer retention costs are less than acquisition costs.	• Yes, if it is cost effective relative to other programs.

important not to alienate them. They may not think of themselves as light or insignificant buyers. The response function is steepest in zone 2. Here the aim is to motivate the midsize buyer to continue buying and to allocate more purchases to the product. These customers are likely to be the most profitable type, big enough to be profitable to serve, but not so big that they request a volume discount. The response function is flat in zone 3, which implies a company should limit the rewards available to super-heavy buyers. The value proposition is already good for these customers, and their current level of buying suggests that it will be difficult to entice them to buy even more, unless the company enhances the value proposition itself or gains wider distribution.

The point here is that whatever reward scheme a company adopts, it should design it with the profitability of different types of customers in mind. Ideally, this will motivate the most profitable customers to give a company a higher share of their business. But realistically, in a competitive market where copycat schemes are inevitable, the aim may be no more than to ensure that the company maintains market share (with the attendant level of loyalty and divided loyalty).

4. *Consider specific market situations in planning.* (For some typical situations, together with comments on whether a customer loyalty program is appropriate, see Table 1. Because the situations are usually interrelated, our comments are guidelines, not inviolate prescriptions.)

Conclusion

There are three primary lessons from the research and examples we cite here.

First, a major reason for the launch of many customer loyalty schemes is competition. Companies may want to preempt a competitor (and possibly secure first-mover advantages) or respond to a competitor's scheme (as in most of the frequent-flyer clubs).

Second, apart from purely defensive reasons, if a loyalty program does not support the product or service value proposition, it might be justified in enticing more distributors to handle the product, a demand-pull effect. As noted earlier, for many products and services, there is a positive relationship between distribution coverage and market share.

Third, the behavioral loyalty research we reviewed here suggests that brand loyalty is more likely to come from the market in which a company operates and the brand it has already than from an add-on customer loyalty program. In other words, in most cases, all that a customer loyalty program will do is cost money to provide more benefits to customers—not all of which will be seen as relevant to the brand's value proposition and/or positioning. The program is unlikely to significantly increase the relative proportion of loyal customers or profitability.

These lessons suggest that customer loyalty programs that (1) neutralize a competitor's program, (2) broaden the availability of the product or service, or (3) directly enhance the product or service value proposition may be worthwhile. But they also suggest that (4) it is probably a mistake for a company to introduce a frequent-buyer program if it is selling a parity brand in a competitive market and merely add a me-too scheme. Competitors are sure to counter the move with something of equal perceived value. If they offer a price cut, the value of such an immediate reward may be more motivating than the promise of a potential but delayed reward. If they counter with a loyalty program, it is likely to be a better program in the hope of winning back defecting customers.

We have reviewed a body of research that indicates that many programs widely discussed in the business press may be seriously flawed. Like some recent management strategies or fads, many customer loyalty programs seem to have been adopted too quickly, without much thought.[31] Our aim here is to generate a more critical analysis of the schemes, especially those added on to prevent the gradual loss of customers.

References

1. T. J. Kearney, "Frequent Flyer Programs: A Failure in Competitive Strategy, with Lessons for Management," *Journal of Consumer Marketing*, volume 7, Winter 1990, pp. 31–40; D. Churchill, "War in the Air: The Scramble for Points Hits Turbulence," *The Sunday Times* (London), 21 November 1993; P. Meller, "Frequent Flyer Offers Fail to Boost Loyalty," *Marketing*, 4 November 1993.
2. D. Peppers and M. Rogers, *The One to One Future: Building Relationships One Customer at a Time* (New York: Currency/Doubleday, 1993); S. Pearson, *Building Brands Directly* (Basingstoke, England: Macmillan Press, 1996); R.C. Blattberg and J. Deighton, "Manage Marketing by the Customer Equity Test," *Harvard Business Review*, volume 74, July–August 1996, pp. 136–144.
3. H. Hakansson, ed., *International Marketing and Purchasing of Industrial Goods* (Chichester, England: John Wiley, 1982).
4. F. F. Reichheld and W. E. Sasser, "Zero Defections: Quality Comes to Services," *Harvard Business Review*, volume 68, September–October 1990, pp. 105–111; F. F. Reichheld with T. Teal, *The Loyalty Effect* (Boston: Harvard Business School Press, 1996); F. F. Reichheld, "Learning from Customer Defections," *Harvard Business Review*, volume 74, March-April 1996, pp. 56–69; R. T. Rust and A. J. Zahorik, "Customer Satisfaction, Customer Retention, and Market Share," *Journal of Retailing*, volume 69, Summer 1993, pp. 193–215.
5. Quote by V. Jenkins, chairman of the direct marketing agency, Clemenger Direct Response, in: A. Biziorek, "Desperately Seeking Loyalty," *Australian Professional Marketing*, September 1994, pp. 15–18; and Reichheld and Sasser (1990).
6. Blattberg and Deighton (1996).
7. A. S. C. Ehrenberg and G. J. Goodhardt, *Understanding Buyer Behavior* (New York: J. Walter Thompson and the Market Research Corporation of America, 1977).
8. For a discussion of behavioral loyalty, see: A. S. Dick and K. Basu, "Customer Loyalty: Toward an Integrated Conceptual Framework," *Journal of the Academy of Marketing Science*, volume 22, 1994, pp. 99–113.
9. W. Gordon, "Retailer Brands—The Value Equation for Success in the 90s," *Journal of the Market Research Society*, volume 36, number 3, 1994, pp. 165–181; and W. Gordon, "Taking Brand Repertoires Seriously," *Journal of Brand Management*, volume 2, number 1, 1994, pp. 25–30.
10. A. S. C. Ehrenberg, *Repeat-Buying, Facts, Theory, and Applications*, 2nd. ed. (London: Charles Griffin and Co.; New York: Oxford University Press, 1988).
11. Ibid.; M. Uncles, A. S. C. Ehrenberg, and K. Hammond, "Patterns of Buyer Behavior: Regularities, Models, and Extensions," *Marketing Science*, volume 14, number 3, 1995, pp. G71–G78; and A. S. C. Ehrenberg and M. Uncles, "Dirichlet-Type Markets: A Review" (Sydney, Australia: University of New South Wales; London: South Bank Business School, working paper, 1996).
12. Ibid.
13. *OAG Business Traveller Lifestyle Survey 1993* (Dunstable, Bedfordshire, England: Official Airline Guides, 1993).
14. M. Uncles, "Do You or Your Customers Need a Loyalty Scheme," *Journal of Targeting, Measurement, and Analysis for Marketing*, volume 2, number 4, 1994, pp. 335–350; M. Uncles, "The Seven Perils of Loyalty Programmes," *The Marketing Society Review*, Autumn 1994, pp. 18–20; P. Hawkes, "The Customer Loyalty Challenge," *Admap*, January 1996, pp. 47–48; and S. Rayner, *Customer Loyalty Schemes: Effective Implementation and Management* (London: FT Retail and Consumer Publishing, FT Management Report, 1996).
15. A. S. C. Ehrenberg, "If You're So Strong, Why Aren't You Bigger," *Admap*, October 1993, pp. 13–14, 20; A. S. C. Ehrenberg, "New Brands and the Existing Market," *Journal of the Market Research Society*, volume 33, number

4, 1991, pp. 285–299; B. Kahn, M. U. Kalwani, and D. Morrison. "Niching versus Change-of-Pace Brands: Using Purchase Frequencies and Penetration Rates to Infer Brand Positionings," *Journal of Marketing Research*, volume 25, November 1988, pp. 384–390.

16. A. S. C. Ehrenberg, G. J. Goodhardt, and P. Barwise, "Double Jeopardy Revisited," *Journal of Marketing*, volume 54, July 1990, pp. 82–91.

17. As the length of the observation period gets longer (e.g., from a month to a year), more people will buy a brand, their average purchase frequency will rise, the percent who are repeat buyers will increase, and rates of 100 percent loyalty will fall. Loyalty, therefore, has to be defined with reference to the observation period.

18. P. S. Fader and D. C. Schmittlein, "Excess Behavioral Loyalty for High-Share Brands: Deviations from the Dirichlet Model for Repeat Purchasing," *Journal of Marketing Research*, volume 30, November 1993, pp. 478–493. See also: N. R. Barnard, A. S. C. Ehrenberg, K. Hammond, and M. Uncles, "Dirichlet Discrepancies: Some Empirical Results" (London: South Bank Business School, working paper, 1995).

19. M. L. Rothschild and W. C. Gaidis, "Behavioral Learning Theory: Its Relevance to Marketing and Promotions," *Journal of Marketing*, volume 45, Spring 198 1, pp. 70–78.

20. L. O'Brien and C. Jones, "Do Rewards Really Create Loyalty?" *Harvard Business Review*, volume 73, May-June 1995. pp. 75–82.

21. R. R. Bootzin, G. H. Bower, J. Crocker, and E. Hall, *Psychology Today* (New York; McGraw-Hill, 1991).

22. *Fly Buys Escape: The Magazine for Members*, August 1995, p. 3.

23. "Fly Buys," *AdNews*, 16 December 1994, p. 24.

24. B. Sharp and A. Sharp, "Loyalty Programs and Their Impact on Behavioural Loyalty Patterns" (Adelaide, Australia: University of South Australia, MSC Technical Report Number 4025, 1996).

25. Reichheld with Teal (1996).

26. Brand loyalty is one of the components in many definitions of brand equity. See, for example: D. A. Aaker, *Managing Brand Equity* (New York: Free Press, 1991).

27. Ehrenberg (1988); Uncles et al. (1995); and Ehrenberg and Uncles (1996).

28. G. S. Carpenter, R. Glazer, and K. Nakamoto, "Meaningful Brands from Meaningless Differentiation: The Dependence on Irrelevant Attributes," *Journal of Marketing Research*, volume 31, August 1994, pp. 339–350.

29. A. S. C. Ehrenberg, K. Hammond, and G. Goodhardt, "The After-Effects of Price-Related Consumer Promotions," *Journal of Advertising Research*, volume 34, July–August 1994, pp. 11–21.

30. "Extra Lift for Airlines," *Asian Business*, August 1993, pp. 44–46.

31. F. Hilmer and L. Donaldson, *Management Redeemed* (New York: Simon & Schuster, 1996).

Customer Switching Behavior in Service Industries:
An Exploratory Study

SUSAN M. KEAVENEY

Customer switching behavior damages market share and profitability of service firms yet has remained virtually unexplored in the marketing literature. The author reports results of a critical incident study conducted among more than 500 service customers. The research identifies more than 800 critical behaviors of service firms that caused customers to switch services. Customers' reasons for switching services were classified into eight general categories. The author then discusses implications for further model development and offers recommendations for managers of service firms.

Services marketers know that *"having customers*, not merely *acquiring customers* [sic], is crucial for service firms" (Berry 1980, p. 25). In terms of having customers, research shows that service quality (Bitner 1990; Boulding et al. 1993), relationship quality (Crosby, Evans, and Cowles 1990; Crosby and Stephens 1987), and overall service satisfaction (Cronin and Taylor 1992) can improve customers' intentions to stay with a firm. But what of *losing* customers? What actions of service firms, or their employees, cause customers to switch from one service provider to another?

The answers to these questions are important to both executives of service firms and service marketing scholars. Service firm executives are concerned about the negative effects of customer switching on market share and profitability (Rust and Zahorik 1993). In the simplest sense, switching costs a service firm the customer's future revenue stream. But the loss is even more damaging when other effects are considered: First, because continuing customers increase their spending at an increasing rate, purchase at full-margin rather than discount prices, and create operating efficiencies for service firms (Reichheld and Sasser 1990), the loss of a continuing service customer is a loss from the high-margin sector of the firm's customer base. Second, costs associated with acquiring new customers are incurred: New account setup, credit searches, and advertising and promotional expenses can add up to five times the cost of efforts that might have enabled the firm to retain a customer (Peters 1988). Operating costs rise as the service firm learns the needs of its new customer and the customer learns the procedures of the firm. Executives need research-based knowledge if they are to avoid the revenue-reducing and cost-incurring impacts of customer switching.

The goal of this research is to help managers and researchers understand service switching from the customer's perspective. Because the topic has not been examined in prior research, exploratory research was conducted among service customers to investigate the following questions: What are the determinants of customers' decisions to switch service providers? What critical events, combinations of events, or series of events cause customers to leave familiar service providers and seek new ones? What roles do service encounters and technical service quality play relative to other functions of the service firm?

Conceptual Background

Review of the services and product literatures reveals a variety of potential, and sometimes conflicting, reasons that customers might switch services. For example, customer switching has been related to perceptions of quality in the banking industry (Rust and Zahorik 1993), overall dissatisfaction in the insurance industry (Crosby and Stephens 1987), and service encounter failures in retail stores (Kelley, Hoffman, and Davis 1993). However, the industry-specific nature of these studies necessarily limits the generalizability of these findings and leads us to adopt the broader, cross-industry perspective endorsed by many services researchers (cf. Berry and Parasuraman 1993; Lovelock 1983; Zeithaml, Berry, and Parasuraman 1993).

Susan M. Keaveney is an Assistant Professor of Marketing, Graduate School of Business Administration, University of Colorado at Denver. The author gratefully acknowledges the valuable comments of Linda Price, Cliff Young, Kass Larson, *JM* editor Rajan Varadarajan, and four insightful *JM* reviewers; the research assistance of Randy Eck; and summer research support from the University of Colorado at Denver Graduate School of Business.

The services literature also examines behavioral intentions variables, such as "intentions to switch" or "intentions to repatronize a service," in tests of the nomological, measurement, or predictive validity of service quality-satisfaction models (cf. Bitner 1990; Boulding et al. 1993; Cronin and Taylor 1992). Those results suggest that satisfaction and service quality are related to service switching. However, direct application of the results is limited by several factors:

1. Behavioral intentions are an imperfect proxy for behavior.

2. In some studies, "intentions to switch" is one item in a composite "behavioral intentions" variable, thereby confounding the contribution of quality or satisfaction uniquely to service switching (cf. Bitner 1990; Boulding et al. 1993).

3. Most studies emphasize intentions to engage in behaviors *beneficial* to an organization rather than intentions to engage in behaviors *harmful* to an organization. Variables and relationships that predict positive outcomes may be asymmetrical with those that predict negative outcomes (LaBarbera and Mazursky 1983).

Perhaps the most limiting factor is that prior work was designed to focus on quality, satisfaction, or service encounters—not on service switching. Although service quality failures and dissatisfaction represent some of the reasons that customers switch services, they do not account for all of them. Bitner (1990) speculates that time or money constraints, lack of alternatives, switching costs, and habit might also affect service loyalty; Cronin and Taylor (1992) suggest that convenience, price, and availability might enhance customer satisfaction and ultimately affect behavioral intentions.

Finally, well-established differences between goods and services lead to a generalized expectation that reasons for switching services would differ from reasons for switching goods. Thus, the degree to which service switching might be caused by price deals (Guadagni and Little 1983; Gupta 1988; Mazursky, LaBarbera, and Aiello 1987) or variety seeking (Kahn, Kalwani, and Morrison 1986), two major causes of brand switching, is unknown.

Method and Procedure

A major goal of this research is to introduce a grounded model of customer switching in service industries that would help managers to understand customer defections and provide researchers with a foundation for future systematic investigation. Research methods and procedures followed recommended guidelines for theory development in marketing (cf. Deshpande 1983; Zaltman, LeMasters, and Heffring 1982). We began by collecting "grounded events," or actual incidents that caused customers to switch services (Glaser and Strauss 1967). The incidents were then analyzed to reveal broader patterns. With grounded theory development, patterns must be allowed to emerge from the data (in contrast to the hypothetico-deductive approach, in which *a priori* theory is superimposed on the data).

Data Collection

Critical Incident Technique The critical incident technique (CIT) has been applied successfully to the study of customer (Bitner, Booms, and Tetreault 1990; Kelley, Hoffman, and Davis 1993) and employee perceptions of service encounters (Bitner, Booms, and Mohr 1994). Reliability and validity of the technique have been demonstrated (Ronan and Latham 1974; White and Locke 1981). The CIT is particularly appropriate when the goals of the research include both managerial usefulness and theory development.

Critical incidents were defined as any event, combination of events, or series of events between the customer and one or more service firms that caused the customer to switch service providers. Critical incidents were defined broadly to cast a wide net: Incidents could include not only employee-customer service encounters but any relevant interface between customers and service firms. Incidents could also involve more than one service firm. For example, the customer might decide that interactions with both the service firm "switched from" and the service firm "switched to" were relevant. The key criterion for inclusion was that, from the customer's perspective, the incident led to service switching.

Data Collection Procedures Interviewers were 50 trained graduate student volunteers enrolled in services marketing classes at an urban university. Interviewers each contacted ten individuals to participate in the study. Because most interviewers were full-time corporate employees, they were encouraged to collect incidents from coworkers, neighbors, and other contacts, but not from other students. Respondents were asked to record their critical incidents on a standardized form in the presence of the interviewer. According to Flanagan (1954, p. 342), asking respondents to write their responses in the presence of an interviewer "retains the advantages of the individual interview in regard to the personal contact, explanation, and availability of the interviewer to answer questions ... [and] the language of the actual observer is precisely reproduced." Moreover, the procedure mitigates certain problems that can arise with multiple interviewers, such as inter-interviewer bias, selectivity in listening and recording, or variation in recording and editing.

Sample size was determined according to Flanagan's recommendations (1954, p. 343): "Adequate coverage has been achieved when the addition of 100 critical incidents to the sample adds only two or three critical behaviors." This *post hoc* method of evaluating sample size necessitated collection and analysis of data in two phases. First, a "classification sample" of 300 responses was collected. Later, two "confirmation samples" totaling 226 additional responses were collected, for a total of 526 responses.

Questionnaire Development The first question asked respondents to indicate which of 25 different services they had purchased during the previous six-month period. The question was included for two reasons: First, because respondents may have been uncertain about what was meant by "services," the question provided 25 different examples of services for clarification. Second, because the population of interest was consumers of services, the question allowed researchers to check whether respondents had purchased services during the prior six months.

The six-month time frame was recent enough for reliable recall yet long enough to include infrequently visited services (such as doctors). Respondents were then asked the following:

> Please think about the last time that you switched service providers. That is, you were a customer of one service provider and you switched to become the customer of a different service provider. What service are you thinking about?

The question was carefully worded to achieve several objectives: (1) It allowed respondents to select service switching incidents of their own choosing, without constraining them to specific industries; (2) It asked for the most recent observation to prevent respondents from describing only the more dramatic or vivid incidents; and (3) The most recent observation should be well remembered. Finally, the question gave respondents time to collect their thoughts and to have incidents clearly in mind.

A series of probing questions encouraged respondents to provide detailed descriptions:

- Please tell us, in your own words, what happened? Why did you switch service providers?

- Try to tell us exactly what happened: where you were, what happened, what you said, how you felt, what the service person said, and so forth.

Note that respondents were not asked to analyze why the incidents occurred; they were asked to tell stories about all the things that had occurred—something people do quite easily (Bitner, Booms, and Tetreault 1990; Nyquist and Booms 1987). Analysis, evaluation, abstraction, and inference were conducted by the researchers.

Data Quality

Validation of the Sample The use of multiple interviewers increased the need to validate the sample. Ten percent of respondents (one chosen arbitrarily from each set of ten) were contacted by telephone and asked (1) to verify that they had personally answered the questionnaire and (2) to identify the service in their "switching story." If a respondent could not verify participation, all surveys by that interviewer were eliminated. One set could not be verified and was eliminated, for a revised subtotal of 516 useable responses.

Quality of the Critical Incidents Flanagan (1954, p. 340) suggests that "if full and precise details are given, it can usually be assumed that this information is accurate. Vague reports suggest that the incident is not well remembered and that some of the data may be incorrect." Judges removed 48 responses in which either the respondent had not switched services or the response was judged to be vague, for a final total of 468 incidents.

Characteristics of the Sample Demographically, 58% of respondents were female and 42% were male, 62% were married, and 52% had at least one child. Respondents worked an average of 38 hours per week and spouses worked an average of 35 hours. The group was well educated, with 67% holding at least a bachelor's degree. Respondents ranged in age from 18 to 79 years; the average age was 36 years. Almost 60% of respondents lived in suburbs, 34% lived in the city, and 6.5% lived in rural areas. All respondents were service consumers, purchasing between 2 and 19 of the 25 services listed in question 1. Service purchase responses were normally distributed with a mean, median, and mode of 10 services.

Forty-five different services were cited in critical switching incidents, including beauty salons (67), auto mechanics (67), insurance agents (54), dry cleaners (50), sit-down restaurants (27), doctors or medical services (27), dentists (16), travel agents (15), banks (14), phone service providers (14), fast-food restaurants

(12), and housekeepers (10). Less frequently mentioned were trash pick-up services (9), day care services (8), real estate agents (7), clothing stores (7), health clubs (6), lawn care services (6), airlines (6), hotels (5), accountants (4), and plumbers (4). Twenty-three other services were cited by fewer than 4 respondents.

Data Analysis

Unit of Analysis Because the term "critical incident" can refer to either the overall story or to discrete behaviors contained within the story, the first step in data analysis is to determine the appropriate unit of analysis (Holsti 1968; Kassarjian 1977). We determined that discrete behaviors would best preserve the specificity of the data. Therefore, two judges independently coded the 468 incidents into 838 separate critical behaviors, as follows: For example, consider a critical incident in which an employee ignored a customer and was rude. That incident would be coded as containing two critical behaviors ("ignored" and "rude"). Synonyms were coded as a single critical behavior ("rude and discourteous" would be coded as "rude"). Upon completing the unit of analysis coding task, the two judges compared their decisions regarding discrete behaviors and resolved disagreements by discussion.

Category Development and Reliability The next step was to sort the 838 critical behaviors into categories and subcategories, following the critical incident technique procedures shown in Figure 1 and described following.

Two judges (A and B) independently developed mutually exclusive and exhaustive categories for responses 1–300 (271 useable critical incidents composed of 462 critical behaviors). Following Weber (1985), but unusual in critical incident studies, intrajudge reliability was examined to determine whether the *same* judges classified the same phenomena into the same categories over time (essentially, test-retest reliability over a one-month period). When intrajudge reliability exceeded the .80 cutoff, Judges A and B compared their categorization schemas and resolved disagreements by discussion.

A rigorous classification system should also be "intersubjectively unambiguous" (Hunt 1983), as measured by interjudge reliability. Interjudge reliability is a measure of whether different judges classify the same phenomena into the same categories. Interjudge reliabilities above .80 are considered satisfactory (Bitner, Booms, and Tetreault 1990; Kassarjian 1977; Nyquist and Booms 1987; Ronan and Latham 1974). When the interjudge agreement between Judges A and B exceeded .80, their results became the benchmarks (Latham and Saari 1984).

Two new judges (C and D) sorted the 462 behaviors into the categories and subcategories provided by Judges A and B. Judges C and D were instructed to create new categories if appropriate. When intrajudge reliability exceeded .80, their classification decisions were compared against the benchmarks. Interjudge reliabilities were very high, averaging .88 overall. Finally, a fifth judge (Judge E) conducted a final sort of responses 1–300. Judge E's interjudge reliability averaged a very satisfactory .85 overall.

Category Confirmation and Reliability A sample is of sufficient size for critical incident analysis when the addition of 100 new incidents does not create any new categories. The two confirmation samples collected in this research (incidents 301–400 and 401–516) yielded 197 useable critical incidents and 376 critical behaviors.

Judges A and B sorted responses 301–400 into the classification system explained previously with an eye to developing new categories. No new categories emerged in this process, indicating that no further analysis was necessary. As a precautionary measure, the confirmation process was repeated with responses 401–516; again, no new categories emerged. Finally, Judges C and E sorted responses 301–516. Interjudge reliability averaged a very satisfactory .88 overall. The final classification schema for service switching incidents is shown in Table 1.

Content Validity Content validity of a critical incident classification system is considered satisfactory if critical behaviors in the confirmation sample are fully represented by the categories and subcategories developed in the classification sample (Flanagan 1954; Ronan and Latham 1974). As shown in Figure 1 and Table 1, no new categories emerged during sorting and classification of either of two confirmation samples. High content validity, intrajudge reliabilities, and interjudge reliabilities provide a high degree of confidence that the schema accurately represents the domain of customer switching in service industries.

Results: A Model of Customer Switching Behavior in Service Industries

The model of customer switching behavior in service industries is shown in Figure 2. Categories and hierarchical subcategories are discussed in detail subsequently.

TABLE 1
Classification of Services Switching Incidents

Service Switching Category	Classification Sample[a]			Confirmation Sample[b]			Total Sample		
	N of Critical Behaviors	% of Critical Behaviors	% of Critical Incidents[c]	N of Critical Behaviors	% of Critical Behaviors	% of Critical Incidents[3]	N of Critical Behaviors	% of Critical Behaviors	% of Critical Incidents[3]
1. Pricing	79	17.1	29.0	61	16.2	31.0	140	16.7	29.9
2. Inconvenience	48	10.4	17.7	49	13.0	24.9	97	11.6	20.7
3. Core service failures	120	26.0	44.3	88	23.4	44.7	208	24.8	44.3
4. Failed service encounters	95	20.6	35.1	65	17.3	33.0	160	19.1	34.1
5. Response to failed service	50	10.8	18.5	31	8.2	15.7	81	9.7	17.3
6. Competition	20	4.3	7.4	28	7.5	14.2	48	5.7	10.2
7. Ethical problems	19	4.1	7.0	16	4.3	8.1	35	4.2	7.5
8. Involuntary switching	11	2.4	4.1	18	4.8	9.1	29	3.5	6.2
9. Other	20	4.3	7.4	20	5.3	10.1	40	4.7	8.6
Total behaviors	462	100.0		376	100.0		838	100.0	

[1]Critical Incidents 1–300
[2]Critical Incidents 301–516
[3]Percents; sum to greater than 100 due to multiple reasons for switching services per incident

FIGURE 1

Critical Incident Sorting and Classification Process

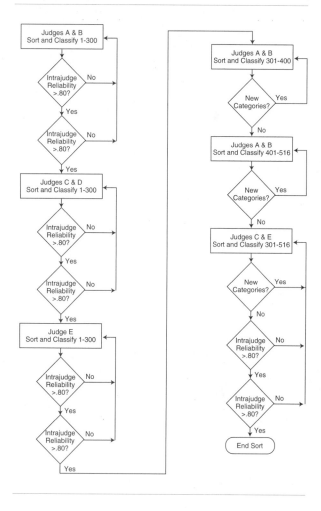

FIGURE 2

A Model of Customers' Service Switching Behavior

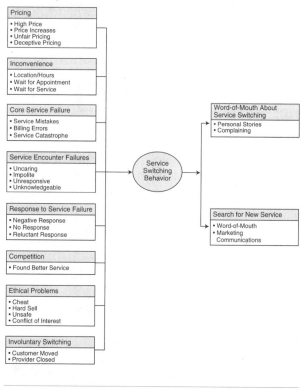

value of the services received ("The national auto mechanic chain was overpriced compared to their services"), or too high relative to competitive prices ("The other telephone service could save me money").

In the second subcategory, customers switched because of a price increase ("[I] never had a claim but every year the car insurance company raised the rates"). The reference price in this subcategory was based on prior experience with the focal service. In the third subcategory, customers felt cheated or believed that the price charged was unfair ("The realtor charged me excessively. I felt cheated"). In the fourth subcategory, customers switched because prices were deceptive, as when a final price greatly exceeded a quoted price ("My original diagnosis was supposed, by a mailing sent to me, to be a 1- to 2-hour visit costing less than $300. It turned out to be a 7.5-hour examination costing over $1,200").

Pricing

The "pricing" category included all critical switching behaviors that involved prices, rates, fees, charges, surcharges, service charges, penalties, price deals, coupons, or price promotions. Price was the third largest switching category, mentioned by 30% of all respondents. Nine percent of respondents mentioned only price as the reason for switching services, and an additional 21% mentioned price as one of two or more causes of switching.

Pricing subcategories included (1) high prices, (2) price increases, (3) unfair pricing practices, and (4) deceptive pricing practices. In the "high price" subcategory, customers switched services when service prices exceeded internal reference prices. Prices were deemed too high relative to some internal normative price ("The cost of the dry cleaner was too great even with coupons in the mail"), too high relative to the

Inconvenience

The "inconvenience" category included all critical incidents in which the customer felt inconvenienced by the service provider's location, hours of operation, waiting time for service, or waiting time to get an appointment. More than 20% of all respondents attributed at least one of their reasons for service switching to inconvenience. Of the respondents who reported inconvenience, 21.6% cited inconvenience as the only reason for switching.

Inconvenient incidents were sorted into three subcategories: The first included customers who switched because of location ("The new auto service was closer to work") or hours of operation ("I switched to a dry cleaner . . . that was open past 6 p.m."); in the second, customers switched services when it took too long to schedule an appointment ("To get an appointment with the medical services doctor I had to wait 4–6 months"); in the third, customers switched when they waited too long for service delivery. "Too long" was determined by comparing the wait against an internal, normative reference point ("It took us 45 minutes to get another beer) or against promises made by the service provider ("The [building] project completion was two months late").

Core Service Failures

The largest category of service switching was core service failures, mentioned by 44% of respondents. Core service failures included all critical incidents that were due to mistakes or other technical problems with the service itself. More than 11% of respondents described only the core service failure incident as the reason for service switching, and another 33% of respondents mentioned a core service failure as one of two or more reasons.

Three subcategories of core service failures represented (1) mistakes, (2) billing errors, and (3) service catastrophes. The first composed the largest subcategory. Core service mistakes included longitudinal problems, in which a series of mistakes ("We had a number of problems with the accuracy of our monthly [bank] statements and with transfers not being completed") or decreases in levels of service ("The level of [banking] service I had grown accustomed to has deteriorated") occurred over time. The subcategory also included multiple mistakes that occurred within the context of a single service encounter ("The travel agent couldn't get accurate information. She couldn't offer me the seat I wanted [it was available]; she couldn't connect my flights. She couldn't come up with a super saver flight according to my schedule"). Other core service mistakes that led to customer switching included single "big" mistakes ("The pharmacist provided incorrect insulin"), incomplete service provision (" . . . dentist started work and did not finish. Left town for three days. The area became infected and I

was sick"), or incidents in which the provider was unable to deliver the service ("the [auto mechanic] was unable to repair my car").

A second subcategory of core service failures grouped billing problems. Customer complaints included incorrect billing ("The dentist billed my insurance company for services not yet provided") and failures to correct billing in a timely manner ("I was unable to get the [health] club to stop taking money from my account (mistakenly) for months").

The third subcategory included service catastrophes. Here, core service failures not only failed to provide the appropriate service but actually caused damage to the customer's person, family, pets, or belongings ("A routine surgical procedure almost killed my dog") or caused the customer to lose time or money ("I had to rent a car [to go] to work").

Service Encounter Failures

Service encounters were defined as personal interactions between customers and employees of service firms. Service encounter failures were the second largest category of service switching, mentioned by 34% of respondents: 9% of respondents mentioned only service encounters as the reason for switching services, and an additional 25% of respondents mentioned service encounter failures as at least one of two or more reasons for switching.

Service encounter failures were all attributed to some aspect of service employees' behaviors or attitudes: If employees were (1) uncaring, (2) impolite, (3) unresponsive, or (4) unknowledgeable, customers switched service providers. Uncaring service contact personnel did not listen to customers ("The doctor was very cut and dry [sic], and I did not feel she listened to me. She didn't validate my concerns and discuss them further with me"), ignored customers ("The waitress was practically nonexistent. She never asked if everything was OK or if we needed anything else"), or paid attention to people other than customers ("The barber spent [more] time talking to her boyfriend than paying attention to what she was doing with her scissors"). Uncaring service personnel rushed ("The accountant only talked to us for 20 minutes") or were not helpful ("The mortgage broker was not helpful to our business at all"), friendly ("The [flight] attendant had as much personality as an ATM machine"), or interested in customers ("The plumber seemed to have a lack of caring about us").

Unresponsive contact personnel were inflexible or uncommunicative. Inflexible service providers refused to accommodate customer requests ("The doctor's office refused to transfer my records to a new physician without first receiving a registered letter requesting such a transfer even though I was standing right there"). Uncommunicative service providers failed to be proactively informative ("The day care service had lots of problems of not being informative on a day-to-day basis"), refused to return phone calls ("We could not get [the stock broker] to return a call—he was too busy"), or neglected to answer questions ("They wouldn't explain what they were doing to my car").

Impolite employees were described by respondents as rude ("Flight staff was rude and uncooperative"), condescending ("The clothing store sales people got snotty when I demanded what I already paid for"), and impatient or ill-tempered ("My daughter needed a shot and was uncooperative. The doctor was very impatient and short-tempered").

Unknowledgeable service employees were described as inexperienced ("Our son was not receiving adequate supervision, training, and instructional time at the chain's day care center [because of] inexperienced new hires"), inept ("The car salesman gave me wrong information about the car"), or not versed in state-of-the-art techniques ("The dentist's practice had not moved forward with newer technology"). Others simply did not instill confidence in the customer ("[The building contractor] made enormous assumptions regarding the works, but I had a lack of confidence in his judgment").

Employee Responses to Service Failures

The "employee responses to service failures" category included critical switching incidents in which customers switched, not because of a service failure, but because service providers failed to handle the situation appropriately. Just over 17% of all service switching incidents were caused in part by unsatisfactory employee responses to service failures.

Employee responses to service failures were sorted into three subcategories that range from bad to worse: (1) reluctant responses, (2) failure to respond, and (3) patently negative responses. In "reluctant responses," customers told of service providers who responded to service failures and made corrections—but did so with obvious reluctance. For example, these customers never returned to this restaurant, despite a service "correction":

> We received two incorrect entrees. We asked the waiter to replace them and he refused. He said we would have to pay for them. The manager reluctantly agreed to replace one entree. We wrote a letter to the owner and never heard from him.

In the second subcategory, customers switched because service employees failed to respond to service problems. Some failed responses were of the "too bad, you're on your own" variety ("I told the receptionist that I couldn't wait that long. She said, "Get another doctor"). Other times service providers did not acknowledge the legitimacy of a complaint ("I thought their prices were high compared with motels in other cities. The response was that they had a 90% occupancy rate so the price must be about right") or ignored a customer's complaint ("No one asked why I wanted to cancel their [credit card) service").

The third subcategory grouped "patently negative responses," in which the service provider attributed blame for the failure to the customer. This incident describes one customer's experience: "The owner said that the original seamstress told her that I had contributed to the first error, as I had personally pinned the jacket sleeves too short."

Attraction by Competitors

The "attraction by competitors" category included critical switching incidents in which customers told stories about switching *to* a better service provider rather than *from* an unsatisfactory provider. Approximately 10% of critical switching incidents were sorted into this category. Customers switched to service providers who were more personable ("new club is well maintained, staff is friendly, greet me by my first name"), more reliable ("Both cars are always ready at pickup time"), or provided higher quality ("switched to a private home [day care provider] that is 20% higher; however, the smaller number of kids, home environment, and personal attention are worth it"). Many customers switched to a better service even when the new provider was more expensive ("We feel the quality [of the haircut] is worth the price, even though it is almost twice the price") or less convenient ("I now travel further to buy my liquor . . . I like the attitude of friendliness").

Ethical Problems

The "ethical problems" category included critical switching incidents that described illegal, immoral, unsafe, unhealthy, or other behaviors that deviated widely from social norms. More than 7% of all critical incidents cited unethical service provider behavior as at least part of the reason for switching services. This percentage increases to almost 9% if deceptive pricing and bait-and-switch practices (categorized with pricing) are added.

Four subcategories of unethical behaviors included (1) dishonest behavior, (2) intimidating behavior,

(3) unsafe or unhealthy practices, and (4) conflicts of interest. Dishonest service providers cheated customers, stole personal belongings or money, charged for work not performed, or suggested unneeded service work ("The major problem was that if we brought our car in and they looked it over they always found a million other things wrong"). Threatening service providers engaged in overly aggressive selling behavior, yelled at customers, or intimidated them ("When I told the original repair shop I would not have the repairs done at this time the mechanic said, 'I can't believe you would drive around with your children in a car needing these repairs'").

The third subcategory included unhealthy or unsafe service practices. For example, one respondent switched restaurants because "most of the tables in the place were dirty. A person who had been cooking handled the trash. A person who handled the food also handled the money." Another switched hotels after being "given a key to a room that was occupied." In the fourth subcategory, customers told of conflict of interest problems. For example, one customer switched after learning that "the travel agent had been booking with the airline giving the best perks and commissions."

Involuntary Switching and Seldom-Mentioned Incidents

The involuntary switching category (6%) included stories that described switching because of factors largely beyond the control of either the customer or the service provider. These included involuntary switching because the service provider had moved, the customer had moved, or the insurance company or other third-party payer had changed alliances. Finally, an "other" category was created for responses mentioned only once or twice. Interestingly, some factors that appear in satisfaction and quality research, such as tangibles, crowding, and problems with other customers, were seldom mentioned. Fewer than 5% of critical behaviors were classified as "other."

Simple versus Complex Service Switching

Table 2 shows categorization of simple (defined as involving one category or factor) and complex (defined as involving more than one category or factor) incidents. Forty-five percent of respondents described switching incidents composed of a single behavior or factor. Although simple switching incidents occurred in all categories (except, by definition, responses to service failures), core service failures, pricing problems, and service encounter failures were the most frequently mentioned simple causes of service switching.

The remaining 55% of critical switching incidents were complex. Critical switching incidents composed of two different categories (two-factor incidents) were reported by 36% of respondents. Of those, more than half described a core service failure compounded by another problem. For example, 15% of two-factor incidents described core service failures exacerbated by unsatisfactory provider responses to the problem ("The color on the jacket was blotched after dry cleaning. The clerk swore up and down that my coat was defective, they were not responsible, and I should return the coat to the store where I bought it"). Another 15% described core service failures combined

TABLE 2

Simple and Complex Switching Incidents: Number of Critical Behaviors per Switching Incident by Category

Switching Incidents and Reasons Cited	Simple Incidents:		Two-Factor Incidents:		Three-Factor Incidents:	
	N of Behaviors	% of Behaviors	N of Behaviors	% of Behaviors	N of Behaviors	% of Behaviors
A. Price	42	19.9	51	15.2	33	15.9
B. Inconvenience	21	10.0	41	12.2	27	13.0
C. Core service failure	52	24.6	96	28.6	45	21.8
D. Service encounters	42	19.9	61	18.1	45	21.8
E. Response to failure	0	0.0	38	11.3	31	15.0
F. Competition	14	6.6	7	5.0	11	5.3
G. Ethical problems	9	4.3	11	3.3	7	3.4
H. Involuntary/other	31	14.7	21	6.3	8	3.8
Number of incidents	211		168		69	
Total behaviors	211		336		207	

Note: The remaining 20 respondents averaged 4.2 behaviors per incident for a total of 468 incidents and 838 behaviors.

with service encounter failures ("[The airline] tickets were . . . missing, seating [was] with partners not together . . . [the travel agent] told us to pick up the tickets, then didn't have them. [The travel agent was] impersonal, not friendly or helpful"). Ten percent of two-factor incidents involved core service failures combined with pricing problems ("I walked out to find that the haircut was uneven, and that I had been over-charged in the process") and another 6% were core service failures combined with inconvenience ("The accounting service was very slow and did make major errors").

A second pattern involved service encounter failures combined with an additional problem. Most common were service encounter failures combined with core service failures (noted previously), service encounter failures combined with inconvenience (8%), and service encounter failures combined with pricing problems (7%).

Fifteen percent of respondents described switching incidents composed of three different categories. Most common were incidents involving a core service failure *and* a service encounter failure combined with a failure to respond to the service problem ("The dry cleaners ruined my comforter . . . they yelled at me when I got upset . . . they would not fix it or replace it"), a pricing problem ("The auto mechanic could not find the problem . . . he had a bad attitude . . . the dealership still charged me $50"), or a convenience problem ("[The medical provider] misdiagnosed a serious medical condition . . . provided very imper-sonal care . . . the doctor never saw you [sic] at the scheduled time").

Finally, 20 respondents reported four or more different critical behaviors in each switching incident. For example, this highly complex switching incident had elements of price, ethical issues (unnecessary work), service encounter failures, and inconvenience:

> My doctor is equipped with a fairly complete office. It seems every time one of my family or myself [sic] goes in, we end up needing an X-ray, blood tests, or some other proce-dure that really skyrockets [sic] our bill. Some of these procedures seem a little pre-mature and/or unnecessary. I also happened to overhear the receptionist at the end of the day tell the doctor that they cleared X amount of hours for that day & took in more than they expected. I happened to be right there at the time. Very unprofessional. There were also scheduling problems in there [sic] office.

Consequences of Service Switching

Once customers switch services, it is likely that they will engage in post-switching behaviors related to the incident. First, respondents were asked if they had engaged in word-of-mouth communications about the service switching incident. Content analysis of responses was conducted as described previously. Interjudge reliability averaged .90 overall. Results showed that 75% of customers had told at least one other person, and usually several other people, about the service switching incident. Proximity was a fac-tor—respondents told family, friends, neighbors, coworkers, and other known customers of the service. Some respondents told the new service provider, in an effort to prevent the problem from occurring again in the future. Only 7% of respondents told the original service provider.

Second, respondents were asked if they had found a new service provider and, if so, how they had identi-fied the new provider. Responses were content ana-lyzed and interjudge reliability averaged .86 overall. Eighty-five percent of respondents reported having already found a new service provider. Approximately half found the new service firm through word-of-mouth communications, references, and referrals. Approximately 20% found the new provider through active external search: that is, shopping around, calling around, dropping in, trial. Another 20% were per-suaded by marketing communications that included direct sales, promotional offers, or advertising media (e.g., yellow pages, newspapers).

Discussion

Implications for Research

The exploratory model of customer switching behav-ior in service industries presented here defines the domain of customer service switching behavior "through the eyes of the participants" (Deshpande 1983). The categories (1) adequately capture the domain (no new categories emerged after the addition of either of two confirmation samples), (2) are inter-subjectively unambiguous (evidenced by high inter-judge reliability), (3) are collectively exhaustive (fewer than 5% of behaviors were sorted as "other"), and (4) are mutually exclusive.

Articulation of a rigorous classification system provides the fundamental first step in developing a comprehensive theory of customer switching behavior in service industries by organizing a standardized vari-able system for understanding the phenomenon.

Specifically, the model of customer switching behavior in service industries proposes eight main causal variables, including price, inconvenience, core service failures, service encounter failures, failed employee responses to service failures, competitive issues, ethical problems, and involuntary factors. The model proposes several two-way interactions among causal variables, including interactions between core service failures and service encounters, responses to service failures, inconvenience, or high price; interactions between service encounters and inconvenience or high prices; and interactions between high prices and competitive service offerings. Results even suggest several three-way interactions based on core service failures and service encounter failures combined with responses to failures, price, or inconvenience.

The proposition that core service failures, service encounter failures, failed employee responses to service failures, and inconvenience cause customers to switch services implies certain extensions to services marketing research. Researchers have examined antecedents of service encounters (Bitner, Booms, and Tetreault 1990), technical quality in service delivery (Shostack 1984), management of service demand fluctuations (Sasser 1976), and waiting for service (Taylor 1994) and their effects on customer evaluations of satisfaction and service quality. The model of customer switching proposes that the consequences of these factors extend beyond cognitive and affective evaluations to actual behavior: Customers not only experience dissatisfaction but may actually take action to switch service providers.

The proposition that price, competition, ethics, and involuntary factors cause customers to switch services implies a need to examine variables in addition to the more frequently researched variables discussed previously. Services literature tends to focus, appropriately, on service quality and satisfaction, service encounters, and service design as antecedents of customer loyalty. The model proposes that such variables, *along with* price, competition, ethical issues, and other factors, should be considered if we are to understand customer defections from service firms fully. Broadening the scope of services research is consistent with the Marketing Science Institute's research priority to study how "service interact[s] with other actions of the firm, e.g., pricing, advertising, etc., to affect customer perceptions" (1992–94, p. 9).

The proposition that combinations of causal factors interact to cause customer switching suggests a need to design services research that focuses directly on customer switching behavior. Research focused on selected antecedent variables (e.g., research focused on

price deals or service encounters or technical service delivery only) will be unable to detect the potentially substantive interaction effects proposed by the model. To measure the total effects of service variables on customer switching behavior, multiple antecedents must be investigated simultaneously.

Implications for Managers

The model of customer switching behavior in service industries offers numerous implications for executives of service firms. Reports of switching activity in 45 different service businesses suggests that few if any services are exempt. The need to develop customer retention strategies may be most compelling in frequently mentioned services such as insurance, auto repair, personal grooming, dry cleaning, and housekeeping. However, even relationship-intensive services were not immune to customer switching—as many respondents reported switching physicians as reported switching restaurants.

An important implication for managers is that six of the eight service switching factors are controllable from a service firm's point of view. The six categories suggest areas in which managers might take action to prevent customer switching: For example, if core service failures cause customers to switch, then a "zero defects" philosophy to deliver a technically correct service every time should be effective in reducing customer defections (cf. Fitzsimmons and Fitzsimmons 1994). The proposition that failed responses to service breakdowns may cause customers to switch suggests the importance of developing policies for effective service recovery (cf. Berry and Parasuraman 1991; Hart, Sasser, and Heskett 1990). The proposition that customer switching may be caused by inconvenience implies that effective queue management, timely delivery of service, and efficient management of reservations systems might reduce defections.

Customer defections caused by unsatisfactory employee-customer interactions might be reduced by teaching employees to listen to customers, return telephone calls promptly, keep customers informed, and explain procedures and by training employees in technical, state-of-the-art knowledge. The proposition that customers may switch services for price-related reasons implies a need for careful management of pricing policies, especially when service firms charge higher-than-competitive prices or are considering increases in fees, service charges, or penalties. Evidence of ethical problems suggests that service firms might develop behavior-based control systems to reward ethical conduct and discourage unethical conduct among service contact employees (Hunt and Vasquez-Parraga 1993).

The predominance of complex switching incidents suggests that service firm managers might benefit by the use of cross-functional teams to solve complex customer switching problems. Marketing managers might be joined by managers from operations (to improve core service delivery), human resources (to improve service encounters), legal department (to address unethical behavior), or finance (to adjust prices).

Managers of service firms should note that some customers switched services even when satisfied with their former providers. This was often the case for service customers who switched because of convenience ("I was very satisfied with the service that [the accountant] provided me in the past; however, I prefer direct access . . ."), competitive actions ("I was relatively happy . . . but the other mechanic worked on my wife's car and did a good job . . ."), or prices (". . . switched long distance phone carriers due to . . . dollar savings—no problems with previous service"). It is impossible to determine whether switching among satisfied service customers approaches the 65%–85% reported in other studies (*Fortune* 1993, p. 58). Still, the issue is important: Although the services literature points out that customers may stay even after a dissatisfactory encounter (Bitner, Booms, and Tetreault 1990; Kelley, Hoffman, and Davis 1993), the present study points out that satisfied customers may be leaving.

The ideas proposed here are implications of the general model of customer switching in service industries. Managers should investigate their own customers' reasons for switching services. A particular advantage of using the CIT for this purpose is its ability to identify specific behaviors for application in training and control systems. For example, knowing that an employee "was talking on the phone while I waited" is more useful information than the more general "the employee was unresponsive:" Moreover, the CIT uncovers behaviors that might not be identified with more traditional methods. Surveys would hardly include items such as "the manager of restaurant x yells at waitresses in front of customers," yet customers switched services when this happened. The use of external researchers to investigate customer switching could be beneficial if in-house researchers inhibit customers from reporting their "real" reasons for switching.

Limitations and Directions for Further Research

We introduce the first model of customer switching behavior in service industries, identifying possible causal factors and proposing interaction effects among them. Further evaluative research, including controlled manipulation of proposed causal variables, is needed to test actual cause and effect. Multiple causes of service switching should be modeled concurrently whenever feasible, but especially in the context of core service failures, service encounter failures, responses to service failures, price, and inconvenience. Further model development is also indicated. Although the model identifies possible causal antecedents, the process of customer switching in service industries remains unknown. For example, what are the roles of cognitive and affective evaluations in the model? Do prior evaluations of service satisfaction or service quality mediate (or moderate) the effects of antecedent factors on customer switching? What is the role of customers' attributional processing of their own actions and the actions of services firms on switching behavior?

Some ideas for further research are suggested by the limitations of the study. For example, questions about service switching may have discouraged stories about simply quitting a service provider, self-provision of the service, or variety-seeking behavior. Probing questions focused on actions and emotions may have neglected cumulative experiences. Respondents' self-reported causes might not reflect "objective" causes of their behavior: Because people tend to make internal attributions for positive outcomes but external attributions for negative outcomes (Folkes 1988; Folkes and Kotsos 1986), for example, explanations of one's own behavior may differ from an observer's explanation of the same event. Researchers in the future might conduct a parallel study among service providers to gain perspective from the other side of the dyad. Finally, generalizability of results is limited by the use of convenience sampling and should be tested in the future.

Additional implications for research are suggested by specific variables in the model. For example, examination of pricing incidents reveals that customers develop service reference prices that range from the specific (competitive prices) to the abstract (internal normative prices). If services are intangible, variable, and difficult to compare, how do customers form service reference prices? The role of competition in customer switching suggests research opportunities to understand the effects of competitive service strategies, new service introduction, or service positioning on customer switching. Evidence of ethical problems in service industries suggests that theoretical models of marketing ethics might be empirically examined in the context of service firms: Do service characteristics, such as the intangible or personal nature of services, influence consumers' perceptions of ethical issues? In addition, research in the future might contribute to the literature by developing a set of deontological norms for service firms (i.e., policies specifying "right" and "wrong" service behaviors).

Implications and recommendations in this study emphasize the costs of customer switching. Yet functional customer turnover (i.e., in which low-margin customers switch from the firm and high-margin customers switch to the firm) might ultimately benefit a service firm. In addition, service firms might track information about customer switching behavior to signal market trends, measure the performance of competitive strategies, or keep current with new customer demands. Much interesting work remains to be done in this area.

In conclusion, the article presents the first model of customer switching in service industries. The number of proposed causal factors and the proposed interrelationships among them suggest a complicated process—possibly even more complicated than brand switching behavior. The services literature has made significant progress in understanding the complex combination of variables that comprise the gestalt of service provision. The model of service switching reveals that an equally complex combination of variables, composed of many but perhaps not all of the same variables, is involved in customers' decisions to switch services. Further specification and testing of the model, including conceptualization and operationalization of proposed variables, experimental testing of proposed causal relationships, structural modeling of the switching process, and identification of other relevant variables, are needed to increase our understanding.

References

Berry, Leonard L. (1980), "Services Marketing Is Different," *Business*, 30 (May), 24–29.

——— and A. Parasuraman (1991), *Marketing Services: Competing through Quality*. New York: The Free Press.

——— and ——— (1993), "Building a New Academic Field—The Case of Services Marketing," *Journal of Retailing*, 69 (Spring), 13–60.

Bitner, Mary Jo (1990), "Evaluating Service Encounters: The Effects of Physical Surroundings and Employee Responses," *Journal of Marketing*, 54 (April), 69–82.

———, Bernard M. Booms, and Mary Stanfield Tetreault (1990) "The Service Encounter: Diagnosing Favorable and Unfavorable Incidents," *Journal of Marketing*, 54 (January) 71–84.

———, ———, and Lois A. Mohr (1994), "Critical Service Encounters: The Employee's Viewpoint," *Journal of Marketing*, 58 (October), 95–106.

Boulding, William, Ajay Kalra, Richard Staelin, and Valarie A. Zeithaml (1993), "A Dynamic Process Model of Service Quality; From Expectations to Behavioral Intentions," *Journal of Marketing Research*, 30 (February), 7–27.

Cronin, Joseph J., Jr. and Steven A. Taylor, (1992), "Measuring Service Quality: A Reexamination and Extension," *Journal of Marketing*, 56 (July), 55–68.

Crosby, Lawrence A., Kenneth R. Evans, and Deborah Cowles (1990), "Relationship Quality in Services Selling: An Interpersonal Influence Perspective," *Journal of Marketing*, 54 (July), 68–81.

——— and Nancy Stephens (1987), "Effects of Relationship Marketing on Satisfaction, Retention, and Prices in the Life Insurance Industry," *Journal of Marketing Research*, 24 (November), 404–11.

Deshpande, Rohit (1983), "Paradigms Lost: On Theory and Method in Research in Marketing," *Journal of Marketing*, 47 (Fall), 101–10.

Fitzsimmons, James A. and Mona J. Fitzsimmons (1994), *Service Management for Competitive Advantage*. New York: McGraw-Hill.

Flanagan, John C. (1954), "The Critical Incident Technique," *Psychological Bulletin*, 51 (July), 327–57.

Folkes, Valerie (1988), "Recent Attribution Research in Consumer Behavior: A Review and New Directions," *Journal of Consumer Research*, 14 (March), 548–65.

——— and Barbara Kotsos (1986), "Buyers' and Sellers' Explanations for Product Failure: Who Done It?" *Journal of Marketing*, 50 (April), 74–80.

Fortune (1993), Special Issue on the New Consumer (Autumn–Winter).

Glaser, Barney and Anselm Strauss (1967), *The Discovery of Grounded Theory*. Chicago: Aldine.

Guadagni, Peter M. and John D. C. Little (1983), "A Logit Model of Brand Choice Calibrated on Scanner Data," *Marketing Science*, 2 (Summer), 203–38.

Gupta, Sunil (1988), "Impact of Sales Promotions on When, What, and How Much to Buy," *Journal of Marketing Research*, 25 (November), 342–55.

Hart, Christopher W. L., W. Earl Sasser, Jr., and James L. Heskett (1990), "The Profitable Art of Service Recovery," *Harvard Business Review*, (July–August), 148–56.

Holsti, Ole R. (1968), "Content Analysis," in *The Handbook of Social Psychology: Research Methods*, Vol. 2, Gardner Lindzey and Elliot Aronson, eds. Reading MA: Addison-Wesley, 596–692.

Hunt, Shelby D. (1983), *Marketing Theory*. Homewood, IL: Richard D. Irwin.

——— and Arturo Vasquez-Parraga (1993), "Organizational Consequences, Marketing Ethics, and Salesforce Supervision," *Journal of Marketing Research*, 30 (February), 78–90.

Kahn, Barbara E., Manohar U. Kalwani, and Donald G. Morrison (1986), "Measuring Variety-Seeking and Reinforcement Behaviors Using Panel Data," *Journal of Marketing Research*, 23 (May), 89–100.

Kassarjian, Harold H. (1977), "Content Analysis in Consumer Research," *Journal of Consumer Research*, 4 (June), 8–18.

Kelley, Scott W., K. Douglas Hoffman, and Mark A. Davis (1993), "A Typology of Retail Failures and Recoveries," *Journal of Retailing*, 69 (Winter), 429–52.

LaBarbera, Priscilla A. and David Mazursky (1983), "A Longitudinal Assessment of Consumer Satisfaction/Dissatisfaction: The Dynamic Aspect of the Cognitive Process," *Journal of Marketing Research*, 20 (November), 393–404.

Latham, Gary and Lise M. Saari (1984), "Do People Do What They Say? Further Studies on the Situational Interview," *Journal of Applied Psychology*, 69 (4), 422–27.

Lovelock, Christopher H. (1983), "Classifying Services to Gain Strategic Marketing Insights," *Journal of Marketing*, 47 (Summer), 9–20.

Marketing Science Institute (1992), *Research Priorities 1992-1994: A Guide to MSI Research Programs and Procedures*. Cambridge MA: Marketing Science Institute.

Mazursky, David, Priscilla LaBarbera, and Al Aiello (1987), "When Consumers Switch Brands," *Psychology and Marketing*, 4,17–30.

Nyquist, Jody D. and Bernard H. Booms (1987), "Measuring Services Value From the Consumer Perspective," in *Add Value to Your Service*, Carol Surprenant, ed. Chicago: American Marketing Association, 13–16.

Peters, Tom (1988), *Thriving on Chaos*. New York: Alfred A. Knopf.

Reichheld, Frederick F. and W. Earl Sasser, Jr. (1990), "Zero Defections: Quality Comes to Services," *Harvard Business Review*, 68 (September–October), 105–11.

Ronan, William W. and Gary P. Latham (1974), "The Reliability and Validity of the Critical Incident Technique: A Closer Look," *Studies in Personnel Psychology*, 6 (1), 53–64.

Rust, Roland T. and Anthony J. Zahorik (1993), "Customer Satisfaction, Customer Retention, and Market Share," *Journal of Retailing*, 69 (Summer), 193–215.

Sasser, W. Earl (1976), "Match Supply and Demand in Service Industries," *Harvard Business Review*, 54 (November–December), 133–40.

Shostack, Lynn (1984), "Designing Services That Deliver," *Harvard Business Review*, 62 (January–February), 133–39.

Taylor, Shirley (1994), "Waiting for Service: The Relationship between Delays and Evaluations of Service," *Journal of Marketing*, 58 (April), 56–69.

Weber, Robert Philip (1985), *Basic Content Analysis*. London: Sage Publications Inc.

White, Frank M. and Edwin A. Locke (1981), "Perceived Determinants of High and Low Productivity in Three Occupational Groups: A Critical Incident Study," *Journal of Management Studies*, 18 (4), 375–87.

Zaltman, Gerald, Karen LeMasters, and Michael Heffring (1982), *Theory Construction in Marketing: Some Thoughts on Thinking*. New York: John Wiley & Sons, Inc.

Zeithaml, Valarie, Leonard L. Berry, and A. Parasuraman (1993), "The Nature and Determinants of Customer Expectations of Service," *Journal of the Academy of Marketing Science*, 21 (Winter), 1–12.

Measuring Service Quality
A Reexamination and Extension

J. JOSEPH CRONIN, JR.
& STEVEN A. TAYLOR

The authors investigate the conceptualization and measurement of service quality and the relationships between service quality, consumer satisfaction, and purchase intentions. A literature review suggests that the current operationalization of service quality confounds satisfaction and attitude. Hence, the authors test (1) an alternative method of operationalizing perceived service quality and (2) the significance of the relationships between service quality, consumer satisfaction, and purchase intentions. The results suggest that (1) a performance-based measure of service quality may be an improved means of measuring the service quality construct, (2) service quality is an antecedent of consumer satisfaction, (3) consumer satisfaction has a significant effect on purchase intentions, and (4) service quality has less effect on purchase intentions than does consumer satisfaction. Implications for managers and future research are discussed.

Service industries are playing an increasingly important role in the overall economy of the United States (Bateson 1989; Ginzberg and Vojta 1981; Koepp 1987). In fact, the proportion of the U.S. population employed in the service sector increased from 30% in 1900 to 74% in 1984 (Bateson 1989). Koepp (1987) suggests that this sector is continuing to increase, as 85% of all the new jobs created since 1982 have been in service industries. Bateson (1989) further suggests that the growing importance of the service sector is not limited to the United States, as services currently account for 58% of the total worldwide GNP. There even appears to be executive consensus in the United States that service quality is one of the most important problems facing management today (Blackiston 1988; Cound 1988; Cravens 1988; Langevin 1988; Sherden 1988).

Interest in the measurement of service quality is thus understandably high and the delivery of higher levels of service quality is the strategy that is increasingly being offered as a key to service providers' efforts to position themselves more effectively in the marketplace (cf. Brown and Swartz 1989; Parasuraman, Zeithaml, and Berry 1988; Rudie and Wansley 1985;

Thompson, DeSouza, and Gale 1985). However, the problem inherent in the implementation of such a strategy has been eloquently identified by several researchers: service quality is an elusive and abstract construct that is difficult to define and measure (Brown and Swartz 1989; Carman 1990; Crosby 1979; Garvin 1983; Parasuraman, Zeithaml, and Berry 1985, 1988; Rathmell 1966). In addition, to date the important relationships between service quality, customer satisfaction, and purchasing behavior remain largely unexplored.

Our research has two objectives. First, we suggest that the current conceptualization and operationalization of service quality (SERVQUAL) is inadequate. The SERVQUAL scale is based on Parasuraman, Zeithaml, and Berry's (1985) gap theory, which suggests that the difference between consumers' expectations about the performance of a general class of service providers and their assessment of the actual performance of a specific firm within that class drives the perception of service quality. However, little if any theoretical or empirical evidence supports the relevance of the expectations-performance gap as the basis for measuring service quality (Carman 1990). In fact, the marketing literature appears to offer considerable support for the superiority of simple performance-based measures of service quality (cf. Bolton and Drew 1991a, b; Churchill and Surprenant 1982; Mazis, Ahtola, and Klippel 1975; Woodruff, Cadotte, and Jenkins 1983). We therefore develop and test a performance-based alternative to the SERVQUAL measure.

The second objective is to examine the relationships between service quality, consumer satisfaction, and

J. Joseph Cronin, Jr. is Associate Professor of Marketing, Florida State University. Steven A. Taylor is Assistant Professor of Marketing, Illinois State University. The research was completed while the second author was a doctoral candidate at Florida State University. The authors express their sincere appreciation to the editor and three anonymous *JM* reviewers for their helpful comments on previous versions of the article.

441

purchase intentions. Though these relationships have been discussed theoretically (cf. Bitner 1990; Bolton and Drew 1991a, b; Brown and Swartz 1989; Parasuraman, Zeithaml, and Berry 1988; Zeithaml, Parasuraman, and Berry 1990), they have not been subjected to a thorough empirical test. In particular, the purpose of the second phase of our study is to provide managers and researchers more information about (1) the causal order of the relationship between service quality and customer satisfaction and (2) the impact of service quality and customer satisfaction on purchase intentions. Simply stated, the managers of service providers need to know how to measure service quality, what aspects of a particular service best define its quality, and whether consumers actually purchase from firms that have the highest level of perceived service quality or from those with which they are most "satisfied."

After presenting theoretical background, we describe our research methods and results. We then discuss our findings and explore their implications for management and for future research. Finally, we examine the limitations of our study.

Theoretical Background

Service quality has been described as a form of attitude, related but not equivalent to satisfaction, that results from the comparison of expectations with performance (Bolton and Drew 1991a; Parasuraman, Zeithaml, and Berry 1988). A close examination of this definition suggests ambiguity between the definition and the conceptualization of service quality. Though researchers admit that the current measurement of consumers' perceptions of service quality closely conforms to the disconfirmation paradigm (Bitner 1990; Bolton and Drew 1991a), they also suggest that service quality and satisfaction are distinct constructs (Bitner 1990; Bolton and Drew 1991a, b; Parasuraman, Zeithaml, and Berry 1988). The most common explanation of the difference between the two is that perceived service quality is a form of attitude, a long-run overall evaluation, whereas satisfaction is a transaction-specific measure (Bitner 1990; Bolton and Drew 1991a; Parasuraman, Zeithaml, Berry 1988). Parasuraman, Zeithaml, and Berry (1988) further suggest that the difference lies in the way disconfirmation is operationalized. They state that in measuring perceived service quality the level of comparison is what a consumer *should* expect, whereas in measures of satisfaction the appropriate comparison is what a consumer *would* expect. However, such a differentiation appears to be inconsistent with Woodruff, Cadotte, and Jenkins' (1983) suggestion that expectations should be

based on experience norms—what consumers *should* expect from a given service provider given their experience with that specific type of service organization.

Thus, the service literature has left confusion as to the relationship between consumer satisfaction and service quality. This distinction is important to managers and researchers alike because service providers need to know whether their objective should be to have consumers who are "satisfied" with their performance or to deliver the maximum level of "perceived service quality." The importance of this issue has led to several recent efforts to clarify the relationship between satisfaction and service quality (c.f., Bitner 1990; Bolton and Drew 1991a, b; Parasuraman, Zeithaml, and Berry 1985, 1988).

Initially Parasuraman, Zeithaml, and Berry (1985, 1988) proposed that higher levels of perceived service quality result in increased consumer satisfaction, but more recent evidence suggests that satisfaction is an antecedent of service quality (cf. Bitner 1990; Bolton and Drew 1991a, b). In particular, Bitner has demonstrated empirically a significant causal path between satisfaction and service quality in a structural equation analysis. In a second study, Bolton and Drew (1991a) used the common assumption that service quality is analogous to an attitude as a basis to suggest that satisfaction is an antecedent of service quality. Specifically, Bolton and Drew posit that perceived service quality ($ATTITUDE_t$) is a function of a consumer's residual perception of the service's quality from the prior period ($ATTITUDE_{t-1}$) and his or her level of (dis)satisfaction with the current level of service performance (CS/D_t[1]). This notion suggests that satisfaction is a distinct construct that mediates prior perceptions of service quality to form the current perception of service quality.

$$ATTITUDE_t = g(CS/D_t, ATTITUDE_{t-1}) \qquad (1)$$

Bolton and Drew (1991a) indicate this relation implies that the disconfirmation process, expectations, and performance all should have a significant impact on consumers' current perceptions of service quality. However, their results suggest that perceived service quality is strongly affected by current performance and that the impact of disconfirmation is relatively weak and transitory.

Finally, Bolton and Drew (1991b) extend the discussion of the relationship between satisfaction and service quality by proposing the following structural equations.

---

[1]CS/D_t = Consumer Satisfaction/Dissatisfaction.

Service Quality = q_o (CS/D_t, Disconfirmation) (2)

$$\text{CS/D}_t \qquad\qquad (3)$$
$$= c(\text{Disconfirmation, Expectations, Performance})$$

To gain more insight into Bolton and Drew's findings, and into how service quality should be measured, we next briefly examine the satisfaction and attitude literatures.

Implications from the Satisfaction and Attitude Literatures

A major problem in the literature is the hesitancy to call perceived service quality an attitude. The literature's position is typified by Parasuraman, Zeithaml, and Berry's (1988) description of service quality as ". . . similar in many ways to an attitude" (p. 15). Researchers have attempted to differentiate service quality from consumer satisfaction, even while using the disconfirmation format to measure perceptions of service quality (cf. Bitner 1990; Carman 1990; Gronroos 1990; Heskett, Sasser, and Hart 1990; Parasuraman, Zeithaml, and Berry 1988; Zeithaml, Parasuraman, and Berry 1990). However, this approach is not consistent with the differentiation expressed between these constructs in the satisfaction and attitude literatures.

Oliver (1980) suggests that attitude (ATT) is initially a function of expectations (EXP) [$\text{ATT}_{t1} = f(\text{EXP})$] and subsequently a function of the prior attitude toward and the present level of satisfaction (SAT) with a product or service [$\text{ATT}_{t2} = f(\text{ATT}_{t1}, \text{SAT}_{t2})$]. Purchase intentions (PI) then are considered initially to be a function of an individual's attitude toward a product or service [$\text{PI}_{t1} = f(\text{ATT}_{t1})$], but subject to modification due to the mediating effect on prior attitude of the satisfaction inherent in subsequent usages [$\text{PI}_{t2} = f(\text{ATT}_{t2}) = f(\text{ATT}_{t1}, \text{SAT}_{t2})$]. Thus, Oliver suggests that consumers form an attitude about a service provider on the basis of their prior expectations about the performance of the firm, and this attitude affects their intentions to purchase from that organization. This attitude then is modified by the level of (dis)satisfaction experienced by the consumer during subsequent encounters with the firm. The revised attitude becomes the relevant input for determining a consumer's current purchase intentions.

If one considers service quality to be an attitude, Oliver's (1980) study suggests that (1) in the absence of prior experience with a service provider, expectations initially define the level of perceived service quality, (2) upon the first experience with the service provider, the disconfirmation process leads to a revision in the initial level of perceived service quality, (3) subsequent experiences with the service provider will lead to further disconfirmation, which again modifies the level of perceived service quality, and (4) the redefined level of perceived service quality similarly modifies a consumer's purchase intentions toward that service provider.

Hence, Oliver's research suggests that service quality and consumer satisfaction are distinct constructs, but are related in that satisfaction mediates the effect of prior-period perceptions of service quality to cause a revised service quality perception to be formed. Satisfaction thus rapidly becomes part of the revised perception of service quality. This logic is consistent with Bolton and Drew's (1991a) findings and also calls into question the use of the disconfirmation framework as the primary measure of service quality, because disconfirmation appears only to mediate, not define, consumers' perceptions of service quality.

If in fact service quality is to be conceptualized as "similar to an attitude," perhaps more information could be generated for managers and researchers alike if the measurement of the construct conformed to an attitude-based conceptualization. A review of alternative attitude models suggests that the "adequacy-importance" form is the most efficient model to use if the objective is to predict behavioral intention or actual behavior (Mazis, Ahtola, Klippel 1975). In this model, an individual's attitude is defined by his or her importance-weighted evaluation of the performance of the specific dimensions of a product or service (see Cohen, Fishbein, and Ahtola 1972). However, experimental evidence indicates that the performance dimension alone predicts behavioral intentions and behavior at least as well as the complete model (Mazis, Ahtola, and Klippel 1975). This finding suggests using only performance perceptions as a measure of service quality.

A study by Churchill and Surprenant (1982) also partially supports the efficacy of using only performance perceptions to measure service quality. They conducted two experiments to examine the effects of expectations, performance, and disconfirmation on satisfaction. The results of one experiment suggested that performance alone determines the satisfaction of subjects. Woodruff, Cadotte, and Jenkins (1983) contribute additional support for performance-only measures of attitude. Again using the "adequacy-importance" model, they indicate that assimilation/contrast theory suggests that consumers may raise or lower their performance beliefs on the basis of how closely perceived performance approximates expected performance. Thus, they suggest that including importance weights and expectations only introduces redundancy. From the results of a field experiment, Bolton and Drew (1991a) also conclude that current performance ratings strongly affect attitudes whereas the effects of disconfirmation are generally insignificant and transitory. This study is particularly significant because the attitude examined is customers' perceptions of the quality inherent in a service.

Thus, the conclusion of the satisfaction and attitude literatures appears to be that (1) perceived service quality is best conceptualized as an attitude, (2) the "adequacy-importance" model is the most effective "attitude-based" operationalization of service quality, and (3) current performance adequately captures consumers' perceptions of the service quality offered by a specific service provider. In addition to the theoretical support for performance-based measures of service quality, practitioners often measure the determinants of overall satisfaction/perceived quality by having customers simply assess the performance of the company's business processes. Furthermore, the performance-based approach may actually be more in line with an antecedent/consequent conceptualization: that is, judgments of service quality and satisfaction appear to follow the evaluation of a service provider's performance. The first objective of our study is to examine these conclusions empirically by testing a performance-based measure of service quality as an alternative to the current disconfirmation-based SERVQUAL scale.

Operationalizing Service Quality

The current measurement of perceived service quality can be traced to the research of Parasuraman, Zeithaml, and Berry. These authors originally identified 10 determinants of service quality based on a series of focus group sessions (1985). They subsequently developed SERVQUAL (1988), which recasts the 10 determinants into five specific components: tangibles, reliability, responsiveness, assurance, and empathy (Figure 1).

The basis for identifying these five components was a factor analysis of the 22-item scale (see Appendix) developed from focus groups and from the specific industry applications undertaken by the authors (see Parasuraman, Zeithaml, and Berry 1985, 1988; and Zeithaml, Parasuraman, and Berry 1990 for a comprehensive review).

The scale development procedures employed appear to support the face validity of the 22 scale items (individual questions) included in the scale, but the issue of how the service quality measure should be constructed and whether the individual scale items actually describe five separate service quality compo-

FIGURE 1

Service Quality as Conceptualized by Parasuraman, Zeithaml, and Berry (1988)

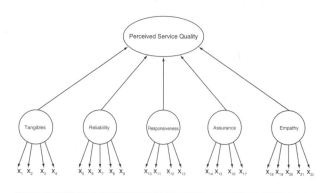

nents is problematic. In fact, some empirical evidence suggests that the proposed delineation of the five components is not consistent when subjected to cross-sectional analysis (Carman 1990). Specifically, Carman found that some of the items did not load on the same component when compared across different types of service providers. However, though the veracity of conceptualizing the SERVQUAL scale as consisting of the five distinct components identified by Parasuraman, Zeithaml, and Berry (1988) has been questioned (Carman 1990), the validity of the 22 individual performance scale items that make up the SERVQUAL scale appears to be well supported both by the procedures used to develop the items and by their subsequent use as reported in the literature (cf. Carman 1990). We therefore conclude that these 22 performance items adequately define the domain of service quality and we use the same performance items to examine the proposed alternative to the SERVQUAL scale and in the analyses of the relationships between service quality, consumer satisfaction, and purchase intentions.

Research Models and Propositions

We investigate four specific questions that correspond to the three research steps identified in the Methods section. The first question is directed at the measurement of the service quality construct. Specifically, the ability of the more concise performance-only scale suggested by the literature review (SERVPERF, equation 6) is compared with that of three alternatives: SERVQUAL (equation 4), weighted SERVQUAL (equation 5), and weighted SERVPERF (equation 7).

$$\text{Service Quality} = (\text{Performance} - \text{Expectations}) \quad (4)$$

FIGURE 2
The Structural Models

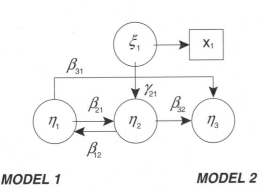

MODEL 1   **MODEL 2**

ξ_1 = SERVQUAL ξ_1 = SERVPERF
η_1 = Consumer Satisfaction η_1 = Consumer Satisfaction
η_2 = Overall Service Quality η_2 = Overall Service Quality
η_3 = Purchase Intentions η_3 = Purchase Intentions

Service Quality = Importance* (Performance
$\qquad$ − Expectations) $\qquad$ (5)

Service Quality = (Performance) $\qquad$ (6)

Service Quality = Importance* (Performance) $\qquad$ (7)

The first proposition provides the basis for our investigation:

P₁: An unweighted performance-based measure of service quality (unweighted SERVPERF) is a more appropriate basis for measuring service quality than SERVQUAL, weighted SERVQUAL, or weighted SERVPERF.

The evaluation P₁ calls for an assessment of whether the addition of the importance weights suggested by Zeithaml, Parasuraman, and Berry (1990) improves the ability of the SERVQUAL and SERVPERF scales to measure service quality and a direct comparison of the two measurement approaches. On the basis of the findings by Bolton and Drew (1991a), and the attitude and satisfaction literatures reviewed previously, the addition of importance weights is not expected to improve either scale and the SERVPERF alternative is expected to outperform the SERVQUAL scale.

The structural models identified in Figure 2 are used to further the consideration of the SERVQUAL and SERVPERF scales as well as to consider the three remaining research questions. As discussed in the literature review, the SERVPERF scale appears to conform more closely to the implications of the satisfaction and attitude literatures. Therefore, we propose that the model incorporating SERVPERF (model 2) will have a better fit (as measured by the chi square statistic and

the measurement model's adjusted goodness of fit) because the performance-only form is more consistent with established theory (cf. Mazis, Ahtola, and Klippel 1975) and hence the SERVPERF measurement model should more closely approximate the theoretical model identified in Figure 2.

The second objective of our study is to examine the relationships between service quality, consumer satisfaction, and purchase intentions. The following three additional propositions identify the questions addressed in this part of the study.

P₂: Customer satisfaction is an antecedent of perceived service quality.

P₃: Consumer satisfaction has a significant impact on purchase intentions.

P₄: Perceived service quality has a significant impact on purchase intentions.

The first question considered is the causal order of the perceived service quality-satisfaction relationship (P₂). This analysis is also based on a consideration of the structural models identified in Figure 2. Specifically, P₂ proposes that the path (B_{21}) showing consumer satisfaction as an antecedent of service quality should have a statistically significant (p ≤ .05) LISREL estimate whereas the estimate of the reverse path (satisfaction as an outcome of service quality, B_{12}) should not be significant (cf. Bitner 1990; Bolton and Drew 1991a, b).

The next question investigated is whether consumers' level of satisfaction with a service provider affects their purchase intentions toward that firm (P₃). Again, the structural models are used to investigate this proposition. Specifically, in models that confirm (i.e., the theoretical model is not rejected), the LISREL estimate for the path linking satisfaction and purchase intention (B_{31}) is examined to determine whether the effect is significant ($p \le .05$).

The final question addressed is whether consumers' perceptions of service quality affect their purchase intentions (P₄). The investigation of this proposition is identical to that of P₃ but the path of interest is between service quality and purchase intentions (B_{32}).

Methods

Organization of the Research

Step 1: Examining the Dimensionality of SERVQUAL In this step, the confirmatory factor analysis capabilities of LISREL VII were used to determine whether the 22 items that define the SERVQUAL scale have the same factor loading pattern for the firms investigated as was found by Parasuraman, Zeithaml, and Berry

(1988). To the extent that similar factor structures are identified (see Figure 1), evidence of the reliability of the SERVQUAL scale is produced. If the five-component structure is not confirmed, the OBLIMIN factor analysis procedure in SPSS-X and a reliability analysis can be used to assess the dimensionality and reliability of the items.

Step 2: Comparison of Alternative Measures of Service Quality

On the basis of the theoretical concerns discussed previously, we assessed three alternatives to the SERVQUAL scale. Specifically, in this step we examined the original SERVQUAL scale (equation 4), an importance-weighted SERVQUAL scale (equation 5), a performance-based approach to the measurement of service quality (SERVPERF, equation 6), and an importance-weighted version of the SERVPERF scale (equation 7). This examination proceeded in two stages. First, the ability of each of the four scales to explain variation in service quality was assessed by regressing the individual items comprising each of the alternative scales against a measure of the respondents' perceptions of the overall quality inherent in the services offered by the eight firms included in the sample (see Appendix, variable 85).

Second, each measure's theoretical support was examined in an analysis of the structural models identified in Figure 2. Specifically of interest were (1) the degree of fit of the respective models and (2) the significance of the effect on service quality attributed to each of the alternative measures (i.e., the significance of the path between the perceived service quality scale used and the overall measure of service quality, path γ_{21}).

Step 3: Analysis of Relationship between Service Quality, Consumer Satisfaction, and Purchase Intention

The third step extended the research beyond the question of which approach to the measurement of service quality is the most appropriate. Here we considered (1) the causal order of the consumer satisfaction-service quality relationship, (2) the effect of consumer satisfaction on purchase intentions, and (3) the effect of service quality on purchase intentions. These relationships were also investigated through the analysis of the structural models identified in Figure 2. Specifically, we investigated each relationship by examining the significance of the LISREL VII estimated path coefficient that links the variables noted.

The Sample

Data were gathered from personal interviews conducted in a medium-sized city in the southeastern United States. A total of 660 usable questionnaires (all questions answered) were gathered randomly from consumers at their residences by trained interviewers

during a two-week period in the summer of 1988. The sampling frame was the entire population of the city. Interviewers were instructed to solicit responses randomly and were assigned city areas to prevent overlap.

Responses were gathered on the service quality offered by two firms in each of four industries: banking, pest control, dry cleaning, and fast food. Because of the length of the questionnaire, respondents were asked to evaluate only one firm. The sample size for each industry was: banking 188 (firm 1, 92 and firm 2, 96); pest control 175 (firm 1, 91 and firm 2, 84); dry cleaning 178 (firm 1, 88 and firm 2, 90); fast food 189 (firm 1, 98 and firm 2, 91). The firms and industries were chosen on the basis of the results of a convenience survey suggesting that these were the four service industries most familiar to the area's consumers. The two firms chosen within each industry were those with the largest sales volume in the city where the sample was drawn (for the banks, the number of depositors was used to qualify the firms included). Respondents were screened to determine whether they had used one of the service providers included in the study within the last 30 days. This screening ensured that the respondents were familiar with the firm whose services they were asked to evaluate.

Measures

The measures needed for the study were expectations, perceptions of performance, and importance measures to construct the four alternative measures of service quality, a direct measure of service quality, a measure of consumer satisfaction, and a purchase intentions measure. The 22 expectation (see Appendix, variables E_1-E_{22}) and performance (see Appendix, variables P_1-P_{22}) items were taken directly from the SERVQUAL scale (Parasuraman, Zeithaml, and Berry 1988). The importance weights were adapted from the wording of the expectation and performance items included in the original SERVQUAL scale (see Appendix, variables I_1-I_{22}). The direct measure of service quality was based on responses to a 7-point semantic differential question (see Appendix, variable 85). In addition, self-report measures of consumer satisfaction and purchase intentions were constructed similarly (see Appendix, variables 87 and 84, respectively).

Results

Dimensionality, Reliability, and Validity of Service Quality Measures (Step 1)

Dimensionality and Reliability The first step was to examine the dimensionality of the current service quality scale (SERVQUAL) by means of a confirmatory factor analysis. Table 1 gives the results of the LISREL VII-based analysis for each of the four types of service firms (banks, pest control, dry cleaning, and fast food). These results suggest that the 5-component structure proposed by Parasuraman, Zeithaml, and Berry (1988) for their SERVQUAL scale (see Figure 1) is not confirmed in any of the research samples. Specifically, the chi square statistic universally indicates a poor fit between the theoretical and measurement models for the 5-component structure. The adjusted goodness-of-fit indices (AGFI) are also not indicative of a good fit as they range from .740 to .831.

Because the 5-factor structure was not confirmed, we decided to assess the unidimensionality of the 22 items. We performed a factor analysis of the SERVQUAL and SERVPERF scales using the OBLIMIN oblique factor rotation procedure in SPSS-X. All of the items loaded predictably on a single factor with the exception of item 19 (see Table 2), which loaded very weakly in the analysis of the SERVQUAL scale and had a negative loading for both scales. It was therefore dropped and coefficient alpha for both scales and all subsamples (each industry) was recalculated. As is indicated in Table 2, the reliability in every case (coefficient alpha in excess of .800) suggests that both scales can be treated as unidimensional. Thus, in the analysis that follows, the 21 retained items are either summed or averaged (to develop the four service quality scales in the LISREL VII analysis of the structural models) or they are considered as one composite set of individual measures (in the stepwise regression analysis).

Validity   The primary threat to the validity of the measures used in this study is construct validity. Carmines and Zeller (1979, p. 23) state, "[f]undamentally, construct validity is concerned with the extent to which a particular measure relates to other measures consistent with theoretically derived hypotheses concerning the concepts (or constructs) that are being measured." They further suggest that the process of construct validation is by definition theory-laden. Churchill (1979) suggests that convergent and discriminant validity should be assessed in investigations of construct validity. Convergent validity involves the extent to which a measure correlates highly with other measures designed to measure the same construct. Therefore, we examined a correlation matrix of all the items tested in models 1 and 2 (see Table 3). A high correlation between the items SERVPERF, importance-weighted SERVPERF, and service quality indicates some degree of convergent validity. Discriminant

TABLE 1

Confirmatory Factor Analysis Parameter Estimates for 5-Factor Conceptualization of Service Quality

Parameter	Banks	Pest Control	Dry Cleaning	Fast Food
Chi square	308.60	486.16	402.60	364.16
d.f.	204	204	204	204
p	.000	.000	.000	.000
GFI[a]	.863	.790	.819	.849
AGFI[b]	.831	.740	.776	.813
RMSR[c]	.309	.466	.381	.515

[a]Goodness of fit.
[b]Adjusted goodness of fit.
[c]Root mean square residual.

validity involves the extent to which a measure is novel and does not simply reflect some other variable. Churchill (1979) suggests assessing discriminant validity by determining whether the correlation between two different measures of the same variable is higher than the correlation between the measure of that variable and those of any other variable. Again, an examination of the correlation matrix in Table 3 indicates discriminant validity of the research variables as the three service quality scales all correlate more highly with each other than they do with other research variables (i.e., satisfaction and purchase intentions). Hence, we suggest that the proposed performance-based measures provide a more construct-valid explication of service quality because of their content validity (i.e., use of importance weights and use of performance-based measures are arguably more theoretically sound approaches) and the evidence of their discriminant validity.

Comparison of Alternative Measures of Service Quality (Step 2)

P_1 suggests that the unweighted SERVPERF scale should capture more of the variation in service quality than any of the other identified alternatives (SERVQUAL, weighted SERVQUAL, and weighted SERVPERF). The stepwise regression analysis summarized in Table 4 affirms P_1. In all of the four service industries examined, unweighted SERVPERF explains more of the variation in the global measure of service quality (see Table 4).

In addition, a comparison of the SERVQUAL and weighted SERVQUAL scales (columns 1–4 and 5–8 of

TABLE 2

Factor Analysis of 22 Individual Dimensions of Service Quality

Variable	SERVQUAL				SERVPERF			
	Banks	Pest Control	Dry Cleaning	Fast Food	Banks	Pest Control	Dry Cleaning	Fast Food
V1	.396	.697	.577	.181	.480	.820	.692	.408
V2	.397	.368	.492	.249	.463	.652	.614	.458
V3	.477	.523	.536	.339	.557	.842	.642	.499
V4	.381	.319	.398	.055	.485	.703	.640	.384
V5	.781	.741	.736	.543	.804	.831	.774	.572
V6	.728	.753	.798	.543	.726	.828	.760	.683
V7	.826	.837	.805	.748	.822	.891	.856	.669
V8	.791	.832	.789	.679	.799	.873	.785	.679
V9	.833	.694	.654	.380	.788	.835	.626	.349
V10	.346	.467	.209	.325	.355	.532	.281	.136
V11	.568	.611	.358	.657	.640	.712	.483	.607
V12	.522	.622	.499	.706	.631	.706	.539	.672
V13	.500	.556	.392	.706	.623	.789	.538	.660
V14	.572	.622	.730	.409	.685	.785	.771	.550
V15	.817	.676	.762	.595	.815	.788	.836	.665
V16	.573	.764	.740	.641	.638	.793	.803	.689
V17	.647	.608	.673	.544	.688	.702	.666	.518
V18	.535	.563	.472	.412	.620	.762	.483	.429
V19	−.337	−.298	−.165	.027	−.677	−.769	−.615	−.474
V20	.459	.502	.399	.422	.580	.685	.490	.485
V21	.502	.571	.522	.464	.552	.670	.703	.573
V22	.272	.420	.399	.156	.345	.598	.403	.280
Eigenvalue	7.472	8.229	7.437	5.194	9.037	12.651	9.378	6.408
% of variation	34.8%	37.4%	33.8%	23.6%	41.1%	57.5%	42.6%	29.1%
Coefficient alpha[a]	.890	.901	.900	.849	.925	.964	.932	.884

[a]Item V19 excluded.

TABLE 3

Correlation Coefficients for Structural Models in Figure 2

	SERVQUAL	Weighted SERVQ-UAL	SERVPERF	Weighted SERVP-ERF	Overall service quality	Satisfaction	Purchase intention
SERVQUAL	1.0000						
Weighted SERVQUAL	.9787	1.0000					
SERVPERF	.8100	.7968	1.0000				
Weighted SERVPERF	.6589	.6307	.9093	1.0000			
Overall service quality	.5430	.5394	.6012	.5572	1.0000		
Satisfaction	.5605	.5559	.5978	.5513	.8175	1.0000	
Purchase intention	.3534	.3613	.3647	.3486	.5272	.5334	1.0000

Table 4) indicates that the unweighted SERVQUAL scale explains more of the variation in service quality in three of the four industries (the exception being dry cleaning). We therefore decided to use only the unweighted SERVPERF and SERVQUAL scales in the structural analysis of the relationships between these scales, service quality, consumer satisfaction, and purchase intentions because they arguably represent the best of each of the two alternative conceptualizations of service quality.

TABLE 4
The Variation Explained by the Alternative Measures of Service Quality

	SERVQUAL				Weighted SERVQUAL				SERVPERF				Weighted SERVPERF			
	Banking	Pest Control	Dry Cleaning	Fast Food	Banking	Pest Control	Dry Cleaning	Fast Food	Banking	Pest Control	Dry Cleaning	Fast Food	Banking	Pest Control	Dry Cleaning	Fast Food
V1[1]																
V2							.164[b]				.157[b]					.256[c]
V3				.143[a]												
V4	.147[a]											.248[c]				
V5					.194[a]	−.227[a]										
V6	.284[c]	−.200[a]	.307[c]	.255[c]	.222[b]	−.186[a]	.277[b]	.282[c]	.350[c]		.380[c]		.267[b]		.240[b]	
V7	.478[c]				.452[c]		.268[b]	.234[b]	.351[b]			.407[c]	.437[c]		.242[b]	.323[c]
V8		.594[c]			.614[c]					.304[b]				.346[c]		
V9	−.216[a]				−.248[b]			−.131[a]	−.231[b]				−.195[a]			
V10														.193[b]		
V11		.158[a]					.268[c]			.256[c]						
V12													.253[c]			.242[c]
V13			.141[a]									.152[a]				.194[b]
V14		.352[c]				.329[c]	−.153[a]									.130[a]
V15										.191[a]						
V16			.235[b]	.187[b]				.318[c]	.175[a]	.349[c]	.165[a]				.189[a]	
V17										−.219[b]				.161[a]		
V18																
V19			−.127[a]	−.163[a]		−.135[a]									−.164[b]	
V20									.158[b]			.141[a]	.181[b]			
V21	.189[b]				.167[b]											
V22		1.42	.		.157[a]											
R²	.46511[2]	.36515	.30747	.41534	.44813	.36316	.36958	.38332	.47895	.38760	.44675	.47585	.40333	.33726	.43166	.46718

Where: a = p < .05,
  b = p < .01,
  c = p < .001.

[1]V1 to V22 are the alternative scale items of service quality (see Appendix A, variables P1 to P22). Entries in the cells represent correlation coefficients. All non-significant coefficients are omitted.

[2]Numbers in each cell are adjusted R²s.

Relationships between Service Quality, Customer Satisfaction, and Purchase Intentions (Step 3)

Figure 2 identifies the two models used to investigate P_2, P_3, and P_4 and to further the comparison of the performance- and disconfirmation-based measures of service quality (SERVPERF and SERVQUAL, respectively). Models 1 and 2 are identical with the exception that SERVQUAL is used to measure service quality in model 1 whereas SERVPERF is used in model 2. The models conceptualize a nonrecursive ("two-way") relationship between service quality and satisfaction in order to test simultaneously the effects hypothesized by Parasuraman, Zeithaml, and Berry (1985, 1988) (service quality is an antecedent of customer satisfaction) and by Bitner (1990) and Bolton and Drew (1991a, b) (service quality is an outcome of customer satisfaction). In addition, the model suggests that both service quality and satisfaction affect purchase intentions.

However, before considering P_2, P_3, and P_4, we assessed the fit of the two respective models to the data (see Table 5). Model 1 (SERVQUAL) had a good fit in two of the four industries (banking and fast food) whereas model 2 (SERVPERF) had an excellent fit in all four industries. Because the only difference in the two models is the measure of service quality used (either SERVQUAL or SERVPERF), these results were interpreted as additional support for the superiority of the SERVPERF approach to the measurement of service quality.

Because of this superiority, we used model 2 to assess the strength of the relationships between service quality, consumer satisfaction, and purchase intention. This analysis suggests that (1) service quality has a significant ($p \leq .05$) effect on consumer satisfaction in all four samples (see Table 5, model 2, path β_{12}), (2) consumer satisfaction has a significant ($p \leq .05$) effect on purchase intentions in all four samples (see Table 5, model 2, path β_{31}), and (3) service quality does not

TABLE 5
Standardized Parameter Estimates for Causal Models

		Banking		Pest Control		Dry Cleaning		Fast Food	
		LISREL		LISREL		LISREL		LISREL	
	Parameter	Estimate	T-Value	Estimate	T-Value	Estimate	T-Value	Estimate	T-Value
SERVQUAL Model (1)									
	B_{21}	−1.796	−1.512	−2.810	−1.341	−8.398	−.408	−.055	−.300
	B_{12}	1.113	14.794	1.099	10.620	1.103	15.256	.904	10.566
	B_{31}	.668	3.712	.646	4.247	.836	4.598	.343	2.774
	B_{32}	.280	1.475	.301	2.033	.099	.542	.296	2.187
	γ_{21}	2.417	2.226	2.289	1.746	7.157	.452	.812	5.235
	Chi square	.000	(p = .972)	5.090	(p = .024)	4.060	(p = .044)	6.020	(p = .140)
	AGFI	1.000		.863		.890		.838	
	RMS	.001		.068		.061		.063	
	SMC-Y_1	.664		.465		.750		.647	
	-Y_2	−3.482		−7.309		−58.200		.254	
	-Y_3	.325		.326		.409		.260	
SERVPERF Model (2)									
	B_{21}	−1.353	−1.595	−1.377	−1.944	−2.904	−.989	−.141	−.845
	B_{12}	1.109	14.156	1.006	11.793	1.065	17.584	.944	12.787
	B_{31}	.550	3.124	.659	4.323	.837	4.598	.362	2.924
	B_{32}	.374	1.979	.285	1.926	.098	.535	.282	2.069
	γ_{21}	2.154	2.585	1.683	3.202	3.644	1.300	1.179	6.122
	Chi square	.080	(p = .781)	.220	(p = .639)	3.290	(p = .070)	.230	(p = .629)
	AGFI	.998		.994		.910		.994	
	RMS	.009		.012		.044		.010	
	SMC-Y_1	.657		.521		.768		.652	
	-Y_2	−2.298		−1.886		−7.799		.278	
	-Y_3	.305		.325		.412		.266	

have a significant (p ≤ .05) impact on purchase intentions in any of the samples (see Table 5, model 2, path β_{32}). Thus, P_2 and P_3 both receive strong support from the results, though the direction of the effect observed in the consideration of P_2 is the opposite of that proposed. The analysis of P_4 afforded no support for the proposed effect.

Discussion

We investigated three main questions:

- How should service quality be conceptualized and measured?

- What is the causal order of the relationship between service quality and consumer satisfaction?

- What impacts do service quality and consumer satisfaction have on purchase intentions?

In answer to the first question, the literature review and empirical results both suggest that service quality should be conceptualized and measured as an attitude.

The literature clearly supports the performance-only (SERVPERF) approach. In the empirical analysis, the first step calls into question the efficacy of the 5-component conceptualization of service quality offered by Parasuraman, Zeithaml, and Berry (1988). The second step indicates that the SERVPERF scale explains more of the variation in service quality than does SERVQUAL. Both the literature review and the analysis of the structural models (see Figure 2 and Table 5, models 1 and 2) suggest that the SERVQUAL conceptualization is in fact flawed: (1) it is based on a satisfaction paradigm rather that an attitude model and (2) the empirical analysis of the structural model suggests that the SERVQUAL model (see Figure 2 and Table 5, model 1) confirms in only two of the four industries. Thus, the weight of the evidence clearly supports the use of performance-based measures of service quality.

The second question investigated is the causal order of the satisfaction–service quality relationship. Much of the recent literature has suggested that satisfaction is an antecedent of service quality (cf. Bitner 1990; Bolton and Drew 1991a, b). However, the analysis of the research model indicates that this may not be the case and provides empirical support for the notion that perceived service quality in fact leads to satisfaction as proposed by Parasuraman, Zeithaml, and Berry (1985, 1988).

The third question pertains to the effects of service quality and satisfaction on purchase intentions (see Figure 2 and Table 5). The analysis of the LISREL estimates (model 2; see Table 5) suggests that satisfaction has a significant ($p \leq .05$) effect on purchase intentions in all four samples whereas service quality does not have such an effect in any of the four industries. From the significance tests summarized in Table 5, satisfaction appears to have a stronger and more consistent effect on purchase intentions than does service quality.

Conclusions and Managerial Implications

The major conclusion from our study is that marketing's current conceptualization and measurement of service quality are based on a flawed paradigm. We present empirical and literature support suggesting that service quality should be measured as an attitude. The performance-based scale developed (SERVPERF) is efficient in comparison with the SERVQUAL scale; it reduces by 50% the number of items that must be measured (44 items to 22 items). The analysis of the structural models also supports the theoretical superiority of the SERVPERF scale (see Table 5); only the model that uses the SERVPERF scale consistently confirmed (model 2). These factors, along with the failure of the 5-component SERVQUAL model to confirm (see Table 1), support the use of a performance-based measure of service quality.

The remaining questions addressed in our study are essential managerial issues. The results suggest that service quality is an antecedent of consumer satisfaction and that consumer satisfaction exerts a stronger influence on purchase intentions than does service quality. Thus, managers may need to emphasize total customer satisfaction programs over strategies centering solely on service quality. Perhaps consumers do not necessarily buy the highest quality service; convenience, price, or availability may enhance satisfaction while not actually affecting consumers' perceptions of service quality.

Finally (see Table 4), the results from step 1 also suggest that the scale items that define service quality in one industry may be different in another. Perhaps high involvement services such as health care or financial services have different service quality definitions than low involvement services such as fast food or dry cleaning. Managers and researchers therefore must consider the individual dimensions of service quality when making cross-sectional comparisons. Managers should also be able to adjust their marketing strategies more effectively when the full set of individual scale items are considered.

Implications for Future Research

Our research has only begun to address the many issues that are important in the management of services. The findings undoubtedly raise more questions than they answer, but the questions we address—how the service quality construct should be measured and how service quality is related to consumer satisfaction and purchase intentions—are arguably among the most important concerns in services marketing.

Future studies should consider other attitude-based conceptualizations and extend beyond the four service industries sampled in our study. The nature of the relationship between consumer satisfaction and service quality appears to be an area in great need of additional exploration. Investigations of the roles of satisfaction and service quality in predicting market share also appear well directed and may enhance our understanding of the role of these constructs in the formation of purchase intentions. The failure of service quality to affect purchase intentions consistently should be a concern for both managers and researchers. Perhaps consumers do not always buy the best quality service. Might they instead purchase on the basis of their assessment of the value of a service? Perhaps future research should develop measures of service performance that utilize other criteria, such as value, or determining whether a service is purchased. Finally, our study was specific to a service context. Generalizing the results to goods industries may not be possible. The ever-increasing magnitude of the service sector simply underscores the need for managers and researchers alike to increase the attention directed at the important issues in the marketing of services.

Limitations

In designing our study, we attempted to minimize its limitations. However, generalizations beyond the four specific service industries investigated are tenuous. Future studies should incorporate multiple measures of all of the constructs examined. Limiting the study to the two highest market share firms in each category may also have affected the variable distributions and, hence, the importance of the predictors. In addition, with the possible exception of banking, the services investigated are all low involvement service categories. Perceived quality may play a bigger role (in comparison with satisfaction) in high involvement situations, where a firm may need to do more than simply meet customers' "minimum requirements." Finally, the number of constructs other researchers could add to the models examined is probably unlimited.

APPENDIX

Expectations

This survey deals with your opinions of _____ services. Please show the extent to which you think institutions offering telephone services should possess the features described in each statement. Do this by using the scale presented below. If you strongly agree that these institutions should possess a feature, place a seven on the line preceding the statement. If you strongly disagree that these institutions should possess a feature, place a one on the line. If your feelings are not strong, place one of the numbers between one and seven on the line to properly reflect the actual strength of your feelings. There are no right or wrong answers—all we are interested in is a number that best shows your expectations about institutions offering banking services.

```
1 - - - 2 - - - 3 - - - 4 - - - 5 - - - 6 - - - 7
STRONGLY                          STRONGLY
DISAGREE                          AGREE
```

____ E1. They should have up-to-date equipment & technology.

____ E2. Their physical facilities should be visually appealing.

____ E3. Their employees should be well dressed and appear neat.

____ E4. The appearance of the physical facilities of these institutions should be in keeping with the type of services provided.

____ E5. When these institutions promise to do something by a certain time, they should do so.

____ E6. When customers have problems, these institutions should be sympathetic and reassuring.

____ E7. These institutions should be dependable.

____ E8. They should provide their services at the time they promise to do so.

____ E9. They should keep their records accurately.

____ E10. They shouldn't be expected to tell their customers exactly when services will be performed.

____ E11. It is not realistic for customers to expect prompt service from employees of these institutions.

____ E12. Their employees don't always have to be willing to help customers.

____ E13. It is okay if they are too busy to respond to customer requests promptly.

____ E14. Customer should be able to trust employees of these institutions.

____ E15. Customers should be able to feel safe in their transactions with these institutions' employees.

____ E16. Their employees should be polite.

____ E17. Their employees should get adequate support from these institutions to do their jobs well.

____ E18. These institutions should not be expected to give customers individual attention.

____ E19. Employees of these institutions cannot be expected to give customers personal attention.

____ E20. It is unrealistic to expect employees to know what the needs of their customers are.

____ E21. It is unrealistic to expect these institutions to have their customers' best interests at heart.

____ E22. They shouldn't be expected to have operating hours convenient to all their customers.

Performance

The following set of statements relates to your feelings about XYZ _____ . For each statement, please show the extent to which you believe XYZ _____ has the feature described by the statement. Once again, placing a seven on the line means you strongly agree that XYZ has that feature, and a one means you strongly disagree. You may use any of the numbers in the middle as well to show how strong your feelings are. There are no right or wrong answers—all we are interested in is a number that best shows your perceptions about XYZ whether you use their service or not.

```
1 - - - 2 - - - 3 - - - 4 - - - 5 - - - 6 - - - 7
STRONGLY                          STRONGLY
DISAGREE                          AGREE
```

____ P1. XYZ _____ has up-to-date equipment.

____ P2. XYZ _____'s physical facilities are visually appealing.

_____ P3. XYZ _____'s employees are well dressed and appear neat.

_____ P4. The appearance of the physical facilities of XYZ _____ is in keeping with the type of service provided.

_____ P5. When XYZ _____ promises to do something by a certain time, it does so.

_____ P6. When you have problems, XYZ _____ is sympathetic and reassuring.

_____ P7. XYZ _____ is dependable.

_____ P8. XYZ _____ provides its services at the time it promises to do so.

_____ P9. XYZ _____ keeps its records accurately.

_____ P10. XYZ _____ does not tell its customers exactly when services will be performed.

_____ P11. You do not receive prompt service from XYZ _____ employees.

_____ P12. Employees of XYZ _____ are not always willing to help customers.

_____ P13. Employees of XYZ _____ are too busy to respond to customer requests promptly.

_____ P14. You can trust employees of XYZ _____.

_____ P15. You can feel safe in your transactions with XYZ _____'s employees.

_____ P16. Employees of XYZ _____ are polite.

_____ P17. Employees get adequate support from XYZ _____ to do their jobs well.

_____ P18. XYZ _____ does not give you individual attention.

_____ P19. Employees of XYZ _____ do not give you personal attention.

_____ P20. Employees of XYZ _____ do not know what your needs are.

_____ P21. XYZ _____ does not have your best interests at heart.

_____ P22. XYZ _____ does not have operating hours convenient to all their customers.

Importance

The following set of statements relates to your feelings about the importance of each feature described in your decision to purchase _____ services. A seven means you consider the feature very important in deciding where to purchase banking services; a one means it is very unimportant. You may place any of the numbers shown on the scale below beside each feature to indicate its importance to you. There are no right or wrong answers—all we are interested in is your perception of how important each feature is to you in your decision where to purchase banking services.

1 - - - 2 - - - 3 - - - 4 - - - 5 - - - 6 - - - 7
VERY   VERY
UNIMPORTANT   IMPORTANT

_____ I1. Up-to-date equipment.

_____ I2. Physical facilities that are visually appealing.

_____ I3. Employees that are well dressed and appear neat.

_____ I4. Physical facilities that appear to be in keeping with the type of service provided.

_____ I5. When something is promised by a certain time, doing it.

_____ I6. When there is a problem, being sympathetic and reassuring.

_____ I7. Dependability.

_____ I8. Providing service by the time promised.

_____ I9. Accurate record keeping.

_____ I10. Telling the customer exactly when the service will be performed.

_____ I11. Receiving prompt service.

_____ I12. Employees who are always willing to help customers.

_____ I13. Employees who are not too busy to respond to customer request promptly.

_____ I14. Employees who are trustworthy.

_____ I15. The feeling that you are safe when conducting transactions with the firm's employees.

_____ I16. Employees who are polite.

_____ I17. Adequate support from the firm so employees can do their job well.

_____ I18. Individual attention.

_____ I19. Employees who give you personal attention.

_____ I20. Employees who know what your needs are.

_____ I21. A firm which has your best interests at heart.

_____ I22. Convenient operating hours.

Other Measures

The following set of statements relates to your feelings about XYZ _____. Please respond by circling the number which best reflects your own perceptions.

(Future Purchase Behavior)

(84) In the next year, my use of XYZ _____ will be

1 - - - 2 - - - 3 - - - 4 - - - 5 - - - 6 - - - 7
NOT AT ALL   VERY FREQUENT

(Overall Quality)

(85) The quality of XYZ ____'s services is

1 - - - 2 - - - 3 - - - -4 - - - 5 - - - 6 - - - 7
VERY POOR   EXCELLENT

(Satisfaction)

(87) My feelings towards XYZ ____'s services can best be described as

1 - - - 2 - - - 3 - - - 4 - - - 5 - - - 6 - - - 7
VERY UNSATISFIED   VERY SATISFIED

References

Bateson, John E. (1989), *Managing Services Marketing*. London: Dryden Press.

Bitner, Mary Jo (1990), "Evaluating Service Encounters: The Effects of Physical Surroundings and Employee Responses," *Journal of Marketing*, 54 (April), 69–82.

Blackiston, G. Howland (1988), "Service Industries: A Renaissance in Quality," *Executive Excellence*, 5 (9), 9–10.

Bolton, Ruth N. and James H. Drew (1991a), "A Longitudinal Analysis of the Impact of Service Changes on Customer Attitudes," *Journal of Marketing*, 55 (January), 1–9.

—— and —— (1991b), "A Multistage Model of Customers' Assessments of Service Quality and Value," *Journal of Consumer Research*, 17 (March), 375–84.

Brown, Stephen W. and Teresa A. Swartz (1989), "A Gap Analysis of Professional Service Quality," *Journal of Marketing*, 53 (April), 92–8.

Carman, James M. (1990), "Consumer Perceptions of Service Quality: An Assessment of the SERVQUAL Dimensions," *Journal of Retailing*, 66 (1), 33–55.

Carmines, Edward G. and Richard A. Zeller (1979), "Reliability and Validity Assessment," Sage Publications Series Number 07-017. Newbury Park, CA: Sage Publications, Inc.

Churchill, Gilbert A., Jr. (1979), "A Paradigm for Developing Better Measures of Marketing Constructs," *Journal of Marketing Research*, 16 (February), 64–73.

—— and Carol Surprenant (1982), "An Investigation Into the Determinants of Customer Satisfaction," *Journal of Marketing Research*, 19 (November), 491–504.

Cohen, Joel B., Martin Fishbein, and Olli T. Ahtola (1972), "The Nature and Uses of Expectancy-Value Models in Consumer Attitude Research," *Journal of Marketing Research*, 9 (November), 456–60.

Cound, Dana M. (1988), "What Corporate Executives Think About Quality: The Results of the 1987 Gallup Survey," *Quality Progress*, 21 (2), 20–3.

Cravens, David W. (1988), "The Marketing of Quality," *Incentive*, 162 (11), 26–34.

Crosby, Philip B. (1979), *Quality Is Free: The Art of Making Quality Certain*. New York: American Library.

Garvin, David A. (1983), "Quality on the Line," *Harvard Business Review*, 61 (September–October), 65–73.

Ginzberg, Eli and George Vojta (1981), "The Service Sector of the U.S. Economy," *Scientific American*, 244 (March), 31–9.

Gronroos, Christian (1990), *Service Management and Marketing: Managing the Moments of Truth in Service Competition*. Lexington, MA: Lexington Books.

Heskett, James L., W. Earl Sasser, Jr., and Christopher W. L. Hart (1990), *Service Breakthroughs: Changing the Rules of the Game*. New York: The Free Press.

Koepp, Stephen (1987), "Pul-eeze! Will Somebody Help Me?" *Time* (February 2), 28–34.

Langevin, Roger C. (1988), "Service Quality: Essential Ingredients," *Review of Business*, 9 (3), 3–5.

Mazis, Michael B., Olli T. Ahtola, and R. Eugene Klippel (1975), "A Comparison of Four Multi-Attribute Models in the Prediction of Consumer Attitudes," *Journal of Consumer Research*, 2 (June), 38–52.

Oliver, Richard L. (1980). "A Cognitive Model of the Antecedents and Consequences of Satisfaction Decisions," *Journal of Marketing Research*, 17 (November), 460–9.

Parasuraman, A., Valarie Zeithaml, and Leonard Berry (1985), "A Conceptual Model of Service Quality and Its Implications for Future Research," *Journal of Marketing*, 49 (Fall), 41–50.

——, ——, and —— (1988), "SERVQUAL: A Multiple-Item Scale for Measuring Consumer Perceptions of Service Quality," *Journal of Retailing*, 64 (Spring), 12–40.

Rathmell, John M. (1966), "What Is Meant by Services?" *Journal of Marketing*, 30 (October), 32–6.

Rudie, Mary J. and H. Brant Wansley (1985), "The Merrill Lynch Quality Program," in *Services Marketing in a Changing Environment*, Thomas Bloch, Gregory Upah, and Valarie A. Zeithaml, eds. Chicago: American Marketing Association.

Sherden, William A. (1988), "Gaining the Service Quality Advantage," *Journal of Business Strategy*, 9 (2), 45–8.

Thompson, Phillip, Glenn DeSouza, and Bradley T. Gale (1985), *The Strategic Measurement of Quality*. Cambridge, MA: The Strategic Planning Institute, PIMSLETTER, No. 33.

Woodruff. Robert B., Ernest R. Cadotte, and Roger L. Jenkins (1983), "Modeling Consumer Satisfaction Processes Using Experience-Based Norms," *Journal of Marketing Research*, 20 (August), 296–304.

Zeithaml, Valarie A., A. Parasuraman, and Leonard L. Berry (1990). *Delivering Quality Service: Balancing Customer Perceptions and Expectations*. New York: The Free Press.

Research Note:
Improving the Measurement of Service Quality

TOM J. BROWN
University of Wisconsin-Madison
Madison, Wisconsin

GILBERT A. CHURCHILL, JR.
Arthur C. Nielson, Jr., Chair of Marketing Research
University of Wisconsin-Madison
Madison, Wisconsin

J. PAUL PETER
James R. McManus-Bascom Professor in Marketing
University of Wisconsin-Madison
Madison, Wisconsin

SERVQUAL, which involves the calculation of the differences between expectations and perceptions on a number of prespecified criteria, is currently the most popular measure of service quality. However, there are some serious problems in conceptualizing service quality as a difference score; these are reviewed and empirically investigated in this paper. An alternative method for measuring service quality is found to have favorable psychometric properties and to be more efficient than SERVQUAL.

The competitive environment in retailing is increasingly hostile and unforgiving. In order to compete, retailers are focusing on areas in their operations that might give them an advantage over their competitors. A prime recent focus is service quality. If service quality is to be a cornerstone of a retailer's strategy, the retailer must have the means to measure it. One of the most popular measures of service quality is SERVQUAL, developed by Parasuraman, Zeithaml, and Berry (1988, 1991). Not only has it been widely cited in the marketing and retailing literatures, but its use in industry has also been widespread.

In their article describing the development of the SERVQUAL scale designed to measure service quality across environments, Parasuraman, Zeithaml, and Berry (1988) measured the quality of service provided by an appliance repair and maintenance firm, several retail banks, a long-distance telephone provider, a securities broker, and credit card companies. Subsequently, SERVQUAL has served as a basis for measuring the quality of the service offered by a hospital (Babakus and Mangold 1989); a CPA firm (Bojanic 1991); physicians (Brown and Schwartz 1989); a dental school patient clinic, business school placement center, tire store, and acute care hospital (Carman 1990); public recreation programs (Crompton and Mackay 1989); and real estate brokers (Johnson, Dotson, and Dunlop

1988). It seems that scholars "throughout the world" are using SERVQUAL and the research surrounding it "as a basis for their own studies" (Zeithaml, Parasuraman, and Berry 1990, p. xi).

Despite its popularity, several analysts have suggested that the measure has serious shortcomings that limit its usefulness. For example, Carman (1990) argues that SERVQUAL needs to be customized to the service in question in spite of the fact it was originally designed to provide a generic measure that could be applied to any service. This may mean adding items or changing the wording of items. He also suggests that more dimensions than the five currently found in SERVQUAL are needed, that the item-factor relationships in SERVQUAL are unstable, and that the measurement of expectations is a problem. Babakus and Mangold (1989), on the other hand, suggest that the SERVQUAL items represent only one factor rather than five. Using confirmatory factor analysis procedures and the LISREL model, Finn and Lamb (1991, p. 487), find that "the SERVQUAL measurement model is not appropriate in a retail store setting" causing them to conclude "that retailers and consumer researchers should not treat SERVQUAL as an 'off the shelf' measure of perceived service quality. Much refinement is needed for specific companies and industries" (p. 489).

Finally, Cronin and Taylor (1992) also took issue with the conceptualization and measurement approach used in developing SERVQUAL. In their research, the perceptions component of SERVQUAL outperformed SERVQUAL itself, which led them to conclude that the disconfirmation paradigm was inappropriate for measuring perceived service quality.

An important issue with the SERVQUAL measure that has not been addressed heretofore is its use of a difference score method of measurement. Difference scores involve the subtraction of scores on one measurement from another measurement to create a new variable which is used in subsequent data analysis. With SERVQUAL, service quality is assessed by subtracting subjects' ratings of expected level of service from their ratings of the actual level of service received with respect to each of a number of specific items representing five dimensions of a service. The average of the difference scores making up a dimension serve as the measure of that facet while the average score across all items serves as the overall measurement of service quality.

Although not generally known in the retailing literature, there are a number of problems with conceptualizing service quality in this manner. The purposes of this paper are to describe several potential problems with SERVQUAL's conceptualization of service quality as a difference score and to offer and empirically compare an alternative approach to the measurement of the service quality construct.

The paper is divided into two major sections. The first section overviews problems with the use of difference scores as measures of marketing and retailing constructs, such as service quality. The second section empirically demonstrates these problems and discusses the performance of a non-difference score measure of service quality that successfully overcomes these concerns. Before proceeding, however, the SERVQUAL approach to the measurement of service quality is briefly reviewed.

The SERVQUAL Scale

The SERVQUAL measure of service quality has been developed following generally recommended psychometric procedures (Parasuraman, Zeithaml, and Berry 1988). The studies supporting its development led to a final measure with 22 pairs of items designed to capture five dimensions of service quality including tangibles, reliability, responsiveness, assurance, and empathy. Respondents are first asked to provide the level of service expected from a service firm (e.g., bank, telephone company) on a set of 22 *expectations* items. Agreement with each item is assessed on a seven-point

scale with end anchors "strongly disagree" and "strongly agree" and no verbal descriptors for intervening scale positions. Next, respondents provide their evaluations of the actual level of service provided by a specific firm on a corresponding set of 22 *perceptions* items. Perceived service quality is obtained by *subtracting* the expectation rating from the perception rating for each of the 22 pairs of items. These SERVQUAL scores may be used individually for diagnostic purposes or may be averaged across the 22 pairs of items to obtain an overall service quality score.

SERVQUAL's Use of Difference Scores

The calculation of a difference score in the SERVQUAL measure can lead to several psychometric problems. Since a complete review of difference score problems is provided by Peter, Churchill, and Brown (1993), only those problems relevant to SERVQUAL will be reviewed and examined here. The three psychometric problems associated with the use of difference scores to measure service quality include: reliability, discriminant validity, and variance restriction problems.

Reliability

Difference score measures often demonstrate poor *reliability*, primarily because any positive correlation between the component scores attenuates the reliability of the resulting difference score. The formula used to calculate the reliability of a difference score (r_D), is a special case of the formula for the reliability of a linear combination, namely:

$$r_D = \frac{\sigma_1^2 r_{11} + \sigma_2^2 r_{22} - 2r_{12}\sigma_1\sigma_2}{\sigma_1^2 + \sigma_2^2 - 2r_{12}\sigma_1\sigma_2} \tag{1}$$

where r_{11} and r_{22} are the reliabilities of the first and second component scores, respectively, σ_1^2 and σ_2^2 are the variances of these component scores, and r_{12} is the correlation between the component scores (Johns 1981). Note that as the reliability of either component score decreases or the correlation between the component scores increases, the reliability of the difference score itself decreases. When two responses are taken from the same respondent and then subtracted to form a measure of a third construct (as with SERVQUAL), only rarely will the difference score components not be positively correlated. In situations where the reliabilities of the component variables are very high, attenuation may be relatively modest, even with a large correlation between components. However, there will be attenuation.

Discriminant Validity

There are two potential problems with *discriminant validity* that can arise through the use of difference scores. Recall that discriminant validity refers to the degree to which measures of theoretically unrelated constructs do not correlate too highly with one another. One problem is common to all measures while the other is unique to measures formed as linear combinations of measures of other constructs. The common problem relates to how the reliability of measures affects discriminant validity. Low measure reliability attenuates correlations between constructs. Thus, a measure with low reliability may appear to possess discriminant validity simply because it is unreliable. Since difference score measures are usually less reliable than non-difference score measures, they can be particularly subject to this phenomenon.

The discriminant validity issue that is unique to difference scores and other linear combinations concerns the degree to which the difference score measure can be discriminated from one or both of the component measures used to obtain the difference. In theory, the difference is supposed to represent a construct that is distinct from the constructs represented by its component measures. In practice though, the difference will always be highly correlated with, and thus not distinct from, at least one of the component measures. Thus, any correlation between a difference score and another variable is an artifact of the relationship between the component measures used to form the difference score and the other variable (Wall and Payne 1973; Johns 1981). Since difference score measures will not typically demonstrate discriminant validity from their components, their construct validity is questionable.

Variance Restriction

Another common problem with difference scores is *variance restriction*, which occurs when one of the component scores used to calculate the difference score is consistently higher than the other component. This is typically the case when one of the variables is a "motherhood" variable for which more is always better. Wall and Payne (1973), for example, emphasize that there is ample evidence that when people respond to "what is desirable" in comparison to "what there is now," they seldom rate the former lower than the latter. Such is the case with SERVQUAL; the expected or desired level of service is almost always higher than the perceived level of actual service.[1]

To illustrate, assume that a group of respondents was asked to respond to a single pair of SERVQUAL items, and that the expected level of service always equals or exceeds the perceived level of service. Respondents who perceive service to be poor (and circle a 1 in response to the perceptions item) have a potential range on the difference score of 0 (if their expected level is 1) to − 6 (if their expected level is 7). Respondents who perceive service to be good (and circle a 6 in response to the perceptions item) have a much more constrained potential range on the SERVQUAL score for that pair of items (0 to − 1). This restriction of range for respondents who evaluate the service highly results in a smaller variance in SERVQUAL scores for these individuals than for those less satisfied with it. This creates a problem in many types of statistical analysis that require equality of variances.

Empirical Investigation

The empirical investigation sought to determine if the problems with inference scores identified above indeed manifest themselves when the SERVQUAL measure is used, and if they can be reduced or overcome by conceptualizing the items differently. The modified SERVQUAL scale (Parasuraman, Zeithaml, and Berry 1991) was used in the investigation. The modified scale is similar to the original SERVQUAL scale except for the substitution of two new items, the change in orientation from the level of service that *should* be provided to the level that *would* be provided, and the transformation of all negatively worded items into positively worded statements.[2] We used financial institutions for the focal service since financial institutions were one of the stimuli used in the development

---

[1] There can be exceptions when the desired level of service is less than the perceived level. In their study evaluating the quality of architectural services, Cravens, Dielman, and Harrington (1985), for example, suggested firms were providing "excessive quality" on four of the 21 criteria examined. However, the exceptions are rare. Moreover, Cravens et al. determined ideal quality and perceived quality using two different types of scales, which departs from the proposed method of measurement for SERVQUAL. Specifically, they determined ideal quality by asking respondents how "important" each of 21 criteria were to them on 10-point scales. They also asked respondents to "evaluate" architectural firms on 10-point scales. An average evaluation rating that exceeded the average importance rating was taken as an indication of excess quality on the criterion.

[2] Parasuraman, Zeithaml, and Berry (1991) recommend these changes because in their original study (1988), the negatively worded items loaded separately from the positively worded items, forming two of the five dimensions. Moreover, the expectation scores were unrealistically high when respondents were asked to indicate the level of service that should provided.

of the SERVQUAL measure and they were relevant to the study's respondents. Respondents completed the expectation items first and then completed the perception items with reference to their own financial institution.

The non-difference score approach involved asking subjects to indicate how their perceptions matched their expectations for the same 22 issues that were examined by the SERVQUAL measure. Each item was rephrased the form of a "how" phrase (e.g., "How willing employees are to help,") and subjects were asked to respond on a seven-point scale with verbal descriptors attached to each scale position. The descriptors ranged from "much worse than I expected," "somewhat worse. . . ," "slightly worse. . . ," through neutral and up to "much better than I expected." Note that the alternative measure asks subjects to make a direct comparison of their perceptions to their expectations.

Data were collected on several other measures in the study to investigate the psychometric properties of the difference and non-difference score measures. The additional measures included (1) a single-item global measure of overall service quality, (2) a five-item global measure containing one item designed to assess each of the five proposed dimensions of service quality, and (3) a three-item behavioral intentions measure. Several single-item measures used in previous research to investigate the nomological validity of SERVQUAL were also included. These items were designed to investigate (1) whether subjects would consider the financial institution first if they were seeking additional services, (2) whether subjects would recommend the financial institution to a friend, and (3) whether they had ever reported a problem with it. The argument for these items is that those who perceive higher service quality for a particular service should be more willing to go there first, to recommend it to a friend, and more likely never to have reported a problem with it.

Finally, two different variations of a consumer discontent measure were included in order to investigate the discriminant validity of SERVQUAL and the non-difference score measure. Both 10-item measures were derived from the consumer discontent scale developed by Lundstrom and Lamont (1976). Items from the scale were rank ordered on their ability to discriminate between contented and discontented consumers as reported in the Lundstrom and Lamont research. Items were then grouped into pairs and one item in each pair was randomly assigned to one version of the scale and the other item to the other version. The first version, Form A, expressed the items in a six-point Likert format with only the end points anchored, a structure similar to the difference score measure. Form B expressed the items in a four-point Likert format with verbal anchors attached to each scale position, a structure similar to the non-difference score method we developed.

Procedure

A total of 230 subjects completed a questionnaire packet containing the SERVQUAL scale, the non-difference score measure, and the other measures designed to assess the validity properties of the two scales. Two forms of the questionnaire were prepared which varied the order of the difference score and non-difference score measures. Approximately half of the participants completed each version. Subjects were undergraduate students enrolled in business courses at a major Midwestern university.

Results

Table 1 presents the intercorrelations, summary statistics, and scale liabilities for the measures of interest. The reliability of SERVQUAL is .94, slightly below the reliability of the non-difference score measure (.96). The component reliabilities for SERVQUAL are high (the reliability of the perceptions component equals .96 while that of the expectations component equals .94), and their correlation is moderate (.34).

The findings also provide evidence for the convergent validity of all of the measures of service quality. The SERVQUAL measure, the non-difference score measure, and both global measures of service quality all correlate .60 or better, suggesting that all are tapping the same construct. Both SERVQUAL and the non-difference score measure demonstrate discriminant validity in terms of not correlating highly with consumer discontent. The correlations of the difference score measure to Form A and Form B of the consumer discontent scale are −.05 and −.03 respectively. The correlation of the non-difference score measure to both Form A and Form B is .06.

However, the discriminant validity problem that is unique to difference scores manifests itself in the SERVQUAL scores. Service quality, as measured by SERVQUAL, correlates highly with perceptions (.79) and moderately with expectations (−.31). Thus, it does not demonstrate discriminant validity from them, even though it is intended as a measure of a separate construct.

There are two important issues bearing on the nomological validity of the measures. First, the perceptions component of SERVQUAL alone performs about as well as SERVQUAL itself, while the expectations comment has small correlations with measures of other theoretically related constructs. In fact, the

TABLE 1
Correlations, Summary Statistics, and Scale Reliabilities

	(1)	(2)	(3)	(4)	(5)	(6)	(7)	(8)	(9)	(10)	No. of Items	No. of Scale Points	Mean	Average Scores			
														Variance	Skewness	Kurtosis	Reliability[2]
(1) Perceptions[1]											22	7	5.30	.86	−.84	1.32	.96
(2) Expectations	.34										22	7	6.12	.36	−2.24	11.95	.94
(3) SERVQUAL	.79	−.31									22	—	−0.82	.85	−1.19	1.87	.94
(4) Non-Difference Score Measure	.65	−.03	.67								22	7	4.51	.68	.39	.29	.96
(5) Global (1-item)	.63	−.05	.67	.63							1	10	7.52	2.79	−1.11	1.66	NA
(6) Global (5-item)	.77	−.02	.79	.74	.80						5	10	7.49	2.55	−.72	.13	.90
(7) Behavioral Intentions	.31	.06	.26	.32	.35	.31					3	6	5.10	1.88	−1.63	1.86	.86
(8) First Choice	.39	−.04	.43	.44	.56	.47	.33				1	6	4.59	1.64	−1.19	.88	NA
(9) Recommend	.50	−.04	.53	.53	.78	.67	.38	.61			1	6	4.78	1.31	−1.28	1.74	NA
(10) Consumer Discontent (A)	−.07	−.03	−.05	.06	.03	−.03	−.08	−.04	−.04		10	6	3.56	.32	.16	.32	.70
(11) Consumer Discontent (B)	−.04	−.02	−.03	.06	.08	.00	−.03	.02	.00	.68	10	4	2.45	.08	.16	.33	.65

[1]Correlation in this table larger than .13 are statistically significant at p ≤ .05.

[2]Reliability for scales (1), (2), (4) was calculated using the formula for the reliability of a linear composite; reliability for scale (3) was calculated using the formula for the reliability of a difference score; other reliabilities are coefficient alpha.

perceptions component outperforms SERVQUAL .31 to .26 in predicting behavioral intentions. This finding is consistent with the findings of Cronin and Taylor (1992). The inclusion of expectations thus leads to a suppressor effect rather than explains variance in this important variable. Moreover, once both expectation and perception scores are taken into account, the part correlation between SERVQUAL scores and behavioral intentions is 0. Thus, measuring service quality as a difference score does not add anything to empirical prediction over and above components.

Second, the non-difference score measure does somewhat better in predicting behavioral intentions than does SERVQUAL (.32 to .26), about the same in predicting the first choice (.44 to .43), and identically in predicting the recommend variable (.53). Also, the difference in means between those who have and who have not reported a problem with their service is slightly larger for the non-difference score than for SERVQUAL, although both mean differences are statistically significant (i.e., $t = -5.730$ for the non-difference score measure and $t = -5.364$ for SERVQUAL). Overall, the nomological validity evidence somewhat favors the non-difference score measure to the SERVQUAL measure.

A *variance restriction* problem is clearly demonstrated in the SERVQUAL data. As shown in Table 1, the mean item score for the expectations component is 6.12 on a seven-point scale, and the variance is .36, by far the smallest variance of any measure taken. Moreover, subjects checked one of the top two positions on 79 percent of the expectation items. With such a high mean and small variance, SERVQUAL scores for subjects who rate their perceptions highly are restricted, so that when the expectation items are used to generate differences, there is a systematic relationship between the difference score levels and variances. More particularly, the SERVQUAL scores have smaller variance when they are high than when they are low.[3] This phenomenon can affect the conclusions drawn from statistical analyses. For example, the SERVQUAL scores would not satisfy the assumption of constant variance if they were being used as a dependent variable in an ordinary least squares regression model. Either generalized least squares would need to be used or the SERVQUAL scores would

need to be transformed so that they satisfied the constant variance assumption. None of the previous studies employing SERVQUAL used generalized least squares or made such a transformation. In contrast, the variance of the non-difference score measure was approximately equal at all levels of the perceptions variable.[4]

The variance restriction problem, caused by the "motherhood" nature of the expectations items, also can cause measure distributions to be other than normal. Table 1 reports skewness and kurtosis measures for perceptions, expectations, SERVQUAL scores, and the non-difference score measure. The distribution for the perceptions component is negatively skewed and leptokurtic as are the SERVQUAL scores. The distribution for the expectations measure is extremely skewed and peaked. However, the distribution for the non-difference score measure is approximately normal, as is required for many statistical analyses.

Another problem with SERVQUAL that arose during the empirical investigation is that its dimensionality did not replicate. While Parasuraman, Zeithaml, and Berry (1988) identified five dimensions of service quality, our factor analysis indicated their 22 items might represent a unidimensional construct, and certainly not a five dimensional one.[5] The first eigenvalue accounted for over 51 percent of the variation in the data. While two other eigenvalues were also greater than one, they were only slightly larger (1.6 and 1.4 respectively), and in combination only accounted for less than 14 percent additional variation. These disappointing results raise serious doubts about the correspondence between the SERVQUAL measure and the theory underlying it. It seems the theory is incorrect in specifying five components of service quality or that the measure is incorrect in only capturing one component of service quality when theory suggests there are five dimensions to it. If future research also finds that SERVQUAL is only assessing a unidimensional construct, then one must question the validity of the theory, or measure, or both. Moreover, while this unidimensionality may enhance the "reliability" of the measure, it calls into question its construct validity. Perhaps the service quality construct is underidentified

---

[3]This can be seen most easily when the SERVQUAL scores are broken into groups. Consider the breakdown of SERVQUAL scores by decile, for example. When the mean and variance of scores are computed for each decile and the variance in scores by group is regressed on the mean score by decile, there is a negative linear relationship between the variance and means ($\beta = -.103$), and the relationship is statistically significant ($R^2 = .496$, $F_{1,8} = 9.84$, $p = .014$). This indicates that as SERVQUAL scores increased, their variance decreased.

[4]The breakup of non-difference scores into deciles, the calculation of variance and means by group, and the subsequent regression of the variances on the means indicated the variables were unrelated ($\beta = .016$, $R^2 = .000$, $F_{1,8} = .562$, $p = .475$).

[5]Babakus and Mangold's (1989) exploratory factor analysis of 15 items from the five dimensions of SERVQUAL also suggested a single-factor solution might be most appropriate. Similar results were reported by Cronin and Taylor (1992).

with the SERVQUAL measure (see Peter and Churchill 1986).

Summary and Conclusions

As service quality has become increasingly important to retailers' strategies, its assessment has become increasingly critical; strides have been made in recent years to measure it. The most popular measure, SERVQUAL, involves the subtraction of subjects' expectations of the service they would receive from their perceptions of the service they actually did get with respect to specific items. The differences are averaged to produce a total score for service quality.

While not generally recognized, the conceptualization of service quality as a difference score leads to a number of potential problems. These problems were reviewed and an investigation was carried out to see if they arose empirically with SERVQUAL. The paper also explored a non-difference score conceptualization of the same facets of service used in the SERVQUAL measure.

The empirical investigation indicated that the problems with SERVQUAL, brought on by its measurement as a difference score, indeed manifest themselves empirically. Although SERVQUAL had high reliability, its reliability was below that of a non-difference score measure of service quality. Moreover, not only did SERVQUAL fail to achieve discriminant validity from its components, but the perceptions component by itself performed as well as the difference score on a number of criteria. SERVQUAL also exhibited variance restriction effects and the distribution of SERVQUAL scores was non-normal.

The non-difference score measure did not exhibit these problems. Moreover, it displayed better discriminant and nomological validity properties. In sum, it was the preferred alternative. It outperformed SERVQUAL on a number of important psychometric and statistical considerations. It did so while requiring subjects to respond to only half as many items, and thus is twice as efficient. The non-difference score measure also allowed subjects to compare directly their expectations and perceptions and did not restrict them to some arbitrary, linear difference.

Cronin and Taylor (1992) also found that their measure of service performance produced better results than SERVQUAL. Their non-difference score measure consisted of the perception items used to calculate SERVQUAL scores. This measure assessed service quality without relying on the disconfirmation paradigm. We have presented a new measure that performs as well as the perceptions component of

SERVQUAL yet includes a comparison of perceptions to expectations. Future research might examine the relative merits of each approach.

However, before this research is conducted, a larger issue that arose during the course of this investigation should be addressed. This issue concerns whether a scale to measure service quality can be universally applicable across industries. In attempting to modify the wording of the SERVQUAL items to fit the alternative conceptualization, we were struck by the omission of items we a priori thought would be critical to subjects' evaluation of the quality of service they receive from a bank (e.g., the convenience of the bank's location or its operating hours). We suspect issues like this did not hold up in the original item pool because of the developers' emphasis on generating a measure applicable across service industries and their consequent focus on items in the analysis that had stable factor loadings across industries. As others have noted though (Carman 1991; Finn and Lamb 1991), it takes more than the simple adaptation of the SERVQUAL items to effectively address service quality in some situations. Managers are advised to carefully consider which issues are important to service quality in their specific environments and to modify the scale as needed. The non-difference score version of the SERVQUAL scale can serve as a useful starting point for these modifications.

References

Babakus, Emen, and W. Glynn Mangold (1989). "Adapting the 'SERVQUAL' Scale to Health Care Environment: An Empirical Assessment," in Paul Bloom, et al. (eds.), *AMA Educators' Proceedings*, Chicago, IL: American Marketing Association.

Bojanic, David C. (1991), "Quality Measurement in Professional Services Firms," *Journal of Professional Services Marketing*, 7 (2), 27–36.

Carman, James M. (1990), "Consumer Perceptions of Service Quality: An Assessment of the SERVQUAL Dimensions," *Journal of Retailing*, 66 (Spring), 33–55.

Cravens, David W., Terry E. Dielman, and C. Kent Harrington (1985), "Using Buyers' Perceptions of Service Quality to Guide Strategy Development," in Robert F. Lusch, et al. (eds.), *1985 Educators' Proceedings*, Chicago, IL: American Marketing Association.

Crompton, John L., and Kelly J. Mackay (1989), "Users' Perceptions of the Relative Importance of Service Quality Dimensions in Selected Public Recreation Programs," *Leisure Sciences*, 11, 367–75.

Cronin, J. Joseph, Jr., and Steven A. Taylor (1992), "Measuring Service Quality: A Reexamination and Extension," *Journal of Marketing*, 56 (July), 55–68.

Finn, David W., and Charles W. Lamb, Jr. (1991), "An Evaluation of the SERVQUAL Scales in a Retail Setting," in Rebecca H. Holman and Michael R. Solomon (eds.), *Advances in Consumer Research*, Vol. 18, Provo, UT: Association for Consumer Research.

Johns, Gary (1981), "Difference Scores Measures of Organizational Behavior Variables: A Critique," *Organizational Behavior and Human Performance*, 27 (June), 443–63.

Johnson, Linda L., Michael J. Dotson, and B. J. Dunlop (1988), "Service Quality Determinants and Effectiveness in the Real Estate Brokerage Industry," *The Journal of Real Estate Research*, 3, 21–36.

Lundstrom, William J., and Lawrence M. Lamont (1976), "The Development of a Scale to Measure Consumer Discontent," *Journal of Marketing Research*, 13 (November), 373–81.

Parasuraman, A., Valarie A. Zeithaml, and Leonard L. Berry (1988), "SERVQUAL: A Multi-Item Scale for Measuring Consumer Perceptions of Service Quality," *Journal of Retailing*, 64 (Spring), 12–40.

———, Leonard L. Berry, and Valarie A. Zeithaml (1991), "Refinement and Reassessment of the SERVQUAL Scale," MSI Working Paper.

Peter, J. Paul, Gilbert A. Churchill, Jr., and Tom J. Brown (1993), "Caution in the Use of Difference Scores in Consumer Research," *Journal of Consumer Research*, 19 (March), 655–62.

——— and ——— (1986), "Relationships among Research Design Choices and Psychometric Properties of Rating Scales: A Meta-Analysis," *Journal of Marketing Research*, 23 (February), 1–10.

Wall, Toby D., and Roy Payne (1973), "Are Deficiency Scores Deficient?" *Journal of Applied Psychology*, 58 (3), 322–26.

Zeithaml, Valerie A., A. Parasuraman, and Leonard L. Berry (1990), *Delivering Quality Service: Balancing Customer Perceptions and Expectations*, New York, NY: The Free Press.

Page numbers appearing in italics refer to tables and figures.

MCI Phone Services
Chapter 8, Article 3.1
www.mci.com

Merck Corporation
Chapter 7
www.merck.com

MTV
Chapter 6
www.mtv.com

NASDAQ
Chapter 8
www.nasdaq.com

National Park Service
Chapter 6
www.cr.nps.gov

Nestlé
Article 3.5
www.nestle.com

Newsweek
Article 2.7
www.newsweek.com

Nick at Nite
Chapter 6
www.nick-at-night.com

Nickelodeon
Chapter 6
www.nick.com

Nielsen Media Research
Chapter 8
www.nielsenmedia.com

Nike
Chapter 5
www.nike.com

Nordstrom
Chapter 7
www.nordstrom-pta.com

North Carolina State University
Chapter 7
www.ncsu.edu

Northwest Airlines
Chapter 7
www.nwa.com

Office Depot
Chapter 10
www.officedepot.com

Olive Garden
Chapter 8
www.olivegarden.com

Paramount Pictures
Chapter 6
www.paramount.com

Parker House Manufacturing Company
Chapter 9
www.parker-house.com

Procter & Gamble
Chapter 1, Article 3.5
www.pg.com

Progressive Corp.
Chapter 1
www.progressive.com

Rainforest Café
Chapter 1
www.rainforestcafe.com

Ritz-Carlton Hotel
Chapter 13
www.ritzcarlton.com

Riverside Methodist Hospital
Chapter 2
www.grmh.org

Royal Scotsman
Chapter 10
www.royalscotsman.com

Safeway Stores
Chapter 2
www.safeway.com

Scandinavian Airlines
Chapter 7
www.sas.se

Sealink Ferries
Chapter 9
www.sealink .com

Sears
Chapters 7, 8
www.sears.com

Shell
Article 3.5
www.shell.com

Sheraton
Chapter 7
www.sheraton.com

Singapore Airlines
Chapter 7, Article 3.1
www.singaporeair.com

Snowshoe
Chapter 10
www.snowshoemtn.com

Southwest Airlines
Chapter 7
www.southwest.com

Southwestern Bell
Chapter 13
www.swbell.com

State Farm Insurance
Chapter 13
www.statefarm.com

Taco Bell
Chapter 7
www.tacobell.com

The Economist
Chapter 1
www.economist.com

Tide
Chapter 1
www.tide.com

Time Magazine
Article 2.7
www.pathfinder.com/time

Toyota
Articles 3.1, 3.5
www.toyota.com

Toys "R" Us
Article 3.1
www.toysrus.com

Tremblant
Chapter 10
www.tremblant.ca

U. S. Air Force
Chapter 6
www.airforce.com

U. S. Army
Chapter 6
www.army.mil

U. S. Navy
Chapter 6
www.navy.mil

U.S. News & World Report
Article 2.7
www.usnews.com

Unilever
Article 3.5
www.unilever.com

United Airlines
Chapters 2, 5, 13
www.ual.com

University of Michigan
Chapter 11
www.umich.edu

UPS
Chapter 7
www.ups.com

US Airways
Chapters 2, 6, 7
www.usair.com

Viacom
Chapter 6
www.viacom.com

The Wall Street Journal
Chapter 6
www.wsj.com

Wal-Mart
Article 3.1
www.wal-mart.com

The Walt Disney Company
Chapters 1, 5, 7, 10, Article 3.1
www.disney.com

Wendy's
Chapters 8, 10
www.wendys.com

Xerox Corporation
Chapter 1
www.xerox.com

Yale University
Chapter 10
www.yale.com

NOTE: Internet Web addresses change frequently. If you do not find the exact sites listed, you may need to access the organization's or company's home page and search from there.